D1524974

SPECIAL EDITION

USING
Crystal
Reports® 10

Neil FitzGerald

Ryan Marples

Naisan Geula

Bob Coates

James Edkins

Michael Voloshko

Previous contributors:

Joe Estes

Kathryn Hunt

Steve Lucas

Roger Sanborn

800 East 96th Street
Indianapolis, Indiana 46240

CONTENTS AT A GLANCE

I Crystal Reports Design
1 Creating and Designing Basic Reports 17
2 Selecting and Grouping Data 53
3 Filtering, Sorting, and Summarizing Data 77
4 Understanding and Implementing Formulas 93
5 Implementing Parameters for Dynamic Reporting 127

II Formatting Crystal Reports
6 Fundamentals of Report Formatting 145
7 Working with Report Sections 167
8 Visualizing Your Data with Charts and Maps 187
9 Custom Formatting Techniques 217

III Advanced Crystal Reports Design
10 Using Cross-Tabs for Summarized Reporting 231
11 Using Record Selections and Alerts for Interactive
       Reporting 247
12 Using Subreports for Advanced Reporting 263
13 Using Formulas and Custom Functions 281
14 Designing Effective Report Templates 295
15 Additional Data Sources for Crystal Reports 313
16 Multidimensional Reporting Against OLAP Data with
       Crystal Reports 323

**IV Enterprise Report Design—Analytic,
    Web-based, and Excel Report Design**
17 Introduction to Crystal Repository 349
18 Crystal Reports Semantic Layer—Business Views 359
19 Creating Crystal Analysis Reports 375
20 Advanced Crystal Analysis Report Design 409
21 Ad-Hoc Application and Excel Plug-in for Ad-Hoc
       and Analytic Reporting 437

V Web Report Distribution—Using Crystal Enterprise
22 Introduction to Crystal Enterprise 461
23 Using Crystal Enterprise with Web Desktop 473
24 Crystal Enterprise Architecture 505
25 Planning Considerations When Deploying Crystal
       Enterprise 541
26 Deploying Crystal Enterprise in a Complex Network
       Environment 569
27 Administering and Configuring Crystal Enterprise 597

**VI Customized Report Distribution—Using
    Crystal Reports Components**
28 Java Reporting Components 653
29 Crystal Reports .NET Components 673
30 COM Reporting Components 695

**VII Customized Report Distribution—Using Crystal
    Enterprise Embedded Edition**
31 Introduction to Crystal Enterprise Embedded Edition ... 713
32 Crystal Enterprise—Viewing Reports 725
33 Crystal Enterprise Embedded—Report Modification
       and Creation 741

**VIII Customized Report Distribution—Using Crystal
    Enterprise Professional**
34 Introduction to the Crystal Enterprise Professional Object
       Model 765
35 Creating Enterprise Reporting Applications with Crystal
       Enterprise Part I 783
36 Creating Enterprise Reporting Applications with Crystal
       Enterprise Part II 801
A Using SQL Queries in Crystal Reports 819
    Index 827

SOMERSET CO. LIBRARY
BRIDGEWATER, N.J 08807

SPECIAL EDITION USING CRYSTAL REPORTS 10

International Standard Book Number: 0-7897-3113-4

Library of Congress Catalog Card Number: 2004104261

Printed in the United States of America

First Printing: July 2004

07   06   05   4   3

Trademarks

All terms mentioned in this book that are known to be trademarks or service marks have been appropriately capitalized. Que Publishing cannot attest to the accuracy of this information. Use of a term in this book should not be regarded as affecting the validity of any trademark or service mark.

Crystal Reports and Crystal Analysis are registered trademarks of Business Objects SA, and Crystal Enterprise is a trademark of Business Objects SA.

Warning and Disclaimer

Every effort has been made to make this book as complete and as accurate as possible, but no warranty or fitness is implied. The information provided is on an "as is" basis. The authors and the publisher shall have neither liability nor responsibility to any person or entity with respect to any loss or damages arising from the information contained in this book.

Bulk Sales

Que Publishing offers excellent discounts on this book when ordered in quantity for bulk purchases or special sales. For more information, please contact

U.S. Corporate and Government Sales

1-800-382-3419

corpsales@pearsontechgroup.com

For sales outside of the U.S., please contact

International Sales

international@pearsoned.com

Associate Publisher
Greg Wiegand

Acquisitions Editor
Michelle Newcomb

Development Editor
Mark Renfrow

Managing Editor
Charlotte Clapp

Project Editor
Dan Knott

Copy Editor
Kate Givens

Indexer
Erika Millen

Proofreader
Kathy Bidwell

Technical Editor
Robert Coates
Dawn Geula

Publishing Coordinator
Sharry Lee Gregory

Designer
Anne Jones

Contents

III Advanced Crystal Reports Design

VI Customized Report Distribution—Using Crystal Reports Components

VIII Customized Report Distribution—Using Crystal Enterprise Professional

34 Introduction to the Crystal Enterprise Professional Object Model 765

FOREWORD

Crystal Reports version 10 was officially launched in January 2004, which is fitting because the month was named for the Roman god Janus. Janus is the god of gates, doors, beginnings, and endings. Crystal Reports version 10 has been released in a time of change marked by a key ending and some exciting beginings.

On December 11, 2003, Business Objects acquired Crystal Decisions. Although Business Objects and Crystal Decisions were perceived as direct competitors, Business Intelligence users knew these companies essentially offered complementary products. Both companies approached the problem of presenting data to users in different manners. Business Objects had focused on empowering end users to develop and manipulate data in an ad hoc interface. Crystal Decisions had focused on providing users with the capability to create highly formatted printed documents. Depending on their end-user needs and data requirements, many organizations use both Business Objects and Crystal Decisions products to meet their diverse reporting needs.

The launch of Crystal Reports 10 represents the end of Business Objects and Crystal Decisions as separate companies. This release marks the beginning of a new company that unites best of breed reporting and analysis solutions to meet the needs of the entire spectrum of Business Intelligence consumers and developers.

Crystal Reports version 10 includes the best of the nine previous versions of Crystal Reports—the de facto standard of report writers—and introduces new technologies to solve new business challenges. The new Java version of the Crystal Reports Print Engine, available in the Developer and Advanced Developer versions, provides developers with the capability to embed Crystal Reports technology in Java applications. Crystal Reports 10 has also significantly improved its integration with Crystal Enterprise and has fully leveraged the metadata and repository services offered by Crystal Enterprise 10. This integration makes Crystal Enterprise 10 a great timesaver for developers who want integrated security, fault tolerance, and scalability in their Web-based reporting applications.

By working closely with the Development and Quality Assurance teams on the Crystal Reports 10 project, I was able to witness the unwavering commitment to ensure new features provided the maximum benefit in meeting user needs. I was amazed at the number and variety of testing scenarios that were inspired by real customers who use Crystal Reports. This experience reminded me that there are things that Crystal Reports does so well that most of us take the depth of the product for granted.

Readers of this book will find that it is the source of information on the features, functions, and capabilities of Crystal Reports 10 from a perspective of what customers want to do with the product. This book has been written by the members of the Business Objects Presales Team who can best apply our technology capabilities to solve your real-world business challenges. These creative and ingenious people will share with you their knowledge to help you meet your customers' needs. Like the mythical reign of Janus, we hope that Crystal Reports version 10 ushers in the beginning of the Golden Age of Reporting.

Nigel Stoodley

Regional Technical Director

Business Objects

About the Lead Author

Neil FitzGerald has more than 9 years' experience working with information delivery, business intelligence, and enterprise reporting products. He has combined this experience with his bachelor of computer science degree from Queen's University in Kingston, Canada, and his MBA from the Ivey School of Business at the University of Western Ontario, to help provide information solutions to Fortune 500 companies across North America. Neil is currently based in New York City and helps Business Objects clients understand the potential of the Crystal suite of products. He can be reached at neil_fitzgerald@hotmail.com.

About the Contributing Authors

Ryan Marples has worked in a variety of roles at Business Objects and formerly Crystal Decisions for six years. His experience in supporting, building, marketing, and selling Crystal-based products makes him an authority on the technology. Today Ryan works with the company's largest customers helping them define and architect successful technology deployments. This is the second book he has helped author for the Crystal community. Ryan resides in Vancouver, Canada.

Naisan Geula manages the Business Objects field sales alliance with Microsoft in North America. He is an avid garage tinkerer, mountain bike mechanic, and gadget-phile, and he lives in rural Washington with his wife and personal zoo. He greatly enjoys the outdoors and watching technology unite humanity and facilitate a more holistic lifestyle.

Bob Coates has been an employee of Business Objects (through the acquisition of Crystal Decisions) for seven years. He is currently a member of the pre-sales department and the Public Sector team in the United States. Bob started working with Crystal Decisions as a technical product specialist and team leader in technical support; he moved on to become a consultant in the professional services organization, and finally moved into his current role in pre-sales. Prior to coming to the technology industry, Bob enjoyed diverse roles as an Infantry Officer in the Canadian Forces Army Reserve (Seaforth Highlanders of Canada), bartender in various bars and restaurants, and a first-aid attendant in a sawmill in Vancouver.

James Edkins is a senior pre-sales consultant for Business Objects. He holds a bachelor's degree in information technology and a post graduate diploma in marketing management. He has been in the information technology sector for more than 10 years and has experience working with the Fortune 500 companies in an ERP, product development, and business intelligence capacity.

Michael Voloshko is a pre-sales consultant for the financial services team at Business Objects and is based in New York City.

DEDICATION

To my new wife and long-time soul mate—Arlene.

—Neil FitzGerald

To every person at Crystal Decisions: Your hard work and passion for our company over the years has not only helped make this book possible, but has also provided me with a lifetime of learning, experiences, and friendships.

—Ryan Marples

To all the young people out there who are playing with technology or dreaming about how they will remake their world using all of these gadgets. It's your world—we just live in it.

—Naisan Geula

First and foremost to my wife Amanda—you inspire me and you make every day an adventure.

—Bob Coates

To my wife Cristine, who during the writing of the book had our second child. Thank you for picking up the slack during those trying times.

—James Edkins

To all the people throughout the years who have inspired me to continue achieving and advancing in life.

—Michael Voloshko

ACKNOWLEDGMENTS

Neil FitzGerald: Thanks to all the authors for delivering on our joint goals of making this book a reality and for truly applying yourselves in tough times—you are all world-class and it was a treat to work with each of you.

Special recognition also goes to the Crystal Product and R&D teams for delivering this world-standard suite of products, and the "old school" Crystal NYC team for having helped make the tough times easier—Bill, James, Mike, Dan, Larry, Vic, Devin, and John.

Ryan Marples: Thank you Neil for being the ringleader for this book; you kept us all going. Thanks to our editor Michelle for believing in us. Also thank you to the many people I have learned from at the company over the years including but not limited to: Steve Lucas, Mani Gill, Tim Wier, Steve Holzgraefe, Fred Tummonds, Dave Galloway, Mandeep Jassal, and Keith Thomson.

Naisan Geula: Thanks, Dawn, for putting up with all my idiosyncrasies and even loving me for them, and for being my true partner in all things.

Thanks to my family (yes all of you, even Moochie) for being the craziest bunch that a man could every want to know, and yet making me very proud to be a leaf of this tree. My parents and grandparents especially—thanks for giving me a sense of the transcendent and teaching me what love is.

Ralph, Debra, and Peter—you yanked me away from all things medical before it was too late, and thanks for giving so freely of your hard-earned knowledge and experience. To all my buddies at Crystal and now Business Objects—we are going to have a fun few years!

And to the Creator, not last nor least, for a bringing me forth out of my disappearance and filling me with wonder every day. Amazing place you built here—let's just hope us humans don't mess it up!

Bob Coates: To my friends and family; thanks for helping me to grow, and for all the great times. And to my peers and co-workers, everyday you make our company great.

James Edkins: To the members of the team, my co-workers, and Neil FitzGerald for making this possible.

Michael Voloshko: I want to thank Kathryn for being there for me and loving me, my brother Alex for helping me throughout the years and always finding the time...you are the best. Thanks to Mom and Dad for giving me life and helping me get to where I am today. Thanks also to the rest of my wonderful family and to my friends for being there for me (you know who you are).

I also want to thank Neil for giving me the opportunity to contribute to this book and the rest of the team members at Business Objects for all the hard work that went into creating this product

WE WANT TO HEAR FROM YOU!

As the reader of this book, *you* are our most important critic and commentator. We value your opinion and want to know what we're doing right, what we could do better, what areas you'd like to see us publish in, and any other words of wisdom you're willing to pass our way.

As an associate publisher for Que Publishing, I welcome your comments. You can e-mail or write me directly to let me know what you did or didn't like about this book—as well as what we can do to make our books better.

Please note that I cannot help you with technical problems related to the topic of this book. We do have a User Services group, however, where I will forward specific technical questions related to the book.

When you write, please be sure to include this book's title and author as well as your name, e-mail address, and phone number. I will carefully review your comments and share them with the authors and editors who worked on the book.

E-mail: feedback@quepublishing.com

Mail: Greg Wiegand
            Associate Publisher
            Que Publishing
            800 East 96th Street
            Indianapolis, IN 46240 USA

For more information about this book or another Que Publishing title, visit our Web site at www.quepublishing.com. Type the ISBN (excluding hyphens) or the title of a book in the Search field to find the page you're looking for.

INFORMATION DELIVERY WITH CRYSTAL PRODUCTS

In this introduction

INTRODUCTION TO INFORMATION DELIVERY

Organizations in the early twenty-first century find themselves increasingly awash in data yet hungering for information to help them meet their business objectives. These corporations, from Main Street and Wall Street alike, have spent large amounts of time and money over the past 10 or so years implementing systems to help collect data on and streamline their operations. From monolithic Enterprise Resource Planning (ERP) systems (SAP, PeopleSoft, Oracle, and so on) through Customer Relationship Management (CRM) systems (Siebel, Pivotal, Salesforce.com, and so on) to Custom Data Warehousing projects, these firms are now looking for ways to extract value from that collective body of data to help them run their businesses more productively and competitively. These firms are looking for a strategic *information delivery* or *business intelligence* solution to help them become more productive and ultimately compete more effectively. The products covered in this book are geared toward meeting that challenge.

The information delivery products and solutions that are presented in this book are often categorized under the *Business Intelligence (BI)* banner. BI is the industry of value-added information delivery based on structured data sources—essentially providing meaningful, business-driven value and information to business endusers by connecting them to data with appropriate tools and products. Figure 0.1 highlights the conceptual divide of Information Delivery Solutions into the structured and unstructured world. Although evidence points to the blurring of the boundaries between these discrete industries over time, the Business Objects products covered in this book most aptly fit under the BI banner.

Figure 0.1
The information delivery industry is broadly divided into structured and unstructured information management.

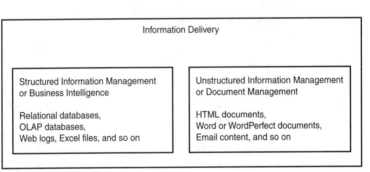

Information Delivery

Structured Information Management or Business Intelligence

Relational databases,
OLAP databases,
Web logs, Excel files, and so on

Unstructured Information Management or Document Management

HTML documents,
Word or WordPerfect documents,
Email content, and so on

Industry analysts in the information delivery area regularly highlight the impressive adoption rates that BI products have witnessed in the last few years as testimony to the value of BI products. The impressive double-digit growth rates for industry leaders like Business Objects and Crystal Decisions are increasingly impressive when the difficult macroeconomic operating environment of the time period is taken into account. Ironically, many suggest, it is this same poor economic environment that has largely driven the increased worldwide demand for BI functionality as firms work to increase their productivity and competitiveness by leveraging existing investments—and doing more with less. This BI industry driver along with a few other drivers are covered in the next section.

SPECTRUM OF BUSINESS OBJECTS PRODUCT USAGE

BI products like those distributed by Business Objects (Crystal Reports, Crystal Enterprise, Crystal Analysis, and WebIntelligence) are deployed and used in about as many different ways as there are product implementations—and there are millions. However, as you become exposed to a broad swath of BI clients and their implementations, you can find definite themes to their deployments. Taking a step back, you can perceive distinctive drivers to the worldwide BI product adoption—and a few of the most common are discussed in the following sections.

CUSTOM INFORMATION DELIVERY APPLICATIONS

Despite the plethora of turnkey software and Web applications in existence today, corporations both large and small still regularly look to custom developed applications to provide them with unique competitive advantages and to meet their proprietary business requirements. These applications run the gamut in size from small business applications through large firm departmental applications to enterprise intranet and extranet applications. One key component of many of these custom applications is the provision of BI functionality such as formatted reporting, ad hoc query, self-service Web reporting, and analytic capabilities. Table 0.1 highlights some typical examples of custom applications using Business Objects Crystal suite of products to help deliver custom applications.

TABLE 0.1   SAMPLE CUSTOM INFORMATION DELIVERY APPLICATIONS

Application	Application Audience	Product Usage
Small retail chain's internal Java-based sales metrics application	Approximately 20 sales employees and managers	Using Crystal Reports Java Engine, the developer provides the sales team with Web access to on-demand metrics reports built into the intranet application.
Large portfolio management firm's client extranet application	10,000+ high value customers of firm	Using Crystal Enterprise, the developer provides access to the scalable Crystal Enterprise–driven reporting infrastructure and facilitates those customers getting online Web access to their portfolio reports.
Asset management firm's report batch of scheduling application	50,000+ clients	Using the Crystal SDKs and an external scheduling engine (or Crystal Enterprise), the developer's application dynamically creates tens of thousands of customized reports daily and automatically emails them to the appropriate clients.

One strength of the Crystal suite of products is that the products lend themselves readily to integration into custom applications. From the inclusion of basic formatted reports in your Java/J2EE or .NET/COM applications and inclusion of rich ad hoc query and self-service reporting functionality in proprietary information product applications to provision of large-scale enterprise BI analytics, scheduling, and security functionality in a globally deployed application, the Crystal suite of products can meet your requirements. Table 0.2 provides a jump-point for those looking for this type of application integration information in this book.

TABLE 0.2   CUSTOM APPLICATION CHAPTERS OVERVIEW

Development Environment	Functionality Required	Section and Chapters
Java/J2EE	Pre-built reports included in custom Java application	Part VI, Chapter 28
.NET/COM	Pre-built reports included in custom .NET/COM application	Part VI, Chapters 29 and 30
Java/J2EE/.NET/COM	All of the above and self service or ad-hoc report creation in custom application	Part VII, Chapters 31–33
Java/J2EE/.NET/COM	All of the above and scheduling, alerting, scalability, Enterprise security, analytics, and more in a custom application	Part VIII, Chapters 34–36

ENTERPRISE BI INITIATIVES

With the proliferation of BI tools and the acceleration of product adoption around the globe, there has been concurrent pressure for the involved companies to standardize on a single set of products and tools—effectively a BI infrastructure or platform. The main arguments for such standardization include the following:

- Reduced total cost of product ownership
- Creation of Enterprise centers of excellence
- Reduced vendor relationships
- Movement towards a BI infrastructure/platform

As BI products have matured from different areas of historical strength and their marketplace acceptance has grown, end-user organizations have found themselves with disparate and incompatible BI tools and products across or even within the same departments in their organization. To eliminate the costliness of managing such a broad set of tools, many firms are now moving to adopt a single BI platform like Business Objects Crystal Enterprise. The infrastructure of Crystal Enterprise provides a single architecture to manage all the content and tools required to serve an organization's structured information delivery requirements. Figure 0.2 shows an end-user map of a typical organization. As you can imagine, each of the different types of end users in a company requires different types of tools to be productive.

A common infrastructure or centrally managed center of excellence such as Crystal Enterprise that can meet all the varying end-user and IT requirements has clear organizational benefits.

Figure 0.2
Organizational end-user requirements map from Business Objects.

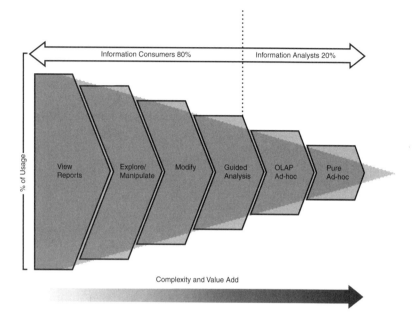

Details of the breakdown of this book are included later in this introduction but to jump-start your learning on this type of BI application, Table 0.3 can point you to the sections and chapters of particular relevance now.

TABLE 0.3   ENTERPRISE BUSINESS INTELLIGENCE CHAPTER OVERVIEW

Enterprise Business Intelligence Focus	Section and Chapters
Out-of-the-box product using Business Objects Crystal Enterprise	Part V, Chapters 22, 23, 27
Setting up and administering Business Objects Crystal Enterprise	Part V, Chapters 24–27
Integrating Crystal Enterprise functionality into applications	Part VIII, Chapters 34–36

ENTERPRISE APPLICATION EXTENSION

In the past two decades, large firms have spent hundreds of millions of dollars on enterprise applications including ERP and CRM applications such as SAP, PeopleSoft, and Siebel. These large organizations are now looking for ways to extract analytic value from these operational data stores to facilitate organizational planning and forecasting through BI products.

The Business Objects suite of Crystal products includes a variety of specialized drivers that provide direct connectivity into these enterprise applications. It is important to note that these drivers are provided for use with the Crystal Enterprise infrastructure and are usually released 3–6 months after the product suite is released. At the time of writing, these drivers were not yet available for version 10 but many have since been released, and data can be found at businessobjects.com or usingcrystal.com.

SPECTRUM OF BI TOOL USERS

Across the usage profiles of the thousands of BI scenarios/implementations, there generally exists a consistency in the types of people that become involved. Figure 0.3 provides a relatively high-level yet accurate graphic that shows a typical distribution of the people involved in BI implementations.

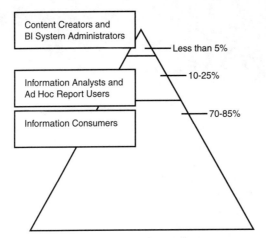

Figure 0.3
Average BI implem
entation user
distribution.

Each of the three communities outlined in the pyramid plays a key role in the ongoing success and operation of any BI implementation. The content creators and system administrators play perhaps the most important role in ensuring the short- and long-term success of any deployment because it is their work to set up the system content and tools from which the other users derive benefit. The information analysts generally come from across an organization's typical functions and are highly demanding users who require rich and highly functional interactive tools to facilitate their jobs as analysts. The last group is by far the largest group and includes employees, partners, customers, or suppliers who rely on the BI implementation to provide timely, secure, and reliable information or corporate truths. This group tends to span the entire corporate ladder from foot soldiers right up to the executive suite—all of whom have the same requirement of simple information provision to enable them to complete their regular day-to-day assignments successfully.

Figure 0.4 provides a schematic highlighting the distinction between the different version 10 content creation tools and the version 10 content delivery tools—Crystal Enterprise,

Report Application Server, or Java/.NET Reporting engines. This book is essentially broken down into two halves covering these two themes—content creation (Parts I–IV) and content delivery in all of its possible forms (Parts V–VIII) using the Business Objects Crystal suite of products.

Figure 0.4
Content creation and content delivery schematic.

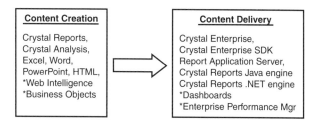

Content Creation

Crystal Reports,
Crystal Analysis,
Excel, Word,
PowerPoint, HTML,
*Web Intelligence
*Business Objects

Content Delivery

Crystal Enterprise,
Crystal Enterprise SDK
Report Application Server,
Crystal Reports Java engine
Crystal Reports .NET engine
*Dashboards
*Enterprise Performance Mgr

*Coming soon to the Business Objects Crystal Enterprise suite of products: You can view the product roadmap at www.businessobjects.com to understand why an investment in the Crystal suite of products and infrastructure is a sound investment in the future of BI.

CONTENT CREATORS (INFORMATION DESIGNERS)

Content creators provide the foundation to any BI implementation. Using content creation tools such as Crystal Reports, Crystal Analysis, Web Intelligence, Excel, and so on, this group of users—primarily composed of IT folks but sometimes complemented with technically savvy business users—creates the report content, dashboards, OLAP cubes, and reporting metadata that facilitates system usage and benefit derivation from the other system users. Because these tasks are of paramount importance in a Business Objects Crystal Enterprise suite deployment, the entire first half of the book is dedicated specifically to providing these folks with a comprehensive tutorial and reference on content creation.

After content has been created, it needs to be deployed in a distribution mechanism such as Crystal Enterprise, the Report Application Server, or a custom application; and then it needs to be managed. Another small but critical group of BI system users—the BI administrators—need to ensure that the system is deployed and tuned correctly to ensure optimal performance for the business end users. Chapters 24–27 provide a detailed guide to enable such administrators to effectively manage a Crystal Enterprise system and the remaining chapters—28 through 36—provide detailed information on deploying Crystal content in a custom home-grown application.

INFORMATION ANALYSTS

Although not the primary group in number, the information analysts in a BI deployment are those who are primarily responsible for the extraction of new business insights and actionable recommendations from the BI implementation. Using such analytic tools as Crystal Analysis or the Crystal Reports Explorer, this group of users spends their time interrogating, massaging, and slicing and dicing the data provided in the various back-end systems until nuggets of business relevance can be gleaned. These users tend to come from a wide variety of functional areas in a company including operations, finance, sales, HR, and marketing and all work with the provided BI tools to extract new information out of the existing corporate data set. Chapters 19–21 in Part IV provide detailed information on using both Crystal Analysis and the Crystal Reports Explorer.

INFORMATION CONSUMERS

This group of users composes the clear majority of those involved with a BI implementation. They are also the most diverse group and come from every rung on the corporate ladder. Executives who view corporate performance dashboards fit into this category as would truck drivers who receive their daily mileage and shipping reports online through a wireless device. The key characteristic of the members of this entire group is that their interactions with the BI system are not indicative of their primary jobs. Unlike the content creators who are responsible for creating the valuable content and tools for the BI system and unlike the information analysts who are tasked with using the system to increase corporate performance, information consumers have jobs outside of the BI implementation and the key measure of success for them is that the BI system helps facilitate their variety of assignments. Chapters 22 and 23 provide instructive overviews of the primary out-of-the-box Crystal Enterprise interface and as the area of information consumer interface is as infinite as the number of implementations, the final sections of the book (Parts VI–VIII) provide you with the customization skills to provide your users with their perfect interfaces.

THE CRYSTAL PRODUCT FAMILY FROM BUSINESS OBJECTS

As Figure 0.4 showed, the Crystal Product family distributed by Business Objects is broken into two major segments, content creation and content delivery. This book is split in two with each half covering one of the topics in great detail. All of the products in the Crystal family are covered in these sections.

In the content creation half of the book, the following Crystal products will be introduced and covered in detail:

- Crystal Reports version 10: The world standard for professional formatted reporting across the largest spectrum of data sources. The Crystal Reports Application Designer benefits from more than 15 years of development and provides an unparalleled combination of powerful functionality and report-design flexibility.
- Crystal Analysis 10: A powerful content creation tool designed to access OLAP data sources and to provide interactive, speed of thought analytic reporting functionality to users across the end-user spectrum. The drag-and-drop design functionality is intuitive and the unique guided analytic functionality enables creation of content that brings the power of OLAP to the masses.

- Crystal add-ins for Excel: Excel is the world's most used BI tool. To enable Excel power users to remain in their familiar Excel interface, the Crystal family includes two Excel add-ins. The first is a Crystal Analysis plug-in for OLAP Cube exploration, and the second is a powerful ad hoc report creation plug-in that can leverage existing Crystal Reports managed in Crystal Enterprise as a data source.

- Crystal Reports Explorer: Based on the Report Application Server object model and used with Crystal Enterprise, this Crystal application provides designers with a subset of Crystal Reports Design capabilities over the Web in a DHTML interface. All the content created in this interface are Crystal Report files.

In the content delivery half of the book, the following Crystal Products and SDKs are covered in detail:

- Crystal Enterprise: A complete end-to-end BI and Enterprise Reporting Platform that provides the infrastructure to support a range of implementations from small internal projects to global extranet deployments supporting tens of thousands of users. Crystal Enterprise provides a wealth of Enterprise functionality including scheduling, security, auditing, alerting, and so on through several turnkey interfaces. Additionally, the functionality of Crystal Enterprise can be embedded in your custom applications through use of its completely open Java and .NET/COM object models and UI code.

- Crystal Reports Engine for .NET Applications: The only third-party tool distributed with Visual Studio .NET, this reporting component enables .NET developers to quickly embed limited but powerful reporting functionality into their .NET applications.

- Crystal Reports Engine for Java Applications: Embedded in Borland's JBuilder and other Java IDEs, this reporting component enables Java developers to embed limited but powerful reporting functionality into their Java applications quickly.

- Crystal Reports Report Designer Components: A legacy object model for the Crystal Reports Designer, this reporting component allows for the integration of reporting capabilities into COM-based applications. Use of this single-threaded object model is being phased out in lieu of the multithreaded, multiplatform Report Application Server object model.

- Report Application Server: Now called Crystal Enterprise Embedded, this multi-threaded object model and scaleable server provides both Java and .NET/COM developers with access to the power of Crystal Reports for integration into their custom applications or for access from within a Crystal Enterprise deployment.

WHAT IS IN THIS BOOK

This book is broken down into several sections to address the varied and evolving requirements of the different users in a BI deployment.

The entire first half of the book (Parts I through IV) is exclusively focused on content creation. Through use of hands-on step-by-step examples and detailed descriptions of key product functionality, you will be able to leverage the powerful report creation capabilities of Crystal Reports version 10, Crystal Analysis version 10, Crystal Business Views version 10, the Web-based Ad-Hoc application, and the Excel-based Ad-Hoc plug-in. Some profiles of people who will find these sections of particular relevance:

- New and mature Crystal Reports designers
- Professional Crystal Reports designers upgrading to version 10
- Existing and new Crystal Analysis designers and analysts
- Existing and new Crystal Enterprise administrators

The second half of the book (Parts V through VIII) is geared toward the distribution or delivery of the valuable content created in the first half. Detailed functionality overviews are provided for all the different distribution mechanisms available in the Business Objects Crystal suite of products. Additionally, detailed and instructive code samples are provided for all the Software Development Kits (SDKs) that are provided with Crystal Reports, Crystal Enterprise, and the Report Application Server. Some profiles of people who will find these sections of high value:

- New or existing Crystal Enterprise administrators
- New or existing Crystal Enterprise users
- .NET/COM-based application developers
- Java/J2EE-based application developers
- Application developers looking to integrate programmatic report design or modification into their applications
- Application developers looking to integrate programmatic report scheduling, security, alerting, viewing, and so on into their applications

PART I: CRYSTAL REPORTS DESIGN

Part I should familiarize you with the foundations of Crystal Reports and get you up and running as quickly as possible. It is critical for someone who is new to Crystal Reports and includes the fundamental report-design concepts that even experienced users will be able to use for the rest of their Crystal Reports writing career. This section also provides powerful exercises and real-world usage tips and tricks that will enable even seasoned reporting experts to become more productive.

PART II: FORMATTING CRYSTAL REPORTS

Part II focuses on some of the more subtle nuances of Crystal Report design: effective report formatting and data visualization through charting and mapping. Improper formatting and incorrect use of visualization techniques can make reports confusing and not user-friendly. This section also provides powerful exercises and real-world usage tips and tricks enabling mature reporting experts to become more productive.

PART III: ADVANCED CRYSTAL REPORTS DESIGN

Part III presents a host of advanced Crystal Report design concepts that involve features such as subreports, cross-tabs, report templates, and alerts. This part also touches on customized data access methods such as EJB and COM objects. This section also provides powerful exercises and real-world usage tips and tricks enabling mature reporting experts to become more effective in their report-design work.

PART IV: ENTERPRISE REPORT DESIGN—ANALYTIC, WEB-BASED, AND EXCEL REPORT DESIGN

Part IV focuses on the Crystal Repository that includes object reusability and the new Business View semantic layer and metadata functionality. Additional coverage is also provided on practical Crystal Analysis Design for use with OLAP data sources, and both the Web- and Excel-based Crystal ad-hoc capabilities for use with relational data sources.

PART V: WEB REPORT DISTRIBUTION—USING CRYSTAL ENTERPRISE

Part V presents the powerful functionality of the turnkey BI and Enterprise reporting product—Crystal Enterprise. In addition to covering the many business benefits of Crystal Enterprise, this part also provides extensive coverage of the end-user interface for end-user training. Extensive architecture, administration, and management best practices are provided for system administrators.

PART VI: CUSTOMIZED REPORT DISTRIBUTION—USING CRYSTAL REPORTS COMPONENTS

Part VI focuses on the Customizable Report Distribution Components that are provided for Crystal Reports Delivery in both the .NET/COM and Java/J2EE worlds. Code samples are provided to help jumpstart your development work.

PART VII: CUSTOMIZED REPORT DISTRIBUTION—USING CRYSTAL ENTERPRISE EMBEDDED EDITION

Part VII presents a detailed look into the Object Model of the Report Application Server (RAS) through Java and .NET/COM code samples and tutorials. This object model and service provide a scaleable means to include Crystal Report Distribution in your custom applications without all the bells and whistles of the full-fledged Crystal Enterprise Professional system.

PART VIII: CUSTOMIZED REPORT DISTRIBUTION—USING CRYSTAL ENTERPRISE PROFESSIONAL

Part VIII provides a detailed look into the object model of the Crystal Enterprise system through Java and .NET/COM code samples and tutorials. All the functionality described in Parts V and VII is included in this rich object model and allows developers to quickly include the powerful functionality of Crystal Enterprise and Crystal Reports in their custom applications.

EQUIPMENT USED FOR THIS BOOK

You can find various supporting material that will assist you in the completion of the exercises in this book, as well as supplemental documentation on related topics.

WEB RESOURCES

You can find all the source code for the examples in the book, as well as the appendix to the book, at an easy-to-find Web site. Just go to www.usingcrystal.com. You'll find report samples to download and code for you to leverage in your report design and sharing efforts. Also, a great deal of additional product-related information on the Business Objects Crystal suite of products including Crystal Reports, Crystal Analysis, and Crystal Enterprise can be found at www.businessobjects.com.

INTENDED AUDIENCE

This book was written to appeal to the full range of Crystal Reports, Crystal Analysis, and Crystal Enterprise users. You'll find this book useful if you've never used Business Objects Crystal Suite of products before, if you are a mature Crystal Reports user looking for some new productivity tips, or if you want to explore some of the new features found in version 10 and their related SDKs.

You don't have to be an expert, but you should have a basic understanding of the following concepts:

- Database systems such as Microsoft SQL Server, Oracle, Sybase, and Informix
- Operating system functions in Windows NT/2000/XP
- General Internet/intranet-based concepts such as HTML, DHTML, ActiveX, and Java

The first four parts of this book build on each other, so skipping around those parts isn't the best approach unless you have some familiarity with Crystal Reports 10. Even if you are familiar with Crystal Reports, many new features have been introduced in version 10, so you are encouraged to read the entire first half of the book so that you don't miss anything. The second half of the book is focused on the different forms of content delivery and each part can be approached independently without loss of context.

REQUIREMENTS FOR THIS BOOK

To get the most from this book, you should have access to a computer that has at least a Pentium II or equivalent processor, 128MB of RAM, and a Windows NT Workstation, 2000 Professional, Advanced Server, or Windows XP Professional.

All reports are based on sample data that is installed with Crystal Reports, so you will have access to the same data that was used in this book. You'll need to install Crystal Reports to get the most out of the examples included in each chapter in the first half of the book.

CONVENTIONS USED IN THIS BOOK

Several conventions are used within this book to help you get more out of the text. Look for special fonts or text styles and icons that emphasize special information.

- Formula examples appear in computer type, and they can be found on the Sams Publishing Web site as well.

- Objects such as fields or formulas normally appear on separate lines from the rest of the text. However, there are special situations in which some formulas or fields appear directly in the paragraph for explanation purposes. These types of objects appear in a special font like this: `Some Special Code`.

- In some cases, we might refer to your computer as *machine* or *server*. This is always in reference to the physical computer on which you have installed Crystal Reports.

- You'll always be able to recognize menu selections and command sequences because they're implemented like this:
  Use the File, Open command.

- New terms appear in *italics* when they are defined.

- Text that you are asked to type in appears in boldface.

- URLs for Web sites are presented like this: `http://www.crystaldecisions.com`.

NOTE

> Notes help you understand principles or provide amplifying information. In many cases, a note emphasizes some piece of critical information that you need. All of us like to know special bits of information that make our job easier, more fun, or faster to perform.

TIP

> Tips help you get the job done faster and more safely. In many cases, the information found in a tip is drawn from experience rather than through experimentation or documentation.

Sidebar

Sidebars spend more time on a particular subject that could be considered a tangent, but will help you be a better Business Objects product user as a result.

Real World sections provide some practical and productivity enhancing usage insights derived from the author's real-world experience designing and deploying hundreds of Crystal Reports.

The Troubleshooting sections provide some quick chapter summary notes and examples that are useful reminders on the product operations.

CRYSTAL REPORTS DESIGN

CHAPTER 1

CREATING AND DESIGNING BASIC REPORTS

In this chapter

INTRODUCING THE CRYSTAL REPORTS DESIGNER

This chapter takes you through the required steps to create your own basic reports in the Crystal Report Designer. After you've installed the Crystal Reports V.10 Designer, you are ready to open it and familiarize yourself with the environment. This section briefly introduces the following components of the application interface:

- Report sections
- Application toolbars
- Application menus

If you have already registered your installation, you should be presented with the Welcome to Crystal Reports screen shown in Figure 1.1. This screen provides quick access to existing Crystal Reports files while also enabling you to begin designing new reports via the Report Expert Wizard or from a blank report template.

Figure 1.1
The Welcome screen provides quick access to existing Crystal Reports files as well as the Report Expert Wizard.

CRYSTAL REPORT SECTIONS

From the Welcome dialog window, select Using the Report Wizard (listed below Create a New Crystal Report Document) and then click OK. You should see the Crystal Report Gallery dialog. Select As a Blank Report and click OK. At this point, you'll see a window labeled Data Explorer; click Cancel. If the Field Explorer window is also displayed, click Close.

You are presented with a blank report template that is divided into numerous report sections. As Figure 1.2 illustrates, report sections are identified by name on the left side of the design area. These sections segment the Crystal Reports design environment into logical areas to facilitate more intuitive report creation—these include the Report Header, Page Header, Details, Report Footer, and Page Footer sections. Each of these sections has unique properties and printing characteristics that you can modify. When creating reports, you place objects (such as data fields) into the various sections according to report requirements. If a report object such as an image is placed in the Report Header section, the image displays and prints only once per report, on the first page. If the same image is placed in the Page Header section, the image then displays and prints once per page. The same holds true for custom sections, such as Group Headers and Group Footers. The Details section implies that whatever is placed in this section displays and prints once for each and every row retrieved from the data source.

Figure 1.2
Report sections provide an intuitive way to create and organize your data when designing reports.

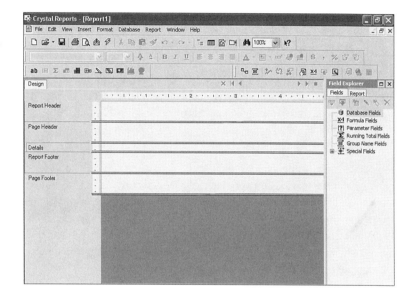

NOTE

Although Crystal Reports is commonly used for Web reporting initiatives, the design environment is built on a paper metaphor with *pages* as a concept to facilitate the presentation of information.

Report sections can contain a variety of different object types, including database fields, text, pictures, charts, and map objects. Additional objects, such as formula and subreport objects, are also positioned within report sections and are covered later in the book in greater detail.

The Section Expert is used to view or modify the properties of the report sections. To access the Section Expert, perform one of the following actions:

- Right-click on the section's label (or name, located on the left sidebar) you want to work with, and then select Section Expert from the pop-up menu.
- Click on the Section Expert button.
- Select the Section Expert option from the Format menu.

NOTE

When designing reports, you should consider the following items when working with report sections:

- It is good practice to print a validating test page of each report you are designing.
- Consider keeping all font sizes the same within each section for maximum eye appeal.
- Print preprinted forms on the same machine to avoid discrepancies in the interpretation of the report layout by different print drivers and printers.

Crystal Reports also provides some more advanced section formatting options, reviewed later in the book, such as underlaying and suppressing sections based on certain criteria (formulas). These features are accessible from the Section Expert dialog.

USING TOOLBARS AND MENUS

Toolbars are the graphical icon bars at the top of the Crystal Reports application environment, containing various buttons that you can click to activate the most frequently used application commands. Toolbars act as shortcuts to access commonly used functions of the design application, and you can enable or disable them to appear or disappear at the top of the application area by selecting Toolbars from the View menu, which is located in the upper-most area of the application. As Figure 1.3 shows, there are four main toolbars that you can use within the Crystal Reports design environment:

- Standard—The most commonly used application functions, including New, Open, Save, Print, Preview, Export, Copy, Cut, Paste, and Help.
- Formatting—Functions that pertain specifically to modifying object properties with regard to Font, Font Size, Bold, Italics, Underline, Alignment, Currency, and Percentage formats.
- Insert Tools—Quick access to the building blocks of all reports including Text Objects, Summary Fields, Groups, Online Analytical Processing and Cross-Tab Grids, Charts, and Maps, and Drawing items such as lines and boxes.
- Expert Tools—Functions that enable you to access the main application experts quickly, such as the Database, Group, Select, Section, Formula Workshop, and Highlighting Experts.

Figure 1.3
The Four Crystal Reports Design Toolbars provide quick and easy access to commonly used application commands during report design.

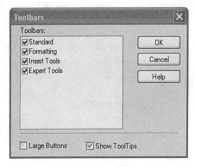

NOTE

> ToolTips are pop-up descriptions that appear when your cursor rests over any of the toolbar buttons. ToolTips are enabled by default. To disable ToolTips on your toolbars, deselect the Show ToolTips check box from within the Toolbars dialog.

In much the same way that the toolbars offer quick and easy access to commonly used commands, the menu items at the top of the application environment provide listings to virtually all the application functions available in Crystal Reports. The menu items act as shortcuts to all the commands within the design application, and they include the following items:

- The File menu includes file-specific commands to create a new report file, open an existing report, close a current report, save a report, save a report with an alternative filename, export to a different file format, save the current data set with a report, and secure a report so that it cannot be opened by other users. In addition, the File menu contains commands that enable you to preview a report before printing, send a report to a printer, select a specific printer, modify the page setup and margins, and add summary information to a report.

- The Edit menu includes commands used to modify various aspects of a report, including commands to undo and redo actions, as well as to cut, copy, and paste report and OLE objects. Additionally, you can edit fields, formulas, summaries, and subreport links.

NOTE

> *Object Linking and Embedding (OLE)* enables you to insert objects (OLE objects) into a report from other applications and then use those applications from within Crystal Reports to edit the objects if necessary. If Crystal Reports did not make use of OLE, you would have to exit Crystal Reports, open the original application, change the object, return to Crystal Reports, delete the object originally inserted, and then insert the newly revised object.

- The View menu includes commands used to customize the user interface of the Crystal Reports application. The View menu commands enable you to navigate between the application's Design and Preview views, access the three main explorers (Field, Report, and Repository Explorers), access the Toolbars dialog, zoom in and zoom out of a report, as well as to turn on and off the application rulers, guidelines, grids, and group tree from both the Design and Preview views of the report.

- The Insert menu includes commands used to insert text objects, summaries (counts, sums, medians, and so on), groups, subreports, lines, boxes, pictures, charts, maps, and other objects into your report. The Insert menu becomes very convenient when designing reports that include a variety of objects, such as a corporate logo and summary figures.

- The Format menu provides easy access to a variety of commands useful in formatting your reports for presentation purposes. This menu includes commands used to change the characteristics of the objects in a report. The Format menu provides quick access to commands for modifying font properties (color, size, borders, background color, and drop shadows for example), chart and hyperlink properties, and formatting for entire sections of the report. The Format menu also provides commands to arrange report objects (move, align, and size) and to specify desired highlighting characteristics via the Highlighting Expert.

- The Database menu includes commands used to access the Database Expert, from which you can add and remove data source tables for use within reports, specify links between data source tables, and modify table and field alias names. This menu also provides easy access to the set database location and enables you to log on and off SQL and ODBC servers, browse field data, and display and edit the report SQL syntax. In general, the Database menu enables you to maintain the necessary specifications for the report with regard to the data source(s) with which the report interacts.

- The Report menu includes commands used to access the main application experts (also referred to as *wizards*), identify the desired records or groups to be included in a report via the Select Expert and Selection Formulas (often referred to as applying report *filters*), construct and edit formulas, create and view alerts, specify report bursting indexes, modify grouping and sorting specifications, refresh report data by executing the query to run against the database, and view report performance information.

- The Chart menu is only visible after selecting a chart or map object and includes specific commands used to customize your charts and maps. Depending on the type of chart you select, the Chart menu includes commands to zoom in and out of charts; apply changes to all instances of a chart; discard custom changes made to the chart; save the chart template to a file; apply and modify template specifications for the chart; change the titles, numeric axis grids, and scales of the chart; and auto-arrange the appearance of the chart. After selecting a map object, the Chart menu then includes additional commands used to configure the overall style of the map, reorganizing the layers of report elements, changing the geographic map, and hiding or showing the Map Navigator.

- The Window menu includes commands used to rearrange the application icons and windows, as well as providing a list of report windows that are currently open and a command that enables you to close all report windows at once.

- The Help menu includes commands used to quickly access the Crystal Reports online help references, commands to register Crystal Reports and locate the Welcome screen, and quick access to the About Crystal Reports dialog and several key Business Objects Web sites for technical support and product information.

REPORT DESIGN EXPLORERS

Several report design explorers, intended to streamline the report design process, compose another key component to Crystal Reports 10. The design explorers are application tools that greatly enhance a report designer's efficiency while working with reports. They are design tools you will use in building reports throughout the remainder of the book.

The report design explorers are dialog windows that display various objects relevant to the report in a hierarchical tree view facilitating quick access to and formatting of each respective object and its properties. The explorers enable you to easily locate and navigate to specific report objects, such as the report header or a corporate logo image, to customize the object for design purposes. All the objects included in a report (report sections, groups, database fields, formulas, parameters, images, charts, and so on) are organized and displayed within one of the design explorers. There are three distinct explorers:

- Report Explorer—Provides a tree view of each report section in the report and each of the report objects contained within each section. You can work with each report object directly from the explorer rather than navigating to each object separately in either the Design or Preview tab of the report.

- Field Explorer—Displays a tree view of database fields, formulas, SQL expressions, parameters, running totals, groups, and special fields. You can add any of these field types directly to a report from the Explorer dialog. Fields that have already been added to the report or fields that have been used by other fields (such as formula fields, groups, summaries, and so on) have a green check mark icon in front of them.

- Repository Explorer—Provides a tree view of each object contained in the Crystal Enterprise report repository. You can work with each report repository object directly from the Repository Explorer rather than locating each object separately for inclusion in the report during the report design process.

NOTE

It is important to emphasize that with Version 10, the centralized Crystal Repository is only available for use with Crystal Enterprise. See Chapter 18, "Crystal Reports Semantic Layer–Business Views," for more details on this topic.

LOCATING AND USING THE REPORT DESIGN EXPLORERS

Each of the explorer dialogs can be *docked* in place or used in a free-floating state. By default, the Report and Field Explorers appear docked on the right side of the report design environment. However, you can manually dock each of them in other locations if you prefer. The explorers can also be used in free-floating mode, in which case each of the explorer dialog windows can be dragged to any location within the report design environment and float in place until you either close or reposition them. To view each of the report design explorers, click the View menu and select each desired explorer individually, as shown in Figure 1.4.

TIP

To save space in the design environment, the individual explorers can be dragged on top of each other and provide their functionality through respective tabs in a single dialog. This is the default position for the Field and Report Explorer in a fresh install but note in Figure 1.4 how the Report Explorer has been dragged into its own dialog with the Repository Explorer exposing itself through a tab in that same dialog.

Figure 1.4
By default, the design explorers are docked on the right side of the report designer application but can be moved about and toggled on and off.

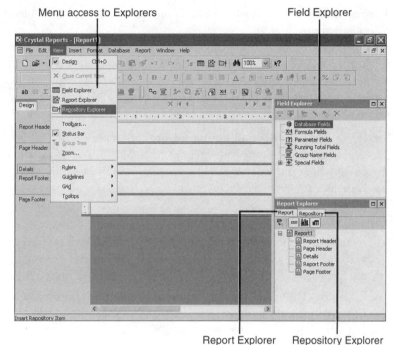

The report design explorers create an intuitive way for report designers to add and format report objects quickly while constructing reports. As you progress through the remainder of the book, you will be using these explorers on a regular basis, so it's important that you understand the basics of these application features.

UNDERSTANDING DATA AND DATA SOURCES

The first step in creating a report is always to identify a data source. Today, Crystal Reports supports more than one hundred different types of data sources. These data sources range from traditional databases such as Microsoft SQL Server, Oracle, IBM DB2, and Microsoft Access to other more abstract forms of structured data such as log files, e-mail, XML, COM/.NET/EJB objects, and multidimensional (OLAP) data. Many of the advanced data sources and their specific nuances are covered in great detail in Chapters 15–18.

To determine which database driver to use to connect to a certain data source, it's best to understand the different types of database drivers. The following sections discuss direct and indirect access database drivers.

UNDERSTANDING DIRECT ACCESS DRIVERS

Direct access database drivers are built solely for reporting from a specific type of database such as Oracle. If a direct access driver (sometimes called a *native* driver) exists for the database that you intend to report from, it is generally the best choice. Although they follow the standard model of a database driver, direct access drivers are tailored for that specific database. For example, if you choose the Microsoft Access direct access driver during the creation of a report, you will be prompted for the filename of the Access MDB file. If you are using the Oracle direct access driver, you will be prompted for a server name. Not only is the user experience more specific to that database, a direct access driver often results in better performance than other methods of connecting to the same data. Table 1.1 lists some of the most common direct access database drivers.

TABLE 1.1 COMMON DIRECT ACCESS DATABASE DRIVERS	
Direct Access Driver	**Description**
Microsoft Access	Used to access Microsoft Access databases and Microsoft Excel spreadsheets
Oracle	Used to access Oracle database servers
DB2	Used to access IBM DB2 database servers

UNDERSTANDING INDIRECT ACCESS DRIVERS

As you might guess from the name, an indirect access driver is one that connects indirectly to an actual data source. Indirect access drivers are not built for any one type of database, but rather are built to read data from a variety of data sources via a standard data access mechanism. The purpose of these drivers is to enable Crystal Reports to use data sources for which direct access drivers do not exist. The two major indirect access drivers provided are ODBC and OLE DB.

ODBC, which stands for *Open Database Connectivity*, is a long-standing technology built to connect various applications to various data sources via a common mechanism called an ODBC driver. Just as Crystal Reports has a concept of database drivers that enables data access to report developers, ODBC has a concept of ODBC drivers that enables data access to any application. The Crystal Reports ODBC database driver communicates with an ODBC driver, which in turn communicates with the actual database. ODBC drivers are generally developed by the database vendors themselves and often come bundled with the database software.

OLE DB, pronounced "*OH-lay-dee-bee*," is the evolution of ODBC. Like ODBC, OLE DB has a concept of database drivers, but calls them OLE DB providers. Crystal Reports can read most OLE DB providers. Figure 1.5 illustrates the various ways to connect to your data.

NOTE

> If appropriate, any necessary database client software should be installed and configured prior to installing Crystal Reports. However, if you've installed Crystal Reports before installing the database vendor's client software, follow the directions located in the Crystal Reports Help files to ensure correct configuration of the Crystal Reports system Data Source Names (DSNs).

Figure 1.5
The Crystal Reports data access architecture provides unparalleled data access.

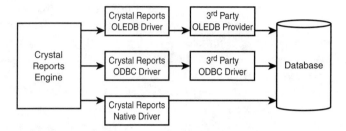

INTRODUCTION TO THE DATA EXPLORER

Now that you've got a basic understanding of what database drivers are and an idea of which one you might use to access a particular data source, let's look at the user interface for selecting the data source for a report. Because this is the first step in the creation of a report, it is only natural that this is the first step in the Report Wizard. This is shown in Figure 1.6. The Data Explorer is a tree control hosted inside the Report Wizard that enables you to identify the following:

- Which Crystal Reports database driver you want to use
- Which data source you want you use
- Which database objects you want to use

Figure 1.6
The Data Explorer provides access to the multitude of supported Crystal Report's data sources.

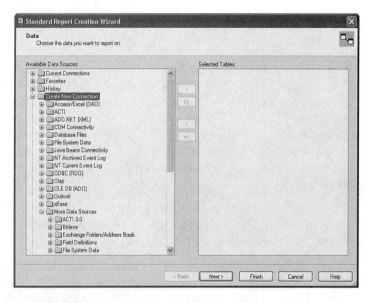

To open the Data Explorer, select File, New and click OK to create a new report using the Report Wizard. The Data Explorer represents data source connections organized into a number of categories. The following sections describe each of these categories, whereas Crystal Repository is discussed in Chapter 18.

CREATING A NEW CONNECTION

To specify a new connection, expand the Create New Connection node in the Data Explorer. As Figure 1.6 shows, you can select from a multitude of data sources in this interface. You will notice a node in this section for each of the drivers selected during the installation process.

NOTE

One node to take special note of is the More Data Sources node. When this is expanded, it lists all database drivers that are available but not installed. Crystal Reports supports *install on-demand*. This means that various features always appear as being available, even if they are not installed. When you expand one of the database driver's node selections under the More Data Sources node, that driver would be installed on-demand. Then the next time the Data Explorer is loaded, it would list that driver directly under the Create New Connection node.

Now that you understand which data sources are listed where, look at the process of creating a connection. To create a connection, follow these steps:

1. Expand the node that corresponds to the appropriate database driver. An easy one to play with is the Xtreme sample database that comes with Crystal Reports 10. To create a connection to this database, expand the ODBC (RDO) node.

2. Notice that when a node is expanded, a dialog is presented that allows for the specification of connection information. In the case of ODBC, the DSN is the only thing required. In this list of available DSNs, Xtreme Sample Database 10 should be visible. This is pre-installed with Crystal Reports. Select this and click Finish.

3. Focus returns to the Data Explorer, and there should be a node below the ODBC (RDO) node called Xtreme Sample Database. Below that node is the list of available tables and views, as well as the Add Command option for adding a SQL command. (This will be discussed shortly.)

The Xtreme Sample Database could also have been used via the OLE DB or direct Access driver. Note that when prompted for connection information when using one of these drivers, the report developer is asked to provide different information. In the case of ODBC, a DSN needed to be selected, whereas with OLE DB, a provider would need to be specified.

USING CURRENT CONNECTIONS

The Current Connection node lists all database connections that are currently open. In other words, if a report is currently open or was recently open, that connection is listed under the Current Connections node. The first time the Crystal Reports designer is opened, the Current Connection node is empty because no connections have been initiated. This is indicated by a "…no items found…" item shown when the Current Connections node is expanded. This is a quick way to select the same connection as another report currently open.

USING FAVORITE CONNECTIONS

The Favorites node lists all connections that have been designated a favorite. This is analogous to favorites and bookmarks in a Web browser. If you have a certain database connection that is used often, adding it to the favorites makes it quick and easy to find in the future.

To accomplish this, create a connection to a database (you can use the Xtreme Sample Database to try this out), and select Add to Favorites when right-clicking on that connection. Be sure to right-click on the connection and not the driver or table name. Figure 1.7 illustrates the Xtreme Sample Database connection being added to a user's Favorites.

Figure 1.7
Add the Xtreme
Sample Database
ODBC connection to
the Favorites node to
locate it quickly.

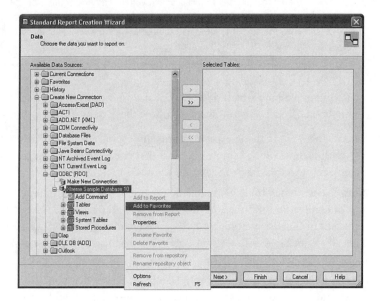

LEVERAGING RECENTLY USED CONNECTIONS WITH THE HISTORY NODE

The History node is situated beneath the Favorites node in the Data Explorer. It lists recent database connections that have been made. This is useful for quickly locating and using a connection that has been recently used, but not added to the Favorites list. The history list stores the last few connections. If you find yourself using connections from the History node frequently, it might be better to add the connection to your favorites list.

ADDING DATABASE OBJECTS TO YOUR REPORT

The term *database objects* is used to describe the various forms of data that can be added to a report. Specifically, Crystal Reports can use the following types of database objects as data sources for a report:

- Tables or system tables
- Views

- Synonyms
- Stored procedures
- SQL Commands

Database objects are listed underneath connections in the Data explorer and are grouped by object type. In Figure 1.8, the various database objects are shown for the Xtreme Sample Database. In this case, there are tables, views, system tables, and stored procedures. The Add Command node gives you the ability to add SQL commands to this report.

TIP

You can control the objects that are displayed in the Data Explorer by setting selection, description, and filtering options accessed from either the Database tab of the Options dialog under the File menu or the Options menu option off the database's right-click context menu. This can be particularly useful when you are reporting off databases with hundreds of tables.

Figure 1.8
The Data Explorer presents database objects in their logical categories.

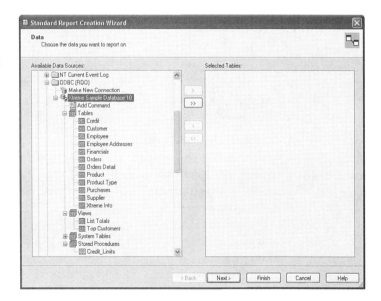

The following sections describe the most common database object types in further detail.

REPORTING ON TABLES

Tables are the most basic form of a data structure. Simply put, a table is a set of fields bound together to represent something in the real world. A Customer table might contain fields that describe all the customers of a given business. An Employee table might store information about a corporation's employees such as name, title, or salary.

To add a table to a report, select the table in the Data Explorer and click the arrow (>) button. The table is added to the Selected Tables list on the right side of the dialog below its corresponding connection. Most database administrators give the tables meaningful names; however, sometimes tables can have quite archaic names, such as RM564_321. A name like this isn't very descriptive, so it would be useful to rename this table to something more meaningful. To rename a table, select it in the Selected Tables list and press the F2 button (F2 is a standard convention for renaming things in Windows). In Crystal Reports, renaming a table is referred to as *aliasing* a table.

REPORTING ON VIEWS

A *view* is a query stored by the database that returns a set of records that resemble a table. Views often perform complex query logic, and good database administrators create them to simplify the job of people (like report developers) extracting data out of the database. For example, the Top Customers view in the Xtreme Sample Database returns all customers who have sales of more than $50,000. From a report developer's perspective, views act just like tables and can be added to the report in the same way.

REPORTING ON STORED PROCEDURES

Stored procedures, in the context of Crystal Reports, are similar to views in that they are predefined queries in the database and return a set of records. The major difference is that a stored procedure can be parameterized. This means that rather than having a preset query that returns the same data every time it is run, stored procedures return different data based on the values of parameters passed in.

Adding a stored procedure to a report works much the same way as tables and views. However, if the stored procedure has a parameter, a dialog appears when you attempt to add the stored procedure to the report. This is shown in Figure 1.9. The dialog asks you to provide values for each of the stored procedures' parameters. After you complete this and click the OK button, focus returns to the Data Explorer and the stored procedure is shown in the list of selected tables. At this time, a parameter is created in the report that corresponds to the stored procedure parameter, and any values that parameter is given are passed to the underlying stored procedure.

REPORTING ON SQL COMMANDS

When reporting from tables, views, and stored procedures, Crystal Reports generates a query behind the scenes using the *Structured Query Language (SQL)*. This is beneficial because the report developer does not need to understand the complexity of the SQL language, but rather can just drop fields onto the report and get data back that matches those fields. However, sometimes report developers are quite experienced with databases and specifically, the SQL language. Because of this, they sometimes prefer to write their own SQL query rather than have Crystal Reports generate it for them. For an introduction to the SQL language, refer to Appendix A, "Using SQL Queries in Crystal Reports."

Figure 1.9
Adding a stored procedure with a parameter invokes the Enter Parameter Values dialog.

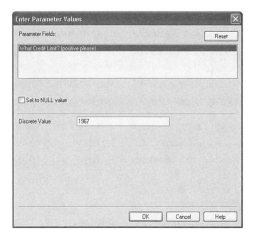

SQL Commands enable you to use your own prebuilt SQL query and have the Crystal Reports engine treat that query like a *black box*. This means that any query, whether simple or very complex, that returns a set of records can be used as a data source for a Crystal Report. To create a SQL Command, select the Add Command item under the database connection, and then click the arrow (>) button. This initiates a dialog that enables the user to type in a SQL query. Figure 1.10 illustrates a typical query.

Figure 1.10
Adding a typical SQL Command to a report.

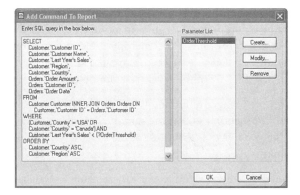

After the query is typed in and the OK button is clicked, focus returns to the Data Explorer, and the newly created command is represented as 'Command' underneath its corresponding connection. As with all database objects, selecting the command and pressing the F2 button enables the user to rename the object.

One key feature of SQL Commands is parameterization. If you had to create a static SQL query, much of the power of SQL Commands would be lost. Fortunately, SQL Commands in Crystal Reports support parameters. Although parameters can be used in any part of the SQL Command, the most common scenario would be to use a parameter in the WHERE clause of the SQL statement to restrict the records returned from the query. To create a parameter, click the Create button in the Add Command to Report dialog. This initiates a dialog that enables the user to specify a name for the parameter, text to use when prompting for the parameter value, a data type, and a default value. After the OK button is clicked, the parameter appears in the Parameter list. To use this parameter, place the cursor where the parameter should be used in the SQL query, and double-click the parameter name. Figure 1.11 illustrates a simple SQL Command with an 'OrderThreshold' parameter.

When a SQL Command is created with a parameter, the report developer is prompted for a parameter value. This works much the same way as parameterized stored procedures in that a parameter is created automatically in the report that maps to the SQL Command parameter.

CAUTION

> Unlike version 9, SQL Commands can no longer be centrally stored and accessed in a centralized Crystal Repository without the Crystal Enterprise product. In fact, the Crystal Repository and all its reusable objects are now only available through Crystal Enterprise. A Repository Migration Wizard is distributed with Crystal Enterprise to facilitate a quick migration from the V.9 Crystal Reports–based Repository.

JOINING DATABASE OBJECTS TOGETHER

Up until this point, only reports based on a single table, view, stored procedure, or SQL Command have been discussed. However, it is quite common to have several disparate database objects in the same report. Crystal Reports treats all types of database objects as peers, which means that a single report can contain multiple tables, views, stored procedures, and SQL Commands. Because all database objects are treated as peers, the term *table* will be used from now on to describe any of these database objects.

Because of Crystal Reports' inherent basis on relational data, any time multiple tables are used, they must be linked together so that the sum of all database objects is a single set of relational records. The good news is that most of the time, Crystal Reports takes care of this automatically, and the report developer need not worry about linking.

To see this in action, create a connection to the Xtreme Sample Database and add both the Customer and Orders tables to the report. When clicking Next in the Report Wizard, the linking between those tables is displayed as shown in Figure 1.11. Each table is represented by a window. In addition to the name, each field in the table is listed inside the window, and those fields that are defined as indexed fields in the database are marked with colored arrows. Any links defined between tables are represented as arrows connecting the key fields from two tables. Based on general database theory, linking to a field that is indexed generally results in a better performing query, and indexing is highlighted in this dialog through the color-coded icons displayed beside the field names.

By default, Crystal Reports creates links based on name. In this case, both tables have fields with a name of Customer ID, so a link is already created. To accept this link, simply click

Next to move to the next step in the Report Wizard. If there were not a common field name, selecting the By Key option and clicking Auto-Link would attempt to create a link based on the fields defined in the database as keys. If neither of these methods of automatic linking work, the link must be manually created. This is very simple to do: Simply drag the field to link from one table and drop it onto the field from a second table.

Figure 1.11
You can link multiple tables together in the Report Wizard.

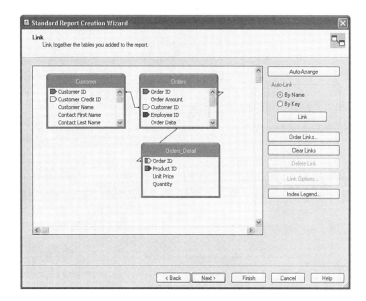

After links are created, you can configure them by clicking on the link arrow connecting two tables (it turns blue when selected), and then clicking the Link Options button. Links have two options: join type and link operator. These settings determine how Crystal Reports matches records from both tables. The default join type is an inner join, which means that only records with a matching key in both tables are included. The default link type is equal. For most cases, these two settings do not need to be modified.

UNDERSTANDING THE DIFFERENT JOIN TYPES

In Crystal Reports, the Link tab of the Report Wizard (and Database Expert) provides a visual representation of the relationship between multiple database objects. Defining the appropriate join strategy for any given report should be reflective of the data within the database objects and of how the report needs to read and display that data. Join type settings enable you to control more precisely the query results based on your unique requirements. The following is a list of the most common types of joins and their associated descriptions:

- Inner: The resultset includes all the records in which the linked field value in both tables is an exact match. The Inner join is the standard type of join for most reports, and it is also commonly known as the Equal join.

- Left Outer: The resultset includes all the records in which the linked field value in both tables is an exact match. It also includes a row for every record in the primary (left) table for which the linked field value has no match in the secondary (lookup) table. For example, if you would like your report to display all customers and the orders they have each placed—including the customers who have not placed any orders at all—you can use a Left Outer join between the Customer and Orders tables. As a result, you would see a row for every customer who has not placed any orders.

- Not Equal: The resultset includes all records in which the linked field value in the primary table is not equal to the linked field value in the secondary (lookup) table. For example, if you needed to report on all orders that were not shipped on the same date that they were ordered, you could use the Not Equal join type to join the OrderDate field in the Orders table with the ShipDate field in the OrderDetails table.

- Full Outer: The resultset includes all records in both of the linked tables—all records in which the linked field value in both tables is an exact match, in addition to a row for every record in the primary (left) table for which the linked field value has no match in the secondary (lookup) table, and a row for every record in the secondary (lookup, or right) table for which the linked field value has no match in the primary table. The Full Outer join is a bidirectional outer join, which essentially combines the characteristics of both the Left Outer and Right Outer joins into a single join type.

NOTE

> The capability to enforce links created in a report is new to version 10. Enforcing a link between two tables ensures that this link will be used in the report's respective SQL, regardless of whether fields are required from either or both of the involved tables. The default setting is Un-enforced links, meaning that the link will only be used if the report's respective SELECT statement requires it. Access to the different enforcing options is provided by right-clicking on a link and selecting the Link Options menu item.

After a report is created, select Database Expert from the Database menu to return to the Data Explorer. Here tables and SQL Commands can be added, removed, and renamed just as they could from the Data Explorer in the report creation process.

USING THE REPORT CREATION WIZARDS

Now that you have been quickly introduced to the Crystal Reports development environment and reviewed data access, a good place to begin creating reports is with the default report wizards. The report wizards are provided to expedite the report design process for report designers of all skill levels, but they are especially useful for new users of Crystal Reports.

The report wizards, also commonly referred to as *report experts*, provide a simplified interface and guided path to constructing the fundamental elements found within most reports.

As a result, designing interactive, professional looking reports can be achieved in a matter of minutes.

This section reviews the Report Gallery and the various wizards available based on the report style you choose. You will then explore these report wizards—the different options available depending on the report requirements you are trying to achieve—and discuss the Report Explorer components. This chapter also provides a tutorial that walks you through the report design process using the Standard Report Creation Wizard to create a useful, professionally styled report.

TIP

> Using the default report wizards as a starting point for beginners on most reports is a good idea. The report wizards offer a shortcut to establishing the core elements required for most reports.

UNDERSTANDING THE CRYSTAL REPORTS GALLERY

The Report Gallery is a special dialog that is presented when you choose to create a new report file. The Report Gallery is a shortcut to various report creation wizards, which facilitate the guided, visual creation of reports.

As Figure 1.12 illustrates, the Crystal Reports Gallery is a dialog that serves as the gateway to accessing and using the various report creation wizards. From the Report Gallery dialog, you can select from one of the four provided report wizards:

- Standard—Used to create traditional columnar-styled reports.
- Cross-Tab—Used to create summary styled Cross-Tab reports.
- Mail Labels—Used to create reports with multiple columns, such as address labels.
- OLAP—Used to create summary styled Cross-Tab reports that are based on an OLAP data source.

Figure 1.12
The Crystal Reports Gallery dialog provides quick access to the various report creation wizards.

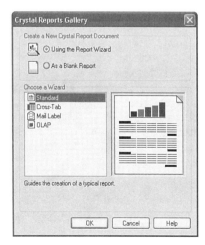

The remainder of this section focuses on exploring and using the Standard Report Creation Wizard. In general, this is the most commonly used report wizard, and it provides a good introduction to the components of the report design process. If your interests lie in either OLAP or Cross-Tab reports, they are covered in later chapters.

USING THE STANDARD REPORT CREATION WIZARD

The Standard Report Creation Wizard is the most frequently used design assistant in Crystal Reports. It provides multiple dialogs common to creating reports that are based on conventional corporate data sources. The Standard Report Creation Wizard guides you through selecting a data source, linking data source tables, adding data source fields to the report, specifying field groupings, identifying summary (total) fields, and setting the desired sort criteria for your report.

Additionally, the Standard Report Creation Wizard walks you through creating chart objects, applying record selection criteria (data filters), and applying predefined templates (layouts) to your report.

NOTE

> The term *filter* is commonly used to describe data selection criteria that narrow the scope of the data being extracted by the report from the underlying data source. For example, by using a filter such as Country = USA, you can easily limit your report to include only the information you are interested in extracting.

The Standard Report Creation Wizard consists of nine dialog screens that enable you to specify the criteria mentioned previously to create a professional-looking report quickly. The sequence of the wizard's dialog screens is dynamic and directly associated with the items selected in each of the progressive screens. For example, if you do not choose to identify any summary items for your report, you will not be presented with a Chart dialog screen. In general, charts apply best to summarized data, so if you have not identified any summary fields, the wizard assumes that you do not want to include a chart object in your report.

NOTE

> Charts can also be created from base-level data, although to do this you must appropriately specify the On Change Of option and use the Advanced settings with the Chart Expert. Generally, it makes more sense to base chart objects on summary-level data, such as regional sales by quarter—where you are charting the total sales for each quarter rather than each sales transaction in each quarter.

The following exercise steps through the wizard and builds a sales report to display last year's sales by country. By making use of the Standard Report Creation Wizard, you include the country, city, customer name, and last year sales database fields, graphically display a summary of last year sales by country, and apply professionally styled formatting to the report. To create the sales report, follow these steps:

1. From the Report Gallery dialog, select Using the Report Wizard in the upper portion of the screen, and then select Standard from the wizard list in the lower portion of the screen. Click OK to initiate the Standard Report Creation Wizard.

2. As shown in Figure 1.13, you should now be presented with the first dialog—labeled Data—as part of the Standard Report Creation Wizard. From the Data dialog screen, expand the Create New Connection node and then expand the ODBC listing as well. This should present the ODBC Data Source Selection dialog.

Figure 1.13
The Standard Report Creation Wizard begins by requesting a data source for your report.

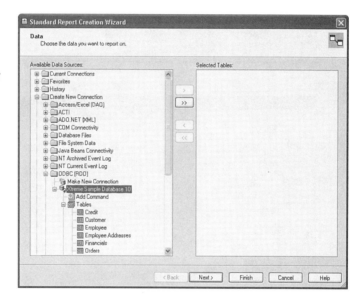

3. From the ODBC Data Source Selection dialog, scroll to the end of the Data Source Name list and select Xtreme Sample Database 10, as shown in Figure 1.14. Click Next to continue.

4. Verify that the Data Source Name is correct and click Finish from the ODBC Connection Information dialog. No password is necessary to access this database.

5. After you have successfully identified and connected to Xtreme Sample Database 10, you should see this item listed under the ODBC node in the Available Data Sources area of the Data dialog screen, as shown in Figure 1.15. Upon expanding the Xtreme Sample Database 10 item, you should see three or four distinct data source items listed: Tables, Views, and Stored Procedures—and possibly System Tables dependent on your options settings (shown in Figure 1.16).

6. Within the Data dialog screen, select the Customer and Orders tables so that they are listed in the Selected Tables area on the right. After these two tables are selected, click Next to continue onto the Linking Dialog.

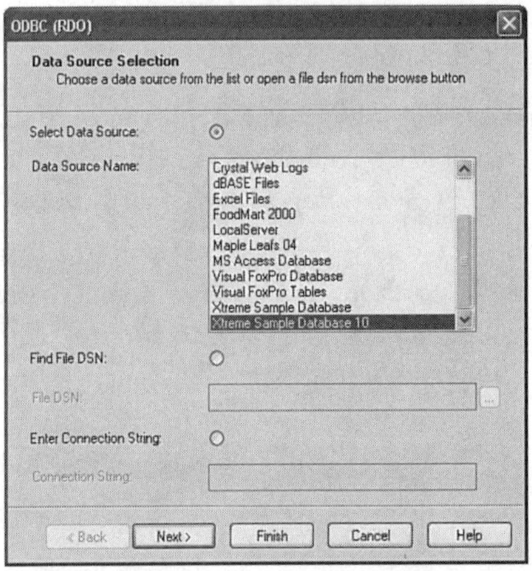

Figure 1.14
The ODBC Data Source Selection dialog enables you to select a valid connection to access your ODBC data sources.

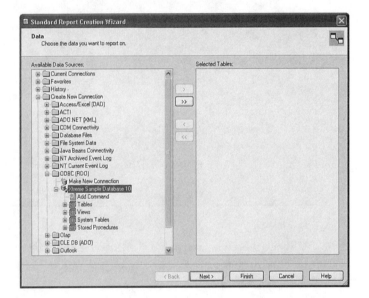

Figure 1.15
The Xtreme Sample Database is listed under the Available Data Sources area of the Data dialog.

TIP

There are multiple ways to include tables in your report from within the Data dialog screen. From the list of available tables on the left side of the dialog, you can perform any one of the following actions to populate the Selected Tables list on the right side of the dialog area:

- Double-click on each desired table item
- Drag-and-drop each desired table item
- Highlight the table item on the left and click on the respective arrow icons (> or >>) between the two listing areas to populate the listing on the right

Figure 1.16
Upon expanding the Xtreme Sample Database 10 item, you will notice multiple database items listed.

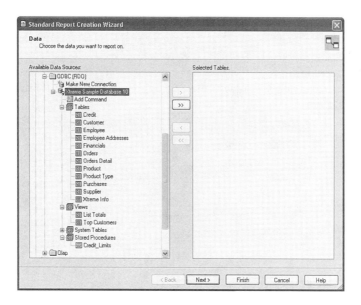

7. The Link dialog screen presents a visual representation of the relationship between these two tables and permits you to modify the defined relationship by specifying the exact *Join* links that you require to accurately report on the data within the selected tables. As shown in Figure 1.17, you should now see the Link dialog screen. For our purposes here, accept the default Join condition. Click Next to continue.

Figure 1.17
The Customer and Orders tables are linked together via the Customer ID field.

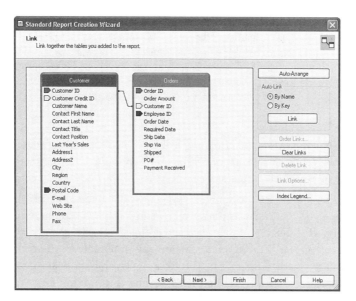

8. After specifying the table linking, you will see the Fields dialog screen, shown in Figure 1.18. Select the Customer Name, Country, and City fields from the Customer table and the Order Amount and Order Date fields from the Order table so that they appear under the Fields to Display area on the right. If necessary, you can use the up and down arrows to modify the order of these fields in the list. Click Next to continue.

Figure 1.18
The Customer Name, City, Country, Order Amount, and Order Date fields should appear under the Fields to Display area.

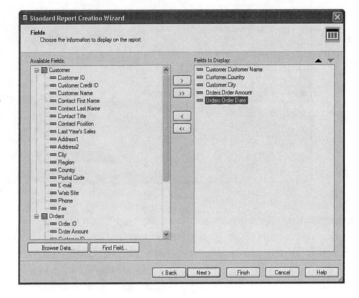

NOTE

If you're not sure of the data contained in any of the respective field items on the left, you can highlight a field name and click the Browse Data button to view a list of values from this field, as shown in Figure 1.19. This can be particularly useful if you are unfamiliar with the database and need to locate a field based on the values it contains, such as account numbers, policy codes, or employee names.

9. You should now see the Grouping dialog screen. This dialog enables you to specify logical groups of information within your reports. For this example, select to group by the Country field only, as shown in Figure 1.20. Click Next to continue.

10. You should now see the Summaries dialog screen. The Summaries dialog screen enables you to identify summary values (such as Sums, Counts, and so on) for your reports. If you have not identified any grouped items in a report, the Summaries dialog does not appear because summaries are only applicable to grouped data. To apply a summary object to the report, select the Order Amount field so that it appears under the Summarized Fields list on the right. This is shown in Figure 1.21. Click Next to continue.

Figure 1.19
The Browse Data button enables you to view a list of values from any of the available database field items.

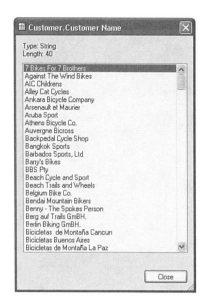

Figure 1.20
The Grouping dialog enables you to create structured groupings of information within your report.

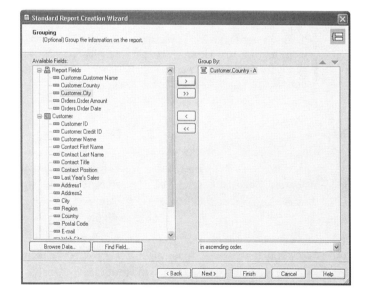

NOTE

As you might notice, Crystal Reports automatically chooses a summary for you if you choose to group your report data. It examines the detail information you've specified for the report and builds a summary on the first available numeric field. However, this default summary criteria is easily modified in the wizard.

Figure 1.21
The Summaries dialog screen enables you to create summarized values that are frequently used in coordination with the grouping structure within reports.

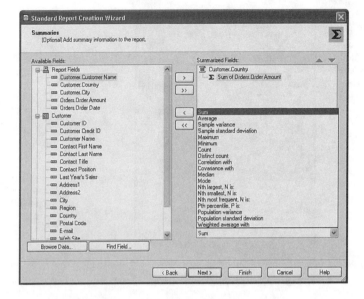

NOTE

> By default, the Order Amount field that appears under the Summarized Fields area on the right is aggregated as a Sum of the actual field value. As shown in Figure 1.21, the drop-down list located in the lower-right area of the Summaries dialog screen enables you to select from a variety of summaries, including Sum, Average, Maximum, Minimum, Count, Correlation, Covariance, and Standard Deviation.

11. Now sort the report based on the total order amounts of the top five countries. The Group Sorting dialog screen enables you to sort the grouped fields based on the summarized totals. From the Group drop-down list, select the Country field (the only option in the example here) and select the Top 5 Groups option from the Group Ordering choices. Also, select the Sum of Order Amount item from the Comparing Summarized Values drop-down list, as shown in Figure 1.22. Click Next to continue.

12. Charting can be added through the wizard to visually display the data already selected. From the Chart dialog screen, you can select a chart object to be included in the report based on the group and summary items you identify here. For this example, add a bar chart and select the Country field from the On Change Of drop-down list and the Sum of Order Amounts item from the Show Summary drop-down list. Change the chart title to read **Total Order Amounts by Country**—see Figure 1.23 for additional guidance. Click Next to continue.

13. Now you'll address the fictitious requirement that you are only interested in customer orders from the year 2000. The Record Selection dialog screen enables you to identify selection criteria, often called *data filtering*, to focus the resultset of the report to

include only the information you are interested in returning. To accomplish this, select Order Date as the Filter Field, choose Is Between from the filter operator drop-down list, and select a data range from the newly created date-range drop-down boxes to incorporate all the dates in 2000 (see Figure 1.24). Click Next to continue.

Figure 1.22
The Group Sorting dialog enables you to sort your report based solely on the Group values that you want to include in the report results.

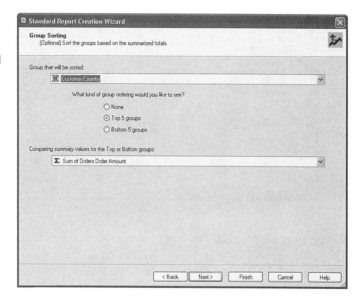

Figure 1.23
The Chart dialog enables you to select a chart object for a report based on the previously identified group and summary criteria.

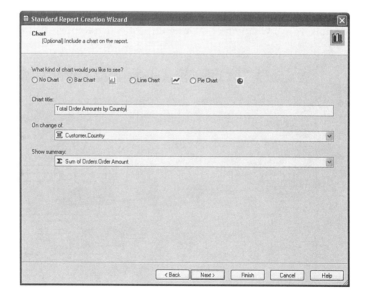

Figure 1.24
The Record Selection dialog permits you to narrow your resultset based on the selection criteria identified here.

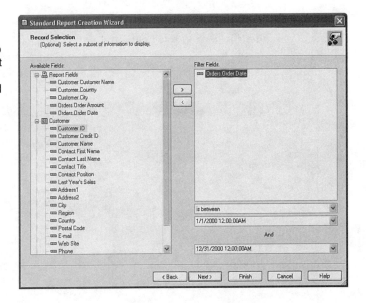

14. Finally, apply a predefined style to your report. From the Template dialog screen, you can select predefined styles to be applied to your report for formatting purposes, as shown in Figure 1.25. The Available Template list includes various sample templates that are included with the Crystal Reports 10 installation. However, you can also create your own templates to be used for report formatting. For this example, select the Corporate (Blue) template. For additional details on how to design and implement your own templates, see Chapter 14, "Designing Effective Report Templates."

Figure 1.25
The Template dialog permits you to select predefined styles to be applied to your report.

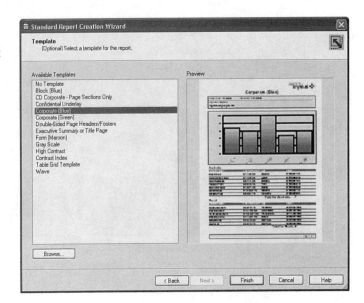

This now concludes the Standard Report Creation Wizard example. After you click Finish, you will execute the report that you have just created and will be presented with the preview of the corresponding resultset. At this point, you can click Finish if you are satisfied with the report design criteria. When you are presented with the preview of your report, save your new report by selecting Save As from the File menu. Name this report **Chap1Wizard.rpt** or anything you would like.

After you select Finish at the end of the Standard Report Creation Wizard process, you will be presented with the executed resultset and a preview of your newly created report. As Figure 1.26 shows, creating a useful and professional looking report is extremely simple when using the Standard Report Creation Wizard. In the preceding exercises, you have connected to a database, identified the tables and fields you wanted to include in your report, linked the tables together, grouped and summarized the data, sorted the data, applied filtering criteria, included a chart object for enhanced visualization of the report results, and applied a report template for quick and easy formatting—all in just a few clicks of your mouse! This process speaks both to the ease of use and power of the Crystal Reports design application.

Figure 1.26
The executed resultset and preview of the report you have just created using the Standard Report Creation Wizard.

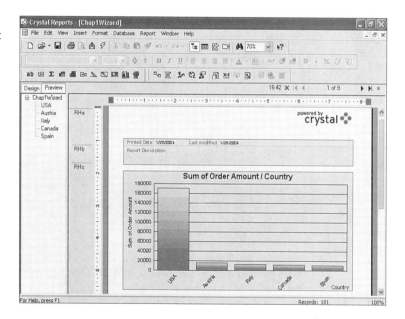

CREATING A REPORT WITHOUT WIZARDS

As with many software tools, educational tools and facilitators like the Report Wizards are often the best way to begin a learning process. They are by their nature, however, limited in functionality and it generally does not take long before maturing students want to roll up their sleeves and discover the raw power and incredible flexibility that lies beneath. This section reintroduces the report just created in the Report Wizard through a manual design process in the Crystal Reports Designer. The beginnings of that same Sales Report are created from scratch with the following steps:

1. Select a report template. After opening Crystal Reports, either click on the New button or access the New option from the File menu. Once in the Crystal Reports Gallery dialog, select As a Blank Report and click OK.

2. Select an appropriate data source. From the Database Expert dialog that comes up, in the Available Data-sources list, browse to Create New Connection, ODBC. As soon as you choose ODBC, the ODBC (RDO) dialog pops up. Scroll until you find the Xtreme Sample Database 10. Select it and click Finish. (There are no other settings to get this database working, so you can ignore the Next button.)

3. Select the appropriate tables. After choosing the appropriate database to connect to, you need to select the tables for this report. Move down in the left list box and expand the Tables item. Choose the Customer and Orders tables by using the right-arrow (>) button, shown in Figure 1.27.

Figure 1.27
The Data tab from the Database Expert dialog shows the two tables you just added to the report.

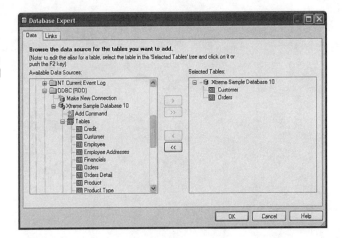

TIP

Remember that you can choose each table separately and click the arrow button or hold down the Ctrl key to select all tables that you want and then press the arrow button only once. Also, if you want to select several tables in a row, the Shift key helps you with that.

4. Link tables from the database. Move to the next tab in the Database Expert dialog by either clicking the OK button or selecting the Links tab. Notice that all the tables have already been linked. Crystal Reports attempts to link tables using similar field names and sizes whenever possible.

TIP

You can enlarge this dialog by using the stretch markers so that you can increase the display area and see more tables at once. The next time you enter this dialog, your adjusted size will be remembered.

You don't need to make any changes at this point, so just click the OK button.

5. Add detail records to the report. First, confirm that the Field Explorer is being displayed so that you can use it to add the fields to the report. If it is not, choose View, Field Explorer. In the Field Explorer that becomes available, open the Database Fields item and then the Orders item to expose the fields that you'd like to add. Select each field separately and drag it to the Design tab using your mouse. Place them side-by-side in the Details Section: Customer Name and Customer City from the Customer table, and Order Amount and Order Date from the Orders table. Figure 1.28 highlights the desired result.

Figure 1.28
This is the Design window after you've added all the fields.

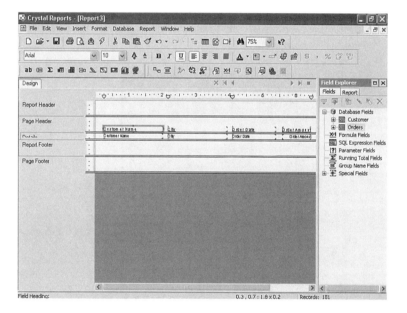

6. Create a logical grouping of data by Country. To accomplish this, choose Insert, Group. When the Insert Group dialog appears, scroll down the first list box until Country under the Customer table is available. Select it, as shown in Figure 1.29, and then click OK.

Notice that in the Design view of the report, two new sections become available called Group Header #1 and Group Footer #1. Within Group Header #1, the Group Name #1 field is also automatically added.

Figure 1.29
The Common tab of
the Insert Group dia-
log with the Customer
Name field selected.

7. Add a summary value of total Historical Order Amount by Country to the report.
Choose Insert, Summary to get the Insert Summary dialog to appear. In this dialog,
select the Order Amount field in the Field to Summarize drop-down box. Next, because
you plan on finding out how much has been ordered in each country, you need to set
the summary operation in the second list box to Sum. Last, because the desired summary is per Country, set the location of the summary to show Group #1, as shown in
Figure 1.30. Click OK.

Figure 1.30
The Insert Summary
dialog with Order
Amount summed by
Customer Name
selected.

TIP

A shortcut to the Insert Summary command (and running total command described
later) is accessible for each field on the report by right-clicking the involved field in the
report designer.

Notice that in the Design view, in the Group Footer #1, the Sum of Order Amount
field has been added.

8. View the report. Take a look at the report by choosing Report, Refresh Report Data or by either pressing the F5 key or clicking the lightning icon refresh/preview button in your Crystal Reports Designer. A report with all the data represented in the last wizard-driven report you created is returned in the Preview tab as shown in Figure 1.31.

Figure 1.31
The resulting report based on steps 1 through 8 in the Preview tab.

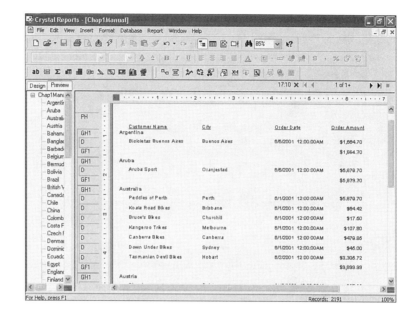

9. Save the report. Choosing File, Save opens the Save dialog. Provide a suitable name for the report, such as Chap1Manual.rpt. You are welcome to explore the charting and report template features now to replicate the Chap1Wizard report but they are covered in detail in Chapter 8, "Visualizing Your Data with Charts and Maps," and Chapter 14, "Designing Effective Report Templates."

> **TIP**
>
> If you are concerned about losing work between manual saves of a report, Crystal Reports has an autosave feature that you can enable. Set this option by navigating to File, Options, and then selecting the Reporting tab. The Autosave Reports After option can be set and the length of time in minutes between saves can be specified in the edit box for this option.

TROUBLESHOOTING

I AM HAVING DIFFICULTY LAUNCHING THE DATA EXPLORER.

To open the Data Explorer, select File, New and click OK to create a new report using the Report Wizard.

CRYSTAL REPORTS IN THE REAL WORLD—SQL COMMANDS

Experienced report developers will notice that the sample database is very simple (only a dozen tables) and that all the fields in the tables have useful names. In practice, it's very common for a database to have many more tables with very complex relationships and that the field names are not descriptive. This is where SQL Commands can help. This section explores the advantages of using SQL Commands to create reports. To take SQL Commands for a test-drive, follow these steps:

1. Open Notepad and type the following lines of SQL exactly as they appear here:

```
SELECT
     'Customer'.'Customer Name' AS Name,
     'Customer'.'City' AS City,
     'Orders'.'Order Date' AS OrderDate,
     'Orders'.'Order Amount' AS Amount
FROM
     'Customer' 'Customer' INNER JOIN 'Orders' 'Orders' ON
     'Customer'.'Customer ID'='Orders'.'Customer ID'
```

This is the SQL statement that will be used in the report.

2. Select a report template. After opening Crystal Reports, either click on the New button or access the New option from the File menu. Once in the Crystal Reports Gallery dialog, select As a Blank Report and click OK.

3. Select an appropriate data source. From the Database Expert dialog that opens, in the Available Data-sources list, browse to Create New Connection, ODBC. As soon as you choose ODBC, the ODBC (RDO) dialog pops up. Scroll until you find the Xtreme Sample Database 10. Select it and click Finish. (There are no other settings to get this database working, so you can ignore the Next button. These additional options will be discussed in a later chapter.)

4. Rather than selecting tables, double-click the SQL Command option. The Add Command To Report window pops up. Copy the SQL Command from Notepad into the box as shown in Figure 1.32.

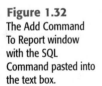

Figure 1.32
The Add Command To Report window with the SQL Command pasted into the text box.

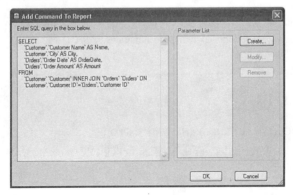

Click OK; notice that there is no need to link the tables because the SQL Command already defines the relationship between the tables. Notice also that there are only four fields to choose from and that the names have been changed.

The SQL Command does three things:

- **Hides database complexity.** Converts many tables into one view with the table relationships defined.

- **Hides unnecessary fields.** Many database fields are ID fields that simply aren't intended to be seen by users. The SQL Command can be constructed so these fields don't pass through.

- **Renames database fields.** Database field names are often unreadable and give no hint about what they contain. The SQL Command can rename these obscure names into something more meaningful.

CHAPTER 2

SELECTING AND GROUPING DATA

In this chapter

INTRODUCTION

The Field Explorer, which was introduced in Chapter 1, "Creating and Designing Basic Reports," provides a quick and easy way to select and display fields on your report and then easily drag and drop them onto the Report Design area. In addition to choosing existing fields from your selected data sources, the Field Explorer enables you to create calculated (formula) fields, parameter fields, running total fields, and group summary fields, as well as choose from a predefined set of default special fields. These additional objects enable a great deal of flexibility and power in the information you can deliver through the reports you create.

In addition to selecting the fields that make up the raw content for a report, it is often beneficial to group base-level data by country, region, or product line. Grouping the data facilitates relevant business user analysis and enables meaningful summarizations in your reports. Crystal Reports provides easy-to-use grouping functionality that enables nested groups, hierarchical grouping, and drill-down analysis into the different levels of grouping selected.

This chapter covers the following information:

- Understanding the different types of field objects
- How to add grouping to your reports
- How to add multiple groups to your report and reorder them
- Hierarchical grouping
- Creating and using drill-down in your reports
- Hiding and suppressing detail records in your reports

UNDERSTANDING FIELD OBJECTS

As described in Chapter 1, the Field Explorer displays a tree view of data fields in your report. It shows database fields, formula fields, SQL expression fields, parameter fields, running total fields, group name fields, and special system fields that you have defined for use in your report. This chapter introduces you to all the standard field types available in Crystal Reports.

To activate the Field Explorer, either select it from the View menu or click on the Field Explorer button in the Crystal Reports Standard toolbar. Figure 2.1 shows the sample Crystal Report created in the last chapter with the Field Explorer activated and docked on the right side of the screen. As previously mentioned, this can be docked on either side of the designer or at the bottom the screen. Alternatively, the Field Explorer can freely float over any part of the design window by simply dragging and dropping it.

Figure 2.1
Crystal Reports Designer with the Field Explorer docked on the right side.

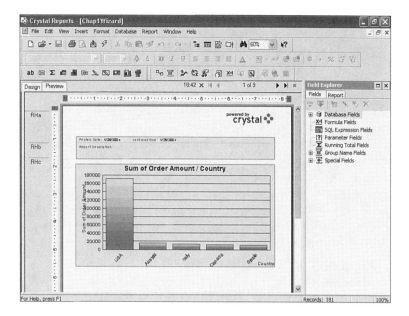

The next seven sections introduce the different types of fields accessible from the Field Explorer and provide ideas on where they might be used in a report. Subsequent chapters in the book cover some advanced uses of these types of fields. Before moving on to explore these different types of fields, here are some common traits shared by all field types:

- Fields that are being used in the report or fields that have been used by other fields (for example, formulas) being used in the report are highlighted with a green check mark in front of them.

- The buttons along the top of the Field Explorer (Insert, Browse, New, Edit, Rename, and Delete) are enabled or disabled based on the availability of the selected Field type.

- Detailed report field formatting, positioning, and resizing are covered in Chapter 6, "Fundamentals of Report Formatting."

ACCESSING DATABASE FIELDS

The Database Fields branch of the Field Explorer tree is used to add database fields to your report. The fields that can be added to your report are those from standard database tables, views, stored procedures, synonyms, and system tables. To add additional tables or other data sources to your report, you would use the Database Expert under the Database menu.

To insert the database fields that are available from the Field Explorer into your report, either click and drag them into the desired location on the report or select them, click the Insert to Report button (or Insert to Report action from the right-click menu), and then select the desired location on the report for the highlighted fields.

TIP

> If you are uncertain of exactly which fields to add to your report because of ambiguous (for example, WERKS, MENGE, LEAFS) or similar (for example, District, Region, Locale, Division) field names, you might be able to determine the appropriate field by selecting the respective field and using the Browse button (or the Browse action from the right-click menu) to view the data type and sample values of data from the table.

Multiple fields can be highlighted simultaneously in the Field Explorer and placed in the report designer window at once. Crystal Reports drops the first of the multiple chosen fields in the selected location on the report and places the subsequent fields in order to the right of the initial field. If the report's layout runs out of real estate on the right side of the report, the subsequent fields are placed one line down and the placement algorithm continues.

ACCESSING FORMULA FIELDS

Formula fields provide a means to add derived fields (that is, those not directly available in your database) such as a calculation into your Crystal Reports. Crystal Reports treats derived formula fields in exactly the same manner as it does original database fields. Some examples of where formulas might be used on the sample report from Chapter 1 would include the following:

- Days Until Shipped: A date formula determining the difference between the two database fields—Order Date and Ship Date

- Next Years Sales Projection: A numeric formula that multiplies the database field Last Years Sales by 110%

- Custom Name Field: To include the first letter of a customer contact's First Name (a database field) concatenated with a space and the contact's last name (another database field)

The formula fields branch of the Field Explorer tree is used to add existing or new formula fields to a report. A listing of previously created formulas appears in this part of the Field Explorer tree. Once created, existing formulas are added to the report by either clicking and dragging and dropping or by selecting the formula and using the Insert functionality—available through the right-click menu or Field Explorer action button—and then selecting the location.

TIP

> Both simple and complex formulas can be created on any type of field including numeric, date, string, Boolean, or memo fields. This is explored in Chapters 11, "Using Record Selections and Alerts for Interactive Reporting," and 13, "Using Formulas and Custom Functions."

If a new formula is required, it can be created directly from the Field Explorer by using the New toolbar button. You are prompted to name the new formula and then select the method of creation. This dialog is displayed in Figure 2.2.

Figure 2.2
The Formula Name dialog requires specification of a formula name.

Using the Xtreme Sample Database and the sample report created in Chapter 1 (chap1Wizard.rpt), one simple formula you might want to add is a Full Name field that comprises both the first and last name of the customer's contact person (Contact First Name and Contact Last Name in the Customer sample table).

To perform this task, implement the following steps:

1. After opening the **Chap1Wizard** report, highlight the Formula Fields branch of the Field Explorer tree.

2. Select New either by using the New button or right-clicking and selecting New from the fly-out menu.

3. Enter the Formula Name **Full Name** in the Formula Creation dialog and select the Formula Editor using the Use Editor button.

4. Scroll down in the Report Fields window (the top-left window in the main frame) to locate and open the Customer table. Select the Contact First Name field by double-clicking on it. The field displays in the main Formula Editing window.

5. Add a space after the Contact First Name field and then type in **+ " " +**. This concatenates the two fields together and also adds a space between the first name and the last name.

6. Scroll down in the Report Fields window (the top-left window in the main frame) to locate and open the Customer table. Select the Contact Last Name field by double-clicking on it. The field is displayed in the main Formula Editing window.

7. When you have confirmed that the main formula window looks exactly like that shown in Figure 2.3, save the Full Name formula by clicking the Save button and then closing the main Formula Editor window.

By selecting Save in the Formula Editor, you return to the Field Explorer and the new formula, Full Name, is now available to be placed on the report. Finish this section by placing the Full Name Formula Field onto the report beside the Customer Name.

ACCESSING SQL EXPRESSION FIELDS

The SQL Expression Fields branch of the Field Explorer tree is used to add existing or new SQL Expression fields to a report. A listing of previously created SQL Expressions appears in this part of the Field Explorer tree. Once created, existing SQL Expressions are added to the report by either clicking and dragging and dropping or by selecting the SQL Expression—using the Insert into Report button or action on the right-click menu—and selecting the location.

Figure 2.3
This is the Formula Editor after you created a String concatenation formula.

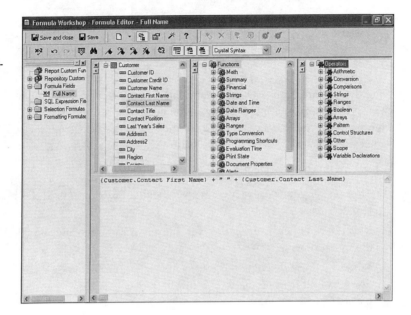

SQL Expressions are created in the same Formula Editor as formulas but use *Structured Query Language (SQL)* statements (rather than the formula syntax). SQL Expressions are used in cases where report-processing efficiency is critical. Using SQL expressions can give report designers greater report processing performance by pushing data processing to the database server instead of the Crystal Reports engine as this is generally most efficient.

→ For more information on SQL, **see** "An Introduction to SQL," **p. 820**

NOTE
The SQL syntax created in SQL Expressions must be appropriate to the source database. Different databases support various syntactical versions of SQL and even diverse degrees of functionality. This is explored in Appendix A, "Using SQL Queries in Crystal Reports."

ACCESSING PARAMETER FIELDS

Parameter fields provide a means to create dynamic reports and provide your business users with an interactive method of driving the report content or layout they view. When a Crystal Report contains parameters, it requests certain pieces of information from the business user before processing. The involved Crystal Report can then use those inputted parameters to filter the data that is presented or even suppress entire report sections. Some examples of where parameters might be used include

- A region parameter on a sales report

- A profit center on a financial report

- Beginning and ending dates on a transactional report

- A department on an HR salary listing report

- A salesperson name on a customer order listing report

The Parameter Fields branch of the Field Explorer tree is used to add existing or new parameter fields to your report. A listing of previously created parameters appears in this part of the Field Explorer tree. Once created, Parameter fields are added to the report by either clicking and dragging and dropping or by selecting the Parameter Field—using the Insert into Report button or action on the right-click menu—and selecting the location.

If a new parameter is required, it can also be created directly from the Field Explorer by using the New toolbar button. You are prompted to name the new parameter and enter some supporting information. This dialog is displayed in Figure 2.4.

Figure 2.4
The Create Parameter Field dialog enables you to specify a parameter name and supporting parameter type information.

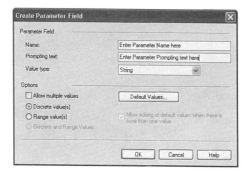

→ For detailed information on parameter creation and use as a means to filter report information, **see** "Creating and Implementing Parameters Fields," **p. 129**

At this point, it is only important to note the location of this field type.

IMPLEMENTING RUNNING TOTAL FIELDS

Running total fields provide a means to incrementally calculate a total on a report as the records are processed. In contrast to the summary fields you will learn about later in the book, running total fields enable you to control how a total is calculated, when it is reset, and when it is displayed. Some examples in which running total fields might be used include

- Running Total of Web site hits over multiple Days/Weeks/Months and so on

- Running Total of sales expenses over Weeks in a Quarter or Fiscal Year

- Running Total of average order amount over time
- Running Total of employee count over time

The Running Total Fields branch of the Field Explorer tree is used to add existing or new running total fields to your report. A listing of previously created running totals appears in this part of the Field Explorer tree. Once created, existing running total fields are added to the report by either clicking and dragging and dropping or by selecting the Running Total Field—using the Insert into Report button or action on the right-click menu—and selecting the location.

If a new running total is required, it can be created directly from the Field Explorer by using the New toolbar button. You are prompted to name the new running total. Select the field to calculate the running total on, the type of running total (for example, sum, average, variance, and so on), and some other supporting information about when the running total is to be evaluated and reset as shown in Figure 2.5.

Figure 2.5
The Create Running Total Field dialog enables you to specify a Running Total Name and its supporting information.

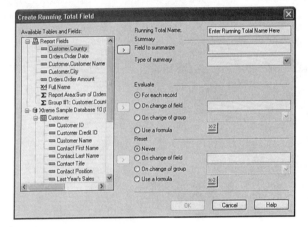

In the sample Customer Order Listing report from Chapter 1, an interesting running total to add would be one on the average order amount over time within each country. This running total tells senior sales management whether the average order size for each country is increasing or decreasing over time. To create this running total, follow these steps:

1. Open the sample report from Chapter 1 (Chap1Manual.rpt). Sort the data by ascending date by accessing the Record Sorting Expert from either the Report menu or the Record Sort icon on the Expert Tools toolbar. Then select Order Date as a secondary sort order after Country.
2. Highlight the Running Total Fields branch of the Field Explorer tree.
3. Select New using either the New toolbar button or by right-clicking and selecting New from the pop-up menu. This opens the dialog shown in Figure 2.5.
4. Enter the name **Avg Order Size** for the Running Total Name.

5. Select the Order Amount field from the Order Table as the Field to summarize by highlighting it in the field selection window and clicking on the Select button (>).

6. Because you want an average summary instead of the default Sum summary, select this from the Type of Summary drop-down box.

7. You want to calculate the average order amount for each order, so select the For Each Record option in the Evaluate section.

8. Because you want to calculate this for each Country, select the Reset On Change of Group option and select the Country group in the Reset section and click OK to finish.

The completed Running Total dialog is shown in Figure 2.6

Figure 2.6
The Edit Running
Total Field dialog with
Average Order Size
Running Total
Information entered.

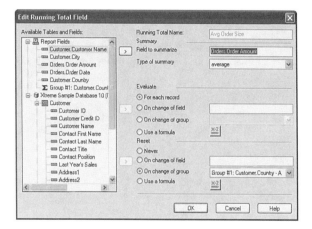

After the running total has been created, it only needs to be dragged onto the report in the appropriate section. In this example, the appropriate section is the Detail section to show a changing average order size for every order. The Updated Sample Customer Order report is shown in Figure 2.7. Notice the changing average order size being calculated for each record. This type of report can now provide increasing value to senior sales management.

TIP

> It's not necessary to place running total fields exclusively in the Details Section of your reports. By placing running total fields in different sections of your report, you can receive very interesting results. For example, if you place a running total in a Group Footer section, the running total displays the selected running total up to and including the current group. This can be very useful when analyzing average order size over time and grouping by month or quarter (for example, where you are only interested in some form of aggregated running total).

As highlighted in the Running Total dialog, it is possible to both evaluate and reset the running total fields based on four different options. The first three are self-explanatory—for each record, on the change of a specified field, or on the change of a specified group. The last option, using a formula, is a powerful and flexible option that should be more fully explored after reviewing Chapter 13, on formula creation. In its simplest description, this option enables the creation of a conditional running total or the reset of that running total based on the results of a formula you have created.

→ For detailed information on using formulas, **see** "Becoming More Productive with Formulas," **p. 282**

Figure 2.7
A sample Orders report with Running Average Total on Order Size for each sales rep.

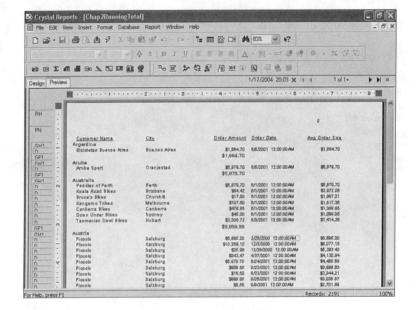

TIP

A good use of this conditional summing is the creation of a running total that calculates the sum of all orders, but only evaluates (or sums in this case) the running total when the total order amount on a given record is greater than a certain amount (for example, 1,000). This running total, in effect, would provide a running total of only large orders so that business analysts can determine the percentage of revenue derived from large orders. Another common usage of this functionality is for financial statements (such as income statements) where a number of General Ledger transactions compose the rows retrieved from the database and different Running Totals are used to conditionally add the associated transaction value to their total if and only if certain conditions are met (for example, a certain account code is associated with the transaction value). The resulting running totals are then placed in a report to present financial statement–oriented information such as Total Revenue, Operating Costs, Investment Income, Taxes, and so on.

USING GROUP NAME FIELDS

Group Name fields only exist in a report after you have specified one or more groups to add to your report. You will read about that functionality later in this chapter. Group Name fields are created at the same time you add a Grouping to a report. Once created, existing Group Name fields are added to the report by either clicking and dragging and dropping or by selecting the Group Name—using the Insert into Report button or action on the right-click menu—and selecting the location.

SPECIAL FIELDS

The special fields in the Field Explorer are a number of system fields that Crystal Reports provides. These system fields and a brief description are presented in Table 2.1. The new fields are suffixed with a *10.

TABLE 2.1   SPECIAL FIELDS AVAILABLE IN CRYSTAL REPORTS V.10

Field	Description	Valid Locations on Report
Current CE User ID*10	The ID number of the current Crystal Enterprise user (if one exists).	Anywhere
Current CE User Name*10	The username of the current Crystal Enterprise user (if one exists).	Anywhere
Data Date	The date the data in your report was las t retrieved.	Anywhere
Data Time	The time the data in your report was last retrieved.	Anywhere
File Author	The author of the report. This is set in Document Properties (File, Summary Info in the menu).	Anywhere
File Creation Date	The date the report was created.	Anywhere
File Path and Name	The file path and name for the report.	Anywhere
Group Number	An automatically created group numbering field.	Group Header or Group Footer sections only
Group Selection Formula	The current report's group selection formula. This is created by using the Select Expert covered in Chapter6.	Anywhere
Horizontal Page Number*10	The current horizontal page number of a report using either a Cross-Tab or an OLAP Grid.	Anywhere

continues

TABLE 2.1   CONTINUED

Field	Description	Valid Locations on Report
Modification Date	Date that the report was last modified (in any way).	Anywhere
Modification Time	Time that the report was last modified (in any way).	Anywhere
Page N of M	Indicates current page on report relative to total number of pages.	Anywhere
Page Number	The current page number.	Anywhere
Print Date	Either the current date or a date specified in the Set Print Date and Time dialog under the Reports, Set Print and Date Time option.	Anywhere
Print Time	Either the current time or a time specified in the Set Print Date and Time dialog under the Reports, Set Print and Date Time option.	Anywhere
Record Number	An automatically created number that counts the records in the detail section of your report.	Details Section
Record Selection Formula	The current report's record selection formula. This is created by using the Select Expert covered in Chapter 7.	Anywhere
Report Comments	Comments summarizing the report. This is set in Document Properties (choose File, Summary Info in the menu).	Anywhere—but only the first 256 characters are printed.
Report Title	The title of the report set in the Document Properties dialog (File, Summary Info in the menu).	Anywhere
Total Page Count	The total number of pages for this report.	Anywhere

These special fields are added to the report by either clicking and dragging and dropping or by selecting the Special Field—using the Insert into Report button or action on the right-click menu—and selecting the location.

WORKING WITH GROUPS

Grouping data in a report facilitates business user analysis and enables meaningful summarizations. Examples of common and useful groupings in reports include

- Sales Reports that group by Sales Rep, Product Line, Sales District, or Quarter
- HR Reports that group by Department, Management Level, or Tenure with the company
- Financial Reports that group by Company Division, Product Line, or Quarter
- Inventory Reports that group by Part Number, Supplier, or Manufacturing Plant

Crystal Reports provides easy-to-use grouping functionality that enables multiple types of powerful and flexible data grouping.

INSERTING GROUPS

Taking either the sample report from this or the previous chapter, you can realize the flexibility and power of grouping in a few short steps. Assume that senior sales management in a hypothetical company is interested in viewing customer order information by Employee/Sales representative, in addition to the existing grouping by Country. The following steps will guide you through an example of how grouping can help this company accomplish this task:

1. Select the Group option from the Insert menu or click on the Insert Group button located on the Insert toolbar. This opens the Insert Group dialog shown in Figure 2.8.

Figure 2.8
The Insert Group dialog requires selecting the field to be grouped on and enables specification of some custom grouping options.

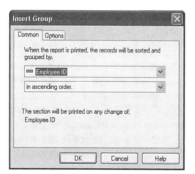

2. The Insert Group dialog prompts for the Data field on which the group is based. The field you select can be an existing database field already on the report, a database field included in your data sources (perhaps not yet on the report), a formula field, or a SQL Expression. For this exercise, select the Employee ID field from the Orders Table for the Grouping field.
3. Select Ascending Order for the Sort Order.
4. Click OK, and the report changes to reflect a new grouping on Employee ID.

The results of this new grouping are shown in Figure 2.9. Note that the Employee ID grouping is automatically selected to be the lowest-level grouping. This is the standard and expected behavior when inserting new groups, but based on the sales management's hypothetical request, you will need to edit the grouping order so that Employee ID becomes the highest level and you can view an Employee's sales across countries. You will do that in the next section.

Figure 2.9
Here is a sample report that has been grouped by Country and Employee ID.

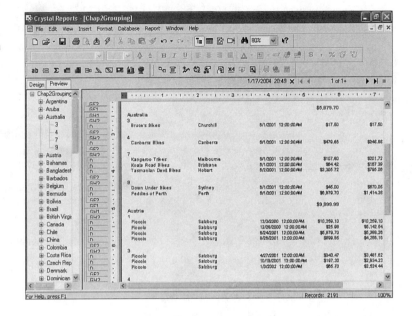

NOTE

The specified order selection of the Insert Group dialog is particularly interesting because of the great flexibility it provides. With this option, you can dynamically create both groups and a custom order of appearance on the report. A related geographic example would be the creation of a Continent grouping based on the country field in the database with the groupings and order of appearance specified in the Insert Group dialog. Notice that when you select specified order, two more tabs appear in the Insert Group dialog (see Figure 2.10). These tabs enable you to specify or create dynamic groupings and also to select a method of handling the other elements that do not fit into your dynamically created groups.

Figure 2.10
The Insert Group dialog displaying the Specified Ordering tab.

A last note on the Insert Group dialog is that options around group naming are available for customization. These options are accessed through the Options tab and facilitate the process of making your reports most presentable. For example, in another situation you might want to group on a country code instead of a country name for report processing efficiency (that is, numeric fields are sorted faster than string fields), but you still want to present the actual Country Name in the report. You could perform this customization through the Options tab in the Insert Group dialog as shown in Figure 2.11.

Figure 2.11
The Options tab of the Insert Group dialog enables you to set some custom Grouping options such as the displayed Group name.

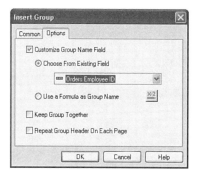

REORDERING GROUPS

As you can certainly imagine, it is quite common to want to group data by different fields within a single report. It is also quite common to receive multiple reporting requests for different views of data by various levels of grouping. Some examples might be

- View sales numbers grouped by product, region, and by sales rep
- View sales numbers grouped by region, product, and by sales rep
- View sales numbers grouped by sales rep, product, and by region

During report design, one of these different grouping orders could be created initially as you did in the last section with the groups Country and Employee ID. If other grouping orders were required, these could be quickly realized through either the Crystal Reports Design window or the Group Expert. Working in the left-most report section area of the Design tab of Crystal Reports (not the Preview tab), the different groups (sections) can be dragged and dropped before or after each other, quickly rearranging the grouping order. To complete the sales management's reporting request from the last section (to group by Employee ID at the highest level and Country below that), follow these steps:

1. Click on the Design tab of the Crystal Reports Designer if you are not already on that tab.

2. After double-clicking and holding the last click on either the Employee ID Group Header or Footer, drag that group to the outside of the Country Grouping to dynamically re-sort the order of grouping. A hand replaces the normal cursor image when you have grabbed a group, and blue lines highlight the intended drop location before you release your click and re-sort the grouping order.

TIP

> To facilitate identification of groups while in the Design tab, hover over a group header or footer section and a descriptive rollover tip temporarily appears.

3. Click on the Preview tab, and you will see the benefits of your work—the same report with the groupings instantly rearranged. Figure 2.12 highlights your intended results.

Figure 2.12
A sample Customer Orders report regrouped by Sales Rep (Employee ID) and then Country.

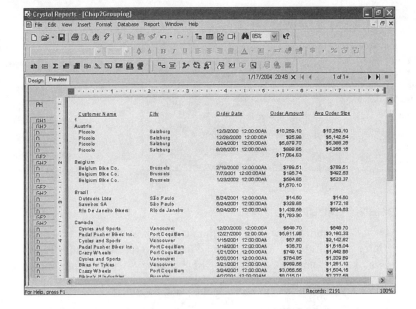

NOTE

> Note the change in the Group Tree as you move back to the edited Crystal Report. This Group Tree provides an easy-to-use navigation system for end users of this report as they can drill into the group tree and then link to the exact location and group they desire.

An alternative and powerful method for reordering groups is provided with the Group Expert. It is accessed from the Report menu, and the different groups can be reordered through the up and down buttons within the Grouping dialog. This quick reordering can present your data in completely different ways, serving multiple analysis requirements with very little report development effort. The next section explores the power of the Group Expert.

USING THE GROUP EXPERT

Crystal Reports provides an easy method to add multiple groups simultaneously and a central location for accessing all your current groups—the Group Expert dialog. Accessed from the Report menu, the Group Expert dialog, shown in Figure 2.13, enables you to add multiple groups at one time and quickly reorder any specified groups.

Figure 2.13
The Group Expert dialog accessed from the Report menu enables macro-level report group reordering and option setting.

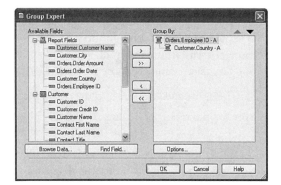

This dialog enables the selection of multiple groups in one location and provides access to the same functionality as the Insert Group dialog through the Options button. The groups can also be easily reordered from within this dialog through use of the up and down arrow buttons, located on the upper right of the dialog area.

GROUPING ON DATE/TIME FIELDS

One type of grouping that is common across most organizations is date-and-time related grouping. Analysts from all industries want to see how numbers (for example, sales revenue, units shipped, units produced, employees hired, and so on) change over various periods of time. To facilitate this type of analysis, Crystal Reports provides some built-in flexibility around date-and-time grouping. When you are creating a group that is based on a Date or Time field, an extra drop-down box appears in the Insert Group dialog (see Figure 2.14). This extra Print by Section box enables the user to group the detail records in the report automatically by any number of time-related criteria. Examples include By Day, By Hour, By Quarter, or even By Second. These automatic grouping options enable quick time-oriented analysis.

Figure 2.14
The Insert Group dialog with the Date/Time grouping drop-down box expanded.

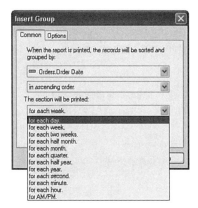

HIERARCHICAL GROUPING

Another type of special grouping that is available in Crystal Reports is hierarchical grouping. This special type of grouping enables your report data to be dynamically grouped on a hierarchy kept within a single table of your database. To enable hierarchical grouping, a group of the base-level data should be created through the standard Group Creation dialogs described previously. The Hierarchical Group option dialog can then be selected from the Report menu. To walk through a quick example, follow these steps:

1. Create a new blank Crystal Report and connect to the Xtreme Sample Database 10.

2. Select the Employee table for the report and Click on the OK button in the Database Expert.

3. Open the Field Explorer, select the First Name, Last Name, Extension, and Position fields from the Employee table, and drop them into the detail section of the report.

4. Insert a Group on Employee ID using the Insert Group dialog (accessed from the Insert menu) and select ascending sort order. Move to the Options tab of the Insert Group dialog before finishing, click on the Customize Group Name Field check box, and select the Employee Last Name field as the field to display. Now click OK in the Insert Group dialog.

5. Select Hierarchical Grouping Options from the Report menu. You are presented with the dialog displayed in Figure 2.15. Click on the Sort Data Hierarchically option and select either Employee Supervisor ID or Employee Reports To as the parent field with an indent of 0.33 of an inch.

Figure 2.15
The Hierarchical Group Options dialog accessed from the Report menu enables specification of hierarchical grouping options such as parent field and indentation.

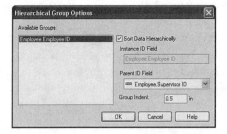

6. Click OK and view your new report. Figure 2.16 displays a report that should be similar and highlights the power of hierarchical grouping.

CAUTION

When creating a hierarchical group, the only eligible parent fields are those fields in the selected data source that have the same field type (for example, number, string, date) as the Grouped On field.

Figure 2.16
A sample report that highlights the hierarchical grouping and indentation functionality.

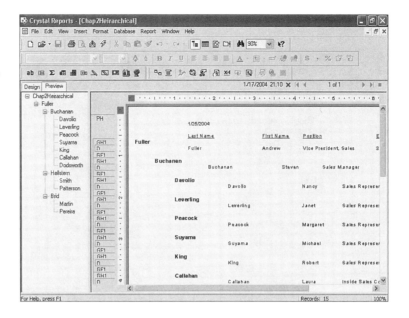

UNDERSTANDING DRILL-DOWN REPORTS

As you have learned, grouping data facilitates data analysis for business users and enables meaningful summarizations in your reports. Having both the group level and the detail level data available in a view of a report enables the simultaneous analysis of both group level summaries and the supporting detail records (for example, database fields, formulas, and so on). There are situations, however, in which a report consumer or analyst wants to view only aggregated group level information initially and then selectively drill-down into detail records where relevant (that is, drill-down only where the aggregated group level information is interesting, appealing, or stands out). This is easily and quickly accomplished in Crystal Reports through the use of the built-in drill-down capabilities in the product.

NOTE

When the term *drill-down* is used, it implies that a business user has the capability to move from an aggregated or grouped view of the data (for example, sales revenue for each sales district) to a more detailed level of the data (for example, sales revenue for each salesperson in a selected sales district). In Crystal Reports, this is as easy as double-clicking on the involved group data or aggregated graphic.

CREATING A DRILL-DOWN REPORT

By default, whenever a group is created within Crystal Reports, an automatic drill-down path is created from the respective group headers into the child groups and Detail records. The drill-down icon, when the cursor icon turns into a magnifying glass, appears in your Crystal Reports Preview tab as you hover over a group header with drill-down enabled. A sample report with Grouping and associated drill-down on Employee ID and Country is shown in Figure 2.17.

Figure 2.17
A sample report with drill-down groups available for end-user navigation/drilling.

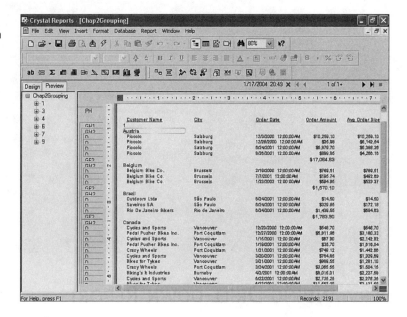

By double-clicking on the involved group header (such as Austria in Figure 2.17), a new viewing tab is opened with only the relevant group header's supporting information. Figure 2.18 highlights one of these views.

Figure 2.18
The Drill-down viewing tab in Crystal Reports Preview mode highlights the drill-down results.

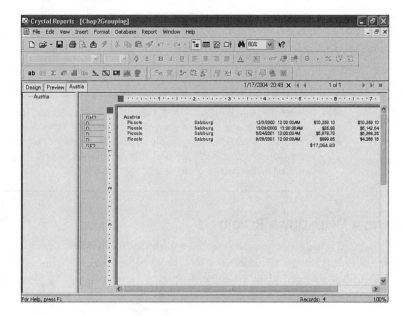

NOTE

An alternative method of navigating through report data is to use the Group Navigation tree that is exposed through all Crystal Report Viewers. The advantage of this is that it does not initiate new viewing tabs like those shown in Figure 2.18. If your report does not have a group navigation tree displayed, click on the Toggle Group Tree button located on the main toolbar. The Group Navigation tree enables report viewers to quickly jump to any point in the report by highlighting the group level that they are interested in viewing.

HIDING DETAILS ON A DRILL-DOWN REPORT

To accomplish the task of only displaying the aggregated group level information in our sample report and not the details, right-click on the Details section—either in the Design or Preview window. Figure 2.19 highlights the resulting right-click menu.

Figure 2.19
The Detail Section right-click menu enables hiding (or even suppression) of the detailed section.

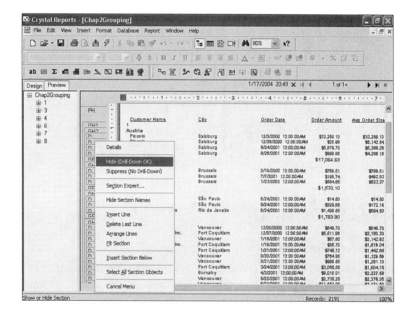

By selecting the Hide (Drill-Down OK) option in this right-click menu, your report now shows the details within the aggregated groups only when a business user drills down into them. Figure 2.20 shows what the report now looks like in Preview mode. From here, the business user can drill-down to the drill-down viewing tabs (refer to Figure 2.18 for an example) by double-clicking on any of the group header rows or data.

NOTE

The Suppress option from the same right-click menu, shown in Figure 2.19, can provide another viewing option to report designers and essentially turn off drill-down in your

continues

continued

> report. If the aggregated group level section data is to be viewed by business users but they are not allowed to view detailed section data, this can be accomplished by suppressing the detail section.

Figure 2.20
A sample report with detail sections hidden, but available in drill-down.

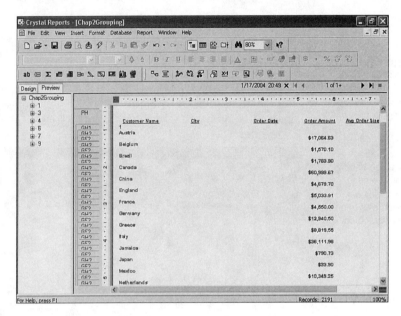

TROUBLESHOOTING

GROUP ON A FORMULA

Sometimes when creating a report, the development database might not be complete or in some cases even in production, there might be a requirement to group elements based on some criteria that is not in the database.

In situations such as these, it can be useful to group on a formula (this will be covered in more detail throughout the book).

CRYSTAL REPORTS IN THE REAL WORLD— GROUP ON A FORMULA

Sometimes when creating a report, the development database might not be complete or might be in production; there might be a requirement to group elements based on some criteria that is not in the database. In these cases, it can be useful to group on a formula. The formula needs to meet some criteria that will be explained in greater detail in later chapters.

1. Open the sample report from Chapter 1 (Chap1Manual.rpt). Create a new formula and name it Group1 and click the Use Editor button.

2. Type the following text into the code window so it appears like Figure 2.21:

```
WhileReadingRecords;
Select {Customer.Country}
    Case "Canada", "Mexico", "USA":
        "North America"
    Default:
        "Outside North America";
```

Figure 2.21
A sample formula to group information on a formula.

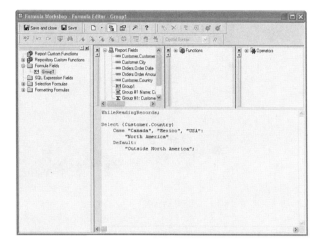

3. With the text entered, click the Save And Close button.

4. From the Report menu, select Group Expert. Find the Group1 formula from the list of Available Fields and add it to the list of Group By fields. Finally, because the Group1 field is a higher level than the For Country field, select it and move it up using the arrow button. The results are displayed in Figure 2.22.

Figure 2.22
The report correctly grouped, highlighting the capability to group on formulas and create increasingly flexible reports.

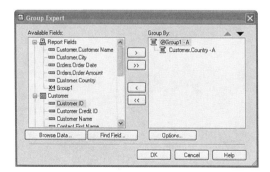

5. Click OK to see the completed report.

CHAPTER 3

FILTERING, SORTING, AND SUMMARIZING DATA

In this chapter

INTRODUCTION

In the first two chapters, you created reports that simply project the rows of data in your database onto the report surface with minimal manipulation of that data. The value of Crystal Reports is its inherent capacity to convert those rows of raw data into valuable information. Information will reveal something about the data that cannot be found by simply poring over pages and pages of records. In the last chapter, you began to take advantage of the power of Crystal Reports by applying grouping to a report to organize the data into categorical groups. In this chapter, you build on that by learning how to create reports that perform the following actions:

- Filter data based on a given criteria
- Sort data based on field values
- Summarize and subtotal data

→ For more detailed information on grouping data, **see** "Working with Groups," **p. 64**

FILTERING THE DATA IN YOUR REPORT

So far, the reports you have created have returned all the records from your database. Sometimes this is appropriate, but often reports need to filter the data based on specified criteria. This is most relevant when you're working with large databases in which there can easily be hundreds of thousands of records returned from a query, especially when joins are applied.

As with many features in Crystal Reports, there are multiple ways to filter data:

- Using the Select Expert—This simple method provides a visual way to specify filtering.
- Using the Record Selection Formula—This more granular, yet powerful, method involves creating a custom formula language expression to determine the filter criteria.

Regardless of the method used to filter your report, you should always make best efforts to filter on indexed database fields. By filtering on indexed fields, you realize the greatest performance on the database server. You can determine the indexed fields in a table by using the Crystal Reports Links tab on the Database Expert accessible from the Database menu. Use the Index Legend button and dialog provided to understand the different index markers in your database tables.

WORKING WITH THE SELECT EXPERT

The Select Expert is a design tool that enables you, the report designer, to specify basic yet powerful filters for the current report using a graphical design dialog. Figure 3.1 shows the Select Expert dialog. Let's work through an illustrative example of filtering using the Select

Expert. Taking what you have learned so far about creating simple columnar reports, create a new report from the Xtreme Sample Database 10, adding the Customer Name and Last Year's Sales fields from the Customer table to the details section of the report. Follow these steps to add a filter to this report:

Figure 3.1
The Select Expert provides access to easy-to-use filtering functionality.

1. To invoke the Select Expert, click its button found on the Experts toolbar or, alternatively, select the Select Expert option from the Report menu.

2. The first step in creating a filter is to choose which field the filter should be created on. Accordingly, the Choose Field dialog is displayed. Both fields that are present in the report and fields from the database are listed. A field does not need to be on the report to create a filter using it. At this point, if you forget which values are stored in any of the fields listed, click the Browse button to see a sample list of values. For this example, choose Last Year's Sales field and click OK. The Select Expert dialog appears, as shown in Figure 3.1.

TIP

Another quick and directed method of accessing the Select Expert is through the right-click menu available on any data field. This method opens the Select Expert directly with the specified field already selected as the filtered field and bypassing the Choose Field dialog.

3. The Select Expert has a group of tabs—one for each filter defined inside that report. In the case of your sample report, there is only one tab for the Last Year's Sales field and another called <New>, which is used to define additional filters. By default, the filter setting on the Last Year's Sales tab is set to Is Any Value. This means that regardless of the value of the Last Year's Sales field, all records are included in the report. To change the filter in a report, change the value of the drop-down list. For this example, change it to Is Greater Than.

4. When this option is selected, another drop-down list appears. If the exact value to filter the field on is known, it can be typed into this list box. However, in this case, you might not know exactly what the values of the field are, so you are provided with the capability to browse that field's values by simply pulling down the drop-down list. Choose $300.00 and click OK.

TIP

> Often when modifying filters and selections in the report designer, Crystal Reports displays a message asking the user if she wants to use the saved data in the report or refresh the data from the database. Using the saved data in the report is usually a good option because it does not incur a new query to the database. However, especially when modifying filters, it can cause some confusing results because the set of saved data in the report might or might not consist of all the records in the database; that is, a filter might have already been applied. So when modifying filters, it's best to refresh the data whenever Crystal Reports asks you.

5. When returning to the report, you should notice that the report now only displays a single record: the Has Been Bikes company that had sales of $300. A more useful filter would be to show all records that were above or below a threshold. To accomplish this, re-open the Select Expert. This time, change the Is Equal To criteria to Is Greater Than and type **100,000** into the list box. When closing the Select Expert and returning to the report, a small collection of records should be returned. In just a few seconds, you've created a report showing your top customers.

Let's look at a few more types of filters that can be applied to a report. The following steps walk you through applying these various types of filters:

1. Open the Select Expert again and change the criteria from Is Greater Than to Is Between.

2. This time, two list boxes are presented, each corresponding to an upper and lower bound. Type in the values **2,000** and **3,000**, respectively (as shown in Figure 3.2), and click OK. The report displays all customers with sales between $2,000 and $3,000.

Figure 3.2
Modify the report to display customers with sales between $2,000 and $3,000.

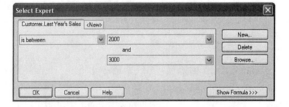

3. So far, only the Last Year's Sales field has been used as a filter. However, any field can be used as a filter, although there are slightly different options for various field types. Go back into the Select Expert and, while on the Last Year's Sales tab, click the Delete button to remove that filter.

4. Add a new filter on the Customer Name field by clicking the New button and selecting the Customer Name field from the subsequent dialog.

5. To have the report only show a single customer's record, leave the criteria as Is Equal To and choose Alley Cat Cycles from the drop-down list. Applying this filter results in the report only showing a single record.

6. Return to the Select Expert and change the criteria to Is One Of. This option enables you to choose multiple values. Each time a value is selected from the drop-down list, it is added to the bottom of the list box. Select Alley Cat Cycles, Bikes R Us, and Hikers and Bikers and notice how the report now reflects those three records.

7. Next, remove the three values previously selected by highlighting them and clicking the Remove button. Now change the criteria to Is Like and type **Wheel*** into the drop-down list. Click Add or press Enter to add this item to the list. Applying this filter results in the report showing all customers whose names begin with the word Wheel.

NOTE

When using the Is Like option, an * acts as a wildcard for any number of characters, whereas a ? acts as a wildcard for only a single character. This can be quite useful when you're searching through textual fields for a specific text pattern.

The last thing this chapter covers with respect to the Select Expert is applying multiple filters. To do so, perform the following steps:

1. Start from scratch and delete any filters you have applied by clicking the Delete button on each tab.

2. Click the New button and add a new filter using the Last Year's Sales field.

3. Change the criteria to Is Less Than and the value to 5,000. This filter would result in showing all customers with sales of less than $5,000, but let's apply another condition.

4. Click the New button and add a new filter based on the Country field. Note that this is slightly different from the previous filters that have been created—not only because more than one filter is being applied at the same time, but also because the filter being created is based on a field that is not present on the report.

5. Change the criteria for the Country filter to Is Equal To and choose Canada from the drop-down list. Clicking OK applies this filter, resulting in a report with multiple conditions: customers from Canada with sales below $5,000. See Figure 3.3 for the output of this report.

Figure 3.3
A filter is applied to show all Canadian customers with sales less than $5,000.

NOTE

The two filters that were just added to the report are concatenated together by default with a logical AND statement, that is, All Customers with Last Year's Sales of less than $5,000 AND from Canada. This can be edited in the Formula Editor accessible from the Show Formula button on the Select Expert. This is discussed in the next section.

THE RECORD SELECTION FORMULA

Although the Select Expert is quite powerful, there are certain situations where you need to define a filter that is more complex than the Select Expert allows. Fortunately, Crystal Reports has a built-in formula language that enables custom expressions to be defined as a filter. In fact, this is one of the strengths of the Crystal Reports product: being able to use the formula language to attain a high level of control in various aspects of report creation.

Although you might not have realized it, even when you were using the Select Expert, a formula was being generated in the background that defined the filter. To see this in action, open the Select Expert and click the Show Formula button. This expands the Select Expert dialog to reveal the formula being generated. This formula is called the *record selection formula*. Notice that the formula's value is as follows:

```
{Customer.Last Year's Sales} < $5000.00 and
{Customer.Country} = "Canada"
```

The formula language is covered in more detail in Chapter 11, "Using Record Selections and Alerts for Interactive Reporting," but the following are the key points to learn right now. In formulas, braces denote a field. For database fields, the table and field name are included and are separated by a period. The rest of the formula is a statement that tests whether the sales value is more than $5,000.

Think of a record selection formula as an expression that evaluates to a true or false result. For each record in the database, Crystal Reports applies the record selection formula, plugging in the current field values in place of the fields in braces. If the result of the statement is True, the record is included in the report. If the result of the statement is False, the record is excluded from the report. Let's look at an example. The first record in the Customer's table is that of City Cyclists who had sales of $20,045.27.

For this record, Crystal Reports evaluates the preceding formula, substituting $20,045.27 in place of {Customer.Last Year's Sales}. Because this value is larger than $5,000, this statement is False and the record is not included in the report. To see what other formulas look like, change the filter using the Select Expert to a few different settings and observe how the formula changes.

WORKING WITH THE FORMULA EDITOR

The formula shown at the bottom of the Select Expert is not just for informational purposes: It can be edited in-place. However, a much better editor exists for formulas. It's called the Formula Editor (shown in Figure 3.4), and it can be invoked by clicking the Formula Editor button in the Select Expert or by selecting the Report menu and choosing Selection Formulas, Record. Although the formula language doesn't change, the process of creating formulas becomes much simpler because of a focused user interface.

Let's work through creating a simple record selection formula. This formula attempts to filter out any customers who owe more than $5,000 in tax. Tax owing will be defined as 2% of their sales figure. To implement this, work through the following steps:

1. To begin, launch the Formula Editor as described previously and delete the existing selection formula.

2. Next, create an expression that calculates the tax owing. To do this, enter the following expression:

   `{Customer.Last Year's Sales} * 0.02`

3. The previous expression now represents the tax owing. To complete the expression to filter out all customers who owe less than $5,000 in tax, modify the formula to look like this:

   `({Customer.Last Year's Sales} * 0.02) > 5000`

4. To complete the formula and apply the filter, click the Close button at the top-left corner of the Formula Editor window, and then click OK to close the Select Expert. Focus returns to the report, and when data is refreshed, only a handful of customers should be listed on the report.

Figure 3.4
The Formula Editor provides quick access to powerful formula creation capabilities.

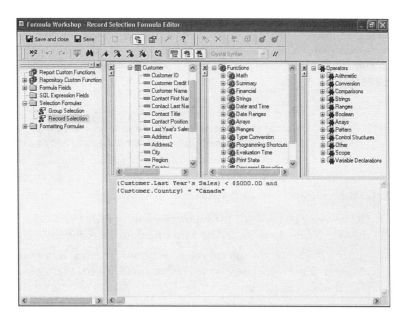

Both the formula language and the Formula Editor are topics unto themselves and will be discussed in more detail in Chapter 4, "Understanding and Implementing Formulas," and Chapter 11, "Using Record Selections and Alerts for Interactive Reporting."

LEARNING TO SORT RECORDS

Although filtering is one of the key components of an effective report, it alone is not enough. Often, to properly see the key pieces of data, a report needs to be sorted. Crystal Reports is quite flexible when it comes to sorting, allowing any field type to be sorted, as well as multiple ascending or descending sorts. Sorting is applied using the Sort Expert.

WORKING WITH THE SORT EXPERT

The Sort Expert is launched from a button on the Experts toolbar, and also via the Record Sort Expert item on the Report menu. Figure 3.5 shows the Sort Expert.

Figure 3.5
The Sort Expert dialog accessed from the Report menu.

To apply sorting to the report, select a field from the list of available fields on the left side of the dialog area, and click the arrow (>) button to add that field to the Sort Fields list. Note that like filters, sorts can use fields both on the report and fields not otherwise used in the report.

> **TIP**
>
> In addition to sorting on report and database fields, you can sort on formula fields. Creating a formula field enables you to sort a report based on a custom expression.

To see this in action, follow these steps:

1. Create a new report using the Employee table of the Xtreme Sample Database and add the First Name, Last Name, and Salary fields to the report.

2. Initially, this report doesn't tell you a lot because the data is in seemingly random order. However, if the report were sorted by last name, it would be more useful. To accomplish this, first launch the Sort Expert.

3. Select the Last Name field from the available fields list and click the arrow (>) button to apply a sort on it. Click OK to return to the report. Notice how the report's records are now sorted in alphabetical order by last name.

The Sort Expert enables you to sort on both alphabetic and numeric fields. To modify this report to sort on salary instead of last name, follow these steps:

1. Return to the Sort Expert and remove the current sort by selecting the Last Name field from the sort fields list and clicking the < button.

2. Now select the Salary field and add it to the sort fields list.

3. Alphabetic fields are usually sorted in ascending order (from A to Z), but numeric fields are often sorted both ways. In this case, select the Salary field in the Sort Fields list and

click Descending for the sort direction. This lists the employees with the top salary first. Click OK to apply the sort and return to the report.

Notice that some employees have the same salary level. If you wanted to perform a secondary sort within duplicates of the primary sort field, you can simply add another sort field. These sort fields can be arranged up and down using the buttons near the top-right corner of the Sort Expert.

CREATING EFFECTIVE SUMMARIES

The third key aspect of a good report after filtering and sorting is summarizing. Summarizing creates totals and subtotals that help the viewer of the report understand the data better. The following sections discuss various types of summarizing.

CREATING GRAND TOTALS

The simplest kind of summary is a grand total. This takes a single field and creates a total at the end of the report. To try this out, create a new report from the Orders table and add both the Order ID and the Order Amount fields onto the report.

Initially, this report is more than 30 pages long. A report of this length would make it very difficult to estimate the total amount of all orders, but a summary does that quite easily. Right-click the Order Amount field and select Insert, Summary from the context menu. This opens the Insert Summary dialog shown in Figure 3.6. To insert a summary, the first thing you need to specify is the field to summarize. Because you right-clicked the Order Amount field, this is already filled in for you. The next piece of information to fill in is the summary operation. The default is Sum, which you'll leave as its default. Finally, Crystal Reports needs to know for which group the summary should be performed. Because there is no grouping in this report, the only option is Grand Total, which is already filled in for you. Click OK to close this dialog.

When looking at the end of the report, you see a grand total of the order amount is now visible in bold text. To edit the summary, right-click on it and select Edit Summary from the context menu. This opens the Edit Summary dialog. Try changing the calculation from Sum to Average. This now updates the summary to show the average order amount. There are various calculations to choose from including minimum, maximum, variance, count, deviation, and median.

Besides the order amount total, it might be helpful to know how many orders there are. To do this, right-click the Order ID field and select Insert, Summary. Change the calculation from Sum to Count and click OK. Now besides the order amount summary, there is a count of all orders.

CREATING GROUP SUMMARIES

Although grand totals are useful, summarizing starts to become really powerful when it is applied at the group level. This enables totaling for each level of a group and tells more about the data than a simple grand total does because it measures the relationships between the various groups. To apply a group summary, a group must first exist in the report.

Figure 3.6
Inserting a summary
based on the Order
Amount field.

Using the same report from the last example with the Order ID and Order Amount fields, insert a group on the Ship Via field. This produces a report showing all the orders grouped by the method they were shipped with, for example, FedEx, Loomis, and so on. To compare the different methods of shipment, right-click the Order Amount field and select Insert, Summary. Previously, when you created a grand total, you accepted all the defaults in this dialog. But this time, the summary location needs to be changed. Change Grand Total (Report Footer) to Group #1: Orders.Ship Via in the Summary Location drop-down box, and click OK.

Now a total field is inserted into the report, which acts much like the grand total except that the total is repeated for each group. By examining these summaries, you can determined that the largest order amount was shipped via UPS. You could also add a group-level summary to the Order ID field to determine the count of orders for each shipping method. Doing this reveals that the most orders were shipped via Loomis. These conclusions would have been difficult to reach without an effective summary.

TIP

> When groups have many records inside of them, it sometimes becomes difficult to compare summaries because they aren't all visible on the page at the same time. A good tip for comparing these values is to hide the details section, which contains all the records, and only display the group header and footer that normally contains the group name and its summary. To hide the details section, move to the Design tab, right-click the Details bar on the left side of the screen, and select Hide.

USING GROUP SELECTION AND SORTING

On the topic of group summaries comes group selection and sorting. This brings together both filtering and summarizing concepts. Group selection and sorting is to groups what record selection is to records. In other words, defining a *group selection* or *sorting* defines which groups are included in the report and in which order, respectively. A key point to understand is that whereas record selection and sorting work from values of individual fields, group selection and sorting work from summary fields.

In the example from the previous "Creating Group Summaries" section, you created a report that displayed all orders grouped by the shipment method but to determine which shipment method shipped the highest dollar value of orders, you had to manually browse through the report comparing the numbers. Applying a group sort would provide an easy way to see the rankings. Also, what if you only wanted to show the top three shipment methods? Group selection provides a way to filter out groups in such a manner.

As you might expect, there is an expert for applying group selection and sorting. It's called the Group Sort Expert, and it can be found on the Experts toolbar, as well as from the Group Sort Expert item on the Report menu. When the Group Sort Expert is launched, it displays one tab for each group in the report. In the previous example, there was only a single group on the Ship Via field so that's what you should see. Inside that tab, there is initially only a single list box with a value of No Sort. Changing this list box to All displays a set of options very similar to that of the Record Sort Expert—except instead of having a list of all report fields to choose to sort on, only summaries are listed.

The Group Sort Expert should have initially selected the Sum of Orders.Order Amount summary field and selected Ascending order. In this case, because it's more useful to see the highest dollar value first rather than last, change the sort order to Descending. Clicking OK closes the Group Sort Expert and returns focus to the report, which should have re-ordered the groups from largest to smallest. It's easy to see now that UPS was the method that shipped the highest dollar amount because it is the first group to appear.

There are only six shipment methods, but you can imagine reports that contain many more groups than six. Even if the groups are sorted, sometimes it's just too much data for the consumer of the report to absorb. To solve this problem, you can apply a group selection. To do this, launch the Group Sort Expert and change the All option on the left to Top N. Notice that the options are different from sorting. Applying a Top N selection implies that the groups will be sorted, but enables you to only display a specified number of the top groups in order. The default value is 5: Change this value to 3.

Another important option is relating to the set of groups that are excluded by the group selection. By default, these groups are all combined under a new group called Others. You might or might not want to include this Others group in your report. If you choose not to, uncheck the option labeled Include Others. Clicking OK returns focus to the report that now should only display the top three shipment methods based on the total order amount.

NOTE

> Like the record selection, the group selection also has a formula that can be defined to use a custom expression to determine which groups to include in the report. The group selection formula can be found on the Report menu, under Selection Formulas, Group.

Some other options available in the group sort expert include Bottom N, which is the oppo-site of Top N, and Top and Bottom Percentage, which allow a filtering of the top *x* percent of groups.

CAUTION

> It is instructive to note that group selection formulas are executed on the second pass of the Crystal Reports Engine. This second pass takes place after grand totals, group subto-tals, and the group navigation tree have been created. To understand the nuances of multi-pass reporting, review the last topic in Chapter 4.

CREATING RUNNING TOTALS

The last kind of summary to be discussed in this chapter is a running total. In some older versions of Crystal Reports, to create a running total, you had to create a collection of for-mula fields, so a feature was added just to handle running totals. To illustrate this, follow these steps:

1. Create a new report using the Orders table. Add the Order ID, Order Date, and Order Amount fields to the details section of the report. You can reformat the order date to a more user-friendly format if you prefer by right-clicking the field and selecting Format.

2. Add a sort based on the Order Date field. This report now shows all orders in the order they were placed. This is a perfect scenario for a running total that would show a cumulative total of orders so that the viewer of the report could see what the current order amount was at any given time.

3. To add a running total, right-click the Order Amount field and select Insert, Running Total from the Context menu. The Create Running Total Field dialog is shown in Figure 3.7.

Figure 3.7
Creating a Running Total field is quickly accomplished through the Create Running Total Field dialog.

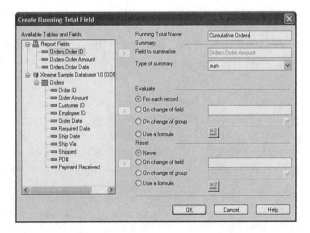

Four pieces of information need to be provided in this dialog, including

- **Name of the running total field.** The default is somewhat cryptic; it's best to give this a more meaningful name.

- **The summary to perform.** The Field to Summarize should be prepopulated for you, but you can change the summary type from the default of sum to other standard summary types. Some of the more useful types for a running total are Count and Average.

- **When to evaluate the running total.** The default and most common setting here is For Each Record, but this can be modified to only be evaluated when the value of another field is changed or a group value is changed, or you can define a custom formula that defines the evaluation criteria.

- **When to reset the running total.** This setting determines whether the running total should reset itself. If no groups are present in the report, you'll likely want to keep the default of Never. But if you have groups, you might want to reset the running total for each group or define more complex criteria with a formula.

4. For our example, give the running total a name of Cumulative Orders and leave all other settings at their defaults. Completing this running total adds this new field to the report next to the Order Amount field and provides a cumulative total of orders. The output of this report is shown in Figure 3.8.

Figure 3.8
A cumulative orders report using a Running Total Field.

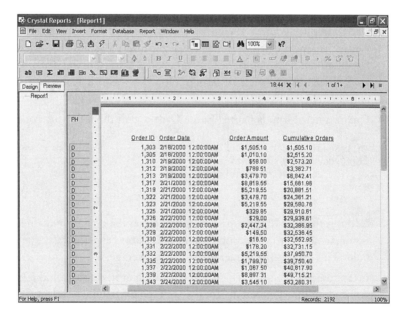

NOTE

> Running totals can also be created from the Field Explorer by selecting the Running Total Field item and clicking the New button or right-clicking and selecting New from the context menu. Creating a field in this way does not automatically add it to the report; you need to place it on the report in a desired location yourself.

TROUBLESHOOTING

GROUP SELECTION FORMULA

Where can I find the Group Selection formula?

The group selection formula can be found on the Report menu, under Selection Formulas, Group.

CRYSTAL REPORTS IN THE REAL WORLD— NESTING FORMULAS

It's common for some more complex formulas to be combined to provide specific insight into report data. For example, a user might need to have a report that lists all customers with their total sales, but also show the average value of sales over a given amount. As described previously, there are many ways that a report design expert can approach this; what follows is one method.

1. Open the report Chap3RunningTotal.rpt. Insert a group on Customer ID. Select the running total field, right-click it, and choose Edit Running Total. Under the Reset section, choose On Change Of Group. Now the report is ready for the new functionality and should look like Figure 3.9.

2. Create a new formula named Large Orders with the following code:

```
WhileReadingRecords;
If {Orders.Order Amount} > 3000 Then
    {Orders.Order Amount}
Else
    0;
```

3. Add this formula to the report. Right-click on the new formula field and select Insert, Summary and for the section Summary Location change this value to your Group 1 field. This creates the numerator for your average.

4. Next, to determine the value for the denominator, right-click the Large Orders formula and choose Insert, Running Total. For Type Of Summary select Count; for Evaluate, select Formula and enter the following code:

```
{@Large Orders}>0
```

Under Reset select Group 1. Check your settings against Figure 3.10.

Figure 3.9
This is the starting point for the new functionality.

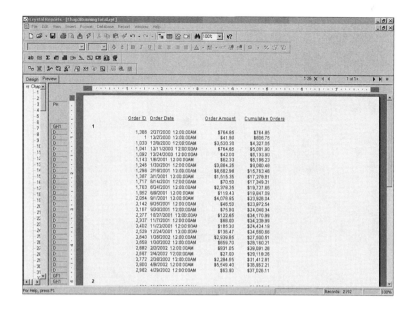

Figure 3.10
Create Running Totals easily using the Running Total Expert.

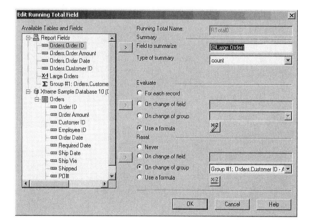

5. Now with the numerator and denominator values defined, simply create a new formula with the following code:

```
Sum ({@Large Orders}, {Orders.Customer ID})/{#RTotal0}
```

6. Insert this new formula onto the Group Footer and the report now has a summary value showing the average of all orders greater than $3,000 (see Figure 3.11).

7. Save the report as Chap3AverageLargeOrder.rpt.

Figure 3.11
A report complete
with complex
formulas.

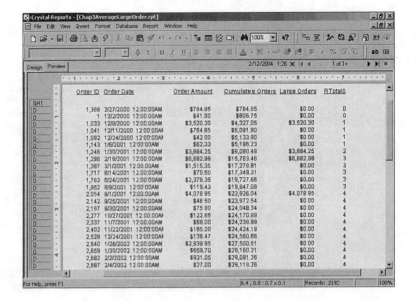

CHAPTER 4

UNDERSTANDING AND IMPLEMENTING FORMULAS

In this chapter

INTRODUCTION

Chapter 2, "Selecting and Grouping Data," introduced the concept of formulas, and you saw how to create them and subsequently drop them into a report from the Field Explorer. This chapter explores the Formula Editor in more detail.

Formulas provide great flexibility and power when creating Crystal Reports by enabling you to create *derived* fields not directly stored in available data sources. Formulas also enable you to create advanced conditional object formatting and use flexible selection formulas in a report.

Crystal Reports has a number of built-in tools that facilitate the formula creation and formula reuse processes, the Formula Editor being a good example. The Formula Workshop provides a single convenient access point to almost all your formula fields within a given report. SQL Expression fields, Record and Group Selection formulas, Formatting formulas, and Custom Report- and Repository-based functions can all be accessed from the new Formula Workshop.

This chapter covers the following topics:

- An introduction to the Formula Workshop
- A review of the Formula Workshop Tree Elements
- Formula Editor
- Arithmetic, Date, and String formulas
- Type conversion
- Variables in formulas
- Formula Expert
- Formula Extractor
- Multi-pass Reporting

USING THE FORMULA WORKSHOP

You have already been introduced to the Record Selection and Group Selection functionality of Crystal Reports that each independently leverages the formula capabilities of the product for enhanced flexibility. As you create more advanced reports, you will come across more functional areas that will exploit the formula capabilities of Crystal Reports. Figure 4.1 displays the familiar Formula Editor within the new Formula Workshop interface.

The Formula Editor can be used in the following functional areas of Crystal Report creation:

- Creation of derived fields (Formulas, SQL Expressions)
- Report Section formatting
- Report Object formatting

- Record Selection formulas
- Group Selection formulas
- Running Total conditions
- Formula-based hyperlinks (covered in Chapter 9, "Custom Formatting Techniques")
- Alert conditions (covered in Chapter 11, "Using Record Selections and Alerts for Interactive Reporting")
- Use of Report Variables (covered later in this chapter and in Chapter 12, "Using Subreports for Advanced Reporting")

Figure 4.1
The Formula Editor within the new Formula Workshop.

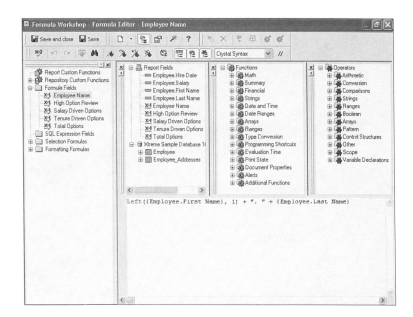

Although the independently accessed Formula Editors for each of these reporting areas provide powerful capabilities, a great new productivity feature introduced in Crystal Reports version 9 is the capability to access almost all the formulas held in a report in a single interface called the Formula Workshop—essentially a one-stop shop for all formulas. At the time of writing, the only exceptions to the rule were Running Total and Alert Condition formulas.

The Formula Workshop consists of a toolbar, a tree that lists the types of formulas you can create or modify, and an area for defining the formula itself either through the Formula Editor or a Formula Expert.

NAVIGATING THE FORMULA WORKSHOP WITH THE WORKSHOP TREE

Figure 4.2 shows some of the new Formula Workshop features you see by expanding the Formula Workshop Tree found in the Formula Editor.

Figure 4.2
The Formula Workshop with expanded Formula Workshop Tree and the Formula Expert displayed.

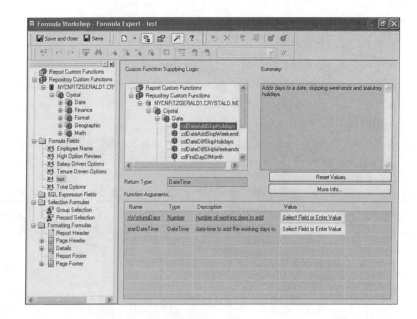

The Workshop Tree is a container for Report and Repository functions, Formula fields, SQL Expression fields, Selection formulas, and Formatting formulas—all of which are explained in more detail in the following sections.

REPORT CUSTOM FUNCTIONS

Report Custom Functions are functions created by Crystal Report Designers that are stored within the current report file. It is important to note that custom functions are accessed from the Formula Workshop along with other types of formulas and functions. New Custom Report functions are created through the Formula Editor by right-clicking on any part of the Report Function section of the Formula Workshop or by selecting Custom Function from the New menu drop-down list.

→ For more information on custom functions, **see** "Creating Custom Functions in Your Reports," **p. 287**

REPOSITORY CUSTOM FUNCTIONS

Repository Custom Functions are functions created by Crystal Report Designers and then stored centrally within the Crystal Enterprise Repository. The repository acts as a central library for these custom functions among multiple other reusable objects. Note that Repository functions are accessed from the Formula Workshop along with the other types of formulas and functions. You upload new Repository functions by creating a Report function and subsequently adding it to the Repository through the Add Repository option accessed by right-clicking Custom Report Function.

→ For more detail on Repository functions, **see** "The Repository Explorer," **p. 364**

CAUTION

> Although the Crystal Repository was introduced and made available in Crystal Reports version 9, it is now only available to Crystal Report designers who are licensed for Crystal Enterprise version 10. When requesting any Repository-related function or activity, a logon prompt for Crystal Enterprise is presented to the designer and must be successfully completed before the functionality is made available.

TIP

> Remember that when you add a custom function to the Central Repository for other report developers to use, you must first create it locally as a Report Custom function and only then can it be added to the Central Repository. Custom functions cannot be directly added into the Central Repository. See Chapters 13 and 18 for more details on Report and Repository functions.

FORMULA FIELDS

As you learned in previous chapters, formula fields provide a means to add derived fields (that is, those not directly available in your database), such as a calculation into your Crystal Reports, as well as provide your business users (report consumers) with additional views of data. Once created, Crystal Reports treats derived formula fields in exactly the same manner as it does original database fields. The majority of this chapter is dedicated to introducing the different methods of creating formulas through two interfaces—the Formula Editor and the Formula Expert. Both of these are discussed next, and Chapter 13, "Using Formulas and Custom Functions," explores some advanced features of formula creation and use.

SQL EXPRESSION FIELDS

SQL Expressions provide a means to add derived fields (that is, those not directly available in your database), such as a calculation into your Crystal Reports, that are based exclusively on *Structured Query Language (SQL)* statements rather than standard Crystal formula syntax. As a reminder, SQL Expressions are used in cases where report-processing efficiency is critical.

Using SQL Expressions facilitates pushing data processing to the database server instead of the Crystal Reports Server, and this is usually most efficient. Like Formulas, SQL Expressions are created in the Formula Editor but provide only a subset of the functionality because of the dependency on the SQL supported by the report's attached data source. Appendix A, "Using SQL Queries in Crystal Reports," provides a good introduction to SQL.

SELECTION FORMULAS

As discussed in Chapter 3, "Filtering, Sorting, and Summarizing Data," selection formulas come in two varieties in Crystal Reports—Group and Record. A Record Selection formula provides a filtering mechanism on records to be included in the final report. Likewise, a

Group Selection formula provides a filtering mechanism on the groups to be included in the final report. Each of these selection formulas can be accessed and edited through the Formula Workshop using the familiar Formula Editor component. The Formula Editor will be described in detail in the next major section and in extended detail with respect to selection formulas in Chapter 11.

FORMATTING FORMULAS

Formatting formulas provide flexibility in the presentation of a Crystal Report's report sections and all the report objects contained within report sections. Examples of object and section formatting options include Background Color, Suppression, ToolTip, Border Color/Style, Section Underlay, and so on. All the formatting capabilities available in the Format Editor dialog (see Figure 4.3) and the Report Section Expert (see Figure 4.4) accessed by the x+2 icon can be set—and be set conditionally—through these Formatting Formulas.

Figure 4.3
The Format Editor dialog provides access to numerous formatting settings and additional access to the Formula Editor for conditional formatting.

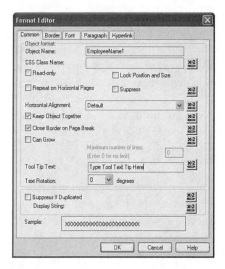

Coverage of the formatting functionality provided through these dialogs is covered in Chapter 8, "Visualizing Your Data with Charts and Maps," but you should note that this is accessed and set through the Formula Workshop's Formula Editor. When you select the New Formatting Formula option by either clicking the New button or right-clicking on a Section or Field element under the Formatting Functions tree, you can access all formatting functions that can be modified through a formula.

Figure 4.4
The Section Expert provides access to numerous section formatting settings and additional access to the Formula Editor for conditional settings.

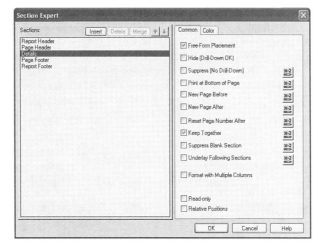

USING THE WORKSHOP FORMULA EDITOR

The Formula Editor, shown in Figure 4.5, is a common tool used across all the different types of formulas accessible through the Formula Workshop. The Formula Editor is composed of five distinct areas:

- The Fields area (at the top-left frame of the Formula Editor) includes all the available report, formula, summarization, and database fields that can be added to the current formula.

- The Functions area (at the top-center frame of the Formula Editor) includes the prebuilt Crystal Reports functions and custom functions that are available to be added to the currently edited formula.

- The Operators area (at the top-right frame of the Formula Editor) includes a number of operators that can be used in the currently edited formula. Examples of operators include +, *, IF/THEN/ELSE, SELECT CASE, AND/OR, and so on.

- The Editing area (the large bottom frame of the Formula Editor) is the free-form text-editing area where formulas are formed through either direct typing or double-clicking selections from the other three Formula Editor frames.

- The toolbar area contains a number of Formula Editor options including toggles on the different frames, a new toggle on the Formula Editor or Expert, some bookmarking options, a formula syntax checking button (x+2), and, importantly, the Crystal versus Basic Syntax drop-down box.

NOTE

> Crystal Reports provides two different formula languages for use in creating formulas. Basic syntax is very similar to the Visual Basic programming structure and provides a natural fit for report designers with a Visual Basic programming background. The other more commonly used syntax—Crystal syntax—has no programming language affiliation, but is highly-evolved and easy to use for nonprogrammers. For the rest of this chapter, the examples are created using the more commonly used Crystal syntax.

Figure 4.5
The Formula Editor provides a one-stop shop for formula development.

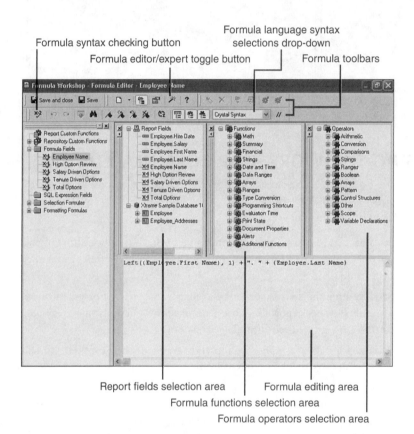

The available elements in each of the top three areas of the Formula Editor vary depending on what type of formula you are creating. For example, when you create a Formatting formula, the Functions frame presents a Formatting section not available while editing or creating other types of formulas. Another familiar example is the limited set of fields, functions, and operators presented when creating SQL Expressions. This is, of course, dependent on the supported SQL for the current report's data source.

To facilitate your understanding of the Formula Editor, the following hypothetical business problem provides a hands-on experience with creating formulas within reports. The CEO of Maple Leaf Bikes is planning an initial public offering (IPO) of his stock to the marketplace.

Having recently acquired another company called Xtreme Cycles, he wants to fairly share the success of the overall company with these new employees. As such, he wants to allocate stock options to them based on tenure with Xtreme Cycles (a metric of loyalty) and their current salary (a metric of expected contribution). Therefore, the CEO has determined that a fair allocation would be 100 shares for each year of tenure and 100 shares for each $10,000 in salary, and he wants a report outlining these allocations so that he can present this proposal at the next board of directors meeting. The following steps demonstrate a solution for this problem:

1. Create a new report based on the Xtreme Sample Database ODBC Connection using either the Standard Report Wizard or through the main Report Design menus.

2. Select the Employees and Employee_Addresses tables to be used in the report. They should be automatically smart-linked on their indexed (noted by the Red Icon in the linking dialog) Employee ID fields.

3. Add the Employee ID, Salary, and Hire Date fields into the detail section of the report.

At this point, the design frame (from the Design tab) for the report should resemble Figure 4.6.

Figure 4.6
The Crystal Reports Design window with a sample report.

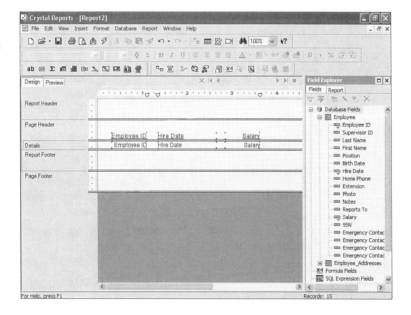

The basic building blocks to the requested report have now been added to the sample report, but there is clearly work to be done to capture the CEO's intent. This report is flushed out through the next few sections as different formula functions are systematically introduced.

ARITHMETIC FORMULAS

Arithmetic formulas are those derived from existing numeric fields (or fields converted into numbers—type conversion information is discussed later in this chapter). These formulas can be simple multiplication or addition operations, or they can be as complex as standard deviations, sums, or correlations. Arithmetic formulas are created within the Formula Editor by selecting any combination of numeric fields, numeric operators, or numeric-oriented functions. Figure 4.7 displays the Formula Editor resized to highlight some common arithmetic functions and operators.

Figure 4.7
The Formula Editor highlighting some arithmetic functions and operators.

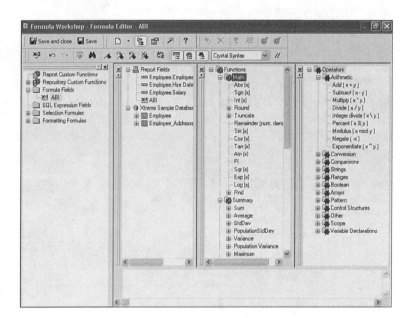

With hundreds of formula functions and operators built into Crystal Reports and the new capability to expand that set with custom functions, it's easy to become overwhelmed with all the available formula possibilities. One very helpful source of information on the many built-in formulas in Crystal Reports is the provided help files accessed through the F1 key. By clicking on the Index tab of the Crystal Reports Help Screen and searching on functions or operators, you can access a detailed description of each of the hundreds of different Crystal Reports functions and operators. Figure 4.8 displays the Crystal Reports Help dialog with an Aging function highlighted.

To create an Arithmetic formula (as any other kind of formula) within the Formula Editor, either double-click on the appropriate elements from each of the Fields, Functions, and Operators frames or select them by single-clicking and dragging and dropping them into the Formula Editing frame. Using either method, a formula begins to be constructed in the Formula Editing Area/Frame. Alternatively, experienced users can create formulas by typing the formula directly into the Formula Editing Area and periodically checking the formula's syntax with the x+2 toolbar button, which provides error-checking functionality.

Figure 4.8
Crystal Reports functions Help—a great reference for understanding the syntax of formula functions.

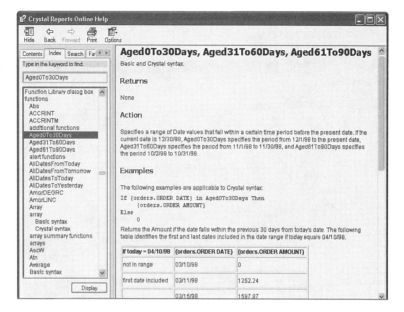

TIP

For users who prefer to work in the Formula Editor and type in their formulas by hand, Crystal Reports provides an Auto-Complete capability accessed by using the Ctrl+Spacebar key combination. A list of formula functions that could complete the most recently typed characters is made available for instant selection.

Revisiting the Maple Leaf Bikes reporting scenario, the CEO has designated two criteria for stock option allocation to the Xtreme Sports employees—Tenure and Salary. The Salary component is based on a derivation from a numeric field (salary) and lends itself to the creation of an Arithmetic formula based on the requirements that each $10,000 of salary contributes to 100 stock options. The following steps, continued from the last section, move toward a reporting solution for the CEO and provide exposure to the Formula Creation process in the Formula Editor:

1. If the Field Explorer is not already open in your Crystal Reports Design window, open that now by either clicking on the Field Explorer icon or by toggling to the Field Explorer option under the View menu. Figure 4.9 displays the Crystal Reports Design window with the Field Explorer displayed.

2. Create a new Formula by clicking on the Formula Fields field and either accessing the New option on the right-click menu or clicking the New button in the Field Explorer toolbar. You will be prompted for a Formula Name—call this formula **Salary Driven Options** and select the Use Editor button to create the formula. If you accidentally click the Use Expert button, have no fear; simply click the Formula Editor/Expert toggle button in the Formula Workshop toolbar. The Formula Expert is explored later in

this chapter, but for now, the Formula Editor is your primary focus. The familiar Formula Workshop (as you saw in Figures 4.2 and 4.5) appears.

Figure 4.9
Maple Leaf Bikes CEO report with Field Explorer displayed.

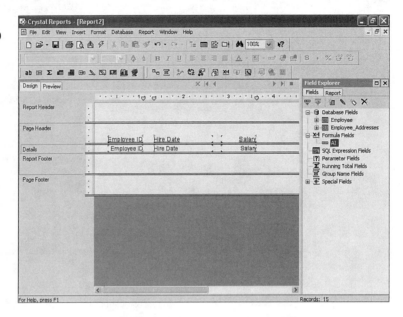

3. Logically stepping through the CEO's request, the first database field you need to access to determine the Salary Driven Component of stock option allocation is Salary, so find the Salary field in the Fields frame and double-click on it.

> **TIP**
>
> More than just providing access to those fields already selected for viewing in the report, the Formula Editor Fields frame provides access to all available database fields for those tables selected as report data sources. Additionally, existing formulas, sums, running totals, and so on can be accessed here, which can be included in other formulas.

Because the CEO wants to provide 100 stock options for each $10,000 in existing salary, you logically need to divide each employee's current salary by $10,000 and then multiply by 100. To do so, you could either access the Arithmetic operators (/ for division and * for multiplication) in the Operators Frame and double-click on those or simply type them in.

4. To accomplish this task, you need to type in the numeric constants regardless, so type the following into the Formula Editor so that it resembles Figure 4.10: **/ 10000 * 100**.

5. Perform error-checking on your report by clicking the x+2 icon. After you confirm that no errors are found and your formula is identical to that in Figure 4.10, save the formula with the Save button and exit the Formula Workshop by clicking Close.

Figure 4.10
Salary-driven options
formula creation
example.

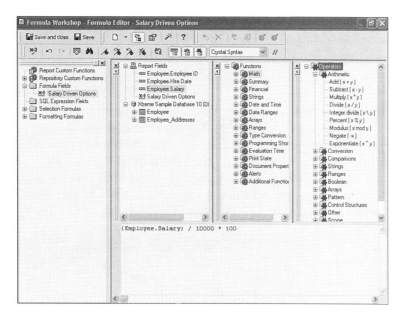

6. Add the new formula into the report beside Salary and try to format it to display zero decimals and no currency symbol (hint—right-click on the object and select the Format option or use the shortcut buttons from the Formatting toolbar). At this point, also remove the original Salary and Hire Date fields from the report by deleting them. Note that the Salary Driven Options field can exist without its underlying support fields (Salary) existing on the report. The Preview tab of the CEO's report should now resemble that shown in Figure 4.11.

Figure 4.11
The interim version of
the Maple Leaf Bikes
CEO sample report.

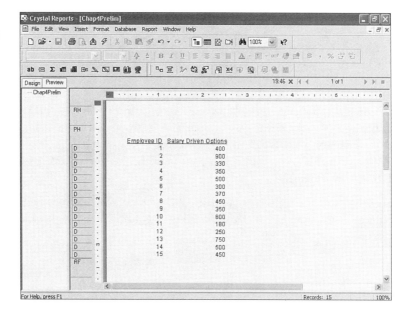

The current version of the report takes the content of the report to about half complete. The tenure-driven component of the CEO's request needs to be taken care of with some date calculations.

DATE AND TIME FORMULAS

Date and Time formulas are those derived from existing date or time fields (or fields converted into dates). These types of formulas can be as simple as extracting a month name from a date field or as complex as determining shipping times in business days (difference between two dates not including weekends and holidays). Date and Time formulas are created within the Formula Editor by selecting any combination of date and time fields, Date operators, or date-oriented functions. Figure 4.12 displays the Formula Editor resized to highlight some common date functions.

Figure 4.12
The Formula Editor highlighting some Date and Time functions.

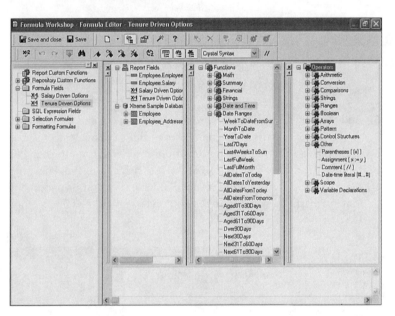

To create a Date/Time formula (as with Arithmetic formulas) within the Formula Editor, either double-click on the appropriate elements from each of the fields, functions, and operators frames or select them with a single-click and drag and drop them into the Formula Editing frame. Using either method, a formula begins to be constructed in the Formula Editing Area/Frame.

Some operators that are commonly used with dates include + and -. Those are displayed in Table 4.1 with some quick examples and their effect. These operators work equally well on time fields and date fields.

TABLE 4.1   COMMON DATE OPERATORS, THEIR FUNCTIONS, AND EXAMPLES

Common Date Operator or Function	Formula Usage Example	Effect
+ operator	`{Employee.Hire Date}+ 365`	Returns the one year anniversary date of the given employee in a date format.
- operator	`{Orders.Ship Date}- {Orders.Order Date}`	Returns a numeric field representing the days taken to ship after receiving an order.
- operator	`{Orders.Warranty Expiration Date} - 365`	Returns a date representing the purchase date of the given item.

Common functions that are used with dates include the use of the prebuilt date ranges and date type conversion formulas in Crystal Reports.

- Conversion functions are found under the Date and Time section in the Functions frame of the Formula Editor.

- Range functions are found in the Date Ranges section of the same Functions frame and provide a number of built-in date ranges that can be automatically created in Crystal Reports and used in comparisons. Range examples include Aged61To90Days, Next30Days, or AllDatesFromTomorrow. These ranges can be used with the control structures introduced later in this chapter (for example, IF statements) to determine if dates fall within certain predefined ranges.

Revisiting the Maple Leaf Bikes reporting scenario, the Tenure component of option allocation still needs to be created in the report. It is based on a derivation from two date fields (hire date and the current date) and lends itself to the creation of a date formula based on the requirements that every 365 days of tenure will contribute to 100 stock options.

The following steps move toward a final reporting solution for the CEO and provide exposure to date-focused formula creation in the Formula Editor:

1. Create a New Formula in the Field Explorer called **Tenure Driven Options**.

   Because the CEO wants to provide 100 stock options for each year (365 days) of tenure, you logically need to determine each employee's tenure in days by finding the difference (with the - operator) between the current date (with a built-in Crystal Reports function) and the hire date (with a provided database field). This employee tenure measured in days will then need to be divided by 365 to find the tenure in years before being multiplied by 100 to determine the number of tenure-driven options.

2. To accomplish this, add the Current Date function (CurrentDate) to the formula by accessing it under the Date and Time section of the Functions frame in the Formula

4

Editor. You could alternatively add this by typing **Cu** in the editor box, clicking on Ctrl+Spacebar, and selecting the CurrentDate function from the list. Add the - operator (found under the Arithmetic section in the Operators frame) after that, and then add the database field Hire Date to the formula by double-clicking on it. Finally, add the / 365 and * 100 formula pieces by typing them in and, more importantly, wrap two round brackets around the CurrentDate—Employee.Hire Date} section of the formula—to ensure the proper order of calculation.

NOTE

> The Crystal Reports Formula Editor respects the standard mathematical order of operations. In order this would be brackets, exponents, division and multiplication, and, finally, addition and subtraction.

3. Ensure that your formula resembles what is displayed in Figure 4.13 and save it before closing the Formula Workshop.

Figure 4.13
A Tenure-Driven Options sample formula highlighting some date formulas.

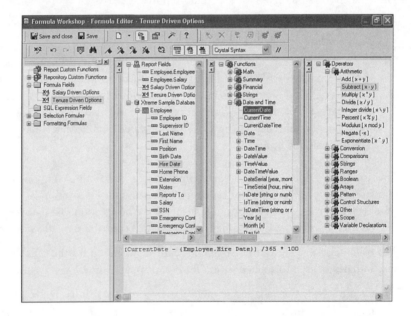

4. Place the new formula on the report beside the Salary Driven Options field and format it to have no decimal places and no currency symbol.

It has likely struck you that most CEOs would not appreciate having to take the two options numbers you have created and add them themselves. It seems like a good opportunity for another formula to sum up those two numbers.

5. Create a new formula called **Total Options** and make that formula be the sum of the two previously created formulas. (Hint: The previously created formulas appear in the

Fields frame under the Report Fields Tree node, and you can use the addition operator.)

6. Add this new field to the report, remove the hire date and salary fields, and reformat it to make your sample resemble that displayed in Figure 4.14.

Figure 4.14
Maple Leaf Bikes CEO report with options formulas.

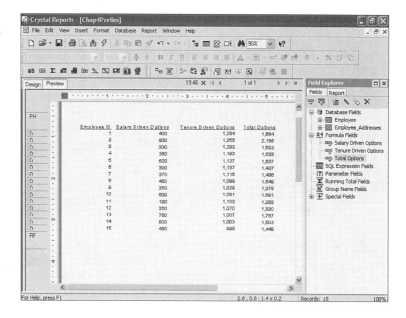

The CEO of Maple Leaf Bikes should be quite happy with the turnaround time on this report. Having created the results so quickly, it might be a good move in career management to spend a little time on the presentation and readability of this report. The next sections and chapters introduce some additional capabilities provided in Crystal Reports and the Formula Editor that increase the presentation quality of this report.

STRING FORMULAS

String formulas are created from existing string fields (or fields converted into strings—type conversion is covered later in the chapter in the section "Using Type Conversion in Formulas"). These formulas can be as simple as concatenating two string fields or as complex as extracting some specific piece of information from a string field. String formulas are created within the Formula Editor by selecting any combination of string fields, string operators, or string-oriented functions. Figure 4.15 displays the Formula Editor resized to highlight some common string functions.

The most commonly created string-based formulas involve the concatenation of multiple existing fields from a data source. This is accomplished through the Formula Editor with either the formal Concatenate function from within the Strings section of the Operators frame or by using the much easier + and & concatenate operators. These last two operators enable the dynamic linking of one or more string fields into one large string field.

Figure 4.15
The Formula Editor
with string-oriented
functions expanded.

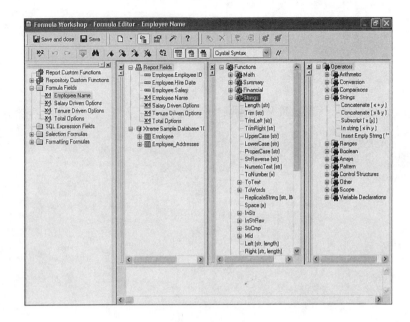

TIP

Although the + operator requires all of its arguments to be of the same string type when concatenating, the & operator performs dynamic conversion to text on any non-string fields included in the operation—a nice timesaving feature.

Revisiting the Maple Leaf Bikes reporting scenario and focusing on increasing the readability of the report, Employee ID can be replaced with Employee First Initial and Last Name. To use the string capabilities of the Formula Editor and enhance the report, follow these steps:

NOTE

When creating a string formula that is meant to join two existing strings (for example, First Name and Last Name, or Address 1 and Address 2), the concatenation features of Crystal Reports dynamically resize the resultant formula to exclude any redundant spaces between the end of the first joined field and the beginning of the next. This is an important presentation feature that prevents the requirement to trim all fields before joining them together.

1. Create a new formula in the sample report called **Employee Name**.
2. Because you only want to present the first letter of the employee's first name, you need to use the Left function under the Strings section of the Functions frame. Add this to

your formula and note that the cursor is automatically placed in the expected location for the first parameter to this function—a string.

3. Without moving the cursor in the Editing area, find the First Name field of the Employee table and double-click it (you will likely need to expand the Xtreme Sample Database section because this field is not currently added to the report). This adds it as the first argument to the Left function.

4. Move the cursor in the Editing area to the location of the second expected parameter for the Left function—after the comma—and type **1** (the number of characters to extract). This creates the entry Left ({Employee.First Name}, 1) in the Formula Editor and instructs the Formula Engine to take the leftmost single character from the First Name field.

5. To concatenate this with the Last Name in a nice-looking manner, type **+ ". " +** into the Editing area and then double-click on the Last Name field of the Employee table. Your new formula should resemble Figure 4.16.

Figure 4.16
String formula sample in the Formula Editor.

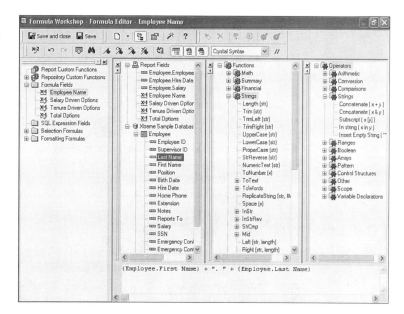

6. Replace the Employee ID field in the CEO's sample report with the new Employee Name formula you just created and re-arrange your report to resemble Figure 4.17.

Having covered the primary data types used in strings, it is useful for operating in the real world to know how to move between those data types. The next section discusses data type conversion.

Figure 4.17
Maple Leaf Bikes CEO report with String formula.

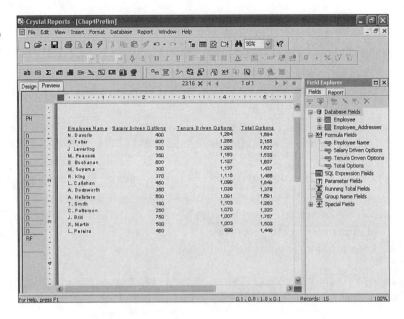

TIP

> Comments can be added to formula statements to better document the formula. To insert comments, use the double forward slash (/ /) at the beginning of a line of code to comment out the entire line. Thus, any text on this commented line would not be processed as part of the formula. There is also a toolbar command within the Formula Editor that enables you to add this syntax into formulas quickly, as indicated with the double slash (//) icon. If you're using the Basic Syntax, the apostrophe (or rem) commands can be used for commenting.

USING TYPE CONVERSION IN FORMULAS

Often, data is not accessible in the format that is required for a particular operation. A common example is when numeric fields are stored in a database as string fields and they are required in an Arithmetic formula. For any number of additional reasons, it often happens that data needs to be converted to and from different data types. The Formula Editor provides numerous built-in functions that facilitate this conversion process. These functions are accessible from the Type Conversion section under the Functions frame of the Formula Editor. Figure 4.18 displays the Formula Editor with the Type Conversion section expanded.

A great deal of flexibility is provided with the numerous type conversion functions built into Crystal Reports and these should enable all required conversions. Additionally, Crystal Reports provides some automatic conversions in the following cases: Number to Currency,

Date to DateTime, and basic type to a Range Value of the same underlying basic type. Some of the most commonly used Type Conversion functions are

- CStr() or ToText(): These identical functions convert Numbers, Currency, Date, Time, and DateTime values to text strings.

- CDbl() or ToNumber(): These identical functions convert Currency, text string, or Boolean values to a Number. Often used in combination with **IsNumeric()** or **NumericText()** to validate input arguments.

- CDate(), CDateTime(), or CTime(): These functions convert their given arguments (numeric, string, and specific fixed formats) to a respective Date, DateTime, or Time value.

Figure 4.18
The Formula Editor provides you with many different Type Conversion functions.

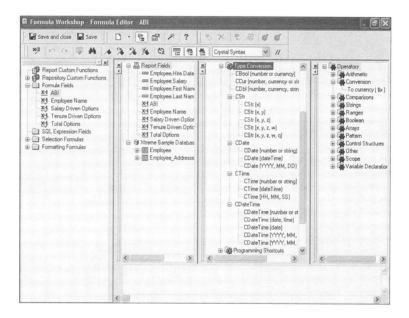

A couple of more interesting type conversion options include the following:

- Roman(): This function converts a number ranging from 0 to 3999 into its Roman numeral equivalent (for example, Roman(2004) = MMIV).

- ToWords(): This function converts a number or currency value to a string representation of that number (for example, ToWords($134.15, 2) = one hundred thirty four and 15/100). This is a nice function for facilitating the delivery of checks.

NOTE

Barcode conversion functions are also available through a third party, Azalea, at: http://www.azalea.com/CrystalReports/index.html. These enable you to convert numbers to standard barcodes that can be embedded on your Crystal Reports.

CONTROL STRUCTURES—CONDITIONAL AND LOOPING STRUCTURES

The Formula Editor provides additional power in formula creation through a set of control structures made available in the Operators and Functions Frames. Figure 4.19 displays the involved sections of those respective frames that include the provided control structures.

Figure 4.19
The Formula Editor provides several Control Structure functions and operators.

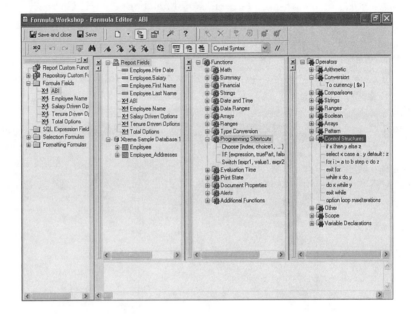

One of the most useful control structures is the If/Then/Else construct. This structure enables the inclusion of conditional logic in Crystal Reports formulas. The If/Then/Else works particularly well when a condition leads to either one of two settings. Although this construct can handle multiple potential settings through nested If statements, creating this type of complicated formula can be avoided with the Select Case operator that allows for multiple settings and multiple potential results.

Revisiting the Maple Leaf Bikes example, assume that the CEO has provided a new requirement specifying that employees with a recommended stock allocation of greater than 1750 stock options need to be highlighted for his personal review. Of course, with Crystal Reports, there are multiple methods of providing this highlighting; to use the If/Then/Else control structure, follow these steps:

1. Create a new formula called High Option Review.

2. Add the If/Then/Else control structure to the formula.

3. Add the condition that the Total Options Formula (the @Total Options field) is greater than 1750 between the If and Then components so that the beginning of the formula text is IF {@Total Options} > 1750 THEN.

4. Now when this condition is met for any employee, you need to highlight that record for the CEO's special review. To do this, add text similar to "** Review **" (with the

double quotes surrounding the text) to the area after the Then part of the If statement construct.

5. When that condition is not met, you can simply print a space or dash. Do this by adding "-" (including the double quotes) after the Else part of the If statement so that your new formula resembles that shown in Figure 4.20.

NOTE

> Carriage returns (via the Enter key) can be inserted into the construction area of the formula, such as between lines and logical breaking points, to make formulas more readable. If you're using the Basic Syntax, you can extend single code lines over multiple lines for readability by using the underscore character (_) preceded by a space.

Figure 4.20
A sample formula with an If control structure.

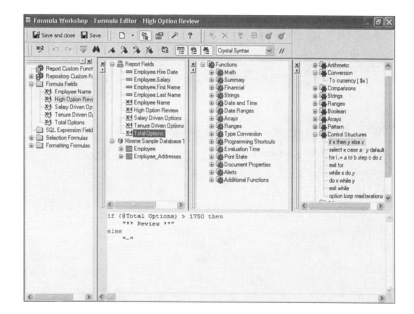

6. Add the new formula to the CEO's report so that it resembles the sample report shown in Figure 4.21.

The conditional logic inherent in the If/Then/Else and Select/Case statements provides clear flexibility in formula creation. Another valuable formula capability that programmers appreciate immediately is the looping functionality. The Formula Editor provides three different looping constructs (For/Step/Do, Do/While, and While/Do), and each of these enable the evaluation of formula logic multiple times for each evaluation of the formula. Table 4.2 describes the most common types of control structures and their usage.

Figure 4.21
The revised sample report includes a High Option Review indicator.

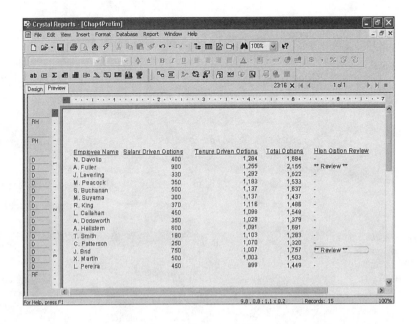

TABLE 4.2	COMMONLY USED CONTROL STRUCTURES	
Control Structure	**Description**	**Usage**
If/Then/Else and IIF()	Conditional structures that select an execution path based on the evaluated conditions.	This construct is best used when evaluating conditions with a minimal set of potential execution options.
Select Case	Conditional structure that selects an execution path based on the evaluation conditions.	This construct is best used in place of the if/then/else construct when evaluating conditions with multiple potential execution paths.
Switch	Another conditional structure that selects a value from a set of expression/value pairs where the expression evaluates to true.	This is especially effective when creating report selection filters because it allows for the pushing of the results down to the database for faster report execution—this is not possible with the other conditional constructs. It is also useful for compact conditional formula creation.
For/Step/Do Loops	For loops enable you to evaluate a sequence of statements a fixed numbers of times. An Exit statement can end this looping prematurely.	This construct is best used when you know the number of times that the expressions need to be evaluated in advance or the loops are dependent on a variable in the report. `For I = X to Y Step Z Do` (*statements*)

Control Structure	Description	Usage
Do/While Loops	Do/While loops execute until the While condition is no longer met. They always execute at least once. The Exit While statement can end this looping prematurely.	While loops can be used to execute a fixed block of statements an indefinite number of times. Do statements While condition
While/Do Loops	While/Do loops execute until the While condition is no longer met. It is possible that not a single iteration takes place if the condition is immediately false. The Exit While statement can end this looping prematurely.	While loop can be used to execute a fixed block of statements an indefinite amount of time. While condition Do (statements)

CAUTION

The Crystal Reports engine has a built-in safety mechanism that displays an error message and stops processing any formula if it includes more than 100,000 loop iterations. This is important to consider when including any of the loop constructs in a formula. It is also important to note that this built-in governor works on a per formula basis and not per loop. This means that if any one formula contains any number of loops that tally more than 100,000 looping iterations, the formula stops processing with an error. Another control structure function called Option Loop can be used for limiting iterations to a number different than 100,000.

VARIABLES

Crystal Reports has included yet another programming construct, variables, in the Formula Editor to provide even further flexibility in formula creation. Variables give you a powerful means to store and retrieve information throughout the processing life of any report—essentially providing a temporary storage space for valuable information. Examples of information that might be useful to store and retrieve later are previous detail section information, previous group section information, or a one-time calculation that needs to be incorporated into many subsequent report formulas.

Several different types of variables can be declared (for example, String, Number, Date, Time, Boolean, and so on) and three different scopes for each of these variables are as follows:

- Local: Accessible only in the same formula within which they are declared.
- Global: Accessible from all formulas in the main report, but not accessible from subreports.
- Shared: Accessible from all formulas in both the main report and all subreports.

Both the Variable Declaration and Scope operators listings are accessible from the Operators frame in the Formula Editor. To use variables in your report formulas, they must be declared first—and this applies to every formula that accesses any given variable—not just the first processed formula.

TIP

> Another important function to remember when using multiple variables in multiple formulas with calculation dependencies is the EvaluateAfter() function. This formula function can force certain formulas (and their variable logic) to be processed after another formula (and its variable logic). This can be very useful when the order of formula calculation is important because of variable and formula dependencies. A good discussion of when things are evaluated in Crystal Report's multi-pass engine is provided in Chapter 12.

It is worth noting that variables can provide significant power in report creation in their capability to maintain persistent information outside the regular processing path of the report. A practical hands-on use of variables is explored in Chapter 12.

CREATING FORMULAS WITH THE FORMULA EXPERT

The Formula Expert is used to create formulas based on existing custom functions—either from the current report or the Crystal Repository. The expert appears when you click the Use Expert button in the Formula Name dialog during the formula creation process or click on the Formula Expert/Editor toggle button (the magic wand). The Formula Expert leverages the power of the custom functions and repository functionality introduced first in version 9. Figure 4.22 displays the Formula Expert dialog.

Figure 4.22
The Formula Expert dialog enables rapid creation of formulas through a wizard type interface.

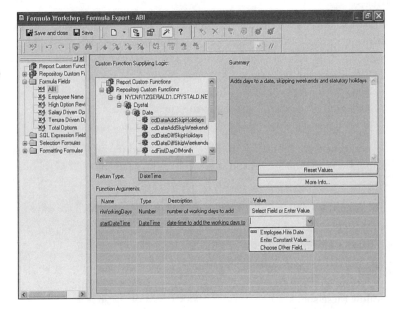

To use the Formula Expert, follow this simple three-step process:

1. Find the custom function that meets your formula requirements by searching through the Report and Repository Custom Function libraries. The supporting Help description and More Info button can aid in this search.

2. For each parameter of the selected function, select a field from your report data source or enter a constant.

3. Save the new formula using the Save button.

The created formula is now accessible through the Formula Editor and can be enhanced or edited with that tool.

USING THE FORMULA EXTRACTOR TO CREATE CUSTOM FUNCTIONS

The Formula Expert enables you to create formulas from existing custom functions. The Formula Extractor does the exact opposite—it enables you to create custom functions from previously created formulas. This functionality is accessible by creating a new Custom Report Function and selecting the Use Extractor button. Figure 4.23 displays the Extract Custom Function from Formula dialog accessed when creating custom report functions.

Figure 4.23
The Extract Custom Function from Formula dialog enables the creation of a custom function from an existing formula.

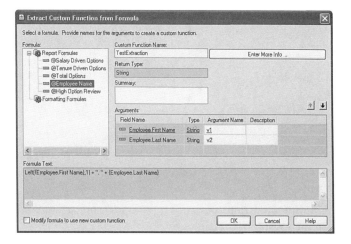

By using the Formula Extractor, it is possible to migrate existing formula logic from a formula field into a custom function. The appropriate part of the migrated formulas can subsequently be replaced with the new custom function and eventually be added to the Crystal Repository.

To create a custom function from an existing formula using the Formula Extractor dialog, follow these steps:

1. In the Formula Workshop, create a new Custom Report Function. Select the Formula Extractor by clicking on the Use Extractor button after you have ensured that the custom function name you have selected follows your personal or organization's standard naming convention.

2. Edit the default argument names (v1, v2, and so on) and descriptions that represent the required parameters for the new function. These argument names and descriptions should communicate the expected information to future users of the custom function. The importance of meaningful information here cannot be underestimated with respect to the future usefulness of the newly created custom function.

3. Add an appropriate summary description to the Summary window so that future report designers using this custom function will understand its proper use.

4. Click on the Modify Formula to Use New Function check box (in the lower-left area of the Extract Custom Function dialog) to place the new custom function into the formula on which you are basing it. This is not a mandatory step, but it is a nice feature that quickly enables you to take advantage of the reusability of your new custom function.

5. Click the Enter More Info button to add additional support information for the custom function. Figure 4.24 displays the More Info dialog.

Figure 4.24
The Custom Function Enter More Info dialog enables the specification of supporting information for the newly created custom function.

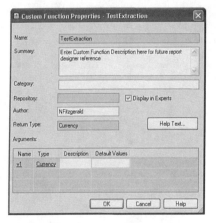

6. Enter the custom function author (likely yourself) and custom function category information in their respective text boxes.

NOTE

> When entering a custom function category, it is possible to create it at more than one level of subfolder depth by using forward slashes in the Category text box. For example, by entering **MapleLeafBikes/HR**, the newly created formula will be added to the Custom Function library under the Maple Leaf Bikes category and the HR subfolder. By adding and maintaining your custom functions in a logical hierarchy, future users will find accessing them much easier.

7. Optionally, set default values for your custom functions arguments by clicking on the default value cells and filling in the Default Values dialog.

8. Add Help text describing the custom function by clicking on the Help Text button. Again, it is important to consider future report designers using this custom function when deciding on the detail that you should include in this description.

THE MULTI-PASS REPORTING PROCESS OF THE CRYSTAL REPORTS ENGINE

Despite all the Crystal Reports functionality covered, to this point, it would be understandable if you assumed that the Crystal Reports reporting engine provides all this power with a single pass through the data it retrieves from the database. This would be a faulty assumption—Crystal Reports actually uses a three-pass reporting methodology to generate reports. Understanding the multi-pass nature of the reporting engine can facilitate effective report design and expedite the debugging of potential reporting challenges. Figure 4.25 from the Crystal Reports online Help file provides a good starting point for understanding the different passes through the data that Crystal Reports makes and what is calculated on each pass.

Figure 4.25
Understanding the Crystal Reports Multi-Pass report engine flow can help in creating and debugging Crystal Reports.

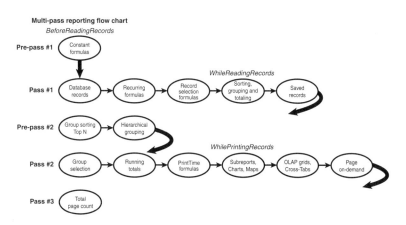

CRYSTAL REPORTS PROCESSING ENGINE—PRE-PASS #1

In the Pre-Pass phase of report creation, only constant formulas are processed. A constant formula example might be 1967*10. These formulas are evaluated at the beginning of the print generation process and are never evaluated again. This process is known as "BeforeReadingRecords."

CRYSTAL REPORTS PROCESSING ENGINE—PASS #1

After the constant formulas have been processed, Crystal Reports begins reading the database records. During the record reading process, known as "WhileReadingRecords," the following occurs:

- **Database connection and Record retrieval**. Record selection and sorting are pushed down to the database in this step if possible.

- **Evaluates recurring formulas**. These formulas are those that contain database fields but do not contain references to subtotals or summary information. This evaluation time is referenced as "WhileReadingRecords" and can be specified within a formula. Formulas that contain references to subtotals or summary information are processed in the second pass.

- **Local Record Selection applied**. If the record selection is too complex to be pushed down to the database, it is applied by Crystal Reports in this step. This is common where the record selection could be not specified in a proper SQL Expression.

- **Sorting, Grouping, and Summarizing**. The data is sorted, separated into groups, and then subtotals and summaries are calculated for each group.

- **Cross-tab, chart, and map generation**. Only cross-tabs, charts, and maps that are based entirely on database fields and recurring formulas are generated in Pass 1.

- **Storage of saved data**. After the totaling process is complete, all the records and totals are stored in memory and to temporary files. Crystal Reports does not read the database again, but instead uses this saved data during all subsequent processing.

CRYSTAL REPORTS PROCESSING ENGINE—PRE-PASS #2

During Pre-Pass #2, groups are ordered in the report for Top/Bottom N and/or Hierarchical Grouping. The reporting engine looks at group instances from Pass 1, and takes the Top N as appropriate, or orders the groups based on the specified Hierarchical Group settings.

CRYSTAL REPORTS PROCESSING ENGINE—PASS #2

Crystal Reports moves through the saved data, if required, to complete any remaining operations and initiates printing of the records in this phase known as "WhilePrintingRecords." During this phase, the following takes place:

- Application of Group selection formula, if applicable.

- Evaluates print-time formulas. These formulas are those that contain any print-time formula functions like Previous() or Next() or explicitly use the "WhilePrintingRecords" function within the formula.

- Running totals calculations, if applicable.

- Charts, maps, cross-tabs and OLAP grids. Cross-tabs, charts, and maps that include running totals or PrintTime formulas, and charts that are based on cross-tabs or OLAP grids are generated.

- Subreports. All in-place subreports are calculated during Pass #2. When you're using variables within subreports and expecting certain behavior in the main report based on these shared variables, keep in mind when they are processed relative to everything else in the main report.

CAUTION

> Subtotals, grand totals, and summaries might appear incorrectly if the report has a group selection formula. This occurs because the grand totals and summaries are calculated during Pass 1, but the group selection formula filters the data again in Pass 2. Running total fields or Formula fields with variables can be used instead of summaries to total data successfully with group selection formulas.

CRYSTAL REPORTS PROCESSING ENGINE—PASS #3

In the third and final pass, the total page count is determined. This applies to reports that use the total page count, or Page N of M special fields.

Understanding the multi-pass reporting paths of the Crystal Reports engine helps in the general development and debugging of your production reports. Additional leveraging of the built-in Formula functions discussed previously (`BeforeReadingRecords`, `WhileReadingRecords`, and `WhilePrintingRecords`) in combination with the `EvaluateAfter()` function enable you to design more flexible reports and formulas. These functions also enable you to leverage advanced variable usage and successful sharing among subreports.

TROUBLESHOOTING

ADDING A CUSTOM FUNCTION

I cannot add a custom function directly into the Central Repository.

Custom functions cannot be directly added into the Central Repository. When you add a custom function to the Central Repository for other report developers to use, you must first create it locally as a Report Custom function and only then can it be added to the Central Repository. With version 10 of the Crystal Suite of products, you must also be licensed for Crystal Enterprise Professional or Premium editions to leverage a Central Repository.

CRYSTAL REPORTS IN THE REAL WORLD— CUSTOM FUNCTIONS

Some examples of custom functions include handling divide-by-zero errors and handling multilanguage text. Both of these examples are described in this section. A common reason for divide-by-zero errors is simply that a field might not be populated. If a given field has not been populated but it is used in the report, Crystal converts it to a default value. Unless modified, the default value for a numeric field that returns NULL is 0. This means that if there is a formula calculating percent of capacity (`Current_Amount/Max_Amount`) but the item is new and therefore no max amount has been set, then the `Max_Amount` field in the database is likely blank. When the preceding formula is applied to the database fields then the result will be an error. `Current_Amount/Max_Amount` would resolve to some real value divided by NULL, the NULL would be converted to the default value of 0, and the result would be some number divided by 0—and a divide-by-0 error is the result.

To avoid this, create a custom function to handle all division. The custom function simply checks for a denominator of 0 and handles it appropriately.

First create the custom function:

1. Open the sample report Chap4Formulas.rpt. From the Field Explorer, select Formula Fields and click New. Type in a name for the formula such as **Source Formula** and click Use Editor.

2. When the Formula Workshop window opens, enter the following formula:

```
If {Employee.Supervisor ID} = 0 Then
    0
Else
    {Employee.Employee ID}/{Employee.Supervisor ID};
```

> **NOTE**
> Although it seems (and is) odd to build a formula using ID fields in a calculation, what is important is the field types. The fields are used to build the custom function based on their data types rather than actual content. The previous fields are abstracted to simply numeric fields named v1 and v2.

3. With the Formula Workshop still open, mouse over the New button near the top of the window and click the down arrow. From the list choose Custom Function, enter the name **DivBy0**, and click the User Extractor button.

4. When the Extract Custom Function from Formula window opens, select the @Source Formula item from the list of formulas. Rename the arguments from v1 and v2 to Denominator and Numerator, respectively (see Figure 4.26).

5. Click OK to close the window and the function is now part of the report. Right-click on the function name and choose Add to Repository. If prompted, enter the logon information for your Crystal Enterprise system and the custom function will be added to the Crystal Enterprise Repository making it available to all the users who have access to the repository.

6. Click Save and Close (see Figure 4.27).

Another example of a custom function might be how to handle some standard text options. For example, it might be useful to have a parameter drive the column header for a field.

1. Keep the report open. Create a new parameter named Language (described in Chapter 5, "Implementing Parameters for Dynamic Reporting") and add a new formula named Country Source (described previously). Add the following formula code:

```
If {?Language} = "English" Then
    "Country"
Else If {?Language} = "French" Then
    "Pays"
Else If {?Language} = "Italian" Then
    "Paese";
```

Figure 4.26
Using the Custom
Function Extractor,
create a custom func-
tion from a formula.

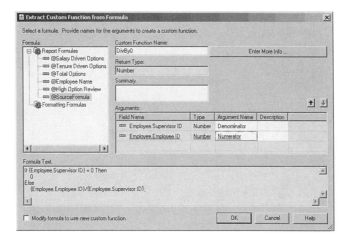

Figure 4.27
The custom function
is now part of the
repository making it
available to users who
have appropriate
rights.

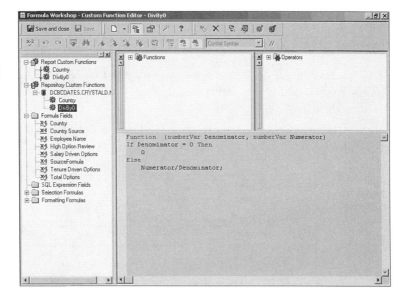

2. Repeat steps 3, 4, 5, and 6 to create a new custom function called Country extracted from the Country Source formula.

3. To use the new custom function, create a new formula named Country. From the list of functions, expand the Custom Functions and double-click the Country formula. The function takes one argument, pass in the Language parameter (see Figure 4.28).

Figure 4.28
The custom function accepting the Language parameter. This parameter determines what the function does.

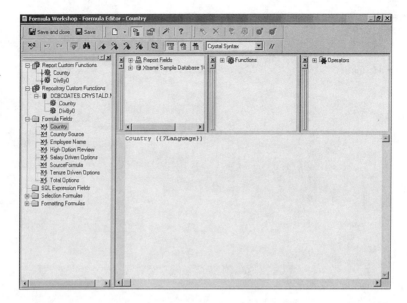

4. Click Save and Close. If prompted, enter the text **English**. Place the new formula in the group header alongside the other column headers and add the country field below it on the detail line.

5. Save the report as Chap4FormulaswithCustom.rpt. Refresh the report passing in "English," "French," and "Italian" to see the effect (see Figure 4.29).

Figure 4.29
The field header changes to display Country in appropriate languages.

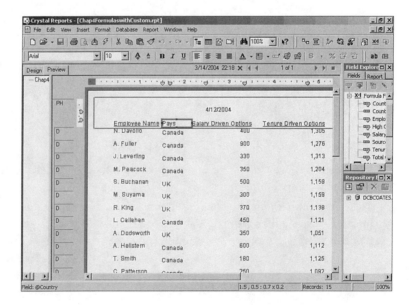

CHAPTER 5

IMPLEMENTING PARAMETERS FOR DYNAMIC REPORTING

In this chapter

INTRODUCTION

A common goal of report design is providing a single report that can service very specific reporting requirements and also accommodate a large audience of business users. Parameter fields enable you to satisfy this requirement and provide three primary benefits:

- *An additional level of interactivity for business users when viewing reports.* A sales report can prompt a business user for her specific district or territory.
- *Ability to segment reports in many different ways to reduce the number of reports necessary to service the demands of the business users.* A sales report can be segmented by district to service the needs of all district-level business users with one report.
- *Greater control over the report query for administrators by filtering the report results to include only the selected parameter value(s).* A sales report can be filtered to include only data for the appropriate district. This also includes the capability to constrain the report query to avoid including excess or sensitive data.

In this chapter, you take a closer look at using parameters in your reports, as well as how parameter fields can be created and implemented. Like many of the Crystal Reports application features, working with report parameters is very logical but understanding the underlying mechanics facilitates the creation of effective reports.

This chapter covers the following topics:

- Understanding the value of parameters
- Creating and implementing parameter fields
- Using parameters with record selections

UNDERSTANDING THE VALUE OF PARAMETERS

By using parameter fields that enable business users to select from a list of one or more parameter field values (such as district, country, or account type), you can make reports more valuable for the business users while limiting the volume of data that the report retrieves. For example, a sales report is likely to be more valuable for a sales professional if it allows him to select his specific territory or district, while the report runs more efficiently because it retrieves only the desired data and not an unnecessarily large data set. Parameter fields can prompt users for a variety of information that can be used in a number of flexible ways within reports—good examples include controlling the sort order, grouping order, record selection (filter), report title and descriptions, report language, alerting thresholds, formula inputs, and so on.

Parameter fields prompt report users to enter information by presenting a question that the user must answer before the report is executed. The information that the user enters determines what appears in the resulting report and also how that report is formatted and presented.

One of the greatest benefits of parameter fields for report designers is the opportunity to have a single report service a large audience while also empowering the users to personalize the information they are viewing within the report. Parameter fields can be used in coordination with record selections so that a single report can be segmented many different ways. Parameter values that business users enter can also be used within record selection formulas to determine what data is retrieved from the database.

For example, consider a World Sales Report for a large organization. This report could potentially include a tremendous amount of data. Not only is the report itself large, but also many of the business users are not concerned with the entire worldwide scope of the sales data. Rather than allow each salesperson to generate the report to include worldwide data, you can include a parameter dialog that asks the salesperson to select from a list of available countries, as shown in Figure 5.1. The report would then return the results for only these specific countries. Thus, by using a parameter field to enable the salespeople to select from a list of countries, the report becomes more valuable for the business users while also limiting the scope of the query by using the selected parameter value(s) to filter the report and reduce the volume of data retrieved.

Figure 5.1
Prompts enable business users to select values to populate the parameter field.

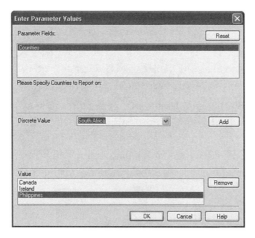

CREATING AND IMPLEMENTING PARAMETERS FIELDS

The process of using parameter fields in reports includes two distinct steps:

1. Creation of the parameter field.
2. Implementation of the parameter field into the report.

The remainder of this chapter uses the example mentioned earlier, the World Sales Report, to create and implement parameter fields into a report. The World Sales Report is one of the many sample reports that are provided by the Crystal Reports installation.

REVIEWING PARAMETER FIELD PROPERTIES

Before you learn how to create and implement parameter fields, it is useful to understand a few common properties associated with creating parameter fields. Each of the following properties is presented within the Create/Edit Parameter Field dialog, shown in Figure 5.2:

- Name—A logical name for the parameter field.
- Prompting Text—A statement or question that is presented to the business user within the report prompt dialog for the parameter field.
- Value Type—A list of available field types that correspond to how you want to use the parameter field within the report, including String (the default option), Boolean, Currency, Date, Date Time, Number, and Time.
- Allow Multiple Values—Enables the business user to enter more than a single value for the parameter field.
- Discrete Values—Enables the business user to enter only a single value for the parameter field.
- Range Values—Enables the business user to specify a range, using start and end values, for the parameter field.
- Discrete and Range Values—Enables the business user to enter specific single values as well as a range, using start and end values, for the parameter field.
- Allow Editing of Default Values—Enables the business user of a report to edit any default values provided in the report parameter dialog or add their own manually.
- Default Values—A dialog that enables the report designer to specify default parameter values based on either a database field, external pick list, or manual entries.

Now that you have been exposed to the primary parameter field properties, you will use these items while creating parameters for a World Sales Report, as referenced earlier in the chapter.

5

Figure 5.2
The primary parameter field properties are presented within the Create/Edit Parameter Field dialog.

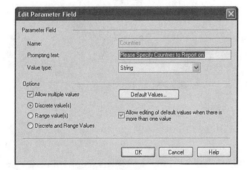

CREATING PARAMETER FIELDS

The first step in using parameters within a report is to create the actual parameter field and define the primary properties associated with it. In the following exercise, use the Field Explorer dialog to create two new parameter fields for the World Sales Report:

- A manual text entry field to use as the report's title
- A database field that prompts the business user to select one or more countries and use this selection to filter the data returned for the report

To begin your exercise, open the World Sales Report within the Crystal Reports designer. This sample report should be installed in the following directory, unless you have chosen an alternative location for the sample reports during the Crystal Reports 10 installation process:

```
C:\Program Files\Crystal Decisions\Crystal Reports
10\Samples\En\Reports\General Business
```

After you have opened this sample report, you can begin the steps necessary to create the parameter field objects in the following way:

1. Remove the existing report title text object. After you have opened the World Sales Report, navigate to the Design tab view, highlight and delete the text object currently used as the report's title that reads World Sales Report, located in the Report Header A section. Use your parameter field to populate the report title.

2. Remove the current Top N sort order because it is not needed for your exercises. From the Report menu, select Group Sort Expert, and within the presented dialog modify the For This Group Sort: drop-down setting to display All as shown in Figure 5.3. Click OK to continue.

Figure 5.3
Use the Group Sort Expert dialog to remove the Top N sort order from the report.

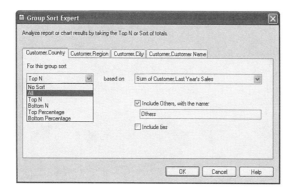

3. Open the Field Explorer dialog by either clicking the appropriate toolbar button or using the View menu.

4. Open the Create Parameter Field dialog. To do this, right-click on Parameter Fields within the Field Explorer and either select New from the pop-up menu or click on the New button at the top of the Field Explorer.

TIP

> In addition to using the right-click menu to create a new parameter field, you can use the Field Explorer's toolbar commands to create, edit, rename, and delete parameter fields. The operations available on this toolbar depend on what you have selected in the Field Explorer dialog.

You first create a manual text-entry parameter field to enable the business user to define a title to display on the report.

5. Define the key properties for the parameter object. Within the Create Parameter Field, enter **Title** in the Name property, and provide a meaningful prompting text so that the business user understands how the entered value is used, such as, **Enter a title to be used for this report**.

6. Select Discrete Values under the Options area and click OK to return to the Field Explorer.

7. You should now see the **Title** parameter field listed under Parameter Fields in the Field Explorer, as shown in Figure 5.4.

Figure 5.4
The Field Explorer is used to access, edit, and create parameter fields.

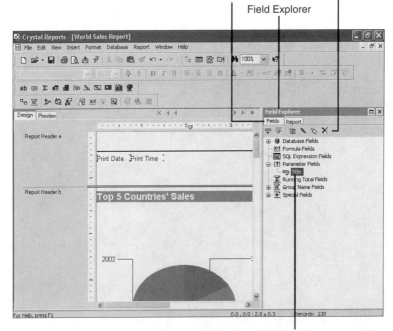

Newly-created "Title" parameter field

You now create a second parameter field to use later in the chapter when discussing how to use parameter fields in coordination with record selections. In this way, you can filter the report data according to the selected parameter values.

8. Open the Create Parameter Field dialog. To do this, highlight the Parameter Fields item and click the New toolbar button inside the Field Explorer dialog.

9. Define the key properties for the parameter object. Within the Create Parameter Field dialog, enter **Countries** in the Name property and provide a meaningful prompting text so that the business user understands how the entered value will be used, such as, **Please select one or more countries for this report**.

10. Select both the Allow Multiple Values and Discrete Value(s) items under the Options area, as shown in Figure 5.5.

Figure 5.5
Use the Create Parameter Field dialog to create and edit parameter fields.

SETTING DEFAULT VALUES FOR PARAMETER FIELDS

You now want to define the Countries parameter field to include all database values within the Country field of the Customer table. Map the parameter field to this database field and quickly import these values, enabling the business user of the report to select one or more country values from the available list.

When setting default parameter values, a list of default values can be read from the database or entered manually to provide the business user with a list of available values from which to choose. The Crystal Reports application enables you to define the default values list only when you are designing reports, and no direct database connection exists to populate the prompting parameter field list when the business users run the report. The following is an overview of various options available within the Set Default Values dialog to make data entry easier for the business users:

■ Browse Table—The database table that contains the default values for the parameter field.

■ Browse Field—The database field that contains the default values for the parameter field.

■ Select or Enter Value—Used to enter values in the Default Values list. You can type new values in the entry box and then click the Add button (>), or select a value from the list and then click the Add button (>). This list is automatically populated when a field is selected through the Browse Field drop-down box.

- Add, Add All—Used to move one (>) or all (>>) values from the Select or Enter Value to Add list (on the left) to the Default Values list (on the right).

- Remove, Remove All—Used to move one (<) or all (<<) values from the Default Values list (on the right) back to the Select or Enter Value list (on the left).

- Import/Export—Used to import or export a text file containing a pick list of parameter values to be used as the default values. (Note: These two buttons are not available when creating or editing parameters in the OLAP Report Creation Wizard.)

- Default Values and Description—The list of values displayed when business users are prompted to populate the parameter field, and a description for each value (optional). To set the optional description for each default value, use the Set Description button and corresponding dialog, located just below the Default Values list. The value list can be populated from any database table included in the report using the Browse Table and Field drop-down boxes. The description can be used to create a more user-friendly label for the business users. For example, the Country field could have been stored as a number in the database, but it would be more intuitive for the user to select it by name.

- Display—Controls whether the prompt to business user displays the Value and Description, or just the Description, for each default value. In either case, only the Value is used within any database interaction, such as with record selection definitions.

- Order—The order that the default values are displayed in the prompt to the business users of the report.

- Order Based On—The order of the default values can be based on either the Value or Description property of these values.

- Length Limit—The minimum and maximum length limits for the parameter field.

- Edit Mask—Used to enter an Edit Mask for string data types rather than specifying a range of values. The Edit Mask can be any of a set of *masking characters* used to restrict the values you can enter as parameter values. (The Edit Mask also limits the values you can enter as default prompting values.) Table 5.1 provides a listing of the masking characters and instructions on how to use them.

TABLE 5.1   EDIT MASK CHARACTERS

Mask Character	Mask Description
A	Requires entry of an alphanumeric character for its place in the parameter value.
a	Enables an alphanumeric character but does not require the entry of a character for its place in the parameter value.
0	Requires a digit (0 to 9) for its place in the parameter value.
9	Enables a digit or a space but does not require such an entry for its place in the parameter value.

Mask Character	Mask Description
#	Enables a digit, space, or plus/minus sign, but does not require such an entry for its place in the parameter value.
L	Requires a letter (A to Z) for its place in the parameter value.
?	Enables a letter but does not require such an entry for its place in the parameter value.
&	Requires a character or space for its place in the parameter value.
C	Enables any character or space but does not require such an entry for its place in the parameter value.
. , : ; - / (separator characters)	Inserting separator characters into an Edit Mask is akin to hard-coding the formatting for the parameter field. When the field is placed on the report, the separator character appears in the field object frame, like this: L0L-0L0. This example depicts an edit mask for a Canadian Postal Code (such as M2M-2L5) with a forced display dash.
< or >	Forces subsequent characters in the parameter to be converted to lowercase (<) or uppercase (>).
\	Forces the subsequent character to be displayed as a literal.
Password	Enables the setting of the Edit Mask to "Password," so that subsequent conditional formulas can specify that certain sections of the report become visible only when certain user passwords are entered.

You now define the default values for your parameter fields (if necessary, refer to the list of options within the Set Default Values dialog while completing these steps):

1. Access the Create/Edit Parameter dialog if you have closed it by highlighting the Countries parameter and clicking on the Edit toolbar button. Open the Set Default Values dialog by clicking on the Set Default Values button, as shown in Figure 5.6.

2. Choose the database table and field from which to set the defaults. Under the Select from Database area of the Set Default Values dialog, select Customer from the Browse Table list, and then select Country from the Browse Field list.

3. Add the actual database values to the default value list. With all the country values listed under the Select or Enter Value to Add area on the left, use the Add All (>>) button to move all these values to the Default Values list on the right, as shown in Figure 5.6.

   Continuing the steps started above, now add descriptions to the default values that you have added to the parameter field.

4. Locate and highlight the USA value in the Default Values list. Click on the Define Description button located just below the Default Values list to present the Define Description dialog.

5. Add **United States of America** as the description for USA, as shown in Figure 5.7, and click OK to close the Define Description dialog. If you want, repeat this step for any additional default values.

5

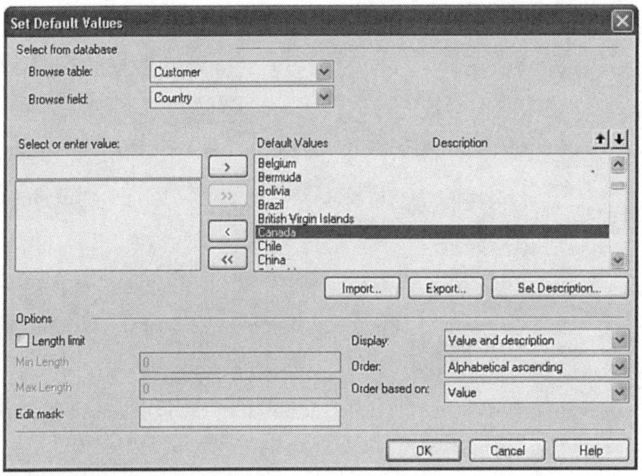

Figure 5.6
The Set Default Values dialog enables you to define the default values for parameter fields.

Figure 5.7
The Define Description dialog enables you to create user-friendly descriptions for parameter selections that can be presented to users instead of potentially cryptic database values.

5

To make the default values friendlier to the business users of the report, you can sort the contents of the display prompt lists based on the Order and Order Based On option settings. Seven distinct options are available to sort the parameter field values that are reflective of the parameter value type, including both ascending and descending for the three data types—alphanumeric, numeric, and date/time—as well as No Sort. Continuing the Parameter Creation example, follow these steps:

6. Sort the Country parameter field in alphabetic order. Select Alphabetical Ascending from the Order drop-down list, and choose Value from the Order Based On list, as shown in Figure 5.6.

> **TIP**
> If you select a sort type from the Order list that does not match the parameter field value type, no sorting is applied.

7. For your purposes here, you can leave the remaining options within the Default Values dialog to their default state and click OK to return to the Create Parameter Field dialog. If desired, peruse the overview of default setting options and use these to modify the desired options for your parameter field.

8. Click OK to return to the Field Explorer. You should now see the Countries parameter field listed under Parameter Fields in the Field Explorer.

TIP

> There are a few considerations to keep in mind when working with parameter fields, such as
>
> - Any parameter field prompting text more than one line in length will automatically word wrap.
> - The creation of a pick list enables the business user to select parameter field values from drop-down boxes instead of needing to enter them manually.
> - A parameter field does not have to be placed in a report to be used in a record or group selection formula. You can create the parameter field and then enter it in your formula as you would any other field.

IMPLEMENTING PARAMETER FIELDS

You have now completed the first task necessary to use parameter fields within a report—creating the actual parameter field objects. This section, and the exercises included here, discuss how to apply these parameter fields and make use of them to provide the business user of the report with a more dynamic and interactive reporting experience.

First, implement the parameter field created earlier, called Title, to serve as the title to the report. This example demonstrates how a manual text entry field can be used to add useful commentary or descriptive information to a report. Continue working with the same report, the World Sales Report and follow these steps:

1. Add and position the Title parameter object onto the report. Open the Field Explorer dialog and expand the Parameter Fields list. Click on the Title parameter field, drag it onto the report, and drop it into the upper-left corner of the Report Header A section, shown in Figure 5.8 in a size 20 Arial font.

2. Preview the report. To view how this parameter is now used within the generation of the report, run the report by clicking on the Refresh toolbar button (represented by the lightning bolt icon). As shown in Figure 5.9, the report now prompts the business user to enter a value that will be used as the report's title.

NOTE

> If you have already run the report at least once and then select to refresh the report, you will also see the Refresh Report Data dialog that asks you to select from the following two options:
>
> - Use Current Parameter Values
> - Prompt for New Parameter Values
>
> To enter or select new values for any existing parameter fields, you need to select the second option–Prompt for New Parameter Values.

5

Figure 5.8
Drag and drop the
Title parameter field
into the upper-left
corner of the Report
Header A section.

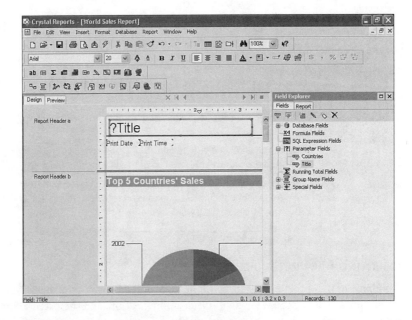

Figure 5.9
Parameter fields offer
a means to add addi-
tional interactivity for
the business users
within the report.

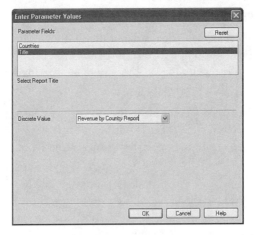

USING PARAMETERS WITH RECORD SELECTIONS

Now that you have completed the task of implementing a parameter field within a report, you learn how a parameter field can also be used to filter the data retrieved by a report. Parameter values that business users enter can be used within record selection formulas to determine what data is retrieved from the database.

In the following exercises, use the same World Sales Report to implement the Countries parameter field (created earlier in the chapter) to filter the report results by including the parameter field within a record selection definition (using the Select Expert dialog). In this case, you enable the business user of the report to select one or more country values to be included in the record selection, thus filtering the report results to include only the desired data. The following steps demonstrate how a single report can be segmented many different ways:

1. Verify that the Countries parameter field is listed below the Parameter Fields group within the Field Explorer.

2. Open the Select Expert dialog by clicking the Report menu and choosing Select Expert.

3. Create a new record selection definition. Within the Select Expert dialog, click on the <New> tab to create a new record selection definition. This opens the Choose Field dialog. Choose Customer.Country from the Report Fields list and then click OK to return to the Select Expert dialog.

4. Define the selection formula. Select Is Equal To from the drop-down list on the left, and then choose the {?Countries} option from the drop-down list on the right, as shown in Figure 5.10.

NOTE

Parameter Field objects are denoted with the question mark, ?, and enclosed in brackets, {}. This convention is used within various application dialogs, including the formula workshop and record selections, to signify that these objects are parameter fields.

Figure 5.10
Parameter fields can be added to record selection formulas quickly via the Select Expert dialog.

5. Preview the report. To view how this parameter is now used within the generation of the report, run the report by clicking on the Refresh toolbar button (represented by the lightning bolt icon). As shown in Figures 5.11 and 5.12, the report now prompts the business user to select from a list of country values that is used to filter the data retrieved by the report and present only the requested values in the report.

Figure 5.11
Business users can now select one or more countries to be included in the report results.

Figure 5.12
Based on the selected parameter field values, the report results display only the desired data.

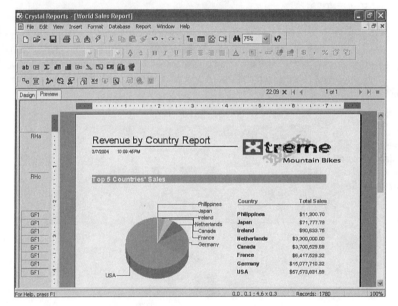

NOTE

After the parameters have been created and implemented into a report, no extra effort is required for parameters to also work within the Crystal Enterprise solution. See Part V, "Web Report Distribution—Using Crystal Enterprise," for more details on Crystal Enterprise.

CRYSTAL REPORTS IN THE REAL WORLD— CUSTOM FILTERING

Sometimes a report needs to return all records for a parameterized field where a record selection filter has been created on this parameter. Although it would certainly be possible to create a parameter and select all valid values for the parameter, there certainly must be a better way—and there is. In this example, a filter is added to a report so that if a user enters a specific value or a list of values, only those values are returned. Alternatively, if the user enters an asterisk (*, or other predefined symbol such as All Values), all values are returned.

1. Open the sample report Chap 5 World SalesParm.rpt created earlier in this chapter.

2. From the Report menu choose Selection Formulas, Record. Remove the following line of text.

```
{Customer.Country} = {?Countries}
```

3. Replace the text with the following (as shown in Figure 5.13):

```
If {?Countries} = "*" Then
    True
Else
    {Customer.Country} = {?Countries};
```

Click Save and Close.

Figure 5.13
The updated Record Selection Formula enables the end user to select All Values with one easy selection.

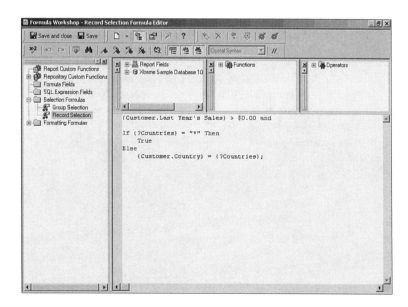

4. When prompted for a new parameter value, remove any existing values, enter the * symbol, click the Add button to add the symbol to the list of values, and click OK. You should see something like in Figure 5.14.

Figure 5.14
The report returns all values when * is passed in as a parameter. In this photo the chart has been removed from the report but the group tree clearly shows many countries being returned.

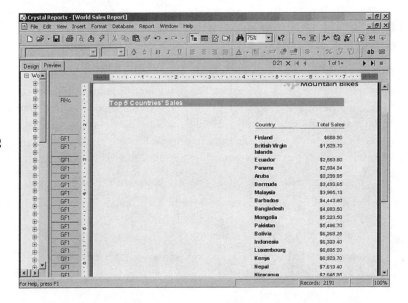

NOTE

Another way to implement an All Values parameter option for the report consumer is to create a record selection through the Record Selection dialog that uses the `is like` operator instead of the `equals to` operator. Using this operator enables you to use the * and ? wildcards in your filter. By having endusers enter '*' or providing that as one of the default parameter selection options, the users can specify All Values without needing to add them all independently. One thing to watch for here is that parameters that allow multiple values do not by default allow themselves to be mapped to in the Record Selection dialog with the `is like` operator. A viable workaround, however, is to map the record selection to the parameter using the `equals to` operator and then edit the formula record selection manually and replace the = operator with the `like` operator.

5

FORMATTING CRYSTAL REPORTS

FUNDAMENTALS OF REPORT FORMATTING

In this chapter

Introduction

To this point, the majority of material you've seen in this book focused on the various functions of the Crystal Reports design application. Equally important, however, is the form (or format) of the report—especially when a report is used as a corporate or industry-standard document that projects a company's image externally (such as an income statement or balance sheet). This chapter focuses on form over function and discusses a myriad of formatting techniques.

You have already reviewed the Crystal Reports 10 development environment and learned about creating a report from a blank canvas, as well as how to select, group, filter, sort, and summarize your report data. Now, you move on to the cosmetic aspects of report design. Working with report formatting and object properties to create professionally designed reports is very straightforward, but does require familiarity with various features of the design-application environment. This chapter reviews the most commonly used object formatting techniques—fonts, borders, page and margin properties, and object layering—and also provides a tutorial to apply these techniques to one of the sample reports created earlier in the book.

This chapter covers the following topics:

- Positioning and sizing report objects
- Modifying object properties for formatting purposes
- Combining and layering report objects
- Configuring report page and margin properties

Positioning and Sizing Report Objects

After you have completed your functional report design tasks—connecting to the data source, adding report objects, and structuring the report—the next step in the report design process is to format the various objects on a report. As demonstrated in Chapter 1, "Creating and Designing Basic Reports," objects can be added to a report via a variety of methods—dragging and dropping objects from the design explorers or selecting objects from toolbar and menu commands and placing them in the desired locations—for quick and intuitive report creation. Upon successfully adding objects to your report, each of the respective objects can be positioned, sized, and formatted for display purposes, as demonstrated in the following exercise.

As a visual example of the difference that report formatting efforts can make, compare the presentation value of the report samples shown in Figures 6.1 and 6.2. These two reports accomplish the same functional tasks, but the report in Figure 6.2 is much more visually appealing.

You will spend the remainder of this chapter reproducing many of the visual transformations from Figure 6.1 to Figure 6.2. By completing the following exercises, you create a Customer

Contact Listing report using a variety of applied formatting techniques, such as adding a group definition to logically structure customers into their respective countries, and formatting the font styles of the report title, column titles, country description, and e-mail address fields to make for a more precise presentation of the report information. By combining the Country database field with a text field, you also provide for a bilingual display of the country description.

Figure 6.1
A customer contact listing report with little to no formatting applied.

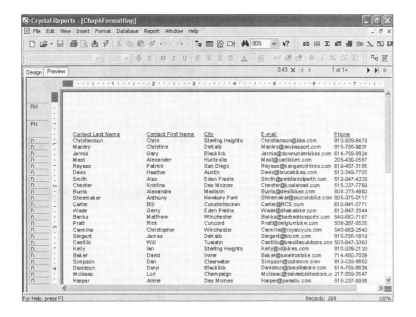

Figure 6.2
A customer contact listing report with a moderate amount of formatting applied.

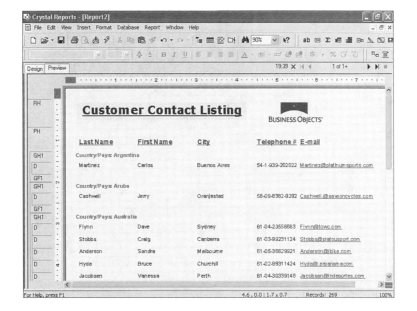

6

To begin designing your report, follow these steps to create your own nicely formatted Customer Contact Listing report:

1. Open the Crystal Reports application and choose to Create a New Report Using the Blank Report Layout from the Report Gallery dialog.

2. From the Database Explorer dialog, expand the Create a New Connection list, and then expand the ODBC (RDO) node to present the ODBC dialog window that lists the available data sources. Select the Xtreme Sample Database from the list of data sources and click Finish to continue to the Database Expert dialog.

3. From the Database Expert dialog, use the arrow (>) button to add the Customer table to the Selected Tables list on the right. Click OK to continue.

4. From the View menu, select the Field Explorer command to open the Field Explorer dialog.

5. From the Field Explorer, click and drag the Contact Last Name field onto the report's design view and place it to the far left of the Details section area, as shown in Figure 6.3.

Figure 6.3
Add the Contact Last Name field to the Details section of the report.

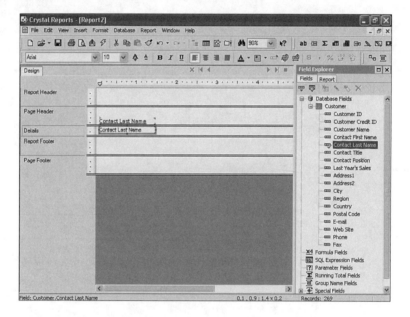

6. Follow the previous step to add the Contact First Name, City, and E-mail fields to the Details section of the report, as shown in Figure 6.4.

7. From the Insert menu, select Text Object and drop the object into the middle of the Report Header section (as shown in Figure 6.4) and type **Customer Contact Listing** in the text field. Click anywhere outside the text object to remove the cursor focus from the text object.

Figure 6.4
The selected fields displayed within the respective sections of the report and a floating Field Explorer dialog.

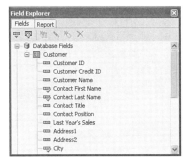

Now that the report includes the field and text objects identified previously, focus on positioning and resizing these fields for display purposes.

8. As Figure 6.4 shows, you might not be able to see the entire text entered into the report title text object because it is not wide enough to display the text entry by default. To resolve this, click once on the report title text object located in the Report Header section so that it becomes highlighted. Using the dark blue handles that encompass the objects perimeters, float over the handle located on the right side of the text object with the mouse pointer; then click and hold the mouse button while dragging the handle farther to the right to widen the text object's display area. Refer to Figure 6.5 to see the result of this action.

N O T E

> Notice that when you float over the perimeter handles of an object with your mouse cursor (or pointer), the cursor icon turns into an alternative shape, such as horizontal or vertical arrows, to illustrate that you can modify the object if you click on the handle.

9. Now that you have widened the display area of your report title object using the concept of object handles, repeat this same step to modify the width of the field objects within the Details report section so that you can insert one additional object into the Details section of your report between the City and E-mail fields.

10. Using the Field Explorer, insert the Phone database field from the Customer table into the Details section of your report. Based on the previous steps, practice positioning and sizing the objects in the Details section to accommodate for all the database fields, as shown in Figure 6.5.

T I P

> Although many formatting activities can be exercised on field objects in both the design and preview tabs, some formatting facilities are only available within the Design tab. One useful feature to take note of is the capability to move a highlighted field (or even a set of fields) and its associated column title with the arrow keys on your keypad. This technique is a great help when you're moving report fields around as you did in step 9.

6

Figure 6.5
The sample report displays five database field objects in the Details section, five database field column header text fields in the Page Header, and one text object in the Report Header section.

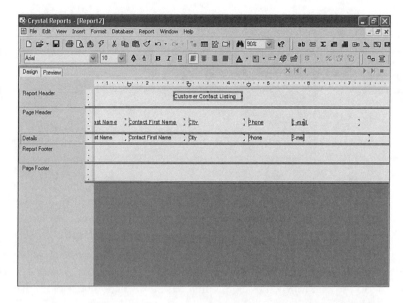

NOTE

As you might have noticed, the field sizes are often large enough to show the entire field name in the Design view of the report. But from the Preview tab view of the report, you see that fields (such as the E-mail or Phone fields here) are cut off from the display area. This is not unusual, and it might require you to resize the field objects to ensure that they are appropriate for the report display area. It is often useful to use the report's Preview tab as the active window when finalizing the formatting and layout of your reports.

11. Now click the Preview tab to see a preview display of what the report actually looks like, as shown in Figure 6.6.

NOTE

If the Preview tab is not displayed in the application, you have not yet run the report against the database. To run the report, click the Refresh toolbar icon to execute the report to run—the Refresh toolbar icon is represented with a yellow lightning bolt.

NOTE

Although it's important to understand the basics of report formatting, you will not necessarily have to go through the often arduous process of formatting reports every time. Report templates can be used to apply predefined and meaningful formatting characteristics in a very quick manner.

→ For more details on designing and using report templates, **see** "Creating Useful Report Templates,"
p. 300

Figure 6.6
To preview your
report, either select
the Preview tab or
click the Refresh
button.

Figure 6.6
To preview your
report, either select
the Preview tab or
click the Refresh
button.

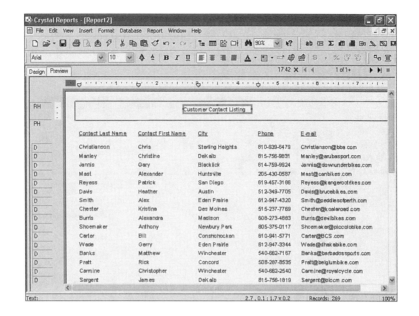

MODIFYING OBJECT PROPERTIES FOR FORMATTING PURPOSES

Now that the foundation of our report is complete, it is time to focus on how to improve the form and aesthetic appearance of the report.

By modifying various object properties, the presentation value of the report can be greatly improved. In doing so, you will be using the Format Editor to access a variety of specific properties, such as fonts, borders, colors, and alignment. The Format Editor is a commonly used dialog to quickly and easily modify all report objects, and its contents are reflective of the specific object type being formatted (text, chart, database field, and so on). To explore these formatting capabilities, follow these steps:

1. Continuing with the report from the chapter's earlier exercise, return to the Design tab of your report and right-click on the report title text object (located in the Report Header section) and select the Format Text option from the list, as shown in Figure 6.7. This opens the Format Editor dialog.

2. The Format Editor dialog (displayed in Figure 6.8) enables you to set and adjust a variety of properties of the object. For this exercise, navigate to the Font tab of the Format Editor and select the Bold font style, a font size of 14, and a font color of Red. Also, select the Paragraph tab of the Format Editor and choose Centered from the Horizontal Alignment drop-down list.

3. Now select the Border tab from within the Format Editor and then select Single from each of the four border Line Style drop-down lists (left, right, top, and bottom). Under Color, click the Background check box and select Yellow from the drop-down list as the

background color. Based on all of your selected properties in the Format Editor, you should now see a representative example of the text object in the Sample area at the bottom of the dialog box. Click OK to save these settings and return to the Design tab on your report.

Figure 6.7
The Format Editor dialog is accessed from the right-click pop-up menu on most Crystal Reports' objects.

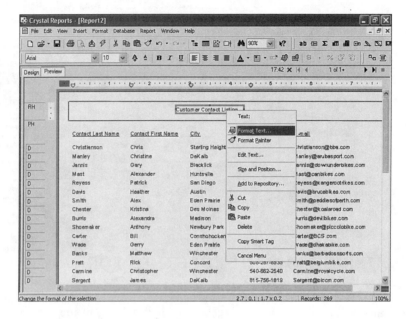

Figure 6.8
The Format Editor dialog provides for quick and easy access to a variety of report object properties.

4. To improve the effectiveness of your report, you can modify the database field column titles to provide more meaningful descriptions for the business users of your report.

Working within the Design tab of your report, double-click on the Phone object in the Page Header section of the report. When the cursor's focus is on this object, you can delete, append, or update the text as you choose. Modify this text to read `Telephone #` and then click anywhere outside the object to remove the cursor's focus from the object.

As an alternative to the Format Editor, you can also use the toolbar and menu commands to quickly apply common formatting techniques, such as font and alignment characteristics.

5. From the View menu, select Toolbars to present the Toolbar dialog. Make sure that the Standard, Formatting, and Insert toolbar items are all selected and click OK.

6. Click on the Preview tab to see a preview display of what the report will actually look like. Again, if the Preview tab is not displayed in the application, click the Refresh toolbar button to execute the report. From the Preview mode, hold down either the Shift or Ctrl key on your keyboard and click each of the five column titles so that they are all highlighted with a dashed perimeter. With all five columns title fields highlighted, click the Bold toolbar button, represented with a large bold letter B on the formatting toolbar. See to Figure 6.9 to see the results of this action.

7. With the five column title fields still highlighted, click the downward arrow located on the Font Color toolbar button, represented with an underlined letter A on the formatting toolbar. Select the bright blue color from the available list, as shown in Figure 6.9. Lastly, remove the contact prefix for the name fields and increase the size of these column titles to font size 12 with either the font size drop-down box or the A+ increase font size button. The fields might need to be stretched vertically to fit the new font size but can eventually be made to look like Figure 6.9.

Figure 6.9
Common formatting properties can be quickly specified via the formatting toolbar commands (such as font styles, font size, colors, borders, and so on).

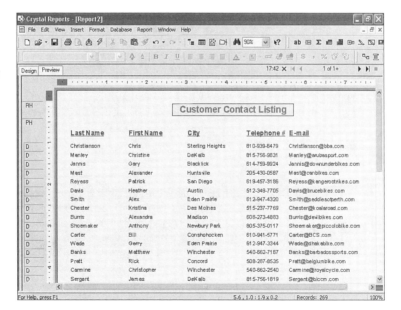

6

To make the E-mail field appear more meaningful to the business users of the report, let's format the E-mail database field values to resemble and behave like standard hyperlink text.

8. To remove the cursor focus from the five column titles fields, click anywhere outside these field areas or press the Esc (escape) key on your keyboard.

9. Click any of the actual E-mail field values to highlight the E-mail database field objects and right-click on the same object to present the pop-up menu. From the pop-up menu, shown in Figure 6.10, select the Format Field item.

Figure 6.10
Right-clicking on any field object presents you with a list of commands for that particular object.

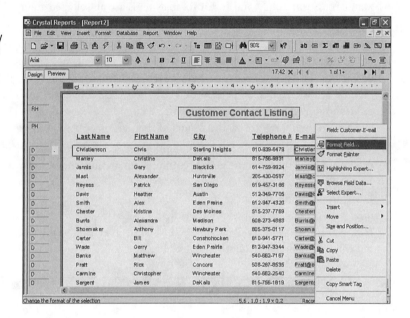

10. Select the Hyperlink tab after you have opened the Format Editor. From the available Hyperlink Types, select Current E-mail Field Value—this option automatically creates a hyperlink based on the values stored within this field in the data source assuming that these values are formatted as proper e-mail addresses in the data source, such as `abc@domain.com`.

NOTE

> You can use the Hyperlink tab within the Format Editor to create hyperlinks to a Web site, e-mail address, file, or another Crystal Report. A hyperlink is saved with your report and is available to other users as a way of linking to additional external information from your report. Hyperlink definitions can also be defined by formulas thus enabling context-sensitive, data-driven hyperlinks—a very powerful feature of Crystal Reports.

11. Now let's make the E-mail field appear as a standard hyperlink value, commonly known to have a blue underlined font style. Select the Font tab within the Format Editor

dialog to apply the blue font color and select the Underline check box. Click OK to return to the report Preview, and then press Esc to remove the cursor focus from all report objects.

12. Based on the completion of the previous step, your mouse pointer should now change into a hand icon as it floats over any of the E-mail field values on the report. This indicates that upon clicking on any of the E-mail values, you initiate an e-mail message to be sent to that address, as shown in Figure 6.11.

Figure 6.11
By applying an e-mail hyperlink, report end users can initiate a context-sensitive e-mail to any of the respective customer contacts.

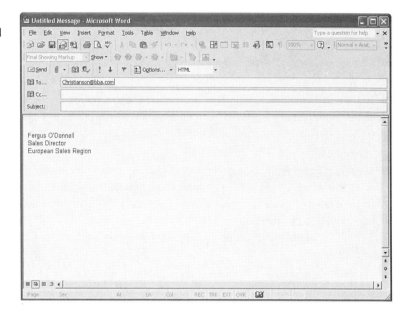

By using the Format Editor, as well as the Toolbar commands, to modify report object properties, you have very quickly and easily enhanced your report's presentation quality. Not only did you enhance this report example visually, but you also easily incorporated hyperlink functionality to add an additional level of interactivity to your report.

For more information on using hyperlink functionality in reports, see Chapter 9, "Custom Formatting Techniques."

6

EXPLORING THE FORMAT EDITOR DIALOG COMMON OPTIONS

The previous exercises introduced the Format Editor—the dialog where the appearance of report fields and other report objects can be manipulated. Different Crystal Reports objects present different tabs within the Format Editor and each provides specific editing functionality for the underlying object types (such as Date and Time, Boolean, Hyperlink, and so on). The next few sections introduce the most commonly used tabs and underlying formatting options.

THE COMMON TAB OF THE FORMAT EDITOR

The Common tab of the Format Editor provides basic functionality for the majority of Crystal Reports' objects. The most commonly used formatting features accessed through this tab include the following:

- Object Name: Assigned by default, this name is referenced primarily for use with Report Part Viewing (that is, when specifying which report parts to view in a report parts viewer).

- CSS Class Name: Provides the capability for Crystal Reports to leverage existing CSS stylesheet classes when deployed in a Web application or with Crystal Enterprise.

- Repeat on Horizontal Page: New in version 10, this option enables the repetition of a report object that does not expand horizontally (such as text objects, field objects, OLE objects, charts, maps, lines, boxes, and so on) for each additional horizontal page that a cross-tab or OLAP grid might create.

- Suppress: Enables the suppression of the selected object in the Preview tab and on any report printing. Often used with formula components that the end user is not intended to view or conditionally through the x+2 formula button to only suppress (or display) the selected field based on certain data conditions being met (for example, Only show "ALERT" text object if Shipping Date is five or more days after Order Date for a specified field).

- Horizontal Alignment: Provides the capability to align the data within an object either Left, Center, Right, or Both Justified.

- Close Border on Page Break: This functionality ensures that borders created on the object close at the bottom of any page and begin again as the object is continued on the next page. This provides for a much slicker looking border format for your reports.

- Can Grow: Enables for variable length fields to grow vertically in the report and word-wrap automatically. A Maximum Number of Lines can be set with this option to control rogue data elements.

- Tool Text Tip: Enables a text bubble to be displayed as the end user hovers over report fields. A common and powerful use of tooltips is to provide the end users with a database-driven description of the involved field from an associated meta-data table. To use this functionality, the Tool Tips option must be turned on under the Layout tab of the Options dialog accessed under the File menu.

- Text Rotation: Enables the rotated display of the involved object by 90 or 270 degrees. This feature is highlighted in Chapter 9.

- Suppress if Duplicated: This option enables the suppression of repeated field names in a report.

- Display String: This Custom String functionality enables the conditional formatting and display of different types of fields (for example, number, currency, date, time, date and time, Boolean, string, running total, formulas, parameters, and so on) as a custom string (for example displaying the number 1,500,000 as the custom string 1.5M).

THE BORDER TAB OF THE FORMAT EDITOR

The Border tab of the Format Editor provides border, background, and drop-shadow formatting functionality for Crystal Report objects. The most commonly used formatting features accessed through this tab include the following:

- Line Style drop-down boxes: The Left, Right, Top, and Bottom drop-down boxes enable specification of the different types of supported borders (Single, Double, Dashed, or Dotted). For Basic borders, this functionality is more easily accessed through the Borders button on the Formatting toolbar.

- Tight Horizontal: This option specifies that a border tightly wraps around the involved object's contents and not the entire field as placed on the report (that is, no spaces are included within the border).

- Drop Shadow: This format prints a drop shadow to the right and below the specified object.

- Border Color: The color of the border and drop shadow is specified here through the drop-down box.

- Background Color: The background check box enables you to specify that a background be displayed for the given field. An additional drop-down box enables you to select the color for the background after the check box has been selected.

THE FONT TAB OF THE FORMAT EDITOR

The Font tab of the Format Editor provides the capability to change the fonts, font size, and font style for text and data fields in your Crystal Reports. The most commonly used formatting features accessed through this tab include the following:

- Font, Style, Size, and Color: Enable the designer to specify a variety of available formatting fonts (such as Arial, Courier, Verdana, Times Roman, and so on), styles (such as Bold and Italics), sizes including manually entered 1/2 sizes and colors.

- Strikeout and Underline: Enable you to specify the selected formatting on the current report object.

- Character Spacing Exactly: Use this option to specify the space that each character in the selected font occupies. The value is defined as the distance in number of points measured from the start of one character to the start of the next. When the character spacing is edited, only the spacing between adjacent characters is changed—not the actual font size of the characters. Using 0 enables the default font character spacing.

6

THE HYPERLINK TAB OF THE FORMAT EDITOR

The Hyperlink tab is used to create hyperlinks to external Web sites, e-mail addresses, files, or other reports and report objects from report objects within the current report. These hyperlinks can be data-driven (that is, change on the data coming back from the database) and provide a rather intuitive method for integrating Crystal Reports into a business work-flow. The helpful hint section of this tab provides in-place coaching for each type of hyperlink that is to be used. The most commonly used formatting features accessed through this tab include the following:

- Web site on the Internet: Enables the specification of an external Web site with or without dynamic context-sensitive components of the URL driven from the database. An example of a context sensitive Web address would be `http://www.google.ca/search?q=` + {Customer.Customer Name} where the link would take the end user to a Google search page full of results based on the current value of the customer name.

- E-mail address: Enables you to add a link to an e-mail address that would need to be typed into the E-mail address text box or through the associated formula editor x+2 button.

- File: Enables the linked upon object to call a specified file and launch its associated application upon end-user activation of this link. Report Designers can specify EXE files with command line parameters through the formula editor accessed by the x+2 button.

- Current Web site or E-mail Field Value: Creates a Web site or e-mail link to the underlying object on which the hyperlink is being created. The formatting of the data for the involved field must be correct (that is, a proper e-mail address or Web site URL).

- Report Part Drilldown: The Report Part Drilldown option lets you define a hyperlink so that the Report Part Viewer can emulate the drill-down functionality of Crystal Reports. The Report Part Viewer displays only destination objects; therefore, to make drill down work, you need to define a navigation path from a home object to one or more destination objects, all residing in the same report section. Initial Report Part specification for a given Crystal Report is set within the Report Options dialog accessed from the main File menu. The drill-down path is then set for each Report Part in the navigation path through this option. Not all Crystal Reports objects have this option available based on their report section location and their type of object.

- Another Report Object: This option enables the definition of a hyperlink to objects in the same or different reports. When defining a hyperlink path to a different report, that report must be managed in a Crystal Enterprise environment. To specify report objects, they must be copied using the right-click Copy command from their source report and then pasted into the current object's Hyperlink tab using the Paste Link button.

OTHER FORMAT EDITOR TABS

The remaining tabs found in the Format Editor are dependent on the type of object selected in the involved Crystal Report. The other tabs that you find and some of the most common formatting options provided in each are as follows:

- Paragraph tab: Enables you to specify formatting for string/text fields including spacing, reading order, and horizontal alignment.

- Numbers tab: Enables detailed formatting on numbers and currency objects including the handling of zeros, decimal point specification, negative number formatting, rounding, and thousands separator specification. The Customize button enables access to the majority of these formatting features.

- Date and Time tab: Provides detailed formatting on dates, times, and `datetime` objects. Many default display options are available with a great deal of granularity provided through the Customize button.

- Boolean tab: Enables the selection of the format for the return values of Boolean field objects.

- Box, Line, Rounding, Subreport, and Picture tabs: Provide for granular level formatting of each of the involved Crystal Reports' objects.

COMBINING AND LAYERING REPORT OBJECTS

The concepts of combining and layering report objects becomes relevant when you need to precisely control the relationship between two or more objects when occupying a common space on the report. For example, assume that rather than having your country field read USA, you would like to combine the Country database field with a text object so that it reads `Country/Pays: USA`—displaying the textual description for country in both English and French. To accomplish this, you can easily combine a text and a database field into one common report object.

The previous exercises can be enhanced by adding a more descriptive text object to your report as that described above. To complete this, start by adding a group definition to your report. The group definition enables you to logically present each customer within the country in which they are located. The following steps will add this grouping:

1. From the Insert menu, select Group to present the Insert Group dialog. Select the Country field (located under the Customer table) from the uppermost drop-down list. Leave the sort order as Ascending and click OK to return to the report.

2. Verify that you are working in the Design view of the report—click on the Design tab if necessary. You should now see two new sections listed in the left column area of the design environment—Group Header #1 and Group Footer #1. From the Insert menu, select Text Object and drop the object to the right of the Group #1 Name field in the Group Header section. Type **Country/Pays:** for the textual content of this new object (including a space after the colon), as shown in Figure 6.12.

Figure 6.12
The Insert menu enables you to quickly add a group and text object into your report.

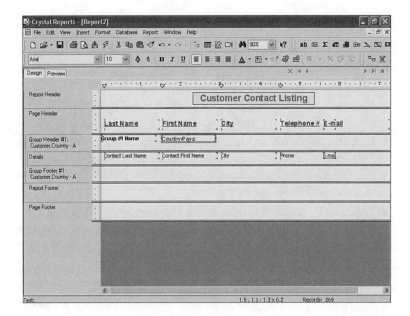

3. Highlight the Group #1 Name field object, click and drag it over the new text object field (you can drag the entire object after the mouse pointer has turned into a four-way cross icon), and drop it onto the text object when the flashing vertical cursor indicates that it falls precisely to the right of the textual description you have entered.

NOTE

Dragging and dropping objects to combine them is a very precise maneuver and might require some practice. If you have dropped the Group Name field in the wrong place, click the Undo button (curved arrow pointing backward) and try again until you are comfortable and successful with this technique.

4. After you have successfully combined these objects together, the design application still references the newly combined object as a Text object. You now need to widen the object's display area. Click this object to highlight it and drag the left-side perimeter handle farther to the left until you reach the left margin of the design area, as shown in Figure 6.13.

5. With the combined text object highlighted, use the steps identified earlier in this chapter to modify the object's properties to present the field values in a bold red font style, as shown in Figure 6.14. Click the Preview tab to see how the report results are displayed. (Use the Refresh toolbar button if the Preview tab is not visible.)

6. Now add a corporate logo to your report and use this to discuss object layering. You need to have a picture file saved in either bitmap, TIFF, JPEG, or PNG format

available for use. Use the Business Objects logo downloaded from its Web site for this example. Select the Picture menu option from the Insert menu. Navigate to and select the Business Objects Logo image and drag it into the Report Header section. Drop the image into the Report Header section so that its left perimeter is aligned directly above the left perimeter of the Telephone Number column, as shown in Figure 6.15.

Figure 6.13
You have now combined a database field object with a text object to form one common report object.

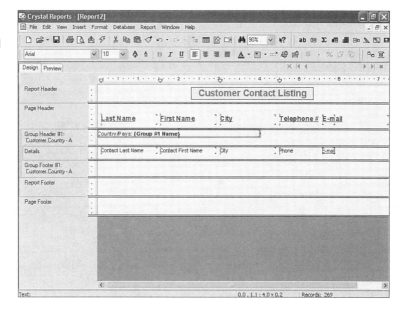

Figure 6.14
After combining two or more objects, you can specify formatting properties for the newly combined report object.

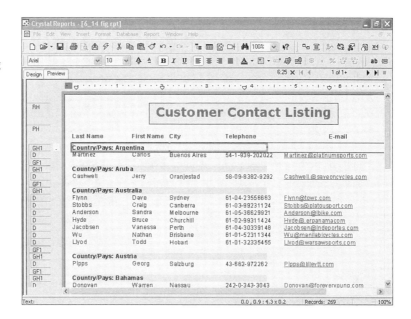

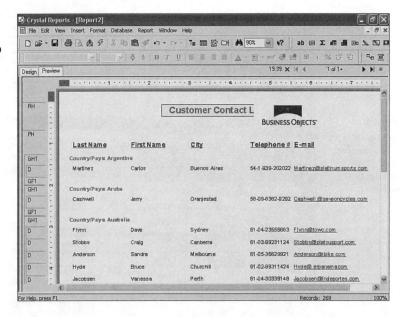

Figure 6.15
Drag and drop the
Business Objects Logo
image object into
place in the Report
Header section.

Notice, as illustrated in Figure 6.15, that you have partially covered the report title object with the new logo image. This could have certainly been avoided by placing the image object farther to the right, but for demonstration purposes, use the Move property of the report title field to once again make it visible.

7. Right-click the report title text object, select Move, and then select To Front from the additional pop-up options. This positions the report title object on top of the logo image, as you can see in the report preview.

8. To resolve the issue of overlapping objects in the Report Header section, adjust the two objects so that the report title is displayed farther to the left of the logo image, as shown in Figure 6.16. Save your report sample if you want.

9. As a final step to re-create the report in Figure 6.2, use the Format Expert dialog to modify the report title text so that it appears in a bold, navy blue, underlined, size 20 Verdana font with no displayed borders.

As a result of these exercises, you now have a very useful report that displays each customer contact record distinctively grouped within the country in which they are located. The formatting that has been applied introduces the capabilities that make Crystal Reports the undisputed champion of professionally formatted reports.

Figure 6.16
By adjusting the objects located in the Report Header, you have resolved the need to layer these objects; however, layering does provide flexible display options.

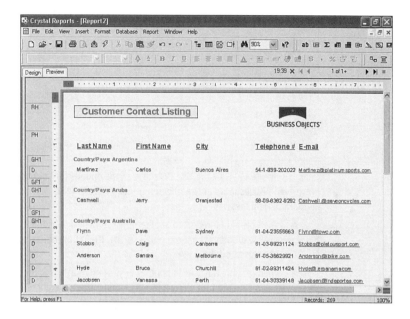

CONFIGURING REPORT PAGE AND MARGIN PROPERTIES

With Crystal Reports, margins can either be set to use specific manually set margin definitions or can be selected to automatically adjust to the report margins. To set your report margins to meet exact specifications, follow these steps:

1. From the File menu, click Page Setup, and the Page Setup dialog appears as shown in Figure 6.17.
2. Modify the default page margins for your exact requirements.
3. Click OK to save your changes.

NOTE

Each of the margin settings is calculated from the paper edge. Consequently, a left margin of .25 inches causes the printing of the report page to start exactly one quarter of an inch in from the left edge of the paper.

As an alternative to specifying exact report margins, you can select the Adjust Automatically check box if you want Crystal Reports to adjust the report's margins automatically when the paper size changes. This option maintains the ratio of the margins to the printable area of the report by enlarging or reducing the left/right and top/bottom margins by the same factor. For example, this setting could ensure that a report designed for a printer that can only print within .5 inches of the paper's edge would maintain the same overall margin ratio when printed on a printer that could print to within .25 inches of the paper's edge.

Figure 6.17
The Page Setup dialog is used to specify report margin settings.

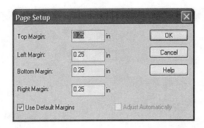

TIP

If you decide to select the Use Default Margins options for your reports, there are two common issues to be aware of when printing reports (also described in the Crystal Reports Help files):

■ When printing a report in another environment in which the printer's default margins are *greater* than the report's setting, the report objects on the right side of the report print off the page.

■ When printing a report in another environment in which the printer's default margins are *smaller* (enabling a larger printing area), the entire report moves to the left side of the page.

As a result, it is recommended that you specify your own report margins. It is encouraged that you do *not* select the Use Default Margins option in the Page Setup dialog to avoid these common problems. It is advisable to set your report margins manually using the Page Setup dialog, even if the margins you want to specify are the same as the default margin settings. This issue becomes especially important when you distribute your reports over the Web and have no idea what type of printer the business user will be using.

CRYSTAL REPORTS IN THE REAL WORLD— REFERENCING EXTERNAL RESOURCES

A very powerful use of hyperlinks is to be able to take advantage of the many resources on the Internet. Many Internet sites make use of what is called a *QueryString*. By knowing the URL and QueryString that drive a particular site, a report hyperlink can be customized to open a Web site and perform some functionality. In the next example, the address of the sample customers can be opened in MapQuest.com by using a hyperlink:

1. Start with opening the report Chap6PostFormat.rpt. From the Insert menu, choose Text Object. Add the text **MapQuest** to the report.

2. Right-click the newly added text object and choose Format Tex. Then click the Hyperlink tab and click the x+2 button. See Figure 6.18 for an example of what the formula should look like. Enter the following code into the text:

```
StringVar URL;

// The prefix of the URL that will not change; it is hard-coded to the USA
URL := "http://www.mapquest.com/maps/map.adp?";
```

```
URL := URL & "country=US&countryid=250&adtohistory=";

// Add the street address
URL := URL & "&address=" & {Customer.Address1};

// Add the city
URL := URL & "&city=" &  {Customer.City};

// Add the state
URL := URL & "&state=" & {Customer.Region};

// Add the ZIP code
URL := URL & "&zipcode=" & {Customer.Postal Code};

// Add the suffix of the URL
URL := URL & "&submit=Get Map";

URL
```

Figure 6.18
Code that builds a
dynamic data driven
URL that will enable
hyperlinks to the
Mapquest Web site
from a Crystal Report

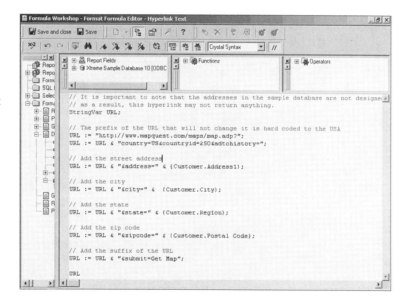

3. Click Save and Close to close the code window. Click OK to close the Format Editor window. Format the hyperlink using the same method used to format the e-mail address to show the user it is an actionable item.

NOTE

The sample data does not necessarily use valid addresses. MapQuest.com might open with only partial information, but the concept remains valid.

6

CHAPTER **7**

WORKING WITH REPORT SECTIONS

In this chapter

INTRODUCTION

You should be familiar with some of the most common formatting features within the Crystal Reports 10 designer. Building on the concepts and techniques covered in Chapter 6, "Fundamentals of Report Formatting," for report object formatting, this chapter explains how you can format entire sections within your reports. Just as any report object has specific modifiable properties available for formatting, report sections also have unique properties.

→ For more information on report formatting, **see** "Exploring the Format Editor Dialog Common Options," **p. 155**

In this chapter, these properties are examined and their use in creating effective professionally styled reports is explored.

This chapter covers the following topics:

- Formatting report sections
- Modifying report section properties
- Using multiple report sections

FORMATTING REPORT SECTIONS

The earlier chapters introduced the concept of report sections such as the detail section and the group header and footer sections. *Report sections* segment reports into logical areas to facilitate logical report design. Report sections are identified by name on the left side of the design environment, and, by default, each report includes a Report Header and Footer, Page Header and Footer, and Details section. If you have inserted any groups into your report, you also have a Group Header and Footer for each defined group item. As reports have been created in the previous chapters, objects such as database fields, text fields, and corporate logo images have been placed into the various report sections and organized based on the report design requirements.

Each section has unique display properties and printing characteristics that can be modified. For example, if a report object, such as an image, is placed in the Report Header section, the image displays and prints only once per report, on the first page. If the same image is placed in the Page Header section, the image then displays and prints once for every single page of the report. The same principals hold true for other custom sections, such as Group Headers and Footers. Finally, the Detail section implies that whatever is placed in this section displays, and prints, once for each and every row retrieved from the data source.

NOTE

The Crystal Reports design environment is built on a *paper metaphor* with *pages* the driving concept in structuring the presentation of report information. This page metaphor applies when referencing report printing and with respect to various presentation characteristics of report formatting.

Using the report created in Chapter 6, take a closer look at how to format report sections. The following exercises demonstrate how to format sections such as the Group Header and Group Footer to improve the overall presentation of a Crystal Report. In addition to modifying display properties, conditional logic is also applied that modifies the behavior of the Page Header section based on the result of the defined condition (format formula). The Section Expert is the central location for working with all report section properties, and it is used to view and modify the properties of each report section throughout the following exercises.

NOTE

> As you might have noticed, long names (descriptive names) of each section are provided to the left of the design environment within the Design tab, whereas only the short names (abbreviated names) of sections are presented while viewing reports from the Preview tab. This maximizes the report viewing space while working in the Preview tab. The long names can, however, be accessed by either hovering the mouse cursor over the section or by right-clicking on the section name (or label).

There are three distinct ways to access the Section Expert; these include

- Right-clicking on the name of the section you want to work with and selecting Section Expert from the pop-up menu.
- Clicking on the Section Expert toolbar button located on the Expert Tools toolbar.
- Selecting the Format menu and choosing Report, Section Expert.

To start the hands-on learning, follow these steps:

1. Open the report you created in Chapter 6. Alternatively, open the report entitled Ch07start.rpt (available by searching for the book's ISBN—0-7897-3113-4— at Que Publishing's Web site, www.quepublishing.com).

2. Open the Section Expert. From either the Design or Preview mode, right-click on the Group Header #1 section and select Section Expert from the pop-up menu. This presents the Section Expert dialog displayed in Figure 7.4.

   Now apply a background color to your Group Header #1 report section so that the report consumers can quickly distinguish between country sections and determine which customer contacts belong to each country.

3. In the Section Expert, select the Group Header #1 item from the Sections list on the left, and then click on the Color tab on the right. Click on the Background Color box so that it is activated and select Navy from the drop-down list of color options. Click OK to continue.

7

TIP

> From within the Section Expert, you can easily navigate from modifying the properties of one report section to another without closing this dialog window. Regardless of how you open the Section Expert dialog window, you can quickly toggle to other report sections, providing a central location to access and modify the properties of all report sections.

4. Select the Preview tab to view your report display.

5. The Red font used for the object in the Group Header #1 does not look good against the Navy background color. To resolve this, highlight the text object—actually a combined object consisting of a text object and a database field object—and change its font color to White, as shown in Figure 7.1.

Figure 7.1
Formatting a report section can make reports more readable and friendly to end users.

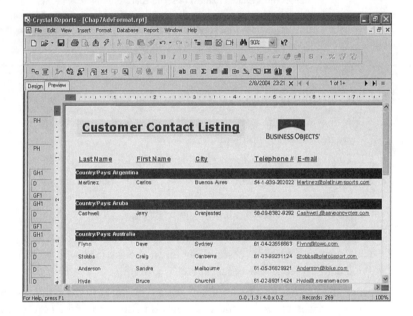

6. To complement the current report grouping on the Country field, add a summary count of the contacts for each country in the Group Footer #1 section. To do this, select Summary from the Insert menu to present the Insert Summary dialog and select the following items:

- Customer.Contact Last Name field from the Choose the Field to Summarize drop-down list
- Count from the Calculate This Summary drop-down list
- Group #1: Customer.Country from the Summary Location drop-down list

NOTE

To access the Insert Summary dialog so that you can add a summary field to your report, you can use the Summary command from the main Insert menu, you can use the Insert Summary button located on the Insert toolbar, or you can simply right-click on any report field already in the report and access the Insert Summary menu option from the right-click menu. This last option prepopulates the Choose the Field to Summarize drop-down box and saves you a few needless steps.

7. After you have made these selections from the Insert Summary dialog, click OK to continue.

8. You should now see the Count Summary field listed in the Group Footer #1 section of your report. To align the field values to the left and make them noticeable, use the Align Left and Font buttons located on the Formatting toolbar to apply the desired alignment and a Red font color.

9. Now add additional report section formatting to the Group Footer #1 section. From the Report menu, select the Section Expert command to present the Section Expert dialog. From the Sections list on the left, select Group Footer #1 and then select the Color tab on the right. Specify a Silver background color for this section and click OK to return to the report preview, shown in Figure 7.2.

10. As a final step, change the font color of the database field column titles. From either the Design or Preview view, right-click on the Page Header section title and choose Select All Section Objects from the pop-up menu. After all the column title objects are highlighted, select Teal from the formatting toolbar Font Color button.

Figure 7.2
Section formatting can be applied specifically to the various sections of your report for a more meaningful report presentation.

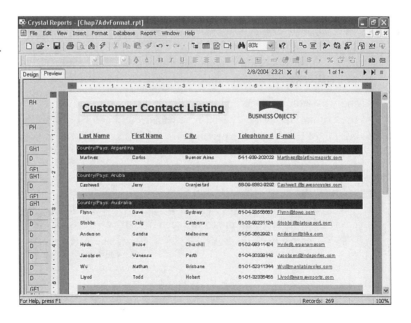

As you have seen, formatting the various sections of your report is very straightforward. Each section has unique and specific properties that can be modified and used collectively to enhance the presentation quality of the entire report.

TIP

> To quickly remove blank space within report sections and tighten up the alignment of the objects positioned within the sections, you can use the Fit Section command. The Fit Section command is available from the right-click menu of each report section. This raises the bottom boundary line and reduces unnecessary space within the section.

MODIFYING REPORT SECTION PROPERTIES

In addition to formatting properties, each section has a variety of general properties that can be used to manipulate the behavior of that section within the overall report. For example, if you would like to suppress a particular section from the report display or just hide a detail-oriented section from the initial display but enable business users to navigate to the underlying details, you can use the Section Expert to accomplish this.

Using the report you created in the previous exercise, relocate the Count summary field into the Group Header and hide the Details section to enable the viewer of the report to access this section only if he double-clicks on the Group Header summary values—commonly known as drilling-down on report data. The following steps guide you through formatting several fields and sections, creating a drill-down report:

1. Highlight the Summary field currently located in the Group Footer #1 section (Count of Contact Last Name) and drag it up in the Group Header #1 section so that it is positioned to the right of the Country/Pays field, approximately under the Telephone # column title. The results are shown in Figure 7.3.

2. While the Summary count field is still highlighted, modify the font properties so that it is underlined and in a bold yellow color.

3. Using what you have learned from the previous exercises, remove the background color of the Group Footer #1 section—the background color property can be located on the Color tab of the Section Expert. Figure 7.3 shows what your report should now look like.

4. To display the listing of customer contacts for each country on a separate and unique page, open the Section Expert and select Group Footer #1 from the section list on the left. As Figure 7.4 shows, the Common tab within the Section Expert provides access to a variety of properties unique to the section that you have selected from the list on the left. In this case, check the box next to the New Page After item and click OK to continue.

7

Figure 7.3
Report objects can be repositioned into the various report sections to change the presentation of the report.

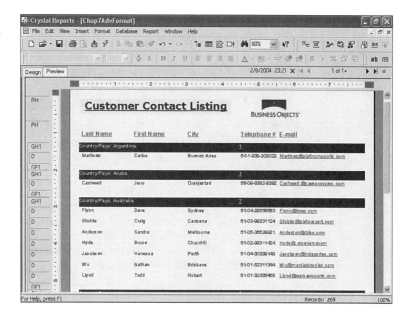

Figure 7.4
The Section Expert provides access to a variety of section formatting properties, as well as enabling the specification of what happens before and after each section is printed.

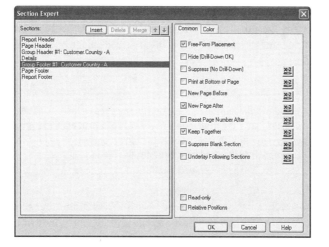

TIP

Common report section commands—such as Hide, Suppress, Delete, Hide Section Names, and Select All Section Objects—are accessible via the pop-up menu when you right-click on the applicable section's name. Some of these commands are also available within the Section Expert dialog, although unlike the Section Expert, the right-click pop-up menu pertains only to the specific section you have selected.

7

5. Looking at the preview of your report, you should now see each country's list of contacts on a separate page. Although this might be desirable for those countries with a considerable number of contacts, such as Canada, France, and the United States in this report, it is not necessarily the most visually pleasing presentation for the countries that have only one or two customer contacts.

Perhaps the majority of the business users for this report are more interested in the total number of contacts for each country rather than the actual list itself. However, a few of the business users also want to be able to access the contact list on occasion. To accommodate both groups of users, you can manipulate the properties of the Details section.

NOTE

> To indicate to the business user of the report that more detailed information is available behind the summary group level, the mouse pointer turns into a magnifying glass icon when it floats over a drillable section (for example, the yellow count field of customer contacts, located in the Group Header #1 section).

6. Disable the New Page After property that was set for the Group Footer #1 section. The Section Expert can be used to remove this setting. Click OK to continue.

7. From either the Design or Preview view of your report, right-click on the Details section title to the far left of the application area and select Hide (Drill-Down OK) from the pop-up menu.

NOTE

> Drill-down functionality is designed to make report viewing easier. You can hide the details of your report and only have the group headers and summaries visible, and, when necessary, the business users of the report can then click on the group header or summary fields to view the report details.

As shown in Figure 7.5, a list of each country with the total number of contacts displayed has now been created. Additionally, upon double-clicking the count of contacts (displayed with the underlined, yellow number) the business user of the report is quickly able to drill-down into the Details section and be presented with the actual customer contact specifications.

As you can see in Figure 7.6, after the business user drills down into a particular group's detail listing (France in this example), that group's detailed contact list is displayed in the Crystal Reports application in a separate tab and is cached so that it can be easily accessed for future reference. When a business user of the report selects a refresh on the report, all cached tabs are removed because there is no guarantee that the data being retrieved from the database would be the same as the previously cached page. The end user would have to drill back down into France if he wanted to view the detailed contact listing again.

7

Figure 7.5
A manager now is presented with a summary list of customer contacts by country and is also able to access the customer contact details through a drill-down.

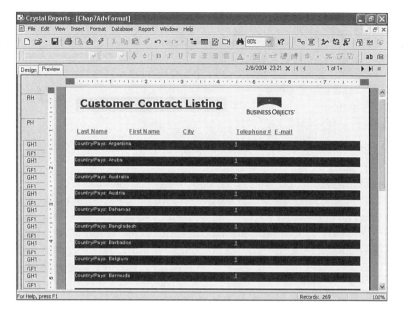

Figure 7.6
The detailed list of customer contacts for France.

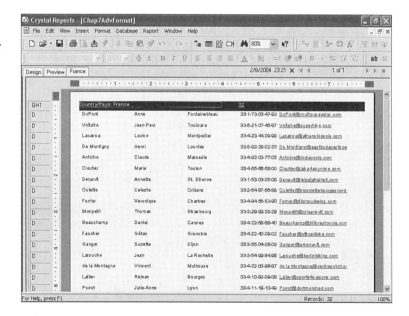

THE SECTION EXPERT SETTINGS AND FUNCTIONALITY

As discussed to this point in the chapter, the Section Expert provides a great deal of powerful report formatting functionality and flexibility. There are two major areas to the Section Expert as shown in Figure 7.4—the Sections area and the Formatting tabs (Common, Color, and Layout). This section presents each of these sections and their associated functionality.

THE SECTIONS AREA

The Sections area is composed of a listing of all the current report's sections and five separate buttons—Insert, Delete, Merge and the up and down arrows. The Sections area takes up the entire left half of the Sections Expert dialog and enables you to create, delete, merge, and reorder entire sections within the involved report. The following list describes each of the Section Expert Sections area components:

- Sections: This box provides a list of all the sections in the current report. When a section is highlighted, the program highlights the other Section Expert properties and buttons that you can set, modify, or use for the selected section.

- Insert button: This button enables you to add sections below the currently highlighted section. The newly added section is based on the type that is currently selected. (For example, inserting a section while on the Detail section creates another Detail section called Detail b, the original Detail section is called Detail a, and they both exist under a parent node called Detail.) Different formatting and display properties are made available for each child section in addition to the parent section. Creating multiple detail (or other) sections dramatically increases the flexibility in which you can display information as each independent child section can have formatting and display properties applied (for example, Only Show Column Titles in Details a Section Every 10th Row).

- Delete button: Use this button to delete existing highlighted sections from the current report. Note that only inserted children sections (as described previously) can be deleted—not original primary sections.

- Merge button: This button enables you to merge two related children sections (for example, Details a and Details b) into one new section.

- Up and Down Arrow buttons: These buttons enable you to reorder children sections within the currently selected report. It is important to note that the original parent sections cannot be reordered in the Section Expert.

THE COMMON TAB

In addition to the Section Expert options that you have already used, the following segment of the chapter provides an overview of the available settings presented on the Common tab of the Section Expert. A subset or all of these options are made available when a section is selected in the Sections area, as described previously. The following options are made available in the Common tab:

- Free-Form Placement: When enabled, this option places objects within a section in a free-form manner, ignoring all program alignment grids and guidelines. When this option is not selected, objects are placed at fixed points using an underlying grid (see the Layout tab of the Options menu for more details on grid display). This option is generally used in combination with report graphics (such as boxes) whose default display mechanism is free-form.

- Hide (Drill-Down OK): This option hides the respective section from the report's initial visual display, but still enables report users to access the section's content upon end-user drill-down.

- Suppress (No Drill-Down): Hides the respective section from the report's visual display and disables any drill-down capabilities such that the section's content is *not* available to report users. This is very useful for eliminating the display of sections that contain no data (such as redundant or empty Group Footer sections).

- Print at Bottom of Page: Causes the current section to print at the bottom of the page. This setting is most useful for printing invoices and other reports where you want summary values to appear toward the bottom of the page in a fixed position.

- New Page Before: Inserts a page break before it prints the section. This option is only applicable to the Group Header, Group Footer, and Details sections.

- New Page After: Inserts a page break after it displays and prints the section. For example, you can use this setting in the Group Footer section to print each group on a separate page.

- Reset Page Number After: Resets the page number to one (1) for the following page after it prints a group total. When this option is used in conjunction with Print at Bottom of Page, a single group prints on a page, the group value is printed at the bottom of the page, and the page number is reset to 1 for the next page. This option is useful whenever you are printing multiple reports from a single file (such as customer invoices), and you want each report to be numbered beginning with Page 1.

- Keep Together: Keeps a particular section together on one page without splitting the section between multiple pages. For example, in a customer list, data on a single customer might extend over several lines. If the standard page break falls within the data for a customer, the data is split—part on one page and the remainder on the next. You can use the Keep Together setting to insert the page break before the record begins so that all the data is printed together on the following page.

- Suppress Blank Section: Hides the report section if it is blank, and only prints it if it is not blank. This is a powerful display control to eliminate unnecessary blank space in reports.

- Underlay Following Sections: Permits the selected section to underlay the following section(s) when it prints, making the current section transparent. This feature is often used for the printing of Watermarks on a report (such as "Internal Use Only," "Draft," or a company logo). It is also often used to display data in different sections beside each other (for example, a summary pie chart from the Report Header underplayed to show beside the actual details of the pie chart kept in the Group and Detail sections).

- Format with Multiple Columns: Only available on the Detail section, this option presents the Layout tab (otherwise hidden from view) within the Section Expert and enables you to use multiple columns in the given report. This powerful feature enables the presentation of row data in the detail section as columns in a report. It is particularly useful when presenting summarized information for comparison or a lengthy list. This is demonstrated later in this chapter.

7

- Reserve Minimum Page Footer (Page Footer section only): Reserves space at the bottom of each page for your Page Footer sections (a default setting). This enables you to minimize the space reserved for your Page Footer sections, thus maximizing the space available for other report information on each page. This option only affects a Page Footer area with multiple sections.

- Read-only: Locks the formatting and position of all report objects within the section so that they can't be formatted or repositioned. The Read-only setting uses password protection to enable the report designer to return to the report to make future changes.

- Relative Positions: Locks the relative position of a report object next to a grid object within a section. For example, if you place a text object one inch to the right of a cross-tab or OLAP grid object, during report generation the program pushes the text object to the right so that the one inch of space is maintained regardless of the width of the cross-tab or OLAP grid object.

The presence of the x+2 buttons to the right of the majority of the options indicates that those options can be set via a formula in addition to setting them via the dialog. When an option is set via formula, this is referred to as *conditional formatting* because the formula typically evaluates a condition.

To implement a conditional option, click on the x+2 button associated with the option and the Formula Editor is presented. Within the Formula Editor, a formula needs to be created that is evaluated for every iteration of the section. If the formula evaluates to a value of True, the involved option is applied; otherwise, it is not. A simple but practical example of conditional section formatting could be a marketing campaign list where the marketing department wants to contact customers in the USA by phone and everywhere else by mail. Two detail sections could be created, one that includes Contact Name and Phone Number, the other with Contact Name and Mailing address. The first section can be conditionally suppressed on the following formula—`{Customer.Country} <> "USA"` to only show that section for USA-based customers. The second details section would be conditionally suppressed with `{Customer.Country} = "USA"` to only show non-U.S.-based customers.

THE COLOR TAB

Use the Color tab to set the background color for the entire highlighted section. This can be done absolutely or conditionally. A good example of a conditionally colored background is when presenting a lengthy list of detailed items. To enable easier reading of the report, every second row can be conditionally colored Silver with the following formula:

LISTING 7.1 ALTERNATE ROW COLORING FORMULA

```
IF RecordNumber Mod 2 = 1 THEN
    Silver
Else
    White
```

THE LAYOUT TAB

The Layout tab only appears when you have the details section selected and the Format with Multiple Columns check box has been selected on the Common tab. This tab enables multi-column formatting. As described earlier, this kind of report enables you to present multiple columns of standard row data and have the data flow from column to column. This tab, shown in Figure 7.7, has four distinct settings:

Figure 7.7
The Layout tab is only available for advanced multicolumn reports.

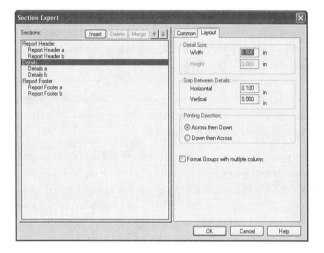

- Detail Size: This box enables the specification of the dimensions (height and width) of each detail column.

- Gap Between Details: This box enables the specification of the empty area between detail columns and rows. The horizontal gap is the distance between the details going across the page and the vertical gap is the distance between rows going down the page.

- Printing Direction: This option enables the specification of the flow path to be followed when printing the detail column and rows on a report page. The Across then Down option prints details across the columns in one row first before moving onto the next row of data. The Down then Across option prints details down an entire column first before moving onto the next column.

- Format Groups with Multiple Column: This option formats groups with multiple columns using the Width, Gap Between Details, and Printing Directions specified for the selected Detail section.

TIP

> When you format a report to show multiple columns, the Crystal Reports engine reviews the fields in the detail section and sizes the columns in the rest of the report based on the width of those fields. As such, if data labels (text fields) are placed in the detail

7

continues

continued

section for row identification, these increase the width of the report's columns and reduce the number of columns that fit onto a page. To place such fields, consider placing them in a Page or Group header and underlaying them onto the Details section. This is presented in a sample format later in the chapter.

USING MULTIPLE REPORT SECTIONS

Including multiple sections within each section area of your report provides for an extremely flexible presentation of your report data. Chances are good that you do not need to create more than one occurrence of any of the existing report sections for basic reporting needs. However, Crystal Reports enables you to define multiple report sections within any given section area and to identify section-specific properties for challenging formatting requirements within more complex reports. Certain reporting tasks are performed most efficiently by creating multiple sections within an area.

For example, multiple report sections would be very useful if you want to create a form letter for your customers and you need to display only one of two possible return addresses on the letter—an American address for customers based in the United States and a Canadian address for the Canadian customers. To accomplish this, you do need to insert two report header sections into your report and use Conditional Formatting to dynamically apply the appropriate return address based on where the customer is located.

To demonstrate how to implement and use multiple report sections, you first need to review the basic operations of resizing, inserting, removing, and merging report sections.

RESIZING REPORT SECTIONS

Report sections might require resizing to accommodate for various sized report objects, such as large database fields, lengthy text objects, or corporate logo images, but they cannot exceed the size of the report page itself. From the Design tab of the report environment, you can drag the bottom boundary of the various sections up and down with the mouse to resize each section. Using the mouse, float the pointer over the horizontal boundary lines of the different sections. When the mouse pointer changes into a double-headed arrow icon, click and hold the left mouse button while dragging the boundary line to the desired position.

INSERTING NEW REPORT SECTIONS

To display only one of two possible return addresses on a form letter based on the country of the customer, you need to insert a second page header onto the report. The following steps walk you through constructing the following report using the Customer table from the Xtreme Sample Database:

1. Create a new Crystal Report using the standard Report Wizard, connecting to the Xtreme Sample database and selecting the Customers table. Do not add any database fields to the report. Click the Finish button at the Fields Selection dialog.

2. Create a Group (by choosing Insert, Group) based on the Customer Name field, but remove the Customer Name field from the Group header section. The Group field should have automatically appeared in the Group Header section when you created the group.

3. Select the New Page After property for the Group Footer #1 section.

4. Ensure that the Report Header section is suppressed.

5. Create and insert text objects in the appropriate report sections, as shown in Figure 7.8.

Figure 7.8
This simple form letter report shows the correct return address conditionally.

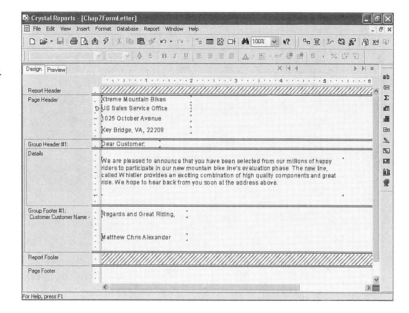

NOTE

Notice that in this sample form letter report, each report object displayed on the report is just a text object inserted into the appropriate section. There are no database fields included in the report yet.

Next you will insert a new Page Header in which to display an alternate return address for Canadian customers:

1. To insert a new Page Header section, locate the existing Page Header section, right-click on the section name (on the left of the design environment), and select Insert Section Below from the pop-up menu.

   The new section is entitled Page Header b and the original section was renamed to Page Header a so that there are now two Report Header sections within your report. The application follows this naming convention whenever multiple report sections are added.

7

2. After you have inserted a new Page Header section (labeled Page Header b), insert text objects to display a Canadian return address to be used for the non-U.S.-based recipients of the form letter, as shown in Figure 7.9.

Figure 7.9
The form letter report now shows two Page Header sections.

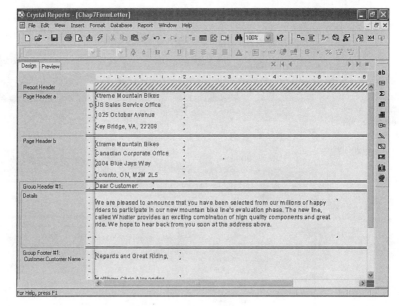

Now that the report has the two different return addresses and report sections created, the logic must be created within the report to implement the appropriate Page Header section based on each customer's location—whether they are based in the United States or Canada. Each customer's mailing address needs to be evaluated—the Country field from the Customer table. For this example, you're only concerned with North American customers, and if this field is equal to USA, use Page Header to display the return address. If it is equal to Canada, use Page Header b.

3. To isolate your report for only North American customers, choose the Select Expert option from the Report menu. From the list of available fields, select the Country field from the Customer table listing and click OK to continue.

4. You should now see the Select Expert dialog. From the drop-down list on the left, select Is One Of and include Canada and USA in the list box.

5. To add additional personalization to the form letter, use the Field Explorer to insert the Customer Name field into the Text Object—located in the Group Header #1 that reads "Dear Customer,"—so that it appears as Dear {Customer Name} in the Design tab of your report. To do this, you'll need to modify the text portion of this combined object to read "Dear " (the word Dear followed by a space), and then followed by the database field object.

Finally, you need to apply the logic to display the appropriate return address on the form letter. To do this, you apply a conditional formatting statement (format formula) to each of the two Page Header sections.

6. Using the Section Expert for Page Header a, click on the x+2 button (with the pencil symbol) located directly to the right of the Suppress (No Drill-Down) option on the Common tab. After clicking this icon, you should be presented with the Format Formula Editor dialog (see Figure 7.10). Here, you can use the Field, Function, and Operator windows (located in the upper area of the dialog) to insert the necessary format formula within this dialog, or you can just type in the statement in the lower area of the Editor dialog so that it reads `{Customer.Country}` = `"Canada"`. After you have inserted this statement, click Save and Close to return to the Section Expert. Note that the x+2 button has changed color (to red) to signify a conditional formula has been created here.

7. You now need to implement a very similar formatting condition for the Page Header b section. Following the same procedure used for the first section, use the Section Expert to insert a statement that reads `{Customer.Country}` = `"USA"`.

Figure 7.10
The report section is suppressed only if the conditional statement defined in the Format Formula Editor is `True`.

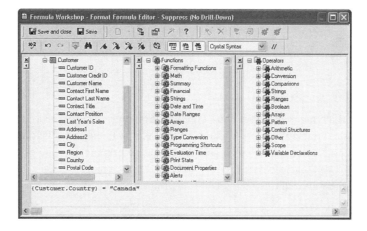

NOTE

> You do not need to check the Suppress (No Drill-Down) check box in the Section Expert dialog for either report Page Header section. By inserting a format formula, you have effectively applied conditional formatting that suppresses the section if the format formula is found to be true. In this case, one of the two format formulas should always be true because the customers are either located in the United States or Canada.

7

8. Close the Section Expert dialog by clicking OK. As shown in Figure 7.11, your report should now display only one of the two possible return addresses on the form letter. To verify that the appropriate return address is being populated on the form letter report

for each customer, you can easily add the Country field from the Customer table into the Group Header #1 section, as shown in Figure 7.11.

Figure 7.11
A simple form letter report is now dynamically formatted with the appropriate return address based on the customer's location.

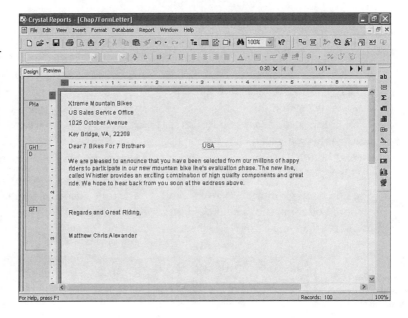

DELETING REPORT SECTIONS

In much the same manner sections were inserted, unused report sections can be removed from reports quickly by right-clicking on the section name and selecting Delete Section from the pop-up menu. Be aware, however, that any report objects positioned within the section are also deleted from the report. If any of the objects within a section that will be removed are required, they will need to be relocated into alternative report sections before deletion.

NOTE

Crystal Reports requires at least one section to be present for certain section types in every report—the Report Header and Footer, Page Header and Footer, and Details sections. These report sections are generated by default when creating new reports. Also, if Group objects exist within a report, you cannot remove the Group Header and Footer sections unless you first remove the Group object itself from the report.

MERGING REPORT SECTIONS

When designing reports, you might periodically want to merge two report sections to simplify the layout of a report. To merge the two Page Header sections from your earlier example, right-click on the Page Header a section title and select Merge Section Below from the pop-up menu. The Merge Section Below command is available from the right-click menu of any report section that meets two criteria:

- There are more than one of the given section type (Page Headers) within the Section Area.

- The section is not last in a series of sections (Page Headers) consisting of the same section types within a common area.

For example, if three Page Header sections are present on a report (as shown in Figure 7.12), the Merge Section Below command would be accessible from the right-click menus of Page Header a and Page Header b, but not from Page Header c.

Figure 7.12
The Merge Section Below command is available from the right-click menu of certain report sections.

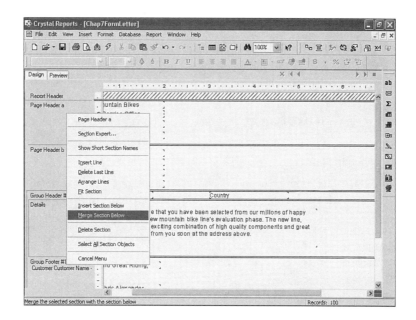

TROUBLESHOOTING

REPORT SECTION FORMATTING

I keep getting blank spaces in report sections, and I need a quick way of removing them.

To quickly remove blank spaces within report sections and tighten up the alignment of the objects positioned within the sections, use the Fit Section command available from the right-click menu of each report section.

CRYSTAL REPORTS IN THE REAL WORLD—ADVANCED FORMATTING

Often, a report section needs to be more than simply one color or another. A report with many rows might need some color to help guide the readers eye and make each line distinctly separate from the next. In the following sample, the report Chap7AdvFormat.rpt created earlier is modified to improve readability:

1. Open the Chap7AdvFormat.rpt report.

2. From the Report menu, select Section Expert. When the Section Expert dialog window opens, select the Details section and click the Color tab.

3. As previously described, checking the Background Color box enables you to set all the Detail lines to a single color. The intent here is to highlight the detail lines so they appear distinctly different from the detail line above and below to improve readability. Click the x+2 button and enter the following text into the code window:

```
If Remainder(RecordNumber,2)=1 Then
    crAqua
Else
    DefaultAttribute;
```

4. Finally, go back to the Section Expert. Select Group Footer from the list of sections and check the box labeled New Page After.

5. Now, each group starts on a new page, and long groups have detail lines defined by color. The color improvement can be seen on page 3 of the report.

Figure 7.13
Records are delimited by color for improved readability.

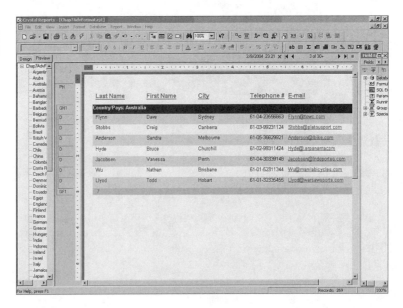

6. Save the report as Chap7AdvFormatPaginated.rpt.

VISUALIZING YOUR DATA WITH CHARTS AND MAPS

In this chapter

8

INTRODUCTION TO CHARTS AND MAPS

Chapter 2, "Selecting and Grouping Data," and Chapter 3, "Filtering, Sorting, and Summarizing Data," introduced the importance of grouping and summarizing in report generation. When doing so for business users, it is often effective to present these groups and summarizations using various visualization techniques. The charting and mapping features in Crystal Reports provide a very effective way to communicate relevant information using powerful visualization techniques.

Charts and maps with Crystal Reports provide an extensive array of data visualization options to report designers. In addition to familiar chart types including bar charts, pie charts, scatter charts, line charts, and bubble charts, new chart types in versions 9 and 10 include the following:

- Funnel charts (version 10)
- Gantt charts (version 9)
- Gauges (version 9)
- Numeric Axis charts (version 9)

Geographic Mapping with color-coding and integrated charting options provides another effective method of conveying macro-level information to report consumers.

This chapter introduces various charting and mapping techniques, including

- Enhancing the sample reports from previous chapters with charts and maps
- A review of the Crystal Reports charting expert
- An introduction to the newer chart types—Gantt, Gauge, and Numeric Axis charts
- A review of the Crystal Reports mapping expert
- Manual chart and map formatting

The Chart Expert is a good place to begin adding visualizations to your reports.

USING THE CHART EXPERT

Reflecting back on the sample reports used in Chapters 2 and 3, you might find that there are opportunities for enhancement through the addition of meaningful charts. As you learned in Chapter 2 with groupings, it is quite easy to summarize the data you collect for a report into meaningful categories or groups. Chapter 2 reviews some examples of grouping based on fields such as country and employee ID. By hiding or suppressing the detail sections of reports, you learned how to bring the meaningful summarizations around these types of groups to the forefront. To further bring this aggregated data to the business user's attention, you can create a chart on this grouped data using the Chart Expert.

To open the Chart Expert, either click on the Chart icon located on the Insert toolbar or select the Insert Chart option under the main Insert menu. Figure 8.1 displays the Chart Expert.

Figure 8.1
The Chart Expert dialog enables the rapid addition of valuable charts to reports.

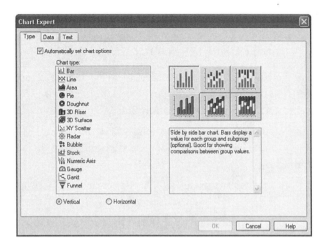

After you access the Chart Expert, several steps are required to actually complete the chart. These are reviewed in the next five sections.

USING THE CHART EXPERT TYPE TAB

The Chart Expert consists of five different tabs. The initial display tab on the Chart Expert is the Type tab, shown in Figure 8.1. On this tab, the type of graphic or chart is selected. In Crystal Reports version 10, there are more than 40 different basic chart types from which to select.

In addition to the classic bar, line, pie, and area charts, new chart types in versions 9 and 10 are listed in Table 8.1.

TABLE 8.1   NEW CHART TYPES IN CRYSTAL REPORTS VERSIONS 9 AND 10

New Chart Type	Chart Type Description
Numeric Axis (V.9)	A Numeric Axis chart is a bar, line, or area chart that uses a numeric field or a date/time field as its On Change Of field. With Numeric Axis charts you can create a true numeric X-axis or a true date/time X-axis.
Gauge(s) (V.9)	A Gauge chart presents data using a speedometer visual and is often used to measure percentage completed against target type metrics.
Gantt Chart (V.9)	A Gantt chart is a project-focused horizontal bar chart used to provide a graphical illustration of a project schedule. The horizontal axis shows a time span, whereas the vertical axis lists project tasks or events. Horizontal bars on the chart represent event sequences and time spans for each task on the vertical axis.
Funnel Chart (V.10)	Funnel charts are most often used to represent stages in a sales cycle and visually depict proportionality of the different phases in that sales process. A funnel chart is similar to a stacked bar chart in that it represents 100 percent of the summary values for the groups included in the chart.

These charts have been added to expand the visual capabilities of Crystal Reports and enrich your report presentations. Let's create a Sample Customer Order Listing report and add a chart to it that highlights the Company's Top 10 Customers in the following steps:

1. Quickly create the basics of this sample report by selecting the Customer Name, Order ID, and Order Amount fields from the Xtreme Sample Database. Then Group by Customer Name and Summarize Order Amount by the Customer Name group.

2. To restrict the data to the Top 10 Customers, access the Group Sort Expert from the Report menu option. Select a Top 10 Sort based on the Sum of Order Amount and do *not* include Others or Ties.

3. Insert a Chart onto the report using the Chart icon or the Chart option from the Insert menu.

4. Select a bar chart as the main chart type in the list box by clicking on it. Then click the Horizontal radio button that is present at the bottom of the dialog.

5. Select the two-dimensional side-by-side bar chart sub-chart type (top left option) by clicking on the associated graphical icon to the right of the Chart Type list box.

6. The last option to set in the Chart Type tab is whether you want Crystal Reports to automatically use the default legend, data-point, color, and axes options for your chart. The automatic option is enabled by default, but it can be turned off by clicking the check box near the top of the dialog. At this point, deselect the automatic check box.

Notice that the Axes and Options tabs appear when this check box is not clicked and disappear when it is selected. These tabs are discussed later in this section. Figure 8.2 displays the result of these six steps. You will continue creating this chart in the next four sections.

Figure 8.2
The Type tab on the Chart Expert dialog for the Sample Top 10 Customers report.

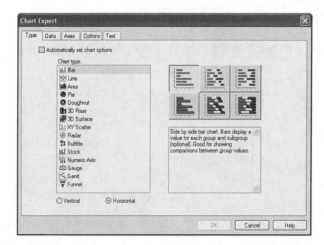

Table 8.2 highlights some common reports, their contained graphics, and the benefits of using them.

TABLE 8.2   COMMON REPORTS WITH CORRESPONDING CHART TYPES

Report	Chart Type	Report and Chart Benefit
Company Sales Report	Pie or Donut Chart	Highlights the regional breakdown of product sales across continents or countries facilitating analysis of revenue contribution.
Product Profitability Report	Horizontal or Vertical Bar Chart	Highlights the profit margin per product that a company sells, facilitating comparative analysis of profitability.
Actual versus Target Report	Gauges	Highlights the progress being made against specified targets through the use of a speedometer visual. When used across projects or divisions, it is relatively easy to compare how they are performing against certain initiatives.

USING THE CHART EXPERT DATA TAB

After a chart type has been selected in the Type tab, click on the Data tab. The Data tab enables the selection of the specific data on which the chart is based and the chart's location on the report. Figure 8.3 displays one view of the second tab of the Chart Expert. This view might vary depending on the different Chart Type options you have selected. The Data tab is composed of three different sections: Placement, Layout, and Data. These sections and corresponding options are discussed next.

Figure 8.3
The Data tab of the Chart Expert enables specification of chart location, layout, and data options.

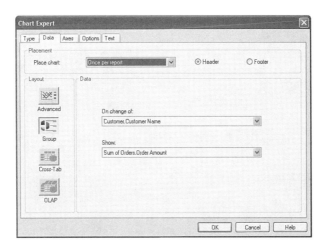

8

SPECIFYING CHART PLACEMENT

The Placement section is used to select the location of the chart on the report and, subsequently, the recurrence of the chart throughout the report. Using the drop-down box, select the section of the report where the chart is to be located (for example, Group 1, Group 2, and so on). The options available in this drop-down box are limited to the groups previously created in the report in addition to the option to create the graphic only once for the entire report. Using the radio buttons located beside the drop-down box, the header or footer of the selected report section can be selected. By making these selections, you also specify the chart's recurrence in the report because the chart repeatedly appears in every section you have specified. For example, if a chart were placed on a report for each country group, a separate chart would appear on the report for each country in the report.

To continue with the addition of a bar chart to the sample report, perform the following steps:

1. Select the Once Per Report option in the Place Chart drop-down box. This should be the only option and is already selected by default.

2. Select the Header button to specify placement in the report header.

NOTE

> When you select the Group Layout button (the second button from the top in the Layout section—see the next section for more details), you are presented with the options in the Chart Placement drop-down box based on what groups and summaries are already created in your report. Alternatively, if you select the Advanced Grouping Layout button, you are not as restricted and can dynamically create summaries across groups not yet in your report.

SPECIFYING CHART LAYOUT

The Chart Layout section specifies the data selection options that the selected chart provides to the report designer. The actual data is selected in the Chart Data section. Note that the options presented in that section are dependent on the specific Chart Layout button you have selected. Table 8.3 lists the different layout buttons and their typical uses.

TABLE 8.3   LAYOUT BUTTONS AND TYPICAL USES

Layout Button	Description	Typical Uses
Advanced	This layout button provides complete flexibility in chart creation by providing you with control of all charting options.	Creation of charts based on summaries not already created in the report or charts to be created for every detail record.

8

Layout Button	Description	Typical Uses
Grouping	Although this button is presented second, it is the default layout. This layout limits the Chart Data Selection options (see the following "Specifying Chart Data" section) to two drop-down boxes specifying the On Change Of and Show Values and expedites the creation of a chart at the cost of some of the flexibility provided by the Advanced layout button.	Quick creation of charts based on summarized fields already in the report and to be displayed at the Report or existing Group level.
Cross-Tab	This layout button appears as an option only when your current report is a Cross-Tab report.	Creation of a chart based on an existing Cross-Tab in the report.
OLAP	This layout button appears as an option only when your current report is based on an OLAP data source.	Creation of a chart based on an existing OLAP grid in the report.

The Cross-Tab and OLAP layout buttons and their related chart creation options are explored in Chapters 10, "Using Cross-Tabs for Summarized Reporting," and 16, "Multidimensional Reporting Against OLAP Data with Crystal Reports," because they relate to very specific report types. The next section explores the detailed data options that the Advanced and Grouping layout buttons enable.

SPECIFYING CHART DATA

Figure 8.3 displays the Data tab with the Group layout button selected. As previously described, this layout option is designed to facilitate the quick creation of a chart with a minimal amount of effort. To accomplish this rapid chart creation, two pieces of information are requested through two drop-down boxes—On Change Of (grouping item) and Show (field to be shown in the chart) selections. The On Change Of field is used to determine where the selected chart breaks the report data to be displayed. The Show field specifies the summary field to be displayed for each break of the data.

To continue adding a bar chart to the sample report, follow these steps:

1. Ensure that the Group layout button from the Layout section is selected.

2. Select Customer Name in the On Change Of field. This indicates that the chart breaks for each different customer.

3. Select Sum of Orders.Order Amount for the Show field. This indicates that the chart reflects this Sum for each customer. Figure 8.3 should reflect the results of these steps in the Chart Data tab. You will continue creating this chart in the next section.

8

NOTE

> When leveraging the Rapid Chart Creation functionality of the Group layout option, it's worth noting again that you are limited to chart creation based on existing summary fields already created in your reports and inserted into existing group sections. For more flexible chart creation, you can use the Advanced layout option described later.

Figure 8.4 displays the Data tab with the Advanced Layout button selected. The additional options presented here give you more flexibility in the charts that you can create.

Figure 8.4
The Data tab with the Advanced Layout button selected.

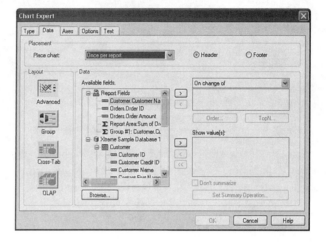

The On Change Of and Show Values fields should be recognizable in this new window although they are selected in a much more flexible manner (see the right side of the Data section beside the Available Fields listing) described next.

The On Change Of field is now only one selection option (among three) in its own drop-down box. If you need to create a chart based on changing a specific field (as you did with the standard group layout), select the On Change Of charting option and then specify the field or fields to break the chart sections on by selecting any of the fields in the available fields listing. Unlike the drop-down box under the Group layout, you can select any of the available report fields in this interface, dynamically order them with the Order button or restrict their display on the report to a specified Top or Bottom N with the Top N button. You can also dynamically select multiple fields for the chart to break on, and none of the selected fields need already be on the report or have summary fields previously existing on the report for them.

The remaining two options in the On Change Of drop-down box are For Each Record and For All Records. These two options enable charts to be created either against all data in a report or for each detailed record in a report.

TIP

When using the For All Records charting option, you can select the field to be displayed for each break by selecting a field from the Available Fields list in the list box beneath the For All Records drop-down box.

After selecting any of these options, you need to select a Show Value(s) field to enable the chart's creation. This selection specifies the summary field to be displayed for each break of the data and can come from any field (database, report, formula, and so on) that is listed in the available field's list. To select the Show Value fields, highlight the intended field and use the selection arrow buttons adjacent to the Show Values list box.

NOTE

You do not need to have an existing summary on your report to use it for a graph in the Advanced Charting layout options. You can add any field to the Show Values list and then dynamically create a summary by clicking on the Set Summary Operation button. These dynamically created summaries are created automatically and used by the chart. This is one of the unique features of Crystal Reports that provides you with more charting flexibility.

USING THE CHART EXPERT TEXT TAB

After a chart type and data have been specified, select the Text tab. This tab on the Chart Expert dialog enables you to specify titles and title formatting that the chart displays when it is placed on the report. Figure 8.5 shows the Text tab of the Chart Expert.

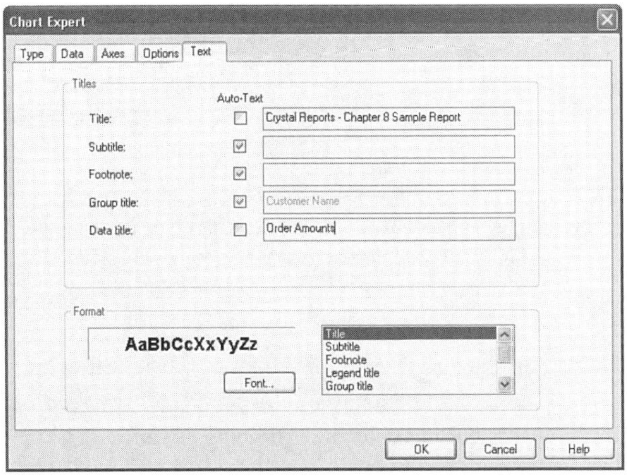

Figure 8.5
The Text tab of the Chart Expert allows specification of Text labels for the associated Chart.

To continue adding the bar chart to the sample report, follow these steps:

1. Deselect the Auto-Text check box beside the Title entry. The text box for the title should now become available for you to modify. Change the title to **Crystal Reports— Chapter 8 Sample Chart**.

2. Deselect the Auto-Text check box beside the Data Title entry. Change the Data Title entry to **Order Amounts**. You will continue creating this chart in the next section.

USING THE CHART EXPERT AXES TAB

The fourth tab in the Chart Expert dialog, the Axes tab, only appears if the Automatically Select Chart Options check box has been deselected on the Type tab. You can then select the Axes tab by clicking it. This tab enables you to customize chart gridlines, data value scales, data value ranges, and data value divisions. Figure 8.6 displays the Axes tab of the Chart Expert dialog for a bar chart.

Figure 8.6
The Axes tab of the Chart Expert allows specification of grid-line display, axis ranges, and divisions.

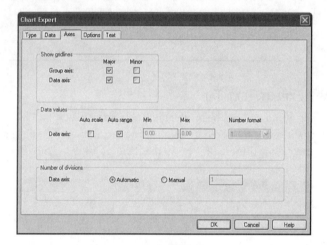

> **NOTE**
> This tab only appears when the selected chart type has axes within it (for example, a bar chart or line chart) and does not display for other chart types such as a pie chart.

To continue adding a bar chart to the sample report, try the following step: Select the Major Gridlines check box for the data axis. This facilitates the reading of the bar charts. You will finish creating this bar chart in the following section.

TIP

> By manually setting both the Min/Max Data Ranges and the Number of Divisions, you are able to customize your data axis gridline display labels.

USING THE CHART EXPERT OPTIONS TAB

The Options tab in the Chart Expert only appears if the Automatically Select Chart Options check box has been deselected on the Type tab. The Options tab enables you to customize chart coloring, data-point labeling, legend placement, legend format options, and several other chart type–specific formatting options. Figure 8.7 displays the Options tab of the Chart Expert dialog for a bar chart.

Figure 8.7
The Chart Expert Options tab allows specification of chart colors, data points, and legends for the involved chart.

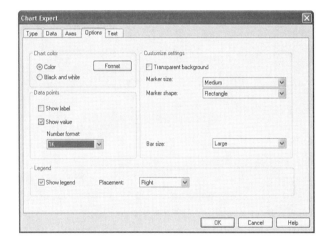

To finish customizing the bar chart you have been adding to your working sample report, follow these steps:

1. Select the Show Value button in the Data Points section.

2. Select the 1K format from the Number Format drop-down box.

3. Click the OK button, and you find a bar chart representing the summarized sales of this company's Top 10 Customers presented. Figure 8.8 provides a snapshot of this report.

If you find your chart is slightly different in appearance or imperfect, that is okay. You have plenty of powerful fine-tuning tools at your disposal, and they will be explored at the end of this chapter.

Figure 8.8
A sample Customer Orders report with a bar chart highlighting the visual benefits of charting.

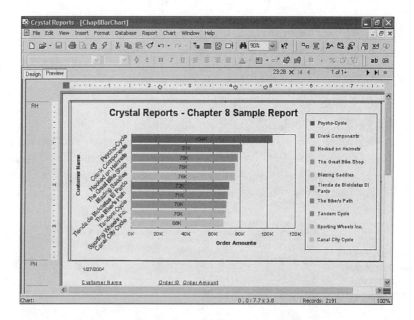

USING THE MAP EXPERT

As you explore the charting capabilities of Crystal Reports, you will discover numerous powerful data visualizations that enhance the productivity of your reports and business users. Another valuable form of data presentation available in Crystal Reports is geographic mapping. This enables you to create reports that are logically grouped by geographically related information and that can communicate meaningful information in a familiar mapping model. When working with geographic data, you can quickly create a map or a map/chart combination on this data using the Map Expert.

TIP

> The maps and mapping functionality provided within Crystal Reports are bundled from a third-party company—MapInfo. Additional map layers and types can be purchased directly from MapInfo and can be made accessible from Crystal Reports by adding them to the mapping folders under \Program Files\Map Info X. You can order additional mapping information from MapInfo at www.mapinfo.com.

To open the Map Expert, either click on the Map Globe icon located on the Insert toolbar or access the Insert Map option under the Insert menu. Figure 8.9 displays the Map Expert dialog.

The next three sections introduce you to the functionality of the Map Expert and also escort you through a brief tutorial on the addition of a map to a sample Order Listing report slightly different than the one you just created.

Figure 8.9
The Map Expert dialog enables the rapid addition of mapping visuals to a report.

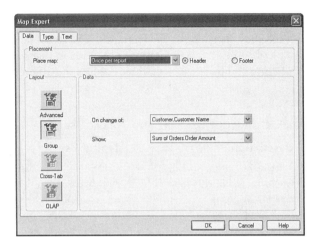

USING THE MAP EXPERT DATA TAB

The Data tab on the Map Expert dialog enables you to select the specific data that the map is based on and where it will be placed on the report. Figure 8.9 displays this tab of the Map Expert. The Data tab is composed of three different sections: Placement, Layout, and Data. These sections, and corresponding options, are discussed next.

SPECIFYING MAP PLACEMENT

The Map Placement section is used in an identical manner as the Chart Placement section for charts. It enables the selection of the location of the map on the report and consequently the recurrence of the map throughout the report.

Using the Place Map drop-down box, select the section of the report where the map will be located (for example, Group 1, Group 2, and so on). The options available in this drop-down box are limited to the groups previously created in the report in addition to the option to create the graphic only once for the entire report. Using the radio buttons located beside the drop-down box, choose the header or footer of the selected report section. By making these selections, you have also determined the map's recurrence in the report because the map repeatedly appears in every section you have specified (for example, for each country in the group based on country).

To begin with a walk-through of an example, perform the following steps:

1. Quickly create a new report based on the Xtreme sample data 10 database, include a few columns of data in the detail section, including Order Amount, and group the report by Customer Country and then Customer Name. Finally, add summary fields on Order Amount for each of the Country and Customer Name groups.

2. Open the Map Expert.

3. Select Once Per Report in the Placement drop-down box and select the header as the map's intended location. The following sections contain more steps for this example.

8

SPECIFYING MAP LAYOUT

The Layout section specifies the data that the map uses. The actual data is selected in the Map Data section (described next), but the options presented in that section are dependent on the Map Layout button you have selected. Table 8.4 lists the different layout buttons and their typical use.

TABLE 8.4   MAP EXPERT LAYOUT BUTTONS AND TYPICAL USE

Layout Button	Description	Typical Use
Advanced	This layout button provides complete flexibility in map creation by giving you control of all mapping options.	Creation of maps based on summaries not already created in the report or maps based on geographic fields not contained in predefined report groups.
Group	Although this button is presented second, it is the default layout if the involved report has predefined groups and summary fields already created. This layout limits the Map Data Selection options (see next section) to two drop-down boxes specifying the On Change Of and Show Values and expedites the creation of a map at the cost of some of the flexibility provided by the Advanced layout button.	Quick creation of Maps based on summarized fields already in the report and to be displayed at the Report or existing Group level.
Cross-Tab	This layout button appears as an option only when your current report is a Cross-Tab report.	Creation of a map based on an existing Cross-Tab in the report.
OLAP	This layout button appears as an option only when your current report is based on an OLAP data source.	Creation of a map based on an existing OLAP grid in the report.

For information on the Cross-Tab and OLAP layout buttons and their related map creation options, see Chapter 10, "Using Cross-Tabs for Summarized Reporting," and Chapter 20, "Advanced Crystal Analysis Report Design."

The next section explores the detailed data options enabled by the Advanced and Group Layout buttons.

CAUTION

> If you attempt to create a geographic map based on a non-geographic field, the Map Expert accepts your request and then displays a blank map when it cannot resolve the selected field values to geographic entities. Make sure you select a valid geographic field in the Geographic Field item of the Advanced layout section or the On Change Of field in the Group layout section.

SPECIFYING MAP DATA

As you saw earlier, Figure 8.9 displays the Map Data section with the Group layout button selected. As described in Table 8.4, this layout option is designed to facilitate the quick creation of a map with a minimal amount of user interaction. To accomplish this rapid map creation, two pieces of information are requested through two drop-down boxes.

The first drop-down box requests you to select the On Change Of field and the second the Show field. The On Change Of field is used to determine where the selected map breaks the report data to be displayed (for example, Country, State, or Province). The Show field specifies the summary field to be displayed for each break of the data.

NOTE

> When using the Rapid Map Creation function of the Group layout option, you are limited to map creation based on existing summary fields already created in your reports and inserted into existing group sections. For more flexible map creation, use the Advanced layout option described later.

Figure 8.10 displays the Map Data tab with the Advanced layout button selected. The additional options presented here provide you with improved flexibility in the maps that you can create.

Figure 8.10
The Data tab with the Advanced layout button selected allows flexible selection of mapping data, layout, and placement.

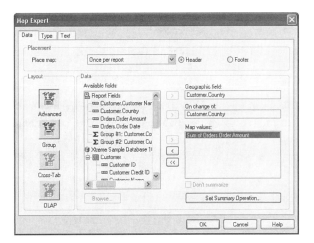

The familiar On Change Of field should be recognizable in this new window although it is selected in a more flexible manner using the selection buttons in the interface. It is selected in exactly the same manner as the Geographic field selection in this interface by selecting any of the fields in the Available Fields listing and clicking on the selection button.

8

NOTE

> The Geographic and On Change Of fields are often the same, but can be set to be differ-ent. These are set to different field values when you want to present pie or bar charts on top of the involved map and for each of the different values in the selected Geographic field. An example of this would be presenting a pie chart for each country that highlights the different order amounts by company—indicated in the On Change Of field.

After selecting your Geographic and On Change Of fields, a Map Values field must be selected to enable the map's creation. This selection specifies the summary field to be dis-played for each break of the data and can come from any field (database, report, formula, and so on) that is listed in the available field's list. To select the Show Value fields, highlight the intended field and use the selection arrow buttons adjacent to the Map Values list box.

NOTE

> As mentioned previously, you do not need to have had an existing summary on a report to summarize on it using the Advanced Mapping layout options. You can add any field to the Map Values list and then dynamically create a summary by clicking on the Set Summary Operation button. These dynamically created summaries are automatically cre-ated and used by the map.

To continue adding a map to your sample report, follow these steps:

1. Ensure that the Advanced layout button from the Layout section is selected.

2. Select Country for the Geographic field. This indicates that the map breaks for each different country. Leave the On Change Of field as Country when this gets populated automatically.

3. Select Order Amount for the Show field and leave the default Sum as the summary operation. This indicates that the map reflects this Sum of Orders for each country. Figure 8.10 should reflect the results of these steps in the Data tab. You will finish cre-ating this map in the next two sections.

USING THE MAP EXPERT TYPE TAB

The Type tab enables you to select from the five different types of maps that are available for presentation. The five map types can be logically broken into two distinct and separate categories—maps that present a summarization based on one variable, and maps that pre-sent a summarization based on two variables. The Type tab with these five map types is depicted in Figure 8.11. All five of the map types are also described in Table 8.5.

The first three map types shown base their maps on the summary of the selected Show Value field and for each Geographic field—the single fluctuating variable. The last two map types base their maps not only on the changing Geographic field, but also on a second fluc-tuating variable selected in the On Change Of field. Based on this second variable changing, either bar or pie charts are displayed on top of each of the involved Geographic fields. Table 8.5 describes the different map types, and includes a sample scenario for each.

Figure 8.11
The Map Expert Type tab enables you to select from the different types of maps available for display in your report.

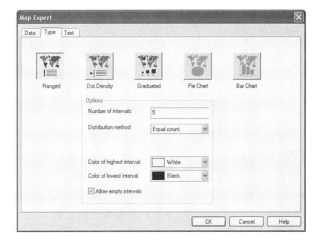

TABLE 8.5   MAP TYPES WITH CORRESPONDING SAMPLE REPORTING SCENARIO

Map Type	Description	Sample Scenario
Ranged	Breaks data into specified ranges and displays geographic areas on the map in different colors.	A U.S.-based firm looking for a Sales Map that highlights the states that fall into a specified number of sales/revenue ranges.
Dot Density	Displays a dot for each occurrence of a specified item.	A growing wireless company in Eastern Canada wants to view the density and point location of new customers and map that to ongoing marketing campaigns.
Graduated	Displays data that is linked to points rather than precise geographical areas.	An Irish beverage company wants a report on geographically dispersed distributors, proportionately highlighting the amount of product being distributed.
Pie Chart	Displays a pie chart over each geographic area. Each slice of the pie represents an individual s ummarization relative to the whole for the given geographic area.	An employee head-count report for the United States with a pie chart over each state that highlights the breakdown of the employees by status including salaried, hourly, or temporary.
Bar Chart	Displays a bar chart over each geographic area. Each bar represents an individual summarization relative to the other summarizations for the given geographic area.	A marketing media report for a U.S.-based company with a bar chart that highlights the amount of advertising and marketing dollars spent in different media in each region: TV, Internet, newspaper, magazine, and so on.

Each Map Type has a small number of associated options that can be set to customize the appearance of that particular map. You are encouraged to explore these options to help you find the maps most useful for your specific design goals.

USING THE MAP EXPERT TEXT TAB

After a map's type and data have been selected, select the Text tab. This tab on the Map Expert dialog enables you to specify titles and legend formatting that the map uses when it is placed on the report.

To finish adding a map to your sample report, follow these steps:

1. On the Type tab, select the Ranged map type.

2. Select Yellow and Blue as the respective low and high range colors.

3. Click on the Text tab and give your map a title such as **Crystal Reports – Chapter 8 Map Sample**.

4. Click OK, and you will find a geographic map added to your report that should look similar to Figure 8.12.

Figure 8.12
A sample Customer Orders Report with a geographic map.

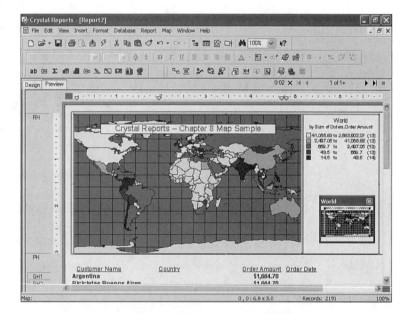

MODIFYING CHART AND MAP PROPERTIES

After you have successfully created a chart or map and placed it on your report, you have a number of post-creation editing options at your disposal within the Crystal Reports Designer. Both charts and maps provide a number of easy-to-use methods to re-visit and edit your charts or maps. Several of the most common editing methods are listed in the following sections.

MODIFYING CHART PROPERTIES

After a chart has been created and placed on your report, you can perform numerous post-creation edits by right-clicking on the chart object while in Preview mode. From the Chart menu that appears, you have both the ability to revisit the Chart Expert and use a number of more finely tuned post-creation editing tools, including the powerful and flexible Chart Option functions.

NOTE

> Versions 9 and 10 of Crystal Reports give you greater abilities to perform numerous in-place edits to chart objects. For example, you can grab a chart title (or other object) and move its location or change its font directly in place in versions 9 or 10. Previous to version 9, this functionality was mostly accessible from a separate tab called the Chart Analyzer. This tab is no longer available.

SPECIFYING CHART SIZE AND POSITION

This option enables you to identify very specific x and y coordinates in addition to height and width measurements for the involved chart. Charts can also be dynamically resized and repositioned by grabbing any of the sizing handles that appear on the frame of the chart after it is selected.

MODIFYING CHART OPTIONS

The Chart Options menu choice enables you to fine-tune the look of your charts at a granular level not available in the standard Chart Expert. The following sections explore the variety of chart customizations and formatting options exposed through the Chart Options menu. These are especially useful where the functionality of the standard chart creation expert does not meet your exact requirements.

SPECIFYING TEMPLATE OPTIONS

This selection provides direct access to the same Report Gallery that is provided in the first step of the Chart Expert.

SPECIFYING GENERAL OPTIONS

This selection provides a rich multitabbed interface with a chart preview window for editing a great number of the presentation components of the involved chart. Figure 8.13 highlights the interface, and the following paragraphs describe the details of the respective tabs.

The *General tab* provides general formatting options for each chart type. The functions give you a great deal of flexibility in controlling the details of the involved graphics (such as Pie Chart tilt, rotation, hole size, and exploding pie characteristics, or Bar Chart shape, overlap, width, depth, and so on).

Figure 8.13
The Chart Options dialog General tab provides advanced chart reporting functionality.

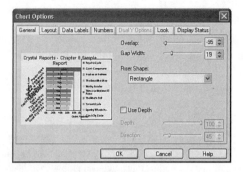

Some common options for pie, bar, and other charts include the following:

- Overlap: Use this slider to change how much risers within each category overlap each other.

- Gap Width: Use this slider to change the gap between the group of bar risers in each category.

- Riser Shape: Use this list box to choose the shape of the chart's bars or risers.

- Use Depth: Use this check box to apply a depth effect or to make a completely flat chart.

- Depth: When Use Depth is selected, use this slider to specify the amount of depth to be applied to the chart risers and frame.

- Pie Tilt: Use this slider to tilt the involved pie chart(s).

- Pie Rotation: Use this slider to rotate the involved pie(s).

- Explode Pie: Exploding a pie or doughnut chart detaches all slices away from its center. Click the Series option tab if you want to attach or detach an individual slice from a chart.

The *Layout tab* provides chart layout options. The options here enable alteration of different display options for different charts (such as 2D versus 3D, Horizontal versus Vertical Bars, and so on).

The commonly edited options for the most common charts include the following:

- Type: Enables you to refine your selection of chart types based on the original (such as Pie or Ring for pie charts).

- Dual Axes: Enables different charts to have two numeric axes (Y1 and Y2).

The *Data Labels tab* provides formatting and display options for data labels. The different options enable you to select the presentation of data labels based on either the underlying value representing the chart graphics, the associated label, or a combination of the two.

For Gauge charts, this functionality is exposed through the Display Options tab.

The *Numbers tab* provides formatting options for data label numbers. This tab is activated when data labels are selected on the Data Labels tab.

The category drop-down box enables you to select a general format for the numeric component of the data labels. After this is selected, more granular options are exposed for control over the display of each format.

The formatting on this tab does not control the numbers displayed on the chart axes. To edit those, access the Grids and Scales dialog by choosing Chart Options, Grids (discussed later in this chapter in more detail).

The *Dual Y Axis tab* provides formatting options for dual axes charts. This tab is only activated when a dual axes chart is selected on the Layout tab.

This tab facilitates the assignment of individual series to each axis and the definition of the location of an axis split line.

Dual Y Axis functionality is not available on Funnel, Gantt, Gauge, Histogram, Stock, Pie, or 3D charts.

The *Look tab* provides options for changing the appearance of the involved chart. The Color Mode drop-down box enables you to select a color scheme for the involved chart components. This is typically a decision between coloring by group or by series although other options are provided for surface charts. The visual effects of these modes are only truly realized when more than one Change By field has been set for the involved chart.

The remaining options surround the display of the legend (available on most charts) and its placement relative to the chart.

The *Display Status tab* provides options for displaying or hiding chart objects. Typical options made here include grid-line display, data label display, legend display (again), pie-chart slice labels, ring-chart total labels, and so on.

SPECIFYING TITLES OPTIONS

This option enables you to specify chart titles, subtitles, footnotes, and so on. Many charts also include axis title specifications such as Group Axis title or Data Axis title here.

SPECIFYING SERIES OPTIONS

This menu option is used to apply formatting options to an individual series in a chart. The Series Option is only available for selection if a series was previously selected in the chart. This series selection is done in place in Crystal Reports (for example, highlighting a pie slice on a pie chart enables the Series Option functionality for that pie slice's series). Figure 8.14 highlights the Series Option dialog, and the following paragraphs describe the different tabs available on the Series option dialog and some common usage scenarios.

The *General tab* shows general formatting options for a selected series. Common display effects enacted here include exploding a pie slice away from its pie chart, selecting markers

8

on a line chart, or altering the visual metaphor for a selected series so it is different than the other series (for example, displaying the U.S. Sales results as an area visual on a bar chart). In certain charts such as 3D Charts, the selection of each series' riser shape is also available.

Figure 8.14
The Series Option dialog provides the capability to specify chart series options such as trendlines, data labels, and number formats.

The *Data Labels tab* shows data label display options for the currently selected series. It enables you to specify series-specific data labels. This functionality is effective for highlighting a series of particular relevance. Unlike the General menu option's Data Labels tab, this series-specific functionality only enables the setting of numeric-based data labels.

The *Numbers tab* shows formatting options for data label numbers. This is only available when data labels have been selected in the Data Labels section of the Chart Options dialog.

This tab enables you to specify a series-specific numeric data label formatting. The category drop-down box enables you to select a general format for the numeric component of the data labels. After this is selected, more granular options are exposed for control over the display of each format.

The *Trendline tab* provides display and formatting options for a trendline selection. It enables you to represent trends in a data series graphically. You can add trendlines to data series in a number of unstacked charts (such as 2D area, bar, bubble, column, line, and scatter charts). Several different automatic trendline creations are possible including Linear, Logarithmic, Polynomial, or Exponential trendlines, in addition to Moving Averages.

SPECIFYING GRID OPTIONS (NUMERIC AXIS GRIDS & SCALES DIALOG)

This Chart Options menu selection is used to format chart axes, gridlines, and scaling. Through the associated dialog, all the axes in a chart can be formatted. The tabs on the left side of the dialog show the available axes in the chart: Group Axis, Data Axis, Dual Y Axis (only for dual-axes charts), X Axis (only for bubble and scatter charts), and Series Axis (only for 3D charts). When a left-side axis tab is selected, the tabs at the top of the dialog reflect the available formatting options for that axis. Figure 8.15 shows the Numeric Axis Grids & Scales dialog, and the following paragraphs describe the different tabs available on the Series option dialog and some common usage scenarios.

Figure 8.15
The Numeric Axis
Grids & Scales dialog
provides granular
level control over
chart axis display
options.

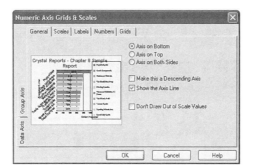

The *General tab* shows general formatting options for a selected axis. You can specify the location of the Axis labels here (for example, top, bottom, left, right, both) through the Location of the Label radio buttons. Additional options of interest are the Descending Axis check box and the Draw Categories in Reverse Order check box.

The *Scales tab* provides options around the scale for the involved axis. The most common options set in this tab are the manually set maximum and minimum scale options. These enable increased control over the range presented on the involved axis. Other options include settings around the logarithmic scale and forcing the inclusion of zero in the axis range.

The *Labels tab* provides control over the involved axis labels. Typical functionality you can access here includes toggling off and on of the following check boxes: Don't Show Maximum Value Label, Don't Show Minimum Value Label, Staggering Labels, and Using Manual Number of Groups.

The *Numbers tab* shows formatting options for data axis numbers. This tab enables you to specify data axis numeric data label formatting. The category drop-down box enables you to select a general format for the numeric component of the data labels. After this is selected, more granular options are exposed for control over the display of each format.

The *Grid tab* provides access to the Gridline formatting options for the involved data axis. This tab enables you to specify the involved axis' displayed gridlines including Custom Gridlines specified at certain values and different grid formats.

SPECIFYING SELECTED ITEM FORMATTING OPTIONS

This Chart Options menu selection enables you to format line, area, and text objects in a chart. It is only available when a chart object has been selected with the mouse or other pointer. Figure 8.16 highlights the Formatting dialog. Different tabs (Font, Line, or Fill) are highlighted and available based on the underlying selected chart item.

SPECIFYING VIEWING ANGLES OPTIONS

This menu option is only available for 3D charts. It enables you to edit the involved chart's viewing angles, position, wall thickness, and so on. The basic options enable you to select a predefined viewing angle template. The advanced options enable you to create new

8

templates and refine the manipulation of the 3D Chart. Figure 8.17 highlights the Viewing Angles Advanced Option dialog.

Figure 8.16
The Formatting dialog provides the capability to format user-selected objects within the involved chart.

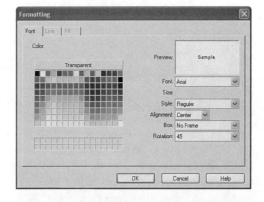

Figure 8.17
The Viewing Angles Advanced dialog provides the capability to specify precise viewing angles for 3D charts.

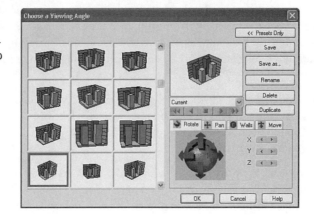

The *Rotate tab* and its X,Y, and Z dimension controls are used to rotate a 3D chart to any angle. There are three different methods or controls to change the rotation of the chart:

- Use the X, Y, and Z left and right control buttons to incrementally rotate the chart in the preview window.
- Use the directional arrows surrounding the globe to affect the rotation.
- Use the preview window itself to click and drag the previewed chart around the different axes.

The *Pan tab* is used to pan and zoom a 3D chart. The same control options exist here as were described for the Rotate tab, with the Zoom option being an additional component.

The *Walls tab* provides a method to increase and decrease the thickness and length of the walls on a 3D chart. The same control options exist for this tab as those mentioned previously for the Rotate tab.

The *Move tab* provides a method to move and set the perspective of the 3D chart. The same control options exist for this tab as those mentioned previously for the Rotate tab.

NOTE

> You will find separate and advanced charting help instructions for these granular options available through the help button present on all the dialogs accessed from the Chart Options menu. This advanced help is provided by 3D Graphics—the third party responsible for the charting in Crystal Reports.

MODIFYING MAP PROPERTIES

After a map has been created and placed on your report, you can perform numerous post-creation edits by right-clicking on the map object while in the Preview mode. From the Map menu that appears when you right-click, you have the capability to either re-visit the Map Expert or use a number of more finely tuned post-creation editing tools such as Zooming, Layer Control, Map Navigation, and Data Mismatch Resolution.

LAYER CONTROL

By clicking on the Layers menu option, you can specify the different layers that display on your map. Examples of this include World Capital Cities and the Mapping Grid. Crystal Reports version 10 is distributed with a number of built-in layers that are accessed through this Layer Control dialog. These layers can be added and removed from Crystal Reports using this dialog and more detail-oriented layers. Additional maps can be purchased separately from MapInfo (a third-party company) and integrated into Crystal Reports.

RESOLVE MISMATCH

The Resolve Mismatch dialog provides two very useful functions for maps. First, the Resolve Mismatch dialog enables you to select a specific map to use for your report. Several maps are provided out of the box with Crystal Reports and others can be purchased separately. Additionally, you can match the field names stored in the Geographic field from which you are basing the map onto the names that the involved map is expecting. This powerful feature enables you to take raw, untransformed data and dynamically match it to a geographical map value that the mapping engine can understand. For example, on a map of Canada, you might have multiple inconsistent data entries in your database for the province of Ontario (for example, ON, Ont, Ontario, and so on). Using this dialog, you can match each of these to the expected value of Ontario, and the mapping engine successfully interprets all of them.

SIZE AND POSITION

This option enables you to specify very specific x and y coordinates in addition to height and width measurements for the involved map. Maps can also be dynamically resized and repositioned by grabbing any of the sizing handles that appear on the frame of the map after it is selected.

ZOOMING AND PANNING

The Zoom In and Zoom Out options enable you to focus on a particularly relevant part of the involved map. The Panning option enables you to horizontally pan the view of the map to what is most interesting to you and your business users. When any of these options have been selected from the Map menu, you are then placed in an interactive mode with the map and your mouse/touchpad. Clicking zooms you in and out and double-clicking and dragging facilitates panning.

TIP

> When selecting from the Map menu, the Map Navigator provides a thumbnail of the entire map you are currently working with. As you saw earlier, Figure 8.12 highlights this Map Navigator in your report sample. The Map Navigator also provides a dotted outline of the area that is currently selected for display. You can fine-tune the area that displays by grabbing this dotted line, double-clicking on any of its corners, and subsequently dragging or expanding them out or collapsing them in while holding down your second click.

TROUBLESHOOTING

I WANT TO CREATE A CHART BASED ON CHANGING A SPECIFIC FIELD BUT DON'T KNOW HOW.

Select the On Change Of charting option and then specify the field or fields to break the chart sections on by selecting any of the fields in the available fields listing. Unlike the drop-down box under the Group layout, you can select any of the available report fields in this interface, dynamically order them with the Order button, or restrict their display on the report to a specified Top or Bottom N with the Top N button.

CRYSTAL REPORTS IN THE REAL WORLD— COMPLEX CHARTS

Charts can be particularly useful when they display data that is different but complementary. Although it is certainly possible to show data in multiple charts, showing complementary data in the same chart allows direct comparison of information and more efficient use of space. The following steps will walk through a good example of this:

1. Start by opening the report Chap8BarChart.rpt. In the chart that will be added, bars represent the individual stores and a line shows the running total across all stores.

2. With the report open, right-click on the field Order Sales and choose Insert, Running Total. When the Create Running Total Field window opens, give the running total a name like Total Sales and leave the remaining values as defaults similar to Figure 8.18. Click OK to close the window.

Figure 8.18
Creating this Running
Total field will help
present a creative use
of charts.

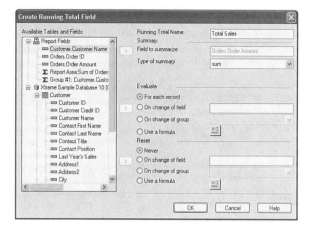

3. From the Insert menu, select Chart. Without making any changes, go to the Data tab and click the Advanced button. Select the Customer Name field and use the upper arrow (>) button to move the field to the On Change Of window. To make this Chart consistent with the rest of the report, you will also need to Specify that you only want to display the Top 10 Customers based on their sales through use of the Top N button. Finally, select the Order Amount and Total Sales fields and add them to the Show Values window using the lower arrow (>) button. The results of this step should resemble Figure 8.19.

Figure 8.19
Creating an advanced
chart with a two sum-
mary fields will
enable some creative
charting.

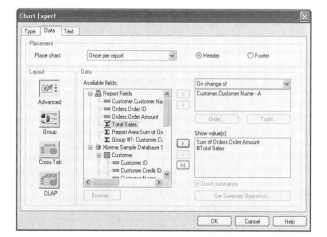

4. Select the Customer Name field in the On Change Of window and click the Top N button. When the Group Sort Expert window opens, select All from the list box and choose Descending. Click OK to close the window.

5. Click the Text tab. Uncheck all the Auto-Text boxes and type **Comparison Chart** into the Chart Title text box. Click OK to close the window and return to the report.

6. Using the handles on the chart object, stretch the chart to fit the page width. Right-click the legend text #Total Sales and select Edit Axis Label. Remove the # symbol, do the same with the text Sum of Orders.Order Amount, and change the text to Sales. This makes the text more readable. Figure 8.20 provides a good benchmark.

Figure 8.20
Bars representing both Individual Client Sales and Total Cumulative Sales are displayed on the same chart, effectively communicating multiple pieces of information in one chart.

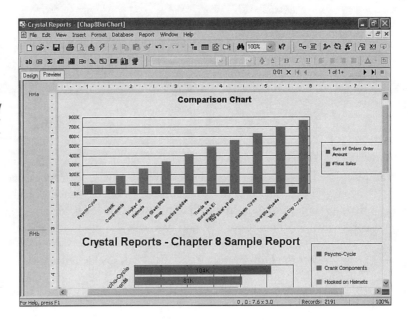

7. Notice that because the Total Sales becomes such a large value, the contrast between individual sales values appears quite small using this scale. To change this, the report will be changed to use a split axis. This enables you to show both sets of values while still highlighting the contrast between individual elements within a set. To change the chart to a split axis, right-click anywhere in the chart and choose Chart Options, Template. Click on the Dual Axes box, and then click OK.

8. Click any of the individual Total Sales bars to select it, and then right-click the bar and select Chart Options, Series. Change the list box from Default for Chart Type to Line and click OK to close.

9. Save the report as **Chap8BarChartComparison.rpt**.

TIP

The preceding example provided a great example of displaying different data sets in the same chart. Another great practical use of this functionality to consider is displaying averages (or running total calculations) over time in the line chart to complement the other bar chart sums by some specified time period (such as a month). Essentially, you could create a chart that represents a moving average laid on top of the monthly sums.

Figure 8.21
Bars represent
Individual Client Sales
and a line represents
Total Cumulative
Sales with two sepa-
rate numeric scales
displayed.

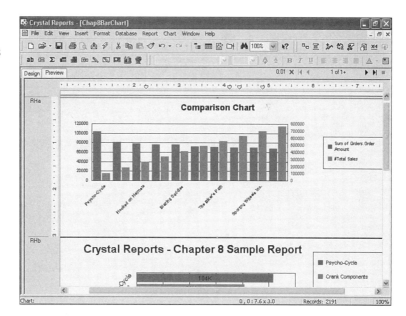

CHAPTER 9

CUSTOM FORMATTING TECHNIQUES

In this chapter

INTRODUCTION

This chapter focuses on more complex formatting to make reports look like high-quality information portals rather than simply paper reports.

MAKING PRESENTATION-QUALITY REPORTS

Up to this point in the book, the focus of the chapters has been on making sure that the data appears as required. The next step, formatting, keeps users coming back to the reports time and time again.

Formatting can take many different forms, from basic font coloring to hyperlinks to conditional formatting (based on the data coming back from the database). This chapter examines a cross-section of all these types of formatting to give the report developer a good basis for report formatting.

This chapter presents a series of tutorials to enable you to actually add formatting to a report started in an earlier chapter. Let's assume that you would like to improve the report that was started in Chapter 6, "Fundamentals of Report Formatting."

COMMON FORMATTING FEATURES

The most common formatting feature is changing font color or font face. This can be done by choosing the features directly on the Formatting toolbar, as shown in Figure 9.1.

Figure 9.1
The Crystal Reports Formatting toolbar lets you change object formatting.

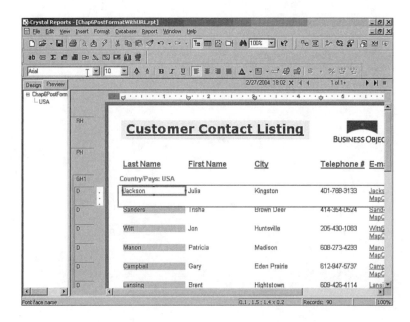

Chapter 6 introduced the Highlighting Expert. I will assume that you have already learned the fundamentals of the highlighting expert.

WORKING WITH TOOLTIPS

All report objects can have rollover text or ToolTips available when the report is viewed. For example, if you would like to use descriptive text to explain why a certain formula was created, you could do this with a ToolTip.

In the example created in Chapter 6, you now want to inform the end user about a formula. The text should appear whenever a user mouses over the Days Until Shipped fields on the report. The following steps create a ToolTip:

1. Open Chap6.rpt, or the report created earlier in Chapter 6. Select File, Open and browse to find Chap6.rpt and open it.

2. Format the e-mail field at the far right. Right-click on it and choose Format Field.

3. Add the ToolTip text. In the Format Editor dialog, select the Common tab. To the right of the ToolTip Text box, click on the formula editor button (see Figure 9.2), and enter the following formula, which makes a custom message for each e-mail address:

```
"Click here to compose an e-mail to " +
{Customer.Contact First Name} + " " +
{Customer.Contact Last Name} + "."
```

Figure 9.2
On the Common tab, click the ToolTip text formula button.

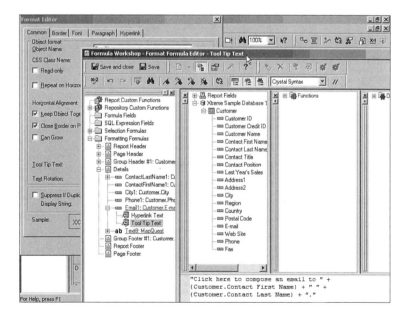

4. Test the ToolTip text. Click OK to finish the formatting. In Preview, scroll the mouse over the e-mail field and see that the rollover text now appears as a custom message, which is different when viewed by each e-mail recipient. Before proceeding, save the report as **Chap9_1.rpt** by choosing File, Save As.

9

LINES AND BOXES

Adding lines and boxes to a report can make it easier to read as well as visually grouping items for business users.

To add lines under each Detail section as well as a box around each group, follow these steps:

1. View Chap9_1.rpt in Design mode. If the report is not already open, open it using Ctrl+O. Make sure that the report is in Design Mode by choosing Ctrl+D.

2. Insert the line by Choosing Insert, Line. The mouse changes to a pencil. Move the mouse to the bottom-left of the fields in the Details Section. Hold down the left mouse button to begin drawing the line. Scroll the mouse to the right until you reach the end of the Details Section. Once reached, release the mouse button.

3. View the result in Preview mode. Select F5 to refresh the report to see the line with the data as shown in Figure 9.3.

Figure 9.3
Use the Preview mode view of a report to show a line under each detail record.

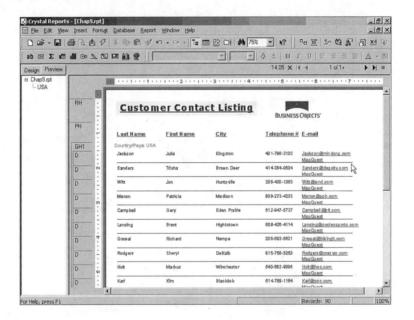

4. Add the box by choosing Insert, Box. The mouse changes to a pencil. Move the mouse to the top-left of the Country/Pays USA data in the Group Header. Hold down the left mouse button to begin drawing the box. Scroll the mouse down to the bottom left of the Summary amount in the Group Footer and then scroll to the right until the end of the Group Footer section. Once reached, release the mouse button. The resulting box should appear similar to Figure 9.4.

5. Choose File, Save As and save the report as **Chap9_2.rpt**.

Figure 9.4
Preview a report to
show lines and boxes.

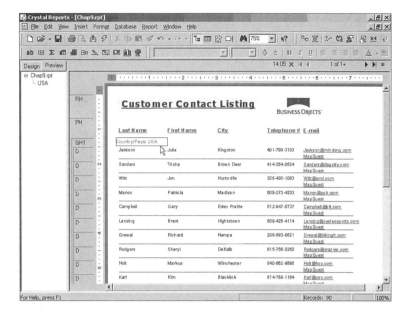

TIP

A feature of boxes is that they can be rounded. To do this right-click on a box, choose Format Box, and select the Rounding tab. The rounding factor can be changed by the slide or the percentage buttons. Figure 9.5 shows how Xtreme's report would look with a rounded box at 30%.

Figure 9.5
Preview of a report
showing rounded
boxes.

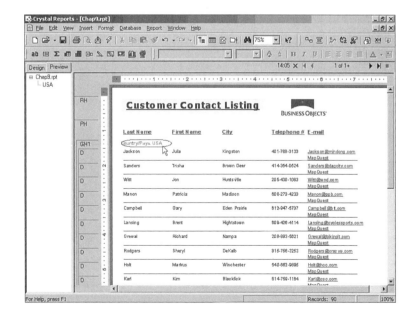

9

CREATING A VERTICAL TEXT WATERMARK

Another visually pleasing feature is the capability to rotate text. This can be very effective when used in conjunction with the Underlay Section property for sections. Follow these steps to make a sample watermark:

1. Start by using Chap9_2.rpt in Design mode. Choose Insert, Text Object to add a text field in the Report Header. Enter **DRAFT** for the text.

2. Right-click on the Text field and choose Format Text. Select the Common tab. Change the Text Rotation to 90 degrees and click OK. Go to the Font tab, where you can change the font size to 48pts. Because you want this watermark to be semi-transparent, choose the More item from the Color drop-down, where you can specify a custom color. Choose a light gray (or silver). Increase the Character font spacing by specifying 70 pts in the dialog, then exit the dialog by clicking OK twice.

NOTE

This color section, common to all objects within Crystal Reports 10, enables you to specify colors using RGB or Hue, Saturation, and Luminance. By choosing corporate colors and adding them to the custom colors, you can extend corporate branding into report presentation.

3. Resize the field. Because the field needs to go down the page, it needs to be resized to be narrow and long. Select the field and choose the rightmost square on the field. Resize the object by holding down the left mouse button. Now choose the bottom square on the field and stretch the height to 5". Figure 9.6 shows how this should look.

Figure 9.6
Design tab with text rotation applied to group name field.

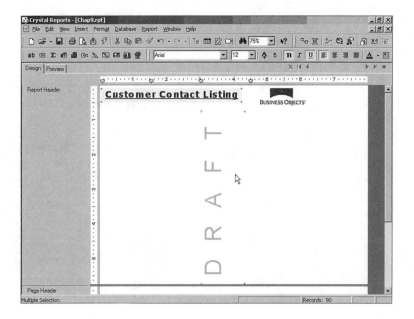

4. Refresh the report to see your progress by pressing F5. It shows the text rotated, although it is not running down beside the records as shown in Figure 9.7.

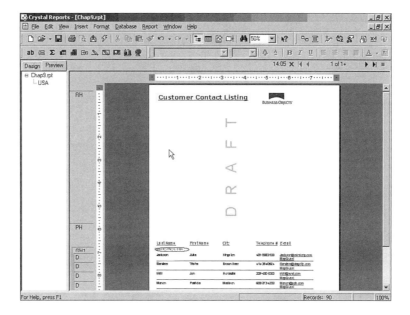

5. Set the Report Header to Underlay. Because the text does not yet flow to the record level, it must be underlayed. This is a section property. Right-click in the Group Header 1 section located on the left side of the report design area, choose Section Expert, select Underlay Following Sections, and click OK. The desired results should appear similar to Figure 9.8.

CAUTION

Realize that when rotating text, the justification rules might be opposite of what would normally be expected. In the case of 90 degrees, the text must be right-justified to have the company name appear to be top-justified, as shown in Figure 9.8.

6. Save as `Chap9_3.rpt`.

Figure 9.8
Preview of the report with rotated text flowing beside detail records.

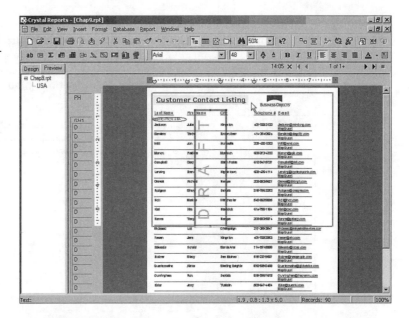

CONDITIONAL FORMATTING—USING DATA TO DRIVE THE LOOK OF A REPORT

Up to now, the focus has been on static formatting. The next step is to apply formatting based on the data that is being returned from a field or even applying formatting on one field based on the value of another.

Conditional formatting relies on formulas. Because the formula language is extensive, complex statements can be created. For this chapter you use relatively simple examples.

The simplest way to add conditional formatting is to use the Highlighting Expert. This feature enables you to apply font face and font color changes to database fields based on their values.

> **TIP**
>
> Almost every formatting option can be conditional. To determine which ones are conditional, look at the x+2 button next to the option in the Formatting Editor dialogs.
>
> If a formatting option has already been set to a conditional format, the button appears with red text. Otherwise, it appears as blue text.

APPLYING FORMATTING FROM ANOTHER FIELD

1. In Design view, right-click the Contact Last Name field, choose Format Field, and then navigate to the Font tab and click the formula button to the right of the Color drop-down. This opens the formula editor, driving your font color choice.

2. Enter the following formula:

```
        SELECT {Customer.Last Year's Sales}
CASE 0 TO 1000: crRed
CASE 1001 TO 100000: crYellow
CASE IS > 100001: crGreen;
```

NOTE

Here you specified a color as the result of the case expression because the formula controlled color. In cases where the formatting option is Boolean (that is, either you turn the feature on or off) there is an assumed IF statement, and all you have to do is enter the condition (for example, `{table.field} > 100`). Entering a full IF statement in cases like this causes an error.

3. Refresh the report by pressing F5 while you're in the Preview tab. Now you see red, yellow, and green last names depending on the amount of last year's sales for that person (see Figure 9.9).

Figure 9.9
Conditional highlighting based on another field.

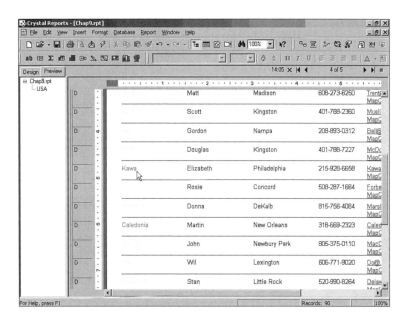

4. Save the report as **chap9_5.rpt**.

CRYSTAL REPORTS IN THE REAL WORLD— ADVANCED CHARTING

Nothing enables users to visualize data better than a chart. With a glance, charts enable users to see relative distribution, peaks, and valleys of values. This section describes how to use charting in creative ways. The following creates a report that charts the sum of sales and distribution of customers by country:

1. Open the World Sales Report from

   C:\Program Files\Crystal Decisions\Crystal Reports 10\Samples\En\Reports\General Business

   and stretch the chart so it takes the full width of the page. In the left margin, right-click on the text Group Footer 1 and from the menu choose Suppress.

2. Right-click on the chart and choose Chart Expert. For Chart Type choose Bar and from the buttons that refine which type of bar chart, choose the lower left option described as Side by Side with 3D (see Figure 9.10).

Figure 9.10
Choosing a chart type.

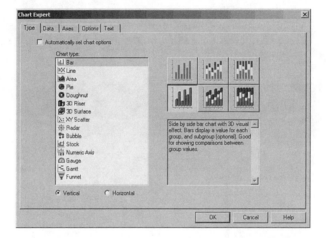

3. Click on the Data tab and the Advanced button. From the list of available fields select Customer.Country and add it to the window below On Change Of. Again, from the list of available fields choose Customer.Last Year's Sales and Customer.Customer Name and add them to the Show Values (see Figure 9.11).

4. Click the Options tab and uncheck the Show Label option. Click OK to close the window.

5. The bar chart is almost complete. It contains the correct data so it is technically accurate, but because the scale of the values is so different it is unreadable for the user. See Figure 9.12.

6. Because the scale of the data is significantly different, the chart needs to be broken into two axes. Right-click on the chart and choose Chart Options, Template. Click the Dual Axis check box, and click OK. The resulting chart should look like Figure 9.13.

Figure 9.11
Selecting data for the chart.

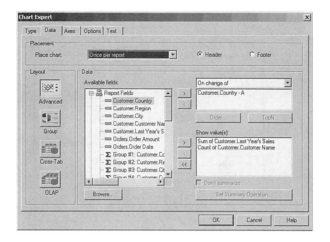

Figure 9.12
Technically accurate but not helpful yet.

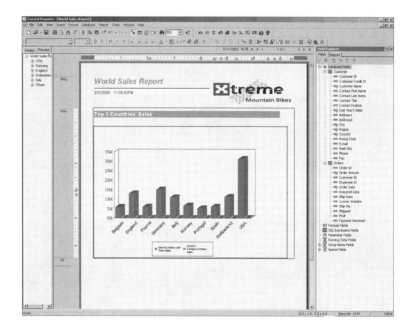

7. Finally, a trend line can be added to the chart to show a trend in the data. Right-click on the customer name bar and choose Chart Options, Series. Click the Trend Line tab and add a check to the Show Trend Lines check box and click OK. The resulting chart should resemble Figure 9.14. Save the report as World Sales Report with Charts.rpt.

Figure 9.13
Chart showing two scales of information.

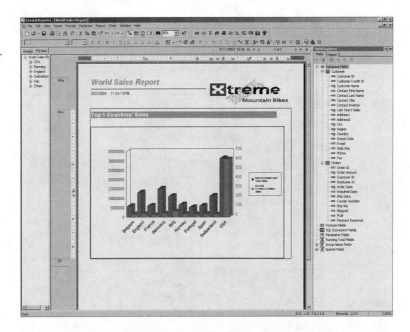

Figure 9.14
Chart showing two scales of information and a trend line.

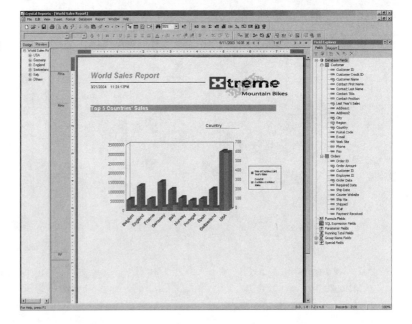

ADVANCED CRYSTAL REPORTS DESIGN

CHAPTER 10

USING CROSS-TABS FOR SUMMARIZED REPORTING

In this chapter

INTRODUCTION TO CROSS-TABS

Cross-tabs are highly formatted and densely populated reports that look a lot like a spreadsheet. This chapter gives you an understanding of how and when to use cross-tabs for your reporting needs.

A *cross-tab* is a fully summarized set of cells in a grid format. It summarizes values both across as well as down. It is a compact representation of information that is grouped on two different *axes*. There can be more than one level of grouping on either axis (row or column).

A *row* goes across the page, whereas a *column* runs down the page. The intersections between the rows and columns are called *cells*. *Cells* are places where a value to be summarized displays. Totals in the cells are summarized for each row and column as well as the break points for the different levels of groupings.

BENEFITS OF CROSS-TABS

Cross-tabs deliver data in a familiar spreadsheet format. They also summarize both vertically and horizontally, have a grid format, and can change size depending on the data.

Several of the most compelling reasons for using cross-tabs are

- Making better use of space
- Leveraging experience with the spreadsheet format
- Horizontal expansion
- Custom formatting

Because cross-tabs are grouped and summarized both vertically *and* horizontally, they are incredibly efficient at saving space as compared to a typical grouping report. They are very good at showing key information if the information required has at least two levels of grouping.

Let's look at an example: school grades for the end of the year. These need to be grouped by course, student, and term. If the report were shown in a standard grouping layout like you've worked with previously, it could be several pages long. Figure 10.1 shows a typical Crystal Report in which three pages display one course with only 10 students in one class.

Cross-tabs replicate the information contained in a teacher's grade book while resembling a spreadsheet. Teachers get a one-stop view of all the students and all their grades. Figure 10.2 shows how the information is more efficiently presented when a cross-tab is used to display the same information. Now the teacher can view all the student grades information at a glance.

LEVERAGING EXPERIENCE WITH THE SPREADSHEET FORMAT

Another benefit of the cross-tab format is its familiarity to many users of spreadsheet applications. Many people use spreadsheets in their daily routines and are accustomed to their look and feel. Because cross-tabs do appear very much like spreadsheets, Crystal Reports offers a familiar format and reporting style for many users.

Figure 10.1
Standard grouping style used on a typical school grades report.

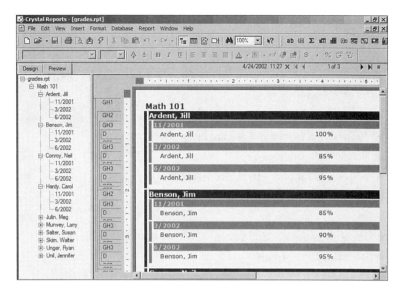

Figure 10.2
Student grades shown in a cross-tab.

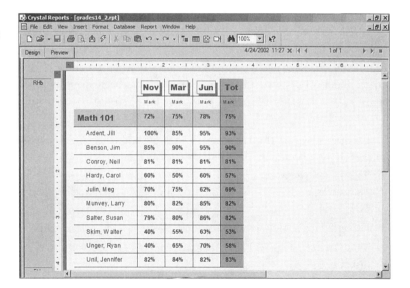

HORIZONTAL EXPANSION

Cross-tabs, like spreadsheets, expand both vertically and horizontally. In Crystal Reports, cross-tabs are one of only two object types that expand across horizontal pages. Crystal Reports handles this expansion automatically. If there is more data to display than the original size of the cross-tab allows for, Crystal Reports doesn't cut off any critical data from the cross-tab area.

CUSTOM FORMATTING

Cross-tab objects are also highly customizable in terms of formatting. Everyone has different needs from their data, so Crystal Reports allows for a great deal of changes to the formatting of these objects. Some of the most highly useful formatting features that are used in cross-tabs are

- Customizable styles (colors, grid lines, and so on)
- Vertical and horizontal placement of summaries
- Formatted grid lines
- Toggle for summary totals (rows/columns)
- Cell margins
- Indented row labels
- Location of totals (beginning or end for both rows/columns)
- Repeatable row labels

USING THE CROSS-TAB WIZARD

Let's work through an example for the Xtreme Mountain Bike Company—the fictitious company that corresponds to the sample database provided with Crystal Reports.

Xtreme management needs a summary report to provide a quick glance at its shipped orders. The managers want to know how much has been spent by country for every six-month period, but they only want to see the top 10 countries. The following steps show you how to create this report:

1. Create a new report by choosing File, New and when the Report Gallery appears, choose As a Blank Report and then click OK.

2. The Database Expert appears. In the Available Data Sources list, expand the following nodes: Create New Connection, ODBC. Select the Extreme Sample database 10, click Next, and then click Finish.

3. Expand Tables, and double-click on Customer and Orders. Click OK.

4. The Database Expert dialog appears again. Click OK again to accept the default linking.

5. Insert a cross-tab by choosing Cross-Tab from the Insert menu, or click the Insert Cross-Tab button on the Insert toolbar (the fourth item from the left). This should present the Cross-Tab Expert dialog.

6. Set up the initial cross-tab. In the Cross-Tab tab of the Cross-Tab Expert, enter the grouping and summarizing fields for the Xtreme report. The rows of the report are the countries, so select Country from the Available Fields and then click the arrow button (>) under Rows. The column grouping is going to be by order data, so choose Order Date from Available Fields and then click the arrow button (>) under Columns. Because the OrderDate is supposed to be by quarter, click on the Group Options drop-down under Columns and change the third list box from Each Day to For Half Year. Finally, choose Order Amount from Available Fields and click the arrow button (>) under

Summarized Fields so that the cell's summary is also selected. The final result looks like Figure 10.3.

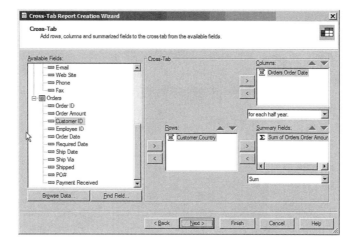

7. Data input is practically done. Now that you've specified the necessary items, click the OK button to close the Cross-Tab Expert. Then place the object connected to your mouse in the top-left corner of the Report Header section. Press F5 to refresh the report and see the result in the report Preview as shown in Figure 10.4.

8. Before continuing, save your work. Choose File, Save As. Call this **cross-tab1.rpt** and then click OK.

Figure 10.4
Cross-tab in Preview.

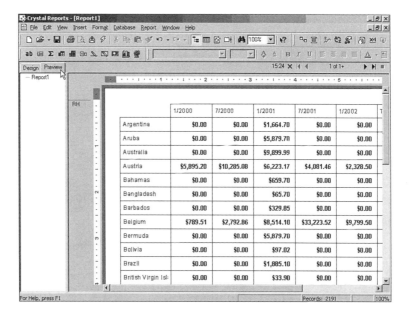

USING TOP N WITH CROSS-TABS REPORTS

Group sorts can be done on a report level so that the records are sorted and removed as necessary. However, there are times when the records are needed in the overall report but not in a cross-tab.

1. Right-click in the top-left corner of the cross-tab where there is no data or words and choose Group Sort Expert. Choose Top N for the primary list box and change 5 to 10 in the Where N Is field. In this example, make sure that the Others option is not selected.

2. Click OK in the Group Sort Expert to view the final result, as shown in Figure 10.5.

Figure 10.5
Cross-tab with a Group Sort applied.

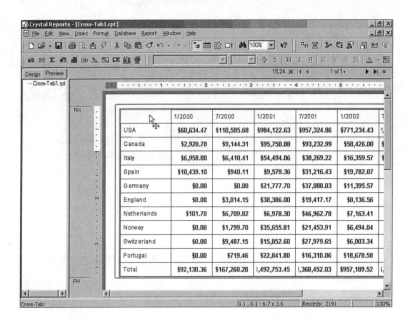

3. Save your work by choosing File, Save As. Call this **cross-tab2.rpt** and then click OK.

USING ADVANCED CROSS-TAB FEATURES

Crystal Reports version 9 introduced significant cross-tab improvements. The advanced features gave cross-tabs improved flexibility and functionality to satisfy even more reporting requirements.

SETTING RELATIVE POSITION

When it comes to planning the width or length of cross-tabs, remember they expand dynamically. With the addition of new information or data, the number of rows or columns can grow or shrink. This makes putting objects at the end of a cross-tab very difficult because it's unclear when the object will be overwritten if new data appears.

For the same issue at the bottom of a cross-tab an easy solution exists. Place the new object in the next report section—even if it means adding a new section. By default, objects in Crystal Reports do not overwrite a section.

However, you often need to specify an item in the far-right column. In this report you might want a logo to be displayed to the right of the cross-tab. But, in Design, the size of the cross-tab doesn't match what you see in Preview. Follow these steps to set the Relative Position:

1. Open crosstab2.rpt. Start with your last saved document by choosing it from the File list on the File, Open menu.

2. Insert a text object by opening the Insert menu, and then selecting Text Object.

3. Preview the report. Click F5 to see the result. It's not exactly as you intended (see Figure 10.6).

Figure 10.6
Design with cross-tab and text field in improper location.

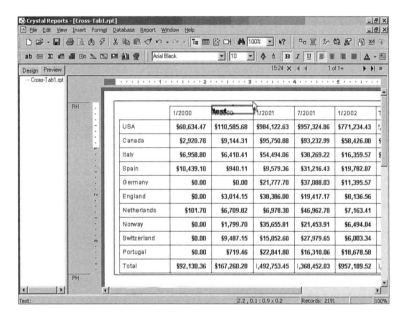

4. Set the Relative Position property. Right-click on the Report Header label (on the left where it says Report Header, or RH, in the gray area). Choose Section Expert. Toggle the Relative Positions check box and click OK. To see the resulting report, refer to Figure 10.7.

The Relative Position property works on the left, top, and right borders of the cross-tab. Remember that the bottom border of the cross-tab is handled by the end of a section.

Relative positions can be used in many situations. For example, showing a chart on the information in the cross-tab can be very useful.

Figure 10.7
Preview of the cross-tab and text field as requested.

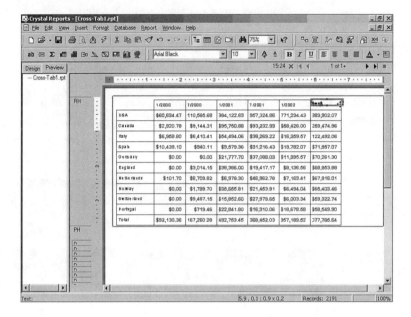

INSERTING A "PERCENTAGE OF" SUMMARY

Summary values can also be displayed as percentages of either the total rows or total columns:

1. Add another summary. Right-click in the top left of the cross-tab where no data appears and choose Cross-Tab Expert. In the Cross-Tab tab, choose to add the Order Amount to the Summarized Fields list box by clicking the arrow (>) button. Notice that it looks like it duplicates the summary above it, so choose the Change Summary button.

2. Change the Summary to a Percentage Summary. In the Edit Summary dialog in the Options box, select Show As Percentage Summary. Notice that it has an option for Row or Column. In this case you want to know by country (row) where the percentage split is, so keep Row selected as shown in Figure 10.8.

3. Preview the results by clicking OK on both dialog windows. It should look like Figure 10.9.

Notice that the USA is consistently the largest percentage of Xtreme's orders. It's very easy to see this when percentages are added to the cross-tab.

Figure 10.8
The Edit Summary dialog.

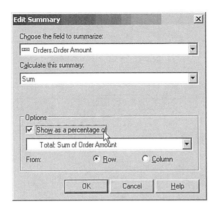

Figure 10.9
Percentages by country.

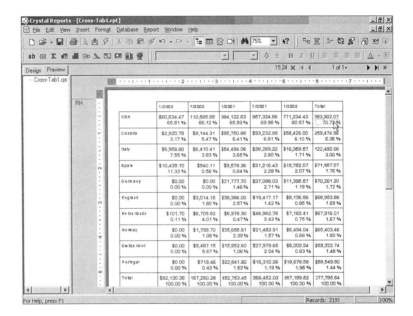

HORIZONTAL AND VERTICAL PLACEMENT

Because the percentages add up to 100% down the page, it would be easier to understand if the summaries could be displayed side by side instead of one on top of the other. That way, the numbers down the page could be added up easily.

Crystal Reports allows the toggle between horizontal and vertical placement of summaries:

1. Launch the Cross-Tab Expert. Right-click in the top-left of the cross-tab again and choose Cross-Tab Expert. Select the Customize Style tab. Under Summarized Fields, choose Horizontal; select the Show Labels option.

2. View the report. Click the OK button to see the changes made to the cross-tab (see Figure 10.10).

Figure 10.10
Horizontal placement
of summaries.

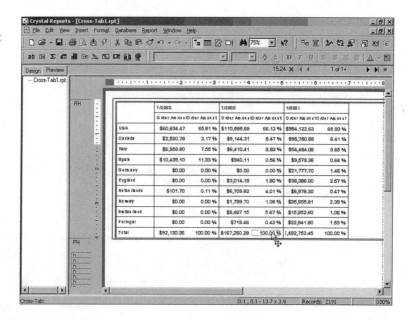

INSERTING SUMMARY LABELS

Notice that on the report in Figure 10.10, both titles for the percentage and the summary
are exactly the same (Order Amount). This is because Crystal Reports is showing the field
that a summary is acting on. In this case, where the field is being acted on twice, it's not a
good choice.

Crystal Reports enables you to edit these labels right on the cross-tab in both Design and
Preview modes:

1. Edit the Summary's Title. Right-click on the first Order Amount field in the cross-tab
   and choose Edit Text. Delete the Order Amount Text and add Sum instead. Then
   choose the Align Center button on the toolbar while the item is highlighted. Click off
   the object and see the result.

2. Edit the Percentage Title. Repeat the previous step for the second Order Amount field,
   but instead of changing the text to sum, change it to %, as shown in Figure 10.11.

ADDING A DISPLAY STRING

Cross-tabs are based on the need for numbers or currency to be summarized, but there are
times when the numbers don't need to be seen to get the point across. Crystal Reports has a
feature for all fields called Display String. This formatting feature allows a different representation for a field than its underlying value. For example, a teacher might want to see a
grade letter beside a percentage mark, as shown in Figure 10.12.

As previously mentioned, cross-tab cells are always an intersection of rows and columns with
a summary because the strings are the visual representation of the underlying summary

being computed in the cross-tab. You can affect this string using the advanced Cross-Tab features of Crystal Reports.

Figure 10.11
Cross-tab with both labels changed.

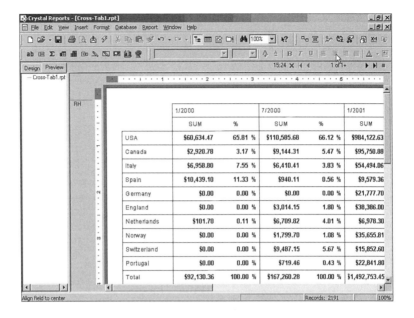

Figure 10.12
Math 101 marks with letter grades as display strings.

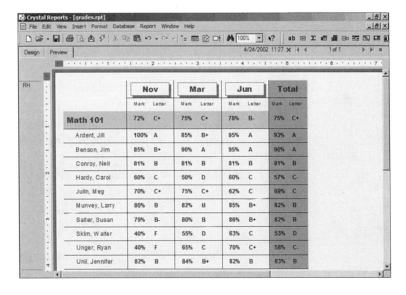

Crystal Reports can now separate the data value from its display. This is a powerful feature and is *not* limited to cross-tabs, although it plays a major role in cross-tabs because of the requirement of summaries.

To complete this report, ensure that all $0.00 amounts be shown as NONE on the report.

1. **Format the Order Amount Summary.** Right-click on one of the $0.00 amounts on the report and choose Format Field. Choose the Common tab and then choose the Conditional Formatting (x+2) button to the right of Display String. The Formula Workshop appears.

2. **Format Formula for strings.** Use an If-Then-Else formula structure to accomplish the task. The final result is If CurrentFieldValue = 0 Then "NONE" Else ToText(CurrentFieldvalue) (see Figure 10.13).

Figure 10.13
Display String formatting formula.

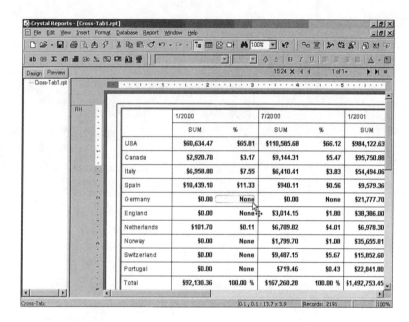

TIP

Try to avoid using explicit field names in these formulas so that they can be reused in other places.

Also, remember that these are string formulas. That's why the ToText is needed around the CurrentFieldValue. Both Then and Else clauses must contain similar data types.

3. **Close the dialog windows.** Choose the Save and Close button on the Formula Workshop and then click OK on the Formatting dialog. The result is shown in Figure 10.14.

4. **Save the report as Crosstab3.rpt** by choosing File, Save As.

Figure 10.14
$0 changed to NONE by using the Display String feature.

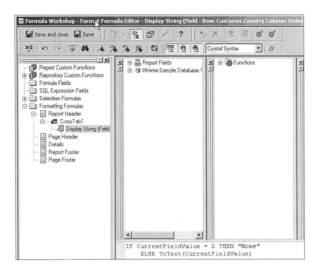

TIP

> The same technique that you used to change the display value of the cell can be used on any area, and you can combine the interactivity provided by parameters and other formula functions to drive any section or field in the cross-tab.

CRYSTAL REPORTS IN THE REAL WORLD— ADVANCED CROSS-TABS

Although a single Cross-Tab that covers all the data in a report can be quite useful, with some large datasets it can be quite unreadable. A simple solution to this is to group the report and place the cross-tab in the group header or footer. Cross-tabs are context sensitive and if placed in a group header or footer will show only data for that group.

1. Using the skills described in earlier chapters, create a new report from the Xtreme Sample Database. Add the Customer table to the report, group the report by country, and remove all fields but the Country field in the group header. See Figure 10.15 for a visual of the report's starting point.

2. From the Report menu, choose Cross-Tab. From the list of available fields, select Customer Name and add it to the Rows window of the Cross-Tab. Select the Region and add it to the Columns window. Select Last Year's Sales and add it to the Summarized Fields window. Check your work against Figure 10.16 for accuracy.

3. Click OK to close the Cross-Tab expert. Add the cross-tab to the group header and preview the report. In Figure 10.17, the completed report can be seen.

4. Save the report as GroupedCrossTab.rpt.

Figure 10.15
Report framework.

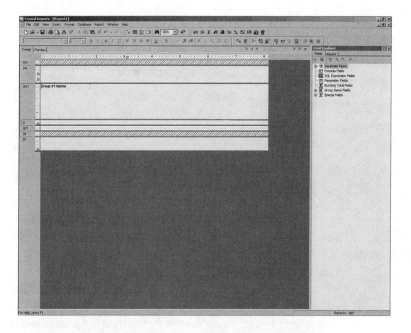

Figure 10.16
Building the cross-tab.

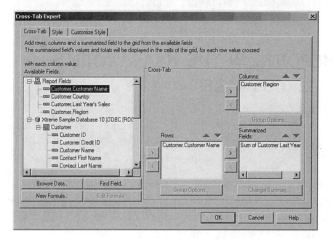

Figure 10.17
Grouped cross-tabs can avoid confusion through improved readability.

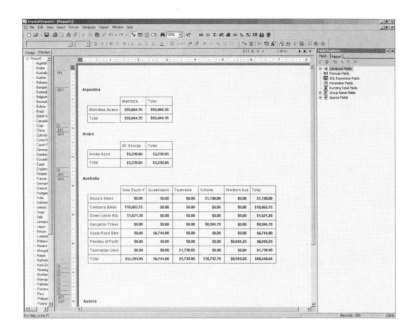

CHAPTER **11**

USING RECORD SELECTIONS AND ALERTS FOR INTERACTIVE REPORTING

In this chapter

CREATING ADVANCED RECORD SELECTION FORMULAS

Although creating a simple report can be very useful for an end user, highlighting notable information can increase the utility of the report because it saves time spent looking for trends and crucial data. *Outliers*, data that falls above or below the average of a specified threshold, often contain key information.

This chapter focuses on drawing attention to key data by using record selections and introducing SQL expressions, and introduces report alerting.

Although many filters are simple enough to be defined using the Select Expert, most real-world reports require editing the record selection formula itself. Before covering the best practices for creating formulas, review the material on record selections introduced in Chapter 2, "Selecting and Grouping Data."

RECORD SELECTION REVIEW

Record selections, or filters, are defined by a record selection formula built using the Crystal syntax of the Crystal Reports formula language. You can build a record selection formula using the Formula Editor by opening the Report menu and choosing Selection Formulas, Record. A simpler way to build record selections is to use the Select Expert icon accessed via the Experts toolbar.

A record selection formula returns a Boolean value indicating whether a given record should be included in the report. It is evaluated for each record in the database. Any time a database field is used in the formula, it is replaced by the actual field value.

After this quick review, the following sections move on to some of the more important topics in creating record selection filters.

DISPLAYING RECORD SELECTIONS

Although the techniques discussed in this chapter allow powerful filtering, this should not be applied without the end user's knowledge in most cases (certainly there are cases where end users should not know of hidden data, but this more often is handled via filters to secure the data in a Business View). In these cases, you can simply display the current selection filter or other special fields by either dragging the fields onto the report from the Field Explorer, Special Fields area, or by using the same fields in a formula to change the way these fields display as per the previous chapter.

DEALING WITH DATES

Use the select expert, which you access by choosing Report, Select Expert, to manipulate dates with the addition of four specific date-related comparators:

- Is between—The selected items fall between these two dates.
- Is not between—The selected items do not fall between these two dates.

- Is in the period—The selected items fall in the periods selected from the drop-down list.
- Is not in the period—The selected items do not fall in the periods selected from the drop-down list.

These date-specific comparators appear when you have selected a field of date type, and prompt for the specific values. However, in more complicated situations, you are forced to create a formula in the formula editor rather than using the select expert to create the formula for you.

One of the most common record selection formulas is {field} = value, where {field} is a database field and value is a corresponding value of the same data type. An example of this would be

```
{Customer.Country} = "Canada"
```

This kind of formula is very easy to create, but becomes more complicated when the data types of the values to be compared are not the same. Filtering data based on dates often causes this type of situation; for instance, this formula:

```
{Orders.Order Date} > "2/25/2000"
```

NOTE

> When clicking the Check button to check the formula's syntax, Crystal Reports provides a message saying "A date-time is required here" and after closing the message box, "1/29/1998" is highlighted. Because the Order Date field has a data type of date-time, the formula attempts to compare a date-time to a string, which is not allowed. Comparisons must always be performed on objects of the same data type. To rectify this, instead of using a string literal to describe a date, the formula could use the DateTime function to return a date-time value. Here is an example of the corrected formula:
>
> ```
> {Orders.Order Date} > DateTime(2000, 2, 25, 0, 0, 0)
> ```

11

Notice that when the DateTime function is used, it takes arguments for not only year, month, and day, but also for hour, minute, and second. This is because in order to compare this value to the Order Date field, it needs to be a date-time value. In this case, you might not care about the time part of the date-time value. The best way to solve this would be to first convert the Order Date field into a date from a date-time, and then use the Date function instead of DateTime. The improved formula follows:

```
Date({Orders.Order Date}) > Date(2000, 2, 25)
```

To make this even simpler, the Crystal Reports formula language also supports dates specified in the following format:

```
#YYYY/MM/DD HH:MM AM/PM#
```

Using this syntax, the following formula is also valid:

```
{Orders.Order Date} > #2000/2/25 12:00 AM#
```

Another nice feature of this syntax is the capability to omit the time portion. When this is done, a default of 12:00 AM is used.

Various functions are available for converting between strings, dates, and date-times. These can be found in the Function Tree window of the Formula Editor, under the Date and Time folder.

Another issue that comes up often is filtering on a field in the database that contains dates but is defined as a string field. The following fictitious formula, although it will not return any errors when checking the syntax, does not accomplish what you might expect:

```
{Shipments.Ship Date} > "1/1/2001"
```

This will not perform a date comparison because both fields are of type string. To correct this formula, you could use one of the functions provided by the DTS (date time string) user function library called DTSToDate.

NOTE

A *user function library* is a library of functions that can be used from the Crystal Reports formula language. Business Objects provides several of these with the product, and others are available from third-party vendors. If you are proficient with Visual Basic or C++, you could even create a user function library yourself. The user function library can be found under the Additional Functions folder in the Function Tree of the Formula Editor.

The DTSToDate function takes a string that is in the proper date format and converts it to a date value. The correct formula is shown here:

```
DTSToDate({Shipments.Ship Date}) > Date(2001, 1, 1)
```

where the Ship Date field contains a date in *DD/MM/YYYY* format.

WORKING WITH STRINGS

As with dates, simple string comparisons are easy to achieve using the record selection expert. Slightly more complex comparisons can easily become tedious unless you are armed with knowledge for effectively dealing with strings. A simple example is a listing of customer data for a set of countries. Creating a record selection formula like the following can become quite tedious:

```
{Customer.Country} = "England" or
{Customer.Country} = "France" or
{Customer.Country} = "Germany" or
{Customer.Country} = "Denmark"
```

Rather than using multiple comparisons, this can be accomplished with a single comparison using a string array.

NOTE

An array in the context of the Crystal Reports formula language is a collection of values that can be referenced as a single object.

The previous record selection formula can be rewritten to look like this:

```
{Customer.Country} in ["England", "France", "Germany", "Denmark"]
```

Notice that there are several differences. First, instead of using multiple comparisons, only a single comparison is used. This is both simpler to read and easier to maintain. The four country values are combined into a string array. Arrays are indicated by square brackets with values separated by commas. Finally, instead of an = operator, the in operator is used. This operator, as its name implies, is used to determine if the value on its left is present inside the array on its right.

NOTE

Although string arrays are described here, arrays can be made holding other data types, such as integers and currency values.

In this example, the countries are hard-coded into the selection formula. Although this makes it easy to read, the report would need to be modified if the country list were to ever change. A better way to handle this would be to create a multiple value parameter and use it in place of the country list. If you did that, the formula would look like this:

```
{Customer.Country} in {?CountriesParam}
```

During the parameter prompting, the user will be allowed to enter multiple values, and you can even provide a list of default values from which to choose.

PUSHING RECORD SELECTIONS TO THE DATABASE

When dealing with large sets of records, performance becomes important. The record selection used makes a significant difference in report performance. Crystal Reports does have the capability to perform database-like operations on the data such as grouping, filtering, summarizing, and sorting. However, in general, asking the database to perform those operations results in a faster overall transaction. Because of this principle, Crystal Reports attempts to ask the database to perform these operations if possible.

In the context of record selections, when Crystal Reports queries the database it attempts to incorporate as much of the logic of the record selection formula as possible into the query. Ideally, all the logic can be incorporated into the query, which means that the database will perform all the filtering and only return the records that meet the criteria. However, because the SQL language doesn't support all the Crystal Reports formula language, there could be certain situations in which some or all the logic of the record selection formula cannot be converted to SQL. In this case, Crystal Reports needs to pull some or all the records from the database and perform filtering itself.

11

When working with a desktop database like Access or FoxPro, the performance difference between the database engine or the Crystal Reports engine doing the filtering would be minimal because it really comes down to which filtering algorithm is faster. Because databases are made for just this purpose and are customized for their own data structures, they will generally perform this kind of operation faster. However, when dealing with client/server databases in which the database resides on a back-end server and Crystal Reports resides in your desktop machine, the difference becomes much more apparent. This is partly because of network traffic. There's a big difference between sending 50 records back over the network and sending 100,000. This performance hit becomes even worse when using a slow connection such as a dial-up modem.

To determine whether the logic you've used in the record selection formula or select expert is incorporated into the query sent to the database, it's helpful to have a basic understanding of the SQL language. You need not be an expert at SQL, but being able to recognize if the query is performing a filter on a certain field makes record selection formula tuning much more effective.

Although there are some guidelines for creating record selection formulas that will be fully passed down to the server, often the best approach is to simply check the SQL statement manually and determine whether the record selection logic is present. To view the SQL statement that Crystal Reports has generated, select Show SQL Query from the Database menu. The resulting dialog is shown in Figure 11.1.

Figure 11.1
The Show SQL Query dialog displays the actual SQL code used to retrieve the results from the relational database.

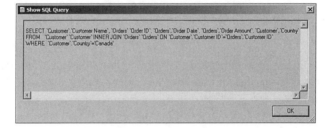

You can infer from the preceding SQL query that this report is based on the Customer table, is using the Customer Name, Web Site, and Last Year's Sales fields, and has a record selection of

```
{Customer.Last Year's Sales} > $20000
```

All the logic of the record selection formula has now been passed down to the database in the SQL query. However, if this report had a formula field that calculated the tax, that formula might consist of the following:

```
{Customer.Last Year's Sales} * 1.07
```

This formula field might be placed on the report to indicate the tax for each customer. A problem occurs when this formula is used in the record selection formula. Although the following formula seems logical, it is inefficient:

```
{@Tax} > $10000
```

If you were to look at the SQL query being generated for this report, you would see that there is no WHERE clause present. In other words, the report is asking the database for all the records and doing the filtering locally, which, depending on the size of the database, could result in poor performance. A better record selection to use—which would produce the same results, but performs the filtering on the database server—would be:

```
{Customer.Last Year's Sales} > $142857
```

This works out because at a tax rate of 7%, $142,857 is the minimum a customer would need to sell to have tax of more than $10,000. Using the previous record selection would result in a SQL query with the following WHERE clause:

```
WHERE 'Customer'.'Last Year's Sales' > 142857
```

Although this approach returns the correct data, a slightly less cryptic approach would be to use a SQL Expression.

AN INTRODUCTION TO SQL EXPRESSIONS

Crystal Reports formulas are useful because they enable you to use the full Crystal Reports formula language as well as a suite of built-in functions. However, as you've learned in this chapter, they can be a factor in report processing performance. SQL expressions provide an alternative to this.

A *SQL Expression*, as the name implies, is an expression written in the SQL language. Instead of consisting of a whole formula, a SQL Expression consists of an expression that defines a single field just like a formula field does. The difference between a formula field and a SQL Expression is based on where it is evaluated. Formula fields are evaluated locally by Crystal Reports, whereas SQL Expressions are evaluated by the database server and thus produce better performance when used in a record selection formula.

To better understand this, look at the example discussed in the previous section. The example had a report with a Crystal Reports formula that calculated tax based on the Last Year's Sales field. Although there certainly are situations in which formula fields need to be used, this is not one of them because the logic being used in the formula is simple enough that the database server is able to perform it. Instead of creating a formula field, a SQL Expression could have been created. SQL Expressions are created via the Field Explorer, which was introduced in Chapter 4, "Understanding and Implementing Formulas." Right-clicking on the SQL Expressions item and selecting New will begin the process of creating a SQL Expression. When choosing to create a new SQL Expression, the SQL Expression Editor is launched (see Figure 11.2).

This editor is, in fact, the same editor used to create Crystal Reports formulas, but with a few small changes. First you'll notice that in the field tree, only database fields are present to be used in the expression. Because SQL Expressions are evaluated on the database servers, Crystal Reports constructs, such as parameter fields and formula fields, do not exist and thus cannot be used in the expression.

11

Figure 11.2
The SQL Expression
Editor.

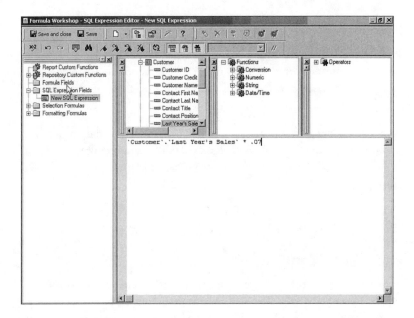

To create a SQL Expression that calculates the tax, the following expression can be used:

```
'Customer'.'Last Year's Sales' * 0.07
```

Notice that instead of using the {Table.Field} syntax for fields, the 'Table'.'Field' syntax is used. This is because the quoted syntax is how you define fields in the SQL language.

When inserting this SQL Expression into the report and checking the SQL query, you will find Crystal Reports has generated SQL similar to this:

```
SELECT 'Customer'.'Customer Name', ('Customer'.'Last Year's Sales' * 0.07)
FROM 'Customer' 'Customer'
```

The SQL Expression that was defined in the report is inserted into the main SQL statement that Crystal Reports generates. This means that you can use any database-specific syntax or function inside a SQL Expression.

Getting back to the topic of performance, you'll remember that using the tax calculation formula field in the record selection formula resulted in all the records being returned and Crystal Reports having to locally perform the filtering. Fortunately, any SQL Expressions used in the record selection are always passed down to the database server. Therefore, a better record selection for filtering out customers who pay less than $10,000 in tax would be the following:

```
{%Tax} > 10000
```

In this record selection formula, {%Tax} is the SQL Expression discussed previously. This record selection formula would result in Crystal Reports generating the following SQL query:

```
SELECT 'Customer'.'Customer Name', ('Customer'.'Last Year's Sales' * 0.07)
FROM 'Customer' 'Customer'
WHERE ('Customer'.'Last Year's Sales' * 0.07)>10000
```

N O T E

> Remember that any formula evaluated after the first pass of the multipass system, for instance grouping criteria or information to prompt a subreport, can cause slow report processing. Again a SQL Expression can retrieve the correct data in the first place, speeding report processing significantly. The next chapter of this book covers the multipass system in detail.

ADDING ALERTING TO YOUR REPORTS

Although calling out outlying values can be accomplished by using conditional formatting, the alerting feature inside Crystal Reports allows for more interactive identification of key data as well as pushing of those alerts to end users via Crystal Enterprise's alerting functionality.

A report *alert* is a custom notification created within Crystal Reports, triggered when a pre-determined condition is met. An alert is comprised of three integral parts:

- Name
- Trigger (condition or threshold)
- Message

Alerts serve the dual functions of bringing end-user attention to a certain condition being met and focusing end-user attention on specifically relevant data in a report—thereby increasing user efficiency. Some examples of reports in which alerts could provide a benefit are outlined in Table 11.1.

11

TABLE 11.1   REPORTS WITH POTENTIALLY USEFUL ALERTS

Report	Alert	Alert Trigger and Result
Product Sales Report	Product Profitability Warning	Trigger: Specific product profitability below 10% Result: A listing of the least successfully selling products
Customer Churn Report	Regional Customer Churn Warnings	Trigger: Specific regions where Customer Churn Rate is higher than 3% in a quarter Result: A listing of regions to increase competitive analysis or to review regional management practice
Income Statement	Company Divisions with Net Losses	Trigger: Company division with net income < 0 Result: A listing of divisions where deeper business analysis is required

Report alerts are triggered when the report is processed and the associated condition has been met. When this condition is true, the alert message will be displayed. Figure 11.3 displays a triggered alert from within the Crystal Reports Designer.

Figure 11.3
A report alert being triggered.

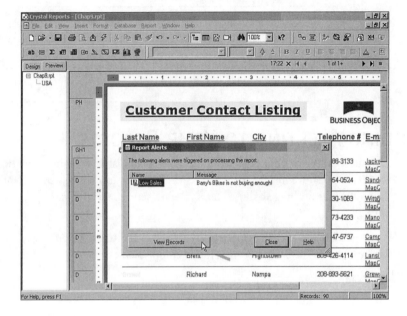

CREATING, EDITING, AND USING ALERTS

To create or edit alerts in Crystal Reports, select the Report, Alerts, Create or Modify Alerts menu items. This dialog (shown in Figure 11.4) enables you to create a new alert, edit existing alerts, and remove existing alerts.

Figure 11.4
Clicking Edit on the Create Alerts dialog opens the Edit Alert dialog.

To create the alert, follow these steps:

1. Give the alert a name. This name should be meaningful and will be displayed to the user when the alert is triggered.

2. Specify a condition for which to trigger the alert. An example of this would be `{Customer.Last Year's Sales} < $10000`. The condition is simply a formula using either Crystal or Basic syntax that evaluates to a true or false result. True means the alert should be triggered; false means that it should not.

NOTE

> You can use other formulas and parameters inside this condition. Using a parameter to determine the threshold on your alert is useful because the report could then be viewed by different audiences with different thresholds, and they could still see the alert triggered for their respective numbers.

3. Give the alert a message to display when it has been triggered. This can be a hard-coded string, or can be a formula such as

```
"Sales are over $" + ToText({Customer.Last Year's Sales})
```

To see your alert in action, refresh the report with data that meets your alert condition, and triggered alerts will be displayed.

Finally, not only are you notified that the alerts have been triggered, you can click the View Records button on the Report Alerts pop-up dialog to filter the report to show only those records that triggered the alert. This is a good way to draw attention to the key outliers in the data.

USING ALERTS IN CRYSTAL ENTERPRISE

The Report Alerts dialog displayed in Figure 11.3 is only available from within the Crystal Reports Designer. If you are delivering your reports via another mechanism such as the Web, alerts are handled differently. To have your end users take advantage of Crystal Reports alerting, you will need to either use Crystal Enterprise for report distribution or exploit the built-in alert functions (`IsAlertEnabled()`, `IsAlertTriggered()`, and `AlertMessage()`) within formulas you create in your report.

For more information on Crystal Enterprise, see Chapter 24, "Crystal Enterprise Architecture."

Typically, alerts can be shown to end users in a portal, which then links back to the report.

TIP

> End users viewing a report from an alert in Crystal Enterprise do not see the items matching the alert conditions—they see the entire report. This leads to some discontinuity both from the Crystal Reports experience and also from the end users' expectation that they should now see values called out in the alert.
>
> To make this more logical for the end user, create a version of the same report (perhaps use a naming convention like ALERT_*reportname*.rpt) with the alert and also a filtering condition *matching the alert condition*. Thus, when end users click on an alert in Crystal Enterprise, they will see a version of the report containing only the relevant values.

PERFORMANCE MONITORING AND TUNING

As reports grow in data size and complexity, ensuring optimal performance becomes increasingly important. This section serves as both a reminder of some performance tips already covered in the book to this point and as an introduction to some other tools and

11

methods provided by Crystal Reports to optimize report performance in demanding environments.

GROUP BY ON SERVER

This Crystal Reports option enables you to push down the Grouping and Sorting activities to the database server. By performing these functions on the database instead of the Crystal server, less data is passed back to the Crystal Report and report-processing time is decreased. This option can be set locally under the Database main menu when the given report is being edited, or set globally on the Database tab of the Options menu accessed under the File main menu.

Some restrictions apply to the use of this option, including the following:

- The data source must be a standard SQL database.
- The report must have groups within it and the groups must be based on database fields—not formula fields.
- The groups cannot contain specified order sorting.
- The details section of the report must be hidden.
- Running Totals must be based on summary fields (that is, they do not rely on detail records for their calculations).
- The report cannot contain Average or Distinct Count summaries, or use Top N values.

When this option is applicable and used, the involved reports will perform faster. In addition, the detail level on these reports is still accessible through the standard drill-down functionality and will make dynamic connections to the database to bring back any user-requested detailed information.

SQL EXPRESSIONS IN RECORD SELECTIONS

As referenced and discussed previously in the book, SQL expressions are SQL statements that provide access to advanced database aggregations and functions. Using SQL expressions wherever possible in record selections and formula creation (versus using Crystal or Basic syntax) optimizes the amount of work that will get processed by the database server (versus the Crystal server)—and this will increase your report's performance.

Some quick examples of SQL expressions that can be used in place of Crystal formula syntax:

Crystal Formula Syntax	SQL Expression (SQL Server Syntax)
IF/THEN/ELSE	CASE [Database Field]
Or	WHEN Condition THEN Value1
SELECT CASE	ELSE Value2 END
Concatenate (x + y)	CONCAT([Database Field1], [Database Field2])
MONTH(datefield)	MONTH([Database Field])

You should investigate the SQL capabilities of the report's database thoroughly when report performance and optimization becomes a critical business issue. Mature databases like Oracle, DB2, SQL Server, and so on have mature SQL capabilities that can often be leveraged in lieu of the Crystal formula language in field selection and record selection. Using SQL expressions can dramatically increase report performance in many instances.

USE INDEXES ON SERVER FOR SPEED

This is another performance option that is set under the Database tab of the Options dialog accessed from the main File menu. This option ensures that the involved Crystal Report uses any indexes that are present for the selected database and for the given report.

ON-DEMAND OR REDUCED NUMBER OF SUBREPORTS

As discussed in the chapter on subreports, these objects are reports unto themselves and maintain their own database connections and queries. As you can imagine, if too many subreports are added to a main report, this can lead to runaway report-processing times. A typical scenario where this might happen is when you want to include the data inside a subreport for every group within the main report. In a large report with hundreds or even thousands of groups, this can lead to that subreport running thousands of times—a palpable performance hit even when the subreport is small and/or optimized.

To minimize this challenge, it is a good idea to ensure that in-place subreports (as opposed to on-demand subreports) are used judiciously and that they are indeed required in performance-sensitive reports. Often times, only a very small subset of the subreports are ever viewed by a user and an acceptable user experience can be provided with On-Demand subreports instead.

PERFORMANCE MONITOR

After a report has been functionally designed, Crystal Reports provides the Performance Information tool to facilitate performance testing. This tool provides information that helps in optimizing the current report for fastest performance. The Performance Information dialog shown in Figure 11.5 is accessed from the main Report menu.

Figure 11.5
The Performance Information window provides detailed report performance metrics.

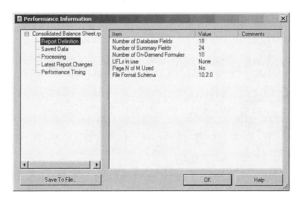

The left side of the Performance window provides a tree structure that facilitates navigation among the different report metrics areas maintained by this tool:

- **Report Definition**: This node provides information about the content of the report: the number of fields, the number of summaries, UFLs (User Function Libraries), Chart objects, and so on. Each of these objects will have some impact on the performance of the report dependent on their quantity and complexity. The Page N of M Used option is relevant because it specifies whether a third pass of the data is needed when processing this report. If not required, this can be eliminated by removing any Page N of M special fields on the report.

- **Saved Data**: This node provides information about the data captured in the involved report: the number of data sources used, the total number of records, recurring database record length, size of saved data, and so on. These metrics are of particular relevance when Group By On Server is properly used but can be generally used to monitor the effects of report changes.

- **Processing**: This node provides information about the processing of the selected report: Grouping on Server?, Sorting on Server? Total Page Count required?, Number of Summary Values, and so on. The metrics provided here have a clear impact on performance and can be used to monitor the effective implementation of the optimization techniques described in this section.

- **Latest Report Changes**: This node provides information about recent changes to the report to facilitate performance monitoring.

- **Performance Timing**: This node provides the timing metrics based on opening the involved report and formatting its pages. These metrics provide the ultimate benchmark to determine the effectiveness of any implemented report optimization techniques.

Additional tree branches and nodes are displayed if the involved report contains subreports—each of these nodes will appear under a new parent node for each subreport facilitating performance analysis at a granular level.

One final note on performance monitoring: to facilitate record-keeping on the progress of any ongoing database or report optimizations, the Performance Information window provides the capability to save the involved report's performance information to a file for future reference and time comparison.

CRYSTAL REPORTS IN THE REAL WORLD— WEB REPORT ALERT VIEWING

There are many creative ways to employ alerting in Crystal Reports to direct the report consumer to information that requires attention. The following scenario helps you understand the use of alerting.

As part of her daily function, a Sales Executive views the World Sales Report multiple times. Although she is familiar with the report, it is easy to overlook an important piece of information if it is hidden in the pages to follow. Simply by looking at the first page of the report, it might not be clear if there is a problem that requires attention. The Sales report that is discussed here is grouped by Country, Region, City, and Customer. The detail section shows the order date and order amount. For the purpose of the example, the problem in the business occurs when a sales order is booked for more than $5,000. An alert will be created that flags this circumstance (see Figure 11.6).

Figure 11.6
Create an alert and set the properties.

This sample report uses two techniques to draw the viewer's attention to the significant records. The first step highlights the Group Header in red if any record in the group sets the alert. To do this, the report will evaluate a built-in function IsAlertEnabled ('Order Amount Alert') and set the highlighting appropriately (see Figure 11.7).

Figure 11.7
Set properties for the group header.

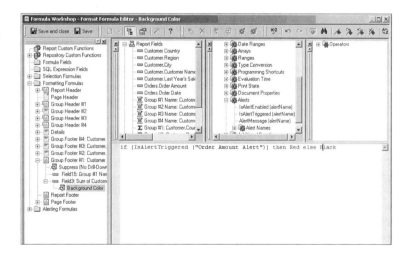

Additionally, to help draw the executive to the order(s) triggering the alert you will highlight the background of the detail record(s) that have triggered the alert. To do this, conditionally set the fill color of the detail section to yellow (see Figure 11.8).

Now, when the executive views the sales report and drills to the detail data, the records highlighted in yellow indicate where the problem occurred.

Conditional formatting techniques described here can be applied to other attributes of report elements such as ToolTips. ToolTips can contain alert messages based on the triggered alerts. You can also conditionally hide or display report sections to highlight (see Figure 11.9).

Figure 11.8
Set properties for the detail line.

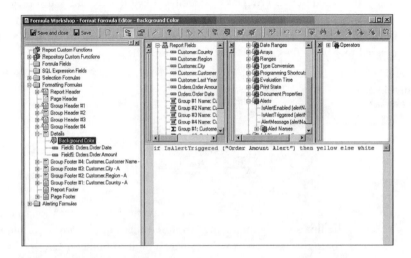

Figure 11.9
Report highlighting draws attention to critical records.

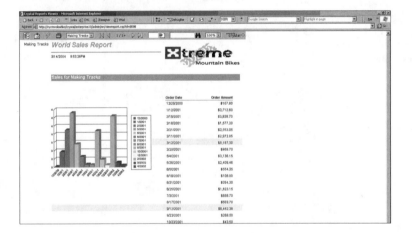

CHAPTER 12

USING SUBREPORTS FOR ADVANCED REPORTING

In this chapter

UNDERSTANDING SUBREPORTS

The first 11 chapters of this book introduced you to the design of individual reports using single aggregated datasets. Crystal Reports provides further flexibility and reporting capabilities through the use of additional reports embedded directly within an original main report. These embedded reports, referred to as *Subreports*, provide enhanced value extending your reporting solutions into an expanded domain that will be explored in this chapter.

This chapter covers the following topics:

- A description of Subreports
- The usefulness and value of Subreports
- Linked versus Unlinked Subreports
- In-Place versus On-Demand Subreports
- Passing data between the main report and Subreports

The next two sections provide you with

- An introduction to Subreports
- An idea of when you might use them
- A lesson on how to use Subreports

Crystal Reports provides the capability to embed multiple Crystal Reports within a single existing main report to allow for increased flexibility in report creation. Think of these Subreports as entire reports within reports, which can contain their own data sources, formatting, and record selections. The embedded Subreports can be created from existing Crystal Reports files or can be dynamically created at report design time using the insert Subreport functionality. When presenting a report that contains one or more Subreports to business users, the Subreports can be displayed either in-place, providing a seamless integration, or on-demand, minimizing the amount of required up-front report processing.

COMMON SUBREPORT USAGE

A few particular reporting problems are difficult to solve without the use of Subreports. Some of the most common problems and a specific example of each are listed here:

- *The presentation of data from two (or more) completely unrelated data sources on a single report.* Specific Example: On a Manufacturing Plant Efficiency report sourced from your internal SAP system, you want to display industry average information sourced from a completely different and unrelated industry or trade database.

- *A report that needs to combine data from different tables with only derived (and not direct) database field links.* Specific Example: On a Customer Profile report, you want to combine Order Information from your ERP (for example, SAP, Oracle, Baan) system with call-center information from your call-center application (for example, Remedy) and your CRM system (for example, Siebel, PeopleSoft), but the employee ID field is stored slightly different in each system. The Subreports enable the linking of the different employee IDs by allowing linking on formulas or derived fields.

■ *The presentation of the same data in two (or more) different ways in a single report.* Specific Example: On a Sales Summary Report, senior management wants to present a high-level summary of sales by region but also wants to present a separate and personalized summary of sales by product for each salesperson who will be viewing the report.

■ *The inclusion of a summary field in the report that is unrelated to the established grouping in the main report.* Specific Example: On an employee HR report, HR managers want to see employee salary information grouped by Business Unit, Division, and Department. Additionally, they want to view a count of the different departments that this employee worked for in the previous year. The main report groups employees by department (and by division and business unit), whereas the Subreport groups departments by employee to determine a department count.

■ *The inclusion of a reusable component like a standard reporting header or footer in numerous reports across an organization that can be dynamically updated for all reports in a single location.* Specific Example: A firm wants to deploy all reports in its organization with a standard header including standard logos and titles. In addition to using the new Report Templates and Repository, Subreports can be used within all the reports as a header and provide a single location for updating the header across all the reports.

Data presented in Subreports is often related to the data presented in the associated main report, but it does not have to be. Subreport data can be a twist on the main report's information or sourced from a completely different database.

ADDING SUBREPORTS TO YOUR REPORTS

Adding a Subreport to your main report is as easy as adding any other Crystal Reports object. After selecting the Subreport option from the Insert menu, you are presented with the Insert Subreport dialog (see Figure 12.1).

Figure 12.1
The Insert Subreport dialog enables you to add a Subreport to your main report.

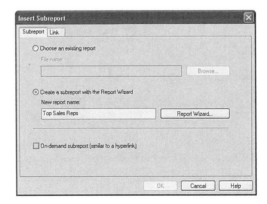

To explore one of the many challenges solved by using Subreports, let's solve the hypothetical reporting problem faced by the Chief Operating Officer (COO) of Maple Leaf Bikes Corporation. This COO wants a single report that highlights the recently acquired company's (Xtreme) top-selling products in one bar chart and additionally highlights the company's top selling sales reps in a corresponding pie chart. The two charts are sourced from the same sales information but have no direct relation or links to each other. To resolve this request, complete the following steps:

1. Create a New Report and point this report at the Xtreme Sample Database 10.

2. Select the Orders, Order Detail, and Product Tables and then select the Product Name and Order Amount Fields to Display on the report.

3. Group the report by Product Name and Add a Summary to the report that sums Order Amount for each Product Name group. Also limit the report to display only the top five groups based on the Summarized Field. (Reminder: You can use the Group Sort Expert under the Report menu option to accomplish this last task and remember to explicitly not include an Others group by selecting that check box.)

4. Add a bar chart in the Page Header to represent the top five selling products, and you should have a report similar to that depicted in Figure 12.2.

Figure 12.2
Preliminary sample report to solve COO problem.

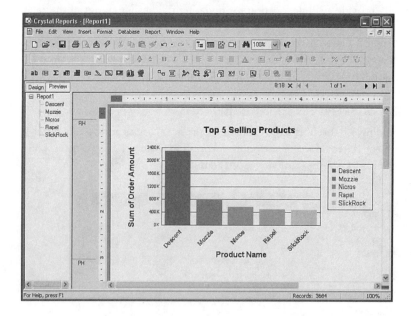

5. Make room for the COO's requested second visual by resizing the bar chart to only take up half of the page header's width.

6. Select the Insert Subreport option by either accessing that option from the Insert menu or clicking on the Insert Subreport icon. The Insert Subreport dialog in Figure 12.1 appears.

7. Select the Create a Subreport with the Report Wizard option by clicking on the associated radio button.

8. Enter a Name similar to Top Sales Reps and click on the Report Wizard button.

9. As you step through the familiar Report Wizard to create this Subreport, select the Xtreme Sample Database 10 and the Employee and Orders tables. From the list of available fields, select the First Name and Order Amount.

10. Group the Subreport on Employee First Name and create a Summary on the Sum of Order Amounts for each Employee Group. Limit the report to display the top five employees based on this sum, add a pie chart to this report, and click the Finish button.

11. Ensure that the On-Demand Subreport check box is unchecked, and then click OK on the Insert Subreport dialog. Drop the Subreport on the right side of the main report so that it does not overlap the existing bar chart. The details of On-Demand reports are described later in this chapter.

12. To clean up the final presentation of your main report and included Subreport, edit the Subreport by right-clicking on it and then hiding all the sections of the report except the report header a. As a reminder, hiding sections is accomplished by right-clicking on the name of the involved sections in the Design or Preview tab and selecting the Hide option. Lastly, delete the report header b section in the Subreport. Figure 12.3 shows the final result of this quick report. If your final result appears slightly different, review Chapter 8, "Visualizing Your Data with Charts and Maps," and revise the charts accordingly.

NOTE

As mentioned in the previous sections, Subreports *are* Crystal Reports in their own right, and as such they have their own Design tab in the Crystal Reports Designer. To format the details of a Subreport, it is necessary to open the Design tab for that Subreport from within the Designer of the main report. This can be accomplished by right-clicking on a Subreport and selecting the Edit Subreport option. Figure 12.3 displays the tabs for both the sample's main report and the Subreport.

With that introduction to Subreports, you should begin to see some of the flexibility and power that they offer in solving difficult reporting (and even dashboard-related) problems. The next few sections explore this in more detail.

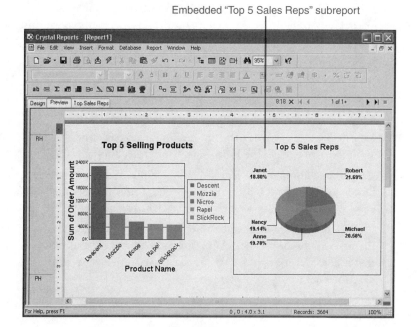

Embedded "Top 5 Sales Reps" subreport

Figure 12.3
Sample report with
Subreport to solve
COO problem.

UNDERSTANDING LINKED VERSUS UNLINKED SUBREPORTS

The hypothetical COO scenario just explored highlights an example of an unlinked Subreport. In Crystal Reports terminology, this means that the parent, or *main*, report did not have any specific data connections (or links) to its related child report (the Subreport). Unlinked Subreports are completely independent from their main reports and do not rely on the main report for any data. Many reporting problems in which multiple views of the same or different data sources are required in a single presentation can be resolved with unlinked Subreports. If a requirement exists to share data between the parent/main report and its Subreport, linked reports provide the answer.

Contrary to unlinked Subreports, linked Subreports are bound (or linked) to the data in their associated main report. The links are defined in the Link tab of the Insert Subreport dialog shown in Figure 12.4.

The Link tab enables you to link report, database, or formula fields in the main report to fields in the Subreport and enables you to filter the Subreport based on the data passed in from the main report.

The Available Fields section of the Links dialog enables you to select the field from the main report to be linked on. More than one field can be selected for linking. After at least one field has been selected, a separate Field Links section appears at the bottom of the Links tab. For each linked field, a parameter in the involved Subreport must be selected to receive and hold that information. These parameters can be pre-existing parameters prede-fined in the Subreport, or they can be a parameter that is automatically created for each field you have selected to link. (These are automatically created in the Subreport with the prefix ?Pm-.)

Figure 12.4
Link tab of the Insert Subreport dialog.

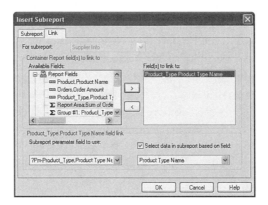

Finally, for each linked field from the main report, a data filter can be created in the Subreport based on that parameter. This is accomplished by checking the Select Data in Subreport Based on Field check box and selecting the report field, database field, or for-mula field in the Subreport that you want to have filtered based on the linked parameter from the provided drop-down box. In effect, checking this box creates a selection filter in your Subreport that is based on the selected filter field and the selected parameter field.

Linking Subreports and Reports with Formulas

The capability to link Subreports and main reports with formulas gives you a flexible method of presenting data from different database tables that is not possible otherwise. The Crystal Reports Database Linking Expert only enables joining of fields from different tables and does not permit joining formulas to fields. By using for-mulas and Subreports, a derived formula can now be linked to another database field in a Subreport.

For example, this would be beneficial if a firm's Order Processing system (SAP, Oracle, Baan, and so on) stored a customer ID as a nine-digit number (999123888), but that same company's Customer Relationship Management (CRM) system (Siebel, Salesforce, PeopleSoft, and so on) stored the same customer ID as a nine-digit number prefixed with a regional code (ONT999123888). These fields could not be joined in the Crystal Reports Database Linking Expert, but they could be linked using a formula that extracts the nine-digit number from the CRM/Siebel Customer ID and links to the SAP Customer ID in a Subreport.

One last point of interest is that the new Business Views does now enable the linking of formula fields in the creation of Data Foundations. Chapter 18, "Crystal Reports Semantic Layer–Business Views," covers this new functionality.

To explore a reporting solution with linked Subreports, solve the hypothetical reporting problem faced by the same COO of Maple Leaf Bikes Corporation. The COO now wants a single report that highlights the company's top-selling product *types* in one bar chart (sim-ilar to the previous example), enables drill-down into the actual products, and produces a list of suppliers for each product type to be available for review—essentially, a Supplier's listing Subreport linked to the main report based on the Product Type Name. To accomplish this, follow these steps:

1. Open the previous sample report from this chapter and delete the previous Subreport containing the Top 5 Sales Rep pie chart. Now add the Product_Type table to this report through the Database Expert under the Database menu option. It is automatically and correctly linked to the Product table. Also, add another Group for Product Type Name on top of the existing Product Name (Hint: You can use the Group Expert under the Report menu.) Then hide the details section of this report.

2. Open the Insert Subreport dialog and create another new Subreport called Supplier Info using the provided Subreport Report Wizard. Connect this new Subreport to the Xtreme sample database, select the Supplier, Product, and Product Type tables (they will correctly smart-link), and add the Supplier Name, City, and Phone Number fields to the report. Finally, click on the Report Wizard Finish button, but do not exit the Insert Subreport dialog.

3. Click on the Link tab in the Insert Subreport dialog. Now, select the Product Type Name field from the Available Fields list as the Field to link on (it can be selected from the Product Type Table). This initiates the Product Type Name ID Link section at the bottom of the dialog. Use the default (and automatically generated) parameter `'?Pm-Product_Type.Product Type Name'` for the link on the Subreport.

4. Select the Select Data in Subreport Field Based On check box and choose the Product Type Name field from the Product_Type table in the drop-down box. Essentially, you have just specified that this supplier's Subreport be filtered on the Product Type Name that is passed in from the main report every time this Subreport is called. Click OK to add the Subreport and place it in the Product Type Name Group Header on the right side of the report.

5. To ensure that the desired results are provided and provided in a clean way, edit the Subreport to remove the default provided date and resize its Report Header Subreport section and hide the report footer b in the Subreport. You also need to specify that this Subreport should only return a *distinct* list of suppliers because the COO is not interested in a repetitive list—this can be done through the Report Options selection under the File menu. Click the Select Distinct Records check box.

6. Lastly, back in the main report, resize the bar chart graphic on the main report and you will have a new sample report for the COO resembling the report depicted in Figure 12.5.

The COO can now make an informed analysis on whether his firm has too much reliance on a small number of suppliers, and you have learned some of the benefits of a linked Subreport.

Figure 12.5
Sample report with Linked Suppliers Subreport.

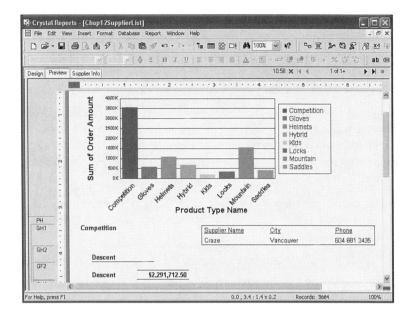

NOTE

> Unlike the initial sample report presented in this chapter where we placed the Top Sales Rep Subreport in the Report Header and it ran once for the entire main report, the Product Suppliers Subreport is run multiple times—in fact, once for every product. This is the case because the Subreport was placed in the Group Header of the main report, and it therefore is executed for each different group in the main report. This is important to note with respect to performance, specifically when your databases and reports become large.

CONSIDERING SUBREPORT EXECUTION TIME AND PERFORMANCE

There are two types of Subreports—In-Place and On-Demand. Both of the sample reports created previously in this chapter have been In-Place Subreports. An *In-Place* Subreport is virtually indistinguishable from the main report components when viewed because it is run at the same time as the main report. In-Place Subreports are displayed as components of the main report like any other report object and require no special business user interaction to view them. *On-Demand* Subreports, on the contrary, are not executed at the same time as the main report and require user interaction to be viewed.

All In-Place Subreports on a main report are run at the execution time of the main report. In the two examples presented in this chapter, this has clearly not caused any performance problems, but as you might imagine, it could on larger databases and reports. Imagine running the last sample report (with the Product Suppliers Subreport in every Group Header) for a large conglomerate with thousands of products. The Product Suppliers Subreport would need to run thousands of times to complete the presentation of the main report. Moreover, the thousands of supplier Subreports would be unlikely to be used by any given business user and would therefore have run extraneously. An elegant solution to that problem is the use of On-Demand Subreports.

Unlike In-Place Subreports, On-Demand Subreports only execute when a user requests them. They lie dormant until that time. The performance benefits to On-Demand reports are clear; however, it does come at the expense of a less seamless integration than In-Place Subreports and a small delay in viewing because the Subreport executes dynamically after being requested.

Taking the last example, follow these steps to make the Product Suppliers Subreport an On-Demand Subreport:

1. Open the most recent sample report if you have closed it.

2. Right-click on the Product Suppliers Subreport and select the Format Subreport option. Many familiar formatting options are available here (see Figure 12.6), but click on the Subreport tab.

Figure 12.6
Format Subreport dialog.

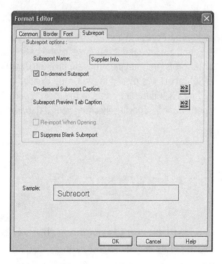

3. Click the On-Demand Subreport check box to turn on that option. Notice that the On-Demand Caption section becomes un-grayed.

4. Click on the On-Demand Caption button (x-2) and type 'Supplier List' (do include the apostrophes) in the Text Editing area. Click on the Save and Close button, and you should now have a main report that resembles Figure 12.7 where the Supplier List link dynamically runs the involved Subreport if and only if a report consumer requests it.

Figure 12.7
Sample report with Linked, On-Demand Suppliers Subreport.

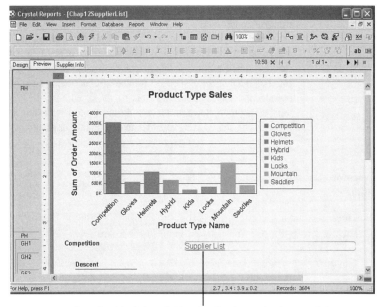

Supplier List link—clicking the On-demand subreport link
dynamically runs the supplier listing report for the end user

TIP

> Careful consideration should be given to report design when deciding between In-Place and On-Demand Subreports. There is a trade-off between the seamless integration of In-Place Subreports and the performance benefits of On-Demand Subreports that must be considered in addition, of course, to the specific requirements of the business users' overall experience.

USING VARIABLES TO PASS DATA BETWEEN REPORTS

The examples up to this point in the chapter that involve passing data between a main report and a Subreport have worked exclusively through the Subreport Linking tab or dialog. Although the functionality provided there is certainly powerful, circumstances might require more flexible passing of data between the main report and the Subreport or the passing of data the other way—from a Subreport to a main report.

With the use of variables, it becomes possible to pass data between the main report and any of the Subreports or even among different Subreports in the same main report. By declaring the same shared variable in formulas in both the main report and at least one Subreport, data can be exchanged back and forth fluidly, and each report can leverage information from the other in a very flexible manner.

TIP

> Using Subreports and variables to pass data back to a main report from a Subreport is an effective way to capture important summarizations or external information to your main report that is not possible otherwise because of the default groupings of the main report. A simple example in this chapter's last sample report would be the inclusion of a count on the number of suppliers for each product. Using only the default groupings provided in the main report (By Product), this count would be impossible to calculate. By using a Subreport, however, that count can be calculated external to the main report (in a Subreport), shared using variables, and eventually displayed on the main report.

To explore the power of shared variables, follow these steps to modify this chapter's last sample report:

1. Open the most recent sample report if you have closed it. Turn the Supplier Subreport back to an In-Place Subreport (versus On-Demand).

NOTE

> When passing shared variables from a Subreport to a main report, the involved Subreport cannot be set to On-Demand. The reason, of course, is that Subreports are not run until specifically requested by the business user. Therefore, their associated variables are not set until that time, making them unusable in the main report.

2. Edit the Supplier's Subreport by right-clicking on the Subreport and selecting the Edit Subreport option.

3. Select the Supplier Name field and insert a summary field that counts the distinct supplier names in this report. (Hint: Right-click on the Supplier Name field and access the Summary menu option.) This summary will shortly be assigned to the shared variable that will be created and used to pass the information back to the main report.

4. Insert a formula into the Report Footer of this Subreport and call it `Assign Supplier Count`. In this formula, declare a shared numeric variable called `SupplierCount` and then assign this variable to equal the Supplier Summary created in the last step. (Reminder: You can access the summary created in step 3 for use in your formula by double-clicking on it.) The formula definition should resemble Figure 12.8.

5. Now click on the Preview or Design tab of the Crystal Reports Designer to take you back to the main report, insert a formula into the Product Group Footer section, and call it `Place Supplier Count`. In this formula, declare the same shared numeric variable—`SupplierCount`—and make this variable the output of this formula. Figure 12.9 shows what this formula should look like.

NOTE

> As the comments in the Formula shown in Figure 12.9 highlight, it is important that this Formula is placed in the Group Footer of the Product Type Name Group. This strategic placement ensures that the Supplier List Subreport for the involved Product Type has already completed (as it is in the Group Header) and has set the shared

SupplierCount variable appropriately. Careful consideration needs to be given when using variables to ensure they are evaluated at the time and in the order desired. In addition to the Top to Bottom and Left to Right default evaluation times of Crystal Reports, the EvaluateAfter() and a few other functions discussed in the Multi-Pass reporting section in Chapter 4, "Understanding and Implementing Formulas," are useful in ensuring the desired reporting results.

Scope and Variable Declaration shortcuts

Summary Report Field used in formula

Figure 12.8
Formula with a shared variable declaration in the Subreport.

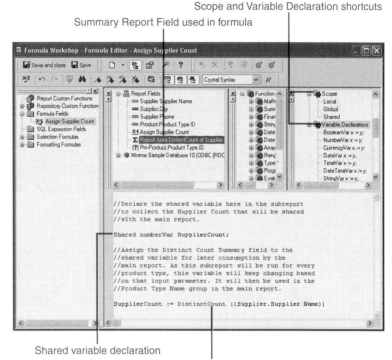

Shared variable declaration

Shared variable assignment to existing summary field

6. Add a text field to the report to complement the Supplier Count field called **Supplier Count**, hide the Details section on the main report and with a little creative formatting and group sorting, the final result should resemble Figure 12.10.

NOTE

As you discover the power of variables, you will begin to leverage this programming feature in increasingly complex ways. The Supplier Count example just provided is a relatively simple example that scratches the surface of the power of variables. Another variable-based technique that can be used to circumvent some common reporting challenges is to use variables to manage Running Totals. The flexibility provided within the Formula Editor and with variables enables you to create flexible condition-based running totals.

12

Shared variable declaration—this must take
place in all formulas referencing a variable

Figure 12.9
Formula with a
shared variable decla-
ration and output in
the main report.

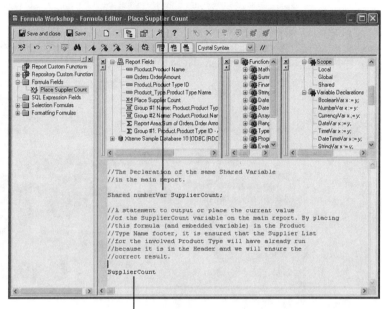

Shared variable specified as formula output

In-place supplier listing subreport that calculates the number of
suppliers per product type and stores the result as a shared variable

Figure 12.10
Sample report with
Supplier Count
sourced from a
shared variable in a
Subreport.

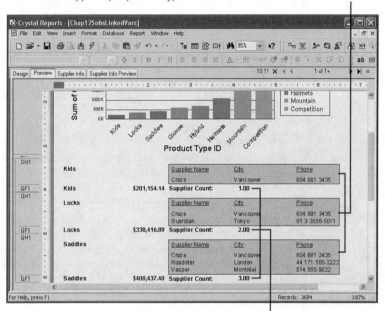

A formula using a shared variable calculated in the listing subreport

Perhaps not the prettiest report ever designed, this quick example does begin to convey the power and importance of shared variables in report design.

EMULATING NESTED SUBREPORTS

Based on the title of this section, you can deduce that it is not possible to nest Subreports—why else would you need to emulate that behavior? Crystal Reports does not currently support Subreports within Subreports. Report Hyperlinks and Report Parts do, however, provide a new and flexible method in advanced navigation between and within reports. This form of flexible navigation can be used to emulate nested Subreports.

→ For more information on Report Hyperlinks and Report Parts, **see** "Making Presentation-Quality Reports," **p. 218**

TROUBLESHOOTING

FORMATTING THE DETAILS OF A SUBREPORT

I can't figure out how to format the details of a Subreport.

Open the Design tab for that Subreport from within the Designer of the main report. This can be accomplished by right-clicking on a Subreport and selecting the Edit Subreport option.

CRYSTAL REPORTS IN THE REAL WORLD— NESTING SUBREPORTS

Often a single report needs to show data from different and often unrelated pieces of information. In the next example, the report shows both customer and supplier information for a given location. This is demonstrated using a main report for the structure of Country, Region, and City hierarchy, one Subreport to show customer information, and another Subreport for supplier information. Because there is no relationship between suppliers and customers, at least one of these pieces of information must come from a Subreport. For this sample, both elements come from a Subreport. Follow these steps to explore this capability:

1. Open the report designer and select Create New Report Using the Report Wizard. Click OK and browse to the datasource Xtreme Samples Database 10 datasource, expand the list of tables, and add the Customer table to the list of report tables by clicking the > button. Click Next.

2. In the Fields window, add the fields Country, Region, and City to the report and click Next. In the Grouping window, add the same fields to the Group By list.

3. Click Finish to complete the report. This builds the hierarchy that is used in the report.

4. Change to Design mode. Move the fields in the group header to the left and indent them slightly at each lower level. Suppress all sections of the report other than the headers and expand each of the header areas below the fields. See Figure 12.11 to view what the framework of the report should look like.

Figure 12.11
Report hierarchy to act as the framework for Subreport content.

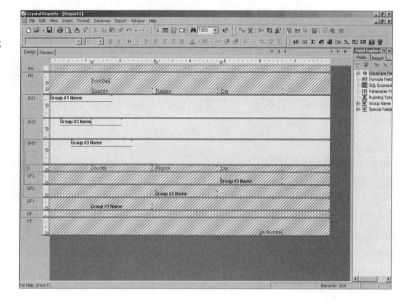

5. With the framework complete, the next step is to create the content. There are different ways to create Subreports; in this instance, the reports are generated as separate files and later imported into the main report. Create the report for supplier information. From the File menu, select New. When the Crystal Reports Gallery window opens, click OK. Find the Xtreme Sample Database 10 connection, browse the list of tables for the Supplier table, and click the > button to move it to the list of selected tables. Click Next. From the Fields window, select Supplier Name and Phone and click the > button to move them to the Fields to Display. Click Finish to close the wizard. Minimize report content by changing to Design mode, moving the fields to the left edge, suppressing sections with no fields, and minimizing whitespace. Figure 12.12 illustrates a sample Subreport.

6. Repeat step 5 for the customer table.

7. Add each Subreport to the report three times, once each for Country, Region, and City. Drill into each of the six Subreports by double-clicking and again suppress blank sections.

8. From the Report menu, select Section Expert. In the list of sections, select Group Footer #1 and check New Page After. Click OK to close the window. Save the report as Chap12SubsContext_Main.rpt. The design of the report should look like Figure 12.13.

Figure 12.12
Supplier information
Subreport, extra
whitespace reduced
to a minimum.

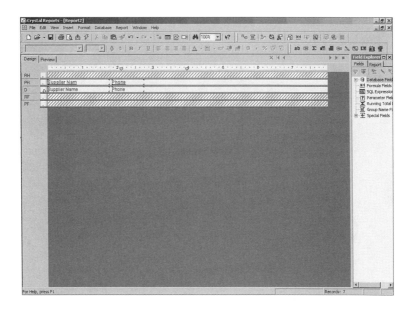

Figure 12.13
Report with hierarchy
and Subreports.

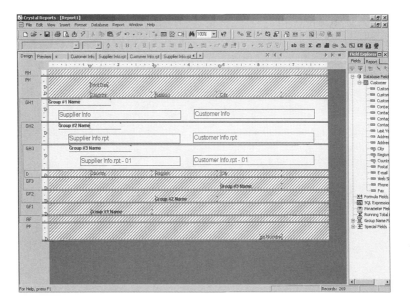

Preview the report and notice on Page 13 (Canada) that there is different and unrelated information for both Suppliers and Customers listed and that the information for both is specific to the location context.

CHAPTER **13**

USING FORMULAS AND CUSTOM FUNCTIONS

In this chapter

BECOMING MORE PRODUCTIVE WITH FORMULAS

This chapter explores the use of advanced formulas and functions to accomplish many mundane and repetitive tasks. Also, you will look at how the formulas and functions can help alleviate redundancy in report design.

Whereas Chapter 4, "Understanding and Implementing Formulas," focused on the basics of formulas, this chapter focuses on some lesser known facts and tricks to make formula work more productive as well as less repetitive.

CHOOSING A FORMULA LANGUAGE: CRYSTAL VERSUS BASIC SYNTAX

In previous chapters, the Crystal syntax was used for all formulas. However, formulas in Crystal Reports can be created, edited, and modified using one of two languages. The Crystal syntax is the most used language, but the Basic syntax is also available.

Both languages are equal in their functionality—meaning that if something was added to Crystal syntax, it was also added to Basic. The reason you're given a choice is for your comfort—you can use whichever language you are more comfortable with using.

UNDERSTANDING SYNTAX DIFFERENCES

The Crystal syntax is most similar to the Pascal or Delphi programming languages. It's not exactly like Pascal, but if you're a Delphi developer or a longtime Crystal Report developer, this syntax is probably your first choice.

The Basic syntax is most similar to Visual Basic as a programming language. If you're a Visual Basic developer, you'll likely find this syntax most beneficial.

Some specific differences between the two languages are described in Table 13.1.

TABLE 13.1 DIFFERENCES BETWEEN CRYSTAL AND BASIC SYNTAX

Description	Crystal	Basic
Variable declarations	`StringVar`	`Dim`
Statement endings	`;`	None required
Comment characters	`//`	`'`
Variable assignment	`:=`	`=`
Formula statement	None required	Required
Formula returns	None required	`Return` statement
Multiline statement indicators	None required	`_`
If statement ending	`;`	`End If`

WHY BASIC SYNTAX WAS ADDED

Many functions and operators provided by the Basic language increase the productivity of Crystal Reports users. By implementing the whole language, the existing Crystal syntax users could benefit from the new operators and functions and at the same time, newer users who are familiar with the Basic language through other development endeavors could easily make the jump to creating formulas in Crystal Reports.

Some of the functions and operators that were added as a result of the addition of the Basic syntax are

■ Date functions such as `DateAdd`, `DateDiff`, and `DateSerial`

■ Financial functions such as Present Value (`PV`)

■ Control structures such as `Do While`, `Do Until`, and `For Next` statements

SELECTING THE BEST SYNTAX FOR YOU

Whether you choose Basic or Crystal syntax, they are both equally capable of doing the job and there is no performance implication in making this choice. The decision is entirely based on the comfort level and familiarity of each language for report designers.

TIP

> Whichever syntax you prefer to use most often, you can set it up as the default for all new formulas by going to File, Options, Reporting, and choosing the desired syntax in the Formula Language list box.

USING BRACKETS IN FORMULAS

Regardless of which syntax is chosen, some fundamental concepts to formula creation are important.

Several variations of brackets are used within the formula language, and it can be confusing to know which one to use at a particular time. To clear up some of the confusion, here is a way to remember them phonetically:

■ {}French = Fields

For example, `{Table.Field}` is used to refer to fields, formula fields or parameter fields in the report definition.

■ []Square = Selected

For example, `{Table.Field}[1]` returns only the first character of a string field. Square brackets are used for indexes on array types (for example, strings or array data types).

■ ()Parenthesis = Parameters

For example, Function (`{Table.Field}`) passes the field to the function. Parentheses are used to define which parts of a calculation or formula should be performed first

13

(that is, defines order of precedence for mathematical and non-mathematical operations).

Using Characters in Formulas

As with brackets, symbols in the formula language (or in the icons) have specific meaning as well. To shed some light on this, check out the listing of symbols that represent different field types in Crystal Reports:

@ = Formula	{@Formula} is a formula field
? = Parameter	{?Param} is a parameter field
# = Running Total	{#RunTtl} is a running total field
[gs] = Summary	[gs]fieldName is a summary field on the report
% = SQL Expression	{%SQL} is a SQL expression field

Recent Improvements to Formulas

Because Crystal Reports has been around for so many years and has released many versions over those years, it's not uncommon to come across users who are still using older versions. To bring those users up to speed this section covers some of the recent additions and improvements to formulas over the past few versions.

Manipulating Memo Fields in Formulas

In the past, Crystal Reports developers had not been able to access string fields that were longer than 255 characters within the formula language other than to find out whether they were null. This limitation has been completely removed.

For our purposes here, let's assume that the Xtreme Mountain Bike Company management needs an HR report that shows only the female employees, but there is no gender field in the Xtreme database. In the Notes field in the Employee table, the word "she" is used for all female employees. However, Xtreme's management has indicated that they might need to search for other words as well, so they want to have a keyword search instead of hard-coding the search values. Follow these steps to create such a report to fulfill this reporting requirement:

1. Open the Employee Profile Report. Press Ctrl+O to open a report. Find the Crystal Reports 9 sample report called Employee Profile. Most installations have it in the following folder: \Program Files\Crystal Decisions\Crystal Reports 10\Samples\en\Reports\General Business.

2. Create a parameter field by selecting View, Field Explorer. Right-click on the Parameter Field item in the Field Explorer and choose New. In the Create Parameter Field dialog, call the parameter **Search-A-Word**. Prompting Text should be **What word would you like to search for?**. The Value Type should be String.

3. Click on the Set Default Values button. In the Set Default Values dialog, add "`<none>`", "`she`", and "`he`" to the default values. The final result should look like Figure 13.1.

4. Click the OK button. The Create Parameter Field dialog should look like Figure 13.2. Click OK.

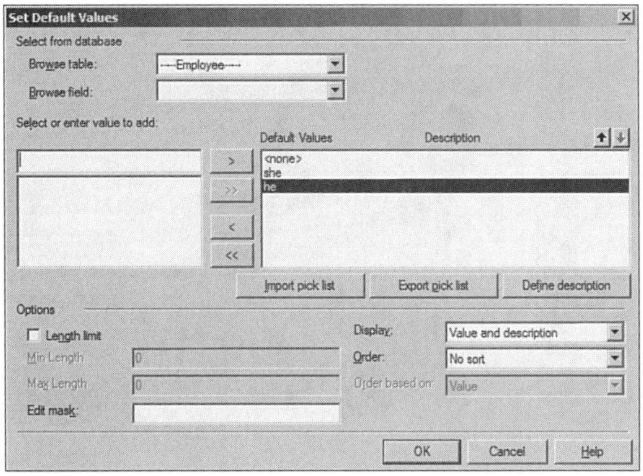

Figure 13.1
The default values for a Search-A-Word parameter.

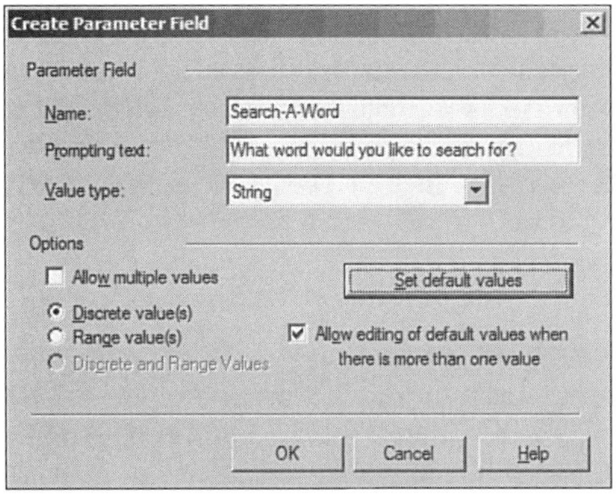

Figure 13.2
The parameter settings for Search-A-Word.

5. Connect the parameter to the Selection Formula. Select the Formula Workshop via Report, Formula Workshop. Then choose Selection Formulas, Record Selection from the Workshop tree. Enter the following selection formula into the editor: **IF {?Search-A-Word} = "<none>" THEN TRUE ELSE ({?Search-a-Word}) IN LowerCase({Employee.Notes})** and click the Save and Close button.

6. Run the report. When prompted, choose she from the Parameter Field prompt and choose to refresh the data. The end result is that only the female employees appear on the report as shown in Figure 13.3. Save the report as **Chap13_1.rpt**.

Figure 13.3
The Employee Profile showing female employees only.

TIP

Notice that you only put the LowerCase() function call around the {Employee.Notes} field and not the parameter. This is because you put the values into the parameter as lowercase by default. However, because you allow the business users to input their own values into the parameter, it might be a good idea to put the LowerCase() function on the parameter as well. This allows Crystal to compare apples to apples when evaluating these exact values. Alternatively, both could have been set to UpperCase() as well.

A keyword search is just one example of how to use a memo field in a formula. The 255-character limit for formulas that was removed in version 9 of Crystal Reports means that practically all database field types can now be accessed in formulas and manipulated. Remember that memo fields are really just long string fields, so they are treated as strings in the formula language. Wherever a string can be called, now a memo field can be called as well.

CAUTION

Not all databases support the capability to search large string fields, so if this type of key-word search is required, more records than necessary might come across the network. For the preceding example, 15 records were returned from the data source but only the 6 that were female were shown on the report. This is because the data source couldn't be passed this selection criteria to handle on the server side.

It is a powerful new feature, but keep in mind that it might bring back more records than you expect.

WORKING WITH THE ADDITIONAL FINANCIAL FUNCTIONS

In older versions of Crystal Reports, the financial functions capability of the formula language was limited to 13 functions. However, version 10 of Crystal Reports provides more than 50 financial functions. With overloads for parameters, these functions count up to about 200 variations.

These functions were implemented to give as much functionality as possible to a highly skilled group of report designers. In the past, they had to hand code the financial functions. By including the standard financial functions that most users have seen in Microsoft Excel, these report developers can now develop their formulas much more quickly.

For more information on the Financial Functions available, refer to the Crystal Reports Help file. In the Index, look up "Financial Functions" for a complete list of what is available.

CREATING CUSTOM FUNCTIONS IN YOUR REPORTS

Custom functions were introduced in Crystal Reports 9 and continue to be a powerful feature of Crystal Reports 10. Although they have been introduced in Chapter 4, "Understanding and Implementing Formulas," this section focuses on some more detailed information on what they are and how they could be used in report development.

Custom functions are packets of business logic that are written in Basic or Crystal syntax. These functions do not have any reference to any database fields at all. Because these functions contain logic that will change values and return a result, the values must be passed in and the results of the logic must be passed out or returned.

Only 10% of a custom function is different from your average formula. As mentioned previously, parameters must be passed in to allow for data manipulation because a custom function is *stateless*. This means that it has no meaning outside the function it has called in. It acts just like all the other formula functions in the formula language. The only difference is that custom functions can be created, edited, and deleted, whereas Crystal formula functions are completely unchangeable.

Here is a custom function that is provided within the sample repository that comes with Crystal Reports:

```
Function cdExpandRegionAbbreviation (regionAbbreviation _
  As String, Optional country As String = "USA")
  Select Case UCase (country)
   Case "CANADA"
    cdExpandRegionAbbreviation _
      = cdExpandRegionAbbreviationCanada (regionAbbreviation)
   Case "USA", "U.S.A.", "US", "U.S.", "UNITED STATES", _
    "UNITED STATES OF AMERICA"
    cdExpandRegionAbbreviation _
      = cdExpandRegionAbbreviationUSA (regionAbbreviation)
    Case Else
        cdExpandRegionAbbreviation = regionAbbreviation
    End Select
End Function
```

13

Some of the things you will notice about the preceding code are as follows:

- It's in Basic syntax. This is not a requirement of custom functions. They can be in either Basic or Crystal syntax.

- It does not reference database fields directly. Any information that is needed from database must be passed in via the parameters in the first statement (`regionAbbreviation`).

- It has an optional parameter (`Optional country As String = "USA"`). This means that this parameter does not necessarily need to be passed in for the function to work. If this parameter is not supplied by the developer in the formula, the value of `"USA"` is used by default.

- It calls other custom functions. `CdExpandRegionAbbreviationCanada` and `cdExpandRegionAbbreviationUSA` are also custom functions. In fact, they are Crystal syntax custom functions. (This shows that Basic and Crystal syntax can call one another.)

- It has a definite end-point (`End Function`). This allows for the final result (the functions return) to be passed back out to the formula making the call.

TIP

> The Enter More Info button takes you to another dialog where you can enter much more descriptive text around the custom function. It also contains fields for categorization and authors. From there, you can also add help text via another dialog. For more information on these dialogs, consult the online help.

SHARING CUSTOM FUNCTIONS WITH OTHERS

Two ways in which you can share custom functions are

- By using them in multiple places in one. Because custom functions are stateless, different parameters can be passed in to allow for instant function reuse.

- By sharing them in the Crystal Repository. Custom functions are one of four report object types that can be shared in the repository.

Custom functions can be used in many ways. Take your existing formulas, convert them, and share their logic with others.

UNDERSTANDING RUNTIME ERRORS

Crystal Reports 10 provides the ability to get more information about variables within formulas when a runtime error occurs. In the past, when a runtime error (such as a Divide by Zero) occurred, Crystal would simply take you to the line of the formula giving the error. However, this was not altogether helpful, especially if the error was because the data being passed in from the database could have been at fault. So, in version 9 of Crystal Reports, there is a new feature that shows all variables and data field values used in all related formulas when an error occurs. You can think of this as a variable stack.

The runtime error stack only appears when a runtime error occurs (when real-time data forces an error). It appears where the workshop group tree normally would in the Formula Workshop.

The runtime error stack shows all variables and all database field data related to the formula in question. If custom functions are called within the formula, their variables will appear above the formula as well. The last function to be called will appear at the top.

TIP

> The idea of a stack (reverse order) is useful in that the last function called most likely will be where the error is. But, of course, that might not always be the case.

This concept is best shown as an example. Assume that Xtreme Mountain Bike Company's management would like to take the Chap13_1.rpt and find out how much money is not accounted for by days when not shipped (`Calculation = Order Amount / Days until shipped`). To see how this works, follow these steps to simulate a formula error:

1. Use the Chap13_1.rpt again. If it's not already open, open it by choosing Ctrl+O.

2. Use the Formula Workshop. Select Report, Formula Workshop. Right-click on the Formula Field branch in the workshop tree and choose New. Name the formula **Unaccounted Amount/Day** and select Use Editor.

3. Add the required logic. In the Editor, enter the following: "`{Orders.Order Amount} / {@Days until Shipped}`". Click the Save and Close button in the top-left corner. Choose Yes when prompted to save. If the report is not already in Preview mode, press F5 to refresh the report. If you don't see any data, choose Report, Section Expert and make sure that the Details section isn't suppressed. If it is, toggle the option and click OK.

4. Drag the field onto the report. From the Field Explorer (View, Field Explorer), select the newly created formula and drag it onto the report to the right of the Days Until Shipped field. Notice that the Divide by Zero error comes up right away. Click OK.

5. View the Runtime Error Stack shown in Figure 13.4. In this case, the formula is quite straightforward. The problem is occurring because some of the orders are on time (zero days wait). Xtreme's management would like to show 0 if the orders are on time, so change the formula to the following: "`if {@Days until Shipped} = 0 then 0 else {Orders.Order Amount} / {@Days until Shipped}`". Click the Save button.

6. Click F5 to refresh the report. See the values of the resulting formula as shown in Figure 13.5 and then save the report as `Chap13_3.rpt`.

13

Figure 13.4
Runtime Error Stack next to the newly updated formula.

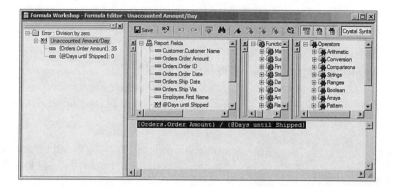

Figure 13.5
Resulting Report with the latest Xtreme requirements added.

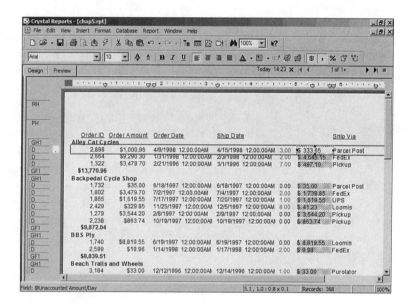

CRYSTAL REPORTS IN THE REAL WORLD— CUSTOM FUNCTIONS

As described in Chapter 4, custom functions can be prepared in advance and can be stateless so they can be used later in a variety of ways. In the next example, a name formula is created in such a way that it builds and formats names in a consistent and reusable manner.

→ For more detailed information on how custom functions can be prepared in advance, **see** "Navigating the Formula Workshop with the Workshop Tree," **p. 95**

1. Open the Employee Profile report. From the Field Explorer, select Formula Fields and click New. Give the formula the name Title and click Use Editor. Enter the following text into the code window of the formula editor:

```
If InStr(LowerCase({Employee.Notes}), " he ")>0 Then
    "Mr."
```

```
Else If InStr(LowerCase({Employee.Notes}), " she ")>0 Then
    "Ms."
Else
    "";
```

2. Click Save and Close. Next, create another new formaula named Suffix and in the code window only type two double-quotes (the string equivalent of NULL); this acts as a placeholder because the table doesn't have a suffix field. Finally, create a formula called Proper Name and add the following text into the code window:

```
Local StringVar strFullName;
strFullName := "";
If {@Title} <> "" Then
    strFullName := {@Title} & " ";
strFullName := strFullName & {Employee.Last Name} & ", " & {Employee.First
➡Name};
If {@Suffix} <> "" Then
    strFullName := strFullName & " " & {@Suffix};
strFullName
```

3. Click Save and Close. From the Report menu, choose Formula Workshop. Click New and give it the name **ProperName** and click Use Extractor. In the list of formulas, select @Proper Name. Your screen should look like Figure 13.6. By default, the Argument Names are v1, v2, v3, and v4 but this won't help users of your formula so change the names to Title, LastName, FirstName, and Suffix.

Figure 13.6
Custom function properties.

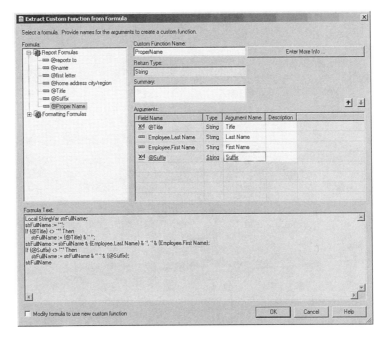

4. Click OK to close the window. Crystal converts the formula from the way it's currently written into a generic custom function for later use. The new custom function is shown in Figure 13.7.

Figure 13.7
Custom function formula.

5. Click Save and Close. The custom function is now available for use.

6. Finally, create the formula that will be used in the report. Create a new formula called Custom Name. From the list of functions, double-click the ProperName function and pass in the following values:

```
Title: @Title
LastName: {Employee.Last Name}
FirstName: {Employee.First Name}
Suffix: ""
```

Your completed formula should look like Figure 13.8.

Figure 13.8
Passing values to a custom function.

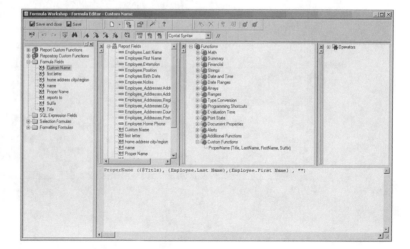

NOTE

> In the sample database there is no Title field, but a formula can be used to generate the Title that will be passed to the custom function. The sample database also doesn't contain a suffix field and because there's no way to determine if the employee name has a suffix, a null string will be passed to the custom function. The custom function can be used later with tables that have both Title and Suffix fields.

7. Add the Custom Name formula to the report and replace the @name formula in the Group Header 2 section. Change the font to Bold and white. Save the report as **CustomName.rpt**. Figure 13.9 shows the completed report.

Figure 13.9
Report using a Name built using a custom function.

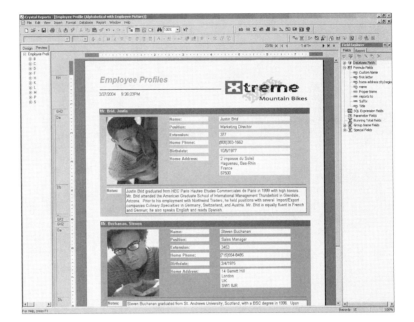

CHAPTER 14

DESIGNING EFFECTIVE
REPORT TEMPLATES

In this chapter

UNDERSTANDING THE IMPORTANCE OF REUSE IN REPORTING

Up to now, you've been creating feature rich reports that are very functional. Most likely, no two of the resulting reports from the previous chapters have a consistent look and feel.

One of the most demanding and time-consuming parts of Report Design is giving all of your reports a consistent look and feel. In many situations, report designers are asked to conform to a corporate standard like letterheads (all page numbers in the bottom right corner, and so on) or perhaps even something as demanding as GAAP or SEC.

In a perfect world that revolves around report designers, less work would be required if you were allowed to focus your efforts on one report and use it as a guide for all other reports that require visual, presentation-focused (yet time-consuming) features. After one report is completed with the appropriate formatting, why not *apply* its contents and format to other reports? Applying an existing report's layout to other reports is very straightforward with Crystal Reports 10. This is made possible through enhancements to the report template's functionality.

UNDERSTANDING REPORT TEMPLATES

A report template is nothing more than a regular report (.rpt) file. It can be any RPT file. Templates are *applied* to other reports so that their formatting and layout can be used as a basis for the other reports. What is useful about the application of templates to other reports is that formatting is applied to the report as well as the layout. An example of this would be a report that has four fields in a detail section, where all sections are "squished" together before applying a presentation-quality template. After the template is applied, the location of the fields in the template would force the fields in the existing report to span out and possibly even change some font information, depending on the specific template.

USING REPORT TEMPLATES

Think of a template as the form that everyone in a company must comply to. Templates can house many types of objects. These objects can be applied to a report after the data-intensive portion of the report design is completed. Applying an existing template to a report can save hours or potentially days of mundane formatting tasks.

Some types of tasks that can be accomplished by (but are not limited to) applying a template to a report are as follows:

- Corporate logos and other images
- Consistent page numbering formatting
- Font style/color/typeface for data fields
- Field border and background formatting

14

- Field sizing
- Group headers and footers formatting
- Summary field formatting
- Watermarks
- Tricky formatting
- Lines
- Boxes
- Repository objects
- Report titles
- Web site links
- Formatting based on data-field type

How Are Templates Better Than Styles in Older Versions?

Templates are better than the Styles in older versions of Crystal Reports in so many ways that it's challenging to explain in a short section. However, because not all report designers have used Crystal Reports prior to version 10, they won't know how cumbersome styles used to be. For those of you new to Crystal Reports 10, feel free to skip this sidebar.

The main problem with the old Report Styles feature in older versions of Crystal Reports (such as 8.5) was that they were not customizable. The styles that one person created when the feature was initially introduced were the only options available. Even if you just didn't like the color red as the group name field and wanted to change it to blue, you were not able to, which was very limiting. This limitation alone made the Styles feature practically useless outside of learning how to create very simple reports.

These styles were also limited to data and group fields. No images or static text objects were included, and again because the styles could not be modified, they could not be updated in this way. The styles were hard-coded into the Crystal Reports designer so that no external .rpt files were used, whereas Templates enable the use of any .rpt file.

USING EXISTING CRYSTAL REPORTS AS TEMPLATES

Now that you've learned the major benefits of Report Templates, apply a template to one of the reports created in Chapter 1, "Creating and Designing Basic Reports." The report (shown in Figure 14.1) as it looked was pretty plain because the focus was on making sure that the data requirements were satisfied. There wasn't a lot of time to play with formatting, so now you are going to apply a template that has some nice grayscale formatting and an underlay applied. These steps walk you through that process:

1. Open the report. Choose File, Open to get the Open dialog box, and browse until the report is found. Choose it and click Open to continue.

2. Look at the report prior to applying the template as shown in Figure 14.1. To get a good view of the application of the template, make sure that the Preview tab is selected. If the Preview tab is not selected or available, choose View, Preview.

14

Figure 14.1
The original report before applying a template

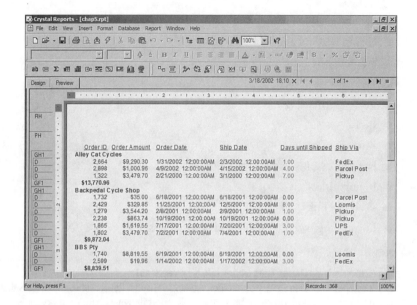

3. Apply the template. To apply some formatting quickly, choose Report, Template Expert. In the Template Expert dialog, feel free to choose each file so that you can see the associated thumbnail. For this case, choose Confidential Underlay, as shown in Figure 14.2, and then click OK.

TIP

For more information on thumbnails, review the Preview Pictures sidebar at end of this chapter.

Figure 14.2
The Template Expert with the Confidential Underlay template chosen.

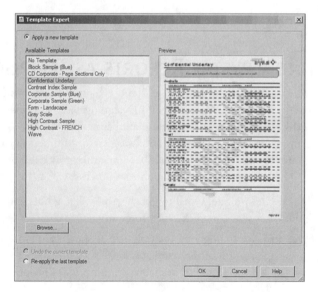

14

4. Save the report. The report will then open with the formatting from the applied template as shown in Figure 14.3. You can now save the report as **CHAP14.rpt**.

Figure 14.3
The target report with the Confidential Underlay template applied.

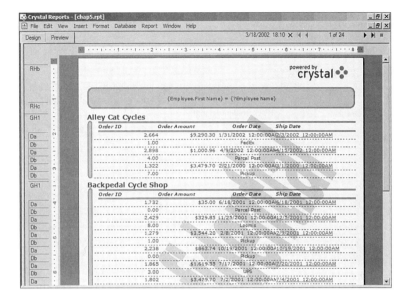

UNDERSTANDING HOW TEMPLATES WORK

A lot of report formatting tasks were accomplished in the two minutes it took to apply the template in the previous exercise, including

- Adding the Powered by Crystal logo to the report (along with its ToolTip and hyperlink) from the Crystal Repository
- Adding an image that says Confidential as an underlay to each page of the report
- Modifying the fonts and positions of all the database fields
- Showing the Record Selection Formula on the report
- Adding dashed lines between all items in the Details Section

14

- Adding a rounded box around the Record Selection Formula
- Using a rounded box to show where groups start and end
- Moving the Field Headings for each data field into the Group Header and formatting them with double lines

> **TIP**
>
> One of the more advantageous features of templates is that even if more fields are in the target report's Details section than the template has, it duplicates the data field formatting for those extra fields. It puts them into a separate Detail Section (usually titled Details B) so that they will all appear together but they won't overwrite each other. You can then move the fields around without having to worry about applying the same formatting by hand.

CREATING USEFUL REPORT TEMPLATES

If a Crystal Report already exists that has been regularly copied in the past or a report that is viewed as the *perfect report*, consider it to be the beginning of an effective template. Because any report can be the basis for a template, you might just need to refine a few functional or formatting characteristics to make the existing report more robust for use as a formal template.

If you don't have any reports to use for creating templates, you don't need to be concerned. Everything you've learned so far (and in the upcoming chapters) will help with effective template design. By creating a nice presentation-quality report, you have also created a likely candidate that can then be used as a useful report.

Keep in mind a few key things when using an existing report for a template.

As previously mentioned, templates can be used to accomplish formatting tasks at lightning pace after data collection is done. Because any report can be used as a template, a Crystal Reports designer might already have a library full of ideas.

Applying one report layout as a template to another could cause some minor issues if the databases that are connected to each report are completely different in terms of schema, structure, or content. However, with some minor adjustments, the template report can be applied more effectively.

Formulas, for instance, can be problematic when applying a report as a template to another report. Because most formulas require database fields to function, they are closely tied to the actual database and structure of the data that is coming in to the report. Because formulas are used to act on database fields, using them in templates is not very effective because errors might occur when applying a template report to another report that accesses a different database. However, some tools are available that can minimize this effect. Using custom functions instead of prewritten formulas can alleviate some of the data dependencies, as can using the CurrentFieldValue evaluator for formatting formulas.

Also, even relatively small things can make a significant difference. Sometimes just focusing on the page headers or footers can go a long way in effective report template design. By reducing the repetitive nature of general page formatting, you will increase your report design productivity.

USING CUSTOM FUNCTIONS AS REPLACEMENTS FOR DATA-DEPENDENT BUSINESS LOGIC

Because custom functions were introduced in the previous chapter, the focus of this section is how to use custom functions to avoid formula errors when applying templates. For more information on Custom Functions, see Chapter 13, "Using Formulas and Custom Functions."

The reason Custom Functions are more useful in templates than straight formulas is that they are *stateless*, which means that they have no direct dependency on the database fields to get their data. Custom Functions see the data only as parameters that are passed in to the report. Instead of searching through an entire formula to find all uses of a given field, by passing it in to a Custom Function once, Crystal Reports effectively does the search and replace repeatedly on the report designer's behalf.

Another advantage to using Custom Functions in a report template is that within the one report—the template report—it might be possible to use one Custom Function more than once because the logic might be used over and over with the only difference being the data that's used.

If a report that contains many formulas is applied as a template to a report that contains a different table name—for example, template.field and target.field—the formulas would not change over correctly. Therefore, all the formulas will result in compiler errors upon the first run of the report to the preview. Because the report designer would have to go through all the lines of business logic and replace each and every database field occurrence, it could be a very tedious process. If the search-and-replace time could be limited to one line per formula, you would be far more productive.

Of course, current formulas in a pre-existing report are already working and you would not want to break them. The task of manually changing all relevant formulas to custom functions would be a big task. However, the Formula Extractor can automate this process for you.

By using the Formula Extractor, you can actually review the existing formula, break it down, find the data-specific pieces, convert them into parameters, and reformulate the formula to accept those parameters and save it as a Custom Function. It even rebuilds the initial formula that created the Custom Function to apply the new Custom Function so that the report designer doesn't have to go back and perform that step manually.

14

TIP

> In general, to make formulas even easier to work with, use the new Formula Workshop as much as possible. This virtual all-in-one workspace for formulas means that navigation between formulas is quick and easy and you don't have to open each one up separately or guess at their names.

Even after formulas are converted, you might need to make adjustments for data-specific fields that would need to be passed in as parameters to those functions. However, because most Custom Functions reduce the lines of code, and pass in the data only once, the search-and-replace tasks are greatly reduced.

TIP

> If you are concerned about losing old formula logic when converting the formula, just comment out the old formula code and put the Custom Function in. Of course, commenting each line by hand can be cumbersome. By using the Comment/Uncomment (//) button on the toolbar, you can highlight all the contiguous lines of code you want to comment out, and then click this button. It will comment them all out in one quick step.

USING THE `CurrentFieldValue` FUNCTION

When using formulas to create conditional formatting, they are usually designed to be data dependent—so much so that the database field name is used at every opportunity. However, to make formatting formulas more portable (and reusable), use the `CurrentFieldValue` formatting function instead of the actual field name that would always change depending on where the formula is located.

`CurrentFieldValue` is a special signifier in the formula language that tells the formatting formula to look at the value of the field it is associated with, without actually having to know the name of the field. This is advantageous in two ways:

- For general formatting, this allows for copying of formatting formulas and reusing the formatting formulas within a single report or within multiple reports without having to replace data-specific field names.

- For template formatting, this is especially useful because you can't be sure that the database field is going to be of the same name, let alone of the same data type.

By keeping the reuse factor in mind when creating and maintaining formulas from now on, creating effective templates will become much easier over time.

USING TEMPLATE FIELD OBJECTS

During the process of designing a report template, you might need to provide some specific formatting for a field not based on its position in the report, but instead based on the type of field it is. For example, a company might require that all date/time fields be displayed in military time regardless of operating system defaults. For example, "6:02 p.m. on March 31, 2004" would have to look like "3/31/04 18:02". Another requirement could be a space as the thousand separator for all numbers (instead of the usual comma).

These requirements could easily be corporate or industry standard requirements, such as the ISO 9000 standard. At the time the template is created, it's unknown where these fields will be located in the report or how many of them there will be. You would have to find another way of handling special formatting requirements. Template Field Objects help in this endeavor.

When designing a report specifically as a template, Template Field Objects take the place of regular database fields in a report. They can be placed anywhere that a database field would normally be placed.

These fields are a special type of formula field that contain no data but allow formats to be applied to them as if they were of any data type. Template Field Objects have a special dialog associated with them that exposes all the Formatting tabs of the Format Editor regardless of type. This provides a one-stop shop for all of your formatting needs regardless of the data type for a given position of a field in a report.

The best way to explain this is by actually performing it, so let's implement the examples given previously in this section:

- Military Time: "6:02 p.m. on March 31, 2004" to appear as "3/31/04 18:02"
- Thousand Separator as a space: `1,000` to appear as `1 000`

Starting with a new report, follow these steps:

1. Create a new report. After opening Crystal Reports, click the New button. Then within the Crystal Reports Gallery dialog, choose As a Blank Report and click OK.

2. Skip the data source step. Because this report is going to be a template, there is no need to have a data source associated with it. Click the Cancel button in the Database Expert to close this dialog.

3. Insert a Template Field object. To insert the first Template Field object, select Template Field Object from the Insert menu. Place the resulting field into the left-most area of the Details section (see Figure 14.4).

4. Add five more template objects. Repeat the previous step five more times and place each new field to the right of the last one. Once completed, the Design tab will look like Figure 14.5.

5. Select all template objects to format. To select all template objects, hold down the Ctrl key while single-clicking on each template object in the Details section. After all six objects are selected, right-click on the last object you chose and select Format Template Fields from the pop-up menu.

14

Figure 14.4
The Design tab with the first template object added to the report.

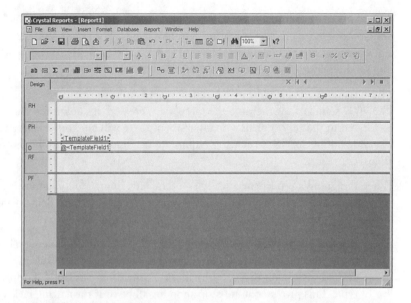

Figure 14.5
The Design tab with six template objects added to the report.

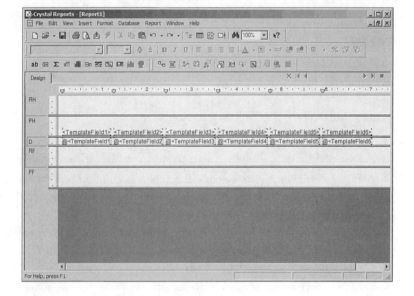

6. Format Date/Time to military time (3/31/04 18:02). After the Format Editor appears, select the Date and Time tab. Choose the third option in the Style list box that represents date/time as 3/1/99 13:23 because this is the option required, as shown in Figure 14.6.

7. Format Number with a space as the thousand separator (1 000) as shown in Figure 14.7. Now select the Number tab in the Format Editor dialog box. Because this style

does not appear in the Style list box, select Customize. In the Custom Style dialog box, change the Symbol to ,. Click OK to return to the Format Editor. Click OK again to return to the Design tab with the changes applied.

Figure 14.6
The Date and Time tab of the Format Editor with Military Date/Time selected.

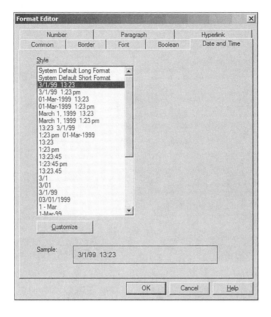

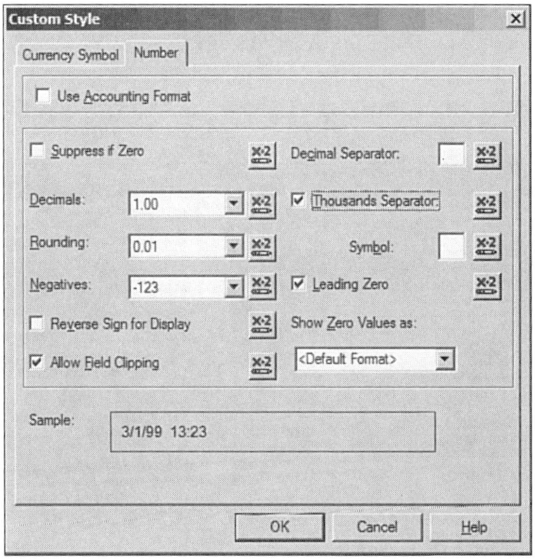

Figure 14.7
The Custom Style dialog box with the space set as the Thousand Separator symbol.

8. Give the template a name and a preview picture. When the report appears in the Template Expert, it will have a name associated with it. The name is saved as the Report Title. To change the Report Title, select File, Summary Info. Input the name

Military Time & Thousands in to the Title property field and select the Save Preview Picture check box as shown in Figure 14.8. Select OK to continue.

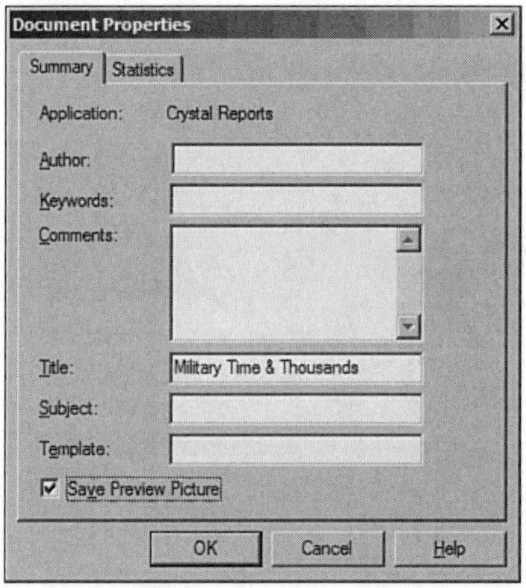

Figure 14.8
The Report Title set to describe the Template report.

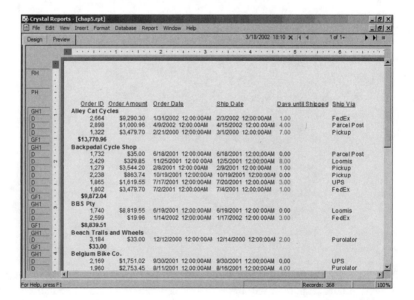

9. Save the report to the template folder. Choose File, Save As to save the report. Call the report **TemplateObjects.RPT** and place it in the Template folder. The Template folder is usually found at C:\Program Files\Crystal Decisions\Crystal Reports 10\ Templates. When it is saved, close the report.

10. Open the report from the previous example. Notice that all the date fields and numbers are in the standard format, as shown in Figure 14.9.

Figure 14.9
The Preview tab showing how the report looked when the original report was created.

11. Select the template. To select the template that was saved earlier, select Report, Template Expert. Select Military Time & Thousands from the Available Templates list, as shown in Figure 14.10.

Figure 14.10
The Template Expert dialog box with a template selected.

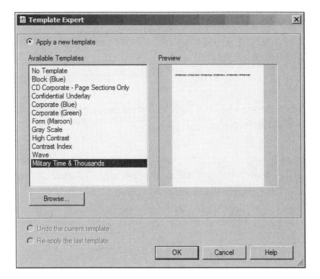

12. To apply the template, simply click the OK button. The report will appear as shown in Figure 14.11. You will notice that the report appears to close. Do not be alarmed because this is standard behavior. Crystal Reports saves a temporary file with the old look of the report and then applies the template during the new open command.

Figure 14.11
The Preview tab showing how the report looked after the template was applied.

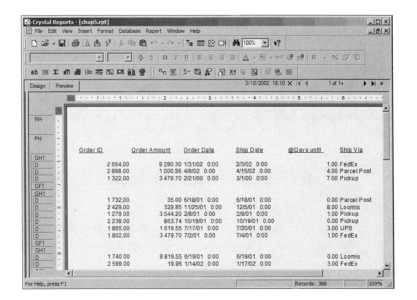

14

> Undoing a template is always an option. If for some reason you do not like the look that the applied template has given to your report, just return to the Template Expert and choose the Undo command at the bottom of the dialog box. Selecting this option and then clicking OK lets Crystal Reports revert to the original report before the template was applied.
>
> Crystal Reports accomplishes this by opening up the temporary backup .rpt that it saved before applying the template file.

13. Save the report. Choose File, Save As, call the report `templateapplied.rpt`, and click OK.

Notice that there was no need to know where the date and numeric fields were located in the report because the Template Field Objects were all formatted to handle the different requirements for the different fields. Using Template Field Objects along with the other template tips mentioned in the chapter will make report design quick and easy.

Preview Pictures

During the previous exercise, you might have noticed that the intended template did not show a preview picture on the right of the dialog window. This can be caused by one of two situations. The Save Preview Picture option in the Document Properties dialog box was not selected. If that option had been checked and the thumbnail still did not appear, it is because the template report was not saved with a Preview.

In the example that you just completed, the template report was not previewed before the report was saved.

Preview Pictures, or *thumbnails* as they are commonly called, are just that—pictures of the Preview of the report. If a report has not been previewed, it will not have the thumbnail to save.

Another key point to notice on Preview Pictures is that if changes are made in the design of the template and then a save is done, the changes will not be reflected in the thumbnail because the Preview tab was not updated with the changes.

Preview Pictures are very useful in the Template Expert because these images provide you with a visualization of what the template does to the existing report. To save them as a default with all reports, select the Save Preview Picture option in File, Options under the Reporting tab.

Preview Pictures are also important to have if the reports will be delivered through Crystal Enterprise because the Web Desktop application uses the thumbnails as a way to show reports in the front-end.

Using Report Templates to Reduce Report Creation Effort

So far this chapter has focused on new features and functions that can be used to create templates. Templates can accomplish many of the more intense designer-related tasks, including

- Conditional formatting
- Field highlighting

- Page headers and footers
- Charting standards
- Lines, boxes, and borders
- Color standards
- Logos and images
- Web sites, hyperlinks, and e-mail addresses
- Standard custom functions
- Repository objects
- Locking size or position of any object
- Special fields

APPLYING MULTIPLE TEMPLATES

Because any report could be used as a template, it is also conceivable that many reports could be applied to any single report as a template.

This can prove quite useful if the templates are doing different things. For example, one template might be applying the standard page headers and footers to all reports within a company, whereas another template could be used to apply department-based colors to the details section. Because both templates are encapsulated separately, they can be applied separately and will not affect each other. The end result is one report with both the corporate style (headers and footers) as well as the specific department's colors (in the Details section) applied.

TIP

Templates can be applied repeatedly, even if new fields are added to the report after the initial template was applied.

Simply choose Reapply Template in the Template Expert to have the template address any new fields.

CRYSTAL REPORTS IN THE REAL WORLD— STANDARDIZED TEMPLATES

Arguably the most powerful use of report templates is simply adding consistent headers and footers. As described previously, the job of placing header and footer information in exactly the right place time after time is time-consuming and boring. A very simple template can give you a head start on basic formatting.

14

To create your template, an image of the company logo will be used. For this example, the Business Objects logo (saved in JPG format) from the corporate Web site is used.

1. Begin by creating a new report without a data source, as described earlier in the chapter. Your starting point should look like Figure 14.12.

Figure 14.12
A blank canvas for the report template.

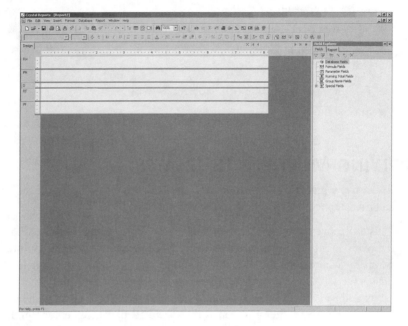

2. From the Insert menu, choose Insert, Picture. Browse for the logo.jpg file and add it to the top left of the report header. In the top right, add a text object and label it **Data as of:** and right justify the text. Add the special field Data Date to the right of the text.

3. Add the special field Report Title to the page header, center justify the text, widen the field so it reaches to both edges of the report, change the font to 14, and add some vertical height so the text fits properly.

4. In the page footer, add the special field Page N of M, centered with the field stretched to both left and right edges of the canvas. The template is now ready to be applied to all reports, effectively standardizing fundamental elements of report look and feel (see Figure 14.13).

NOTE

To maximize flexibility, ensure that objects (like the logo) used in the template make full use of the repository. Not only is it important to standardize the look and feel, it should also be easy to update.

14

Figure 14.13
A sample standard-
ized template.

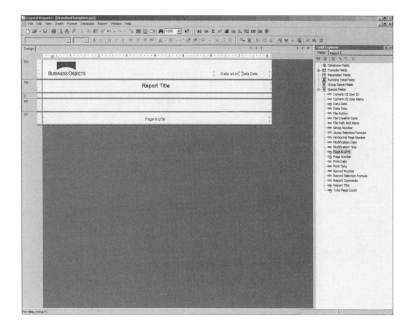

5. Save the template as **StandardTemplate.rpt**.

ADDITIONAL DATA SOURCES FOR CRYSTAL REPORTS

In this chapter

15

UNDERSTANDING THE ADDITIONAL CRYSTAL REPORTS DATA SOURCES

When thinking about data sources for Crystal Reports, most people tend to think about popular databases such as Microsoft SQL Server, Microsoft Access, Oracle, IBM DB2, and so on. However, the extent of Crystal Reports reaches far beyond these traditional relational databases. You've already learned about how Crystal Reports can use OLAP-based data sources in Chapter 16, "Multidimensional Reporting Against OLAP Data with Crystal Reports"; this chapter describes a few more advanced data sources that give you even more flexibility than you already have. The data sources discussed in this chapter are as follows:

- COM-based data sources
- Java-based data sources
- XML as a data source
- Solution kits

→ If you would like a review how Crystal Reports can use OLAP-based data sources, **see** "OLAP Concepts and OLAP Reporting," **p. 324**

CONNECTING TO COM-BASED DATA SOURCES

Crystal Reports provides *direct access*, or *native*, drivers for some databases. These drivers are written specifically for a particular database and are often the best choice. However, because hundreds of types of databases exist, Crystal Decisions can't possibly write direct access drivers for all of them. So often, users turn to using standard data access layers such as ODBC or OLEDB to connect to their databases. Often, the vendor of a database provides an ODBC driver or OLEDB provider so that other applications can access the vendor's database. Sometimes though, even this is not enough. Customers have data that they would like to report off of that is not accessible by any Crystal Reports data source driver or via ODBC or OLEDB. To accomplish this, customers often turn to the COM Data Source driver or the Java Data Source driver. This section describes the COM version of the driver, but much of the theory applies to the Java Data Source driver as well.

NOTE

The *Component Object Model*, or *COM*, is a Microsoft-based technology for software component development. It's the underlying technology that runs Visual Basic and Active Server Pages. A *COM object* is a piece of code that adheres to the COM specification and is easily used by other components, either inside a single application or between disparate applications.

Because COM is a popular technology, Crystal Decisions decided to leverage it to create an extensible data source driver mechanism. This COM Data Source driver doesn't connect to a database—rather it gets data from a COM object written by you. This means that if you are somewhat savvy in the Visual Basic world, you can write your own "mini data source driver" (called a *COM Data Provider*) that enables access to data that would otherwise be unavailable.

NOTE

> The COM and Java Data Provider scenarios are only possible with the Advanced Developer edition of Crystal Reports 10. The other versions do not include the appropriate Crystal Reports driver.

To better understand the concept on writing your own COM Data Provider, look at a few scenarios in which this can be beneficial.

LEVERAGING LEGACY MAINFRAME DATA

Although new technologies are surfacing at an alarming rate, many companies still have data held in legacy mainframe systems. Often, the nature of these systems doesn't allow for any kind of relational data access, and thus lowers the value of the system. However, these systems can often output text-based files called print files or spool files that contain the data held in the mainframe system. These text-based files are often more complicated than a set of simple comma separated values and thus require a "bridge" between the files and a data access and reporting tool like Crystal Reports. Writing a COM Data Provider can serve just this purpose. The Data Provider would read the text files, parse out the required data, and return it to Crystal Reports for use in numerous reports.

HANDLING COMPLEX QUERIES

Often, companies have a database that is accessible via standard Crystal Reports data access methods. However, the process of connecting to the database and performing a query can be quite complex. Sometimes this is because the database servers are constantly changing, queries are becoming more complex, and other business processes affect the complexity of the query. By writing a COM Data Provider, a clever person can abstract the location and complexity of the database interaction away from the user designing a report. The user simply connects to the Data Provider, and the rest of the logic is done transparently in the background.

RUNTIME MANIPULATION OF DATA

Performing a simple query against a database that returns a set of records is often all that is needed. However, sometimes logic needs to be incorporated into the query that cannot be expressed in the database query language (using SQL). Other times, per-user manipulation of data needs to be performed, such as removing all salaries stored in a database for all other users than the currently logged in user for confidentiality purposes (often called data-level security). This runtime manipulation can be performed by a COM Data Provider.

15

These three scenarios outline just a few of the reasons why you might want to use the COM Data Source driver and create your own COM Data Provider. The following sections describe the technical details of doing this.

CREATING A COM DATA PROVIDER

COM Data Providers can be written in any development language or platform with the capability of creating COM objects. Most commonly, they are created in either Visual Basic or Visual C++. The following example uses Visual Basic, but it can easily be translated to other development languages. To create a simple COM Provider, follow these steps:

1. Open Visual Basic and create a new project. Instead of choosing the standard project type of Standard EXE, choose ActiveX DLL (see Figure 15.1). ActiveX is another name for COM technology. Choosing this creates a project that contains a COM object (by default called Class1).

Figure 15.1
Creating a new Active DLL project in Visual Basic.

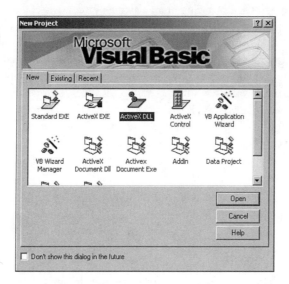

2. The interface between the COM Data Provider that you create and the Crystal Reports COM Data Source driver is based on *ActiveX Data Objects*, or *ADO*. To use ADO in your project, you must first create a reference to it. From the Project menu inside Visual Basic, select References. From the list on the ensuing dialog, look for Microsoft ActiveX Data Objects. You might have just a single version of this on your machine, or you might have several. It's usually easiest to just select the latest version. Figure 15.2 illustrates this.

3. After that is done, the only thing left to do is create a function inside your class that returns an ADO recordset. The basic outline for this function is shown here. See the next section for more information on returning an ADO recordset.

```
Public Function GetRecordset() As ADODB.Recordset
    Dim rs As New ADODB.Recordset
```

```
        ' Populate the recordset
        Set GetRecordset = rs
    End Function
```

Figure 15.2
The Visual Basic Project References dialog is shown here referencing the ADO Library.

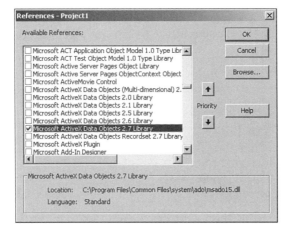

4. By default, the class is named `Class1`. It's best to give this a more meaningful name, such as `DataProvider`. Do this by selecting the Class1.cls file in the Project Explorer and changing the `(Name)` property from the Property Browser.

5. Also, the project name is Project1 by default. It's best to give this a more meaningful name such as the company name or type of data name: for example, Xtreme or Sales. Do this by selecting Project1 Properties from the Project menu and changing the Project Name setting.

6. Build the dll by selecting Make from the File menu; the name is not important.

7. Open the Crystal Reports designer and create a new report. From the data explorer, choose Create New Connection and then expand the More Data Sources item, and then choose COM Connectivity. This presents a dialog asking for you to enter the Program ID. To identify your COM Data Provider, enter the ProjectName.ClassName: for example, Xtreme.DataProvider.

8. You'll receive a table list just like from a traditional database, but the table list is actually a list of methods on your COM object that return ADO recordsets.

RETURNING AN ADO RECORDSET

There are generally two ways to obtain an ADO recordset: performing a database query and constructing it yourself. The following code example illustrates how to perform a database query and obtain a recordset—in this case using a query against the Xtreme sample database.

```
Public Function CustomerOrders() As ADODB.Recordset
    Dim rs As New ADODB.Recordset
    Dim sql as String
    sql = "SELECT * FROM Customer, Orders WHERE Customer.'Customer ID'"
```

```
    sql = sql & " = Orders.'Customer ID'", "DSN=Xtreme Sample Database 10"
    rs.Open sql
    Set CustomerOrders = rs
End Function
```

The question you might be asking yourself is how this query could be parameterized. The COM Data Source driver handles this nicely. It maps any arguments you have defined to your method into report parameters. The following code example illustrates a Data Provider function that has a parameter:

```
Public Function Customers(CountryParam As String) As ADODB.Recordset
    Dim rs As New ADODB.Recordset
    rs.Open "SELECT * FROM Customer WHERE Country = '" & CountryParam & "'", _
            "DSN=Xtreme Sample Database 10"
    Set Customers = rs
End Function
```

When a Data Provider with a parameterized method is used from the report designer, the user is prompted for a parameter value.

As was mentioned previously, one way to obtain a recordset is to perform a query. Listing 15.1 illustrates how to construct a recordset on the fly and read data out of a text file.

LISTING 15.1 A COM DATA PROVIDER THAT PARSES DATA FROM A CSV FILE

```
Public Function CSVText(FileName As String) As ADODB.Recordset
    Dim rs As New ADODB.Recordset

    ' Open the text file
    Dim FileSystem As New IWshRuntimeLibrary.FileSystemObject
    Dim fileText As IWshRuntimeLibrary.TextStream
    Set fileText = FileSystem.OpenTextFile(FileName)

    ' Read the first line of text to grab the field names
    Dim buffer As String
    buffer = fileText.ReadLine()
    Dim fields() As String
    fields = Split(buffer, ",")
    Dim i
    For i = LBound(fields) To UBound(fields)
        ' Add a field in the recordset for each field in the csv file
        rs.fields.Append fields(i), adBSTR
    Next

    rs.Open

    ' Read the contents of the file
    While Not fileText.AtEndOfStream
        buffer = fileText.ReadLine()
        rs.AddNew
        For i = LBound(fields) To UBound(fields)
            ' Grab the field values
            fields = Split(buffer, ",")
            rs(i).Value = fields(i)
        Next
        rs.Update
```

```
    Wend

    Set CSVText = rs
End Function
```

This code could be used as is or adopted to meet the needs of other kinds of files or data sources. Using the COM Data Source driver gives you complete flexibility and control over the data source.

CONNECTING TO JAVA-BASED DATA SOURCES

The COM Data Source driver is targeted at Visual Basic and Visual C++ developers. Because Crystal Reports 10 has a full Java SDK, an equivalent Java Data Source driver provides equivalent functionality of the COM driver for developers using the Java platform.

The process of creating a Java Data Source driver is conceptually similar to that of creating a COM Data Source driver. A Java class needs to be created that has a public function with a return type of `ResultSet` or `CachedRowSet`. A `ResultSet` is the standard object returned from a JDBC-based query, whereas the `CachedRowSet` is a disconnected recordset useful for parsing out things like XML. Listing 15.2 shows a simple Java Data Provider that returns a `ResultSet`.

LISTING 15.2   A JAVA DATA PROVIDER THAT RETURNS DATA FROM THE SAMPLE DATABASE

```
import java.lang.*;
import java.sql.*;

public class XtremeDataProvider
{
    public ResultSet Employee()
    {
    // connect to the database
    Class.forName("sun.jdbc.odbc.JdbcOdbcDriver");
        String url = "jdbc:odbc:Xtreme Sample Database 10";
        Connection con = DriverManager.getConnection(url, "", "");

    // run a SQL query
        Statement stmt = con.createStatement(ResultSet.TYPE_SCROLL_SENSITIVE,
ResultSet.CONCUR_READ_ONLY);
        String query = "SELECT * FROM Employee";
    ResultSet rs = stmt.executeQuery(query);

    // return the results of the query
        return rs;
    }
}
```

To identify a Java class, instead of typing in its name, place the .class file into a given directory, and add that directory's name to the following Registry key of your Windows operating system:

```
HKEY_LOCAL_MACHINE\Software\Crystal Decisions\Crystal Reports
10\DatabaseOptions\JavaUserClassPath
```

During the process of creating a report, Crystal Reports searches through all classes contained in the folder(s) specified in the Registry key discussed previously. It then provides a list of methods with return types of ResultSet. The same rules about function arguments apply. Any arguments to the Java method are mapped to report parameter fields. Using Java code, you can control exactly what data comes back.

UNDERSTANDING SOLUTION KITS FOR CRYSTAL ENTERPRISE

Beyond relational databases, Crystal Reports also has the capability to access data held inside major ERP (Enterprise Resource Planning) and CRM (Customer Relationship Management) systems. Crystal Decisions has produced solution kits for SAP, Baan, and Siebel. The Solution Kits are designed to work with large scale ERP and CRM deployments and are therefore based on Crystal Enterprise. These solution kits contain Data Source drivers for each of these systems, as well as documentation on how to create and edit reports based on these data sources. Also included are packages of prebuilt reports that can be used against your real data.

TROUBLESHOOTING

PUBLISHING WITH A COM OR JAVA PROVIDER

I've published a report using a COM (or Java) data provider to Crystal Enterprise, but I am getting errors when the report is run.

Whenever one of these types of reports is published to Crystal Enterprise, you need to make sure you copy the COM or Java component to the machines running the Page and Job servers. This component needs to be installed and registered properly before the report can invoke it.

I am receiving errors when I try to connect to the Java data provider.

Make sure that you have installed a Java Virtual Machine (JVM, also called the Java Runtime Environment). The JVM is required to connect to Java data providers.

CRYSTAL REPORTS IN THE REAL WORLD— LEVERAGING XML AS A DATA SOURCE

With the emergence of XML as a data interchange format, many customers wanted to create reports on XML documents. So in Crystal Reports 8.5, a new driver was released that allowed just this scenario. This ODBC driver reads certain types of XML documents. Version 10 of Crystal Reports provides the capability to read multiple XML files, most commonly a folder of XML files that have the same schema. When using this driver, you specify either a folder name or a file path to an XML file. Once connected, XML elements at the first level are represented as fields that you can place on a report.

If you require more flexibility around reading XML files, a good approach to take is to write a COM or Java Data Provider to read the XML. This Data Provider can use one of the many readily available XML parsers to read in the XML and choose exactly what fields to return to Crystal Reports. Listing 15.3 is a sample Visual Basic COM Data Provider that reads in a simple XML file.

LISTING 15.3   A COM DATA PROVIDER THAT READS XML DATA

```
' Loads an XML document with the following structure:
' <employees>
'   <employee>
'     <name>X</name>
'     <dept>X</dept>
'     <salary>X</salary>
'   </employee>
' </employees>
Public Function SimpleXML(fileName As String) As ADODB.Recordset
    Dim rs As New ADODB.Recordset

    Dim xmlDoc As New MSXML2.DOMDocument
    xmlDoc.Load (fileName)

    rs.fields.Append "Name", adBSTR
    rs.fields.Append "Dept", adBSTR
    rs.fields.Append "Salary", adCurrency
    rs.Open

    ' Loop through each employee element
    Dim employeeNode As MSXML2.IXMLDOMElement
    Dim childNode As MSXML2.IXMLDOMElement

    For Each employeeNode In xmlDoc.documentElement.childNodes
        rs.AddNew
        For Each childNode In employeeNode.childNodes
            rs(childNode.nodeName).Value = childNode.Text
        Next
        rs.Update
    Next

    Set SimpleXML = rs
End Function
```

CHAPTER 16

MULTIDIMENSIONAL REPORTING AGAINST OLAP DATA WITH CRYSTAL REPORTS

In this chapter

INTRODUCTION TO OLAP

Through the first 15 chapters, you have been exposed to a wide variety of the reporting capabilities found in Crystal Reports. Up to this point, however, all the reports you have created were based on relational data sources—often known as *Online Transactional Processing (OLTP)* databases—where most organizations generally keep their operational data.

In many organizations and for many people today, data reporting ends with Crystal Reports pointing at existing relational data sources such as Microsoft SQL Server, Oracle, DB2, Sybase, or even Microsoft Access. All these relational databases have been designed for the efficient storage of information. These databases were not designed optimally, however, for the efficient extraction of data for aggregated analysis across multiple dimensions—that is where OLAP databases excel.

OLAP stands for *Online Analytical Processing* and is designed to enable business users to quickly identify patterns and trends in their data while reporting against multiple dimensions at once. Examples of dimensions for analysis include time, geographic region, product line, financial measure, customer, supplier, salesperson, and so on. Crystal Reports provides powerful OLAP-based formatted reporting capabilities and these will be introduced in this chapter.

This chapter covers the following topics:

- Introduction to OLAP concepts and OLAP reporting
- Recently added OLAP features in Crystal Reports
- Creation of OLAP-based Crystal Reports

OLAP CONCEPTS AND OLAP REPORTING

OLAP is an analysis-oriented technology that enables rapid analysis of large sets of aggregated data. Instead of representing information in the common two-dimensional row and column format of traditional relational databases, OLAP databases store their aggregated data in logical structures called cubes. These OLAP cubes are created around specific business areas or problems and contain an appropriate number of dimensions to satisfy analysis in that particular area of interest or for a specific business issue. OLAP is a technology that facilitates data viewing, analysis, and navigation. More than a particular storage technology, OLAP is a conceptual model for viewing and analyzing data. Table 16.1 highlights some common business areas and typical sets of related dimensions.

TABLE 16.1   BUSINESS AREAS AND COMMONLY ASSOCIATED OLAP DIMENSIONS

Business Area	Associated Business and Common OLAP Dimensions
Sales	Sales Employees, Products, Regions, Sales Channels, Time, Customers, Measures
Finance	Company Divisions, Regions, Products, Time, Measures
Manufacturing	Suppliers, Product Parts, Plants, Products, Time, Measures

OLAP cubes pre-aggregate data at the intersection points of their associated dimension's members. A *member* is a valid field value for a dimension. (For example: Members of a time dimension could be 2000, 2001, Q1, or Q2; and members of a product dimension could be Gadget1, Gizmo2, DooDah1, and so on.) This pre-aggregation facilitates the speed-of-thought analysis associated with OLAP.

Precalculating the numbers at the intersection points of all an OLAP cube's associated dimension members enables rapid high-level analysis of large volumes of underlying data that would not be practical with traditional relational databases. Considering the example of analysis on several years of sales data by year, quarter, and month and by region, sales manager, and product, the pre-aggregated nature of OLAP facilitates quick speed-of-thought analysis on this data that otherwise would not be practical working with the phenomenal amount of data and involved calculations required on a traditional relational (OLTP) database system to provide those answers—it would simply take too long.

When a Crystal Report uses an OLAP cube as a data source, it presents the multidimensional data in a two-dimensional OLAP grid that resembles a spreadsheet or cross-tab. The focus of Crystal Reports when reporting against OLAP cubes is to present professionally formatted two-dimensional (or flat) views of the multidimensional data that will be of particular business use for report consuming end users and not necessarily analysts requiring interactivity—the more traditional OLAP end users.

The concepts of OLAP usually become more understandable after they are actually explored. To that end, later sections in this chapter step you through a Crystal Reports report creation example against an OLAP cube.

RECENTLY ADDED OR CHANGED OLAP FEATURES IN CRYSTAL REPORTS

This section is specifically targeted for users of previous versions of Crystal Reports. Table 16.2 lists the new OLAP-oriented features of versions 9 and 10 and their practical use or benefit. If you are a new user to Crystal Reports or you have not previously used the OLAP reporting features in the product, you might want to skip directly to the next section.

TABLE 16.2 NEW OLAP FEATURES IN CRYSTAL REPORTS 9 AND 10

OLAP Feature	Feature Benefit and Value
Row/Column Dimension Parameter links	Enables the direct linking of report parameters to member. Selection in the column and row dimensions of the selected cube. The feature is accessed either through the OLAP Report Creation Wizard or the OLAP Report Settings option under the Report menu.

continues

16

TABLE 16.2 CONTINUED	
OLAP Feature	**Feature Benefit and Value**
Slice/Page Dimension Parameter links	This Productivity feature enables the direct linking of report parameters to pages and slices in the OLAP grid. This enables the end user to dynamically specify the values of slices and pages in the OLAP grid. The feature is accessed in either the OLAP Report Creation Wizard or the OLAP Report Settings option under the Report menu.
Interactive OLAP Worksheet (Analyzer) in new Cube tab	The New OLAP Analyzer feature (a Cube tab in Crystal Reports Designer) is accessed by right-clicking on an existing OLAP grid object and selecting the Launch Analyzer option. The Cube tab provides a fully functioning drag-and-drop OLAP worksheet that enables rapid selection of the most appropriate OLAP viewpoint for the Crystal Report. All changes made in the Analyzer worksheet are reflected in the associated Crystal Reports OLAP grid, where advanced format ting can be applied.
Interactive drill-down of OLAP grids in Preview tab	The OLAP grid presented in the Crystal Reports Preview tab has now been made more fully functional. In addition to having access to advanced OLAP grid functionality from the right-click button including calculations, exception highlighting, sorting, filtering, and member reordering, the OLAP grid now enables the report designer to expand (drill-down) and contract members directly from within the Preview tab.
New and improved data sources	At the time of writing, Crystal Reports 10 provides OLAP access to multiple versions of Hyperion Essbase, DB2 OLAP, SQL Server Analysis Services, Holos, and SAP BW.

The following sections explore the creation of an OLAP report through the OLAP Report Creation Wizard, the added value of the OLAP Expert, and the advanced interactivity features of Crystal Reports.

USING THE OLAP REPORT CREATION WIZARD AND OLAP EXPERT

Crystal Reports provides two easy ways to create reports against OLAP data sources. As introduced in Chapter 1, "Creating and Designing Basic Reports," Crystal provides several report wizards to step you through the creation of some popular types of reports—one of those is OLAP. The OLAP Wizard involves five steps and walks you through the process of creating an OLAP grid and an optional supporting graphic based on an existing data source. The OLAP Wizard is accessible when you are creating a new report.

The second method of creating an OLAP-based report is through the OLAP Expert that is accessed from the Insert OLAP Grid on the Insert menu. This expert provides six tabs that step through the creation of an OLAP grid to be placed anywhere on a report.

The two methods of creation offer very similar degrees of functionality, and their respective dialog screens and tabs are almost identical. The OLAP Report Creation Wizard does provide a built-in Charting screen not found in the OLAP Expert, whereas the OLAP Expert provides Style Customization and Label tabs not found in the OLAP Wizard.

NOTE

> Although Crystal Reports has been designed to report off of numerous multidimensional\OLAP databases including Hyperion Essbase, Microsoft SQL Server Analysis Services, and SAP BW, for the purposes of demonstration in this chapter, examples will be based on the SQL Server sample HR cube–FoodMart. If a different OLAP Database is available, the general principles should be followed against that native OLAP cube.

SPECIFYING AN OLAP DATA SOURCE

The OLAP Data tab (or screen in the OLAP Wizard) requests the OLAP data source on which the report is to be based. This wizard and its associated dialog screens are to multidimensional data sources what the data explorer, introduced in Chapter 1, is to relational data. Figure 16.1 shows the OLAP Data screen from the OLAP Wizard.

Figure 16.1
The OLAP Data dialog from the OLAP Report Creation Wizard.

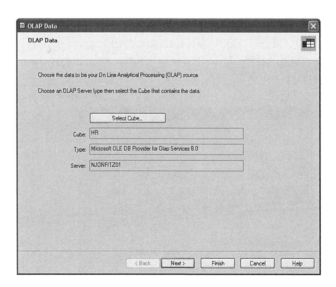

When this screen is first displayed, a cube will need to be selected with the Select Cube button. Clicking on this button opens the Crystal OLAP Connection Browser, which is displayed in Figure 16.2. From the tree control presented in this dialog, select the desired cube.

Figure 16.2
The Crystal OLAP Connection Browser enables the specification of an OLAP data source for the involved Crystal Report.

→ For detailed coverage of the Crystal OLAP Connection Browser and the functionality it provides, **see** "Accessing OLAP Data with Crystal Analysis," **p. 378**

To help you learn about the creation of an OLAP-based Crystal Report, here are the introductory steps to doing exactly that against SQL Server's sample FoodMart cube. Other steps will follow these initial steps after subsequent screens have been explained. Start the OLAP Report Creation process with the following steps:

1. Create a New Crystal Report and select the OLAP Wizard from the Crystal Reports Gallery dialog.

2. Click the Select Cube button from the OLAP Data dialog.

3. Assuming that the location of the OLAP Server has not already been identified to the Crystal OLAP Connection Browser, click the Add Server button and identify the location of your SQL Server Analysis Server and the sample HR cube. Figure 16.3 shows the New Server dialog.

Figure 16.3
The New Server dialog is used to connect to new OLAP data sources.

4. Enter a caption for the OLAP Server you are adding. This caption will appear in the Crystal OLAP Connection Browser. Enter the name of the SQL Server Analysis Server for the server name and click OK.

5. Back in the Crystal OLAP Connection Browser, navigate into the presented list of servers (there will likely only be the one you just added) and double-click on the sample HR cube.

6. Click the Next button to proceed.

NOTE

A Select CAR File button exists on the Data screen of the OLAP Report Creation Wizard, in addition to the Select Cube button. CAR files are *Crystal Analytic Reports (CAR)* and are created with the sister product to Crystal Reports–Crystal Analysis. This product is an OLAP-focused reporting and application tool and will be briefly introduced in Chapter 19, "Creating Crystal Analysis Reports," and Chapter 20, "Advanced Crystal Analysis Report Design." These CAR files can be treated as multidimensional data sources because they themselves contain connectivity information to an underlying OLAP data source.

SPECIFYING OLAP ROWS AND COLUMNS

The Rows/Columns dialog screen enables you to select both the dimensions and fields to be presented along the columns and rows of the OLAP grid. All the available dimensions in the selected cube/data source are listed in the Dimensions list box depicted in Figure 16.4.

To select a dimension for placement in the rows section or the columns section of the OLAP grid, highlight the desired dimension and click either the column or row arrow (>) button. It is possible to select multiple dimensions to be displayed and have these nested in the OLAP grid by successively selecting multiple dimensions for either the rows or the columns section. It is also possible to remove dimensions from the existing row or column list boxes; however, the column and row dimension list boxes cannot be left empty.

After the desired dimensions are selected, a subset of the fields (also known as *members*) for those dimensions can be selected using the Select Row Members or Select Column Members buttons. Examples of this might be selecting only a certain subset of provinces or states in a region dimension or, alternatively, selecting only a certain year's worth of data in a time dimension. By highlighting a dimension in either of the Rows or Columns list box and then selecting the appropriate Selection button, a subset of the members for the involved dimension can be selected from the Member Selector dialog as shown in Figure 16.5.

The last and newest feature of the Rows/Column screen is the Create/Edit Parameter functionality provided for each of the Row and Column dimensions. This capability provides the business user or report consumer with the capability to interact with the report and control its content by entering parameters that directly affect the dimension members displayed in the OLAP grid(s) on the report.

Figure 16.4
The Rows/Columns dialog of the OLAP Report Creation Wizard.

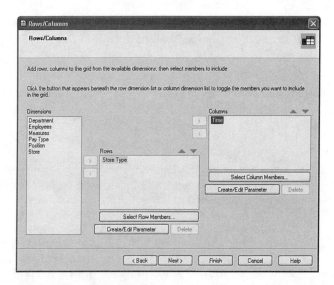

Figure 16.5
The Member Selector dialog is used to select default Column and Row Dimension members.

Because Chapter 5, "Implementing Parameters for Dynamic Reporting," covered parameters in detail, you are likely familiar with this topic already. Of significance for this wizard screen is that the parameter creation process is directly accessible here, and this facilitates the rapid development of formatted and interactive OLAP reports. If necessary, review Chapter 5 for a refresher on creating and editing parameters.

TIP

> The Member Selector dialog provides some powerful shortcuts for the selection of certain logical groups of members. These selection shortcuts are accessed through either the Select drop-down box or by right-clicking on any part of the Member Selection list box. Sample selection shortcuts include the capability to select all base level members or all members at a highlighted level.

Continuing with the creation of the sample report started in the last section, the following steps walk through the Rows/Columns screen part of this report creation example and allow for the refinement of the data to be viewed in the OLAP grid. Follow these steps to add rows and columns to your OLAP-based report:

1. Select the Store Type Dimension from the available dimensions list as the Row Dimension using the Row Dimension arrow button. (Note: It will likely be necessary to remove a default dimension to ensure that this is the only dimension in the Row Dimensions list view.)

2. Using the Select Row Field's button, select all the Store Types (for example, Supermarket, Headquarters, and so on) from the Member Selection dialog, but deselect the aggregated top level All Stores field. This enables the OLAP grid to present all the different store types down the side of the grid as rows.

3. Select the Time Dimension from the available dimensions list as the Column Dimension using the Column Dimension arrow (>) button. (Note: It will likely be necessary to remove a default dimension to ensure that this is the only dimension in the Column Dimensions list view.)

4. Using the Select Column Field's button, select the years 1997 and 1998 from the Member Selection dialog, but ensure that no children members have been selected. This enables the OLAP grid to present a comparison of the two years of data in two side-by-side columns.

5. Click the Next button to proceed.

At this point, you will review the concept of OLAP dimension filters and pages in your OLAP report.

SPECIFYING OLAP DIMENSION SLICES (FILTERS) AND PAGES

The Slice/Page dialog of the OLAP Report Creation Wizard, shown in Figure 16.6, enables you to select values or members for the dimensions that were not selected to be row or column dimensions. In the OLAP world, these dimensions are often called *paged or sliced dimensions*.

The Slice list box lists all the paged dimensions and their current member settings. The default setting is usually all members for any given dimension. An example is that for the Store Dimension, the default slice setting is All Stores. To change the member selection (slice) for a particular dimension, that dimension must be selected in the Slice list box and the Select Slice button must be used to open the familiar Member Selection dialog (refer to Figure 16.5). This dialog is identical to the Member Selection dialog used previously except that only one member from the selected dimension can be selected. If multiple members from a slice dimension are required in a report, the Page list box should be used and separate pages/grids will be created for each value selected.

The Page list box is initially empty but can contain any dimensions outside the row and column dimensions that require multiple member selection. An example could involve selecting the three countries of North America as store regions. The selection of multiple values for a

16

paged dimension creates completely separate grids (based on the same preselected rows and columns) for each selected member value. To select multiple members for a dimension, the involved dimension needs to be selected in the Slice list box and moved to the Page list box using the transfer arrow buttons between the list boxes. Once moved to the Page list box, the Select Page Values button enables multiple member selection through the Member Selection dialog.

Figure 16.6
The Slice/Page screen of the OLAP Report Creation Wizard allows manipulation of the dimensions not selected for use on either the rows or columns.

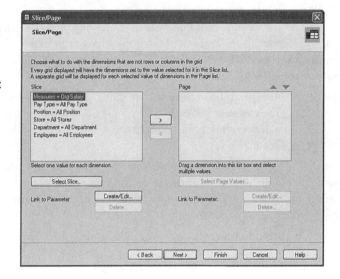

The last, but perhaps most powerful, feature of the Slice/Page screen is the Link to Parameter functionality provided for each of the Filtered and Paged dimensions. This capability provides the business user or report consumer with the capability to interact with the report and control its content by entering parameters that directly affect the information displayed in the OLAP grid(s) on the report.

Of significance for this wizard screen is that the parameter creation process is directly accessible here, and this facilitates the rapid development of formatted and interactive OLAP reports.

→ For more information on creating and editing parameters, **see** "Creating and Implementing Parameters Fields," **p. 129**

Continuing with the creation of the sample report, the following steps walk through the Slice/Page dialog part of this report creation example and will enable you to select the measure that will be displayed in the OLAP grid. Follow these steps to select measures on the page/slice dimensions:

1. Select the Measures dimension from the Filter list box.
2. Instead of selecting a specific filter using the Select Filter Value button, click the Link to Parameter Create/Edit button to enable the business user to dynamically select this

slice every time the report is run. The Create Parameter Field dialog, shown in Figure 16.7, appears.

Figure 16.7
The Create Parameter Field dialog called from the Slice/Page screen.

3. In the Prompting Text text box, enter the text that you want your user to be prompted with when this report is run. In this case, it could be something similar to `Please select the Measure to be used in your report`. Also, ensure that the Discrete Value(s) radio button is selected because a range of entries is not required (or allowed) here.

4. To avoid requiring users to type in any text, defaults can be set so that selection from a drop-down box is possible. To do this, click the Select Default button and the dialog in Figure 16.8 appears.

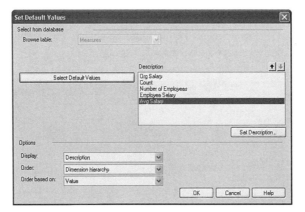

Figure 16.8
The Set Default Values dialog for the OLAP Slice Parameter.

5. The Measures table is preselected because the report respects the association with the previously highlighted dimension. Move all the available member values for the Measures dimension to the Description list box by clicking on the Select Default Values button and selecting all the members through the familiar Member Selector dialog.

16

6. Ensure that the Display drop-down box has Description selected and that the Order drop-down box has no sort selected. Click OK twice to get back to the Slice/Page dialog of the OLAP Report Creation Wizard.

7. Once you return to the Slice/Page dialog, highlight the Pay Type dimension in the Slice list box and click the arrow transfer/select button to move this to the Page list box. The Member Selection dialog will immediately appear with the Pay Type Dimension Hierarchy presented.

8. Select the Hourly and Monthly pay types (children of All Pay Types) and deselect the All Pay Types field. Individual OLAP grids are now created for each of the monthly paid employees and the hourly paid employees. If this isn't clear now, it should make more sense when you are visualizing the report.

9. Click OK and then Next to proceed.

CAUTION

> After Parameters or Multi-Value Paged Dimensions have been set in the OLAP Report Creation Wizard, you can only access them for editing through the OLAP Design Wizard under the main Report menu. These settings are not configurable in the OLAP Expert.

ADDING REPORT STYLES IN THE OLAP REPORT WIZARD

The Style dialog in the OLAP Report Creation Wizard enables you to select any one of a predetermined number of styles for OLAP grids available in Crystal Reports. Figure 16.9 displays the Style dialog. The styles are often considered a good starting point for formatting the OLAP grids on your reports and can be enhanced through both the Customize Style tab of the OLAP Expert (described later in the chapter) and using many of the advanced formatting features you have already learned about.

Figure 16.9
The Style dialog of the OLAP Report Creation Wizard.

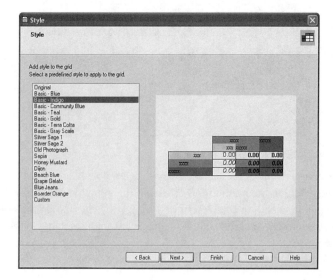

ADDING CHARTS VIA THE OLAP REPORT WIZARD

The Chart dialog provided in the OLAP Report Creation Wizard enables you to add graphics quickly to the OLAP report being created. The graphics available in this wizard, shown in Figure 16.10, are only a subset of the graphics available in Crystal Reports (refer to Chapter 8, "Visualizing Your Data with Charts and Maps," for a refresher), but they do enable the rapid visualization of your OLAP data without the need for using the Chart Expert.

Figure 16.10
The Chart dialog of OLAP Report Creation Wizard enables you to select between different basic chart types.

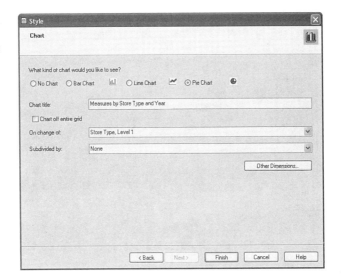

Aside from selecting the type of chart (bar, line, or pie) and specifying a title on this screen, an On Change Of field must be specified with an optional Subdivided By field before this screen is complete. As Chapter 8 discussed, the On Change Of field is the field in your data source that provides the breaking point for the involved graphic. Examples could include country, region, year, store, product, and so on. The Subdivided By field can provide a second variable to base your charts on. An example of a two-variable OLAP Chart using the FoodMart sample cube would be a chart showing salary information by year and then subdivided by store type. Using pie charts, Figure 16.11 shows what that might look like.

Now, to complete the OLAP report creation process, the following steps will take you through the addition of a style, a chart, and the creation of the finished report:

1. On the Style dialog, select any style that suits your preference and click the Next button.

2. On the Chart dialog, select Pie Chart as the Chart Type by selecting the radio button associated with that chart type. This provides a nice way of visualizing comparables across different store types.

3. Provide your chart with a title similar to **Measures by Store Type and Year** by entering this into the Chart Title text box.

4. Select Store Type as the On Change Of field. This facilitates the comparison of the six different store types. Leave the Subdivided By drop-down field empty.

5. Click Finish on the OLAP Report Creation Wizard. You will be prompted to select a parameter for the Measure dimension. After selecting Average Salary (or another field if you prefer), a report is generated that looks similar to Figure 16.12.

Figure 16.11
A two-variable OLAP Chart showing Avg Salary based on Year and subdivided by Store Type.

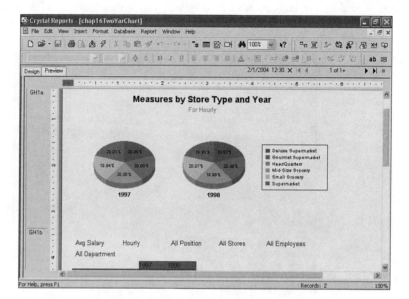

Figure 16.12
The sample OLAP report created using the OLAP Wizard.

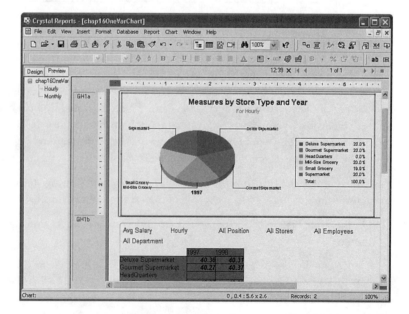

The OLAP Report Creation Wizard provides an efficient and effective method to getting value out of OLAP data in a short timeframe. After an OLAP grid or OLAP chart has been placed on your report through the wizard, further formatting and analysis can be performed through a variety of built-in Crystal Reports formatting tools. The next two sections explore further customization options and the three subsequent sections discuss the powerful new interactivity available in Crystal Reports OLAP objects.

CUSTOMIZING STYLES IN THE OLAP EXPERT

After an OLAP grid has been added to a report, with or without a selected style, Crystal Reports provides the capability to enhance and customize the formatting of that grid through the Customize Style tab accessed on the OLAP Expert. The OLAP Expert dialog is displayed in Figure 16.13 and is accessed by right-clicking on an existing OLAP grid object and accessing the OLAP Grid Expert, or by selecting the Insert OLAP Grid option from the Insert menu.

Figure 16.13
The OLAP Expert dialog provides the capability to edit many of the OLAP Grid display properties including the customization of styles.

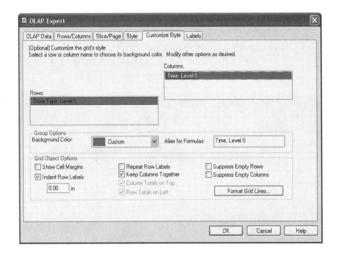

Four of the tabs in the OLAP Expert have identical functionality as presented in the previous Report Wizard sections. The Customize Style tab shown in Figure 16.13 is unique to the OLAP Expert and provides the capability to fine-tune the formatting of the row and column dimensions selected for the involved OLAP grid. By selecting any of the column or row dimensions from the presented list boxes, custom colors can be selected for the backgrounds of the OLAP grid row and column headings. This tab also provides a number of formatting options for the presentation of the grid including indentation, blank column/row suppression, margins, and labels. Also provided is an option to format grid lines, shown in Figure 16.14. This dialog enables granular level formatting and selection of grid lines for display on the OLAP grid's layout.

Figure 16.14
The Format Grid Lines dialog is accessed from the Customize Style Tab of the OLAP Expert dialog and enables granular level control of the OLAP grid's grid lines.

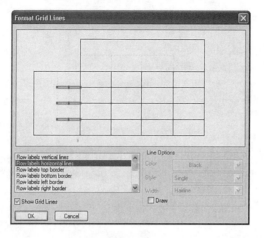

CUSTOMIZING LABELS IN THE OLAP EXPERT

The Labels tab of the OLAP expert, shown in Figure 16.15, provides the capability to customize the display of the paged-dimension (non row/column dimensions) labels on the OLAP grid.

Figure 16.15
The Labels tab of OLAP Expert enables you to specify display properties around the OLAP grid's dimensions.

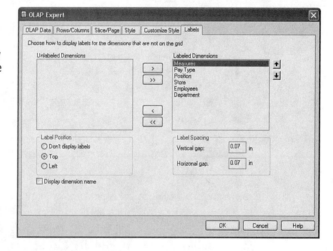

Paged/Sliced Dimension member values for the display grid can be displayed or hidden by simply moving the selected dimension between the unlabeled dimension and labeled dimension list boxes using the transfer arrow (>, >>, <, <<) buttons. Additional labeling options—such as label location, label spacing, and dimension names—can also be selected in this tab.

ADVANCED OLAP REPORTING

Up to this point, the OLAP Expert and OLAP Report Creation Wizard have demonstrated the capability of Crystal Reports to rapidly create OLAP-based reports. More than these capabilities, Crystal Decisions provides advanced analytic capabilities against OLAP data sources through some advanced OLAP-oriented features in Crystal Reports and through a sister product called Crystal Analysis. The last four sections of this chapter introduce some of these advanced features for Crystal Reports; Crystal Analysis is introduced in Chapters 19 and 20.

INTERACTING WITH THE OLAP GRID

Crystal Reports provides some powerful interactive OLAP features from directly within the Crystal Reports Preview and Design tabs. Figure 16.16 displays the right-click menu that appears when right-clicking on the year 1998 member in this chapter's sample report.

Figure 16.16
Advanced OLAP features are provided in the right-click menu.

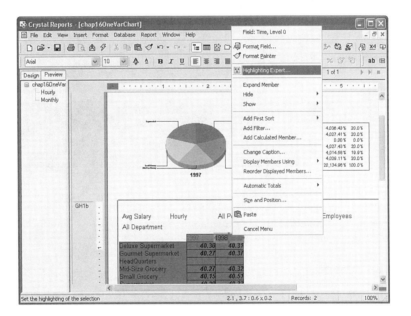

Advanced features made available here include conditional member highlighting, hiding and showing members for asymmetrical reporting, adding calculations, adding filters, reordering members, changing the member caption, expanding members (that is, drilling into the children members), adding sorts, and adding automatic totals to the OLAP grid. Although exploring these features in detail is beyond the scope of this chapter, it is important to note their availability for enhancing your OLAP grid presentations and reports. For detailed information on all these functions, review Chapters 19 and 20 where the same functionality for Crystal Analysis is presented.

One feature of note for now is the active nature of the column and row dimensions in the OLAP grid. By double-clicking on any member in either the row or column headings—and assuming that the selected member has lower level members (children)—the OLAP grid dynamically expands to include that member's children in the grid. In OLAP parlance, this is called *drilling-down*. Figure 16.17 shows the result of drilling-down on the 1998 Header in this chapter's sample report.

Figure 16.17
Sample OLAP-based report with 1998 member's children expanded.

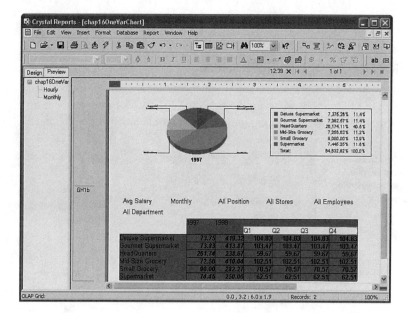

A dimension member can subsequently have its children contracted by double-clicking on the parent member. This feature enables you to interactively determine the best static viewpoint to provide to the business user audience for the report.

PIVOTING OLAP GRID

After an OLAP grid has been added to a report, as in this chapter's sample, Crystal Reports provides the capability to easily swap the grid's columns and rows. In OLAP parlance, this is referred to as *pivoting* the OLAP grid. Figure 16.18 highlights this chapter's sample report after being pivoted with this function. To access this function, right-click on the OLAP grid and select the Pivot OLAP Grid option. Pivoting the OLAP grid does not affect any OLAP charts or maps already on the report.

This function is particularly useful when attempting to decide which viewpoint of the involved OLAP grid will be most useful to the business users of the report.

USING THE CUBE VIEW FUNCTIONALITY

The Cube View (previously called the OLAP Analyzer) is a powerful worksheet analysis tool first introduced in version 9 of Crystal Reports. The Cube View is initiated through the View Cube option on the right-click menu of the OLAP grid (make sure that you don't have any specific grid objects selected) and is accessed through a new tab, titled Cube View, in the Crystal Reports Designer (see Figure 16.19). Report designers and analysts familiar with other OLAP interface tools will be instantly comfortable with the Analyzer because it provides access to the OLAP cube through a traditional OLAP worksheet.

Figure 16.18
A preview of the sample report after pivoting the OLAP grid. Notice how the chart has changed.

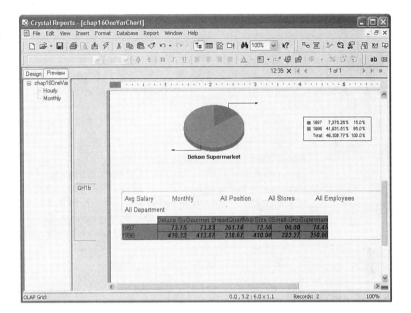

Figure 16.19
The Cube View tab launched by the OLAP Analyzer provides a powerful analytic tool for report designers and power users.

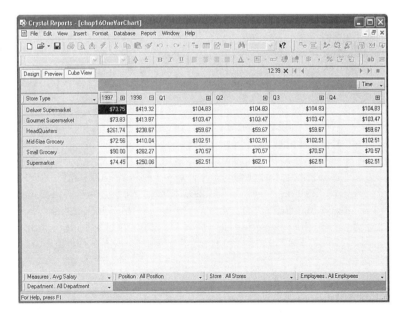

16

Unlike the OLAP grid presented in the Crystal Reports Preview tab, the Cube View tab's worksheet is designed for rapid analysis of the underlying OLAP data through a rich and interactive interface not available in the OLAP grid. Dimensions can be rapidly shifted, swapped, and nested by double-clicking on them and dragging them into any of the row, column, or paged dimension areas. Dimension members can be quickly expanded and contracted by clicking on their associated + or – icons. Additional calculations, sorts, filters, automatic totaling, exception highlighting, and custom captions can also be accessed through a right-click menu in the OLAP Analyzer view of the cube.

The Cube View is a powerful new report design tool because it lets Crystal Reports developers create some very powerful flat views of the underlying multidimensional/OLAP data in a very short timeframe and subsequently format the created OLAP grid in the Preview tab.

CAUTION

> Although both the Cube View tab and the In-Place OLAP Grids within the Crystal Reports Designer offer much of the same functionality, not all the work handled in the Cube View is necessarily translated back into the related OLAP grid on Crystal Reports. Exception Highlighting and Field Formatting are two good examples of functionality that does not cross over. It is generally recommended that the majority of formatting work be done in-place within the Crystal Report's Design or Preview tabs and that cube and dimension orientation be the primary focus of the Cube View tab.

USING CHARTS AND MAPS BASED ON OLAP GRIDS

As described in Chapter 8 and discussed briefly in the "Adding Charts via the OLAP Report Wizard" section earlier in this chapter, OLAP grid data can be presented through visually appealing charts and maps. To create either a chart or a map based on OLAP data, an OLAP grid must pre-exist on your report as a data source for the chart/map to be based on. Selecting the Insert Chart or Map command from the Insert menu (or the respective icons on the Insert toolbar) enables the creation of an OLAP-based visualization.

The creation process for both charts and maps requires the specification of an On Change Of field. This is the field that the chart or map will break its summaries on (for example, country, state, product, sales rep, and so on). An additional optional Sub-divided On field can be specified as well. The results of specifying an extra variable to divide the data on will have different results for various chart types. Explore these different charts to find those most suitable for your business problem. Using the Sub-divided On field with a map adds either a bar or pie chart to every main region on the selected map. An example of this might be a pie chart depicting the breakdown of sales for each country.

CAUTION

> It is imperative that the On Change Of field be a geographic-based field when creating a map. Otherwise, the mapping component returns an empty map.

INTRODUCTION TO CRYSTAL ANALYSIS

Crystal Analysis Professional is a new reporting tool from Crystal Decisions that enables organizations to deliver action-based OLAP analysis to business users. It enables better insights to help decision makers affect business performance through interactive analysis. Crystal Analysis Professional takes OLAP reporting to the next level by enabling you to create intuitive and highly interactive reports that offer a guided analysis approach to business issues.

Power users implementing Crystal Analysis can create analytic reports, based on OLAP data, using a powerful designer (similar in concept to Crystal Reports). Crystal Analytic Reports can contain many pages, each presenting a different predefined view of the OLAP cube. Data can be presented in tables or visualized through a wide range of charts, exception highlights, data sorts, filters, and analytic transition buttons. Business managers can use the resulting analytical reports to drive the business decisions they need to make every day. Figure 16.20 displays a sample analytic report created in Crystal Analysis Professional. These reports, in the same manner as Crystal Reports files, can be published to, secured, managed, and distributed by the Crystal Enterprise solution—also available from Crystal Decisions.

Figure 16.20
A Sample Crystal Analysis report that includes an OLAP grid, chart objects, and several transition buttons for guided analysis.

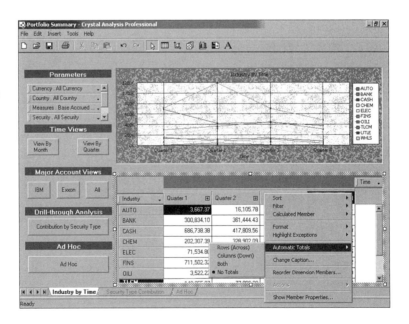

Details of Crystal Analysis are beyond the scope of this chapter but are covered in detail in Chapters 19 and 20.

CRYSTAL REPORTS IN THE REAL WORLD— OLAP SUMMARY REPORT WITH DRILL-DOWN

The scenario discussed here describes the flexibility behind accessing multidimensional and relational data sources in one report. The benefit of this type of functionality is to enable the user to see aggregated information coming from a cube while allowing drill-down on the relational data to provide greater detail. By using parameters in this report you let the user decide which information elements are displayed.

1. Start by creating a simple sales report against the sample Xtreme data source. For the data, select the Customer table. Group the Report by Region, City, and then Customer. Hide the City and Customer groups and enable drill-down on these sections. The report at design time should look like Figure 16.21.

Figure 16.21
Framework for drill-down.

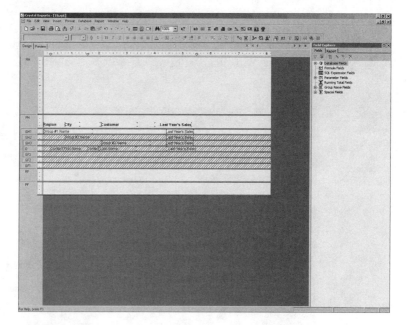

2. Now add an OLAP grid to this report that will go against an offline cube file. Using the steps described earlier in this chapter, point the grid at the xtreme.hdc file located in C:\Program Files\Crystal Decisions\Crystal Reports 10\Samples\En\ Databases\Olap Data. Keep the defaults assigned by the grid expert except in the Rows/Columns tab; here, you will change the Customer Rows to only include AZ, CA, and MA to limit the number of rows displaying in the report. Perform the same task in the report select expert so that both data sources return the same information.

3. Drop the OLAP Grid in the Report Header area. Now split the Report Header area into A and B sections using the Insert Section Below right-click menu function from

the Report Header Title area. The OLAP Grid remains in Report Header A. Insert a pie chart based on the relational source that displays Last Year's Sales on change of values in the Region and City fields and place the chart in Report Header B to enable the user to also visually understand what the contribution of sales is from each of the selected regions. The report in design view should look similar to Figure 16.22.

Figure 16.22
A Report using both OLAP and Relational data sources. The pie chart based on the Relational Data enables drill-down into the relational data details.

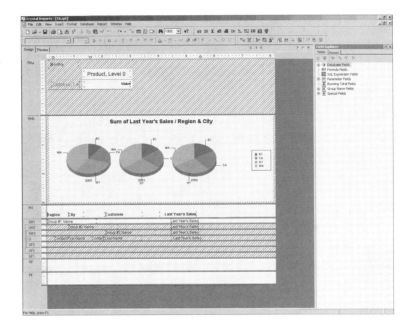

16

4. If the user viewed this report he would currently see both the chart and the OLAP grid at the top of the report. Create two parameter fields, which will specify whether to display the grid or chart or both. This enables the users to decide how they want to look at information in the report.

5. Create a parameter of Boolean type called Display Grid and a parameter of the same type called Display Chart.

6. Next conditionally suppress sections containing the grid and the chart based on the values supplied to the parameters. To do this, right-click on Report Header A and select Section Expert from the Report Explorer. Make sure Suppress is checked and then click next to the suppress option on the formula sign. Inside the formula editor type in

    `{?Display Grid}=false`

and close the editor. Highlight Report Header B and repeat this step using the parameter you created before called Display Chart. Now if the user runs the report he will be prompted to select whether he wants to see the chart, the grid, or both. Save the report as chap16OLAPLinkedToDetail.rpt. On Display, it should look similar to Figure 16.23.

Figure 16.23
Report showing both
the OLAP grid and
charts.

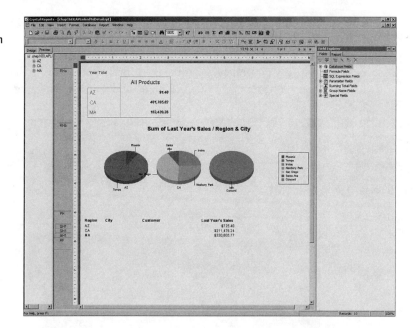

This example illustrates combining relational and multidimensional data in one report to allow for different views based on the same underlying data. This allows drill-down on relational elements and provides aggregate information for views on summary OLAP data.

ENTERPRISE REPORT DESIGN— ANALYTIC, WEB-BASED, AND EXCEL REPORT DESIGN

CHAPTER 17

INTRODUCTION TO CRYSTAL REPOSITORY

In this chapter

WHAT IS THE CRYSTAL REPOSITORY?

The Crystal Repository is a database of commonly used components that report developers can share between Crystal Reports. These components include:

- Text objects: Reusable text, such as company addresses or confidentiality text.
- Images: Bitmaps, metafiles, Tiff, JPEG, and PNG image formats.
- Custom functions: Business logic that could be reused by passing in new fields as variables.
- SQL Commands: Encapsulated SQL Commands that enable you to write free-form SQL for data access, including parameters. The results are seen as a table by Crystal Reports.
- Business Views: New functionality that allows for the complexity of the datasource(s) to be abstracted, allowing for more productive report development. This is explained in more detail further in the chapter.

This repository was separated in the Crystal Decisions version 9 product suite into a repository for Crystal Reports 9 and an Enterprise object repository attached to the Automated Process Scheduler or APS. In Crystal Enterprise version 10 these two repositories are merged and are simply known as the Crystal Repository, which is attached to the CMS.

→ For more information on the Crystal Enterprise architecture, **see** "Crystal Enterprise Architecture Overview," **p. 506**

The Crystal Repository not only stores all the information regarding Crystal Enterprise, such as users, folders, events, and user group information, but now includes the Crystal Report components listed previously. For performance reasons, the report objects themselves are not stored in the Crystal Repository but rather in the File Repository.

WHY IMPLEMENT THE CRYSTAL REPOSITORY?

Imagine the real-life situation where an organization has thousands of Crystal reports, some of which have a copyright notice on the bottom of each page. The legal department decides it wants to change the verbiage on this copyright notice. The administrator faces three problems: which reports have this notice, how to make this change in a timely fashion, and how to effectively make these types of changes in the future.

Without the repository the administrator would have the unfortunate task of checking each individual desktop and any shared drives to locate the reports. Each report would have to be checked for the copyright notice and the change made.

This is the exact problem that the Crystal Repository will resolve. The report developers would publish the report to Crystal Enterprise, which would control where the reports are stored and provide security as to who can see which reports. The publishing process is explained in Chapter 23, "Using Crystal Enterprise with Web Desktop." The administrator could then create, using the Crystal Report Designer, a Text object with the correct copyright notice. This object is saved in the Crystal Repository. These managed reports could then be opened in Crystal Reports and the old copyright notice replaced by the newer one.

Should the organization want to make changes at a later date to the notice or any other shared objects, there are utilities that the administrator would run that would cycle through the reports and update all reports with the new object. For instance, the Publishing Wizard provides the facility of updating repository objects, as does the Crystal Management Console.

INSTALLING THE CRYSTAL REPOSITORY

The Crystal Repository is installed by default and is included in the CMS database that is required to run Crystal Enterprise. This database includes all information regarding the users, groups, managed objects such as Crystal Reports, various Crystal Servers, and also all the Crystal Repository information such as text, bitmap, functions, SQL Commands, and Business Views. To install the Crystal Repository samples, the user needs to open the Business View Manager and from the Tools menu, run the Install Repository Samples option, shown in Figure 17.1.

17

Figure 17.1
From the Business View Manager, the user can install both sample Business Views and sample repository objects.

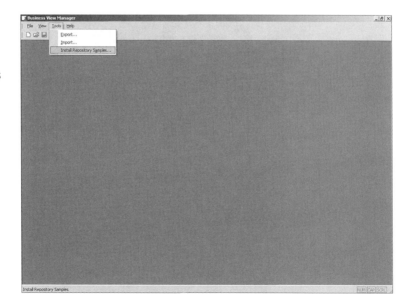

CAUTION

One component that was not included in the Crystal Repository is report templates. Although it is possible to secure the template via Crystal Enterprise security, it is not possible to automatically loop through all the reports that reapply a new template. This task is possible but it is a manual process or requires that an administrative script be written. For more information on writing these scripts, refer to Chapter 36, "Creating Enterprise Reporting Applications with Crystal Enterprise Part II."

ADDING OBJECTS TO AND FROM THE REPOSITORY

Different object types have different methods required to add the object to or from the repository.

ADDING TEXT OBJECTS AND IMAGES

To add text and image objects from the repository, the repository explorer should be open in Crystal Reports. To open the repository explorer, you need to authenticate with Crystal Enterprise. After this occurs, you can see all the folders and objects available in the repository. To add a text or image field, simply drag the field onto the report. You will notice that the object is read-only. To modify the object, right-click the object and select Disconnect from Repository (see Figure 17.2). You will then be able to modify the object. If the changed object is saved back into the repository with the same name, the original version will be replaced and all Crystal Reports that use this object can be updated.

17

Figure 17.2
To modify the object, the user needs to disconnect the object first.

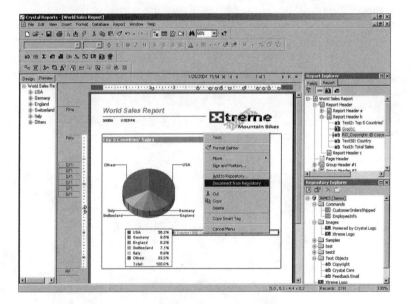

To modify the object, you need to disconnect the object first. If the changed object is saved back into the repository with the same name, all objects that use this object can be updated.

To reconnect a text object or image to the repository, simply drag and drop the object from the Design or Preview tab on Crystal Reports back to its original repository object name in the Repository Explorer. A dialog will appear to confirm that you want to update the original object or add a new one. The user can then set the properties of the object by adding the required information.

→ For information on how to set the security around the object explorer, **see** "Business View Manager,"
p. 364

CAUTION

> The capability to store objects from Crystal Analysis reports in the repository was not supported at publication time.

SQL COMMANDS

With the introduction of SQL Command objects to Crystal Reports, developers have been able to write custom database SQL to access data. The repository enables the developers to share these objects with others who might not have that skill set or those developers who do not want to reinvent the wheel.

To select a SQL Command from the repository, select the Repository from the Data Explorer or the Data step of the Report Wizard. Once again, Crystal Enterprise will ask you to authenticate to ensure you are a valid user. Select the required SQL Command from the repository (see Figure 17.3). If the command has any parameters associated with it you will be required to populate the parameters. This enables the SQL statement to run and populate the report with data, to give the report designer some data to work with.

17

Figure 17.3
The command objects as displayed by the Data step of the Report Wizard.

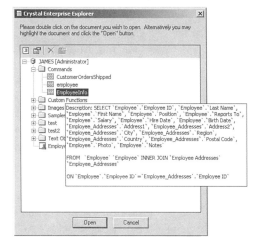

TIP

> If you hover your mouse pointer over the SQL Command, it will display the SQL statement, enabling you to review the statement before selection.

To add a new SQL Command object to the repository, use the Data Connection, and then connect to the database desired in the Available Data Sources list box and choose Add Command from the list of available options. Select Add Command by double-clicking on it. This opens the Add Command to Report dialog. Then follow these steps:

1. Enter the SQL statement you want into the query box. If parameters are required, you can use this dialog to create them as well.

2. Before leaving this dialog, right-click the newly created SQL objects.

NOTE

> For more in-depth information on Structured Query Language, see the supplemental material at the end of this book.

CUSTOM FUNCTIONS

Custom functions are reusable procedures that enable you to share logic across reports (see Figure 17.4). To allow for this sharing, the function needs to be data- and report-independent and specific guidelines must be adhered to:

- No User Function Libraries (UFL) can be used because these are machine dependent.
- No report or data source fields.
- You cannot associate a particular state with the function, such as Evaluation Time or Print State.
- You cannot use recursion, that is, the function cannot call itself.
- You cannot use variables, either shared or global, because these are report-specific.

CAUTION

> Custom functions are not editable from the Repository Explorer because they are housed inside of Formulas. To view custom functions available in the Repository, go to Report, Formula Workshop. In the group tree, the Crystal Repository branch can be seen and all custom functions can be viewed from there.

Adding a new custom function to the repository needs to be done from within the Crystal Reports designer. The user can select the drop-down list from the new icon in the Formula Workshop. The function is then created and the user can select the Add to Repository icon, which adds the function to the desired location in the repository.

ORGANIZING THE REPOSITORY

The Repository Explorer represents the repository database as a tree structure made up of folders and objects. It is up to the report designer how he wants to organize it. For example, the sample Crystal Repository that ships with Crystal Enterprise 10 is sorted by object types. The folders are named to indicate their contents (Images, Text Objects, and Commands). However, the content creator or report designer can use folders to his organizational advantage.

To add new folders to the repository, right-click on the desired folder where the intended subfolder is to be placed. If the folder is intended to be at the root, right-click on the repository name. Choose New Folder from the context menu.

Figure 17.4
A custom function in the repository displayed in the Formula Workshop; the summary shows a brief description of the custom function, return types, and function arguments.

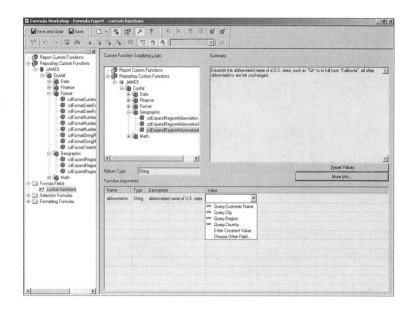

17

To move objects or folders, drag and drop the object to the desired location. To rename a folder, simply choose the folder to be renamed, right-click on it, and choose Rename from the context menu.

MIGRATION OF THE CRYSTAL ENTERPRISE REPOSITORY

There are numerous circumstances whereby an administrator might want to migrate the Crystal Repository, for example, during an upgrade, moving from different instances of Crystal Enterprise, or the possible merging of two repositories.

MIGRATION FROM EARLIER VERSIONS OF CRYSTAL ENTERPRISE AND SEAGATE INFO

Prior to version 9, no Report Object repository existed. The Crystal Import Wizard migrates the Crystal Enterprise repository from versions 10.x and below (see Figure 17.5). The Import Wizard is a Windows-based utility that enables users to import users, groups, report objects and instances, associated permissions, events, and server groups.

NOTE

Although the utility is Windows-based, it can be used to connect to Crystal Enterprise systems hosted on Unix.

CAUTION

With any migration of data, you should perform any necessary backups. Contact Business Objects technical support for assistance.

Figure 17.5
The Crystal Import Wizard showing the versions from which the user can import objects.

MIGRATIONS FROM CRYSTAL ENTERPRISE 9

In version 9 of Crystal Enterprise and Crystal Reports, the repository was split into two databases. This consisted of the Crystal Reports repository that stored the text, bitmaps, SQL Command objects, and custom functions and the Crystal Enterprise 9 repository that consisted of objects such as the users, folders, and so on.

To migrate the Crystal Enterprise 9 repository, the Migration Wizard would be used as described previously in this chapter.

To migrate a Crystal Reports 9 repository to Crystal Enterprise 10, use the Crystal Repository Migration Wizard (see Figure 17.6). This Windows-based utility is found on the Crystal Enterprise CD and can be installed on the local Administrators workstation. It requires the administrator to create a connection to the Crystal Reports 9 repository. After this connection is established, the administrator can connect to the Crystal Enterprise 10. This requires a valid user with the correct permissions.

Figure 17.6
The Crystal Repository Migration Wizard enables the user to choose the exact objects she might want to import.

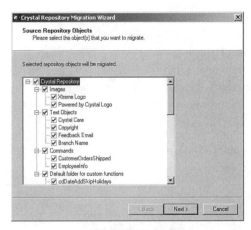

CAUTION

> With any migration of data, you should perform any necessary backups. The Migration Wizard does not move the data, but rather copies it, leaving the existing database intact.

NOTE

> If an object exists with the same name, the Crystal Reports Migration Wizard does not copy over the database, but rather informs the user that there is a duplicate object and the original has not been migrated.

TROUBLESHOOTING

EDITING CUSTOM FUNCTIONS

I can't seem to edit my custom functions from the Repository Explorer.

Custom functions are not editable from the Repository Explorer because they are housed inside of Formulas. To view custom functions available in the Repository, go to Report, Formula Workshop. In the group tree, the Crystal Repository branch can be seen and all custom functions can be viewed from there.

BUSINESS VIEWS ARE GONE

When creating a new report I see my available Business Views; however, after I open the Repository Explorer in Crystal Reports, the Business Views disappear.

The Repository Explorer in Crystal Reports is context-sensitive and only displays objects that can be used within the report itself.

MIGRATING THE REPOSITORY

In Crystal Reports 9, the sample Repository database was in Microsoft Access format. Can I migrate this to Microsoft SQL Server database for use with version 10?

In Crystal Enterprise version 10, Microsoft Access is not a supported Repository database. The Access database will need to be migrated to a support database such as SQL Server. The Crystal Repository Migration Wizard will connect to the Access database and transfer all the data to the SQL Server database for the user. However, for this to be successful, it assumes the user has not modified the Access database.

CHAPTER 18

CRYSTAL REPORTS SEMANTIC LAYER— BUSINESS VIEWS

In this chapter

INTRODUCTION TO BUSINESS VIEWS

Business Views are new to Crystal Enterprise 10. Business Views enable the user to abstract the complexities of the data source by creating a layer on top of the data source layer that abstracts the complexities of the data joins and fields. The end user only sees a logical grouping of available, well-named fields for use and does not have to concern himself with the intricacies of database design.

You do not have to use the Business Views as your data source. You can still connect to the data source directly and create the joins inside Crystal Reports. Using Business Views is contingent on the requirements. For example, if you are building a data warehouse with complex joins and technical field names, Business Views might be the recommended approach. If the requirement is to report from an Access database and you know the data structures and the end users will simply be consuming static reports, the additional effort of building the Business View might not be justified.

NOTE

Although previous versions of Crystal Reports had functionality similar to this in the form of Dictionaries and Query files, Business Views require Crystal Reports 10 and will not function with earlier versions of Crystal Reports.

NOTE

At the time of this writing, Business Views were available for the Professional and Premium editions of Crystal Enterprise. Contact Business Objects for further licensing information.

WHY IMPLEMENT BUSINESS VIEWS?

Business Views offer tremendous advantages over traditional Crystal Report design processes by removing the most difficult data-intensive tasks from report design. This facilitates a change in the way that report creation occurs, as less database-savvy report designers can take on the bulk of report designing, leaving developer or DBA-oriented tasks to the specialists. This approach also results in less re-work and speeds report creation, which is arguably the most costly aspect of owning a Business Intelligence solution. Business Views provide a variety of benefits:

- Abstracting the complexities of the database
- Putting report design in the hands of business people
- Facilitating object reuse
- Dynamically switching data sources
- Simplifying report transportability
- Providing data security at the row and column level

With large complex data warehousing projects using many tables and complex joins, the report designer might not have the requisite knowledge. If the report designer is required to join the tables for the reports, he might not use the most efficient join resulting in poor performance. Business Views allow for a division in labor, whereby the more technical database administrators and developers can create the joins between tables and data sources and the business-oriented report designers can concentrate on designing reports to satisfy the business requirement.

As a result of this division of labor and the reuse of the Crystal Repository, business people do not have to be as technically savvy, effectively resulting in less technical skill required to develop reports.

One of the major drawbacks when having to specify the data joins in each report is that this creates a large amount of redundant work. Should the database change, there is no way to reflect this other than modifying each of the individual reports. Business Views enable you to create the join once and if the join changes, you only need to change it once.

Data in corporations typically sits in multiple data sources. A requirement might exist to pull information from multiple data sources and consolidate this information in a single report. A Business View enables you to join disparate data sources together. The data connectivity uses the same connectivity available in Crystal Reports and Crystal Enterprise themselves. For example, this means that the administrator can join SQL-oriented databases to ERP data sources and finally to a JavaBean. All you would see is the list of available fields and you would not have to concern yourself with the joining of the fields.

18

Organizations typically have two or three environments. Most would have at least a Test/Development environment and a Production Environment. In some cases the Test/Development environment is split into separate environments. During the development process, reports are designed against the development environment, tested against the test environment and finally put into production. In prior versions of Crystal Reports, the report had to be opened and the data source mapped to a new data source. Business Views, through the use of dynamic data connections that create a Crystal Report parameter to dynamically switch the data connection, can dynamically change the data source. In the previous example, you might have test, development, and production as parameters that would drive the data source selection in each environment.

Another aspect of this dynamic data connection switch is that it can be easily incorporated to switch databases based on business logic. For example, many organizations archive data to keep their production databases efficient. However, users often need to view data from the archive. Using dynamic data connections, users can easily switch data sources at runtime yet maintain a single report.

Business Views enable you to set up security such that data is filtered based upon who the user is. This can be based off security within an "entitlements" database or the Crystal Enterprise user model can be used to create the security model. This way, rows and columns can be secured by users or groups.

You can also determine who is able to see a particular Business View. This results in users only reporting off Business Views to which they have access. For example, it is generally accepted auditing practice that accounts receivable personnel should not be able to see accounts payable information and vice versa. By using the user group functionality in Crystal Enterprise, the accounts receivable group would be given access to only the accounts receivable Business Views.

The Business View Manager provides the capability to export a Business View to an XML file and this file can then be easily imported into another Crystal Enterprise repository. This simple form of transportability makes swapping of Business Views a simple exercise. For example, the organization has a Crystal Enterprise system in Europe and one in North America. Administrators might want to share their Business Views or split the development task between the two continents and swap various components of the Business Views. It also simplifies the storage of source code, should the organization have a source code storage requirement.

In certain circumstances the cost of building the Business View outweighs the benefit. Crystal Enterprise 10 gives you the capability to use Business Views, or to access the data source directly without using Business Views. For example, an organization upgrading its reports from earlier versions might be satisfied with the current state of its implementation and hence might never use Business Views. Crystal Reports 10 even allows for a combination of Business Views and direct data source access, via subreports.

PERFORMANCE AND IMPLEMENTATION CONSIDERATIONS

There are certain factors that an organization should take into account before implementing Business Views. Because many people will likely use each Business View, care should be taken when building the query to ensure that performance meets expectations. Additionally, because of the increased functionality (such as joining two data sources), you might be tempted to simply create a structure that fulfills business requirements but sacrifices performance. Although most of the performance considerations are exactly the same as those for Crystal Reports design, some of the most common pitfalls are considered in the following sections.

JOINING LARGE DATA SETS

It is recommended to keep disparate data source joins to a minimum for large data sets to keep performance satisfactory. Because Crystal Enterprise must, based on the Business View, link the data on the Crystal Enterprise server, both data sets must be transferred to that system before they can be joined. Further, joining large data sets can tax the memory resources of the Crystal Enterprise server.

CAUTION

> With the use of disparate data sources, Business Views do not allow the Crystal Report option of grouping on the server. To concatenate the disparate data sets, most of the processing is performed within Crystal Enterprise and not the database.

To ameliorate performance concerns, users or administrators can schedule reports at off-peak hours and cached into the system; the user is not waiting for the report at view time. Another solution might be to combine the disparate data sources into one data source.

For more information on scheduling, see Chapter 23, "Using Crystal Enterprise with Web Desktop," and Chapter 27, "Administering and Configuring Crystal Enterprise."

BUSINESS OBJECTS UNIVERSE

Prior to its acquisition of Crystal Decisions, Business Objects provided Business View functionality in the form of Universes. Business Objects has released a roadmap with migration information that indicates that Business Objects Universes and Crystal Business Views will be merged at some future point. Contact Business Objects for more information.

VERSIONING

The Crystal Repository does not provide version control. Although there are alternatives to achieving versioning, the user cannot simply revert to a prior version, for instance.

USING OTHER METADATA

Other applications generate metadata layers; for example, ETL tools have their own metadata layers. One advantage is to be able to use this metadata so that the number of metadata layers is kept to a minimum. Currently Business Views do not support using other metadata layers or the importing of these layers. Please contact Business Objects for more information.

BUSINESS VIEWS ARCHITECTURE AND IMPLEMENTATION

The architecture provides multiple tiers with each tier performing a different function. This multitiered system is broken down into three layers: Client, Business, and Data Tiers.

CLIENT TIER

The client tier consists of the applications that interact with Business Views, in particular, Crystal Reports 10 and the Ad Hoc Application 10. The Ad Hoc application is based on the Report Application Server (RAS), hence this object model has changed to incorporate Business Views.

See Chapter 32, "Crystal Enterprise—Viewing Reports," and Chapter 33, "Crystal Enterprise Embedded—Report Modification and Creation," for information on the RAS object model.

BUSINESS TIER

The business tier consists of the components to create and manage the Business Views:

- Data Connections (optionally Dynamic Data Connections)
- Data Foundations

- Business Elements
- Business Views

At each component level different security rights can be applied to the components and security setup. This provides great flexibility as to who controls which component. For example, a database administrator can set up the data connections and data foundations but have no rights to view the business element and Business View layers.

CAUTION

> There is functionality within certain components that might give users access to view the data. For example, when creating a data foundation, users can browse the data, which gives them a better understanding of the field. If you do not want users to be able to do this, you need to explicitly remove their rights.

BUSINESS VIEW MANAGER

The tool used to manage the Business Views and the Crystal Repository is the Business View Manager, a Windows-based development tool that can be installed locally (see Figure 18.1 for the installation screen) on the developer's or administrator's Windows workstation.

Figure 18.1
To install the Business View Manager, select that option from the Crystal Enterprise 10 Setup menu that appears when you insert the CD-ROM.

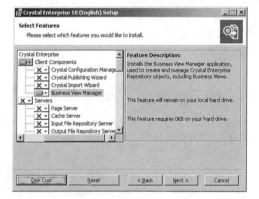

THE REPOSITORY EXPLORER

The Repository Explorer allows the user to manage the Crystal Repository. To reiterate, the objects that can be stored in the Crystal Repository are

- Business Views
- Command objects
- Custom functions
- Images
- Text objects

To show the explorer, click the View menu and then check the Repository Explorer.

It is worth describing some of the functionality of this explorer because the repository can become quite large in larger projects, with multiple users adding objects simultaneously. There are certain features that might simplify navigation and security when dealing with many objects.

As a content creator, you need to navigate quickly and effectively through the repository to reduce content development time. The following list includes some techniques to aid in the organizing of the Crystal Repository:

- The View Setting icon enables the user to filter objects by item type and then sort the object by name or by type.

- The advanced filtering icon turns on filtering by owner or finds a text object by name, as in Figure 18.2.

- Users can add or delete objects or folders depending on their permissions. Creating your own folder structure can be an efficient way of organizing the repository.

- Before deleting and after adding objects, a user can check the dependencies; both from a standpoint of what might be dependent on that object or what that object might depend on. For example, if the user creates a data foundation, they can check what data connections this depends on by clicking the Show Referenced Objects icon or, alternatively, by clicking on the Show Dependent Objects icon.

Figure 18.2
Advanced filtering available in the Business View Manager assists the user when working with large repositories.

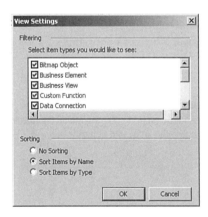

The repository security is controlled via the Repository Explorer found in the Business View Manager. It works on an inheritance mechanism whereby an object inherits the security settings from its parent and is designed so that administrators do not have to set the security for every object. For example, you might have an administrators group that has View, Edit, and Set Security rights, another group called Content Creators that only has View and Edit rights, and a third group called Everyone that only has View rights.

→ For more information on how groups are created in the Crystal Management Console, **see** "Managing Groups," **p. 603**

TIP

> A planning session before jumping in and creating folders and groups is well worth the investment.

Alternatively, reports can inherit security from the folder to which they are published. This is particularly useful to apply security to an organizational structure. For example, the organizational structure might be set up in the following fashion:

Directors

    Managers

    Employees

If the folders are set up accordingly, the managers inherit the rights of the employees, and the directors inherit the rights of both the managers and employees, effectively mirroring what is happening in the organization.

The security model takes the least-privileged approach—should a conflict exist, the user's right will be denied. In the previous example, a user might be part of the Everybody group, which has view rights, and might be a member of the Employee group, which is denied from seeing the Managers folder. In this case, the denial takes precedence over the view right that the Everyone group had and the user's net rights will be one of denial.

The more granular security setting generally takes precedence over the more generic setting. For example, a user belongs to a group that has modify rights to an object, but at a user level, these rights have been denied. The user's net rights will be such that no modify rights exist to the object.

CAUTION

> If multiple developers on different workstations are changing related objects at the same time, the changes might not be replicated through to all the developers. If this is the case, it is recommended to save the related objects, exit the Business View Manager, and re-enter the application.

DATA CONNECTIONS

In the Data Connection, the user establishes a connection to the data source. Setting up the Data Connection is similar to setting up a connection in Crystal Reports and in most cases uses the same drivers and dialog boxes. The user can enter a username and password. These are the data source credentials. The username and password are stored in the repository.

DYNAMIC DATA CONNECTIONS

The Dynamic Data Connection is an optional component that enables the user to switch data sources dynamically through the use of Crystal Reports parameters. If the Dynamic Data Connection component is used, the Crystal Report automatically has a read-only parameter created. The parameter's name consists of the data connection's name concatenated with the Dynamic Connection Parameter. The parameter is populated with the various database options.

Dynamic data connections are useful for quickly moving from Development to Test environments. Also, they can be used to change languages dynamically; if there are English and French databases, the user can switch between the two. However, bitmaps and text objects, for example, do not automatically switch and the report designer needs to have one for each language.

TIP

> If the database is designed in such a way that there is a column that designates language—for example, there is a row in the table for each language—a row level filter is required as opposed to using a Dynamic Data Connection, which applies in the case that there are different databases for each language.

DATA FOUNDATION COMPONENT

The Data Foundation component enables the user to join the various tables exposed by the data connection(s) or dynamic data connection(s). The user would typically have knowledge of the data structures and correct joins. To join a table to another table, simply drag the field from one table to the corresponding field in the other table (see Figure 18.3). The data fields need to be of the same type for the join to be successful. Right-clicking on the join and selecting Link Type enables the user to change the join type. The correct joining of the tables, especially when there are multiple disparate data sources involved, is vital from a performance standpoint and ensuring the correct data is returned. Related to this is the capability to order the links. The linking order in which the Business View links the tables can be set by the user by selecting Order Links from the Linking Diagram menu. In addition, link enforcement can be vital to correct implementation of security filters. For instance, the filter that determines row-level permissions might require information from a particular table. However, if that particular table is not used in the report, you need to force the use of that table to ensure correct filtering. In that case, you can set join enforcement to result in the correct behavior. Please refer to the Business Views documentation on the Crystal Enterprise CD for a complete discussion of the join types.

TIP

> Joining data is similar to joining tables in the Crystal Reports Designer.

Data warehouses can have hundreds, sometimes thousands of tables. The Data Foundation component can become complex to manage. The following list provides some pointers to help you manage the foundation.

- Only map the tables you require information from
- Keep it simple

- Use indexes
- Keep the number of retrieved records to a minimum
- Use the tools available in the Business View Manager

Figure 18.3
The Data Foundation showing a right-click menu and some complex joins.

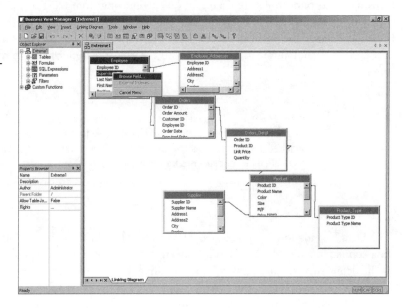

A common mistake is to try and map all the tables in the data warehouse. This might sound obvious, but you might only require information from certain functional areas of the data warehouse and hence you only need to map those tables.

It generally requires less effort to go from simple to complex than complex to simple. Bite off as much as you can chew, work out the relationships, test, check performance and expected data results, and then take another bite.

For performance reasons, try to join indexed fields (indicated by a colored icon to the left of the field) and have the database do the work as opposed to the Business View. Because indexed fields are much faster to find at the database level, the database can return data much faster, especially in large tables, if the fields used for the join are indexed.

TIP

> In some cases the index pointer does not appear next to the indexed field. Select the Fetch Table Indexes from the Linking Diagram menu to make these appear.

The Data Foundation enables the user to create SQL expressions and formulas. SQL expressions are evaluated at the database level, whereas in many cases the formula is evaluated by the Crystal Enterprise server. The number of records retrieved can be reduced significantly by having the database filter the records based on a SQL expression rather than a formula, effectively pushing the filter into the query itself rather than retrieving all the data and then discarding the unnecessary portion.

There are a number of tools applicable to the data foundation that enable you to manage the tables within the Business View. All of these can be found under the Link Diagram menu:

- Locate Tables—User can select the table name from a list and will be taken to that table in the data foundation. This saves the user from having to search by scrolling.
- Rearrange Tables—This arranges the tables so the user doesn't need to move tables around.
- Select Visible Tables—Enables the user to hide tables and only show required tables. The other tables are still linked; they just do not show up in the window.
- Fetch Table Indexes—Show what fields are indexed. Related to this is the index legend.
- Change Linking View—To allow more tables to be visible, the view can be changed so that only the table name is displayed and not all the fields.

SQL EXPRESSIONS   Within the data foundation components, the user can create a SQL expression. A SQL expression is a SQL statement that is executed on the database. These are typically used to create data fields that do not exist in the database. A good example of using SQL expressions is to join disparate data sources where one of the data sources is missing a relevant field to join on. For example, I have a database where I want to join a numeric Vendor Number ID field to a Vendor Number field that is of type string in the other data source. In this case, I could create a SQL expression that converts the Vendor Number to a numeric field so that the field types can be joined.

The administrator has the capability to set security on the SQL expression by right-clicking the SQL expression and selecting Edit Rights.

FORMULAS   In some cases the SQL database might not support the required functionality or a calculation might be required using fields from disparate data sources. In this case, a formula can be used instead of a SQL expression. For example, you might have a quantity shipped number coming from a shipping database and a price field from an Orders database. To see the total value of orders shipped, these values could be calculated in a formula.

The administrator has the capability to set security on the Formula, and any other object, by right-clicking the Formula and selecting Edit Rights.

NOTE

> The SQL formula editor is very similar to the one found in Crystal Reports. However, there is one change in that if you are using Basic as the syntax, you must start a formula with `formula=`.

PARAMETERS   The user can create parameters to be used for filtering. These function exactly like Crystal Reports Parameters except that the report designed does not create or maintain them. Implementing a parameter can be extremely helpful in ensuring that runaway queries do not occur.

For more details on creating and using parameters, see Chapter 5, "Implementing Parameters for Dynamic Reporting."

FILTERS   Business Views use filters to select the data based upon a particular logic. In some cases the logic prevents too much data from being returned to the user. For example, the user might only be interested in seeing data from one particular division. Another case might be that the user is not allowed to see the row of data based upon some business security requirement. This is commonly called row-level security. In addition to this, the security might be such that a certain column of data might not be displayed to a user or group. This is commonly called column-level security.

By default the system creates a Full Data Access Filter and a No Data Access Filter. These are the two extremes; an organization's security typically falls somewhere in between.

Row-level security enables certain users to see certain rows while other rows are filtered out based upon business logic.

For example, if sales representatives should not be allowed to view certain data in the report, the first level of security is at the Crystal Enterprise layer, whereby you could deny access to the Sales Representative group. In this case, the report would not show up and the Sales Representatives would not even see the report show up in their Web Desktop. See Chapters 23 and 27 for information on the Web Desktop and administering Crystal Enterprise.

Alternatively, within the data foundation, a filter could be applied to the Sales Representative group. In this case you could use the No Data Access filter that is created by default by the system. A Sales Representative would be able to see the report, but no data would be returned.

To achieve this, a filter would be created. After the Business View Manager is satisfied that the logic is correct, the user right-clicks the filter and selects either the user or the group that the filter needs to apply to (see Figure 18.4).

Most organizations require more sophisticated business logic. Filters allow for complex logic concatenated together using either AND or OR logic. Users can filter data using fields, SQL expressions, formulas, other filters, parameters, Boolean logic, or a special Crystal Reports field called Current CE User. This special field can be used an alternative to filtering data by group; however, it is based on a user basis and hence might require more setup.

For instance, assume that there is a user field in the database that contains the user's last name, and another field with the user's first name, and that these two fields in the database are in a table where you have the user's department. Also assume that the Crystal Enterprise system uses Active Directory authentication, which has usernames composed of the user's initial from the first name and the entire last name, so Ruhi Nuri's username is RNuri. If you want to filter the report's data so that each user only sees data for his own department, you would apply a filter so {CurrentCEUserID} is set equal to a SQL expression that concatenates the first initial (typically you would use the LEFT command for this) and the last name.

Figure 18.4
The user selects the group or user that the filter is applied against.

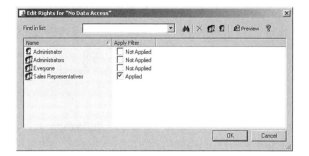

TIP

> If the organization is not using Business Views or wants to quickly filter a report without having to set up a Business View, this {CurrentCEUserID} field can be used with the Record Selection formula of Crystal Reports.

Associated with row-level security is the concept of column-level security. In this case the column data is displayed or not displayed based upon certain business logic.

Depending on who is running the report, the user might want to hide a column of data. For example, if I belong to the Human Resources group I might have permission to see the Identity Number or Social Security column. All other groups would not have access to that column; however, they might be able to see the rest of the report.

To enable the column-level security, right-click on the field in the Object Explorer and select Edit Rights. Select the group or user you want to deny or grant. Click the preview button to see the net rights (see Figure 18.5).

Figure 18.5
Right-clicking on the SSN field in the object explorer opens this dialog to set the rights on the column.

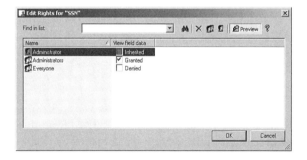

If the user has been denied rights to the column, the Business View returns a NULL from the database. How the Crystal Report is set up to handle the NULL value determines what is displayed.

Remember that security is determined using the least-privileged model. To illustrate this, you might have row-level security applied that returns a column of data; however at the same time, you have column-level security applied that hides the column. In this case the net right for that column is one of denial and the column is not displayed to the user.

CUSTOM FUNCTIONS   The user can import Custom Functions from the Crystal Repository for use within his data foundation. Custom Functions are described earlier in this chapter.

BUSINESS ELEMENTS

Business Elements provide a layer on top of the Data Foundation. It is at this level that the developer can further abstract the complexity of the database by aliasing the fields with business terminology, creating business hierarchies and logically grouping these fields around business requirements. At this level the division of labor might occur between technical- and business-oriented focus. In other words, the business-oriented person might want to start renaming the fields to business terms. The hierarchical nature of the fields can also be shown; for example, a company consists of divisions and those divisions consist of departments and so forth. Putting data into hierarchies does not have an immediate impact in version 10 of Crystal Enterprise, but might be used later with Analytical Business Views to speed relational to OLAP processes.

When creating a new Business Element, the Business View Manager prompts the user for a data foundation. Select the required one. Insert the required fields for the Business Element. The Business Element allows for a logical grouping of the fields. For example, the Business Elements might be designed based upon a division or department or might be a field from the Data Foundation to the Business Element.

APPLYING SECURITY AT THE BUSINESS ELEMENT LEVEL

Applying security at the Business Element level allows for different security definitions to be used by different groups. For instance, should you have one Data Foundation that could be used by multiple groups, but requires that some logical grouping of columns be hidden from certain user groups, you could gather a number of fields into a certain Business View and secure that for viewing only by certain groups. This enables flexibility without creating multiple similar data foundations.

BUSINESS VIEWS

Finally, you can collect Business Elements into Business Views. A primary consideration is that a Business View must contain Business Elements derived from the same Data Foundation. Stated differently, a Business View can contain data from only one Data Foundation.

At this stage in the architecture, the appropriate filtering has been performed and the Business View is a cumulative view of all the underlying components.

For example, assume the database contains multiple company numbers, each representing a separate organization as part of a large conglomerate. The administrator could set up the

Data Foundation and filter by each company number, assigning only that company the rights to the Data Foundation. Within that specific company, there might be multiple sales departments. This could be defined in a Business Element; once again a filter is applied at this level so that only the associated sales department is seen by the relevant personnel. The Business View combines the Business Elements to provide a view of data. This view is filtered by relevant company and by relevant sales department, that is, the cumulative effect of the layers.

To create a new Business View the user can select the New icon, and select a new Business View or from the File menu, choose the Business View. Select the Business Elements that are going to be part of the view and save the view.

By right-clicking on the view in the object explorer, the user can set the rights to the Business View. In this case the rights refer to who has rights to edit, view, and set security on the Business View.

The Rights Test View (shown in Figure 18.6) allows the content creator to check each user's net rights as far as the visible fields are concerned. If column-level security is applied, the field has a Red Cross associated with it; in other words, the field will still be visible but for this user will return no data. As far as the filters are concerned or row-level security, the cumulative total of all the filters are applied, separated by AND statements.

Figure 18.6
The Rights Test View enables you to see user's net rights. In this case both row- and column-level security are applied. The row-level security is defined by the Final Filter Text and the column-level security is defined by the Supplier ID column that has a red cross associated with it.

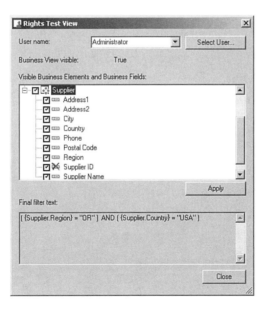

TIP

To create Business View quickly and to become familiar with the steps required, use the Business Element Wizard. This walks you through the creation of a Business View.

DATA TIER

The final tier of the architecture is the data tier. This consists of all the data sources available to the Business View. The available set of data sources changes depending on the platform that Crystal Enterprise is installed on.

Please check the documentation, specifically platforms.txt found on the Crystal Enterprise CD for a list of available data sources for your install.

TIP

> Check http://support.businessobjects.com/library/docfiles/cps10/ doc_en.asp for the latest versions of documentation to check for database support.
>
> http://support.businessobjects.com/ provides a knowledge base to search for related patches (hot fixes), knowledge base articles, and Technical Papers.

TROUBLESHOOTING

CHANGING RELATED OBJECTS AT THE SAME TIME

Multiple developers on different workstations are changing related objects at the same time, and the changes are not being replicated to all the developers.

You should save the related objects, exit the Business View Manager, and re-enter the application.

CREATING CRYSTAL ANALYSIS REPORTS

INTRODUCTION

The concept of OLAP was introduced in Chapter 16, "Multidimensional Reporting Against OLAP Data with Crystal Reports." With OLAP it is relatively easy to create professionally formatted Crystal Reports based on multidimensional data sources. These types of formatted reports are targeted for end users who require only one clean viewpoint into the OLAP Data. Crystal Analysis provides a more interactive end-user environment with the reports so that speed of thought interactive viewing is available to end users. This chapter introduces Crystal Analysis and the richness of interactivity it can add to your reporting environment.

One of the key challenges facing organizations today is providing actionable information to business managers, enabling them to make decisions in a timely manner based on concrete data. This chapter shows how Crystal Analysis Professional can be used to deliver compelling analytical reports to end users.

This chapter covers the following information:

- Introduction to Crystal Analysis
- Data connectivity options for Crystal Analysis
- Introduction to the powerful Worksheet object
- Introduction to the Charting object

INTRODUCING CRYSTAL ANALYSIS

Crystal Analysis is another type of reporting tool provided by Business Objects that enables organizations to deliver action-based analysis to end users. More than the flattened views of OLAP and multidimensional data sources that Crystal Reports provides, it offers a rich, interactive interface that facilitates the discovery of business insights and helps decision-makers affect business performance at the speed of thought. The two primary groups of end users for such reports would be Power Users and General Information Consumers.

Power Users can create *analytic reports* (often called applications) based on OLAP data, using the powerful thick-client designer Crystal Analysis. These reports or applications (which will be called reports from here on) can contain many pages, each representative of a different predefined view of the underlying data source. Data can be presented in tables or through a wide range of charts, as shown in Figure 19.1.

General Information Consumers can also leverage the powerful multidimensional functionality of Crystal Analysis by taking advantage of the guided analytics provided in the product. These single-click analytic buttons used in combination with the other compelling presentation features (such as exception highlighting, sorting and filtering, and drop-down boxes) enable you to provide multidimensional analysis to less sophisticated users. Business managers can use the resulting analytic reports to inform the daily decisions they need to make with less technical skill required.

Figure 19.1
Design an analytic report with Crystal Analysis Professional.

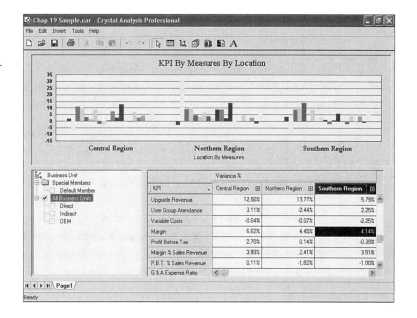

Analytic reports can be delivered to users in two ways: either through distribution of the Crystal Analysis file (.car extension) to users with the thick-client application installed, or, more popularly, through a Web browser by using Crystal Enterprise. The reports in Crystal Enterprise can be viewed using either Dynamic HTML (DHTML) (see Figure 19.2) or ActiveX. Both viewers are fully functional and provide all the analytic capabilities of the desktop tool in a Web browser.

Figure 19.2
An analytic report viewed using the DHTML Viewer of Crystal Enterprise.

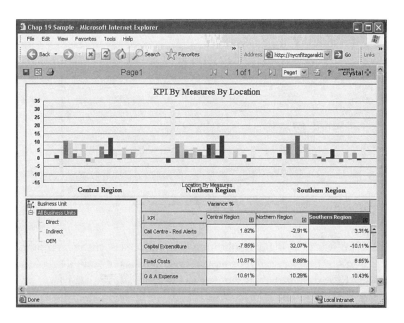

19

Crystal Analysis is suitable for a wide range of analytic business requirements, including sales and marketing analysis, financial reporting and analysis, key performance indicator reporting, supplier performance and billing analysis, click-stream analysis, and HR analysis. When combined with Crystal Enterprise in providing Web Analytic solutions, Crystal Analysis is also suitable for delivering analytic reports and applications to both employees inside an organization and to those outside—customers, suppliers, and business partners.

NOTE

Before using Crystal Analysis it is necessary to have OLAP cubes created. The OLAP cubes supported include

- Microsoft SQL Server 2000 Analysis Services SP2 and SQL Server 7 OLAP Services SP3
- DB2 OLAP 8.1, 7.1.7, 7.1.6, 7.1.5, 7.1.4, 7.1.3, 7.1.1, 7.1.0, and 8.1
- Essbase 6.5.x, 6.2.x, 6.1.4, 6.1.3a, 6.1.2, 6.0.3, 6.0.2, 6.0.1, and 6.0.0
- SAP BW 3.x and 2.0B
- Holos 8.x and 9.0

ACCESSING OLAP DATA WITH CRYSTAL ANALYSIS

After starting Crystal Analysis through the Application Designer option on the Start Programs Crystal Analysis menu, you can create new Crystal applications by choosing File, New. Similar to Crystal Reports Report Gallery, Crystal Analysis provides a set of application templates and wizards as potential starting points in addition to the option of starting from a blank application (see Figure 19.3). This chapter focuses on the manual process of creating analytic applications from the ground up but you are encouraged to review the application templates and their associated wizards to determine if a fit exists.

Figure 19.3
You can select a template in the New Application dialog.

After you select the Blank Application option, Crystal Analysis prompts you with the OLAP Connection Browser shown in Figure 19.4. This is the equivalent of the Data Explorer in Crystal Reports and enables the user to select an OLAP data source on which to base the report.

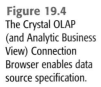

Figure 19.4
The Crystal OLAP
(and Analytic Business
View) Connection
Browser enables data
source specification.

From the Crystal OLAP Connection Browser window, you can add new OLAP servers to the tree using the Add Server button. This then displays the New Server dialog shown in Figure 19.5. There are several ways to connect to a cube, all of which can be defined through this dialog.

Figure 19.5
Add an OLAP server
connection to the
Crystal OLAP
Connection Browser.

CREATING AN OLAP SERVER DATA SOURCE

After you select the Add Server button, the New Server dialog appears. The first option in this window is OLAP Server, which defines a regular client/server connection to the OLAP Server and does not change across the different versions of supported cubes. This is the most common type of connection and is compatible with thin-client delivery when Crystal Enterprise and the OLAP Database Server are on the same side of the firewall.

Figure 19.5 shows this type of server being defined in the New Server dialog for a SQL Server Analysis Services cube. Select Microsoft OLE DB driver for OLAP Services as the Server Type, and then type the server name into the Server Name box and ensure the caption is appropriately filled in. The caption can be changed to give the server a more descriptive name.

ADDING LOCAL CUBE (.CUB) FILES AS DATA SOURCES

SQL Server Analysis Services enables a user to create an offline cube file containing a subset of the data held in SQL Server. These cubes can be accessed using Crystal Analysis Professional when the user is away from the network—for example, when traveling with a laptop. Figure 19.6 shows a .cub file being selected in the New Server dialog. The Browse button (ellipses) enables users to navigate through their directories to locate the .cub file. A caption has been defined to make the entry in the OLAP Connection Browser more readable.

Figure 19.6
Add a .cub file to the OLAP Connection Browser.

ADDING HTTP CUBES DATA SOURCES

HTTP cubes, which are sometimes called *iCubes*, enable the transport between PTS and Microsoft SQL Server to be tunneled through HTTP, allowing connections through fire-walls and proxy servers. Figure 19.7 shows an HTTP connection selected in the New Server dialog. To establish a valid connection to an HTTP Cube server you must specify the full URL, including the http or https prefix. A username and password can optionally be specified. For HTTP cubes, the server checks the authentication of the user who requests the connection. If the password or username is incorrect or blank, the server defines how an anonymous user is logged on.

NOTE
> HTTP cubes were introduced in Microsoft SQL Server 2000 and require Microsoft Internet Information Server (IIS) to be used as the Web server. For more information, see Microsoft's documentation for Analysis Services, which is available either as part of your Microsoft OLAP installation or on the MSDN Web site at http://msdn.microsoft.com/library/.

Figure 19.7
Add an HTTP cube server to the OLAP Connection Browser.

ADVANCED DATA SOURCE CONNECTIVITY

On the New Server dialog, an Advanced Data Source connectivity button is presented that enables you to specify a connection type. Figure 19.8 shows the Advanced Settings dialog, which provides three different options for connectivity to cubes. The Direct to OLAP Server option is almost exclusively used at this time, but the other two forms of connectivity are used currently for connectivity to legacy Holos cubes.

NOTE

If you need more information on this type of legacy connectivity, please consult your Crystal Analysis and Holos help files.

Figure 19.8
The Advanced Settings are almost exclusively set to Direct to OLAP Server.

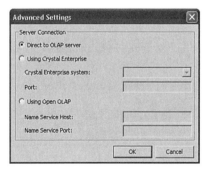

FAVORITE CUBES

Favorite cubes are a feature of Crystal Analysis that enables users to create shortcuts to frequently used cubes. You create shortcuts by simply dragging a cube into the Favorites folder from within the Crystal OLAP Connection Browser window (see Figure 19.9). Once defined, a shortcut can be renamed if required.

Figure 19.9
Create a shortcut to a favorite cube.

DESIGNING CRYSTAL ANALYSIS REPORTS AND APPLICATIONS

This section describes how Crystal Analysis can create compelling analytic reports that enable users to extract valuable insights from their data. It shows how the Guided Analytic techniques provided by Crystal Analysis can be used to identify and prioritize problems, and ultimately extract actionable information and value from the underlying OLAP data.

NOTE

> The examples in this section use Crystal Analysis version 10 and the Key Performance Indicators cube from the Crystal Samples collection. The sample cubes can be installed by running setup.exe located in the Samples subdirectory on the CD-ROM in the back of the book. You might need to look in the appropriate language subdirectory under which you installed the product (for example, en for English).

DESIGN ENVIRONMENT OVERVIEW

Think of the Crystal Analysis Design Environment as a painter's canvas. The Report Designer uses this canvas and a palette of available analytic objects to create an analytic report (often called an analytic application). The point-and-click, free-form designer environment for creating the analytic reports is ultimately flexible and the power of the available analytic objects is impressive. Figure 19.10 shows the major features of the Crystal Analysis Professional designer.

At the top of the window is a toolbar divided into the following three sections:

- File manipulation tools including New, Open, Save, and Print
- Editing tools including Cut, Copy, Paste, Undo, and Redo
- Object manipulation tools including a Selection tool, Worksheet, Chart, Dimension Explorer, Slice Navigator, Analysis Button, and Text Label

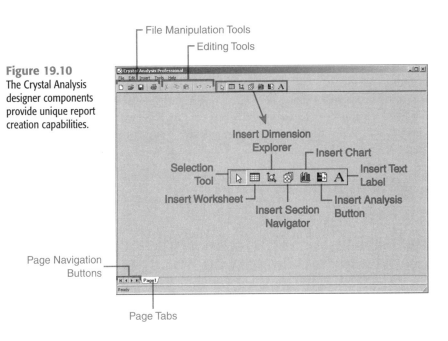

Figure 19.10
The Crystal Analysis designer components provide unique report creation capabilities.

At the bottom of the designer window, there is also a group of controls for managing the pages in the Crystal Analysis report in much the same way that you would in Excel.

CONNECTING TO AN OLAP CUBE

Whether using an expert or creating a blank report, the first step is to connect to a cube. The cube is selected using the OLAP Connection Browser dialog, shown in Figure 19.11.

19

Figure 19.11
Select the OLAP server and Key Performance Indicators cube.

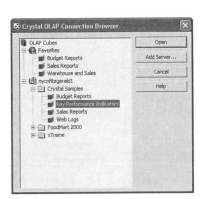

→ For more information on adding cube servers, **see** "Accessing OLAP Data with Crystal Analysis," **p. 378**

ADDING PAGES

The design paradigm of Crystal Analysis is similar to that of an Excel workbook with respect to pages. A Crystal Analysis report or application can contain multiple pages and each page can provide an entirely unique viewpoint on the same underlying data source. New pages are added to the report by either choosing Insert, Page Menu or right-clicking on any existing Page tab and then accessing the Insert option. A New Page template dialog, shown in Figure 19.12, enables pages to be created quickly. If none of the page templates are suitable, a blank page can be inserted.

Figure 19.12
Use templates to create pages quickly.

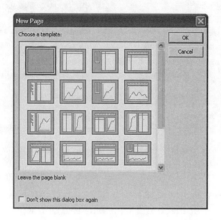

TIP

> If the New Page template dialog is not displayed when pages are inserted, it can be re-enabled through the Tools, Options menu.

New pages are automatically inserted at the end of the report and named Page 1, Page 2, and so on. A page can be renamed by right-clicking its tab and selecting Rename from the menu. You can change the order of the pages by dragging the tabs to a specific destination or by right-clicking and choosing Move or Copy. Creating analytic reports with multiple pages provides the power of a custom application because it provides varying perspectives of the cube and facilitates guided navigation between them. This guided navigation is explored in the next chapter.

ADDING CRYSTAL ANALYSIS OBJECTS TO A REPORT

After a page has been added to the report, individual analytic objects can be added, deleted, and manipulated on those pages to create meaningful report and application content. All the analytic components can be added by using either the Insert menu or any of the toolbar icons previously shown in Figure 19.10. After you select the component, the mouse pointer turns into a cross-hairs pointer. You specify the size and placement of the selected object by locking in one corner of the object with a mouse click and then holding that click while dragging the mouse to the desired opposite diagonal corner. Each of the analytic components, including Worksheets, Charts, Dimension Explorers, Slice Navigators, Transition Buttons, and Text Boxes, is described in detail later in this chapter.

While in Design mode, the currently selected object is indicated by a hatched border and object selection handles, as shown in Figure 19.13.

Figure 19.13
A hatched border shows which object is currently selected.

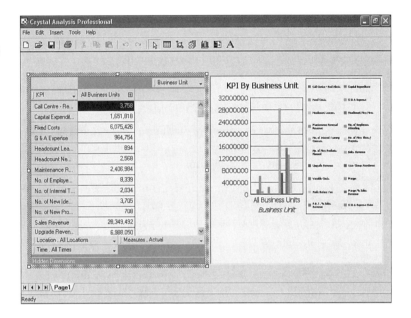

In Design mode, the currently selected object is the only active object and the only object that responds to mouse clicks. To change the active object, simply click a different object until it receives focus as indicated by the hatched border.

NOTE

> The Lock option in the Tools menu prevents users from moving, adding, or deleting report objects. This is useful for finished reports because all the objects become simultaneously active, making the report much more intuitive to use. A locked report can optionally be protected with a password that subsequently must be typed in before the application can be unlocked.

MOVING, RESIZING, AND FORMATTING OBJECTS

After the report objects have been placed on a page, Crystal Analysis allows a significant amount of freedom in defining the appearance, placement, and formatting of the objects. The appearance and formatting properties belonging to any object can be retrieved and edited by right-clicking on the hatched border of any active object. The formatting details of each object are described in the followed sections. Objects can be moved within a page using the mouse to drag the hatched border. As the mouse is moved over the border the cursor indicates when dragging is possible.

TIP

> When dragging objects, the designer snaps the objects to a grid for easier alignment. Using the cursor keys in conjunction with the Ctrl key enables finer adjustments to be made.

Objects can be resized by dragging the select handles on each corner and on each side of its hatched border.

WORKSHEET OBJECTS AND WORKSHEET DIMENSIONS

The most common object and the one that forms the core of most Crystal Analysis reports is the worksheet. Similar in appearance to a Microsoft Excel worksheet, this analytic object provides two key benefits to Crystal Analysis users:

- A numeric-based view into the underlying multidimensional/OLAP data for end-user consumption
- A set of dynamic and interactive tools that enable powerful analysis and exploration into the same data

Figure 19.14 highlights the Worksheet object and the key dimension categories. All the row, column, and slice dimensions can be changed, swapped, or nested by simply dragging and dropping them into the different sections of the worksheet or by right-clicking on any of the dimension toolbars and accessing the various swapping and nesting options.

NOTE

> A chart on the same page as a worksheet always reflects the current column, row, and sliced dimension settings and dynamically changes as the worksheet does. Also note that although you can have two or more worksheets on the same page, they always provide the exact same viewpoint and changes in one are always immediately reflected in the others.

As mentioned previously, a worksheet can display several row and column dimensions at once. This technique highlighted in Figure 19.15 is often referred to as the nesting of dimensions and enables multiple dimensions to be displayed in the row or column positions.

Sliced dimensions can be set to two different states—active and hidden—by accessing their right-click context menu and the Dimension State menu option. When active, the sliced dimension is available for manipulation by the end user. When hidden, the report consumer sees neither the dimension nor its default value. The default value for a hidden dimension is set identically to that of an active dimension—through the use of the member selector. The member selector is introduced later in this chapter.

Row dimension(s)   Column dimension(s)

Figure 19.14
Row, column, slice, and hidden dimensions in a worksheet provide a multidimensional paradigm for viewing OLAP data and reports.

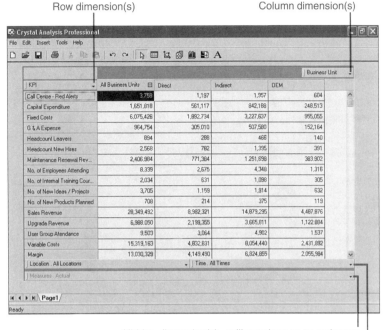

Hidden dimension(s)—will not show up to end users
Sliced (or paged) dimension(s)

Figure 19.15
A page showing two dimensions nested in the columns.

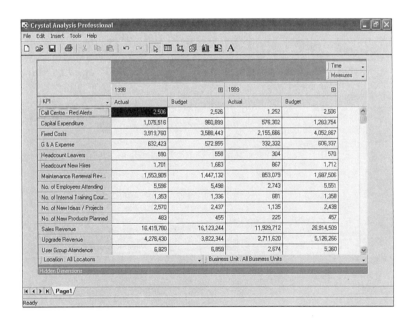

19

SETTING WORKSHEET PROPERTIES

The Properties dialog of the worksheet object shown in Figure 19.16 provides the Report Designer with the capability to selectively turn off some of the powerful functionality within the Worksheet for a specific report. The worksheet properties are displayed by right-clicking on the hatched border and choosing Properties from the menu.

For a complete listing of the worksheet properties, see the Worksheet properties table later in this section.

Figure 19.16
The Worksheet Properties dialog enables you to toggle end-user features of the worksheet.

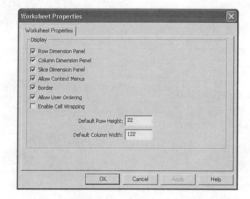

Table 19.1 provides an overview of each of the Worksheet properties and a use case scenario for enabling and disabling the specified property.

TABLE 19.1   WORKSHEET PROPERTIES AND USE CASE SCENARIOS

Worksheet Property	Description	Usage Case Information
Row Dimension Panel	Toggles the Row Dimension title bars and access to their Member Selector dialogs.	This would be turned off if you wanted to provide a fixed list of members in the row dimension and not enable end users to edit those interactively. Turning this off also restricts the end user from swapping the row dimension with any of the other sliced or column dimensions through the drag-and-drop interface—they still might have access to this if the Context menus are toggled on.

Worksheet Property	Description	Usage Case Information
Column Dimension Panel	Toggles the Column Dimension title bars and access to their Member Selector dialogs.	This would be turned off if you wanted to provide a fixed list of members in the column dimension and not enable end users to edit those interactively. Turning this off also restricts the end user from swapping the column dimension with any of the other sliced or row dimensions through the drag-and-drop interface; users still might have access to this if the Context menus are toggled on.
Slice Dimension Panel	Toggles the Sliced Dimension title bars and access to their Member Selector dialogs.	This would be turned off if you wanted to provide a fixed set of row and column dimensions and not enable end users to edit those interactively. Turning this off also restricts the end user from swapping the column and row dimensions with any of the other sliced through the drag-and-drop interface, although the end user still might have access to this if the Context menus are toggled on. Also note that individual sliced dimensions can be hidden without turning off the entire Slice Dimension Panel.
Allow Context Menus	Toggles the right-click menu option on the Worksheet for end users. Access to a multitude of dimension-, member-, and cell-related functionality can be accessed through the right-click menus.	This would be turned off if the end user were not intended to access the variety of dimension-, member-, and cell-related functionality. Details of this functionality are covered later in this chapter but include dimension swapping, member selection, filtering, sorting, calculations, and so on. One important note here is that the menus are either on or off; there is unfortunately no means (yet) to restrict access to a subset of the context menu items.
Border	Toggles the display of a border on the worksheet object.	This is left to the report designer's discretion.

continues

19

TABLE 19.1 CONTINUED

Worksheet Property	Description	Usage Case Information
Allow User Ordering	Toggles the capability of the report user to swap, nest, and move dimensions.	This would be turned off if you wanted to present a fixed view of the data and do not want the user to be able to interactively edit that. It is important to note that although this sounds similar to the Reorder Dimension Members menu option on the row and column members context menus, it is not related. The Reorder Dimension Members is introduced and discussed later in this chapter.
Enable Cell Wrapping	Toggles cell wrapping in individual cells.	This is left to the report designer's discretion.
Default Row Heights and Column Widths	Sets the global default for column heights and row widths.	Report Designer Preference and the Global settings can be overwritten by dragging and dropping the individual member cell borders.

CHOOSING MEMBERS TO DISPLAY

Worksheet objects enable you to navigate through dimensions by expanding (drilling down) or collapsing (drilling up) through the dimension hierarchies. Any member name with a + displayed next to it can be expanded, whereas those member names with a – displayed can be collapsed. You can enact both traditional drill-down and drill-up functions by clicking on the + or – sign. Alternatively, these forms of traditional drill-down in addition to variant forms called Focused Drill-down and Focused Drill-up are available when you right-click any drillable dimension member. Figure 19.17 shows the Drill menu available through the right-click context menu, and Table 19.2 describes four quick examples of the different drilling functions.

TIP

> Focused Drill-down is different than standard drill-down because it displays only the children of the member drilled on instead of the children and the already displayed members. To access Focused Drill-down, you can simply double-click any drillable dimension member. To drill back up, however, you need to use the right-click context menus.

Figure 19.17
The Drill context menu provides access to the different types of end-user drilling.

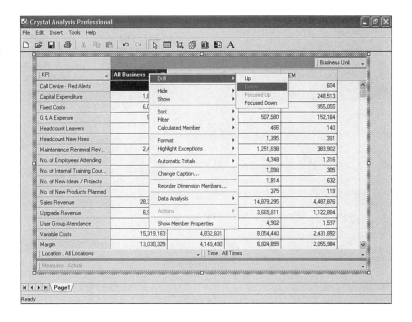

TABLE 19.2   BEFORE AND AFTER DRILLING SCENARIOS

Type of Drill	Sample Time Dimension Before Drill on Quarter 1 Member	Sample Time Dimension After Drill on Quarter 1 Member

Drill-down through context menu or clicking on the + icon	All Times -
	 2002 -
	    Quarter 1 +
	    Quarter 2 +
	    Quarter 3 +
	    Quarter 4 +
	 2003 +
		2003 -
		    Quarter 1 +
		      January
		      February
		      March
		    Quarter 2 +
		    Quarter 3 +
		    Quarter 4 +
		 2003 +

Focused Drill-down through context menu or double-clicking on the member name	All Times -
	 2002 -
	    Quarter 1 +
	    Quarter 2 +
	    Quarter 3 +
	    Quarter 4 +
		January
		 February
		 March

continues

19

TABLE 19.2   CONTINUED

Type of Drill	Sample Time Dimension Before Drill on Quarter 1 Member	Sample Time Dimension After Drill on Quarter 1 Member

Drill-up through context menu or through the – icon on the Quarter 1 Parent—2002	All Times -
	2002 -
	  Quarter 1 +
	  Quarter 2 +
	  Quarter 3 +
	  Quarter 4 +
	2003 +
		All Times -
		2002
		2003

Focused Drill-up through the context menu only	All Times -
	2002 -
	  Quarter 1 +
	  Quarter 2 +
	  Quarter 3 +
	  Quarter 4 +
	2003 +
		2002
		2003

The member selector is another powerful and flexible means to choose members to display. A member selector can be invoked for any dimension through the downward pointing triangle displayed on the dimension heading, as shown in Figure 19.18. Check boxes are presented next to each member, and selection edits are reflected in real time on the page as members are selected or deselected.

Figure 19.18
The member selector provides the end user with the capability to select members of the involved dimension.

The member selector enables end users to find the data of greatest relevance to them expeditiously. Two of the most useful tools in the Member Selector dialog are the Select menu and the Search tool. Both of these tools (along with a few others) are accessible through icons on the Member Selector toolbar. The Select menu, shown in Figure 19.19, provides a number of shortcuts that facilitate quick and efficient member selection. This shortcut menu is also accessible from each member displayed within the member selector.

Figure 19.19
The member selector's Select drop-down box provides shortcuts for adding displayed members.

The Search Wizard, shown in Figure 19.20 and accessed through the binoculars icon, provides both standard and advanced filtering mechanisms to enable report users to productively search through a dimension with a large number of members. Because it is not uncommon in industry today to have dimensions (such as Product or Employee) that have thousands or tens of thousands (or many more) of members contained within them, this search mechanism enables you to find sought-after members efficiently. Figure 19.20 depicts a search for KPIs within a KPI dimension that contain the text Sales. After a search has been completed, you can add the entire search result list or a subset of it to the existing member selection or you can completely replace it.

Figure 19.20
Search the KPI Dimension for members containing the word Sales.

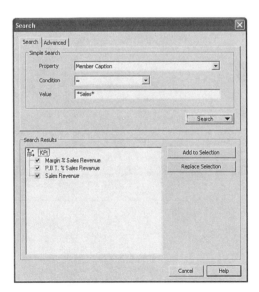

TIP

> When using the Member Selector Search dialog, you can use the * wildcard to find member names or captions quickly that contain a certain word. For example, typing ***Sales*** produces all KPIs that contain the word sales, and typing ***Coffee*** produces all products that contain the word coffee.

If a dimension has multiple hierarchies defined in the underlying data source, the Select Hierarchy button on the Member Selector toolbar is enabled. This enables you to choose the active hierarchy to be displayed.

ASYMMETRICAL MEMBER SELECTION AND DISPLAY

New to version 10, Crystal Analysis supplies an out-of-the box method to provide asymmetrical dimension member views. An asymmetrical viewpoint is one where different members of a nested dimension can be displayed for each parent member. By default, when a dimension is nested as shown in Figure 19.21, the nested members are symmetrical in display—that is, whatever members are selected for the nested dimension are displayed for all parent dimension members. Figure 19.22 shows a sample asymmetrical viewpoint that can be created through the right-click context menu Hide and Show commands on the member fields.

Figure 19.21
Symmetrical reporting viewpoint–the default display shows all nested members for each parent dimension member.

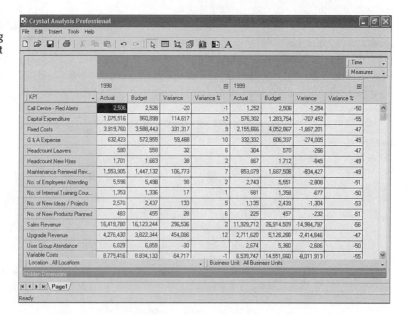

Figure 19.22
Asymmetrical reporting viewpoint enables varied and specific selection of nested members for each parent dimension.

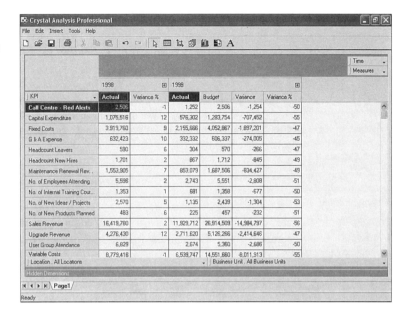

Table 19.3 reviews the commands associated with setting up and removing asymmetrical viewpoints.

TABLE 19.3   ASYMMETRICAL ACTIONS AND DESCRIPTIONS

Right-Click Action	Description
Hide Selected Member	Removes the selected member from the current view. This is different than deselecting a member in the Member Selector—that removes all instances of a member from the view.
Hide All Occurrences	Hides all instances of a member from the current viewpoint. This is identical to clearing a member in the Member Selector.
Show Selected Member	Shows the selected member and hides all other instances of that member.
Show All Occurrences	Shows all instances of a member in the current viewpoint, and hides all other members. This restores symmetry to the view and displays any hidden instances, but also hides all other members on the dimension.

CHANGING THE DISPLAY ORDER OF MEMBERS

By default, members are displayed in a worksheet in the natural dimension order—the order in which they are returned by the OLAP server. Because this might not always be preferred,

19

the shortcut menu for any row or column dimension member contains the option Reorder Dimension Members. Selecting this option displays a dialog where the order of the dimension members can be changed through drag-and-drop operations or using the up and down arrow buttons within the dialog.

> **NOTE**
> The chosen order is lost if a drill-down or drill-up operation is performed on the dimension. This feature is best suited to flat dimensions, such as measures, where the display order tends to be more critical.

NUMBER FORMATTING

You can apply number formatting to individual rows and columns by choosing Format, Add from a dimension member's right-click context menu. This displays the Format dialog, shown in Figure 19.23.

Figure 19.23
Change the display format of data for a selected member.

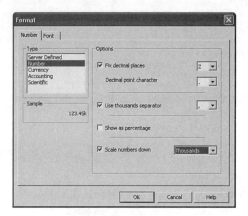

Once added, formats can be edited and removed through the right-click context menu.

CHANGING THE DISPLAYED CAPTION FOR A MEMBER

By default, each member is displayed using the name defined for it on the OLAP server. In some cases a different name might be required. Crystal Analysis enables you to change the caption by right-clicking on a member and choosing Change Caption from the menu.

AUTOMATIC TOTALS

The worksheet can generate a sum calculation for either the rows, columns, or both directions simultaneously, and automatically update it as the worksheet changes. This is useful when an arbitrary selection of members is made, such as a group of products. Figure 19.24 shows the sum of profit margin for the different store locations and for a number of time periods, with the calculation labeled Total on the worksheet.

Figure 19.24
You can display automatic totals down the columns of a worksheet.

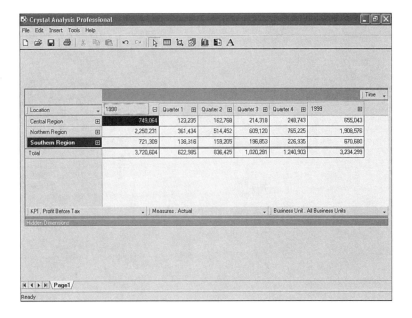

The shortcut menu (right-click menu) of any row or column dimension member in the worksheet controls the display of the automatic totals.

The behavior of the total calculations changes when a filter is added to the column dimension. In Figure 19.25, a Top 3 filter has been added to sales, so the worksheet is now showing just the top three locations. The automatic totals now display the following:

- The sum of the displayed members
- The sum of the members that have been filtered out
- The total of all members considered by the filter

USING CALCULATED MEMBERS AND DATA ANALYSIS

Additional calculations and data analytics not provided in a report's underlying data source can be added to the data presented in the worksheet through the Calculations and Data Analysis menu options accessible through the right-click context menu on any member title. The Calculated Members dialog provides a number of the most common examples and include shortcuts for contribution, variance, ratio, and growth calculations. Additional shortcuts are provided under the Data Analysis tab on the same Calculated Members dialog and include Linear Regression, Trend Lines, and Moving Averages. To add a calculation or data analytic in Crystal Analysis, right-click on a member or a dimension name, and then choose the Calculated Member menu item. This opens the Calculated Members dialog shown in Figure 19.26.

Figure 19.25
Automatic totals with a filter applied display numerous pieces of valuable summary information.

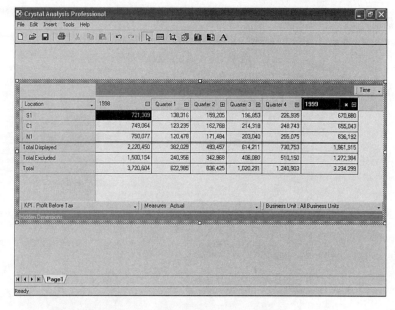

Figure 19.26
The Calculated Members dialog enables creation of advanced members not found in the underlying OLAP data source.

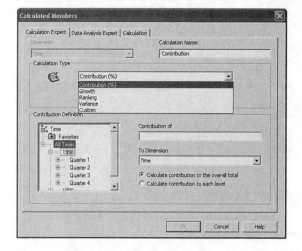

In addition to the Calculation Experts highlighted in Figure 19.26, Crystal Analysis also enables you to create custom calculations that can leverage a rich set of Multi-Dimensional Expressions (MDX) on SQL Server Analysis Services cubes or Crystal OLAP Syntax on other data sources. This advanced functionality is introduced in more detail in Chapter 20, "Advanced Crystal Analysis Report Design."

SORTING AND FILTERING

You can sort and filter reports to isolate important information. These functions help you answer questions such as "What are my top five variances?" and "Which products have the highest sales growth?"

Sorts can be applied to any row or column simply by right-clicking on its heading and using the Sort submenu items, shown in Figure 19.27.

Figure 19.27
The worksheet Sort menu enables the end user to sort the report's data.

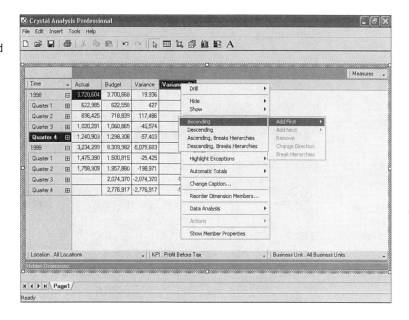

Adding an ascending sort to the variance % column highlights the poorest performing time periods for a given KPI by moving them to the top of the worksheet (see Figure 19.28). Note that the Q3 and Q4 members for 1999 have been removed because they have no actuals in the sample data set.

A sort is indicated by an arrow displayed next to a member name. The arrow points up to indicate an ascending sort and down to show a descending sort. Clicking on the arrow changes the direction of the sort.

By default, a sort respects any dimension hierarchies; that is, the members are sorted within their hierarchical groupings. This behavior is changed through the Sort menu and the result of changing the sort to a "breaks hierarchies" sort is shown in Figure 19.29. The hierarchical relationship between All Time and its children has been broken, and it now appears as the second row.

Figure 19.28
You can sort the variances in the worksheet.

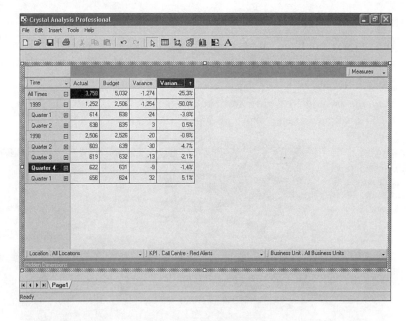

Figure 19.29
Use the Break Hierarchies option to change the order in which the sorted values are displayed.

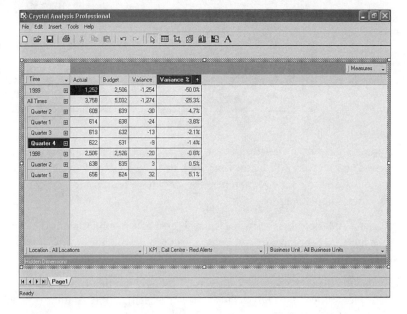

NOTE

Sorts can be nested up to three deep. To add further sorts use the Add Next option in the Sort menu. Nested sorts are indicated by a 1, 2, or 3 displayed next to the sort arrow.

Filters can be applied to any row or column, and also can be applied to the whole work-sheet. Filtering the whole worksheet enables null rows and columns to be removed. Access this by right-clicking in the gray area at the top-left corner of the worksheet and selecting from the resulting menu list, as shown in Figure 19.30. This is a common requirement when using sparsely populated OLAP cubes.

Figure 19.30
Applying a filter to the whole worksheet, removing null rows and columns.

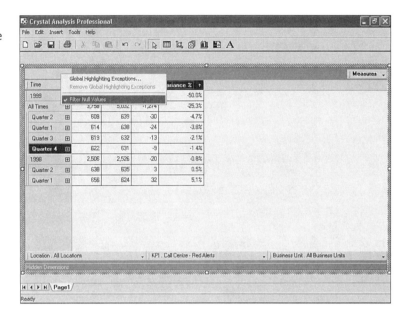

Filtering a specific row or column can be used to pick out the important information in a report. Figure 19.31 shows a filter being added to the variance column, with the aim of iso-lating time periods with variances less than negative 5.

The Define Filter dialog enables the type of filter to be set or changed. In this example the filter hides variances that are less than negative 5. These settings appear in Figure 19.32, and the results are shown in Figure 19.33.

NOTE

An x displayed in the Variance column heading indicates the presence of a filter. The fil-ter can be edited by clicking on the x icon.

In this example the filter was applied based on the displayed data values. Other types of fil-ters are available from this dialog:

- Top/Bottom n: Used to highlight exceptionally good or bad performance; for example, the top or bottom 10 selling products.

- Top/Bottom n%: Used to answer questions such as "Which products contribute the top 5% of sales?" and "Which stores contribute the bottom 5% of margin?"

Figure 19.31
Apply a filter to a column in the worksheet.

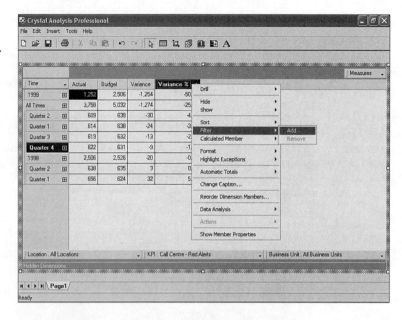

Figure 19.32
Apply a filter to hide variances less than negative 5.

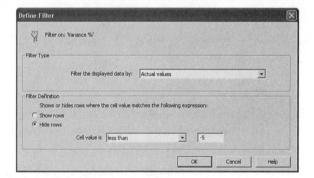

TIP

> A filter considers only members that were displayed in the worksheet. To apply a filter that identifies the top five products, first select no members and then select base members in the Member Selector dialog. As a result, the filter considers only the base-level members.

EXCEPTION HIGHLIGHTING

Exception highlighting, also known as conditional formatting or traffic lighting, is a technique using color to draw attention to values that are out of the ordinary. It might be used on the entire worksheet or only for selected rows or columns of the worksheet.

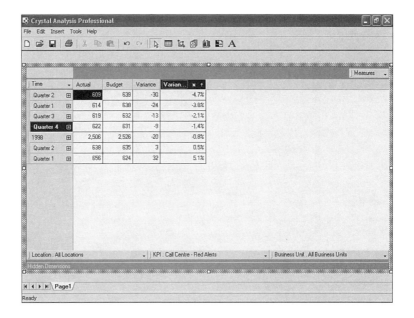

Figure 19.33
A filtered worksheet provides increasingly focused report data for end users.

Access exception highlighting for the whole worksheet by right-clicking in the gray area at the top-left corner of the worksheet and selecting the Global Highlighting Exceptions option.

Highlighting exceptions can also be applied to a single row or column simply by clicking on its heading. Doing this displays the Highlight Exceptions dialog (see Figure 19.34). This enables the definition of the upper and lower limits for highlighting and the formatting to be applied. In this example the involved KPI has been changed to No. of New Products Planned and the recently applied filter has been removed. Here, any values less than 0% are highlighted in red, whereas values more than 5% are highlighted in green. Those values between 0% and 5% are highlighted in yellow. The result appears in Figure 19.35.

Figure 19.34
Apply exception highlighting to a column in the worksheet.

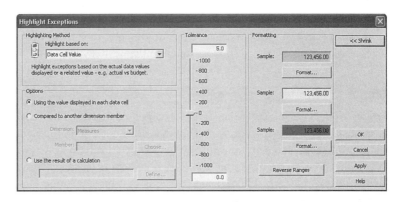

Figure 19.35
Here is an example of exception highlighting, showing adverse variances in red.

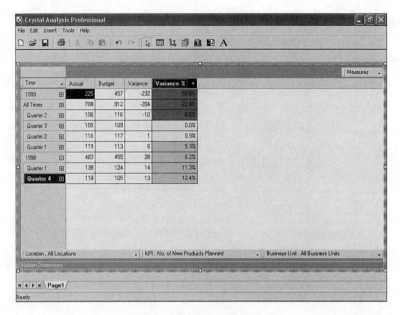

In this example, the exception highlighting is applied based on the displayed data values. This works well where the data value is a percentage but is problematic for absolute values, which change magnitude as the user drills down. To cater to these situations, other types of exception highlighting are available from the Highlight Exceptions dialog:

- **Compared to Another Dimension Member.** Highlights the displayed values according to their relationship to another member on the same dimension. For example, color-coding could be applied to Actual values based on their relationship to Budget. This comparison is valid at all levels of the hierarchy.

- **Based on a Calculation.** Enables more sophisticated situations to be catered to, such as "bubble up" reporting, where the number of exceptions below a parent member is used to highlight members higher up the hierarchy. This method also works well when drilling down. Additional typical uses of this type of exceptional highlighting are to compare current members against recent averages, moving averages, or growth rates. Calculations are covered in more detail in the next chapter.

ACTIONS

Actions are a powerful feature of Crystal Analysis version 10. They enable you to extend the functionality of your applications in a number of ways through the right-click context menu off the worksheet object. Actions provide impressive flexibility to Crystal Analysis Reports and Applications through external application launching (such as Crystal Reports), redirection to external URLs or HTML code, sending of e-mail, opening files, and so on. This advanced functionality is covered in detail in the next chapter.

ADDING CHART OBJECTS TO CRYSTAL ANALYSIS REPORTS

Similar to the Crystal Reports Report Design environment, Crystal Analysis provides a visualization capability to facilitate meaningful data analysis on top of the numerically presented data. To the Crystal Analysis Design Environment, a chart is simply another object that can be added to the report through either the Insert, Chart menu option or the Charting icon. When a chart is added to a report page, the product assumes a number of defaults around the chart's properties that can be edited through the right-click context and properties menus.

NOTE

Unlike the Crystal Reports Design Environment, there is no Charting Expert to step you through the initial chart set-up process. Instead, the chart automatically reflects the current viewpoint of the cube and Crystal Analysis makes default chart option selections that can be edited using the powerful right-click chart editing options—the same ones available in Crystal Reports after a chart has been created with the Chart Expert.

Because the Charting functionality for Crystal Analysis is the same as the Chart Options functionality for Crystal Reports, covered in Chapter 8, "Visualizing Your Data with Charts and Maps," please reference that chapter for details on chart editing and manipulation.

TIP

As mentioned previously, the Chart on any given page reflects the underlying viewpoint (that is, alignment of dimensions) for that page. To change a viewpoint on a given page that only contains a chart, temporarily add a worksheet object and manipulate the dimensions there until the chart reflects the appropriate view, and then delete the previously inserted worksheet.

CAUTION

Because Charts reflect the current viewpoint of any given page and all of a viewpoint's currently displayed row and column dimension members, it is instructive to pay close attention to the data that is intended to be visualized in a chart. If, for example, a meaningful Visualization on Variance % over different KPIs was required but both the Actual and Budget numbers were still part of the viewpoint, the graphic would appear meaningless because the Magnitude of the Actuals and Budgets would change the scale of the graphic; it would be meaningless for projecting information on Variance %. Figures 19.36 and 19.37 show the differences in visualization. A good workaround here involves setting up a page with only the Variance % viewpoint and chart, and providing navigation buttons (covered in Chapter 20) to that page from the other report pages where Actual and Budget are displayed.

19

Figure 19.36
A Variance % Chart that shows Actuals and Budget members.

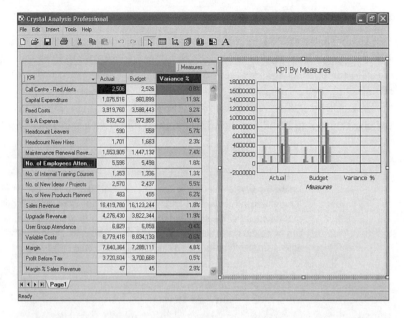

Figure 19.37
A Variance % Chart that does not show Actuals and Budget members.

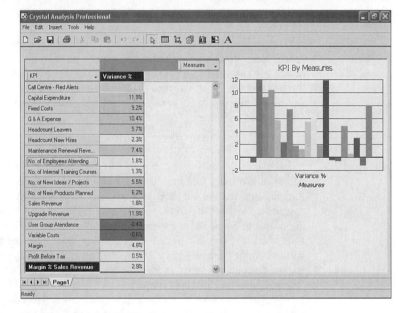

TROUBLESHOOTING

CREATING A CHART BASED ON A SPECIFIC FIELD

I want to create a chart based on changing a specific field but don't know how.

Select the On Change Of charting option and then specify the field or fields to break the chart sections on by selecting any of the fields in the available fields listing. Unlike the drop-down box under the Group layout, you can select any of the available report fields in this interface, dynamically order them with the Order button, or restrict their display on the report to a specified Top or Bottom N with the Top N button.

CHAPTER 20

ADVANCED CRYSTAL ANALYSIS REPORT DESIGN

In this chapter

INTRODUCTION

Crystal Analysis provides even more power and greater flexibility for report designers than the powerful Worksheet and Charting functionality introduced in the last chapter. Several additional Analytic Objects are available for use in report design and the Crystal Analysis Designer provides advanced parameter capabilities that facilitate end-user interactivity with the underlying report. These parameters enable end users to specify a number of different parameters within a report, including but not limited to the actual underlying cube, the member-sets, and the dimension members.

Other advanced capabilities provided within Crystal Analysis include Crystal Analysis Actions and Data Analysis. Actions provide a flexible and powerful method of extending the reach of Crystal Analysis applications outside of the existing report. Data Analysis provides some out-of-the-box statistical functions to enable rapid report design and end-user analysis—these include Trend Line, Regression Analysis, and Moving Average calculations in addition to Best Fitting Curve and Summary Statistics functions.

This chapter covers the following advanced Crystal Analysis capabilities:

- Crystal Analysis Advanced Designer Objects
- Crystal Analysis parameters
- Crystal Analysis actions
- Data Analysis and Calculations including an introduction to Multi-Dimensional Expressions (MDX) and Crystal OLAP Syntax (COS)
- Report Options menu

ADVANCED CRYSTAL ANALYSIS DESIGNER TOOLS

Chapter 19, "Creating Crystal Analysis Reports," introduced the most traditional and common multidimensional or OLAP analytic objects with the Worksheet and Charting objects. Crystal Analysis provides four other analytic objects that can be used to enhance and extend end-user interactivity with the involved reports past the traditional boundaries of other OLAP Client products. The next few sections introduce their powerful capabilities.

USING DIMENSION EXPLORER OBJECTS IN CRYSTAL ANALYSIS

The Dimension Explorer gives users direct control of the view of a cube from outside of the worksheet. This object, shown in Figure 20.1 with all options turned on, enables users to dynamically change cube orientation (that is, which dimensions or on what axes) and member selection across one or all dimensions.

Changes that take place within Dimension Explorer directly affect the other analytic objects on the same page (such as a Worksheet or Chart). Table 20.1 highlights the different components of the Dimension Explorer, and their functions and typical uses. Configure these by right-clicking to access the Properties menu of the involved Dimension Explorer.

Dimension root node   Dimension Explorer toolbar

Dimension selection drop-down

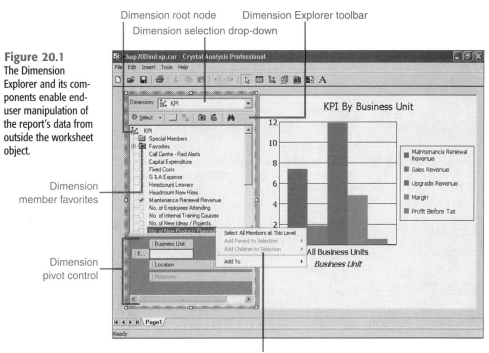

Figure 20.1
The Dimension
Explorer and its com-
ponents enable end-
user manipulation of
the report's data from
outside the worksheet
object.

Dimension
member favorites

Dimension
pivot control

Dimension Explorer right-click context menu

TABLE 20.1   DIMENSION EXPLORER COMPONENTS AND SAMPLE USAGE CASES

Dimension Explorer Component	Function	Sample Usage Case
Favorites	Toggles the display of the Favorite node and the Favorite set-up function on the toolbar.	Favorites provides report end users with the capability to create their own custom favorite groups. These groups are then subsequently available for rapid personalized access. This would likely be only turned off for a novice user group that might become overwhelmed with too much power too quickly.
Dimension bar	Enables users to select the different dimensions in the data source including all non-hidden and hidden row, column, and sliced dimensions.	You can turn this off if you only want the end user to be able to affect a designer-specified dimension. Alternatively, it can be left available to give an end user a single place to select members and member-sets from all dimensions—even hidden dimensions.

continues

TABLE 20.1	CONTINUED	
Dimension Explorer Component	**Function**	**Sample Usage Case**
Pivot control	Provides a compact area where the end user can reorient the row, column, and slice dimensions.	Generally provided as a compact alternative to the same capability in the worksheet. Open to the report designer's preference.
Toolbar	Provides numerous user tools to expedite member-set selection on involved dimensions. These include user shortcuts to member-set selections, display modes, favorite group set-up, and an advanced search utility.	You can turn this off if you do not want to provide end users with the access to the advanced member selection capabilities. It should be left on when the end users will be selecting their own member-sets.
Border	Toggles the display of a border on the Dimension Explorer object.	This is an aesthetic decision made according to the report designer's preference.
Root node	Toggles the display of the dimension's root node.	Can be safely turned off based on report designer preference as long as the dimension bar is displayed to highlight the current dimension.
Allow Context Menus	Toggles the right-click menu option on the Dimension Explorer for end users. Access to a multitude of dimension functions can be accessed through the right-click menus.	This would be turned off if the end user was not intended to access the variety of provided dimension-related functions. This includes dimension swapping, member selection, favorite group creation, and display options. One important note here is that the menus are either on or off; there is unfortunately no means (yet) to restrict access to a subset of the context menu items.

As you might have surmised, the Dimension Explorer does not provide any new functionality over the worksheet introduced in the last chapter but it does provide another method of deploying a good degree of dimension exploration and reorientation functionality to the end user. Figure 20.2 highlights a Crystal Analysis report presenting a Dimension Explorer based off the sample KPI cube provided by Crystal.

TIP

The Pivot Control and Member Selection capabilities of the Dimension Explorer can provide a report design option for designers who want to restrict end user's capabilities. By including these within a Dimension Explorer on a report page, end users will be able to manipulate dimensions and member selections in a report but will not be able to access any of the remaining worksheet functionality covered in the previous chapter (such as Calculations, Filtering, Sorting, Exception Highlighting, Formatting, and so on).

Figure 20.2
A Crystal Analysis report showing a Dimension Explorer with three Favorite groups defined and one selected to drive the appearance of the corresponding Chart object.

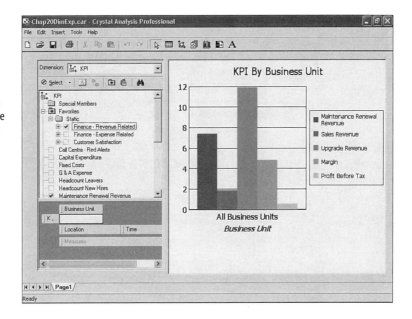

As discussed in Chapter 19, the chart in Figure 20.2 reflects the viewpoint of the page on which it is located. With the Dimension Explorer, you relieve the requirement of needing a worksheet on the same report page as a chart to make it interactive because the content of the chart can be driven exclusively through the Dimension Explorer. Try to re-create this report yourself, complete with new Favorite Groups called Customer Satisfaction and Finance—Revenue Related.

NOTE

In addition to enabling end users to create favorite member groupings and selections, Crystal Analysis provides support for Server-side Named Sets created in Microsoft SQL Server Analysis Services. The Named Sets, which are themselves server-defined custom member groupings (such as Top 10 Selling Products), appear under a new Server node found under the Favorites node in the Member Selector.

Using the Slice Navigator Objects

The Slice Navigator object enables users to explore and edit the current viewpoint's slice dimensions and their associated members. The Slice Navigator, shown in Figure 20.3, is best thought of as an in-line parameter selection mechanism for the Crystal Analysis Report.

Figure 20.3
The Slice Navigator object and its components.

Hidden dimensions panel available in design mode
Slice Navigator dimension panel buttons
Slice Navigator right-click context menu

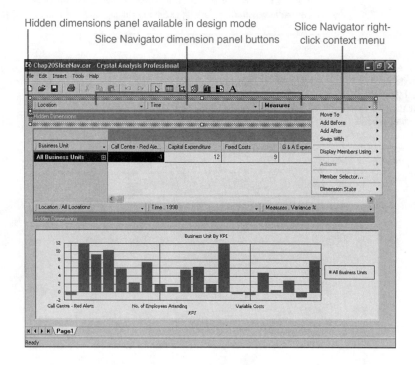

Changes that take place within the Slice Navigator directly affect the other analytic objects on the same page (such as a Worksheet or Chart). Table 20.2 highlights the different components of the Slice Navigator and their functions and typical uses. These are configurable by right-clicking the Properties menu of the involved Slice Navigator.

TABLE 20.2   SLICE NAVIGATOR COMPONENTS AND SAMPLE USAGE CASES

Slice Navigator Component	Function	Sample Usage Case
Panel Button	Toggles the display and function of the Panel Button drop-down icon. This button provides access to the same member selector dialog covered in Chapter 19 and related to the Worksheet object.	Generally turned off if the Slice Navigator is only being used to display the sliced dimension current members (that is, the non-row or -column). Often turned on to enable end users to access member selection from this object.

Slice Navigator Component	Function	Sample Usage Case
Member Names	Toggles the display of the currently selected member names beside the actual dimension name.	Generally turned off only if the member name was visible elsewhere on the report.
Border	Toggles the display of a border on the slice navigation object.	This is an aesthetic decision made according to the report designer's preference.
Tile Panels	Toggles the display of the Slice Navigator Dimensions as either horizontally or vertically stacked.	If the Report Page has limited vertical space, use the Tile Panels option to stretch the slice navigator horizontally. If there is limited horizontal space, turn the Tile Panels off to stack the sliced dimensions panels vertically.
Allow Context Menus	Toggles the right-click menu option on the Slice Navigator for end users. Access to a multitude of dimension- and member-related functions is available through the right-click menus.	This would be turned off if you don't intend for the end user to access the dimension- and member-related functions. This includes dimension swapping, member selection, and display options. One important note here is that the menus are either on or off; unfortunately, there is not yet means to restrict access to a subset of the context menu items.

Use the Slice Navigator on Crystal Analysis Report Pages when you want to present a locked-down worksheet or chart view (that is, no dimension reorientation) yet still want to enable the end user to edit the parameters around the fixed display (that is, edit the sliced dimension members). Figure 20.4 highlights a report page based on the Crystal Sample KPI cube with the slice navigator providing a parameter selection capability that drives the chart and worksheet display.

USING ANALYSIS BUTTON OBJECTS

Analysis Buttons enable end users to rapidly analyze data and move between different analytic viewpoints at the click of a button. The simple user interface that Analysis Buttons provide brings the power of OLAP and multidimensional data sources to the masses.

Analysis Buttons enables single-click provision of any of the following capabilities to end users:

- Changing the current viewpoint of the Worksheet and chart objects on a single report page.
- Moving to another page in the application and controlling the viewpoint of the Worksheet or chart objects on the new report page.

20

- Flexible Drill-down on user-selected members from the worksheet object.

- Executing actions that can open other Crystal Analysis or Crystal Report reports, third-party applications, Web pages, e-mail notes, and so on. The Actions section later in this chapter covers these capabilities.

Slice Navigator driving the content of the associated worksheet and chart

Figure 20.4
Here is a Crystal Analysis report with the Slice Navigator driving a Viewpoint reflected on the corresponding Chart and Worksheet objects.

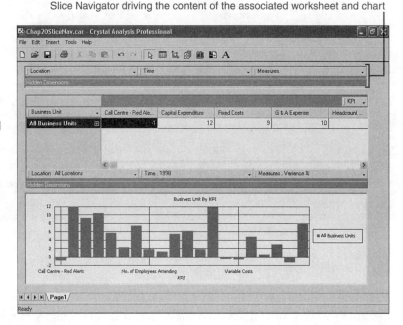

Figure 20.5 shows a familiar sample report that has been enhanced with the provision of three Analysis Buttons—Customer Satisfaction, Finance—Revenue Related, and All KPIs.

Each of the three Analysis Buttons provides the end user with a single-click method of changing the viewpoint on the associated worksheet and chart objects (after the Crystal Analysis report has been locked down or published to Crystal Enterprise). The report designer provides this capability by right-clicking on the Analysis button after it has been added to a report page. Figures 20.6 and 20.7 highlight the Analysis Button Properties dialog accessed by right-clicking on an Analysis Button and selecting Properties.

Figure 20.5
This is a Crystal Analysis report with three Analysis Buttons driving the viewpoint reflected on the corresponding Chart and Worksheet objects.

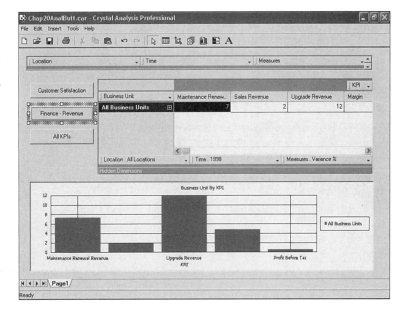

Figure 20.6
The Analysis Button Properties dialog is where you name the Analysis Button and select a transition page or action.

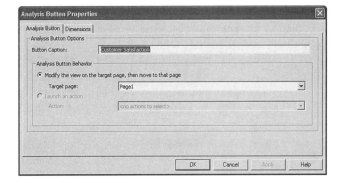

Figure 20.7
On the Dimensions tab of the Analysis Button Properties dialog, you can select a dimension member based on the involved analysis button.

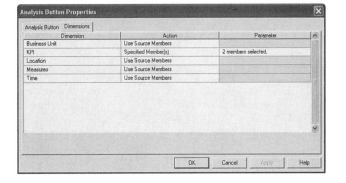

Table 20.3 describes the various properties, functions, and uses that can be set for Analysis buttons.

TABLE 20.3   ANALYSIS BUTTON COMPONENTS AND USAGE CASES

Analysis Button Component	Function	Sample Usage Case
Analysis Button Tab—Button Caption	Enables you to specify the label to be displayed on the Analysis Button.	To present the end user with a clear button label that indicates the button's purpose.
Analysis Button Tab—Modify the View on the Target Page, then move to that Page	Enables you to specify the report page onto which the involved action button takes the user when he or she clicks it.	By specifying the same report page that the Analysis Button resides on, the end user can change the viewpoint of a single report page dynamically and rapidly. By specifying a different page, the end user can navigate among the different report pages in a Crystal Analysis report and pass data context amongst them—and have all that logic wrapped up within the button.
Analysis Button Tab—Launch an Action	Enables you to specify the action that is launched when the user presses the involved Analysis Button. Actions are covered in detail later in this chapter.	When actions are defined for a report, Analysis Buttons can be used to launch them. This powerful function enables you to link to external applications (such as a product ordering system), email systems, other Crystal Analysis Reports, or formatted Crystal Reports.
Dimensions Tab—Action	The Dimensions tab enables you to specify the members for each of the dimensions in the Targeted Viewpoint (the new Viewpoint after the Analysis Button has been clicked). There are many options for specifying these Members:	Use these specifications to encapsulate selection logic for the target viewpoint of an Analysis Button. These Analysis Buttons are then used to provide easy-to-use interfaces for non-power analyst end users.
	Use Source Members—Copies the member selection from the originating viewpoint.	Useful when you intend to keep a dimension's members the same both pre- and post-Analysis Button press. This is often the case because it is common to embed the logic to change only one dimension at a time in an Analysis Button.

Analysis Button Component	Function	Sample Usage Case
	Use Target Members—Uses the viewpoint of the targeted report page.	Useful when the targeted report page contains a predefined set of members for a dimension that should not be affected.
	Drill Down (Single, No Parent)—A Focused Drill-down on a selected member from the worksheet.	Useful for encapsulating focused drill-down functionality into an Analysis Button.
	Drill Down (Single, Keep Parent)—Similar to a Focused Drill-down with the exception that Parent member is kept in the viewpoint.	Useful for encapsulating the combination of focused drill-down functionality with keeping the Parent member into an Analysis Button.
	Drill Down (Multiple, No Parent)—A Focused Drill-down on selected members from the worksheet.	Useful for encapsulating focused drill-down functionality on multiple members into an Analysis Button.
	Drill Down (Multiple, Keep Parent)—Similar to a Focused Drill-down on multiple members with the exception that Parent members are kept in the viewpoint.	Useful for encapsulating the combination of focused drill-down functionality on multiple members with keeping the Parent members into an Analysis Button.
	As Selected (only one accepted)—Displays only the selected member (selected by the end user from the worksheet).	Useful for providing users with focused user-driven Analysis Buttons.
	As Selected (multiple accepted)—Displays only the selected members (selected by the end user from the worksheet).	Useful for providing users with focused user-driven Analysis Buttons. An example might enable the end user to select which products to analyze more deeply.
	Specified Member(s)—Displays a predefined (by the report designer) set of members.	Useful for providing users with focused Analysis Buttons based on predefined views (such as Product Sets or Time Periods).

20

continues

TABLE 20.3   CONTINUED

Analysis Button Component	Function	Sample Usage Case
	Range based on Selected Member—Displays a predefined range of members on either side of a user-selected member.	Useful for providing users with a navigation mechanism to move through time dimensions in a user-driven focused method (for example, showing three months of data on either side of a selected member).
Dimensions Tab—Parameter	The Dimensions Tab Parameter Column enables you to specify parameters for both the Specified Member(s) and Range Based on a Selected Member Dimension Column options. Specified members are selected through a traditional Member Selector dialog and ranges are specified by X:Y where X specifies the number of periods before the selected member and Y afterward.	Both parameter selection options enable you to provide predefined viewpoint navigation logic embedded within an Analysis Button.

CAUTION

> Unlike the Member Selector dialogs accessed through the Worksheet, Dimension Explorer, and Slice Navigator, the Member Selector dialog box accessed from the Specified Members option does not provide access to Favorites or Named Sets (a Microsoft SQL Server capability described earlier in this chapter). As such, be careful when re-creating these lists through this Member Selector to ensure they reflect the member lists you are targeting.

TIP

> Often, a report contains multiple Analysis Buttons all providing only slightly different functions to the end user. To facilitate Report Design, make sure to use the Copy and Paste functions accessible from the right-click menu on the Analysis Buttons.

USING TEXT BOX OBJECTS

The Analytic Objects covered to this point have highlighted the powerful function that Crystal Analysis provides on top of multidimensional (for example, OLAP) data sources. The last object available for use in Report Design is the text box and is exclusively focused on report formatting. Figure 20.8 shows a variation of the sample reports worked on in this chapter with some strategically placed text boxes added for aesthetic affect.

Figure 20.8
Add text objects to a
KPI report.

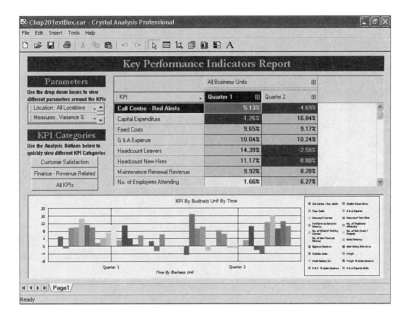

Standard formatting capabilities are provided through the Text Box properties dialog, which you can access by right-clicking on the involved text box.

CREATING PARAMETERS WITH THE PARAMETER MANAGER

Similar to the Crystal Reports parameters discussed in Chapter 5, "Implementing Parameters for Dynamic Reporting," Crystal Analysis also provides you with a rich parameter capability. These parameters enable you to re-use a single report/application across multiple user groups or users with different filtering requirements. Crystal Analysis parameters can be set for the following:

- The underlying cube (for example, the report data source)
- The selected member of an active or hidden sliced dimension
- The selected set of members ('member-set') for any of the row or column dimensions
- The opening page of the report

→ For more information on Crystal Reports parameters, **see** "Creating and Implementing Parameters Fields," on **p. 129**

To add any of these parameters to a report, first use the Parameter Manager shown in Figure 20.9 to define the parameters. You can access this from the Tools menu.

Each parameter is specified through five pieces of information in the Parameter Manager: a parameter name, the chosen parameter type (Cube, Member, Memberset, or Page), the default value for the parameter, a prompting toggle, and prompting text (description). All of these are rather intuitive except for the prompting toggle that is used to specify that end users should be prompted for the report when they view it through Crystal Enterprise. If this is turned off, users will not be prompted for a parameter and the last saved value for that value in the report will be used.

Figure 20.9
The Crystal Analysis Parameter Manager enables you to add parameters to their Crystal Analysis reports.

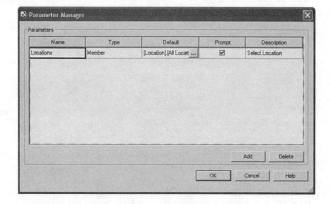

The second step to using parameters in a Crystal Analysis Report is to configure any dimensions that are to use the incoming parameters (Members or Memberset parameters only) as filters for their associated member selection. You specify this in the Member Selector for the involved dimensions. Figure 20.10 shows this selection for the Location Dimension on the sample report from this chapter. The parameters that have been created previously are found and selected under the Special Members node.

Figure 20.10
Existing parameters can be specified as active filters in the Dimension Member Selector of the involved dimensions.

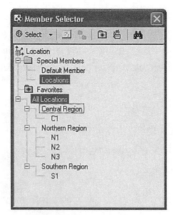

CAUTION

Be careful to test the parameters that you have implemented both in the Crystal Analysis Design Environment and in the Crystal Enterprise Web Delivery environment. Often, the product behavior can be somewhat surprising when you use prompting.

After a parameter has been configured, you make it active for end users by either locking the report in the designer or publishing to Crystal Enterprise. Figure 20.11 displays a report that has been published to Crystal Enterprise and selected by the viewer for viewing. Note the selection screen that has prompted the user for parameter input that is used for filtering the underlying Crystal Analysis report.

Figure 20.11
The Set Parameters dialog and Associated Member Selector dialog on a Web-published Crystal Analysis Report within Crystal Enterprise.

TIP

When publishing Crystal Analysis reports in Crystal Enterprise to maturing or beginning users, it is often instructive to select the ActiveX Viewer for Report Viewing because the DHTML Crystal Analysis Viewer requires typed input for the parameters in special OLAP syntax that new users might find confusing. If ActiveX is against corporate policy or preference, an alternative implementation option is to customize a parameter selection interface and programmatically call the Crystal Analysis reports with the user-selected parameters.

CREATING ACTIONS WITH THE ACTIONS MANAGER

Crystal Analysis actions are a powerful new feature of Crystal Analysis version 10. They enable a Crystal Analysis designer to predefine named operations for report users accessed from four different areas: from dimension headings, from individual members of a dimension, from specific data cells, or from Analysis Buttons. Actions enable end users to kick off other Web pages, link into other applications, initiate e-mail to colleagues, and launch other applications such as Crystal Reports or other Crystal Analysis reports. These links can be made with flexible context awareness of exactly where on the report they were kicked off from (that is, which product member the cursor was on when the action was kicked off).

NOTE

In previous versions of Crystal Analysis, actions defined on a Microsoft SQL Server were supported in much the same way that these new Crystal Analysis actions are supported. In version 10, both SQL Server actions and the new Custom Crystal Analysis actions are supported and accessed in the exact same way. More information on SQL Server actions can be found in the documentation for Microsoft SQL Server Analysis Services.

Actions are accessed in Crystal Analysis by either right-clicking any dimension, dimension member, or data cell, or by clicking an Analysis Button tied to an action, as described earlier in this chapter. If an action is available on the right-clicked report section, the Actions menu option is enabled and access to all defined actions is provided.

A good example of an action could be based on a product dimension and be called Display Detailed Product Information. This might display a detailed Crystal Report based off some relational data from the product master tables and be nicely formatted for printing. An alternative example on the same dimension could be an Order Inventory action based on a product dimension's member. This action would link into the corporate procurement Web site and dynamically pass in the Product ID or Name.

In both the Crystal Analysis designer and the ActiveX Rich Client Web Viewer of Crystal Enterprise, each action appears in the Actions submenu. In the Web (DHTML) client the actions are displayed in a dialog. Figure 20.12 shows an action being called in the DHTML Web Viewer, using the KPI dimension of the sample KPI cube.

Figure 20.12
Invoke an action from the DHTML worksheet in Crystal Enterprise.

Actions are created in the Crystal Analysis Designer using the Action Manager accessible from the Tools menu. The Action Manager shown in Figure 20.13 enables you to Add, Delete, Copy, Edit, and Import Actions from other existing Crystal Analysis reports. Figure 20.13 shows the New Action dialog and Table 20.4 describes the key components of an action.

Figure 20.13
Create a new action in Crystal Analysis with the Action Manager, which you access from the Tools menu.

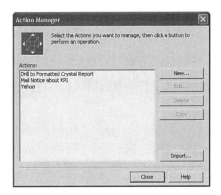

TABLE 20.4   ACTION COMPONENTS AND DESCRIPTIONS

Action Component	Description
Name	The name of the action that shows up to end users in their Action menus. Clear and active descriptions of actions are recommended.
Applies To	There are five options where actions might apply: Nothing—These actions might only be launched from a Crystal Analysis button and cannot include any MDX or Crystal OLAP Syntax Cube—These actions might also only be launched from a Crystal Analysis button but can include any MDX or Crystal OLAP Syntax for dynamic context pass-through Dimension—The action can only be launched from a specified dimension heading Dimension Members—The action can only be launched from member titles within a specified dimension Data Cells—The action can only be launched from a Worksheet Data Cell
Dimension	Enables you to specify the Dimension where the involved action is available. This option is only available for Dimension and Dimension Member actions.
Type	HTML or URL. URL actions open the specified URL in a Web browser. HTML actions render the specified HTML in a Web browser.
Template	The HTML or URL content is the template. The Check Template button on this dialog checks the validity of any involved MDX or Crystal OLAP Syntax in the template. It ignores everything that is kept within double quotes—it does not check URL or HTML syntax. Lastly, the Syntax Editor provides an easy-to-use interface for adding MDX and Crystal OLAP functions and fields into the template. MDX

continues

20

TABLE 20.4 CONTINUED

Action Component	Description
	and Crystal OLAP Syntax are introduced later in this chapter. A few examples shown here highlight the use of the context wildcard '*'.
	URL with MDX:
	`"http://finance.yahoo.com/q?d=t&s=" + *.Name`
	URL with Crystal OLAP Syntax:
	`"http://finance.yahoo.com/q?d=t&s=" + GetName(*)`
	HTML with Crystal OLAP Syntax:
	`"<HTML><P>KPI = " + GetName(*) + "</P></HTML>"`
	E-mail URL with MDX:
	`"mailto:MakeMeRich@broker.com?subject=Buy Some" + [Equity].*.Name`

NOTE

> Remember that actions that apply to nothing cannot use any MDX or Crystal OLAP Syntax within their HTML or URL template. This means that these actions cannot take data context with them to their launched application. To pass in data-driven context at a report level, use the Applies to Cube option.

As alluded to in the last entry of Table 20.4, you can use an asterisk to make an expression context-aware. The use of the asterisk and context depend on where the action was launched. The most common usage of the context asterisk is on Member and Data Cell actions.

For actions launched from a Member, the context asterisk holds the place of the Member from which the action was launched. For example, with MDX, `*.Name` returns the name of the Member from which the action was launched. With Crystal OLAP Syntax, the expression would look like this: `GetName({*})`.

For actions launched from a data cell, the context asterisk specifies the column or row member to which the data cell belongs to. Each cell belongs to multiple dimensions, so you must specify the dimension you want. For example, with MDX, `[KPI].*.Name` returns the name of the member in the Products dimension that corresponds to the cell from where the action was launched. With Crystal OLAP Syntax, the expression would look like this: `GetName({KPI@*})`.

Finally, the following HTML example shows how to specify the column, row, and sliced dimension members corresponding to a specific data cell:

LISTING 20.1 HTML CODE HIGHLIGHTING CONTEXT PLACEHOLDERS FOR ALL DIMENSIONS

```
"<HTML><P>
KPI  = " + [KPI].*.Name +
"</P><P>
```

```
Business Unit = " + [Business Unit].*.Name +
"</P><P>
Time Period = " + [Time].*.Name +
"</P><P>
Measures = " + [Measures].*.Name +
"</P><P>
Location = " + [Location].*.Name +
"</P></HTML>"
```

The calling interface and the results of this action, known as Display Data Cell Context in the samples, are displayed in Figure 20.14.

Figure 20.14
Calling a Data Cell action and the resulting HMTL page showing the context of the selected cell. This context could be used to drive external applications.

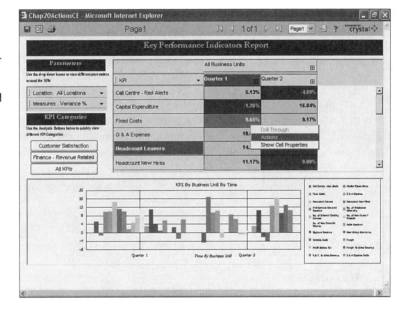

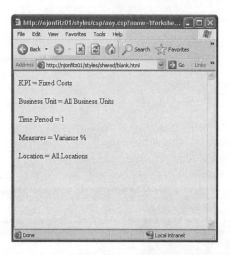

Although the Edit, Delete, and Copy commands in the Action Manager are quite intuitive, the Import Action option is a little more novel. The Import capability enables you to copy actions from any other Crystal Analysis report maintained in the Crystal Enterprise system. To complete an import, log on to Crystal Enterprise and navigate to the desired Crystal Analysis Report. Upon selection of the report, you are prompted to select one or more of the actions that exist in that report to import. The imported actions now become part of the current report.

CUSTOM CALCULATIONS AND ADVANCED DATA ANALYSIS

Additional Calculations and Data Analytics not provided in a report's underlying data source can be added to the data presented in the worksheet through the Calculations and Data Analysis menu, which you access by right-clicking on any member header. These are available at Design time and at End-User Delivery time if context menus have been enabled on the involved Worksheet object. A number of the most common calculations are provided in the Calculated Members dialog and include drag-and-drop parameter-based experts. Additional experts are provided under the Data Analysis tab on the same Calculated Members dialog. To add any of these default calculations or to create a completely new calculation, right-click on a member or a dimension name, and then choose the Calculated Member option. This opens the Calculated Members dialog shown in Figure 20.15.

NOTE

> Crystal Analysis automatically chooses a name for any of the predefined calculations. You can change this by typing the preferred name in the Calculation Name edit box.

Figure 20.15
The Calculated Members dialog provides the report designer and end user with the capability to create custom calculated members not available in the OLAP data source.

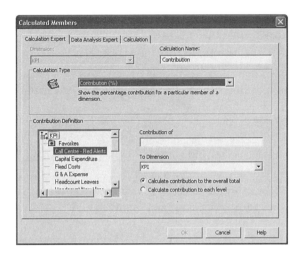

THE CALCULATION EXPERTS

The Calculation Experts provided by Crystal Analysis on the Calculation Expert tab are

- Contribution: Calculates how much each member of a hierarchical dimension contributes to its parent. For example, how much does each week, period, and quarter contribute to total sales?

- Growth: Calculates how much a value has changed from one period to the next. For example, what is the percentage growth in sales week on week, period on period, and quarter on quarter?

- Ranking: Calculates the rank of each member in a dimension, usually based on a measure. For example, rank each product based on sales.

- Variance: Compares the value of one dimension member with a target value; the resulting variance can be expressed as an absolute value or a percentage variance.

Each of the Calculation Experts requires the specification of a different set of parameters in the Calculated Members dialog. These parameters can be set by either clicking and dragging the appropriate members to the involved parameter field or right-clicking on the chosen member and selecting the appropriate destination from the subsequent pop-up menu.

THE DATA ANALYSIS EXPERTS AND SUMMARIES

The Data Analysis Experts provided by Crystal Analysis under the Data Analysis Expert Tab are

- Trend Line: The Trend Line Expert calculates the straight line that best fits all members of the dimension specified in the Series Dimension list. This is done for the measure specified in the Trend Of box. The least squares method is used: minimizing the sum of the squares of the differences between the actual values specified and the regression line values.

- Moving Average: The Moving Average Expert calculates a centered moving average over all the members within each level of a specified dimension. This is done for the measure specified in the Moving Average parameter box.

- Linear Regression: The Linear Regression Expert calculates the straight line that best fits all the members within each level of the dimension. The members of this dimension form the columns of the Worksheet (assuming you are adding a calculated member as a row) where the X and Y values of the points are given by the members specified in the X Values box and Y Values box, respectively. The least squares method is used: minimizing the sum of the squares of the differences between the actual Y values specified and the regression line values. The regression line is evaluated at these same X values as specified by the member in the X Values box. Use the Linear Regression Expert when the data values you want to regress are not evenly spaced.

Each of the Data Analysis Experts requires you to specify a different set of parameters in the Calculated Members dialog. For a more thorough discussion on these calculations and how they are derived, please consult the Reference section of the Crystal Analysis User Manual provided in the docs directory of your install CD.

CAUTION

> It is very important to understand the scope under which the Data Analysis Experts operate. When you select any of these experts, they operate across the entire set of members for the dimension that has been selected regardless of whether they are displayed on the current worksheet or viewpoint. Not taking this into account can lead to suspicious looking data when not all members are displayed. For scenarios where this assumed scope needs to be modified, the underlying MDX or Crystal OLAP Syntax created by the Data Analysis Expert can be modified under the Calculation tab of the Calculated Members dialog. This is introduced later in this chapter.

In addition to the predefined Data Analysis Experts, Crystal Analysis also provides analytic summaries such as Mean, Variance, Standard Deviation, and Best Fitting Curve. Access these summaries by right-clicking any member header and choosing Data Analysis. Figure 20.16 shows the Best Fitting Curve dialog and associated calculations.

Figure 20.16
You access supporting statistics in the Best Fitting Curve dialog box by choosing the Data Analysis menu option.

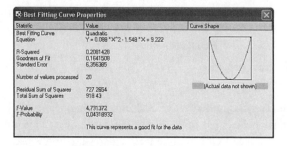

For detailed insights into the statistics behind the Data Analysis summaries, review the Algorithms.pdf document distributed on the product CD.

CUSTOM CALCULATIONS WITH MDX OR CRYSTAL OLAP SYNTAX

In addition to all the experts introduced in the previous two sections, there are times when additional calculations are required to meet a designer or end user's need. The Calculations tab highlighted in Figure 20.17 enables you to create such calculations—or, as is often the case, modify existing calculations (for example, to change the scope of application for a Moving Average or Other Calculation).

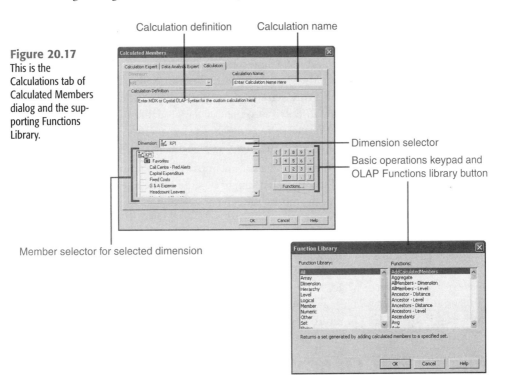

Figure 20.17
This is the Calculations tab of Calculated Members dialog and the supporting Functions Library.

Crystal OLAP Syntax and MDX

Crystal OLAP Syntax and MDX (**M**ulti-**D**imensional E**x**pressions) are related but different syntaxes that support the definition and manipulation of multidimensional objects and data. They can be conceptually thought of as a parallel to Structured Query Language (SQL), which is used for querying relational data, but for multidimensional data sources. There is, however, no direct relationship between SQL and either MDX or Crystal OLAP Syntax. Crystal Analysis uses MDX to access SQL Server cubes and Crystal OLAP Syntax for the remaining supported data sources. Thorough descriptions can be found online for MDX at www.msdn.com (search on MDX) and in the Crystal Analysis Help file (look up Crystal OLAP in the Index tab).

Similar to an SQL query, each MDX or Crystal OLAP query requires a data request (the SELECT clause), a starting point (the FROM clause), and a filter (the WHERE clause). These and other keywords provide the tools used to extract specific portions of data from a cube for analysis. Crystal Analysis uses MDX and Crystal OLAP queries to capture data from the underlying multidimensional data sources. When using MDX (against SQL Server cubes), these queries can be viewed and edited through the Edit MDX option on the Tools menu. Additionally, both these syntaxes support extension through use of calculated members. This is generally the focal area for the report designer's exposure to MDX or Crystal OLAP and is covered through some practical examples later in this section.

The Calculations Tab consists of the four major components, shown in Figure 20.17. These components facilitate the creation of Crystal OLAP or MDX statements that can be converted into meaningful fields usable by Crystal Analysis designers and end users:

- Calculation Definition: This is the actual MDX (if you're using SQL Server) or Crystal OLAP Syntax that is calculated by or through Crystal Analysis against the underlying data source.

- Dimension and Member Selectors: These components facilitate the selection of Dimensions and Dimension Members to be used in creating the custom calculation. When dimensions or members are selected through a double-click, the appropriate syntax for referencing them is transposed into the calculation definition for future editing. It is worth noting that the transposed text might not always reflect the exact user-friendly member syntax displayed in the Member Selector.

- OLAP Functions Library: Clicking on the Functions Library button provides a library of MDX or Crystal OLAP functions that might be used in the creation of the involved custom calculation. A few of the most common and useful functions are described in the next section.

- Basic Operations Keypad: A keypad providing and basic math operations and numerics for use in creating the calculation definition.

Once created, a resultant MDX or Crystal OLAP definition created through the Calculations tab appears as just another member in the involved Crystal Analysis report-- which could even be used in future custom calculations.

SETTING REPORT OPTIONS

The one menu option from Crystal Analysis not covered to this point is the Report Options menu, shown in Figure 20.18.

Figure 20.18
The Options dialog, which you access from the Tools menu.

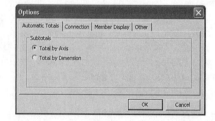

There are four tabs on the Options dialog that control some global behavior on the involved Crystal Analysis report:

- Automatic Totals: The Automatic totaling function accessed by right-clicking on the worksheet can be applied either at the axis or dimension level. This is clearly of relevance in reports with nested dimensions only.

- Connection Passwords: This option enables you to specify the degree of database security you want to implement around your Crystal Analysis report.

- Member Display: Enables you to set a global variable on whether a Member's name, caption, or both are displayed in reports.

- Other: Two toggles are provided here. One shows the Welcome Screen when Crystal Analysis starts that enables report file selection, and the other provides a Report Template Selection dialog for every inserted page in a report. Both options are generally worth keeping turned on.

TROUBLESHOOTING

CALCULATED MEMBERS DIALOG

I can't seem to set the parameters in the Calculated Members dialog.

Don't double-click and drag the parameter, but rather click once and drag it.

CRYSTAL ANALYSIS IN THE REAL WORLD—MDX

As mentioned in the previous section, the primary exposure that a Crystal Analysis designer has to MDX or Crystal OLAP Syntax is in the creation of custom calculations not already available in the data source. This section provides some real-world examples of MDX in action to facilitate some quick learning. Table 20.5 highlights a few sample calculations, their purpose and a quick explanation of their components.

TABLE 20.5   MDX SAMPLES

Calculation	Description	MDX and/or Crystal OLAP Syntax
Member Name	Often in Financial Reporting, the repetition of the Member Name is required in the middle of the worksheet (see Figure 20.19). This can be accomplished using the MDX CurrentMember and Name functions. In Figure 20.19, the caption has been changed to dashes for cosmetic reasons.	`KPI.CurrentMember.Name` Crystal OLAP provides similar functionality with the `GetName` function.

continues

TABLE 20.5 CONTINUED

Calculation	Description	MDX and/or Crystal OLAP Syntax
Variance	The Variance function provided in the Calculation Expert uses the conditional IIF MDX function to check for null values and basic member syntax and math to calculate the variance.	```IIf([Measures].[Budget] = NULL, NULL, ((([Measures].[Actual]-- [Measures].[Budget]) / [Measures].[Budget]) * 100)``` Note that the sample OLAP cube already had a Variance calculation created but was re-created here to demonstrate the MDX.

Growth	The Growth function provided in the Calculation Expert provides a default growth calculation based on the growth of the current member (Q2 1998 in Figure 20.19) over the immediately previous member (Q1 1998) at that member's level in the hierarchy. In the example shown in Figure 20.19, this will not do because a Year over Year comparison is required. The default MDX provides a good starting point for modification. The original calculation used the PrevMember MDX function to capture the last Quarter. This needed to be replaced in the new calculation with a cocktail of MDX functions including Cousin, CurrentMember, Parent, and PrevMember MDX functions.	The Default Growth Function MDX:
		```IIf([KPI].&[1] = NULL, NULL, IIf(Count({ ([KPI].&[1], [Time].PrevMember) }) > 0, 100 * (([KPI].&[1]--([KPI].&[1], [Time].PrevMember)) / ([KPI].&[1], [Time].PrevMember)), 0))```
		
		The Edited Growth Function to Reflect Year over Year Growth:
		```IIf([KPI].&[1] = NULL, NULL, IIf(Count({([KPI].&[1], Cousin([Time].CurrentMember,[Time]. CurrentMember.Parent.PrevMember))}) > 0, 100 * (([KPI].&[1]--([KPI].&[1], Cousin([Time].CurrentMember, [Time].CurrentMember.Parent. PrevMember))) / ([KPI].&[1], Cousin([Time].CurrentMember,[Time].CurrentMember.Parent. PrevMember))), 0))```
		
		Note that Cousin looks for the member at the same level of the first argument in the same relative position underneath the second argument's hierarchy.

Calculation	Description	MDX and/or Crystal OLAP Syntax
Parent Company Sales	The LookUpCube function enables you to process an MDX statement on a separate cube within the same SQL Server database. In this hypothetical example, the Sales Report cube is accessed and Sales for All Products in the most recent year (using the LastChild MDX command) is reported back into this report. Now, you have the ability to perform more interesting financial calculations such as Contribution to Parent Company's revenues.	LookupCube("Sales Reports", "([Products].[All Products], [Year].[All Years].LastChild)") Note that members in the Sales Reports Cube that are not explicitly specified are set to their defaults. Ensure these are appropriate before completing a calculation. External Table Look-ups are *not* available in Crystal OLAP syntax—only in MDX and SQL Server Analysis Services.

Default variance calculation with exception highlighting

Customized MDX calculation displaying member name

Figure 20.19
This sample report available for download at UsingCrystal.com highlights the additional power MDX Calculations can provide to Crystal Analysis reports.

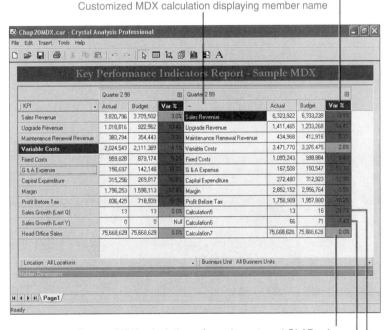

Custom MDX calculation referencing external OLAP cube

Customized growth MDX calculation (quarter versus same quarter previous year)

Default growth calculation (quarter versus previous quarter)

From the few examples highlighted, it should be clear that MDX and Crystal OLAP Syntax add a great deal of flexibility to your Crystal Analysis Reports. It also should have become evident that all the existing calculation experts are based on underlying MDX or Crystal OLAP syntax, and this is a great place to begin exploring the differing capabilities of these query languages.

CHAPTER 21

AD-HOC APPLICATION AND EXCEL PLUG-IN FOR AD-HOC AND ANALYTIC REPORTING

In this chapter

INTRODUCING AD-HOC REPORTING CONCEPTUALLY

Too many competing definitions of ad-hoc reporting exist to dispense with any introduction. This chapter does not pretend to address the larger question of defining ad-hoc as a concept, but rather seeks to place the Crystal Enterprise Ad-Hoc tool into context. Simply put, Ad-Hoc reporting or queries are impromptu questions you put to the data to extract answers. Although many permutations exist, from systems that enable the end user to directly query source data in raw form to accessing OLAP cubes, from tools for very SQL-savvy users to point-and-click tools, from preformatted or unformatted query tools to tools that enable pixel-level formatting, many tools and definitions exist in the marketplace.

Crystal Enterprise's Ad-Hoc tool most facilitates end-user Crystal Reports development and modification through a Web browser. Whether the data source is a database, prebuilt Business View, or another Crystal Report, the result is always a Crystal Report. Although Crystal Analysis provides end users great interactivity, its exclusive connectivity to an OLAP data source helps you categorize it as an Analytic rather than Ad-Hoc tool.

Most organizations debate the amount and type of deployment of various types of Business Intelligence, from reporting to ad-hoc reporting, to query and analysis, to analytic workbooks, to purpose-built applications. Briefly, a typical organization, after reaching a mature stage of Business Intelligence deployment, finds that roughly 80%–90% of information distribution takes place with preformatted reports. Roughly 10%–15% might be ad-hoc queries and another 5% analytics. Every organization varies, but a balance between the time and training necessary for end users to interact with data and the value they derive in the process should be fundamental.

Many organizations actually adopt ad-hoc reporting as a method to reduce IT workload/spending and to provide increased end-user access to data. The Ad-Hoc tool facilitates this approach by enabling end users to develop a Crystal Report themselves. This Crystal Report can then be saved into the Crystal Enterprise system and viewed at any time, or even passed to IT for special features to be added. This concept that end users can do more themselves provides significant cost-savings, but recognition that IT will always play a role in Business Intelligence marks a mature approach to the problem at large.

The remainder of this chapter focuses on how to use the Ad-Hoc application as well as the Excel add-ins for Crystal Reports and Crystal Analysis.

INTRODUCING THE CRYSTAL ENTERPRISE AD-HOC REPORTING APPLICATION

The Crystal Enterprise Ad-Hoc Reporting Application uses the capabilities of Crystal Enterprise to present report modification and creation capabilities via a Web browser. HTML and CSP pages make up the application itself. These CSP pages interact with the COM CE-SDK and interact heavily with the Report Application Server (RAS), which provides the server-side report modification capabilities. Through heavy use of JavaScript in the browser, the Ad-Hoc application interacts with the end user more in the fashion of an application rather than a static Web page.

Because of the heavy level of interaction expected with usage of the Ad-Hoc application, administrators should carefully project and monitor usage at the Web server, Crystal Enterprise, and database levels.

The Ad-Hoc application consumes Business Views, Crystal Reports, or ODBC data sources, so database credentials, Crystal Enterprise credentials, and a data access policy should be in place to maximize effective use of the application. For organizations that have determined to use Business Views for all data access, appropriate Business Views should be in place to enable end users to create reports in the Ad-Hoc application, and appropriate permissions on those Business Views granted. For organizations that choose to enable direct access to the databases, again permissions should be granted.

INSTALLING THE AD-HOC APPLICATION

Installation of Crystal Enterprise, along with either the version 10 Premium bundle or Crystal Enterprise Professional with the appropriate "report modification and creation" keycode, are required before installing the Ad-Hoc application.

Note that the Ad-Hoc application supports the same platforms as Crystal Enterprise 10 with the exception of Netscape/Mozilla browser support—the heavy use of JavaScript precluded the compatibility between Internet Explorer and Netscape/Mozilla.

Two versions of the Ad-Hoc program exist and require different installation methods: a CSP version and a JSP version, and a variant of the CSP installation where a Unix Web server works with a Windows Crystal Enterprise server. Depending on your environment and preferences, the proper version should be selected. The install.pdf file on your distribution of the Ad-Hoc application contains detailed instructions on the various installations.

CONFIGURATION OF THE AD-HOC APPLICATION

Several areas must be configured before deploying the Ad-Hoc application. Because the application heavily uses the RAS service/daemon, the settings for the RAS server should be specified for optimal performance. Also, because the Ad-Hoc application enables you to create and modify reports and save them back to the Crystal Enterprise system, you must modify or write appropriate rights to grant to the user or group on the particular folders affected.

→ For more information on optimizing the RAS server performance, **see** "Sizing the Report Application Server," **p. 559** and "Servers and Processing Options," **p. 618**

Further settings inside the Crystal Management Console, under Home, Crystal Applications, Ad-Hoc Report Creation and Modification determine which folders should be used for the default report templates and data sources. The actual contents of those folders display on the right side. In the displayed tree on the left, which shows Crystal Enterprise's folder structure, right-clicking a particular folder opens a menu to manage the folders

21

(see Figure 21.1). At the bottom of the context menu the two options particular to the Ad-Hoc application let you designate the default folders to be used in the application for Data Sources (which displays the folder icon in red) and Templates (in blue). These folders, respectively, contain reports whose data definition provides a starting point for ad-hoc reporting and which you can use to re-format reports by using the template functionality. Often, for simplicity's sake, administrators create a root folder labeled Ad-Hoc and subfolders labeled DataSources and Templates, and then designate them accordingly using the right-click functionality.

Figure 21.1
The Crystal Management Console's Ad-Hoc application management display.

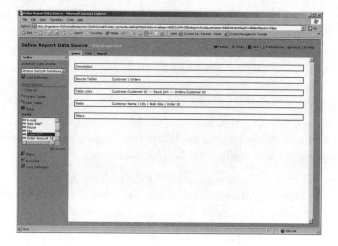

Checking the boxes to enable/disable Business Views or Reports as data sources determines what types of data sources the end users have access to. Business Views, a new feature of Crystal Enterprise 10, provides an easy way to define data in business terms, enabling end users to create reports in the Ad-Hoc application and provide self-service end-user scenarios.

The Manage Groups and Users tabs are identical and manage permissions for the Ad-Hoc application at the group and user level, respectively (see Figure 21.2). Using the group-level permissions enables more efficient management as fewer groups exist than users. You can then set individual user permissions by changing group permissions. If current groups do not map cleanly to the rights appropriate for this particular application, new groups can be created that map existing users or user groups to groups specifically created to manage Ad-Hoc application permissions. The permissions on the right part of the management screen manage which capabilities the end user can see in the toolbar that appears in the end-user application at the left side, the control buttons along the application's top right, and the tabs in the center of the application. Each of these capabilities is considered in the following sections.

REPORT SOURCE SETUP

The Ad-Hoc application enables an end user to create a report from either a Business View or a Crystal Report. Business View creators create and store the Business Views in the

Crystal Enterprise system (refer to Chapter 18, "Crystal Reports Semantic Layer—Business Views"). Creating an Ad-Hoc report from an existing Crystal Report requires a Crystal Report be in the Data-Sources folder as defined previously. You can either design this report in Crystal Reports and save it into the appropriate folder in Crystal Enterprise, move an existing report into that folder, or create it in an administrative area of the Ad-Hoc application itself. Exercise caution when moving an old report into the report definition folders because groupings and table names might confuse end users creating new reports from that definition. Testing in this situation is mandatory to ensure end user success.

Figure 21.2
The Ad-Hoc Application Manage Groups/Manage Users area in the Crystal Management Console.

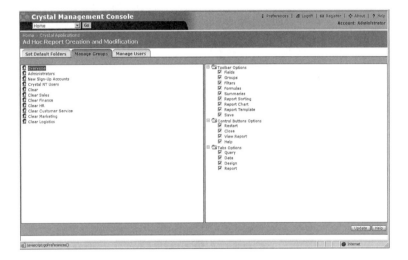

To set up this report definition, start the Ad-Hoc application interface, which has two modes: an Administrator's mode and an end user's mode. Access the application by the application URL (by default, `http://Machinename/crystal/enterprise10/adhoc/`). Logging on to this page with Administrator's credentials provides two options: to Define Report Datasource or to Create Ad-Hoc Report. The Create option refers to the end-user capability covered in the next section. The Define capability refers to the capability to create a report definition that can be used as a data source for an end user creating an Ad-Hoc report at a later time.

Set the report data source definition by choosing to either select an ODBC connection via the Select DB Data Source drop-down on the left under the toolbar, or by clicking on the Load Definition option immediately below it. The Load Definition accesses Crystal Reports stored in the Default Datasources folder designated earlier. Choosing a report here enables you to modify the way that this report's data definition is displayed to an end user creating an Ad-Hoc report. The drop-down list displays the data sources you can connect to if you want to create a Crystal Report from scratch. Typically it contains only the ODBC option. Choosing that option opens a dialog box asking you to select an ODBC connection existing on the server machine that hosts the Report Application Server service/daemon of the Crystal Enterprise system. By choosing the ODBC connection name (DSN), and then

21

supplying the database credentials (username and password), and optionally any connection strings for the ODBC connection, you establish a connection to the database. Keep in mind that because this is a Web application, the dialog to choose the ODBC connection often has an approximately five-second lag, so wait for default values to show in the top line before clicking.

NOTE

> After a data definition loads, you commence moving down the rest of the toolbar—the application design concept has the user start at the top of the toolbar and proceed down by first choosing the definition, selecting tables, linking them, choosing fields, determining filters and then formulas, and then saving this definition. Each of these items on the left is first single-clicked initially, displaying either a dialog box or a simple modification section immediately below it.

Because the dialogs and modification sections in the Ad-Hoc application behave very consistently, a short detour to discuss how you interact with them helps you move through the rest of the material smoothly—especially because this Web application interacts with the end user so much and differs from many Windows conventions and Internet conventions for clicking and maneuvering. Note that the mere inclusion in this book of the following descriptions should trigger the thought that end users require training to successfully use this application. Although quite simple, the application does require some training even if this is only 15 minutes of introduction for the savvy user.

Each item in the toolbar on the left should be clicked *once* only to open it or its dialog box, and then clicked again to hide details that have displayed beneath it. Many users double-click on the toolbar items and wonder why they see nothing! Close dialog boxes by clicking OK or Cancel once. Most dialogs have a list on one side and another list on the other side (see Figure 21.3). In these cases, a single-click selects an item, Ctrl+click adds each clicked item to the current selection, and Shift+click selects everything between the item first selected and the item Shift+clicked. Moving items can be accomplished by double-clicking them, dragging a selection from one area to another, or by clicking the single chevron (>) to move a selection in that direction. Clicking the double-chevron (>>) moves all items in that direction, effectively clearing one area. Remember that response is always slower in a Web application and that clicking multiple times usually results in strange behavior because the application catches up with the user. Counsel end users to wait until they see the desired reaction visibly before going on to the next click or action so that they do not inadvertently cause strange behavior.

This cannot be stressed enough as a crucial part of the education process because end users also often click on an item to open a dialog box, and then click again somewhere else in the same window before the dialog box has opened, causing the dialog box to open *behind* the main window, effectively freezing the application. In cases like this, a savvy user simply minimizes the foreground window and finds the dialog waiting there. However, many times a frustrated user compounds the situation by clicking away in the vain hope that something will happen because he is clicking more, and eventually calls tech support with a frozen

21

application. End users must be carefully instructed that although this application seems like a Windows application, it is still a series of Web pages, and that Web technology has these limitations. You gain by extending the capability to modify and create reports with nothing installed on the machine—you also must live with the resultant limitations.

Figure 21.3
The Data Source Table dialog.

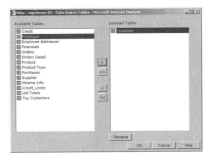

Users might notice a similarity between the items in the toolbar and the Report Creation Wizard in Crystal Reports itself. This similarity is purposeful and makes migration to the concepts in the Ad-Hoc application simple for the user familiar with Crystal Reports. In addition, the underlying functionality of the Ad-Hoc application mirrors that of Crystal Reports, now presented more simply and over the Internet. Thus in an effort not to repeat information here about actual feature behavior, the reader can refer to the appropriate chapter on Crystal Reports for a more detailed understanding of the underlying concepts such as table linking, filter and formula creation, and the like.

The toolbar itself, incidentally, can be moved by clicking and dragging the Toolbar label on the top left, and restored by clicking on the × on the right of the toolbar. The original position of the toolbar on the left side, described as docked, also enables the end user to close it by clicking on the ×, and then restore it by clicking on the triangle icon at the top left.

Returning to the flow of designing a report source, you click once on the Select Tables item to open the select tables dialog box (refer to Figure 21.3). Moving tables to the right includes them in the definition. After you've moved them to the right, you can rename tables by selecting them and clicking once on the Rename button. When you're finished choosing tables to include, choose OK. Again there is a pause after clicking OK as the page re-draws after a round-trip to the server. End users have to be instructed not to click before the page loads again.

After selecting tables, you link them by clicking Link Tables in the toolbar, which opens the Table Linking dialog box (see Figure 21.4). To link tables, select a table on the left, another table on the right, and then the columns in the tables that will make up the link underneath the tables, respectively. Select the desired type of join from the drop-down list, and finally click the Link button once to create the link you have selected. This link now shows up in the Links area of the dialog box. Selecting a join and then clicking the Delete button deletes that join, and clicking the Smart Link button replaces *all* the current joins with joins

21

that the server believes are the best based on column names and index and key positions in the database, if that information is available. Best practice recommends that if you want to use Smart Link functionality, attempt that first, and then examine the results. This way you save work if the joins are correct and can simply delete the incorrect links. When finished, click OK and move to the next item: field selection.

Figure 21.4
The Table Linking
Dialog Box.

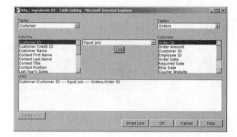

Clicking once on the Field item in the toolbar opens a mini-dialog box underneath the Fields item. Clicking again on Fields hides the mini-dialog. Each time you click on a field in the mini-dialog, an asterisk appears next to that field, and it appears to the right in the Fields area of the Query tab (see Figure 21.5).

Figure 21.5
The Field Selection
mini-dialog.

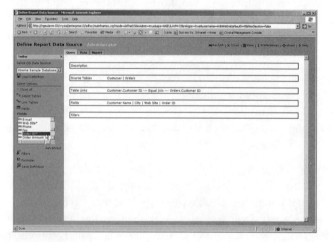

Clicking on the Advanced label underneath the Fields mini-dialog opens an advanced Field dialog box. This dialog enables you to bulk move items and arrange them left-to-right on the report by moving them up or down (up means to the left, and down to the right) in the Fields to Display area by selecting a field and then clicking the up or down arrows at the far right of the dialog box. This advanced dialog arranges available fields by table, but enables you to search for fields by clicking on the Find Fields button, as well as rename fields by selecting the field in the Fields to Display area, and then clicking on the Rename button (see Figure 21.6). Again click the OK button to finish this area and return to the main window.

Figure 21.6
The Advanced Field
Selection dialog.

Clicking on the Filters item opens the Filter mini-dialog, which can be hidden by single-clicking on the Filters item in the toolbar. The process of adding a filter mirrors that in Crystal Reports. Choose the field to filter on in the top drop-down list and choose the operator in the next drop-down list. Then enter the value, or click the Browse button (this is represented by an ellipses [...] on the button), which retrieves values from the database for that field, enabling you to select a particular value from the database if you do not remember the correct value. The Browse button might disappear if the field data type changes to a field type with limited values. For instance, a Boolean field type with only True and False values simply shows True and False in the Value drop-down list, and no longer includes a Browse button.

Remember to click the Add button on the left to add the filter to the top area of the dialog before clicking OK. Clicking OK before adding the filter is like clicking Cancel and results in no filter being applied. Once added, a filter can be modified or removed by highlighting it and then clicking on the proper button at the bottom left of the dialog box (see Figure 21.7).

Figure 21.7
The Filter dialog box.

After creating the appropriate filters, you can add a formula. The formulas appear to end users as fields, and they will not know that these are calculated items. Thus if a database does not contain a necessary field for a query, but the field can be created in a formula from existing database values, the formula here can present the desired value. Clicking on the Formulas button opens a dialog (see Figure 21.8). After it opens, initiate the process by clicking on the New button on the bottom left, which enters a default formula name above at the top right that you can overwrite with the chosen field name for the formula you are about to create. By typing in a valid Crystal Reports formula in the Formula Text box, you create the desired expression. Double-clicking on either a field name or a Function name in the Fields or Functions boxes enters that value into the Formula Text dialog at the point where the cursor was last positioned in that box. For a more detailed discussion of formula

21

syntax, refer to Chapter 4, "Understanding and Implementing Formulas," because the formulas here are exactly the same as formulas in Crystal Reports. In fact, should the report definition require very complicated formulas, the designer should either use Crystal Reports to create the report definition and save it into the correct data sources folder in Crystal Enterprise, or use the Business Views tool to create the formula in a Business View, as both Crystal Reports and Business Views feature a full formula editor. At the bottom of the left side of the dialog box are buttons to check the formula syntax and give a status on whether the formula is valid, and a Remove button, which deletes the formulas highlighted above on the left-hand side. When you've finished entering the desired formulas, choose OK.

Figure 21.8
The Formula
dialog box.

Next save the definition you have created into the Crystal Enterprise system. The name you choose for the definition will be presented to end users who want to create reports based on that definition.

Although there are Query, Data, and Report tabs along the top of the screen, they are not important at this stage and are detailed in the next area. Additionally, at the top right, you have buttons to (from the left to right):

- Restart the process and clear any work you have just done
- Close the application window altogether
- View the report on which you are working
- Change preferences
- Give version information (About)
- Show the application help

The preferences enable you to do the following:

- Select default colors
- Determine which tab opens first
- Determine how the toolbar behaves in terms of whether it is docked at the left, floats in the window, or does not show up at all
- Choose whether to display mini-dialogs or the advanced dialogs initially

- Reset to default preferences
- Choose whether to use a report template to format the reports by default
- Choose how many values to show initially in the data grid
- Choose which areas to show in the Design tab.

Alternatively, creating a Business View provides much of the same capability, and should be the first method used to create data definitions for Ad-Hoc report design. However, in cases where the database administrator cannot access the Business Views tool, or where a Crystal Report has already been created and there is a need to quickly modify it into a data definition for Ad-Hoc report creation, the Report Definition process can be extremely useful.

REPORT CREATION AND MODIFICATION

With the data definition or Business View in place, end users create reports by logging into the Ad-Hoc application, selecting the Create Ad-Hoc Report option, and then choosing the appropriate data source (see Figure 21.9). An examination of the application screen shows that the top-right area is identical to the section detailed previously, and behaves in exactly the same way. Again, most of the items on the left are also exactly the same as the section just covered, except that they do not include the same starting point. The assumption that the end user does not have database skills or desire to optimize the database query precludes those items from this end-user oriented section.

Figure 21.9
Choosing a Business
View as a data source.

After choosing a Data Source, you choose Fields in exactly the same way that you chose them above. You then create groups by clicking on the Groups item on the toolbar, which behaves exactly as the Fields chooser, except the order of the groups might be more important because groups nest inside one another. Moving items up or down within the Advanced Groups dialog enables you to change the grouping order.

Again, the Filters and Formulas items mirror the previous section.

The Summaries area enables you to create summaries of values for each group and behaves exactly as the Filters dialog, except that the result is the summation of fields rather than filtering them (see Figure 21.10). You choose the field to be summarized, the type of summary desired (note that the options displayed depend on the field-type so string fields have

21

different options than numeric and the like), and the level of the report (for example, the group name) at which the summary is desired. Again, make certain to click the Add button before clicking OK to add the summary to the report.

Figure 21.10
The Summaries
dialog box.

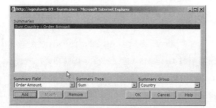

The Report Sorting item on the toolbar defines sort orders for the report details or groups. You can enter a simple definition by selecting the field to sort on and the order (for example, ascending) in the mini-dialog. The advanced item opens a dialog box allowing more advanced sorting on groups or summaries in addition to sorting on fields. Note that multiple sorts can be created here (see Figure 21.11).

→ For more information on sorting options, including Top N and the like, **see** "Using Group Selection and Sorting," **p. 86**

Figure 21.11
The Advanced Sort
dialog box.

If you want a chart, click on the Report Chart item in the toolbar to open the Report Chart dialog box, which enables you to choose a chart type (Bar, Line, or Pie), provide a title for that chart, place it either in the report header or footer section, and if there are multiple groups or summary values, choose the appropriate values for the chart.

The Report Template item in the toolbar opens the door to one of the most advanced features in Crystal Reports—the capability to format a report in one step. The report template dialog asks you to choose a template from several default templates, which will format the report accordingly. As you select any item in the template list in the dialog, a preview thumbnail image appears on the right giving you an indication of what the report might look like. Even more powerful is the capability to create your own templates, store them in your designated Report Templates folder (see the beginning of this chapter for more information), and then by clicking on the Templates button at the bottom left of the dialog (see Figure 21.12) apply the formatting in that report to the report you are designing, including fonts and other field formatting, headers and footers, and chart formatting.

→ For a more complete discussion on templates, **see** "Understanding Report Templates," **p. 296**

Figure 21.12
Choosing a template
to apply to the report.

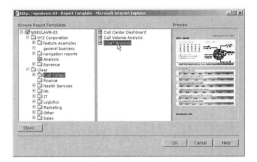

Again, as per the previous section, end users can save this report into the folder of their choice, assuming that they have write permissions on that folder. Often end users save into their Favorites folders.

At any stage in the process end users can move to a different tab than the Query tab that you have used so far to work through different views of the material. Now this chapter takes a closer look at the Data, Design, and Report tabs.

THE DATA TAB

The Data tab shows you a data grid of the values selected in the report. Note that you can use this, or any other tab, while creating the report and see things develop as you add fields, filters, and the like to the report. When a report includes groups, a group tree shows on the left side of the view. This can be toggled on and off by clicking the group-tree icon at the top left of the report viewer toolbar (see Figure 21.13). Clicking on an item in the tree shows the values for that group in the display grid. The rest of the report viewer toolbar is a standard Crystal Reports toolbar with export and navigation capabilities, with two exceptions. Because the view includes row numbers, the white page with the red arrow icon (near the right side of the toolbar) enables you to navigate to a particular row number, and the Flat View icon (the second from the left) toggles between a grouped view, which enables drill-down by clicking blue-underlined values and a flat view, which has no grouping applied.

21

TIP

You can select information right from the grid and copy and paste it into Excel and it falls into the right row-and-column structure, which saves time for simple data transfer.

Figure 21.13
The Data tab of the Ad-Hoc application showing a group tree with several countries.

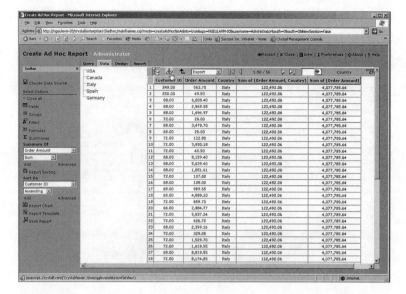

THE DESIGN TAB

Much like in Crystal Reports, the Ad-Hoc tool offers a Design tab for formatting the report in a detailed fashion. Many of the basic formatting options are available here. To move a field, click and drag it to the desired location. To select a field, click on it. You will know you have selected it when you see small gray blocks appear at the visible corners of the field. You can then move your mouse over the blocks and resize the field, or right-click on the field to access a menu that gives you formatting and alignment options. The formatting options are a subset of those in Crystal Reports and behave in exactly the same way (see Figure 21.14).

→ For more information on the options in the format dialog or the right-click menu, **see** "Exploring the Format Editor Dialog Common Options," **p. 155** and "Modifying Object Properties for Formatting Purposes," **p. 151**

Figure 21.14
The Format dialog in the Design tab.

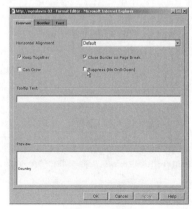

21

Right-clicking in a whitespace not occupied by a field, but still in the report sections, enables you to enter a text field or open the section expert. Like the section expert in Crystal Reports, you can determine here how sections should behave, and for instance, create a drill-down report section on the Web (see Figure 21.15). For a complete discussion of sections and section behavior, refer to Chapter 7, "Working with Report Sections."

Figure 21.15
The Section Expert dialog in the Design tab.

AD-HOC REPORT DESIGN SUMMARY

The Ad-Hoc tool provides powerful report creation and modification over the Web, with many of the core features of Crystal Reports exposed to an end user without any desktop installation. Coupled with the power of Business Views to simplify database interaction, most users can create or modify reports quite easily. Although out of scope in this chapter, the Ad-Hoc application can easily be modified to open existing reports for modification as well as the report creation capability detailed previously. The end users of this application can then share the newly created value with their colleagues by publishing their newly created or modified reports back into Crystal Enterprise directly from the Ad-Hoc application.

With the overview of the Ad-Hoc application completed, you now move to the second major Ad-Hoc tool in Crystal Enterprise, the Crystal Reports Add-in for Microsoft Excel.

CRYSTAL REPORTS EXCEL PLUG-IN

Because so many information workers today use Microsoft Excel extensively for worksheet applications and data manipulation, it follows that enterprise report data should also be accessible in Microsoft Excel. The Crystal Reports plug-in for Excel creates the facility in Excel to connect to Crystal Enterprise and retrieve data in an interactive fashion from within the worksheet itself.

ARCHITECTURE AND DEPLOYMENT SCENARIOS

The Excel plug-in requires installation on the local machine, and so requires administrative rights on the local machine.

The connection between the Excel plug-in and Crystal Enterprise uses TCP/IP over the local area network. Because of the direct connectivity between Excel and Crystal Enterprise, an Internet connection does not easily support the plug-in; usually a LAN connection to the Crystal Enterprise server is required.

21

ADMINISTRATION AND SETUP

The installation commences by executing the setup executable on the client machine. Because the plug-in opens Crystal Reports, the Crystal Enterprise server should be configured to grant View, Edit, Refresh, and View instances permissions to the end users who would use this application. Also, from the Start menu the plug-in must be activated by navigating to Programs, Crystal Enterprise, Add-In, and then enable or disable.

CONNECTING TO A REPORT

The following steps connect to a report:

1. From Excel, highlight a cell where you would like to display the report values, and then choose the Crystal menu, and the New Report View item.

2. Then provide credentials to log on to Crystal Enterprise, and see the Crystal Enterprise folders, from which you can choose a report as a starting point for your query.

3. This in turn opens the Report View Expert, which starts with the Select Fields item. Like the Ad-Hoc application and the Crystal Reports Wizard, you simply move items to the right to include them in the view. Note the origin button at the bottom left: This enables you to choose to report off of the underlying data source of that Crystal Report, saved data in a historical instance previously scheduled in Crystal Enterprise, or saved data in the latest instance of the Report (see Figure 21.16). This dialog also enables you to specify or change report parameters if required for the report.

Figure 21.16
The Select Fields dialog of the Excel add-in for Crystal Reports.

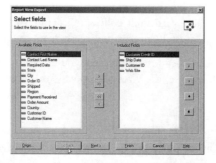

This is particularly interesting for creating time-series analysis, as many different Crystal Report views can be created within one Excel worksheet, not to mention across many tabs. Of course, any Excel calculation can be applied to these values as well, facilitating the creation of summarized and formatted dashboard views that might refer to many worksheet tabs in a workbook.

1. By clicking the Next button you navigate to the Filters dialog. If you had no need to filter the content, you could simply click Finish to populate the data into Excel starting from where the cursor was placed before you chose the menu item. The Filters dialog asks you to choose a field on the left, and then working from the top on the right,

choose an operator (for example, is one of, equals) and appropriate values beneath to filter the returned data (see Figure 21.17).

2. Once finished adding appropriate filters, you choose Finish and populate the data into Excel.

Figure 21.17
The Filter the Data dialog of the Excel Add-in for Crystal Reports.

MODIFYING THE REPORT VIEW

The data then displays in Excel. Should you then want to modify the report display, both right-click menus and the Crystal menu enable you to manipulate the data view in real time. To activate the right-click menu, you have to right-click a cell that contains data populated by the Crystal Reports view (typically cells with a light yellow background).

The right-click menu has several choices. The Insert choice enables you to insert a blank row or column in the display. The Filter submenu enables you to only see data where the value includes the value you clicked on (the Focus On choice), everything other than the value you have right-clicked on (the Exclude This option), and the Add/Modify option, which opens the Filters dialog. This enables you to simply right-click a value like USA for country, choose Filters and then Focus On, and see only values for the USA. Choosing the right-click option for Remove All Filters does exactly as advertised and restores an unfiltered view of the data.

The Field choice on the right-click menu enables you to remove the selected field or open the original Filters dialog box.

The View choice exposes the options available on that report view. The Refresh choice connects to the database and refreshed the data from the database at that moment. The Properties opens a dialog with details on the report view like the Report Title, the Crystal Enterprise system supplying the view, the connection ID (useful for troubleshooting), the type of data source connected to (such as Data source versus Report instance), whether the particular instance is the latest and when it was run, if this data comes from an instance at all. The Remove option removes the entire report view from the worksheet. The Set Origin choice takes you back to the Set Origin dialog as previously mentioned. The Cell Properties choice gives you information on the value, field title, and data type of the cell. Finally, the Add/Modify Parameters opens a dialog to change the parameter values in the report.

21

Lastly, the Crystal menu in Excel offers one option not available from the right-click menu: the Options dialog. This dialog exposes many of the default behaviors of the plug-in. The View tab enables you to specify default data values through the Data Defaults button, and also specify whether you want to conceal the data retrieved when saving the workbook. Should you want to change the right-click behavior or how cell widths or cell protection occurs, you accomplish this from the General tab. The Connection tab governs how and when you connect to the report data source, and the Enterprise tab enables you to set a default login for convenience.

The Excel plug-in, although simple in terms of usage, results in powerful interactivity. Users value this particular method of accessing report data very highly, as they are accustomed to doing data manipulation in Excel, and the value of having enterprise data from a variety of sources available in this format increases knowledge worker efficiency greatly.

CRYSTAL ANALYSIS EXCEL PLUG-IN

Similar to the Crystal Enterprise Add-in for Excel covered in the previous section, the Crystal Analysis Add-in for Excel exposes the power of Crystal Analysis (CA) from within Excel. However, the CA Add-in differs in that it does not report directly from existing CA workbooks stored in Crystal Enterprise—instead it connects to a cube and works from there. The Crystal Enterprise ActiveX viewer for Crystal Analytic reports and the thick client CA designer also enable exported CA views to the Excel Add-in and enable continued analysis from within Excel.

End users find that the CA plug-in offers very much the same interface that they are accustomed to within the CA worksheet, and offers the capability to massage a view, or several views, at a time, and then tie them together using standard Excel formulas and functionality. This flexibility facilitates much more self-service. The user interface, although powerful, uses simple concepts that enable data manipulation that most users prefer to Excel's own pivot tables, which require quite a bit of training to properly use.

ARCHITECTURE AND DEPLOYMENT SCENARIOS

Note from the previous paragraph that the add-in connects directly to the data source. The direct connection from Excel to the data cube uses either the appropriate drivers or Microsoft's Pivot Table Services when connecting to a Microsoft SQL Server Analysis Services cube. Similar to using the Crystal Analysis Rich Client, these drivers sit on the client machine and connect directly to the data source, compared to using the HTML viewer that directly connects to Crystal Enterprise, which in turn connects to the data source. So direct connectivity to the data source—usually in the form of a LAN connection—must be available for the Add-in to function properly.

SETTING UP AND ADMINISTERING THE CRYSTAL ANALYSIS EXCEL PLUG-IN

The installation requires that an actual set of files install on the local machine, which again requires local administrative rights during the install process. Should a distributed installation be required, a command-line interface for the installer should be used to specify that only the CA Excel add-in should be installed. Please see the Install.pdf document on the CA installation disc for further details.

Lastly, most Excel users must actually open the Excel Tools menu, and then select Add-ins, and check the Crystal Analysis Add-in to enable it. This results in a new menu appearing to the left of the Window menu, called Crystal_Analysis. A toolbar might also appear, and initially the CA splash screen loads, and continues to load every time Excel starts.

Because the add-in directly connects to the data cube, you should not have to set up special permissions within Crystal Enterprise to enable the add-in.

CONNECTING TO A WORKBOOK

This section pre-supposes that you have already read Chapter 19, "Creating Crystal Analysis Reports," and Chapter 20, "Advanced Crystal Analysis Report Design," which cover CA in depth. You should also be familiar with the concepts in OLAP and in CA. Thus the following discussion of the Excel Add-in focuses on how these are implemented, not on the actual functionality.

To begin with, the user either exports a view from Crystal Analysis viewer, rich client, or designer, or starts a new connection from within Excel either through the Crystal Analysis menu or the Crystal Analysis toolbar (on the left in Figure 21.18). Then you open a new Cube View, connect to a cube using a dialog identical to the one in CA, and then orient the view in a dialog screen identical to the Worksheet tool in CA.

Figure 21.18
The Crystal Analysis toolbar and menu in Excel.

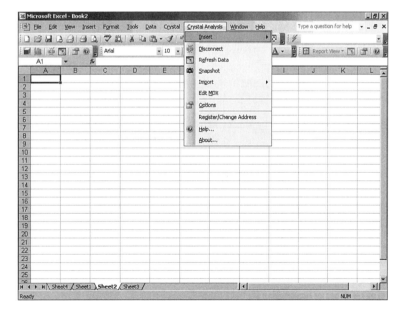

After orienting this view, you choose OK to return to the worksheet with your new view. Here you also have the option to save or open a viewpoint file (an XML file ending in *.cvp), which describes a particular orientation. This creates a cube view in Excel where your cursor was last positioned (see Figure 21.19).

Figure 21.19
The Crystal Analysis cube view within Excel.

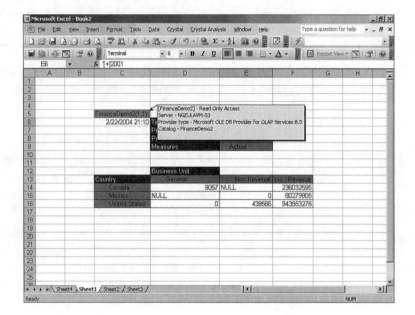

MODIFYING THE WORKBOOK VIEW

After the view has been established within Excel, you can manipulate it just as you did in CA. Because this is Excel, however, the right-click command menus are a bit different. To access the CA right-click menu, you must right-click on a cell (see Figure 21.20), and then hover over the Crystal Analysis item in the menu to expose the right-click menu.

Once again we discuss the menu with respect to how it differs from CA. The Reorient Cube selection navigates back to the worksheet element discussed previously to enable you to swap, pivot, and use an interface like the one in CA's worksheet. The Member Selector exposes the same Member Selector as in CA. The Copy to OLAP Formula copies a formula which refers back to the location of that data in the cube. This formula can be pasted elsewhere and resolves to the data in the cube. The Cube View menu enables you to remove the OLAP view, clone the current view to a new worksheet, select the entire OLAP view (to be able to easily copy it), select the data grid which this time selects only the data area of the OLAP view, and access the properties that are visible via a dialog enabling you to specify properties like which formats you want to have and how the cube view behaves (see Figure 21.21).

21

Figure 21.20
Right-clicking on a cell will display the Crystal Analysis option, which you must hover over or click on.

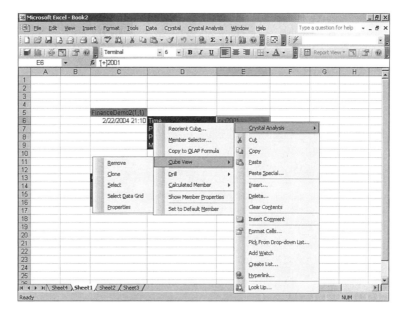

Figure 21.21
The Properties Data tab.

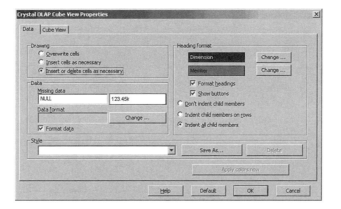

The remainder of the right-click menus are largely the same except that you can right-click on a dimension member in the slice selector area, navigate to the CA menu, and within the drill submenu you find the options to go left and right, which move the selected member to the next value in the cube either left or right of the current value. For instance, choosing Right when the 2001 value is selected would change the value to 2002.

Also unique to this OLAP view in Excel is the capability to drill up and down by double-clicking on the cells with a [+] or [-] cell. Double-clicking on a dimension label (which is blue by default) opens the Member Selector as well. Clicking and dragging an item, however, does not have the effect of swapping or pivoting dimensions within Excel—instead you

21

will find an area of the worksheet selected. Use the right-click menus to choose Re-orient Cube, which opens the worksheet dialog that supports the click-and-drag operations you are accustomed to within CA.

Web Report Distribution—Using Crystal Enterprise

INTRODUCTION TO CRYSTAL ENTERPRISE

In this chapter

22

WHAT IS CRYSTAL ENTERPRISE?

With the explosion of databases and ERP/CRM/SCM functionality in the eighties and nineties, organizations have been increasingly been creating and storing data about their business. One of the major complaints about these implementations is that although a substantial effort was made to capture the data, in a lot of cases, the reporting and analysis of this data was often overlooked.

When speaking with the majority of companies out there, most of them understand what a Crystal Report is and have heard of Crystal Enterprise, but are not sure exactly what it does.

Crystal Enterprise provides a prefabricated, extensible infrastructure for creating, managing, and distributing information to a wide variety of information consumers.

The reason Crystal Enterprise is referred to as a prefabricated infrastructure, rather than an application, is that Crystal Enterprise is extensible. This means Crystal Enterprise provides a number of application programming interfaces, or APIs, that enable users to change the functionality of Crystal Enterprise. The look and feel of one Crystal Enterprise system might be totally different to the look and feel of another; it depends upon the user requirements and how the Crystal Enterprise infrastructure was modified to suit them.

The content creation tools come to you in the form of Crystal Reports and Crystal Analysis. Crystal Enterprise also enables you to create content, either via its APIs or using some of the Business Objects prebuilt applications such as the Ad-Hoc Application.

Crystal Enterprise provides a central place to store and manage content. This can apply not only to Business Objects native file format such as Crystal Reports (.rpt) or Crystal Analysis (.cap), but now also applies to third-party file formats such as Microsoft Excel (.xls) or Adobe (.pdf).

TIP

> Chapter 23, "Using Crystal Enterprise with Web Desktop," includes a full listing of files that can be hosted by Crystal Enterprise and how to publish them.

Related to this is Crystal Enterprise's capability to manage not only the hosted files, but also an interface and API to manage the infrastructure itself. The Crystal Management Console, or CMC, enables you to start and shut down Crystal Enterprise components or apply security to prevent a user from running reports.

→ For more information on the Crystal Management Console, **see** "Using the Crystal Management Console," **p. 598**

How Crystal Enterprise distributes the information depends on the requirement. Crystal Enterprise provides a wide variety of viewers from zero client Web-based Dynamic HTML (DHTML) viewers to thick-client viewers installed on the client desktop. The distribution of information is not limited to reports but can be anything from XML files to Excel spreadsheets. Furthermore, the device on which the information is distributed is not limited to the PC. It can be a cell phone, printer, or PDA. In some cases, the information from Crystal Enterprise might not be viewed by a human at all, but uploaded into another computer system.

The last statement brings up the topic of what is an information consumer. For the most part, an information consumer is a human who is reading (consuming) the information. However, the information consumer could be another computer system that requests that a file be transferred to it, or it could request the information via a Web service. For example, a nightly scheduled job could transfer a file to another system and this file is then uploaded (consumed) by that system.

The key word in all of the above is information. The value that Crystal Enterprise and its content creation tools, Crystal Analysis and Crystal Reports, bring is the tools they provide to transform data into information. This transformation enables users to ask questions about how much inventory they have or what were their share trades for the day. This easy and efficient transformation of data to information is the real value of Crystal Enterprise.

WHY IMPLEMENT A CRYSTAL ENTERPRISE SOLUTION?

Having defined what Crystal Enterprise is, the following sections describe some of the reasons why an organization would want to deploy a Crystal Enterprise infrastructure.

Leverage existing infrastructure. The underlying objective of Crystal Enterprise is that is designed to be an open system and hence leverage existing infrastructure; for example, Enterprise can be installed on a variety of different operating systems. The open nature of Crystal Enterprise is illustrated by its use of industry-standard programming languages, authentication methods, and application servers. The infrastructure can be extended using either the COM, .NET, or Java SDK, running on some of the more commonly found application servers. This effectively means that one set of developers could be using .Net and another group could be using Java, but they need only a single instance of Crystal Enterprise running.

Crystal Enterprise supports Active Directory, NT, and Lightweight Directory Access Protocol (LDAP) authentication and includes some preconfigured attribute mapping for iPlanet Directory Server, Lotus Domino Directory Server, IBM Secureway, and Novell Directory Services. If your LDAP server is not listed here, Crystal Enterprise was built to support the Version 3 LDAP standard and if your LDAP server supports this standard, integration could be achieved via custom mappings.

Authentication is also available against common ERP packages, like SAP. This authentication is enabled via the installation of a solution kit available from Business Objects.

Crystal Enterprise supports an out-of-the-box authentication known as Enterprise authentication (see Figure 22.1). Here the user is created and supported only within the Enterprise infrastructure. This is useful when the user is not supported on an LDAP or third-party authentication system, for example, an employee of the organization might have an Active Directory or Windows account; however, an external user, like a customer, most likely will

22

not. Crystal Enterprise could be configured in such a way that the internal user has single sign-on and Crystal Enterprise authenticates itself against the Windows authentication and the external user is authenticated against the Enterprise authentication.

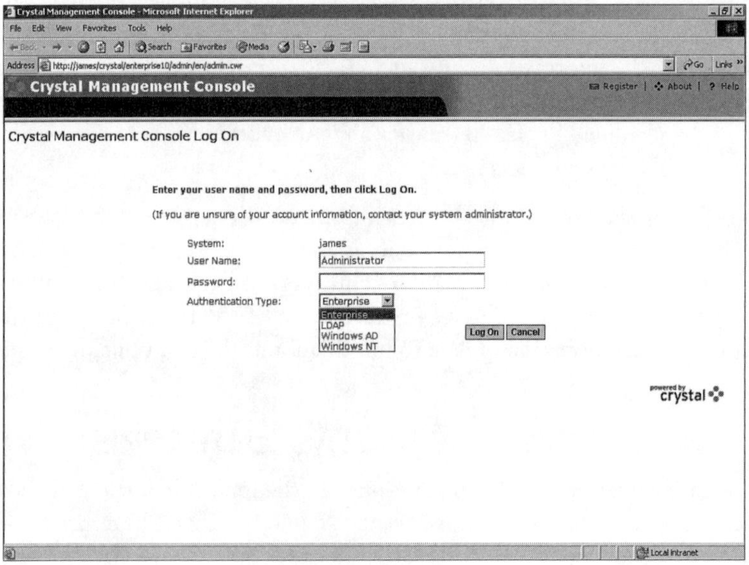

Figure 22.1
The various forms of authentication within Crystal Enterprise.

TIP

> Please see `http://support.businessobjects.com/communityCS/TechnicalPapers/ce10_supported_platforms.pdf.asp` for a listing of supported platforms. An alternative source of supported platforms is `Platforms.txt`, which can be found in the Platforms folder on the Crystal Enterprise CD.

Leverage existing skill sets. At the time of this writing, Business Objects has more than 14 million registered copies of Crystal Reports. Furthermore, the organization stated that the Crystal technology is embedded in more than 350 third-party software products. Crystal has a wide installed base and if an organization does not already have Crystal skills, they can be readily attained or existing staff members trained.

Leverage your existing Crystal investment. Crystal Enterprise allows for an easy and efficient way to consolidate all your existing Crystal Reports into one manageable infrastructure. For example, the Publishing Wizard enables users to easily point to multiple reports and publish them all in a single step.

No more HTML reports. HTML reports take a long time to create and are generally static and not easily maintained. Crystal Enterprise provides a complete DHTML viewer allowing the user to either embed the report into an application or run the report in an external window. Furthermore, the capability of Crystal Enterprise to hyperlink easily between content or to extract a single object such as a chart or cross-tab and embed just that object reduces the need to create static HTML within applications.

One tool—many data sources. Crystal Reports is well known for is its capability to connect to not only standard relational databases such as Oracle or SQL Server, but through its wide array of partners Crystal Reports can connect to ERP applications like SAP or PeopleSoft using specific drivers. As you might have discovered in the earlier chapters, Crystal Reports can also report off of a data objects, such as JavaBeans or ADO.NET.

This great range of connectivity results in organizations only requiring one tool to access their information versus possibly multiple software tools and hence many different skill sets.

Simplified content creation. Crystal Enterprise 10 incorporates a new feature called Business Views, a metadata layer that abstracts the complexity of the data source. Databases typically have complex joins between tables, technical field naming conventions, and complex security requirements. To complicate matters further, all the data might not sit in one data source and can be spread over multiple data sources. The combination of these factors makes report design challenging without detailed knowledge of the data source. This layer allows, for example, a database administrator to join, filter, and secure different data sources, providing the content creator a listing of user-friendly field names, formulas, and parameters that she can make use of in her content. For example, the administrator could join multiple disparate data sources and provide the content creators a business view. The creator does not need to concern herself with the complexities of the data source, rather with meeting the business requirement.

This division of labor speeds report development as the content creators can focus on their task of report development. Furthermore, this reduced dependency on database knowledge enables more business-oriented people to become content creators.

→ For more detailed information on Business Views, **see** "Business Views Architecture and Implementation," **p. 363**

Reuse of components. The capability to change a component and have this change cascade through all content makes reuse a valuable proposition. For example, the organization wishes to change how it calculates a formula—say "Days Sales Outstanding." In this example, the designer could simply make one change to the formula in the repository and have this change cascade through all reports that use this formula. If the user just had a bunch of reports on a shared drive somewhere, he would need to sort through these reports and determine which reports had this formula and then make changes to all the affected reports.

The Crystal Reports repository that was available in the version 9 product has been migrated to Crystal Enterprise 10. This repository allows sharing of commonly used content such as formulas, text, image files, and custom SQL statements. One of these objects can now be updated and any content using the object will be updated, saving a large amount of maintenance work.

22

Another example of reuse is the capability to have multiple reports using a single Business View as its data source. If the Business View is changed, for example, its data connection is pointed at another data source, all reports that use this data source are updated.

CAUTION

> One of the main components missing from this reuse and update functionality is the capability to do version control. In other words, it is difficult to go back to the old version after an update has taken place.

For more detailed information on Business Views and the Repository, see Chapter 17, "Introduction to Crystal Repository," and Chapter 18, "Crystal Reports Semantic Layer—Business Views."

Where-used components. Related to the reuse of components is the concept of where is a component used. For example, a Database Administrator wants to make a database unavailable for a period of time; however, he is uncertain what reports are using this database. Crystal Enterprise would provide him a listing of reports that would be affected should he take the database down.

Information flow. Information flow refers to the flow of information from the bottom of an organization to the top. With the increased focus on corporate accountability, it is vital that senior management know what is actually happening at lower levels. Crystal Enterprise, through its security model, allows for inheritance of permissions, enabling senior employees to see data and reports that subordinates are using. This same information can be summarized ensuring consistent information flow from the bottom of the organization to the top.

Scalability and reliability. Reliable and timely access to information is not something that should be taken lightly. Performance and downtime are difficult to predict in real world situations. Crystal Enterprise provides an infrastructure that is designed to scale and enables fault tolerance.

Crystal Enterprise takes the process required to create and deliver a report and breaks it down into various services (processors on Unix). Auditing tools enable you to determine over/under usage and you can then take the appropriate action. For example, when scheduling a job, there is a service (or process on Unix) called the Job Server that performs this task. If the jobs are taking too long to run, another Job Service can be registered with the framework. This new service could run on the same server as the initial service or another server on the network. By adding this service on the second server, a level of fault tolerance is achieved and should the initial Job Service fail the second one will take over.

NOTE

> There are specific guidelines for the optimal performance of the Crystal Enterprise framework and for establishing a fault-tolerant infrastructure—please contact Business Objects regarding this.

→ For a more detailed discussion on Crystal Enterprise Architecture, **see** "Crystal Enterprise Architecture Overview, " **p. 506**

VERSIONS OF CRYSTAL ENTERPRISE

Crystal Enterprise comes in multiple versions, each with its own set of functionality. In general, the versions build upon one another; for example, the Premium Edition includes all the functionality of the Professional Edition, but includes added functionality that is not included in the Professional Edition.

EMBEDDED

The Embedded edition (previously called the Report Application Server or RAS version) provides the capability to embed Crystal Enterprise inside of applications. It provides little in the way of user and report management but allows for report processing with a Web application. The reporting engine allows for on-demand report processing with smaller data sizes. It includes a report creation and design SDK and an SDK to embed the engine and viewers inside of an application. It is available only on the Windows platform.

EXPRESS

The Express edition (previously called Crystal Enterprise Standard) is best suited to handle a smaller number of users, such as a department or user group within the organization.

It does not provide any modification capabilities or scalability over multiple machines but does allow for report and user management and on-demand and scheduled Crystal Reports. It is available only on the Windows platform.

PROFESSIONAL

Crystal Enterprise Professional is a true enterprise platform designed to provide scalable, centralized management of information delivery. This version includes all the functionality of the Express and Embedded versions but adds scalability and clustering, enabling the user to distribute the infrastructure over multiple servers.

For report and application development, reports can be embedded in an application, processed on the Professional Edition, and then sent back to the application or alternatively the framework can be used to develop the application.

The Professional Edition also provides access to the Crystal Enterprise Repository, introduced in Chapter 17—a single repository that provides object reusability across reports. In addition, it includes a rich semantic layer to facilitate report creation and provides secure data access as described in Chapter 18. It is available on both Unix and Windows platform.

PREMIUM

This edition includes all functionality, including Crystal Analysis Reports and new auditing functionality. It includes the capability to create and modify Crystal Reports over the Web and the capability to create Excel Spreadsheets from a Crystal Report stored within Crystal Enterprise.

NOTE

> The packaging of Crystal Enterprise is subject to change. Contact Business Objects regarding packaging.

DETERMINING WHICH VERSION BEST SUITS YOUR REQUIREMENTS

When trying to determine which version is best suited to your requirements, the following factors should be considered:

- Data source—Different data sources are available for different versions; for example, the solution kits are available for the Professional and Premium Editions only.

- Scalability—The number of users, type and size of reports are just some of the factors that should be considered. The capability to scale Enterprise is different for the various editions.

- Fault tolerance—Related to scalability, fault tolerance is the capability to provide full fault-tolerant systems. Professional and Premium Editions are the two editions that provide for fault tolerance.

- Infrastructure—The capability to run Enterprise on different operating systems and to integrate with various LDAP data stores is reserved for the Premium and Professional Editions.

- User and report management—The capability to manage reports and users and set security accordingly differs from edition to edition.

UNDERSTANDING THE CORE FUNCTIONS OF CRYSTAL ENTERPRISE

In the previous chapters, some of Crystal Enterprise's functionality has been exposed; however, it is the three core functions of content creation, content management, and content distribution.

CREATING CONTENT

The majority of content creation is developed using Crystal Reports and Crystal Analysis; however, the definition of content has been expanded to include third-party applications such as text files, Microsoft Office, program files, Word documents, or Adobe PDF.

The previous sections of the book describe the process required to create reports. However, as you might have discovered, there are numerous tools available within Crystal Enterprise to create content. The ad-hoc report application and the Excel plug-in, as described in

Chapter 21, are just two of the applications that require the Crystal Enterprise infrastructure to create content.

CONTENT CREATION USING EMBEDDED CRYSTAL REPORT ENGINES

At the time of this writing, Business Objects had a partnership with Microsoft, BEA, and Borland, such that the Crystal Reports engine had been embedded in Microsoft's Visual Studio, BEA Weblogic Workshop (as seen in Figure 22.2), and JBuilder X.

Figure 22.2
The Crystal Report viewer java tag libraries embedded inside BEA's Weblogic Workshop.

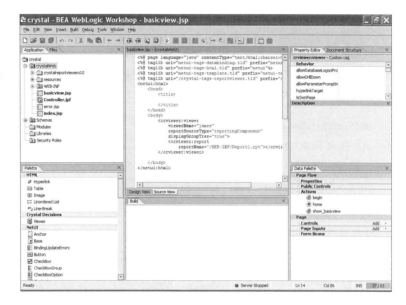

Although the integration of the Crystal Report designer into IDE has made report design a far simpler task, the embedded reporting engines might not be suitable for production environments. This point is further illustrated by the thread governance placed by Business Objects on these engines, making them better suited to development environments. The objective is to migrate the reports from this development environment to a far more robust infrastructure—namely Crystal Enterprise. See Chapters 28, 29, and 30 for more information on these reporting engines.

CONTENT CREATION TOOLS AVAILABLE WITH CRYSTAL ENTERPRISE

There are tools within the Crystal Enterprise framework that enable users to create content. These tools enable the user to create or modify Crystal Reports over the Web or create other file types such as Excel spreadsheets using Crystal Reports as a data source.

THE REPORT APPLICATION SERVER API   The Report Application Server or RAS proves an SDK that exposes Crystal Reports and enables developers to build applications that create, modify, and view Crystal Reports over the Web. This service plugs into the Crystal Enterprise Professional or Premium infrastructure framework or can exist on its own in the form of Crystal Enterprise Embedded. The SDK is available in Java, COM, or .NET versions. See Chapters 31, 32, and 33 for more detail.

NOTE

> This SDK is not exposed in the Crystal Enterprise Express version.

EXCEL ADD-IN   The Excel Add-in enables the user to download and install an Add-in to Microsoft Excel. This Add-in enables the user to import data directly into an Excel spreadsheet. The add-in is available from Business Objects directly as a download.

From this toolbar, the user can then connect to Crystal Enterprise and generate Excel spreadsheets by connection via a Crystal Reports Object or a report instance. When the user is satisfied with the spreadsheet she can save it back to the Crystal Enterprise framework.

→ For more detail on the Excel Plug-in, **see** "Crystal Reports Excel Plug-in," **p. 451**

THE AD-HOC REPORTING TOOL   The Ad-Hoc reporting application is a Web-based application that enables the user to create new or modify existing reports over the Web. Think of it as Crystal Reports but for the Web. The user can select a Business View, an ODBC connection, or an existing report as a data source. After this has been selected, the user walks through the steps of formatting the report. See Chapter 21 for further information on the Ad Hoc application.

NOTE

> The Ad-Hoc Reporting Tool is based upon the Report Application Server API; hence it requires the Report Application Server component of Crystal Enterprise to be running.

CONTENT MANAGEMENT

The capability to take reports, Excel spreadsheets, and other business intelligence content and centrally control and manage these pieces of information is one of the key functions of the Crystal Enterprise infrastructure. Consider all the Crystal Reports, Adobe PDF files, or Excel spreadsheets that are saved locally on an employee's workstations. Now consider what the organization stands to lose should a virus destroy this or what happens when an employee leaves and his hard disk is reformatted to make way for a new employee.

The process of getting content into Crystal Enterprise is commonly referred to as publishing content. The publishing of a report results in the report being copied to the Crystal Enterprise infrastructure. An object ID and description, among other fields, are populated and the content is then referenced either using the object ID or the description.

CRYSTAL ENTERPRISE SDK

The Crystal Enterprise infrastructure provides a Java, COM, or .NET SDK for managing content within the infrastructure. For example, the type of functionalities that are exposed are tasks such as scheduling, exporting, and viewing of reports. Additional tasks could include the management of users, folders, objects, and the related security between these objects. The SDK also provides server management calls for managing the Enterprise infrastructure and security.

For example, a common request is to schedule Crystal reports via a third-party scheduler. It is this SDK that would allow a developer to accomplish this.

This topic is discussed in further detail in Chapters 34, 35, and 36.

CONTENT MANAGEMENT USING THE WEB DESKTOP

Chapter 23 references the Web Desktop—a Web-based application that enables the end user to manage and view their content stored in Crystal Enterprise. It is based upon the Crystal Enterprise SDK and provides users the capability to organize, view, and schedule content. This application provides personalization features permitting users to change the look and feel of their desktop.

CONTENT MANAGEMENT USING THE CRYSTAL MANAGEMENT CONSOLE

The Crystal Management Console, or CMC, is a Web-based application that gives administrators further control over published content. It also provides the interface to manage the infrastructure, the users, and their related security. The CMC exposes two new pieces of functionality, the capability to audit the infrastructure through the auditing module and the migration of the Crystal Reports repository into the Enterprise infrastructure. Like the Web Desktop, this application is based on the Crystal Enterprise SDK and can be extended within this object model.

Further management capabilities regarding the infrastructure can be found in the Crystal Configuration Manager, or CCM (see Figure 22.3). This application is designed to manage the Crystal services running on Windows servers or the Crystal processors that are running on Unix servers. It allows an administrator to, for example, start or shut down a service or add an additional service to a machine.

The CCM and CMC are described in Chapter 26, "Deploying Crystal Enterprise in a Complex Network Environment," and Chapter 27, "Administering and Configuring Crystal Enterprise."

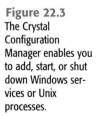

Figure 22.3
The Crystal Configuration Manager enables you to add, start, or shut down Windows services or Unix processes.

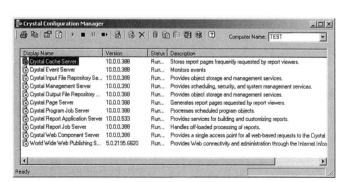

CONTENT DELIVERY

The third component of the Crystal Enterprise infrastructure is that of content delivery. This is the process of delivering the content in the requested format and requested destination.

This process consists of running the reports, checking associated security to determine what data the requestor is allowed to see, transforming the data to the requested format, and lastly, sending the information to the request destination.

Content delivery can take two forms—the data pull method and the data push method.

THE DATA PULL METHOD

The *data pull method* consists of viewing reports on demand. In this case the user requests that the report be run against a data source and the data is "pulled" from the data source, using a viewer.

Crystal Enterprise supports a wide variety of viewers, both server-side, pure DHTML and client side, that require a download.

The functionality between the viewers is similar and determining the required viewer is a matter of determining the requirements of the user. For example, if this is for an extranet application, the Crystal Enterprise administrator would have no control over what the external user's firewall allows or disallows. The recommendation may be to assign the DHTML viewer to that user.

THE DATA PUSH METHOD

Crystal Enterprise gives administrators and users the capability to push information to specific users and locations, in specific formats and, if required, as a result of specific data changing.

For example, an administrator could set up a Crystal Report to run on the last day of the month and e-mail the user the link to his information. Another example could be that a user subscribes to an alert whereby if sales fall below $200,000 for a particular product, she wants the report in PDF format in her e-mail inbox.

In both of these cases, Crystal Enterprise is pushing the information to the information consumer, based upon some event, scheduled to some destination and in a required format.

THE VIEWER SDK

Like the Report Application Server and Crystal Enterprise SDKs, the server-side DHTML viewer is exposed via a Java, COM or .NET SDK. Depending on the language used for development and the requirement, different viewers should be used. For example, if the user needs to see the data independent to the layout in the report, a grid viewer could be used to display this. This viewer removes the banded formatting and displays the data in a grid.

USING CRYSTAL ENTERPRISE WITH WEB DESKTOP

In this chapter

INTRODUCTION

The Crystal Enterprise infrastructure from Business Objects comes with a number of standard applications that can be used to operate and administer Crystal Enterprise from both an end-user and administrator's perspective. Chapter 22, "Introduction to Crystal Enterprise," provided an introduction to the Crystal Enterprise infrastructure and building on that, this chapter describes the tools available to use and administer the Crystal Enterprise system.

These Web-based applications are the starting point for accessing the Web information delivery functionality of Crystal Enterprise.

All the sample applications provided by Business Objects are based upon the application programming interface (API) described in Part VII of the book, "Customized Report Distribution—Using Crystal Enterprise Embedded Edition." This means that the highlighted applications are customizable and, in fact, the source code for the applications ships with the Crystal Enterprise application. The two applications installed by default are the Crystal Enterprise User Launchpad and the Crystal Enterprise Admin Launchpad.

NOTE

> In versions of Crystal Enterprise prior to version 10, both the User Launchpad and the Admin Launchpad applications were found under the Crystal Enterprise Launchpad.

CRYSTAL ENTERPRISE USER LAUNCHPAD

The User Launchpad is a Web-based application that provides a broad range of functionality and enables the end user to interact with the Crystal Enterprise infrastructure. The HTML page provides links to documentation, samples, Web-based help, and the Admin Launchpad (see Figure 23.1).

The Launchpad is broken down into the following components:

- Crystal Enterprise Web Desktop: Provides a feature-rich application for users to interact with reports and other objects. (Crystal Enterprise Web Desktop was known as ePortfolio in prior versions.)

- Crystal Offline Viewer: Enables the user to download a Crystal Reports viewer to his local machine.

- Crystal Enterprise Add-in for use with Microsoft Excel: Enables the user to download the Excel plug-in, as previously described in Chapter 21, "Ad-Hoc Application and Excel Plug-in for Ad-Hoc and Analytic Reporting."

- Documentation: Web-based user and getting started guides.

- Client Samples: Various samples that demonstrate different sample applications that provide the user with a different look and feel. It also gives developers ideas how to build upon the API.

- Mobile Samples: Mobile desktop launches a sample interface for developing content to be delivered on a mobile device such as a cell phone or PDA.

- Administrative Applications: A link to the Administrative Launchpad.

- More on the Web: Web-based support and information on where to go to find patches and updates.

Figure 23.1
Crystal Enterprise User Launchpad provides the entry point for a user.

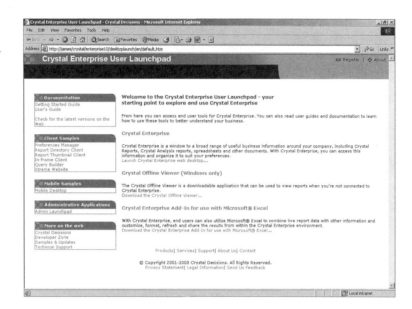

NOTE

> By default, for the English and CSP version, the application is installed under
>
> `http://<server>/crystal/enterprise10/desktoplaunch/en/default.htm`
>
> The application is also available in a JSP version and packaged in the desktop.war file. For procedures on deploying a .war file, refer to your Java Application Server instructions.

Although all the applications provided on this page are useful, the most feature-rich application, and the one explored in this chapter, is the Crystal Enterprise Web Desktop.

CRYSTAL ENTERPRISE WEB DESKTOP

Upon clicking the Crystal Enterprise Web Desktop link, the user is logged onto Crystal Enterprise with a Guest account. This means that the user has whatever rights the Guest account has been granted. This functionality enables anonymous logon to the enterprise system. A common usage scenario is if reports need to be delivered via an extranet system and the administrator does not want to establish an account for every user accessing the system; the Guest account could allow for this. This account can be disabled if you want by using the Crystal Management Console as described in Chapter 27, "Administering and Configuring Crystal Enterprise." If the Guest account is disabled, the user is taken directly to the logon screen. Alternatively, the user can log on by clicking the logon icon shown in Figure 23.2.

Figure 23.2
By default, the Guest account automatically authenticates.

23

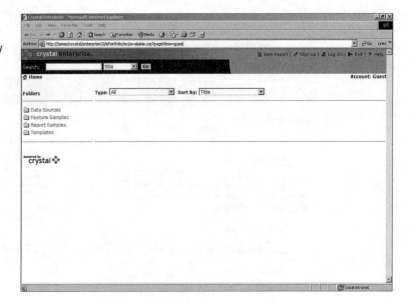

After a user has successfully logged on, a session is established and available folders and reports are shown based upon the security assigned to the user. Crystal Enterprise allows for multiple folders and subfolders, each with their own security assigned, either at the folder level or the individual object level. Only the folders or individual objects to which the user has access are displayed.

Every user created within Crystal Enterprise is assigned a Favorites folder and by default, only that user and the group Administrators have rights to the user's Favorites folder.

The user can then navigate the folder structure by simply clicking on the folder names. As the user moves down the tree structure, her chosen path is displayed, enabling the user to easily navigate forward or backward. In addition, the top-level folders can be displayed. These provide a starting point to each path in the tree structure, shown in Figure 23.3. This piece of functionality can be turned on and off in the preferences section, described later in this chapter.

The Web Desktop also enables the user to search for a required object. The user can search for reports or any hosted object, based upon title, description, folder title, or all these three fields at once. If the search is successful, the Web Desktop returns a listing of all the found objects.

Figure 23.3
Listing of available
objects found in the
folder.

After the desired object is located, the user clicks on the object to determine the available actions, as shown in Figure 23.4.

NOTE

By hovering the mouse over any object, the object's folder and description are displayed. If they do not appear, ensure that these fields are populated in the object properties under the Crystal Management Console (see Chapter 27 for more details).

Figure 23.4
Available options are
displayed when the
user clicks on the
object.

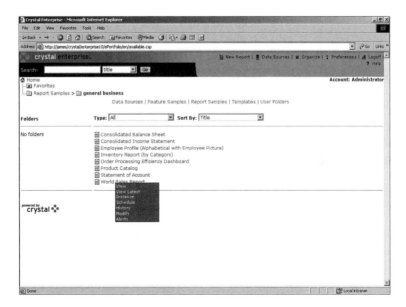

23

Table 23.1 lists the default actions that can be defined for the different objects within Crystal Enterprise. The available actions are partially defined by the security set against the object for the current user (that is, different users might have access to different actions against the same object or report). This security is defined in the Crystal Management Console or CMC and explained in Chapter 27.

The type of object also determines the available actions—for example, a text file cannot be scheduled because the Crystal Enterprise framework does not support scheduling text files. A list of all currently supported object types is presented in the next chapter but the most common are Crystal Reports, Crystal Analysis objects, Crystal Object Packages, Excel, Word, Adobe Acrobat (PDF), PowerPoint and going forward, WebIntelligence objects. The object type also determines the action's result—for example, if the object is a Crystal Report, view executes the report. However, if the object is an object package, view displays the contents of the package.

TIP

> A Crystal Report could be scheduled and then converted to a text file to overcome this limitation.

TABLE 23.1   CRYSTAL ENTERPRISE OBJECT ACTION LIST

Action	Description
View	The object is run live against the data source. For example, if the object were a Crystal Report, the report would execute against its data source and the most current data would be retrieved. If the object were a text file, the text file would be displayed. If the object were an object package, it would display the contents of the package.
Saved View	This applies to Crystal Analysis reports only. A specific view of the data can be saved, enabling the user to return to those specifically aligned dimensions and dimension members.
View Latest Instance	This action enables the user to view the most recently scheduled instance. This is useful if a user wants to view the most recent version of the scheduled report. Often this action is provided to the majority of end users with the ability to View (On-Demand against the database) being provided to only an elite segment of users.
Schedule	The user can schedule the object against the data source. If the object is a Crystal Report, the user might need to enter information such as when the report should be run, any required database logon, any parameters that might need to be entered, filters to further limit the data, and destination of the output. See the following section, "Scheduling a Crystal Report from Within the Web Desktop," for more detail.

Action	Description
History	The history shows the user a listing of all attempts to schedule the report and the status of those attempts, that is, whether they succeeded or failed. The user can click on the status to view reasons for failing or succeeding. If the report succeeded, the user can click on the instance to view the report instance.
Modify	If Crystal Enterprise has been installed with the Report Application Server (available by default with Crystal Enterprise Premium or as an add-on to Crystal Enterprise Professional), the modify button launches a report modification wizard and enables the user to modify the given report and then save the modified report as a new object.
Alerts	Should the report have an alert that has been triggered, the report appears in the alerts page. The user can go directly to the alerts page and see if there are any reports that have triggered an alert.

The scheduling capability requires further detail, as there are a number of options.

SCHEDULING A CRYSTAL REPORT FROM WITHIN THE WEB DESKTOP

With the required permissions, the user can schedule the report, specifying the following input to ensure the report runs appropriately.

SCHEDULE RUNTIME OPTIONS

The runtime options presented under the Schedule selection of the Schedule dialog drop-down box enable specification of the recurring schedule for the involved report. Each of the different potential runtimes presents its own set of parameters:

- Now: The report runs once (immediately) after the schedule action is initiated.
- Once: The report runs once at the time specified by the required start time parameter.
- Hourly: Report instances are created on a recurring schedule matching the parameters entered. The first instance is created at the start time specified.
- Daily: Report instances are created on a recurring schedule matching the parameters entered running once every N days at the time specified.
- Weekly: Report instances are created on a recurring schedule matching the parameters entered running each week on the selected days and at the time specified.
- Monthly: Report instances are created on a recurring schedule matching the parameters entered running on the specified date and time, every N months.
- Nth Day of Month: Report instances are created on a recurring schedule matching the parameters entered with new report instances being created each month on the specified day and at the start time specified.
- 1st Monday of Month: Report instances are created on a recurring schedule matching the parameters entered with new report instances being created on the first Monday of each month and at the time specified.

- Last Day of Month: Report instances are created on a recurring schedule matching the parameters entered with new report instances being created on the last day of each month and at the time specified.

- X Day of Nth Week of the Month: Report instances are created on a recurring schedule matching the parameters entered with new report instances being created monthly on the specified day of the specified week.

- Calendar: This option enables the selection of a calendar of dates. Created by the Crystal Enterprise administrator, calendars are customized lists of schedule dates. A report instance can then be scheduled to run each day specified in the calendar.

Using the various runtimes and their associated runtime parameters is fairly intuitive—the one exception perhaps being the Calendar (see Figure 23.5), which is new to Crystal Enterprise version 10. This functionality enables administrators to create calendars that run reports based on the dates defined in the calendars. Crystal Enterprise allows for multiple calendars, for example a month end closing and a quarter end closing. Calendar creation is covered in Chapter 27.

Figure 23.5
The Calendar displays the schedule runtime days. If a calendar is selected at schedule time, Crystal Enterprise will schedule the report only on the highlighted run days.

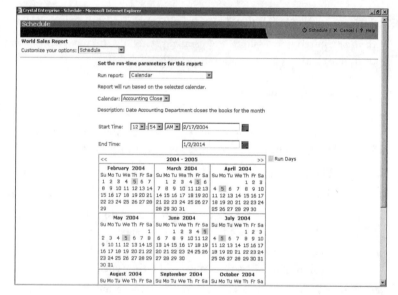

PARAMETERS

If a specified report contains parameters, a parameters option appears in the scheduling dialog and the user is expected to enter the required parameters. If a report does not contain parameters, this option is not available.

DATABASE LOGON

If the report requires a data source logon, the user specifies this under the database drop-down option screen here in the Schedule dialog.

NOTE

> The database logon is the user who is required to access the database; in other words, if the report accesses an Oracle database, the user entered here would be the user that Oracle authenticates against. However, should the Oracle database reside on a different physical server and network authentication is required to access the Oracle server, the user account used for this network authentication is the user account that starts the Job Server or service. If this user does not have the correct permissions, the report will fail.

FILTERS

Any row or group filters that were created in the associated Crystal Report appear here. The user can add or change the filter accordingly, ensuring that he saves the update by clicking on the update field.

TIP

> The filters setting and editing functionality can be withdrawn from end-user access by changing a setting in the Web Desktop Administration. See the section "Customizing the Web Desktop and Report Viewers" later in this chapter.

DESTINATION

The information can be sent to any of the following destinations:

- Default: The instance is stored in the Crystal Enterprise infrastructure, namely the File Repository Server.
- Unmanaged Disk: Accessible disk that is not managed by the Crystal Enterprise infrastructure. The disk needs to be specified via its UNC path or alternatively, if it is a Windows system, via a mapped drive.
- E-mail SMTP Server: Report can be sent as an attachment or as a URL by e-mail. The URL is better suited for internal personnel because this method does not clog the internal network if the attachments are large. If the recipient is outside the firewall, a link might not be the best approach as the recipient might not be able to pass through the firewall to get to the Crystal Enterprise infrastructure.
- FTP Server: Useful for sending reports across the Internet or across dissimilar operating systems. This is particularly useful when interacting with other systems, for example, a customer's shipment report could be sent to her FTP server, whereby this file is automatically uploaded into her system.

DEFINING A FORMAT

The report can be converted to a specific file format upon scheduling, namely

- Crystal Report: This is the default and maintains the original formatting of the report.
- Excel: This Excel option tries to maintain the original format of the report and translates this to an Excel spreadsheet.

- Excel (Data Only): This option removes the formatting in the Crystal Report and sends down the data only, with each field in the report representing a column in Excel.

- Word: Preserves all formatting and attempts to keep the pages consistent with the Crystal Report; for example, if there are three pages in the report, the Word document should have three pages. Any graphics appear as Word pictures.

- Acrobat: Similar to Microsoft Word formatting. Enables the user to specify export by page.

- Rich text: Similar to Microsoft Word formatting.

- Plain text: User needs to specify the number of characters per inch (millimeter).

- Paginated text: User needs to specify the number of characters per inch (millimeter) and the number of lines per page.

- Tab-separated text: The export process forces a tab between fields.

- Tab-separated values: Each value in the field is separated by a tab.

- Character separated values: A specified character separates each value in the field.

Unique features that are specific to Crystal Reports, such as drill down and the group tree, are lost when the report is converted to another format.

Another point to note is that these formats work typically on a "what you see is what you get" paradigm. In other words, if the report is using multiple groupings and the latter groups are hidden in the report, when it comes time for exporting, the user only gets the first group and the hidden sections are not exported. The user gets a similar result with on-demand subreports and with conditionally suppressed sections in a report.

> **TIP**
>
> If a business requirement is such that the users are going to do a lot of exporting, determine the format beforehand and how the user wants to view the exported format before designing the report as this export requirement has an effect on the design of the report.
>
> Check http://support.businessobjects.com for technical papers on preferred formatting and export limitations when you intend to export a report to another format.

PRINT SETTINGS

Users can print a copy of the Crystal Report while scheduling the report.

The desktop application gives the user a choice of either specifying a printer or selecting the default printer, which is the default printer associated with the Crystal Enterprise server.

> **CAUTION**
>
> The server on which Crystal Enterprise is installed would need access to the device or shared printer and not the user's desktop access.

Related to specifying the printer, the user can also specify the Crystal Report page layout settings. These settings affect the Crystal Report page layout; for example, if the page size is changed, the total number of pages for the report changes.

CUSTOMIZING THE WEB DESKTOP AND REPORT VIEWERS

The Web Desktop enables the user to make modifications as to how he might want to view the reports. These settings can be based on a per-user basis or set globally by the system administrator with no user privilege being provided for self-selection.

In the default Web Desktop, each user is allowed to self-select a number of display preferences through the preferences page accessed through the Preferences link and icon in the upper-right corner of the Web Desktop. In addition to being able to change passwords on this page, the end user can specify a number of display preferences. The Preferences Page highlighted in Figure 23.6 is broken down into three tabs, namely General Preferences, Crystal Analysis Preferences, and Crystal Report Preferences. Each is discussed in succession in the following sections.

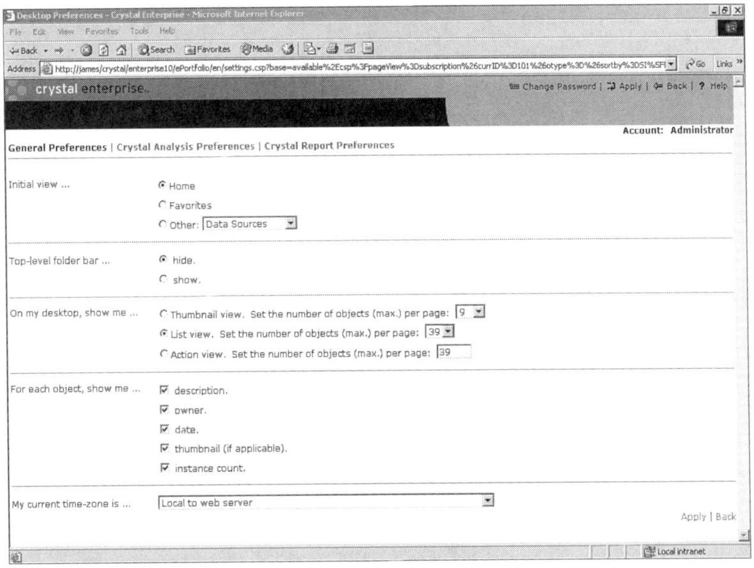

Figure 23.6
General Preferences Page accessed from the Web Desktop. Here users can customize their Web Desktop.

NOTE

The administrator via the Crystal Management Console has the right to remove the preferences icon from the page, effectively removing the user's right to change this.

GENERAL PREFERENCES

The General Preferences tab of the Preferences screen provides access to a number of customizable user-display settings for Crystal Enterprise. Table 23.2 presents a description of each of these settings.

TABLE 23.2 GENERAL PREFERENCES OPTIONS

Options	Description
Initial View	Web Desktop navigates to and opens the folder selected. In the default interface, end users can only select Home, their personal favorites folder, or any other top-level folder in the system. They cannot set a subfolder as the default initial view. This can be provided through a customized edit of the underlying settings.csp page if you want.
Top-level Folder Bar	By selecting Show, the top-level folders are displayed, enabling the user to navigate to folders higher up the folder tree easily.
Views	The user can see various views of how the reports are displayed.
Thumbnail View	Crystal Reports can capture a thumbnail of the first page of the report. The user can associate the look of the report with the thumbnail without having to remember what the report is called.
List View	Lists the objects whereby the user must click on the object to determine the allowed actions.
Action View	Lists the objects but instead of just showing the objects, this shows the available actions allowed.
For Each Object, Show Me	Users can select what they find applicable for display purposes among report description, report owner, report date, report thumbnail, or report instance count.
Time Zone	This is important for users who are going to schedule reports at a particular date and time. The time entered to start the scheduling process is by default local to the Web server (not the CMS). For example, if the user schedules the report and his time zone is PST and the Web server is running in EST then the report runs three hours sooner than expected. This issue is further emphasized when the system has anonymous or guest access enabled because the guest user can only have one time zone associated with it but might be used by many users around the world. If this is the case, it is recommended to establish an account for each of the scheduling users.

CRYSTAL ANALYSIS PREFERENCES

If Crystal Enterprise is licensed for Crystal Analysis, the user can choose between running the Active X (sometimes called the rich client) or the DHTML versions of the viewer under the Crystal Analysis Preferences tab (see Figure 23.7).

Figure 23.7
The Crystal Analysis
Preferences tab.

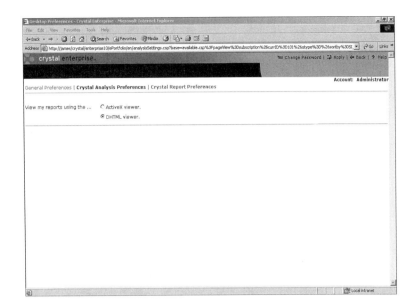

CRYSTAL ANALYSIS DHTML VIEWER

This is the default viewer for Crystal Analysis reports (see Figure 23.8). It does not require any download to the browser and all that is sent to the browser is DHTML.

This viewer gives you the capability to

- Export to Excel: The current view of data is exported to Excel; however, this is a static link and if the current view changes, no data changes in Excel until another export is initiated (see Figure 23.9).

- Save views: The viewer enables the user to save the current view of data back to Crystal Enterprise. This enables the user to return to that exact view of data, or to share this view with other users.

- Navigate between the pages: If the Crystal Analysis application has multiple pages in the application, these viewers enable the user to navigate between these pages either by selecting the page or through the use of transition buttons.

NOTE

In addition to using the DHTML and ActiveX viewers to view OLAP-based data, Business Objects provides an interactive Excel add-in for Crystal Analysis that provides rich multi-dimensional analytic capabilities from within the Excel environment. This is covered in Chapter 21 and should be explored for organizations with a large number of Excel power users. Additionally, when an export is completed from the ActiveX Viewer, it automatically uses the Crystal Analysis Excel plug-in if it has been installed on the client's desktop version of Excel.

Figure 23.8
Crystal Analysis
Report as viewed in
the DHTML viewer.

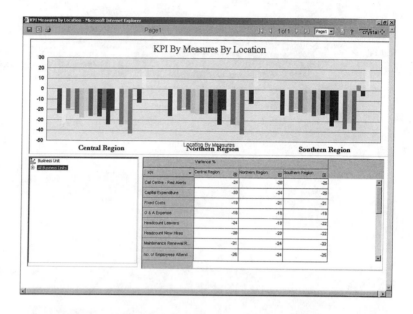

Figure 23.9
View of the report
exported to Excel.
There is no active link
established with the
database and should
the data change, the
report would have to
be exported again to
reflect the change.

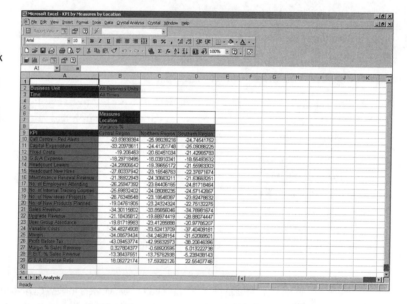

CRYSTAL ANALYSIS ACTIVE X VIEWER

Although the Active X or Rich Client viewer (see Figure 23.10) requires an initial download
to the browser, there is some added functionality that you get with this Rich Client viewer:

- Performance: Some of the work can now be performed on the client.
- Enhanced Excel integration: An active link is maintained between the Excel spreadsheet and the data cube that you are reporting off of. This connection makes the spreadsheet far more dynamic (see Figure 23.11).

Figure 23.10
Active X or Rich Client viewer offers some performance gains over the DHTML viewer but requires an initial download.

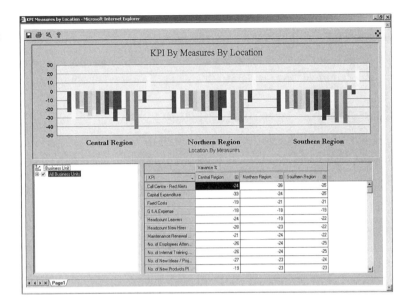

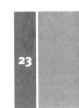

Figure 23.11
This view of the data in Excel includes the Crystal Analysis plug-in. Users can right-click a cell and perform functions because an active link is maintained between the cube of data and the spread-sheet.

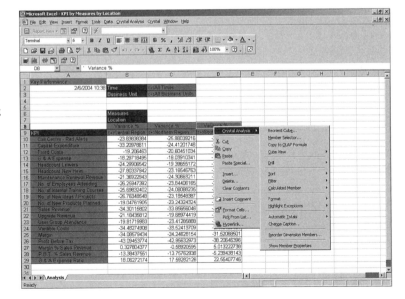

CAUTION

> One concern about the Crystal Analysis viewers is their printing and export capabilities. Crystal Analysis viewers cannot export to formats other than Microsoft Excel. Furthermore, the printing is tricky and it is often difficult to get an Analysis page to reflect accurately on a printed page.

CRYSTAL REPORT PREFERENCES

This page (see Figure 23.12) enables the user to set preferences specifically around the Crystal Report viewers. Table 23.3 highlights the different options available.

TABLE 23.3   CRYSTAL REPORTS PREFERENCES

Option	Description
Display My Reports	In a single window, this makes each report appear in the same browser window. This is well-suited to small reports that are executed quickly because multiple browsers are not opened.
	Multiple Browsers are useful for large reports where there is some wait time before the report is rendered. This way a user can run other reports while she waits for the first to complete.
View My Reports Using	Enables the user to specify the type of viewer. There are additional viewers other than the four mentioned on this page (ActiveX, DHTML, Advanced DHTML and Java Viewers)—see the following section, "Crystal Report Viewers," for further information.
DHTML Viewer Printing Uses	If the user has selected the DHTML viewer, when printing the user has two options—either export the report to PDF and use the Acrobat reader printing control or download an ActiveX printing control.
Preferred Measuring Units	Determines what the preferred unit of measure is defining the reporting page layout.

Before continuing, it is worth investigating these Crystal Reports viewers in a little more detail.

CRYSTAL REPORT VIEWERS

The Crystal Report viewers take the data from the Crystal Enterprise framework and format the data into a report such that it can be viewed.

Table 23.4 provides a listing of the base functionality that the Crystal Report viewers provide.

Figure 23.12
The Crystal Report Preferences page describes the Crystal Report options a user can set regarding printing and viewing reports.

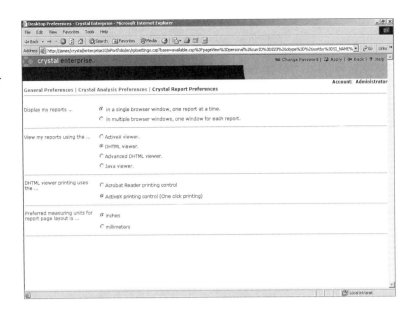

TABLE 23.4   VIEWER FUNCTIONALITY

Viewer Option	Description
Group Tree	The group tree icon enables the user to either display or hide the group one exist in the report. By default, this is set to display the group tree.
Export	Should the user want to export the report to another format, this enables the user to export the report.
Refresh	The report can be refreshed against the data source. This means that it is rerun against the data source.
Print	Depending on how the DHTML viewer printing parameter is set, the DHTML viewer either uses a small ActiveX print control to print the document or exports the report to Adobe PDF before using the Adobe client to print it.
Drill-down viewer name	If the report enables drill-down, the section of data displayed.
First Page	User is taken to the first page of the report.
Previous Page	Pages up the report.
Next Page	Pages down the report.
Last Page	User is taken to the last page of the report.
Go to page	User can go to a specific page.
Find	User can search for any text inside the report and any associated match is highlighted. It is not case sensitive, however; if the text is located in a hidden drill down, the Find might not work.
Zoom	Scale the report by setting the percent.

23

The drill-down functionality provided in the designer is honored by the viewer and users can drill down on charts, group sections, and the group tree.

The look and feel of the DHTML viewer can be customized via the viewer SDK and any of these functions can be turned on or off depending on the requirement.

The Crystal Report viewers are either client-side or server-side reports—hence the process of viewing a report is different depending on the viewer used.

SERVER-SIDE VIEWERS

The Server-Side viewers run within the application server framework; for example, the Java DHTML viewer consists of Java classes that run within the Java Application Server. The COM DHTML viewer processes the request within the Web Component Server or WCS. Upon receiving a report request, the Crystal Enterprise framework sends the data in Encapsulated Page Format (EPF) to the application server. A viewer object is instantiated and the application server processes the EPF pages. DHTML consisting of both the data and the viewer controls are then sent through to the Web server.

DHTML VIEWER   The DHTML viewer is one of the most commonly used report viewers in Crystal Enterprise, see Figure 23.13. It provides a rich functional interface for viewing and navigating Crystal Reports in a zero client interface. This zero client viewer is implemented via viewreport.csp, that requires the Web Component Server to be running or in a Java environment via viewreport.jsp that requires a Java application server to be running. This viewer can be manipulated via a COM, .NET, or Java API—all explored in the later sections of this book.

Figure 23.13
Report viewed in the DHTML viewer. Both the viewer controls and data are sent in DHTML format.

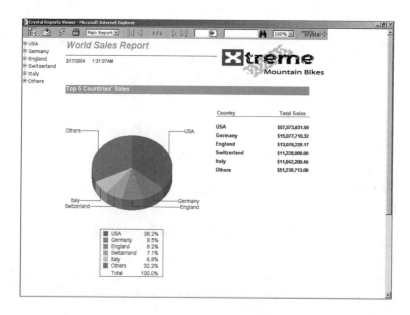

Advanced DHTML Viewer   The advanced DHTML viewer includes all of the functionality of the DHTML viewer but also includes an advanced search wizard that enables you to search for data by setting conditions and to return the data in a table form.

Use the Advanced Search Wizard icon to toggle the report to display the Advanced DHTML viewer options that are described in Table 23.5.

TABLE 23.5   ADVANCED DHTML VIEWER TABS

Tab	Description
Fields tab	Shows all the fields that were available in the original report, including any formulas and summaries. Select the fields required and sort them by changing the sort order; the field at the top of the list appears first on the list.
Conditions tab	Apply any filtering to the report as deemed necessary by selecting the fields and setting the conditions that apply. Add as many conditions as required and separate them using an AND or OR condition. The free-form button enables you to write free-form conditions or to check your condition statement. Figure 23.14 shows the Conditions tab.
Results tab	The Results tab provides the search results (if any) associated with the fields selected in the Fields tab and after application of the filters set in the Conditions tab. These results are provided with active hyperlinks to their respective position in the associated report. Additionally, some quick export functionality is provided to Excel, Word, or HTML. Of further interest is that the active hyperlinks back into the main Crystal Report are maintained through the export and can be used within the newly exported environment.

NOTE

When searching for strings, keep in mind they are case sensitive.

CAUTION

The Advanced DTHML viewer requires the Report Application Server to be installed and running.

Discussions Viewer   The Discussions viewer enables the user to make notes or annotations associated with the involved report or report instance. It enables users to make notes Public or Private, to associate attachments with the notes, and to forward the note to another interested party via e-mail. For example, the sales manager might want to post a note specifying that sales were below what he had expected. Sales representatives could then post their responses to the relevant sections of the report, attaching, for example, a forecast in Excel spreadsheet format. Users can add notes as a follow-up to an existing note, creating what is called a *discussion thread*, or they can create a new note, starting a new thread (see Figure 23.15).

Figure 23.14
This report is viewed in the Advanced DHTML viewer. The user could enter a date to show all orders for a partic ular day.

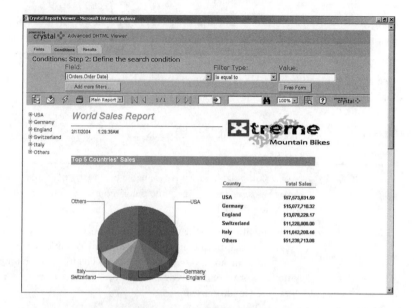

Figure 23.15
The Discussion viewer showing the beginnings of a discussion thread.

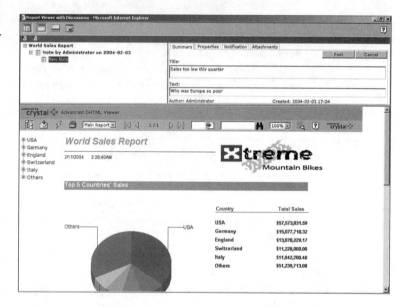

Table 23.6 describes the various Discussion viewer tabs.

TABLE 23.6   THE DISCUSSIONS VIEWER TABS

Tab	Description
Summary tab	Enables the user to add new notes and to view the associated text with an exiting note. It also displays the author of the note and a creation timestamp of the note.
Properties tab	This tab enables the user to set the importance of the note. Highly important notes have a red flag associated with them and notes of low importance have a blue flag associated with them. Notes of normal importance have no flag. Permissions can be public or private. A *private* permission means only you having access to the note; in other words, it's a note to self. *Public* means that anybody who has access to the report can see the note.
Notification tab	Users can send an e-mail notifying other users that a note has been posted.
Attachments tab	Supporting documentation can be added to the note. Supported attachments can be of file types .doc, .txt, .pdf, .ppt, .xls, .htm, .html, and .zip.

23

NOTE

> The user needs to select the root of the thread to insert the note. For the initial thread, the report itself needs to be highlighted.

MOBILE VIEWER   The Mobile viewer enables the user to simulate viewing reports over a WAP-enabled mobile phone or Web-enabled PDA. The design paradigm is simple with only a certain number of characters enabled across the page for fitting into the device. Additionally, these devices typically have limited bandwidth so transferring large reports with thousands of rows would not be an acceptable end-user experience. The Mobile viewer requires that the involved report contain a report part that enables the user to see the critical piece of the report. For example, Figure 23.16 displays the chart of the world sales report as a report part.

CLIENT-SIDE VIEWERS

The Client-Side viewers require some components to be downloaded and executed on the client (browser). The Client-Side viewers do offer some enhanced printing and processing capabilities. Additionally, these viewers require an initial download to the client and hence some of the report processing is performed on the client.

ACTIVEX VIEWER   This viewer is available using Microsoft Internet Explorer supporting ActiveX controls. Over and above the standard viewer functionality described previously, this viewer enables users to freeze the pane; in other words, the users can scroll across or down the report and "frozen" sections remain part of the viewable area. This is achieved by right-clicking on a field where you want the panes to the left and above to be frozen. This enables the user to scroll while headings and other sections remain frozen, shown in Figure 23.17.

Figure 23.16
The Mobile viewer enables the user to simulate viewing reports via a WAP-enabled phone or Web-enabled PDA. Only the initial chart from the World Sales Report is displayed.

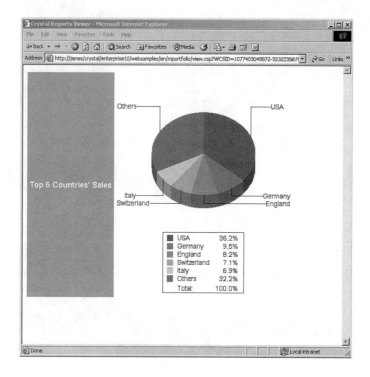

The user can also copy a cell value from a report by right-clicking the cell and selecting the copy function.

Figure 23.17
ActiveX viewer provides additional capabilities allowing sections of the viewer to be frozen. The user can scroll across the remaining sections.

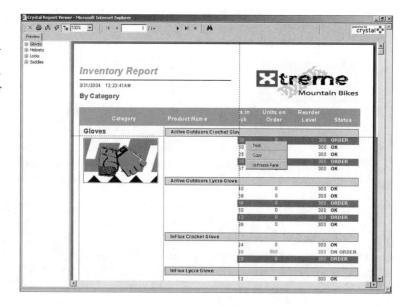

JAVA VIEWER   The Java viewer (see Figure 23.18) is a Client-Side viewer that is downloaded. It requires that a suitable Java Virtual Machine (JVM) be running on the client. If one is not available, the user is prompted to install one.

Figure 23.18
World Sales Report sample as viewed within the Java viewer.

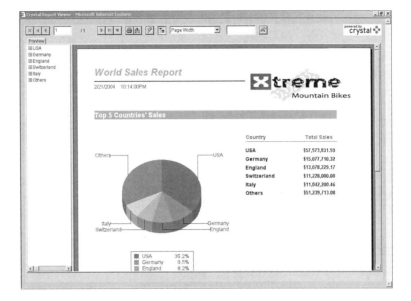

CRYSTAL OFFLINE VIEWER   What makes the Offline viewer different is that you can view Crystal Reports in an offline mode. In other words, the user does not have to be connected to the Crystal Enterprise infrastructure and just needs access to the Crystal Report, that is, the .rpt file. Figure 23.19 displays the World Sales Report in an offline mode.

Figure 23.19
The Offline viewer provides the strongest report manipulation capabilities compared to all the previously mentioned viewers; however, this viewer is not browser-based and requires a Windows desktop download.

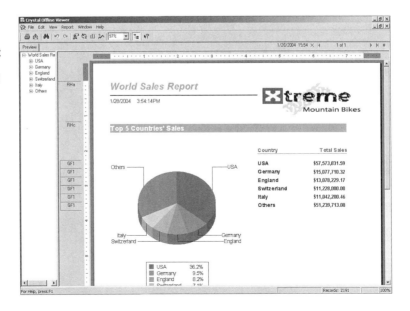

NOTE

> To use the Offline viewer, you must save the involved report with data. You can accomplish this by using the Save With Data option directly from Crystal Reports or by exporting from Crystal Enterprise to the client's machine.

The Offline viewer itself is the most powerful report viewer with respect to data manipulation. It provides functionality over and above the other viewers and gives you the capability to

- Include a larger number of format options.
- Perform improved search capabilities, enabling partial or whole word text search and case matching.
- Create multiple filters.
- Sort data based on the top or bottom value; for example, show the top five countries in sales.
- Change chart types and format the charts.

The biggest drawbacks to this viewer are the following:

- It is not a Web-based viewer.
- Users cannot refresh data live against the database.

To refresh the data the report would have to be refreshed using the Crystal Reports designer and resaved with data.

OBJECT PACKAGE VIEWING

Object packages are new to Crystal Enterprise version 10. They require special mention because viewing a package is different than viewing a report object.

Object packages enable the user to schedule a package as opposed to scheduling the individual components. For example, if the user had reports that were related to one another via hyperlinks without object packages, the user would have had to schedule each individual report making sure the parameters were consistent and accurate information was displayed. With object packages, the package of reports can be scheduled as a whole and any common parameters propagated through the package. If three individual reports were run and each report had a date parameter, the user would need to ensure that the date values were consistent across all reports or else the data would not be consistent. With object packages you can run these as one object and propagate the date parameter for each report to ensure consistency.

For more information about setting up an object package, see Chapter 27.

When viewing an object package, Crystal Enterprise displays a list of the objects that are within the package. This tells the user what the package consists of. To view the individual components, click the individual object within the package. The object type opens with its own individual viewer, which is dictated to by the preferences set by the individual user.

ORGANIZING OBJECTS WITHIN THE WEB DESKTOP

Within the Web Desktop the user can organize the objects, given the appropriate permissions (see Figure 23.20). This functionality effectively means that users who have the rights can copy, move, rename, create shortcuts, and delete objects and folders to which they have access.

Figure 23.20
Users can organize the objects to which they have access.

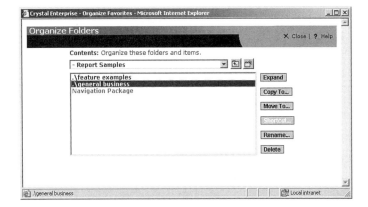

The user would click the Organize icon and the screen in Figure 23.20 would appear. She could then navigate through the objects, copying or moving them to the desired location. The Create Shortcut option enables Crystal Enterprise to have one object, but enables multiple users to access that object. This simplifies maintenance because the administrator or user can update a single object and all users that have access see the change. The Update buttons are also context-sensitive; for example, if the user has a report object selected, only available report functions are available.

PUBLISHING TO THE WEB DESKTOP

Publishing content into Crystal Enterprise refers to taking content in the form of reports or other object types such as spreadsheets and saving them to a specific folder within Crystal Enterprise. The reason it is called publishing content is that once saved, any user with the appropriate authority can then view the content.

There are three ways to publish content into Crystal Enterprise:

- Push method
- Pull method
- Crystal Publishing Wizard

Push Method

The Push method uses the File Save As method available with Crystal Reports and Crystal Analysis Professional. This is illustrated in Figure 23.21.

As an alternative to selecting a local drive, the user can select the Enterprise icon. Crystal Enterprise then forces the user to log in. A listing of folders becomes available to which the user can publish content. This list is secured by the user's rights so the user can only access and publish content to folders to which she has access. This method then pushes the file from her local workstation and saves it within the Enterprise infrastructure.

Figure 23.21
Using File, Save As, the user can select the Enterprise icon. The report is then pushed from the desktop to the Enterprise infrastructure.

NOTE

This is a Windows-only method and users cannot use this if their Crystal Enterprise is hosted on a UNIX platform. Also note that to use this method the publisher needs to have rights to the Windows domain, in which the Crystal Enterprise infrastructure resides.

Pull Method

For the Pull method, the user logs on to Crystal Enterprise, specifically the Crystal Management Console and then "pulls" the file from the local system to the Crystal Enterprise Infrastructure.

In the Crystal Management Console, navigate to the Objects section. Click the New Object button and navigate to the report or object you want to publish to Crystal Enterprise.

For Crystal Reports only, a thumbnail can be saved as an image of the first page of the report. To achieve this, save the report with data and choose File, Summary Info options; the Save Preview Picture needs to be checked.

The user browses for the objects and then specifies which folder to publish the object to. Notice the different object types that can be published to Crystal Enterprise as displayed in Figure 23.22.

Using the method, the user pulls the object into Crystal Enterprise. The user needs to have authority to do this and access to the Crystal Management Console.

Figure 23.22
The Crystal Management Console displaying the various object types that can be published to Crystal Enterprise.

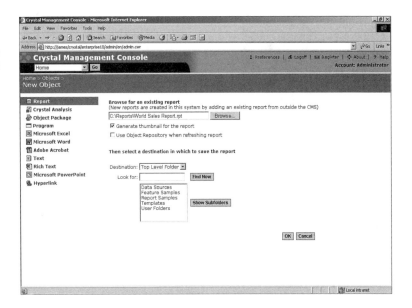

CRYSTAL PUBLISHING WIZARD

The Crystal Publishing Wizard, shown in Figure 23.23, is a locally installed Windows application that doesn't need to be installed on the Crystal Enterprise server. This publishing method is best suited to publishing a large number of files into the system.

The wizard authenticates you first to determine your publishing rights. It then walks you through locating the files you want to publish. You need to specify the Crystal Enterprise folders where you want to publish the files. You can set file properties for each of the files, such as a description or what database logon information should be used as a default when this file is run.

NOTE

In version 10 of this application, the multiple publishing wizards have been consolidated into one. Also, please note the new object types that the wizard enables you to publish.

CRYSTAL IMPORT WIZARD

Although this tool is primarily used to upgrade a set of objects from one Crystal Enterprise system to another or from an older Crystal Enterprise system to the current version, this tool is sometimes used for publishing content. The wizard walks you through selecting a source and destination Crystal Enterprise environment, as illustrated in Figure 23.24. You then select users and objects to import into the destination system.

Figure 23.23
The Publishing Wizard walks the user through publishing an object.

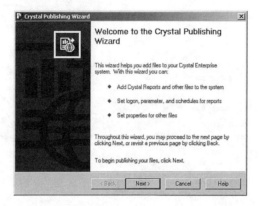

Figure 23.24
The Crystal Import Wizard showing the various source versions that the system can import from.

The source versions include

- Seagate Info (Crystal Enterprise's predecessor) 7.5
- Crystal Enterprise 8
- Crystal Enterprise 8.5
- Crystal Enterprise 9
- Crystal Enterprise 10

Objects that you can migrate

- Users and User Groups
- Folders and Favorites Folder for specified users
- Objects and related instances
- Events
- Server groups
- Calendars
- Repository objects

NOTE

Although the wizard is Windows-based, you can still import from Unix-based Crystal Enterprise systems.

Crystal Reports or Crystal Analysis Professional enables a content creator to design reports while not connected to Crystal Enterprise. This flexibility means that the Crystal Enterprise infrastructure does not have to be established before a report developer can start creating content. However, when publishing the report, the connection information—the information required to connect to the data source—is published with the report. Crystal Enterprise looks for a data source name when executing the report and if one is not found, the report fails.

The solution is that the connection information can be changed in the Crystal Management Console by selecting the object icon and changing the information on the Database tab to a connection that resides on the server. An alternative is to keep the connection information consistent between the Enterprise infrastructure and the publisher's workstation.

Another alternative is to create and publish reports using the ODBC connection string. This effectively removes the need for a DSN.

Because the page or job service/process is executing the report, these services need to have access to the data source server. For example, if the report is using the native Oracle driver to connect, the page and job server need to have rights such that they can connect to the Oracle Server.

CUSTOMIZING THE WEB DESKTOP

During the implementations of the Web Desktop, an organization might want to make a few changes to the standard Desktop application to tailor the application to suit their needs. This might include a cosmetic change such as adding their logo or security changes that remove certain functionality from the users.

The changes made to the desktop are global settings and affect all users using the Web Desktop. This differs from users setting their preferences section because those preferences are saved on a user-by-user basis.

To access the Web Desktop Administration page, the administrator can click the Crystal Applications via the Crystal Management Console and then select the Web Desktop. This page is shown in Figure 23.25.

HEADER

These options, as described in Table 23.7, enable changes to be made to all page headers of the Web Desktop.

Figure 23.25
The Properties page of the Web Desktop.

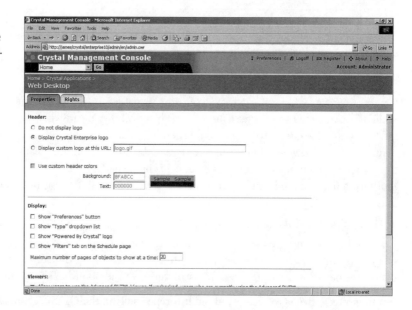

TABLE 23.7   WEB DESKTOP PAGE HEADER OPTIONS

Option	Description
Do Not Display Logo	No logo is displayed
Display Crystal Enterprise Logo	Displays the Crystal Enterprise logo. This is the default and the image can be located at `<server>/program files/ crystal decisions/enterprise 10/web content/ enterprise10/eportfolio/<language>/images/ eportfolio_default.gif`.
Display Custom Logo	Specify the URL where the custom logo is located. This is used when organizations want to display their own logo. Figure 23.26 displays the new Business Objects logo, as opposed to the Crystal Decisions logo.
Use Custom Header Colors	Change the default colors on the header.

DISPLAY

Changes made in this section, as described in Table 23.8, affect the body of the page. Some of the settings are purely cosmetic, like showing the Crystal logo. Others affect the users' functionality, such as allowing a user to filter a report.

Figure 23.26
Example of changing the logo on the Java Web Desktop. The default Crystal Decisions logo has been replaced with the Business Objects logo. Note that the Powered by Crystal logo has also been removed.

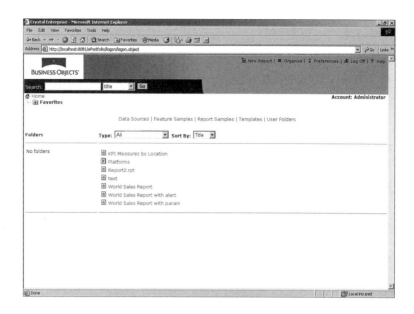

23

TABLE 23.8   DISPLAY OPTIONS

Option	Description
Show Preferences Button	If checked, displays the Preferences icon. If this is not displayed, users have no control over setting their preferences.
Show Type Drop-down List	Removes the capability to filter the page by object type, and all objects are displayed.
Show Powered by Crystal Logo	Adds or removes the powered by Crystal logo at the bottom of the available .csp or jsp.
Show Filters Tab on the Schedule Tab	The logic behind this is that Administrators might not want users applying filters to reports. The Filters tab enables users to write their own filter or modify the existing one, which might not filter correctly if written incorrectly.
Maximum Number of Pages of Objects to Show	Pages of objects are created by the number of objects the user chooses to display on a page.

VIEWERS

The only option here is to allow users to use the Advanced DHTML viewer, should the user want to change and filter the report. However, the Advanced DHTML viewer enables report modification, and this requires further processing power. If report modification is not a requirement, this can be disabled and the users can use the DHTML viewer.

TROUBLESHOOTING

REPORTS DO NOT SAVE TO CRYSTAL ENTERPRISE FROM CRYSTAL REPORTS

When using the Push method, reports aren't saved to Crystal Enterprise. The user get an error message or nothing happens.

There are certain criteria that must be configured correctly for this method to work:

- Check to ensure that you can access the Crystal Enterprise server. Try logging into the Crystal Management Console of the Web Desktop application.

- Make sure the Windows domain that the user is logged into is the same as the one that the Crystal Enterprise Server belongs to or the user has cross-domain access.

- This is a Windows-only method. It will not work with Enterprise Systems hosted on Unix systems.

- The user needs to have sufficient rights to be able to publish. If this is the case, the system will notify the user accordingly.

THUMBNAIL ISN'T WORKING

The user sets her Web Desktop to display as the thumbnail view; however, the reports do not display a thumbnail, rather a generic blue and white logo.

If Crystal Enterprise cannot find an associated thumbnail, the system will display this logo. In the Crystal Management Console locate the incorrect report by clicking the Objects icon. The Properties tab should display a thumbnail of the report; however, if this is not the case, try the following:

- Check Show Report Thumbnail on the properties page of the report in the Crystal Management Console.

- When saving the report, the data needs to be saved with the report. Select the Save Data with Report option from the File menu in Crystal Reports.

- Ensure that the Save Preview Picture option is checked. This is located under Summary Info from the File menu in Crystal Reports.

DISPLAYING OBJECT INFORMATION

In the Web Desktop, an object's folder, title, and description can be displayed by hovering the mouse over the object, but all three pieces of information are not displaying.

Check the following:

- Ensure that these fields are populated in the object properties under the Crystal Management Console.

- Alternatively, the description field can be populated in Crystal Reports by completing the comments field found under Summary Info from the File menu in Crystal Reports.

CHAPTER 24

CRYSTAL ENTERPRISE ARCHITECTURE

In this chapter

INTRODUCTION

This chapter introduces the Crystal Enterprise Framework and the components that make up its architecture. It describes how each of the services or daemons that are part of the Crystal Enterprise Framework operate and what role they have in an information infrastructure. The chapter also discusses the benefits of having a distributed architecture: vertical scalability, horizontal scalability, innate load balancing, failover, high availability, and tune-ability—the capability to tailor the system to a particular environment and type of load.

This chapter uses a progressive approach: considering the highest level first, and then approaching each part of that whole in more detail.

CRYSTAL ENTERPRISE ARCHITECTURE OVERVIEW

At the highest level, Crystal Enterprise has four main tiers: the client tier, application tier, Crystal Enterprise Server tier, and database tier (see Figure 24.1):

Figure 24.1
The client, application, server, and data tiers compose an enterprise business intelligence infrastructure.

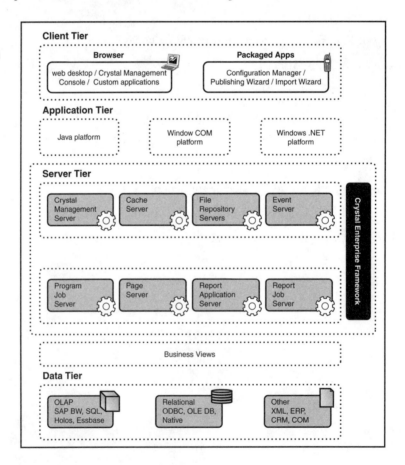

- The *client tier* consists of Web-based and installed applications. You can alternatively categorize these applications into end-user applications such as the Web-based Web Desktop, which enables end users to access data, management applications such as the Web-based Crystal Management Console, and content creation applications such as Crystal Reports or Crystal Analysis. In the majority of cases, the client tier for a Crystal Enterprise user is his Web browser.

- The *application tier* consists of application processing—typically on an application server, using the Crystal Enterprise Software Development Kit (CE-SDK). The CE-SDK provides a programmatic interface to the Crystal Enterprise server tier. These server-based programs are processed on an application server, such as BEA WebLogic, IBM's WebSphere, a Servlet container like Apache Tomcat or Microsoft .Net server. This application tier could provide an application centered on Crystal Enterprise functionality, like the Web Desktop, or an application that uses Crystal Enterprise functionality as part of a greater application (for example, an online banking application that provides full-service banking for customers, and provides detailed statements via Crystal Enterprise).

- The *server tier* consists of services (in Windows) or daemons (in Unix) registered with the Crystal Enterprise Framework. (They are generically referred to as either services or daemons as these terms are interchangeable.) Although this chapter uses the term "service" or "daemon" for technical accuracy, you might see references to these services as "servers" as well, for instance the Crystal Management Server. The server tier is usually subdivided into the intelligence and processing tiers.

- The *data tier* is composed of all data sources from which an organization can pull data. This data can be in a database, an application, a programmatic data source, XML, a Web service, or a variety of other sources.

With a high-level understanding of the role of the client, application, server, and database tiers, you now consider each one in depth.

THE CLIENT TIER

The client tier is the "face" that you associate with Crystal Enterprise. A particular end user might think of the Web Desktop application page that shows up in her Web browser as Crystal Enterprise. However, Crystal Enterprise has many faces, each distinct and useful. By adopting a flexible approach toward potential client applications, Crystal Enterprise offers a system architect diverse means of sharing information with diverse audiences: an executive receives a text message on his cellular phone with the latest profitability statistics; a shipping clerk receives an order on the workgroup printer; a supplier company receives an XML file with detailed order specifications. These are but a few faces of Crystal Enterprise.

To begin categorizing the client tier, define three groups of audiences that will use client applications: the end user, content creator, and administrator. Although these groups are not mutually exclusive (a particular person can have all three roles), this distinction helps to explore important dimensions of each.

24

END-USER CLIENTS

The most common end-user client for Crystal Enterprise is a Web browser. Many of the client applications that are included with Crystal Enterprise, such as the Web Desktop, use a Web browser as their client. Additionally, most custom application development targets the Web browser.

With the proliferation, adoption, and maturation of the Internet as a communications medium, additional client tools offer diverse venues for end-user experiences. Internet-connected phones and mobile devices already grace the belts and briefcases of the more tech-savvy.

With each client targeted for an end-user community, specific considerations take the fore. For instance, most Internet-connected phones have small screens—they can only display a few lines of text at a time. Because Crystal Enterprise is so widely experienced within the Web browser, several browser-related considerations merit your attention. Web browsers such as Internet Explorer and Netscape or Mozilla are page-oriented: They display one page at a time. Users expect these pages quickly and become frustrated at what they consider long waiting times for pages to display. The benchmark hovers at between 5 to 10 seconds for the patience of a typical Web user.

The Web experience also is by and large a simple one. You see a blue-underlined word, and know that you can click on it to go somewhere. Originally, Web browsers were simple text display programs. The capability of today's browsers to render complex graphics and reflect exact positioning represents a tremendous maturation of the technology, but you must remember that a Web browser was not initially designed for this, and even today limitations, most notably around printing, reflect these origins. For content such as Crystal Reports, where pixel-level formatting is vital, and for content such as Crystal Analysis Workbooks, where interactivity is vital, Crystal Enterprise provides special facility for overcoming the limitations of the Web browser.

The Crystal Enterprise report viewers were presented in Chapters 22, "Introduction to Crystal Enterprise," and 23, "Using Crystal Enterprise with Web Desktop." For each type of object managed in Crystal Enterprise, there are specific viewers made available. These viewers appear in the browser and include buttons for exporting, printing, navigating, searching, and so on. These viewers provide pixel-level positioning, tremendous interactivity, and graphical capability. Crystal Enterprise 9 implemented a new viewing architecture, now improved and deepened in version 10. The viewer object in the CE-SDK renders reports and provides a simple interface for the Web developer to embed a Crystal Report or Crystal Analysis Workbook. The developer sets the properties of the viewer to determine the capabilities an end user has. For instance, the report export capability might be inappropriate for a certain end-user population, and so can be turned off by setting the `HasExportButton` property to 0.

The Web browser receives only DHTML and images, with the exception of the optional print control. Should a user choose to print a report, either an ActiveX print control or an Adobe Acrobat file is used to print while maintaining pixel-level formatting and fidelity.

In earlier versions of Crystal Enterprise, reports were rendered via a URL request to the viewrpt.cwr page, which was processed by the Web Component Service provided by Crystal Enterprise. The new control enables a developer to embed a viewer control wherever they want in a Web page, to be platform independent, and to fully secure and control the report viewing experience.

Crystal Enterprise supports the following browsers:

- IE 5.x
- IE 6
- Netscape 6.2
- Netscape 7.0
- Safari 1.0 on OSx (not including Japanese)

CONTENT CREATION APPLICATIONS

Applications, such as Crystal Reports or Crystal Analysis, install on the report developer's machine and create and publish content to the Crystal Enterprise Framework. These were introduced and covered extensively in Parts I through IV.

ADMINISTRATIVE CLIENT APPLICATIONS

Applications such as the Crystal Management Console (CMC) allow administrative users to manage the Crystal Enterprise system. Administrators might also use the Crystal Configuration Manager (CCM) for server-level management. The CMC is a Web-based application, but the CCM is an installed application. Coverage of these administration tools is provided in Chapter 27, "Administering and Configuring Crystal Enterprise."

THE APPLICATION TIER

Various applications dynamically create end-user pages, most typically in HTML. These applications are processed on an application server. In the past few years, the Enterprise application server market has consolidated dramatically, with two main camps now extant: the Microsoft .Net technologies and the Java technologies.

Crystal Enterprise provides a Software Development Kit in three formats for each of the three most popular development environments: COM, Java, and .Net. These allow an organization maximum flexibility in integrating Crystal Enterprise into its applications.

The COM CE-SDK includes a set of COM objects that interact with Crystal Enterprise via the Crystal Enterprise Framework. Typical installations that use the COM CE-SDK include a Crystal Enterprise Web Connector on each of the Web-server machines, and a Crystal Enterprise Web Component Server within the Crystal Enterprise Framework. A typical example of a COM technology is Microsoft's Active Server Pages (ASP) technology. When Crystal Enterprise is installed in a Windows environment, the basic applications such as the Web Desktop are written in Crystal Server Pages (CSP), a technology analogous with ASP, except that processing takes place within the Crystal Enterprise Framework on the Web Component Server.

The Java CE-SDK includes a set of Java classes that communicate with the Crystal Enterprise Framework. In a Java application server environment, no Web Connector (WC) or Web Component Service (WCS) is required. Instead the Java CE-SDK is processed on the Web application server, which communicates via the Java SDK directly with the Crystal Enterprise Framework. In addition, the Crystal Enterprise Web Component Adapter (WCA) installs on the Web application server and provides the capabilities that you expect from the WCS: CSP processing and specific application support.

Microsoft produces the .Net Framework. Applications written within the .Net Framework are supported by Crystal Enterprise via the .Net format of the CE-SDK. This SDK includes primary interop assemblies and visual development controls for visual application development in Microsoft Visual Studio .Net. In a .Net application, there is no WCS, WCA, or WC required, as the native .Net assemblies are loaded into the .Net framework and communicate with Crystal Enterprise via the COM SDK.

The current state of support for the CE-SDK is both a reflection of the marketplace and a reflection of the historical progression of Crystal Enterprise in response to the maturation of the Web server market. Because Crystal Enterprise was introduced before the Web application market had matured, Crystal Enterprise included its own application server: the WCS. Now that the Web server and Web application server markets have consolidated and matured, the WCS is gradually being replaced by the capabilities of those application servers. Generally, all custom applications should be developed using the technology that is most appropriate: the Java or .Net SDKs. Although COM technology is supported in Crystal Enterprise 10, with Microsoft's migration to .Net from COM, it is recommended that development take place in .Net over COM where possible.

THE SERVER TIER: INTRODUCTION TO THE CRYSTAL ENTERPRISE FRAMEWORK

The Crystal Enterprise Framework, the backbone of Crystal Enterprise, provides a distributed mechanism that manages the interaction and communication of the Crystal Enterprise services that make up the server tier, as well as communication between this server tier and the CE-SDK. Each Crystal Enterprise service uses the framework to describe the capabilities it offers and to discover other services that are registered with the framework. The framework treats each of the registered services as equals, which enables one service to use the capability of another Crystal Enterprise server directly, thus enhancing scalability.

The Framework's foundation is a communication bus that handles dialogue between the various services and facilitates automatic load-balancing and fault tolerance. This communication bus registers each service, categorizes the type of service, and maintains a tally of the status of each service. For scalability reasons, much of this service interaction is distributed and decentralized. This is one of the reasons Crystal Enterprise leads the industry in scalability.

The Crystal Enterprise Framework uses programmatic components, known as plug-ins, to represent each object type within Crystal Enterprise. Plug-ins contain the appropriate properties and methods needed to handle a particular object within Crystal Enterprise, and determine how Crystal Enterprise should treat it. For instance, a service might require information about a Crystal Report, and will use the properties of the Crystal Report plug-in to retrieve the information. The Crystal Report plug-in properties include things like the report title, the database login information for that report, and the report thumbnail image. In contrast, a user plug-in might have the username, the type of login, and the group membership as its properties.

Although plug-ins become much more important as you start to explore application development using the CE-SDK, they are a great way to start to explore the capabilities of Crystal Enterprise. Figure 24.2 shows how a plug-in is used. They help you to categorize the types of objects you find in Crystal Enterprise, and understand what you can do with each of them.

Figure 24.2
A plug-in is the way Crystal Enterprise exposes the services of a server on the framework.

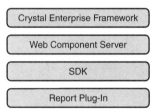

The object types that are part of the Crystal Enterprise Framework are classified in the following groups:

- Administration
- Authentication
- Content
- Distribution

ADMINISTRATION PLUG-INS

Administration plug-ins provide a way to manage the Crystal Enterprise servers. Each plug-in exposes the control and configuration properties of a server within the Crystal Enterprise system so that you can configure the behavior of each Crystal Enterprise server. These plug-ins also provide activity metrics for each server.

AUTHENTICATION PLUG-INS

Authentication plug-ins provide a mechanism for Crystal Enterprise to interact with external security systems and treat these systems as native authentication sources. The authentication plug-ins provided with Crystal Enterprise are

- Crystal Enterprise
- Windows NT
- LDAP
- Windows Active Directory

These authentication types are discussed in more detail in "The Server Tier: Overview of the Crystal Enterprise Services," later in this chapter.

CONTENT PLUG-INS

Content plug-ins describe the types of objects that end users (report viewers) would typically interact with, such as, but not limited to, a Crystal Report. The content types that are provided as part of Crystal Enterprise are

- Folder
- User folder
- Shortcuts
- Crystal Reports
- Crystal Analysis
- Microsoft Word
- Microsoft Excel
- Microsoft PowerPoint
- Rich Text Format
- Adobe Acrobat
- Text
- Users
- User groups
- Servers
- Server groups
- Events
- Connections
- Licenses
- Calendars
- Object packages
- Program objects

DISTRIBUTION PLUG-INS

A *distribution plug-in* allows anyone who is scheduling an object such as a Crystal Report to be able to send that report outside the Crystal Enterprise environment. This facility enables the application to schedule reports to destinations such as e-mail. Distribution plug-ins that are provided with Crystal Enterprise are

- Disk location
- FTP server
- E-mail (SMTP)

NOTE

> Crystal Enterprise also provides the capability for a Crystal Report to be scheduled to a printer. The printer object is not exposed as a distribution object, but rather as a function of the Crystal Report content plug-in.

These plug-ins play a fundamental role in the Crystal Enterprise Framework by encapsulating and exposing the knowledge of the object type that they represent. The remainder of this chapter discusses how these plug-ins are used by the Crystal Enterprise servers within the Crystal Enterprise Framework.

THE SERVER TIER: OVERVIEW OF THE CRYSTAL ENTERPRISE SERVICES

Now that it's clear that the functionality of individual Crystal Enterprise servers is exposed through plug-ins, it's important to understand exactly what that functionality is. The Crystal Enterprise servers are designed to register themselves with the Crystal Enterprise Framework and provide one or more services that can be consumed by other servers or by the plug-ins described in the last section. The services offered by each of the servers is dependent on the type of task that the server is expected to perform.

The following list shows the servers that are delivered with Crystal Enterprise. These servers can be thought of as *core servers*:

- Crystal Management Server
- Web Component Server or Adapter
- Cache Server
- Page Server
- Report Application Server
- Report Job Server
- Program Job Server
- Event Server
- File Repository Server

These servers can be seen in the architecture diagram in Figure 24.3.

Figure 24.3
The core server architecture for Crystal Enterprise.

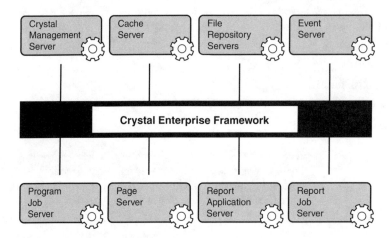

With these servers in place, Crystal Enterprise manages reporting and business intelligence content (such as Crystal Reports, Crystal Analysis Reports, Excel, Word, PDF, and PowerPoint documents) and offers rich customization services allowing organizations to deeply embed and integrate Crystal Enterprise into their already established applications or Web services.

It's important to note that multiple instances of the same server operating in the Crystal Enterprise Framework at the same time are fully supported. This provides a scalable, reliable, and fault-tolerant system.

CRYSTAL MANAGEMENT SERVER

The Crystal Management Server (CMS) provides a number of the core services that the Crystal Enterprise Framework uses. These services include allowing other servers to register with the framework, allowing users to be authenticated with the system, and providing a storage mechanism for maintaining the metadata about each object. The services provided by the CMS fit into four main categories:

- Controlling access to content
- Managing objects and scheduling
- Managing servers
- Managing system auditing

The CMS provides for the following:

- System security
- Object metadata storage
- Object management

- Object scheduling
- Event handling
- Name-server capabilities
- Server clustering
- License management
- Auditing

SYSTEM SECURITY

The security service breaks security down into three main elements:

- Authentication
- Authorization
- Aggregation

AUTHENTICATION   Crystal Enterprise provides mechanisms to allow for third-party authentication services to be used as the basis of user and group/role definition. The CMS interacts with these third-party authentication mechanisms by using the following authentication plug-ins, described earlier in the chapter:

- Crystal Enterprise security plug-in
- Windows NT security plug-in
- LDAP security plug-in
- Windows Active Directory plug-in
- Application authentication such as PeopleSoft or SAP

The Enterprise security plug-in enables organizations to define users and groups directly within Crystal Enterprise and restrict use of an external source for those users. This is useful if an organization has chosen not to use an external security source or has not yet defined one. All authentication information is stored in Crystal Enterprise and does not rely on an outside source to determine whether a user is valid.

The NT and Active Directory security plug-ins enable a customer to map any number of users and groups into Crystal Enterprise. Although these two are separate plug-ins, they function in similar manner and so are discussed here together.

An administrator is required to go into the Crystal Management Console (see Chapter 26, "Deploying Crystal Enterprise in a Complex Network Environment") or use an application written using the SDK and define the default NT or Active Directory (AD) domain as well as any user groups that might need to be mapped into Crystal Enterprise. After this initial mapping is complete, Crystal Enterprise will dynamically query for users within that group and establish those users as Crystal Enterprise users. When a user logs on for the first time, the security service using the NT or AD security plug-in asks the NT or AD security database if this is a valid NT or AD user and whether the user belongs in any of the mapped groups. If the user is indeed a valid user, he will be granted access to Crystal Enterprise. If at any time in the future that user is removed from that NT group, he will not be granted access to Crystal Enterprise (and, hence, reports within the system) because the security service would be told that this user is no longer a valid NT user. There's no requirement for the administrator to manually inform Crystal Enterprise that the user is no longer a valid NT user.

The LDAP security plug-in operates in a similar manner to the NT security plug-in; however, instead of talking to the operating system for a list of valid users or groups, this security plug-in communicates with a directory server using the LDAP protocol. Crystal Enterprise does not require the LDAP schema in the directory server to be modified in any way for use with Crystal Enterprise. This security plug-in provides default mappings for several directory servers, including

- iPlanet Directory Server versions 5.0 and 5.2
- Lotus Domino versions 5.0.12 and 6.0.2
- IBM Secureway 5.1
- Novell Directory Services eDirectory 8.7
- Custom

When the Crystal Enterprise solutions kits for PeopleSoft and SAP are installed, they provide additional authentication plug-ins for each system, respectively.

Users and groups are queried by leveraging attributes within the LDAP schema, such as InetOrgPerson, which is an attribute used by iPlanet Directory Server. If the directory server that is to be used with Crystal Enterprise is not in the preceding list, it's also possible to create a custom mapping of LDAP attributes. The attributes that are used to define a group or user must be mapped to the LDAP security plug-in for these attributes to be used when querying for a user or a group.

Application-specific authentication plug-ins enable Crystal Enterprise to validate a user's credentials against an ERP system such as SAP or PeopleSoft. Installing a Crystal Enterprise Solution Kit installs the respective plug-in, which then appears next to the default authentication tabs in the Crystal Management Console. Each of these application-specific plug-ins requires configuration to enable Crystal Enterprise to interact with the application, and require information on group mapping.

AUTHORIZATION   After configuring Crystal Enterprise with external users and groups, it's necessary to determine which objects within the system an end user has the authority to view. This central mechanism of controlled access to certain reports is a key component of the system. Setting up authorization rules or access control is straightforward after users and reports have been added to the system. Chapter 27 reviews how to apply access control on objects in the system.

NOTE

> Authorization within Crystal Enterprise is enforced through a strong inheritance model throughout the system. This enables you to set desired access levels at a root folder for a large group and have that setting be respected, regardless of how many new subfolders are created or objects are added to those folders (as well as any new users added to groups or subgroups).

AGGREGATION   Crystal Enterprise can aggregate or group users in two ways, as Chapter 27 reviews in some detail. A group can be created directly in Crystal Enterprise or it can be mapped from one of the external authentication sources. The grouping within Crystal Enterprise is quite powerful because native and mapped groups can be used at the same time. If this method of user aggregation is implemented, a native group would contain a mapped group. The use of mapped groups simplifies administration: As users are added or removed from groups in the external systems, this will be automatically reflected in Crystal Enterprise. It's also possible to create a hierarchy of groups to better organize the end users of the system.

OBJECT METADATA STORAGE

Among other tasks, the CMS stores a repository of information about each object in the Crystal Enterprise system. After this information is stored, it becomes available to other objects or servers within the system. This persistent data describes an object (such as a Crystal Report) and makes it possible to dynamically query the system and discover the properties of that object. This repository expanded in version 10 of Crystal Enterprise to include storage of objects used to design Crystal Reports as well as Crystal Business Views Objects (see Chapter 18, "Crystal Reports Semantic Layer—Business Views").

This information is stored in a repository to enable scaling; to do otherwise would require dependence on the information being stored in memory on a physical server—not scalable. The CMS stores this information by writing it to a relational database. Version 10 uses database-querying capabilities more than in previous versions of Crystal Enterprise, resulting in even faster request processing and enhanced scalability. However, this changed functionality also requires that more attention be paid to database optimization than in previous versions.

The CMS service is able to access these databases by using ODBC or by a direct, also known as native, interface to the database. Because the CMS also provides auditing capability, the database compatibility is the same for the auditing database (you will consider the auditing capability itself later in this chapter). Although the Crystal Enterprise system database and the audit database can be on the same or separate database servers, the actual databases are separate.

The following list shows databases supported by the CMS and how they are accessed by Crystal Enterprise 10 when the CMS is operating on Windows NT:

- Direct IBM DB2 8.1
- Direct IBM UDB DB2 7.2

- Direct Oracle 8i(8.1.7) with Oracle 9.2 client
- Direct Oracle 9.2
- Direct Sybase System 12.5
- ODBC-MSDE
- ODBC-MS SQL Server 2000
- ODBC-MS SQL Server 7

The databases that the CMS can access on Unix are a subset of what is available on Windows. If the CMS is operating on Unix, it's able to use the following databases:

- IBM DB2 8.1
- IBM UDB DB2 7.2
- Oracle 8i(8.1.7) with Oracle 9.2 client
- Oracle 9.2
- Sybase System 12.5

All database connections for the CMS repository are done by a direct interface.

The default Windows-platform database that the CMS will use if one is not provided is the MSDE, a simple implementation of Microsoft's SQL Server. Because performance of the CMS database can dramatically affect system performance, MSDE is used to provide an organization a useful out-of-the-box experience. The repository is set up and configured without the need for interaction with a database administrator. If Crystal Enterprise is initially configured to use the default repository database and the need arises to move the repository to a different database server, Crystal Enterprise provides tools (the Crystal Configuration Manager) to easily migrate the data from one server to another.

NAMESERVER CAPABILITIES

The CMS allows all other Crystal Enterprise servers to register with the Crystal Enterprise Framework. After each service has registered through the CMS, it is able to discover the other servers active within the framework and use any services it needs from those servers.

New Crystal Enterprise services can be added to the system from either the Crystal Management Console or the Crystal Configuration Manager. The addition of these new services provides additional scalability and higher availability.

OBJECT MANAGEMENT

One of the key benefits of Crystal Enterprise is how it manages objects. After an object (such as a Crystal Report) is published to Crystal Enterprise, the properties of that object are read and added to the repository. The object is then represented by metadata in the repository, which makes it possible for other services to interact with the object, and the object is formally considered a "managed object" by the system.

Managed objects facilitate simplified administration of an Enterprise Business Intelligence system and represent a principal benefit of Crystal Enterprise. After an object is managed by the system, all of that object's properties become managed from a single access point. For instance, if a server needs access to an object, it asks the CMS for an ID to the object. Additionally, if you want to maintain a certain number of reports in the system, or only keep objects more recent than a certain date, this can be automated within the system. If you want to schedule a report, or organize similar reports into folders, or control access rights, or link reports, or change database properties of multiple reports—all of this and other similar actions are possible when you manage the objects within Crystal Enterprise.

By having objects managed, a Web application developer can use Crystal Enterprise to manage and provide access to all objects. Rather than requiring knowledge of object filenames or network share locations, or even which objects or reports are available at all, developers can simply query Crystal Enterprise for the desired objects—perhaps those kept in a certain folder or of a certain type. Each time a user accesses the Web application, the content might be different, depending on the actual reports (objects) published by or scheduled into Crystal Enterprise. Web developers are not required to make changes such as adding and maintaining reports. This can be done by a report developer or system administrator through delegated administration and provides a logical separation of tasks.

Managed objects can be categorized into folders, which themselves are managed objects. This categorization adds to the manageability of Crystal Enterprise because content can be easily organized into something that is meaningful to end users.

Crystal Enterprise 10 adds several new types of objects to the system, such as program objects and third-party objects such as Microsoft Word objects (please see "The Server Tier: Introduction to the Crystal Enterprise Framework" earlier in this chapter for a complete list). The system database also includes a report component repository that simplifies access to corporate objects such as logos, images, disclaimers, and so on, and a rich semantic layer called Crystal Business Views.

If you were to look at the database directly, you would see that these additional capabilities have altered the database tables from previous versions of Crystal Enterprise, and you now see four tables in the system database instead of the previous two. The two additional tables represent the report component repository.

For performance and security reasons, the vast majority of the information about objects is stored in a binary format in the database, making it unreadable to direct database access. Instead, the CMS provides access to database objects via the CE-SDK via a SQL-like query language. This system ensures authenticated and authorized access only; the application provides access to objects based on their authenticated identity only.

OBJECT SCHEDULING

The scheduling service of the CMS makes it possible for objects such as Crystal Reports to be processed at a particular time or on a recurring basis. This service determines when a report object gets processed using the Report Job Server, or a program object gets processed using the Program Job Server. When a scheduled event occurs, the two main servers that interact with the object are the relevant Job Server and the Event Server. Additionally, an object package combines objects such as reports or programs for simplified scheduling.

When scheduling a job, the scheduling service gathers information from various objects before running. It needs information from the report object regarding how to connect to the database, the desired format to output the report to, where it might be delivered (such as an e-mail address), and which server is going to process it (if there are multiple Job Servers). An object can be scheduled to run at a particular date or time, on a recurring basis, or perhaps according to a custom calendar. This information is then stored in the system as a scheduled instance of the object. This is known as a `ProcessingInfo` object.

The `ProcessingInfo` object contains all the properties set on the report object when it was scheduled. It knows when the job will run as well as all the data-connection information and all the formatting and distribution settings.

A scheduled object can be made to be dependent on an event occurring within or outside the Crystal Enterprise system before it will run. By using events with schedules, it's possible to provide meaningful control around when a schedule should actually run. If an object is due to run every day but the databases that it queries are updated sporadically, an event can be used to initiate the running of the scheduled job and eliminate unnecessary scheduled jobs or reports.

New to Crystal Enterprise 10, a notification capability provides the capability to send e-mail upon a scheduled job completion, either in the case of success or failure. Common use cases include an administrator receiving notification of a report processing failure, or an end-user group being notified of the latest quarterly results.

In some instances, batch scheduling can take place via a custom program. In these cases, report instances might be distributed to many users. The scheduling service makes this possible by allowing a job to be scheduled on behalf of another user. This is useful when an organization wants to configure its system to only show instances of objects to a user if she "owns" that instance. This is exposed in the CE-SDK in the `ScheduleOnBehalfOf` property of the `SchedulingInfo` object.

EVENT HANDLING

Events make it possible for users to ensure that scheduled jobs are processing only when external systems, like a database, are ready to be accessed. All events interface with the CMS Event service.

Crystal Enterprise supports three types of events. The first event type is a *scheduled event*. The scheduled event allows an organization to create dependency chains when scheduling reports. This enables the user to determine the schedule of a report based on a preceding report successfully completing or failing. Users can easily configure scheduled event conditions such that if report 1 is successful, run report 2. If report 1 is not successful, run program object 3. This can continue so that a process flow is established.

NOTE

> With the inclusion of Program Objects in version 10 of Crystal Enterprise, it should become apparent that these scheduling daisy chains could now include workflow that reaches outside of the Crystal Enterprise environment and could affect external systems or applications.

The next event type is a custom event. The *custom event* is sometimes also called a *generic event* in the predecessor to Crystal Enterprise, known as Seagate Info. This event requires application developer interaction to trigger the event by using the `Trigger()` method via the Crystal Enterprise SDK. This event type gives an organization a great deal of flexibility. Having an event that can be triggered by code makes it possible to have an external system determine when the event is triggered and the scheduled jobs that are dependent on it will run. A good example of this would be a database update trigger user event for Crystal Enterprise.

The third type is a *file-based event*. These events are managed by the Event Server and are discussed later in the chapter.

SERVER CLUSTERING

As a Crystal Enterprise system grows and access to information that it contains becomes increasingly mission critical, it's important that the system be fault tolerant, ensuring that end users are always able to access their information.

The CMS can be clustered to provide load balancing and fault tolerance for the services that it provides. When two or more CMSs are clustered, they perform as an active-active collection of servers. By being active-active, they are sharing the workload and this translates into increased scalability and performance.

AUDITING

New to Crystal Enterprise 10, the auditing capability simplifies gathering statistics on system performance and enables administrators to profile the usage of reports or system resources. Because the auditing database is separate from the CMS/system database, you must create the "blank" database and any necessary ODBC DSN first. From within the Crystal Configuration Manager (CCM) you then stop the CMS, click on the Specify Auditing Source icon (the fourth icon from the right in the toolbar), specify the database or DSN you want to use, and then restart the CMS, whereupon the CMS creates the auditing database structure and connection. On Unix platforms you take the same approach, except that you stop and start the CMS with the ccm.sh script and use the cmsdbsetup.sh script with the selectaudit option to specify the audit database, including the connection port (which is 6400 by default).

After the CMS starts and connects to the audit database, you can specify which items you want to audit. The administrator enables auditing of each of the following items by entering the Crystal Management Console (CMC), navigating to the Servers, choosing the particular server you want to affect, and then checking the appropriate boxes in the Auditing tab. Table 24.1 shows each server's auditing features. Note that the table does not include the Page Server; the Page Server's auditing occurs through the Cache Server, which takes reports from the Page Server and passes them to the appropriate viewer. Note also that although the Job Servers are treated as one, they must be specified on each server. Additionally, you must specify auditing on each instance of a server if multiple instances exist.

TABLE 24.1   DETAILED AUDITING CAPABILITIES BY SERVER

Server	Audit Feature
CMS	Folder creation, deletion, modification User logon (concurrent and named) User password change, logon failure, logoff Report or Program Job communication lost (that is, timeout on Program/Report JobServer)
Cache Server	Report view success/failure
RAS	Report open success/failure and which viewer was used Report creation success/failure, and which viewer/application was used Report save success/failure and which viewer/application was used
Event Server	Event registered, updated, or unregistered Event triggered
Job Servers	Job success/failure, failure-retry state

Note that the CMS periodically broadcasts a request to all system services requesting audit information to be returned for writing to the database. The default is every five minutes. Your Crystal Enterprise documentation describes several command-line flags to specify this and other audit-specific CMS parameters. You must specify the same command lines on all CMSs if clustered.

WEB COMPONENT SERVER

The Web Component Server (WCS) is an *application server* provided by Crystal Enterprise that delivers seamless integration of Crystal Enterprise content into any Web application. This integration can be hosted on a variety of Web servers and provides a robust scripting interface known as Crystal Server Pages that enables the creation of rich server-side Web applications.

At the time Crystal Enterprise was introduced many organizations already had licensed and installed Web servers, but did not possess an application server. Crystal Decisions found it necessary to provide this application server so that applications could be written against the CE-SDK on any operating system platform. With the maturation and consolidation of the Web server market many of the functions that the WCS provides are now supplanted by the combination Web and application servers common in the marketplace, rendering the WCS application-serving capabilities unnecessary for most organizations.

However, the WCS did provide some capabilities in addition to CSP processing, and these functions, if desired in an installation, are now provided by the Web Component Adapter. In summary, the WCS capabilities include the following:

- Processing of CSP
- Report parameter prompting at report view time
- Report database logon requests at report view time
- Crystal Management Console server processing
- Rendering of Crystal Analysis Workbooks

To provide these capabilities, should they be required by the use case, Crystal Enterprise includes the Web Component Adapter (WCA) that provides all the above, except the processing of CSP pages.

Crystal Enterprise 10 no longer requires the WCS for all installations. A typical installation on a Unix system, for example, would use client applications such as the Web Desktop written in Java Server Pages (JSP), rather than in Crystal Server Pages (CSP), and so would not require the WCS to process CSP pages but would use a Java application server to process the JSP against the Java version of the CE-SDK. On a Unix installation, then, you use the WCA to take over the functions listed above that might be required on that platform, given that you no longer install the WCS.

A custom application written using the Microsoft .Net version of the CE-SDK would also not require the WCS as the application-processing functions would be carried out by Microsoft Internet Information Services (IIS) Web server and the .Net Framework application serving capability, along with the Crystal Enterprise Primary Interop Assemblies.

WEB CONNECTORS

The Web Component Server interacts with Web servers through a component known as the Web Connector. So whenever a WCS is required, the Web Connector also must be installed. The Web Connector typically operates as an in-process extension of the Web server. The only exception to this rule is the CGI engine.

Crystal Enterprise provides Web Connectors for

- iPlanet Web Server Enterprise Editions 6 and 7
- Microsoft IIS 5 and 6
- Apache 1.3.20 and 2.0
- IBM HTTP Server 2.0
- Lotus Domino 5.0.12 and 6.0.2

The Web Connector redirects certain Web requests from a Web server to the Web Component Server (WCS). By having the Web Connector reside on the Web server and communicate with the WCS, possibly on another physical server, it allows the deployment of the WCSs in a way that will facilitate *scaling out*, or adding additional physical servers to the Crystal Enterprise architecture.

The Web Connector is listening for several potential requests, including Crystal Server Pages and accessing certain objects.

CRYSTAL SERVER PAGES

The first of these requests is for a Crystal Server Page (CSP). The CSP is analogous to Microsoft's Active Server Pages (ASP) but runs on the WCS rather than directly on a Web server. This capability was initially developed and included as part of Crystal Enterprise to allow for application processing in a platform-neutral manner. CSP can process either JavaScript (which is different than Java) or VBScript (which again is different from Visual Basic). Most of the applications provided with Crystal Enterprise implemented in CSP, such as the Web Desktop, are written using JavaScript on the server side.

For future application development, most organizations will derive benefit from using an alternative development approach such as coding against the CE-SDK in Java or a .Net language, rather than developing applications in CSP. Although CSP is not specifically deprecated in the version 10 release of Crystal Enterprise, Business Objects has indicated in the help file that CSP will be deprecated in a subsequent release.

ACCESSING OBJECTS

Another request that the Web Connector will send to a Component Server is known as a Crystal Web Request, or CWR. A CWR is a server-side object that exists on the WCS and provides access to managed objects contained within the Crystal Enterprise Repository.

Support for URL-based requests to directly view a Crystal Enterprise object such as a report is deprecated within Crystal Enterprise 10 because the report viewing model has changed to a Crystal Report viewing control within the Application tier. Certain legacy applications might still use .cwr requests, but this method is not recommended for new installations to ensure forward-compatibility.

WEB COMPONENT ADAPTER

In configurations on Unix, or where an organization wants to use a Java application server (or servlet container like Tomcat) in conjunction with Crystal Enterprise, a Web Component Adapter replaces the Web Connector and WCS. No WCS or Web Connector is required in this configuration. Specifically, the Web Component Adapter

- Processes CSP pages
- Services Crystal Management Console requests
- Handles viewrpt.cwr requests (legacy support)

The Web Component Adapter supports the following Java application servers:

- BEA WebLogic 7(SP1), 8.1
- IBM WebSphere 5.0 (Fix-pack 2) (**JVM 1.4 is not supported on AIX)
- Tomcat 4.1.27

JOB SERVERS (REPORT AND PROGRAM)

The Job Servers process scheduled jobs. Job Servers are informed about the content that they process by loading a Job Server plug-in. This plug-in, like all other Crystal Enterprise plug-ins, describes what capabilities it exposes to the service using it. In Crystal Enterprise 10, there are two different Job Server plug-ins: one for Crystal Reports and one for Programs. When the system administrator adds a new Job Server to the Crystal Enterprise system, he must choose which type of plug-in, and thus which type of Job Server it will be.

REPORT JOB SERVER

The Report Job Server allows scheduled objects to access the necessary data source required, provides row-level data security services, and distributes the content to a location chosen by the user.

Essentially, the Job Server provides three main services to Crystal Enterprise:

- Database access
- Distribution of objects
- E-mail

DATABASE ACCESS

When a scheduled job is about to be processed by the Job Server, it gathers the appropriate information from the ProcessingInfo object mentioned earlier. This information includes database connection information and any filters or parameters required that determine what the final query is. After it has this, it opens the object and queries the database for the appropriate information. The data is retrieved, compressed, and stored back into the system as a report instance.

DISTRIBUTION OF OBJECTS

It's the Job Server's responsibility to distribute the object to the destination set by the user scheduling the job. To do this, the distribution service interacts with the distribution plug-ins mentioned earlier and receives the information appropriate to each plug-in type. For example, if a user scheduled a job to be delivered by e-mail, the distribution service would get the To:, Cc:, subject, and body properties as well as the SMTP server that is configured for use with Crystal Enterprise. Chapter 26 shows how to configure the distribution service.

This service enables a user to send a report outside the Crystal Enterprise environment and deliver it to one of four destinations using the distribution plug-ins mentioned earlier.

E-MAIL AS A DESTINATION

Crystal Enterprise supports SMTP as its e-mail distribution protocol. Virtually all Internet mail servers support SMTP, so it's easy for an organization to integrate Crystal Enterprise into its mail system, regardless of platform. By supporting standards such as SMTP, organizations are not restricted in the e-mail server types that can be used with Crystal Enterprise.

FTP SERVER AS A DESTINATION

Organizations send objects directly to an FTP server location so that it's available for other users or applications. This is useful for getting information that can be used offline by customers, partners, or suppliers. A report can also be scheduled to update information at an FTP location on a regular basis to drive another application or business process. For example, a report could be designed to provide a product pricing list, including dynamic calculations of discounts that vary by customer, and then deliver it automatically to an FTP folder on a customer's Web server. Another example might be a scheduled Crystal Report output to an XML document sent via FTP to an external server for a business partner's application to pick up.

UNMANAGED DISK AS A DESTINATION

The unmanaged disk distribution service is used in the same fashion as the FTP server except that this service distributes the scheduled report to a disk location that is available on an organization's internal network. Building on the preceding example, an organization could have Crystal Enterprise distribute a general pricing list to a location on disk and have this information populated on a purchase form or as a way of populating values into a Web service.

PRINTER AS A DESTINATION

Distributing reports to a printer available on the network is as simple as deciding which printer is to be used when the report is processed. Printing reports often is necessary when the information on the report needs to be shared with people who don't have access to a computer during analysis of that information. Situations such as team or board meetings often require that each member have a printed copy of the information to be covered.

INTERACTING WITH EXTERNAL SYSTEMS

Sometimes, it's necessary for a job to be intercepted before being run. Typically, organizations choose to do this so that information from an external entitlement database can be queried, and they can determine what data the user is allowed to view and modify the filter to reflect their restrictions. This is done in Crystal Enterprise using a component called a *processing extension*. The processing extension is loaded by the Report Job Server during a schedule or by the Page Server or Report Application Server if being viewed. This extension allows for row-level security. Row-level security makes it possible for organizations to have content, such as a Crystal Report, shared by many users but the actual data that they see is targeted to them. It's also important to note that defining row-level security does not affect the content template but rather filters the view that the user sees based on the data that user has the right to see. There is no need to go into Crystal Reports and modify the report to affect which pages a user can see.

NOTE

> With the inclusion of Business Views in version 10 of Crystal Enterprise, it is now possible to directly include external entitlement databases into Business Views and easily provide both column- and row-level security through that mechanism.

Processing extensions are just that, an extension of Crystal Enterprise. Some examples of processing extensions are available for Crystal Enterprise with the product.

PROGRAM JOB SERVER

Much in the same way that the Report Job Server processes Crystal Reports, the Program Job Server processes programs. These programs consist of three types:

- Executable
- Java
- Script

These objects are published to the Crystal Enterprise Framework, scheduled to be run by the Program Job Server, and executed. The goals of the programs differ as organizations can write programs according to their needs. Although processing a report results in a report instance, processing a program results in only a record that the program was run. The results of the program will depend on the program itself. Some programs might do maintenance on the Crystal Enterprise system and some programs might have functions totally unrelated to Crystal Enterprise—a powerful new capability to integrate Crystal Enterprise functionality into an organization's workflow.

PAGE SERVER

The Page Server is responsible for delivering three services to the framework. The primary service is to generate pages for viewing reports. This capability is relevant for performance and the scalability of viewing reports because it only ever sends a single page of a report to the viewers. It does this by using a service known as Page on Demand. Other services performed by the Page Server are refreshing a report's data using a service known as on-demand viewing as well as the capability to export a report to another format for end-user download.

PAGE ON DEMAND

The Page on Demand service receives a request to view a certain page of a report and then generates just enough information to have the report viewers display that page. As described previously, it's much more efficient in a multiuser or low bandwidth environment to have pages of a report rather than the entire report sent to the viewer. This service not only ensures a positive user experience by getting them the view of the report they're after quickly, it also is important to administrators.

Page on Demand minimizes demand on network bandwidth. Each page of the report generated by the Page Server is approximately 2KB in size. A report is usually much larger than this, especially if it's many thousands of pages containing thousands, if not millions, of rows of data. It should now be apparent why Page on Demand is a useful service. This service goes one step further by ensuring a positive user experience through a technology known as *report streaming*.

Report streaming builds on Page on Demand by determining which objects in the page might take longer to calculate than others and then delivering them to the viewer slightly behind objects that can be generated quickly. For example, the report might contain summaries or charts that require additional calculations to be performed before rendering for the end user who is viewing the report. Report streaming will ensure that the rest of the information, such as the details making up the chart or summaries, is sent to the user right away. The remaining portions of a report are sent as soon as they are calculated on the server. Report streaming is similar to the placeholder technologies that browsers use when loading images.

On-Demand Viewing

The Page Server allows a user to refresh the view of the report dynamically instead of scheduling the report. To take advantage of this service, users first must be granted the proper access level for the object that needs to be updated.

If a user has this access level, he has the capability to force the report to connect to the database upon his request. When the user refreshes the report, he will be prompted to enter any relevant information the report requires, such as database connection information or parameter values. Before enabling on-demand viewing for all users, the use of the system and size of reports must be taken into consideration. If many users are querying the database at the same time, are they asking for similar information? If so, the report could be run once and then shared among many users. What amount of data is expected to be returned or how long is the report expected to run? Often, a report might be too complex to enable all users in an organization to run it themselves. Based on the amount of time spent in the database, on the network, and in the report engine, a report can take several seconds, or even minutes, to complete. If this situation occurs, it makes sense to schedule any complex reports that spend a lot of time processing and allow that report to be shared among the users.

Exporting to Other Formats

The Page Server makes it possible for users to request to have the report presented to them in a format other than Crystal Reports. These formats are Crystal Reports, Microsoft Word, Microsoft Excel with formatting, Microsoft Excel data only, Adobe Acrobat, Rich Text Format, text, or Comma Separated Value (CSV) format. The user can request these formats typically by selecting the Export button in the report viewers.

ROW-LEVEL SECURITY

In the same manner as the Job Server, the Page Server is able to restrict information presented to users based on a row restriction set by a processing extension. The main difference here is the Page Server is providing this capability at view time rather than at schedule time. Each method has its benefits. If a report has a row restriction applied to it during scheduling, the amount of data being returned to the report is filtered during the query. This means that the report instance only contains data that is relevant to the user who scheduled it. Another method is to apply the row restriction at view time.

If restrictions are applied at view time, the report instance contains the data necessary for the report, regardless of who is viewing it. When a user requests the report, the Page Server communicates with the processing extension to determine the row restriction to be applied for the user viewing the report. The data is then dynamically filtered so that the user is seeing only the data that he is able to see.

CACHE SERVER

The Cache Server is an integral component to the overall scalability of Crystal Enterprise. It establishes a cache of report pages generated by the Page Server, which are called *encapsulated page format* (EPF) files, and promotes the sharing of this information. This is an important facet of the Crystal Enterprise Framework because, instead of having the report page regenerated for each user who requests it, the Cache Server determines whether the page can be shared among users. If it can, it will return the cached page. The Cache Server receives these requests from the report viewer and when the request is received, it checks to see whether the page requested is available in cache. If it is, the page is returned to the report viewer to complete the request. If it is not, the request is sent to the Page Server to have it generated.

In the case that the Report Application Server serves the view request, caching occurs inside the Report Application Server itself, and the Cache Server does not interact with it. The Report Application Server would service view requests requiring interaction; for instance, when using the Interactive Viewer, the Report Application Service renders reports, as it has the additional capabilities that the Interactive Viewer requires.

CACHE MANAGEMENT

The Cache Server is responsible for maintaining a cache of report pages generated by the Page Server on disk. When a request for a page is received, the Cache Server checks to see whether the page is available in its cache and whether it can be shared. If it is a sharable page, the server returns the page to the user. If the page cannot be shared, the request is sent to the Page Server to generate a new page.

CONSTRAINTS

Sometimes, pages are not sharable. The Cache Server determines that a report page is not sharable if it meets one of these conditions:

- Row-level security is being enforced—If row-level security is being used, the page of information is valid only for the user who requested it; therefore, the Cache Server is unable to pass this page onto another user.

- The query within the report has changed—The query for the report can change if a user chooses to view a report and change the filter already previously defined or change a parameter value. When this occurs, the cached page is invalidated and must be regenerated.

EVENT SERVER

The Event Server provides a way for Crystal Enterprise to monitor and use events that are occurring outside of its environment. It enables an organization to trigger the running of Crystal Enterprise scheduled jobs dependent on external events.

The Event Server monitors the operating system for the existence or modification of a file. Using a file to trigger an event is a useful way of determining when an event is triggered because the generation of a file is a simple thing to achieve. For example, an organization might perform a nightly data warehouse update, and have the same program that does the database load create a file after finishing the load. Upon file creation or update, the event server then reports to the CMS that the required trigger is present, allowing the scheduled job to be processed.

FILE REPOSITORY SERVERS

The File Repository Server provides the Crystal Enterprise Framework with two core services. The first is the capability to provide a centralized content storage facility, and the second is the capability to abstract the location of these objects from other services within the framework.

CENTRALIZED STORAGE OF CONTENT

Crystal Enterprise provides two File Repository Servers (FRS). An input FRS is used to store any content that has been published to Crystal Enterprise by the Publishing Wizard or from the content creation tools. When content is published to Crystal Enterprise, the object is copied from the client to a location in the FRS. This location is set by the installation of Crystal Enterprise but can be controlled by the administrator through modification of the FRS root directory. The objects are placed into unique folders on the server and are given unique names to ensure that there will not be any conflicts with other objects.

An output FRS is used to store the content generated by a scheduled job. The output server operates in the same manner as the input server by generating a unique name and location for each object.

ABSTRACTION OF CONTENT LOCATION

Now that the content is centrally stored and managed, the FRS abstracts the actual location of the objects from the other framework services. By using Uniform Resource Identifiers, or

URIs, the framework sees a virtual "location" for the content. This makes it easy for services to request an object from the FRS without the need to ensure that it has access to the actual physical disk location. From a deployment and administration perspective, the job is much easier if objects are referred by URI. There is no need for complex network configurations, such as setting each service to run as a user account so they can access network shares.

However, this means that the system administrator must ensure that the account privileges of the FRS daemon or service include access to the disk location(s). This concept, of appropriate privileges for services, echoes throughout the entire system. The various services or daemons all interact with the operating system in different ways, and each requires the appropriate rights to function.

REPORT APPLICATION SERVER

The Report Application Server is a powerful add-on server to the Crystal Enterprise Framework. It enables organizations to take their Web reporting a step or two further than the simple viewing of report content over the Web. The Report Application Server provides three new components for the framework: an alternative processing component for the report, a full object model for creating and modifying a Crystal Report, and a dedicated server for handling the creation and modification requests.

24

NOTE

> Although Crystal Enterprise includes the Report Application Server, appropriate licensing must be purchased to use the report modification and creation capabilities within the Crystal Enterprise Framework. This license can be purchased in addition to Crystal Enterprise licenses, or as part of a Crystal Enterprise Premium bundle.

CRYSTAL REPORT MODIFICATION AND CREATION CONCEPTS

One of the main benefits of adding the Report Application Server to the Crystal Enterprise Framework is that organizations can quickly and easily add Crystal Report creation and modification capabilities to their Web applications. The Report Application Server makes it possible to connect to a server-side data source, query for information, and then display that information, all within a zero-client Web viewer. By using any of the built-in clients that are delivered with the Report Application Server or using the object model to create a custom user interface, it's possible to provide ad hoc Crystal Report creation and modification to the system end users—and essentially provide self-service reporting.

WEB REPORT DESIGN

The Report Application Server can take the data returned as part of the previously mentioned ad hoc report query issued by an application user and allow her to begin to format the report. The user is able to modify the query in many ways to format it into a quality report. Many people, after seeing these capabilities within a Web browser, remark that the experience is similar to a Web-based version of Crystal Reports. The Report Application server enables the making of database connections, selecting and joining tables, choosing fields, grouping and summing, creating formulas and charts, and formatting fields and sections.

INTERACTIVE REPORT VIEWING

In addition to the capabilities of the Crystal Enterprise report viewer connected to the Page Server, a benefit of connecting to the Report Application Server from a report viewer is that it provides an object model that enables the report to be manipulated on the server. You can modify the viewer to provide a flexible viewing experience.

The viewer supports an event model that provides you with the information selected by the user in the viewer. This makes it easy for organizations using the Report Application Server to make closed loop systems.

This means that when the event model is used, a report can become much more interactive and drive more business value. For example, a retail organization uses Crystal Enterprise to present its product catalog to its users. The reports are very useful and allow users to browse the catalog or drill in for more details on items. If the user wants to order something, he needs to navigate to another form to enter his order and he has to keep looking back to the catalog report to remember the part number he wants to order.

Using the event model of the Report Application Server this organization can, without changing its catalog report, enable the user to click on the item he wants right within the view of the catalog. This event captures the data that the user clicked on and enables the Web developer to populate the order screen with this information with no user interaction. If the report also displayed inventory counts, the report could be updated as soon as the user finished his transaction.

RICH OBJECT MODEL

The Report Application Server provides a powerful object model (covered in detail in Chapters 31–33) that allows an organization to control any aspect of how a user performs an ad hoc query or formats it. In typical ad hoc tools the users are given the same tool and the organization deploying the tool has no say in how the user is able to perform her tasks.

THE DATA TIER

Every organization has data in a wide variety of sources: databases, applications, XML files, Excel spreadsheets, EJBs, and so on. Crystal Enterprise provides unparalleled access to data in a wide variety of formats. Although data access was covered in Chapter 1, "Creating and Designing Basic Reports," several architectural concepts around this topic merit our attention. First, Crystal Enterprise 10 includes Crystal Business Views, which provide a level of abstraction above data sources, greatly simplifying report writing and data security. Second, you will explore some of the most common sources of data.

CRYSTAL BUSINESS VIEWS

Rather than connect directly to data sources, an organization can use Crystal Business Views to simplify data access. Using the Business Views (BV) Semantic layer speeds report development because the report developer bypasses several typical steps of report development: connecting to the data source, choosing tables, joining tables, and adding calculations. Instead, by choosing the BV, the report developer sees a complete set of fields logically organized around business problems and areas.

During development of a BV, a database administrator or subject matter expert with database skills chose the appropriate data sources and tables or other constructs, joined them together, selected the necessary fields, created any formulas or functions, and applied security at row and column levels against Crystal Enterprise User groups.

Architecturally, this can be seen as a separate layer between the processing services in the server tier and the data sources. BVs are not required to access data because direct connections to data sources remain. BVs are covered in greater detail in Chapter 18.

DATA SOURCE TYPES

Although available data sources were discussed in Chapter 1, a brief summary helps to understand some key architectural concepts when connecting to different types of data sources. The following few sections cover some of the most popular data sources in the enterprise computing environment.

DATABASE SYSTEMS

Databases are the prototypical data source. There are several ways that the Server tier connects to databases. An ODBC connection uses an ODBC driver to communicate with the Database Management system (RDBMS), which returns the relevant data. Every machine hosting report processing services from the Crystal Enterprise Framework, namely Page Servers, Report Job Servers, and Report Application Servers, must have the requisite ODBC Data Source Names (DSN) configured. ODBC connections require special support on Unix-based machines, often in the form of an ODBC driver that must be purchased in addition to the operating system.

Using a direct connection to a database most often requires a database client application installed on any machines. Most RDBMSs that support native connections ship with their respective database client applications, which then must be installed on machines hosting Crystal Enterprise report processing services.

APPLICATION DATA SOURCES

Crystal Enterprise offers a variety of Solution Kits that include application-specific integrations to provide data access to those applications. For instance, the SAP Solution Kit facilitates access to SAP's R/3 and Business Warehouse.

These Solution Kits represent a high level of integration, usually providing single-sign on so end users can use their application credentials to log on to Crystal Enterprise. They are also notable in that data access does not proceed directly from the Crystal Enterprise processing services or daemons to the application databases, but rather connects to the applications themselves, which subsequently manage queries and security and often data transformation to simplify data access. So application data sources present an additional level of abstraction from the underlying data source. These are covered in detail in Chapter 15, "Additional Data Sources for Crystal Reports."

PROGRAMMATIC DATA SOURCES

A data source might not be accessible in the correct format, or might require some transformative or conditional logic. In these cases a software developer can write a program using the appropriate logic, and then expose the resulting data to Crystal Enterprise. Crystal Enterprise supports connectivity to these programmatic, or Active, data sources. Typical programs would expose a JavaBean, ADO (COM), or ADO.NET data provider, which would be consumed by Crystal Enterprise.

→ For more information on this, **see** "Understanding the Additional Crystal Reports Data Sources," **p. 314**

THE CRYSTAL ENTERPRISE ARCHITECTURE IN ACTION

This section takes a look at how all the Crystal Enterprise services come together and which of the services are used when a user requests objects. Each scenario is based on the following situation: Over a corporate intranet site, a user is browsing a Web page that connects him to a Crystal Enterprise system. The user has provided proper login credentials and is logged into Crystal Enterprise. He has been presented with a list of report objects that he has rights to access.

For this scenario to occur, a browser has connected to a Web server, and in turn the Web server passes the processes the Web page. For instance, if the page is written in JSP, the Java application server passes a request to the Crystal Enterprise Framework via the CE-SDK classes loaded on that application server. The continued interaction between the user and Crystal Enterprise Framework occurs through the facility of the CE-SDK on the application server.

If you are using the CSP pages provided in a COM environment, the Web Connector running on the Web server intercepts the file request because it has a .csp extension, and passes this request to the WCS for processing. The .csp is processed and in this scenario, the page asks the user for logon credentials and is returned to the user to complete. The credentials are submitted and passed to the WCS. The WCS now takes this information and attempts to log on to the CMS using the security service. After the user is logged on to Crystal Enterprise, the CMS is queried to present a list of folders and reports to the user. (The query is generated within the CSP page as well.) This scenario diagram can be seen in Figure 24.4.

For simplicity, the following examples will use the COM environment. To determine how this would relate to the Java or .Net environments, the role of the WCS and Web Connector would be replaced with the CE-SDK running on the appropriate server. The CE-SDK, loaded into the server, communicates directly with the Crystal Enterprise Framework.

Figure 24.4
The login process for a user validated by Crystal Enterprise.

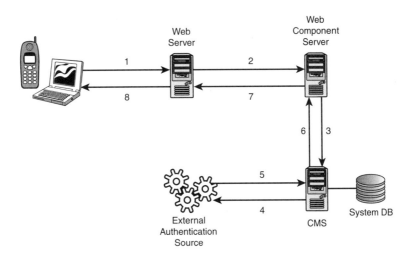

NOTE

The numbered flow in Figures 24.4, 24.5, 24.6, and 24.7 represents the flow of information and requests to get a report processed and delivered to the end user. Dashed lines in the figures represent optional steps.

REQUESTING A CRYSTAL REPORT

The user in the preceding scenario has two methods of viewing a report.

The first method is to view an instance of a previously scheduled job. If an instance is chosen, the report contains cached data from when the job was run. When the request to view the report is received, the WCS asks the Cache Server if the first page of this report is available in cache. If the first page is available, the Cache Server returns the page to the WCS so it can be delivered to the report viewer. The report viewer then displays the report for the user. If the page is not in the cache, the request is forwarded onto the Page Server to generate the page.

As Figure 24.5 shows, when the Page Server receives the request, it loads the report from the output File Repository Server. After the Page Server loads the report, it generates the page that has been requested and then passes it back to the Cache Server. The Cache Server sends the page onto the WCS to be given to the report viewer.

The second method for viewing a report is to view the report itself, which is also known as on-demand viewing. If a user selects the report itself, she must first have the "view on demand" access level. When the report is requested it goes through the same process as shown in Figure 24.5; however, because the report does not have any cached data within the report like the instance has, the Cache Server passes the request directly onto the Page Server.

Figure 24.5
The report-loading process in Crystal Enterprise.

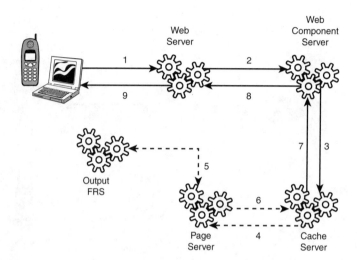

Figure 24.6 shows the extra steps required for on-demand viewing. The Page Server queries the input FRS for the report and loads it. After the report loads, the user will be asked to enter the database logon information and any parameters for the report to run. The Page Server then passes this information to the Crystal Reports engine through the report plug-in. The Crystal Reports engine connects to the database and queries for the necessary data. After the data has been returned to the report engine, the report is recalculated and page information is determined. The Page Server now generates the first page of this report and sends it to the Cache Server, which in turn passes it to the WCS and then to the report viewers.

In both scenarios of viewing a Crystal Report, if a processing extension is being used with this report, the cache is then not sharable. The Cache Server will pass the request directly to the Page Server. The Page Server will load the report from the FRS. During the time that the report is being loaded, the processing extension is engaged to determine the proper row-level restrictions that need to be applied to the cached data within the report. The cached data is then filtered and the page is generated with information that is viewable by that user only.

SCHEDULING A CRYSTAL REPORT

When a report is scheduled, Crystal Enterprise requires the appropriate information so that the scheduling service knows what tasks are to be performed. Figure 24.7 depicts a typical scenario where an end user schedules a report with the appropriate criteria set. This information is passed to the WCS, which in turn forwards the information to be stored in the

CMS. The schedule is set to run at a particular point in the future. When the schedule time occurs, the CMS loads the information from the repository and submits the request to a Job Server. The Job Server asks the input FRS for the report and then loads it into the report Job Server plug-in.

Figure 24.6
The report loading process for on-demand viewing.

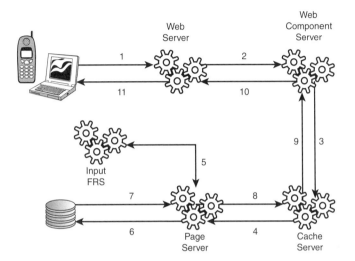

Figure 24.7
The process for scheduling reports.

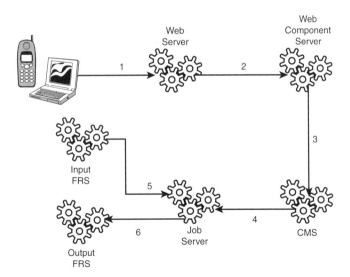

With the report loaded, the Job Server applies any of the parameters set when the user scheduled the report earlier. These parameters might be filters that affect the overall data query. If a processing extension is in use, the report would be further manipulated. After the processing extension is finished with the report, the Job Server connects to the database and completes the processing of the report.

When the job has completed, the Job Server checks two remaining pieces of information the user would have set when scheduling the report; the format in which the report is to be delivered and where it will be delivered. At this stage, the Job Server would output the report into a supported Crystal Enterprise format, including Crystal Reports, Microsoft Word, Excel, Adobe Acrobat, Rich Text Format, or text.

NOTE

> The default output format for all Crystal Enterprise servers is Crystal Reports.

Next, the Job Server needs to distribute the report to the desired location. As previously mentioned, these locations can be a location on disk, an FTP server, or an e-mail address, or remain in the managed Crystal Enterprise environment by distributing it to the output FRS as a report instance object. Regardless of where the user decides to distribute the object, a copy is always stored in the output FRS so that it can be shared between users.

REQUESTING A CRYSTAL ANALYSIS REPORT

If an organization is using Crystal Analysis Professional, it's important to note that report viewing is handled differently from a Crystal Report. Requesting a Crystal Analysis report starts by the user clicking on a link to the report in a Web browser.

The request is delivered to the WCS, and it asks the CMS for the object that was asked for. The object is returned to the WCS and then is loaded by the Crystal Analysis engine. The reports created in Crystal Analysis are dynamic queries to a multidimensional cube of data—the CA engine must connect to the cube referenced in the report.

After a connection to the cube is made, data is retrieved and populated into the .car file, which is an XML document. This XML document is transformed through a style sheet into DHTML and delivered as the first view of the report. This information is sent from the WCS to the Web browser along with the Crystal Analysis DHTML viewer. The viewer makes additional requests for data from the cube via the WCS as it is needed to populate the view of the report.

TAKING ADVANTAGE OF THE CRYSTAL ENTERPRISE DISTRIBUTED ARCHITECTURE

This section of the chapter discusses how the Crystal Enterprise Framework and all the services that it provides are most effectively deployed. As mentioned earlier, Crystal Enterprise is designed as an n-tier distributed system for information delivery. This distributed nature gives an organization a great deal of flexibility in how it might want to deploy Crystal Enterprise in its environments. How Crystal Enterprise is deployed will depend on the way in which the system is expected to be used, how many users are expected to be active in the system at any given time, and how many objects are expected to be processed at any given time.

SCALING UP

The term *scaling up* implies that a software product is able to take full advantage of the physical hardware resources it has access to and ultimately increase its performance as the hardware increases. Crystal Enterprise was designed from its inception to effectively scale up.

All the Crystal Enterprise servers are multithreaded components that are able to scale to take advantage of available physical hardware resources. They have been designed to operate on multiprocessor machines efficiently.

When a system is under high load, even being multithreaded isn't enough. If the load on the servers is high enough, I/O might start to become the limiting factor. Crystal Enterprise deals with this by allowing an organization to configure multiple instances of a server on the same physical piece of hardware. This makes it possible for additional servers to share in the load and remove any I/O bottlenecks. A benefit in doing this is that automatic load balancing kicks in, making the system that much more efficient.

SCALING OUT

Building on the scalability in Crystal Enterprise for scaling up, the capability to distribute report processing loads to multiple physical machines is also available. This is beneficial in many ways.

As an example, an organization can scale its systems to very large levels by adding physical servers to the environment when needed. If an organization chooses to license Crystal Enterprise using named or concurrent access licenses, additional hardware resources can be added to the environment as needed without purchasing additional Crystal Enterprise user licenses. If processor licenses are initially purchased, new processor licenses must be purchased when the additional hardware is added. This is why it's important to understand the expected usage of the system as well as project the future growth of the system so that the appropriate license model is chosen.

The second benefit is the capability to assign tasks to certain computers. For example, the Job Server, Page Server, and File Repository Server could be grouped together on the same physical computer. The Page Server and Job Server both connect to databases and both communicate with the File Repository Server. Locating them on the same computer makes sense in many situations.

The next benefit of scaling out with Crystal Enterprise is fault tolerance. Crystal Enterprise provides the capability not only to have multiple instances of the same service running on the same computer, but also allows for those servers to be spread across multiple machines. Crystal Enterprise has automatic fail-over support in each of its servers to complement the automatic load-balancing capabilities. This means that if a server goes offline for any reason, other servers registered to the Crystal Enterprise Framework will automatically pick up the workload without user interruption.

SCALING ACROSS PLATFORM BOUNDARIES

Some deployments of Crystal Enterprise might require a distributed system on different operating systems. Crystal Enterprise makes it possible for an organization to deploy Crystal Enterprise across any of its supported operating system platforms. This provides a way for organizations to decide what deployment scenario best fits their needs, given the hardware available to them. A key benefit to being able to do this is that organizations might want to seamlessly mix functionality available from different operating systems. For example, an organization might require that reports process on Unix but still want the users authenticated using Windows NT accounts.

There might be situations in which it's necessary to have certain servers running on one operating system and the rest of the system running on another. For example, an organization might have the majority of Crystal Enterprise operating on Unix, but want to seamlessly integrate the SQL Server Analysis cubes being used in the Crystal Analysis reports created by the finance department. These reports can easily be added to the Crystal Enterprise system running on Unix, as long as a WCS is running on Windows so that the Crystal Analysis reports have access to SQL Server Analysis Services.

CAUTION

> Although a mixed-platform deployment can solve problems, do not put clustered CMSs on different platforms. Because they both work together connected to a single database, and because drivers on platforms differ, database corruption can occur on some platform combinations.

EXTENDING CRYSTAL ENTERPRISE

An important aspect of information delivery is how the information is presented to the user community. Crystal Enterprise enables organizations to easily customize how information is presented to end users by providing a rich object model for Web application developers to tightly integrate Crystal Enterprise into their Web applications. Developers can present content to end users, as well as provide Web-based administration applications to their organization, using the Crystal Enterprise SDK. The upcoming sections detail the flexibility of the entire Business Objects suite of Crystal Products and how they can be easily integrated into any environment.

CHAPTER 25

PLANNING CONSIDERATIONS WHEN DEPLOYING CRYSTAL ENTERPRISE

In this chapter

ENSURING A SUCCESSFUL CRYSTAL ENTERPRISE IMPLEMENTATION

The time spent planning a deployment of Crystal Enterprise directly relates to the success of that deployment. In other words, failing to plan is planning to fail. This year in North America, 77% of IT software deployment projects will fail due in part to inaccurate requirement gathering, inexperienced project team members, and insufficient executive interest and sponsorship.

All too often, the average scenario when deploying Crystal Enterprise consists of placing the Crystal Enterprise application CD into the CD drive, double-clicking setup.exe, crossing fingers, and hoping for the best. Whether the person in charge of deploying Crystal Enterprise is an experienced system administrator or a novice at deploying applications to a small or large group of users, certain steps can be taken to increase the deployment success and adoption of Crystal Enterprise.

With its flexible system architecture and SDK, Crystal Enterprise provides organizations with the capability to build uniquely customized information delivery environments scaling from a single-user or workgroup to enterprisewide deployments with tens of thousands of users. Because of this broad scope of functionality, project teams will find themselves planning to deploy an enterprise reporting environment as well as providing application development support to customize the user interface. This is, of course, assuming an organization chooses not to use one of the out-of-the-box Crystal Enterprise end-user interfaces.

The first part of this chapter defines a project management *planning* approach that will enable a Crystal Enterprise system administrator or deployment manager to form a framework around which a Crystal Enterprise deployment project can be successfully built and delivered, thus increasing the rate of success.

The second portion of the chapter focuses on the specific topics related to actually *deploying* Crystal Enterprise, from organizational reporting requirements to server sizing and architecture.

APPROACHING THE PROJECT

Many organizations have standard application development practices and methodologies that are followed with every project that involves system deployment efforts and some level of programmatic customization. These methodologies can trace their ancestry to a simplistic methodology that was used with the invention of the wheel.

The "invention of the wheel" approach goes something like this: Ug is bored of carrying his mammoth tusks on his back all day (business pain); he needs something that will help reduce his effort and allow him to carry more, increasing his efficiency and keeping his boss happy (requirements). After he finds and refines the solution (development) and tests it (pilot), Ug can show his colleagues and find out what they think (user acceptance testing). After this is completed, he can manufacture it and allow his colleagues to carry their tusks more efficiently (deployment). After his colleagues have their tusk carriers, Ug will monitor what they think of it and make changes where necessary (support and maintenance). Needless to say, Ug used this process to develop a cart with wheels, and the rest is history.

Things have changed somewhat since then, but the concept remains the same. This process can help any person responsible for a Crystal Enterprise software project, or any project for that matter:

- Identify business pain
- Establish project requirements
- Develop the application
- Complete user acceptance testing
- Deploy the technology
- Support and maintaining the application

IDENTIFYING BUSINESS PAIN

Necessity is the mother of invention. Most organizations implement new policies, systems, processes, and applications for good reasons: to improve efficiency; save money, time, and effort; and to improve work environments, for example.

Companies have their own processes for discovering business pain. Regardless of how it's discovered, business pain drives the success of the project. In the case of enterprise reporting, existing user interface and application restrictions or data source connectivity requirements and limitations help define the business pain. Crystal Enterprise can be customized to suit most Web delivery GUI requirements and connect to virtually any data source—hence, the reason Crystal Enterprise and its associated report design tools (Crystal Reports) are looked to when solving these types of problems.

Business pains should be documented, concrete, specific, describe the business issue rather than any technical analysis, and taken directly from as many key stakeholders as possible. That way any project success can be evaluated against the initial pain. Key stakeholders feel themselves more involved in the project and therefore more interested in its success when they are directly interviewed regarding their needs. Business Intelligence pains are particularly sensitive to end-user pains, as one of the key benefits of the system is increased decision-maker efficiency, which is very dependent on how end users perceive data.

The project administrator should take pains to explore the root of the business pain: business pains are typically confused with project requirements or generalized statements of need, leading to inappropriate solutions. For example, "We need a reporting solution" exemplifies a solution looking for a problem, rather than a business pain. A business pain might be: "It takes all 10 people in the finance group three hours each Monday to calculate and distribute the latest budget versus actuals variances." Note that the business pain naturally leads into a Return on Investment (ROI) analysis: a great foundation for any project.

ESTABLISHING PROJECT REQUIREMENTS

Without question, the number one reason for a software project's downfall is the failure to gather adequate requirements, and gather them correctly. Anyone undertaking a project to deploy Crystal Enterprise must take the time to discover exactly what the tool is required to accomplish. This need is initially defined by the business problem. Remember, the business problem should be considered the starting point for a Crystal Enterprise solution, allowing the enterprise reporting technology to be embraced and extended to an entire organization.

CAUTION

> Don't get caught stating technical solutions as requirements rather than the true requirements. For example you might state a requirement that: "I want to produce .pdf files from a report." This is actually a solution statement! If you examine why you made this statement, you might see that you thought an Adobe Acrobat (.pdf) file would enable you to share information over the Web. In that case, your requirement should state: "End users can all see the information on Internet Explorer and Netscape browsers on the corporate network." The technical solution to this problem arrives in the next phase, and stating technical solutions instead of actual requirements is a typical and costly mistake.

25

With these points in mind, some of the key questions that need to be considered when defining the requirements for a deployment of Crystal Enterprise involve four concepts: users, user interfaces, reports, and environments. The following lists show the important questions that should be considered:

Users

- How many users will you have?
- What are the skill sets of these users: business/end users; power users; administrators; developers?
- How many concurrent users will you have?
- Where will your users be located?
- How many users will be viewing reports only?
- How many users will design reports?
- How many users will modify/create reports online?
- How many users will schedule reports?
- Will customers be using this application?
- What are the training requirements for administrators? Report designers? Users?

User Interface

- What look and feel is required for the user interface?
- Is this look and feel supposed to inherit the company's intranet appearance and functionality?

■ Will users need to input data or will data extraction and delivery be sufficient?

These questions will help determine whether an out-of-the-box Crystal Enterprise interface, such as the Web Desktop, will meet end-user requirements, or if customization to the Web Desktop will be necessary. Some organizations develop a completely custom front-end to Crystal Enterprise based on end-user feedback to the previous questions. In the case of the latter scenario, some organizations integrate Crystal Enterprise information delivery as a portion of a larger application, which can involve data entry as well.

■ Do users need alert notification via e-mail? What merits e-mail attention?

The alerting capabilities of Crystal Enterprise call out values that merit special attention and can e-mail end users regarding that value.

■ Do end users need to discuss reports or record reactions to reports?

Reports

■ Are legacy reports in use? If so, in which application environments were they created?

Identifying any requirements for support of legacy reports will help identify the extent of the Crystal Enterprise solution. Use of the Crystal Enterprise SDK might be required to link new reports to legacy reports.

■ What type of database(s) will be used with reports in Crystal Enterprise?

■ What is the planned or preferred method of data connectivity, ODBC, OLE-DB, native, Business Views, or something else?

■ Are any existing Crystal Reports connected to the target data sources?

It's also important to consider the data source connectivity methods provided with Crystal Enterprise. They might or might not match up with organizational requirements. Native drivers provide for many data sources, but some data sources can be connected to only through ODBC.

■ Is a DBA available that is familiar with the required data sources?

■ Do any reports cross data sources? Are complex row- or column-level security filters required? Is the report developed on one database, and then run in production on another? Does the data source contain complexity that should be hidden from the end user or even report developer?

All the questions in this bullet point indicate that Business Views should be developed to ease issues around accessing data.

■ How many reports are required?

■ Are enough human resources available with the skill set to develop all the initial reports required by end users?

When setting out to develop reports, consider whether sufficient human resources are available to develop the reports to meet end-user requirements. If not, a third-party consulting organization might be leveraged here to complete report design. One of the biggest challenges organizations have when deploying Crystal Enterprise has nothing to

25

do with Crystal Enterprise itself. It's with the data source. Understanding the database schema and *where* the actual data is can be the most complex portion of the deployment. This area is one where Business Views can dramatically improve report writing efficiency because a skilled DBA works with the database, allowing less skilled resources to develop reports. This both lowers costs and speeds development.

- How frequently will reports be scheduled?

- How many total report instances will be maintained in the Crystal Enterprise system?

- What is an acceptable length of time for reports to process, from initial user request to completion?

Also consider how many report objects Crystal Enterprise will store and manage. A report object in Crystal Enterprise doesn't hold any data. The report instances, reports that have been scheduled, actually contain the data. Chapter 27, "Administering and Configuring Crystal Enterprise," discusses this in more detail. Consider that each report instance occupies space in the File Repository Server. If an organization has 1,000 unique reports and allows 25 scheduled historical instances to be held in Crystal Enterprise for each report, that's 25,000 instances! If each instance held a large amount of data, the File Repository Server would clearly need an ample amount of disk space to manage those instances.

Determining the target length of time for a report to run might not necessarily be achievable, but should be established nonetheless. If a report is based off a database stored procedure that takes 12 hours to run in the database, it's unrealistic to blame Crystal Enterprise for the report taking a long time when, in fact, Crystal Enterprise has nothing to do with the long report runtime.

Bear in mind that ODBC and native drivers affect report runtime; sometimes ODBC is faster and vice versa.

Environment

- What are the current software and hardware configurations on client workstations?

Although Crystal Enterprise delivers information through a Web browser, there are many mechanisms by which this can be accomplished. For example, choosing to deploy the ActiveX viewer with Crystal Enterprise rather than the DHTML viewer can exclude Netscape viewers from using reports. Perhaps the client workstation is actually a mobile device or phone.

- Where will the database servers be physically located?

The specialized roles of Crystal Enterprise servers, such as the Page and Job Servers, can be maximized through effective placement of physical servers. The Page and Job Servers should be placed close to the actual database servers to which reports connect. *Close* is a subjective word, in that it implies a substantial amount of bandwidth and low latency available between the services and database if reports contain a large amount of data. This reduces the impact to an organization's WAN traffic by isolating communication between the database and report processing services.

- Will OLAP data sources be required?

- If so, which OLAP server types are required?

  OLAP servers imply that another type of report object, Crystal Analysis Professional reports, will be stored in Crystal Enterprise. Although Crystal Reports connects to OLAP data sources, version 8.5 of Crystal Reports does not provide the same robust OLAP report and application creation that Crystal Analysis Professional does. Using Crystal Analysis Professional reports with Crystal Enterprise also implies that the Web Component Server will require OLAP server connectivity because this is the hosting point for the Crystal Analysis Professional server-side services.

  If, for example, an organization were using Microsoft's OLAP server, SQL Server Analysis Services, to stage data in OLAP cubes, Crystal Analysis Professional would be required, and the Web Component Server service would require some level of network access to the SQL Server.

- What type of physical network is in place?

  Although most organizations use standard networking components and protocols, such as 10/100 Ethernet and TCP/IP, the speed of a physical network can affect where Crystal Enterprise server components are placed on the geographic network topology.

- What is the projected growth of the Crystal Enterprise system?

- What, if any, dedicated hardware resources are available for Crystal Enterprise?

- Will additional hardware be required?

  Planning considerations must be made not only for an imminent Crystal Enterprise deployment, but also for how the system might look one year from now. Most deployments of Crystal Enterprise grow quickly because end users like to share the new source of information they have accessed.

- What are the security requirements for the reporting environment?

  Determining a strategy for security can be a daunting one because many options are associated with Crystal Enterprise. Crystal Enterprise provides a native security model where users, groups, and objects can be created and managed without the need for any third-party security components. Crystal Enterprise also supports Windows NT or Active Directory security integration, as well as support for a host of major directory servers through LDAP. As a final option, an organization could use the Crystal Enterprise SDK to link in or create a homegrown security model for Crystal Enterprise.

  Crystal Enterprise also allows the creation of custom administration modules using the administrative portion of the SDK, which allows for certain users to be restricted to various portions of the product for system administration.

- What Crystal Enterprise licensing model is the best fit?

  Several licensing models are available for Crystal Enterprise, so understanding the current licensing program for Crystal Enterprise can save your organization some money when it comes time to purchase.

- On what operating system will Crystal Enterprise be deployed (Windows, Solaris, or both)?

  Although Crystal Enterprise is available on the Windows, AIX, and Solaris platforms, some organizations will deploy a "mixed mode" environment, meaning some Crystal Enterprise services or daemons will be installed on different platforms. The Unix versions have a few minor variations from the Windows version.

- What bandwidth and latency exist between LAN/WAN sites that will participate in the Crystal Enterprise deployment?

  As mentioned earlier, different server components of Crystal Enterprise benefit through close physical proximity to database servers. It's important to understand the various functions of the individual Crystal Enterprise servers and what data traffic is passed between them. Chapter 24, "Crystal Enterprise Architecture," covers this in some detail. Understanding this will help the Crystal Enterprise system planner or administrator effectively place server components within a corporate LAN/WAN environment to maximize system performance.

- Will a firewall be incorporated in the solution?

  Crystal Enterprise was designed with a "DMZ" or firewall deployment in mind. This means that Crystal Enterprise can be effectively deployed in a multiple-firewall network environment with minimal impact to security because all information and reports delivered by Crystal Enterprise can be DHTML. This means Port 80, HTTP delivery of data out to the Internet. For more information on deploying Crystal Enterprise in a complex network environment involving firewalls, refer to Chapter 26, "Deploying Crystal Enterprise in a Complex Network Environment."

- Will users require dial-up to access the Crystal Enterprise system?

  This might seem like a trivial consideration because Crystal Enterprise delivers reports that essentially amount to Web pages to an end user through a browser. If, for example, an organization chooses to deliver all reports from Crystal Enterprise as .pdf files rather than Crystal Reports as Web pages through the DHTML viewer, a significant feature is sacrificed: page on demand. *Page on demand* means that only one page of a report is delivered to an end user at a time. If a report contains 3MB worth of data, the user won't notice this because the server opens the report and delivers the requested page of the report to the viewer. This provides a responsive environment for end users, even in a dial-up session at less than 56Kbps.

- What is the current load and performance of existing Web servers that Crystal Enterprise will use?

  Crystal Enterprise is not a Web server. It works with most major Web servers or application servers. Although Crystal Enterprise doesn't place a significant load on a Web server, there is some load nonetheless, especially if an organization decides to install Crystal Enterprise on the physical Web server itself. It's always preferable to have a dedicated server for Crystal Enterprise and offload processing onto a dedicated set of servers for Crystal Enterprise.

- What is the current skill set of system or network administrators that might support Crystal Enterprise?

Crystal Enterprise is a complex enterprise reporting and information delivery product that involves many systems, from databases to operating systems and development platforms. Troubleshooting issues with Crystal Enterprise might not have anything to do with Crystal Enterprise at all. More often than not, issues with reports often lie with database access, operating system permissions, and the like. It's of paramount importance that system administrators understand the spectrum of these issues.

The previous list of questions is by no means complete. It is meant to be a solid foundation from which to formulate an implementation plan. Ideally, the temptation to install any software until after this stage is complete can be resisted.

Each answer should lead a Crystal Enterprise deployment manager to create an action item for delivery before, during, and after the project. For example, the answer to the question "What is the projected growth of the Crystal Enterprise system?" might be "Company A currently derives about $100M in annual revenue and has 200 employees. During the next two years we hope to double in size." This can lead to the deduction that, although current hardware availability will allow for an initial implementation of the project without further hardware and software purchase or budgeting, scalability planning should be performed or at least considered for future growth.

It might be useful to build these questions into a questionnaire format, breaking the organization down into management, users, and IT department members. Submitting a questionnaire or having interviews with the end-user community are exceptional ways to get buy-in from all project stakeholders.

DEVELOPING THE APPLICATION (CUSTOMIZING CRYSTAL ENTERPRISE)

Although Crystal Enterprise comes with several out-of-the-box client applications such as the Web Desktop, this doesn't exclude the customization of one of those applications or development of a completely custom solution from the ground up. The good news is if an organization is deploying the Web Desktop without any customizations, this section can be skipped entirely.

The development of a Crystal Enterprise application can be very personal. Whatever the approach, it should follow these guidelines:

- *Pick the proper project manager.* Someone must be in command. This is not necessarily going to be a promotion for someone into the lofty ranks of a management position; instead, the person in this role must have the authority, knowledge, and character to implement command and control. The size of the project determines how many members compose the team, but their actions should be managed and they must have someone to refer to for information and direction. If possible, the project manager should be able to focus on the application without having to double hat on other jobs.

- *Plan, plan, plan.* There are many project planning tools on the market. A company will probably have its own standard. Whether planning is done on a piece of paper, on a spreadsheet, or in an application, it is another cornerstone of a successful project. No plan survives the first shot of battle, so it is important to keep in mind that this is a work in progress. Without a plan, coordination is impossible, chaos prevails, and the project stands a good chance of going off track. A project plan should involve the following:

- Tasks
- Delivery timelines
- Specification as to who is responsible for delivering those tasks
- A definition of task weightings

■ *Build the project team.* The project team's skill set must be put together very carefully. If internal team members cannot be found, outsourcing should be considered as a very cost-effective way to improve chances for success. In most cases, consultants with proven track records using the technologies surrounding Crystal Enterprise increase the chance of the project's success.

■ *Keep an eye on the prize.* Begin with the end in mind. After the project has started, the project manager and team members must be sure that they understand what the end goal is.

■ *Control change.* Change is inevitable, and the longer a project goes on and the more complex it becomes, the more likely change will occur. Change is a good thing. Without change you would be back where Ug started his tusk movement improvement project. The important thing to remember is that change must be controlled. Team members need to be encouraged to share their ideas and think outside the box.

However, a process must be in place to manage this and be sure that any new changes are implemented with the support and knowledge of the project team, management, and end users. Another result of ignoring change management is the bane of any project, *scope creep*. Scope creep occurs when a project's deliverables, functionality, or look and feel extend past the project plan and definition. Scope creep can blow budgets away, extend project timelines dramatically, and can lead to bad morale on the project team.

One good example might be a specification to customize the look and feel of the DHTML viewer. A corporate logo is to be applied to the background of the viewer. After the addition of the logo, the end users ask whether each individual icon image in the viewer can be changed to match other images the company has, such as product images. Although this might seem trivial and seems to add little value to the overall solution, it could set the deployment timeline back at least half a day.

Table 25.1 is an example of a change control matrix.

TABLE 25.1 CHANGE CONTROL MATRIX

Change Number	Description	Requestor	Assigned to:	Completed on:	To Test (date)	Tested by:	Released to and Date:
1	Provide top 10 customers parameter	Dawn Gugoi	Paul Kooker	4/24/04	4/26/04	Tess Tor	5/5/04

DEPLOYING BUSINESS VIEWS

Although the use of Business Views might at first seem a technical decision which most affects development time, business requirements drive the utilization of Business Views more than any other requirement. First, you must understand end-user requirements with regard to how end users view data: If data is organized to the end user in one way, but captured in the database in another, Business Views bridge the gap and show end users data as they see it. For instance, you might want to see revenue per headcount, which requires the headcount value from an HR system and the revenue total from a finance application. A Business View can connect to both databases and present a unified logical view of revenue per headcount.

The two most significant impacts of business views, however, have everything to do with end users:

- Extending report authoring to a wider audience
- Using Crystal Enterprise to broker database access

Through the development of browser-based report modification and creation capabilities, Crystal Enterprise now offers end users greater possibilities in interacting with data. By encapsulating the database connection and query aspects of the reporting process, end users can now be shielded from the more technical aspects of report creation and instead focus on what to show and how to show it.

The development of Business Views allows organizations to extend this model to develop a more efficient business intelligence model. Most organizations use developers to build the vast majority of reports, referred to as the developer-centric model. End users can now develop more reports themselves instead of a developer-centric model of report development, usually resulting in trivial work for developers, long wait time for end users, poor communication of end-user requirements, and a high opportunity cost. In the end-user centric model, developers and DBAs handle database connectivity, database and table joins, filtering and security, parameterization, formulas, and the like. Report creators then start designing by placing fields on the report and formatting the data. This separation of tasks into distinct roles of DBA versus end user facilitates more efficient report creation and a lower total cost of ownership. It places those who know the business uses of the data closer to report creation, yet allows for tight organizational control over data sources.

Using Crystal Enterprise to control access to data via Business Views tightens and secures access to databases, even for report creation, by asking users to connect to Crystal Enterprise, which provides access to Business Views according to a particular user's permissions. Because Business Views can secure the row- and column-level access to data sources, very fine control over data access can be attained.

Although this model might not be practical for all organizations, it yields cost savings and speeds time-to-market when implemented. In addition, because total security can be attained while still allowing appropriate access to data, confidentiality requirements can be met across organizations.

25

USE CASES FOR SCHEDULED REPORTING

As alluded to previously, Crystal Enterprise allows two modes of report execution: on-demand and scheduled. In the scheduled reporting case, a report template is scheduled to run either right now or at a future point in time or possibly on a recurring basis. When it is time for the report to run, the Crystal Report Job Server accesses the report template, the report is processed against the reporting database, and then the report is saved with data under a different file. This report with saved data is commonly referred to as a *report instance*. This instance is a snapshot of the data in a moment of time. End users can then view an instance to see the report's data from when it was run.

The advantages of scheduling reports and creating instances are numerous. The most important advantage of report instances is that when a user views an instance, the report loads almost instantaneously in the report viewer because the report does not need to execute the database query. In addition, because instances are a snapshot of data in time, you can leverage them as historical reports. For example, when reporting against a transactional information system, the database often contains volatile data. Consequently, running the report with the exact same parameters on different days might return different data because the database contains fewer records because of deletion and so on.

DETERMINING SCHEDULING PERMISSIONS AND REPORT RUNTIMES

If scheduled reports are the preferred method of reporting in Crystal Enterprise, you must determine who will be allowed to schedule reports and when those reports can actually be scheduled. In a tightly controlled environment, a system administrator individually schedules reports either singly or on a recurring basis (for example, weekly, monthly). End users are not allowed to run reports; they can only view instances. Thus, by having a central scheduling authority, you can govern what and when database queries will be executed from your reporting application.

Additionally in this scenario, if scheduling is completed with regards to end-user viewing use, hardware use can be minimized. For example, if end users view reports only during the day, reports could be batch scheduled to run only at night or on the weekend. This means that report execution and report viewing are mutually exclusive, which they are. Report execution is processor-intensive and primarily the responsibility of the Crystal Enterprise Job Server component. Report viewing can be processor-intensive and a major responsibility of the Crystal Enterprise Page Server component.

In this scenario, common hardware can be shared between the Job and Page Servers because their functions will be used mutually exclusively. Otherwise, if report execution and report viewing occur at the same time, and the Job and Page Servers are on the same shared hardware, they might contend with one another for CPU or operating system resources. Because the Page Server plays a key part in report viewing, report viewing responsiveness might be negatively affected during this period.

Although administrator-controlled scheduling makes for a tightly regulated system, it can be constrained by its potential inflexibility. For example, if the report has parameters, these parameters must be determined by the administrator. Thus, report instances might contain too much data or too little data for end users. In addition, if the database is updated and a user wants to see the latest data, he will have to wait until the next scheduled runtime because he cannot run the report manually. As a result, timely access to data can be an issue.

If these issues of data scope and timeliness can be acceptable or managed, controlled scheduling is an excellent solution for organizations with tight server access or hardware restrictions. For example, some data warehouses are updated at fixed intervals (weekly, for example), so the administrator can schedule the reports to run after the update process is complete. Thus, in this case, if data scope is also not an issue, it doesn't make much sense to allow end users to run reports because the data is unchanged between database update periods.

NOTE

> *Data scope* is the specific range or breadth of the data. For example, some reports are useful only if the user provides parameters. If you're checking frequent flyer points you're only interested in data related to you. Thus, a prescheduled report with all data for all customers in this case would not be relevant to you because you're only concerned with your personal data.

On the other end of the spectrum is the scenario where end users are allowed to schedule reports on their own, whenever they want. This allows for maximum flexibility for the end users because they can run reports at their leisure with the parameters they choose. However, if the parameters are unchecked, poor parameter selection (because of user inexperience) can cause rogue database queries that tie up the DBMS if they become unnecessarily large or complex. This can lead to the scheduling queue backing up as other jobs waiting to execute are idling for a free spot on the Job Servers. If the Job Servers are configured to run too many concurrent jobs, this can overrun the DBMS with too many simultaneous queries. Thus, the Job Servers should be scaled back so that the number of concurrent jobs allowed is small enough that DBMS access is appropriately managed. If the Page Server and Job Server are on the same shared hardware, the issue might arise where these processes contend for server resources (CPU time, memory, file system, network bandwidth, and so on).

ON-DEMAND REPORTING

The second mode with which reports can be executed is called *on-demand* reporting. When used correctly and in the right situation this can be a very powerful function in a Crystal Enterprise deployment. To determine which situations should use on-demand reporting, apply the eight-second rule as a guideline: "Users have eight seconds worth of patience while waiting for a Web page to load." To use this measurement, run the report on a test system or in the Crystal Reports designer and determine how long the report takes to execute. If it takes fewer than eight seconds, that report will be a good candidate for on-demand reporting in Crystal Enterprise.

25

Another consideration with on-demand reporting is whether the database driver and database client are *thread safe* (meaning that multiple threads can access the driver at the same time without unwanted interaction). If these components are not thread safe, database queries from the Page Servers will be serialized. Using the ODBC database drivers that ship with Crystal Enterprise will ensure this concurrency because they are thread safe and thoroughly tested.

COMPARING SCHEDULED VERSUS ON-DEMAND REPORTING

Even if reports are ideal candidates for on-demand reporting, scheduling reports still might offer additional benefits. For example, scheduled reporting helps set the right expectations and context for a report. When end users schedule a report, even if it is scheduled to run right now, they will expect the report to take some time to process. Thus, they can better tolerate delays. Users who are utilizing on-demand reporting typically don't understand that doing so actually requires the database query to execute. They expect the report to come up in the viewer instantly and are less tolerant of delays and might become frustrated when the only feedback they get is the spinning Web browser logo.

DETERMINING DATA ACCESS CONTROL METHODS

If the Crystal Enterprise reporting system is designed so that users can schedule reports or run reports on demand, you must decide how to control access to the database. That is, what database user account is used to access the reporting database? With some implementations, individual users are given distinct database accounts that they would provide before running the report. In other implementations, a generic data reader account is used as the default database login for all reports. Having individual users with separate database accounts allows for better auditing if auditing is done at the DBMS level. You can easily track who is running what type of queries against your database. However, this comes with some costs.

First, more database administration is required because these user accounts must be managed. Second, users will potentially have to remember an additional set of usernames and passwords. Additionally, by providing individual users with database credentials, they do not necessarily need to use Crystal Enterprise to access the database. They could freely use any database access tool to communicate directly with the DBMS.

By using a generic database reader account, the shortcomings of individual accounts are eliminated. Database administration is simpler because only one account must be managed. The password for this account is abstracted from the end user, so she won't be able to use any other database tool to access the DBMS directly.

However, this data access model might not be able to leverage databases that have data-level security invoked for users. For example, some databases have data-level security in that different users see different data from the same query based on who they are. This security often is based on which credentials were used to access the database. If an organization were using a generic database account for Crystal Enterprise, such a security model would not integrate well. As part of designing the Crystal Enterprise system, this determination of data access authentication should be agreed upon by all project stakeholders.

NOTE

> The deciding factor for using a generic database user account or individual user accounts typically is the data access level to be enforced.

Using Business Views can alleviate much of this complexity because Business Views can secure the data at the column and row level, and even apply at report development time. The use of Business Views can also alter the development process because the Crystal Enterprise logon becomes the paramount logon, giving access to the databases, via Business Views, as well as the Crystal Enterprise objects, even during the design process.

PLANNING A CRYSTAL ENTERPRISE ARCHITECTURE

Crystal Enterprise is a system that can scale up on a single server by adding processors and memory. In addition, adding servers can scale Crystal Enterprise out. Scaling Crystal Enterprise provides benefits such as greater performance, high availability, fault tolerance, and redundancy. However, determining how to scale a system can be a bit of a challenge. A few best practices and rules of thumb can be followed to guide you. Ultimately, scaling will be determined by usage profile and behavior of the Crystal Enterprise system. One key point is for system administrators to not be fearful of experimenting and trying different configurations to achieve better performance. Different architectures each have benefits and considerations. The idea is to choose those that have the best fit for the given requirements.

25

DETERMINING PROCESSING REQUIREMENTS

The four key Crystal Enterprise server components that require some considerable thought in sizing are the Cache Server, Page Server, Report Application Server, and Job Server. Additionally, because most Crystal Enterprise actions query the CMS, optimizing the CMS database can greatly speed overall system response.

TIP

> Crystal Enterprise 10 relies more heavily on the database for key data retrieval functions than in previous versions. Paying attention to tuning the system database and DBMS will result in faster system response.

This section focuses on how many instances of the services, processors, and physical servers are required and what the settings for these system services should be. The first step in sizing a Crystal Enterprise environment is to answer a few important questions:

- How often will there be on-demand report and report instances viewing?
- When will scheduled reports be processed?

- Is there a report processing time window?
- Is redundancy required?

One key metric also needs to be determined: What is the number of concurrent users of Crystal Enterprise? Even if you have an overall Web application into which Crystal Enterprise will integrate, it is important to remain concerned only with the number of concurrent Crystal Enterprise users when sizing Crystal Enterprise. A concurrent user of Crystal Enterprise can be described as someone who is interacting with Crystal Enterprise. This includes logging into Crystal Enterprise, processing CSP or other pages that utilize the SDK, scheduling reports, querying the system, or viewing reports. If the number of concurrent users is unknown but the size of your total user base is known, a rule of thumb to estimate what the number of concurrent users might be is about 10% to 20% of the total application user base. For example, if your application has 1,000 total users, you can estimate the number of concurrent users for Crystal Enterprise to be between 100 and 200. Often you can use Web logs of previous applications to determine utilization as well.

When reports are processed on-demand or report instances are viewed, a complex chain of processes takes place involving the Web browser, Web server, Web Connector, WCS or WCA, Cache Server, and Page Server or Report Application Server. When sizing the system for on-demand reporting and viewing, the last two components in the process are the most critical for consideration.

SIZING THE CACHE SERVER   The Cache Server is responsible for storing and forwarding epf cache pages created by the Page Servers. The Page Servers are primarily responsible for generating epf cache pages either from reports that are opened from report instances or opened and processed from report templates.

Consider one individual viewing request or on-demand reporting request to be equivalent to one thread being used by the Cache Server and one thread being used by the Page Server. This is an oversimplification of the viewing process but is a good starting point when making considerations and conservative considerations for sizing. Thus, if 200 concurrent users will be running on-demand reports or viewing report instances, then ideally 200 Cache Server threads and 200 Page Server threads should be available. Typically, 100 cache server threads per processor are recommended with up to a maximum of 400 threads per physical cache server service. Thus, on a quad processor server, a single cache server service could be set to 400 threads whereas with an eight-way server two cache server services would need to be installed, each set to 400 threads for a total thread count of 800 threads.

It is important to note that Crystal Enterprise allows a physical server to host multiple copies of the same logical server service for the same or different Crystal Enterprise system environments. This further increases the scalability of Crystal Enterprise. In the preceding example with the eight-way server, two cache server services were configured.

SIZING THE PAGE SERVER   Whether viewing reports or running reports on-demand, Page Servers can optimally manage 75 threads per Page Server service per processor, so if a quad processor is available for the Page Server, a maximum of four Page Server services with 75 threads each for a total of 300 threads should be used. Also, keep the total number of cache server threads exactly equal to the total number of Page Server threads in the entire system for optimal performance.

Consider the following example.

A particular environment has a requirement for 300 concurrent users all running on-demand reports with some redundancy also built into the architecture. Because this is more than a single cache server can optimally handle, two cache server services will be needed. A good choice would be to have two cache server services set to 150 threads each. Because this requires two processors per service, at least a server with four processors will be needed. However, because a level of fault tolerance was required, the cache server services will be split over two dual processor servers. Therefore, the final architecture for the cache servers would have two dual processor servers each with a cache server service set to 150 threads each.

For the Page Servers, six Page Server services (300 threads/50 threads) will be required. This would also require six processors. Although you could use a single eight-way server to handle the Page Servers because you would like some fault tolerance, two quad processor servers will be used instead. Therefore, the final architecture for the Page Servers would be two quad processor servers with three Page Server services each set to 50 threads per service.

SIZING THE REPORT APPLICATION SERVER   The Report Application Server (RAS), much like the Page server, handles 75 threads. However, some important additional configurations affect RAS performance due to its high level of interaction with the reporting database. You can set these values by going to the Crystal Management Console and locating the Servers section, in the Report Application Server area, within the Database tab.

Setting the Maximum Number of Records to read prevents end users from inadvertently creating runaway queries. Specifying a Batch Size determines the number of records to be retrieved from the database at a time; for instance a batch size of 100 means that to retrieve 1,000 records 10 batches will need to be run. Setting this value very high will allow large amounts of data to be processed quickly, but might slow retrieval of smaller data sets. Because report creation and modification can often call for browsing data, for instance when choosing a data value to filter results, you set the browse data size to determine the number of sample values brought back from the database. Although setting a smaller number can speed retrieval, this will also constrain the possible values returned, which might affect some end-user scenarios.

Because the RAS caches report data itself instead of using the Cache Server, setting the Data Refresh value determines the oldest data that should be returned to an end user. Setting a value of 20 minutes means that no query will return data older than 20 minutes old. Higher values speed performance but might show old data, whereas low values show very recent data, but at the cost of report performance.

Setting the Report Job Database Connection determines when to close the connection to the database. Keeping the connection open, by selecting the When the Job is Closed option,

25

saves the time required to reconnect to the database for subsequent queries, but uses additional database connections, which might require additional database licenses with some database licensing methods.

Additionally, RAS processes should be monitored for usage patterns. A typical report modification session might retrieve and format many records from the database and have high processor utilization, For instance, a user can group, filter, and re-format results, causing another full retrieval of records from the database and high processing load on the RAS machine. Additionally, certain types of viewers—such as the Interactive Viewer—also use the RAS. Thus you cannot simply equate RAS use with Page Server use, but must instead monitor the RAS from time to time to ensure that your projects are correct.

SIZING THE JOB SERVER   If scheduled reporting is part of the Crystal Enterprise deployment, it will be necessary to determine how many Job Servers will be required to support the total Crystal Enterprise end-user base.

Optimally, a Job Server service can process roughly five concurrent jobs per CPU. Given a quad processor server, no more than four Job Server services should be installed on a single server. Having too many Job Servers in the Crystal Enterprise system can overwhelm the DBMS because too many jobs try to process concurrently. Alternatively, having too few Job Servers could mean that users have to wait a long time as their job gets queued up waiting for other jobs to complete processing. If the Crystal Enterprise environment has a fixed reporting time window in which all reports can only be processed, the following formulas can be used as a rough guide to determine how many servers to dedicate as Job Servers:

> Total Processing Time required = Average Process Time (per job) * number of jobs
>
> Total Time to Process (per processor) = Total Processing Time Required / Number of Concurrent Jobs (per Job Server service)
>
> Number of Job Servers Required = Total Time to Process / Time Window for Processing

Here's an example applying these formulas:

A company needs to run 58 reports where each report takes on average 20 minutes to run. Because they will be reporting off a production database, they will be given a time window of only one hour nightly. How many Job Servers and processors will they need?

> Total Processing Time required = 20 minutes/report * 58 reports = 1,160 minutes
>
> Total Time to Process (per processor) = 1,160 minutes/5 concurrent jobs/Job Server service = 232 minutes
>
> Number of Job Servers Required = 230 minutes/60 minutes = 3.87 Job Server services

Therefore, for Crystal Enterprise to process 58 20-minute reports in one hour, four Job Server services set to process five concurrent jobs each on four processors would be required.

Given the fact that four processors are required for the Job Server services, a single quad processor server, two dual processor servers, or four single processor servers could be used with the Crystal Enterprise system.

The option to use a single server does not provide any logical Job Server redundancy; that is, if a report processing job fails on one server it isn't picked up by another. Only physical hardware "high availability" is achieved. The four-server implementation also requires added administration and maintenance. In this situation, it would be advisable to use two dual processor servers because it provides a good balance between a level of physical fault tolerance, less resource contention/conflicts, and ease of maintainability. As mentioned before, if report processing of scheduled reports happens during office hours, it is advantageous if the Job Server services reside on dedicated physical servers. If report processing of scheduled reports occurs off-hours, the Job Server services can potentially reside on the same physical servers as the Page Server services, given that the number of processors required is also satisfied.

MONITORING THE CRYSTAL ENTERPRISE SYSTEM: AUDITING

A new feature of Crystal Enterprise 10, auditing, can provide feedback on the current configuration of the system. With the results of the auditing captured in an auditing database, system performance can be examined to determine if services are operating outside of requirements and also to determine how resources are being used. For instance, if you see that a particular report is being viewed many times by many different users, you might elect to schedule that report so that users will not be causing high load on the reporting database.

In addition to the auditing capabilities of Crystal Enterprise, the operating system's native monitoring can help you determine how a system is performing. For instance, in Windows environments, perfmon (the Windows Performance Monitor) can trace the amount of processor time a particular server uses and thus whether a particular server is over- or underutilized.

SAMPLE CRYSTAL ENTERPRISE DEPLOYMENT SCENARIOS

This section describes several different classes of Crystal Enterprise configurations. The first is a centralized Crystal Enterprise architecture followed by a distributed architecture and then a fault-tolerant architecture.

A CENTRALIZED, SINGLE-SERVER DEPLOYMENT

A centralized architecture (see Figure 25.1) has all Crystal Enterprise system components installed on the same server. This is the simplest configuration and the easiest to manage because the entire system is self-contained.

This also is the easiest configuration to maintain; for example, it takes the guesswork out of performing backups because Web pages, report templates, and the system database all reside on this server. This is advantageous for smaller implementations and yet it still allows for outward scalability by adding more servers when and if they are required. This setup is perfect for workgroup applications, small projects, or Web applications that have modest and light report processing and viewing needs. Such a configuration can be very CPU-intensive because all the Crystal Enterprise components, as well as the DBMS and Web server, are running concurrently.

Figure 25.1
Centralized architecture: single-server configuration.

Machine1:
Crystal Management Server (CMS)
Web Component Server and/or Adaptor
Cache Server
Page Server
Report Job Server
Program Job Server
Input File Repository
Output File Repository
Web Connector
Web Server (e.g. IIS)
CMS System Database (e.g. SQL Server DBMS)

25

A system administrator must be proactive in identifying potential system bottlenecks and thus scale those components out onto other separate servers accordingly. Also, this configuration offers little in terms of fault tolerance because all components are centralized.

DISTRIBUTED COMPUTING: THREE-SERVER IMPLEMENTATION

The benefits of distributing components over multiple servers are numerous. By separating Crystal Enterprise components onto separate physical servers, contention for resources that would normally have to be shared in a single server configuration is reduced. For example, components on the same server usually contend with CPU time, context switching, memory substructure, and the disk subsystem sharing.

Admittedly, there are considerations involved with such a configuration. Although separate physical servers help resolve resource conflicts, components now must inter-communicate across the local area network. This adds network traffic and introduces network latency to the whole equation. Although this probably is a negligible issue when compared to the benefits, it is worthwhile to point out that there is always a trade-off. Additionally, adding more servers to the Crystal Enterprise architecture increases server operation and maintenance costs.

This three-server configuration (see Figure 25.2) is the most commonly used deployment by most organizations. The main feature of this configuration is the separation of the intelligence components from the report-processing tier. By separating these processes, user interaction processes have the highest priority and are not affected by CPU contention issues. Server 1 is responsible for Web server interaction, such as processing of Web scripts and presentation of Web pages, as well as caching of repetitive requests. Server 2 handles system database inquiries. Server 3 processes reports and stores processed results.

Figure 25.2
Distributed computing: three-server configuration.

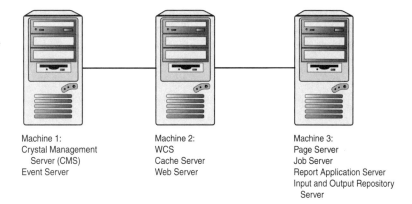

Machine 1:
Crystal Management
    Server (CMS)
Event Server

Machine 2:
WCS
Cache Server
Web Server

Machine 3:
Page Server
Job Server
Report Application Server
Input and Output Repository
    Server

Server 3 is tasked mainly with report-processing duties. Report processing is a highly CPU-intensive activity. It's advisable to assign the best performing hardware for this server. As an example, most companies use a dual-processor server for Server 1 and 2 and have a quad-processor server for Server 3.

In this simple example, Server 3 is processing on-demand reports, generating epf cache pages, and processing scheduled reports. Processing on-demand reports and cache page generation are also response time–sensitive tasks and should have high CPU-processor precedence. Thus, if these tasks are not mutually exclusive with the processing of scheduled jobs, it is advisable to separate Page Servers from Job Servers onto separate servers.

Notice that with this configuration, Server 1 houses only the Web server and the CMS is on a separate server. Often companies already have a Web server and DBMS in place that they would like to leverage. In these cases, these Crystal Enterprise components can be offloaded from Server 1 and 2 (see Figure 25.3).

Figure 25.3
Three-server configuration with offloaded system database and Web server.

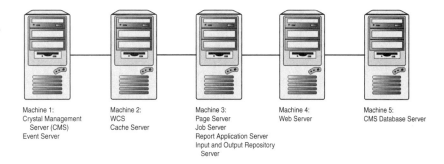

Machine 1:
Crystal Management
    Server (CMS)
Event Server

Machine 2:
WCS
Cache Server

Machine 3:
Page Server
Job Server
Report Application Server
Input and Output Repository
    Server

Machine 4:
Web Server

Machine 5:
CMS Database Server

Depending on hardware availability, this can have either a positive or negative effect on system performance (that is, network traffic, shared Web, and DBMS services). The CMS database must be highly available to the CMS. Thus, it is advisable not to put the CMS database on the same DBMS as reporting databases (the databases that report access for end-user data). For those reasons it's also advisable not to place the CMS database on the same server that houses either the Page or Job Servers because of their CPU-intensive activities. The Crystal Enterprise system administrator must examine issues such as leveraging of existing services, performance, and maintainability to determine which route to go.

A CRYSTAL ENTERPRISE DISTRIBUTED ARCHITECTURE: MULTIPLE REPORT PROCESSING SERVERS

Future growth commonly comes from more concurrent users and thus more report processing and viewing. In most Crystal Enterprise environments the report processing servers are the first to be "extended" (see Figure 25.4). If this is the case, additional Page, RAS, or Job Servers can be added to the architecture without impact or major change to the rest of the system.

Figure 25.4
Configuration with multiple report processing servers.

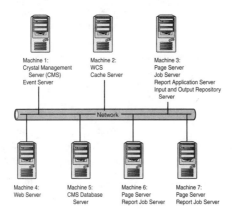

NOTE

Page and Job Servers must access the Input File Repository to find the report template to process. The Job Server must access the Output File Repository to write out the completed processed reports.

When duplicating Crystal Enterprise components onto different physical servers, it is ideal if those servers have reasonable server affinity. That is, it is suggested that the servers with duplicated components should have similar hardware and run the same applications and services as their other counterparts. In addition, duplicated Crystal Enterprise components should all have the same configuration settings (number of threads, timeouts, and so on) to better use the Crystal Enterprise load-balancing algorithms.

The fault-tolerant configuration (see Figure 25.5) is for organizations that are looking for a highly available, reliable, and robust system architecture. This configuration can tolerate a higher level of server failures than previous configurations, thus eliminating single points of failure.

Figure 25.5
Crystal Enterprise in a fault-tolerant configuration.

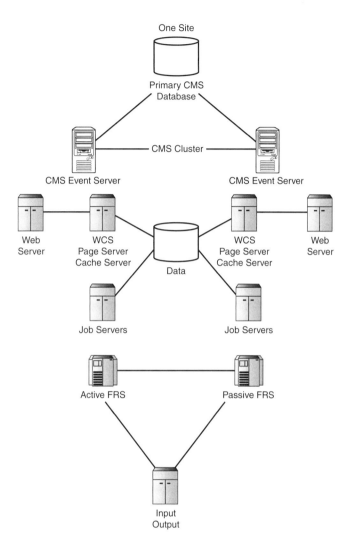

The key design feature of a fault-tolerant Crystal Enterprise architecture is each Crystal Enterprise service or daemon has a minimum of two separate instances running on physically separate servers. With the distribution of each component over two or more servers rather than just a single server, fault tolerance is gained. If one server becomes unavailable but the other is still functioning, your entire system is effectively functioning. In this configuration, additional fault tolerance is gained by using a separate fault-tolerant RDBMS for the CMS database, and a SAN (Storage Area Network) or other fault-tolerant file system for the File Server storage location. However, the price paid for this redundancy is the increase in number of servers and maintenance of those servers.

For the File Repository Servers, all the services should be clustered and pointed to the same file locations for Input and Output respectively. The File Repository Servers would also be installed onto this second server; however, they are running but dormant by default. These File Repository Servers will become "active" only if the primary server fails.

Note that this implementation also has redundancy at the Web server level; however, some method of redirecting Web requests to either Web server is required. This can be accomplished through the use of any Web farm load-balancing mechanism (such as Hardware load balancer, DNS round robin, or Microsoft Network Load Balancing [NLB]).

CAUTION

> Although using Microsoft's Network Load Balancing (NLB) on a Web server works very well, using NLB on any machine that has any Crystal Enterprise services running on it will damage the Crystal Enterprise Installation. NLB acts by changing effective IP addresses on several machines, which allows external requests to one IP to contact several machines. Crystal Enterprise, however, expects that a particular service on a particular machine will *always* have the same IP address. Using NLB results in system corruption such that the system must be totally uninstalled and reinstalled, losing all system data. Remember that Crystal Enterprise automatically load balances, so an external load balancer is unnecessary and indeed can make the system unstable.

TROUBLESHOOTING

As with any form of troubleshooting, the main goals are first to be able to replicate the problem and second to be able to isolate the issue. Sometimes this sounds easier than it really is. However, keeping this philosophy in mind when troubleshooting will be very helpful. This troubleshooting section discusses solid troubleshooting techniques with regard to Crystal Enterprise rather than specific troubleshooting issues.

Crystal Enterprise systems in a production environment can be quite complex. System components might be duplicated and spread across various servers, and these servers also can span firewalls and DMZs. Throw into the mix a custom-developed Crystal Enterprise Web application and it becomes obvious that the domain of the problem can initially appear quite large. By removing this "noise" from a Crystal Enterprise implementation, most issues can be distilled into one key issue. Many companies have separate development, QA, or test environments. If the problem also exhibits itself in these environments it makes troubleshooting much easier than having to tinker with a production system.

Often the most crucial information regarding problem replication seems too trivial to be verified or checked. Additionally, factors that are taken for granted, or assumed, can raise their heads as essential to solving the problem. So documenting, if possible, *all* the factors contributing to the environment improve greatly the chances for success. This includes documenting the operating system, patch levels, virus checking systems, disk quota control systems, backup programs, any logs or error reports, and the like.

After documenting and reproducing the problem, preferably in a test environment, you move on to problem isolation where the goal is to simplify the issue. For example, if issues arise when viewing a report instance through a Web application, try to remove the Web application from the equation by verifying that the report instance can be viewed in the Web Desktop or through the Crystal Management Console (CMC). Another tip in simplifying a problem is to remove duplicate services from Crystal Enterprise. For example, ensure that during troubleshooting only one CMS, WCS, Cache, Page, and Job Server service are running. Isolation of the problem usually consists of reproducing it given one set of circumstances and not experiencing it in another. For instance in this scenario, seeing a problem when viewing a report with the Web application but not with the Web Desktop indicates an issue with the Web application.

When you troubleshoot Crystal Enterprise, having Crystal Reports Designer installed onto the servers where the Page and Job Servers reside provides tremendous value. Often, when a scheduled report fails in Crystal Enterprise, the properties of the instance display the infamous statement: Cannot open SQL Server. This is a very generic statement that can mean a multitude of error conditions.

With Crystal Reports installed on the Page and Job Servers, the report can be run interactively in Crystal Reports so a more meaningful error message can be viewed. If a report doesn't run correctly in Crystal Reports on the physical Job Server, there is certainly no chance of successfully scheduling the report in Crystal Enterprise. Should a report not run in Crystal Enterprise, you should run the report on the Crystal Enterprise server machine within Crystal Reports as your first step. If the report runs, you can look elsewhere for issues.

DEPLOYING CRYSTAL ENTERPRISE IN A COMPLEX NETWORK ENVIRONMENT

In this chapter

INTRODUCTION

One key design consideration for Crystal Enterprise was for the delivery of information to be deployed as part of any Web-based delivery platform—intranet, extranet, or Internet. Increasingly, organizations are looking to standardize the access to corporate information within a Web-based infrastructure. Companies are now able to support a close relationship with their external constituents—be they customers or suppliers—through the delivery of information over the Web. Furthermore, considerable economies of scale can be realized by using the same architecture to deliver information internally.

Often, the means by which information can be rendered is through the display of a Crystal Report (or multiple Crystal Reports) as an integral part of a Web page executing on a client browser. Such integration with a company's Web-based information delivery system requires that the vehicle for providing that information (for example, a Crystal Report managed by Crystal Enterprise and integrated completely into a Web page) can also conform to the company's security requirements. In a nutshell, no matter what firewall standards a company chooses to adopt, Crystal Enterprise not only must be able to be configured within these standards, it also must do so without compromising the integrity (or performance) of information management and delivery.

This chapter concentrates on how the architecture of Crystal Enterprise allows for complete integration into complex networks with firewall systems to provide information delivery across intranets and the Internet without compromising network security. More often than not, providing examples of how Crystal Enterprise works with complex firewall scenarios produces enough information to relate this chapter to other network deployment scenarios.

To understand how Crystal Enterprise works in a complex network environment, a review of several server and system processes is provided in this chapter, extending discussions put forth from earlier chapters in this book.

Essentially, this chapter concentrates on firewalls and illustrates how Crystal Enterprise can be deployed within the various firewall architectures commonly available. First, however, you start by learning to understand firewalls and looking at the supporting technology.

A *firewall* is a set of related programs located at a network gateway server (that is, the point of entry into a network), which protect the resources of a private network from users of other networks. It restricts people to entering and leaving your network at a carefully controlled point. A firewall is put in place to protect a company's intranet from being improperly accessed through the Internet. Additionally, firewalls can be used to enforce security policies and to log Internet activity.

UNDERSTANDING NETWORK PROTOCOLS

To have a clear understanding of how firewalls operate (and how Crystal Enterprise is configured within a firewall), review the major protocols used within the Internet.

MAJOR INTERNET PROTOCOLS AND SERVICES

A standard number of Internet services work in conjunction with firewalls. These services are the primary reason for firewalls because companies want to control who and what goes over these services to their internal network.

HYPERTEXT TRANSFER PROTOCOL

HTTP is the primary protocol that underlies the Web: It provides users access to the files that make up the Web. These files can be in many different formats (text, graphics, audio, video, and so on). This protocol is in clear text and usually operates over TCP/IP. So a typical command in HTTP asking for a red picture might look like `192.168.0.16 ->` `naisan.net GET /~bigdir/agenmc/red.gif HTTP/1.0`.

SIMPLE MAIL TRANSFER PROTOCOL

SMTP is the Internet standard protocol for sending and receiving electronic mail. The most common SMTP server on Windows NT is Microsoft Exchange. Although SMTP is used to exchange electronic mail between servers, users who are reading electronic mail that has already been delivered to a mail server do not use SMTP. When they transfer that mail from the server to their desktop they use another protocol, POP (Post Office Protocol). SMTP is also a clear text protocol, so you could send an e-mail by connecting to a SMTP server, and then entering this:

```
MAIL From:ruhi@abha.net
RCPT To:arsel@futbol-khoreh.org
DATA Dude! Who stole my soccer ball?
.
QUIT
```

FILE TRANSFER PROTOCOL

FTP is the Internet standard protocol for file transfers. Most Web browsers support FTP, as well as HTTP, and automatically use FTP to access locations with names that begin `ftp.` so many people use FTP without ever being aware of it. FTP was the initial transfer protocol used for the Internet before the advent of the World Wide Web. FTP is also an open text protocol.

REMOTE TERMINAL ACCESS

Remote terminal access is most commonly known as *Telnet*. Telnet is the standard for remote terminal access on the Internet, and enables you to provide remote text access for your users.

DNS HOSTNAME/ADDRESS LOOKUP

A naming service translates between the names that people use and the numerical addresses that machines use. The primary name lookup system on the Internet is Domain Name System (DNS), which converts between hostnames and IP addresses.

26

TCP/IP

TCP/IP (Transmission Control Protocol/Internet Protocol) is a family of basic communications protocols used on the Internet. TCP/IP uses what is termed a *data packet* to transfer information over the Internet from one computer to another. Packets contain the data that your browser shows when it is surfing the Net. Each packet is small, so many packets are needed to transmit the data contained on one HTML page. As more and more people access the Net and transmit data, more and more packets are being transferred. This increases the need to make sure all the packets that arrive at your door (Web server) are really supposed to come in.

THE TCP/IP PROTOCOL STACK

The TCP/IP protocol stack, which makes up each packet, is constructed of the following layers, from the highest to lowest:

- Application layer (FTP, Telnet, HTTP)
- Transport layer (TCP or UDP)
- Internet layer (IP)
- Network Access layer (Ethernet, ATM)

Packets are constructed in such a way that layers for each protocol used for a particular connection are built atop one another.

At the Application layer the packet consists simply of the data to be transferred, such as an HTML page, which is simply text. As it moves down the layers, trying to reach the wire (network cable) that it needs to go out on, each layer adds a header to the packet; this preserves the data from the previous level. These headers are then used to determine where the packet is going and to make sure it all gets there in one piece. When the data packet reaches its destination, the process is reversed. In the end, therefore, all that TCP/IP is responsible for is specifying how data can make its way from one computer to another. These computers might reside on the same network or in completely different locations. As far as firewalls are concerned, the main thing to remember is that it is not so much about how the packet physically gets to its destination but what is in that packet and whether it is supposed to be there.

TCP/IP RULES

TCP/IP is ideally suited to being the standard protocol for the delivery of information through both external and internal network architectures for the following reasons:

- TCP/IP is packet-based. There are no set limits to the size of a given message because long messages are broken down into multiple (and linked) packets.
- TCP/IP provides for decentralized control. After you own the domain name/number (businessobjects.com) you can assign anything in front of it to expand your domain.

`Support.businessobjects.com` is an expansion to route traffic specifically to technical support within the Business Objects organization.

- Communicating devices are peers; every computer on the network is a peer. Each device can take on the role of either requester or server in the flow of information across multiple computers.

- TCP/IP is routable and easy to transmit between networks. The same rules apply whether communicating through an external or internal network.

- TCP/IP is an open free standard, an important consideration because this, combined with the other reasons detailed in this list, has led to widespread adoption.

NETWORK PORTS

A typical server sets up services to listen on ports. A *port* is a "logical connection place" and specifically, using the Internet's protocol, TCP/IP, the way a client program specifies a particular server program on a computer in a network. Higher-level applications that use TCP/IP, such as the Web protocol HTTP, have ports with preassigned numbers. These are known as *well-known ports* that have been assigned by the Internet Assigned Numbers Authority (IANA). Other application processes are given port numbers dynamically for each connection. When a service starts (or is initialized), it is said to *bind* to its designated port number. Any client program that wants to use that service must issue its request to the designated port number.

Port numbers range from 0 to 65536. Ports 0 to 1024 are reserved for use by certain privileged services. For example, for the HTTP service, port 80 is defined as a default. When a client makes a request, the server will assign that request to a port above 1024. Two pieces of information need to be passed in the TCP/IP header: the originating address of the source request, and the target address of the destination computer. This establishes the connection points for message exchange. You typically use the shorthand *IP:port* to denote an address, such as 192.9.0.95:1844, which refers to IP address 192.9.0.95 and port 1844 of that IP address.

26

UNDERSTANDING FIREWALL TYPES

Firewalls primarily function using at least one of three methods: packet filtering, Network Address Translation (NAT), and proxy services. Crystal Enterprise works with each of these firewall types. Packet filtering rejects TCP/IP packets from unauthorized hosts and rejects connection attempts to unauthorized services. NAT translates the IP address of internal hosts to hide them from outside access—NAT is often referred to as "IP masquerading." Proxy services make high-level application connections on behalf of internal hosts to completely break the network layer connection between internal and external hosts. Let's look at these different types in more detail.

PACKET FILTERING

Packet filtering inspects and selectively deletes packets before they are delivered to the destination computer. Packet filtering can delete packets based on the following:

- The address from which the data is coming
- The address to which the data is going
- The session and application ports being used to transfer the data
- The data contained by the packet

Typically, there are two types of packet filtering: stateful and stateless. *Stateful* packet filters remember the state of connections at the network and session layers by recording the established session information that passes through the filter gateway. The filter then uses that information to discriminate valid return packets from invalid connection attempts. *Stateless* packet filters do not retain information about connections in use; they make determinations packet-by-packet based only on the information contained within the packet.

UNDERSTANDING NAT

NAT converts private IP addresses in a private network to globally unique public IP addresses for use on the Internet. Its main purpose is hiding internal hosts. It makes it appear that all traffic from your site comes from a single IP address. NAT hides internal IP addresses by converting all internal host addresses to the address of the firewall as packets are routed through the firewall. The firewall then retransmits the data payload of the internal host from its own address using a translation table to keep track of which sockets (connections) on the exterior interface equate to which sockets on the interior interface. This is also a simple proxy.

There are several NAT types including the following:

- *Static translation (port forwarding)*—This is when a specific internal network resource has a fixed translation that never changes. If you're running an e-mail server inside a firewall, a static route for port 25 of the external address can be established through the firewall that maps to the right machine internally.
- *Dynamic translation (automatic, hide mode, or IP masquerade)*—This is where a large group of internal clients share a small group of external IP addresses for the purpose of expanding the internal network address space. Because a translation entry does not exist until an interior client establishes a connection out through a firewall, external computers have no method to address an internal host that is protected using a dynamically translated IP address.
- *Load balance translation*—In this configuration, a single IP address and port is translated to a pool of identically configured servers—a single IP address serves a group of servers. This allows you to spread the load of one very popular Web site across several different servers by using the firewall to choose which internal server each external client should connect to on either a round-robin or balanced load basis. This is somewhat similar to

dynamic translation in reverse—the firewall chooses which server each connection attempt should be directed to from among a pool of clones.

- *Network redundancy translation*—Multiple Internet connections are attached to a single NAT firewall. The firewall chooses and uses each Internet connection based on load and availability. The firewall is connected to multiple ISPs through multiple interfaces and has a public masquerade address for each ISP. Each time an internal host makes a connection through the firewall, that firewall decides, on a least-loaded basis, on which network to establish the translated connection. In this way, the firewall is able to spread the internal client load across multiple networks.

UNDERSTANDING PROXY SERVERS

Proxy servers were originally developed to cache Web pages that were frequently accessed. As the Web went supernova the proxies became less effective as caching mechanisms, but another asset of proxy servers became evident: Proxy servers can hide all the real users of a network behind a single machine, and they can filter URLs and drop suspicious or illegal content, or hide the identity of a user. The primary purpose of the majority of proxy servers is now serving as a sort of firewall rather than Web caching.

Proxy servers regenerate high-level service requests on an external network for their clients on a private network. This effectively hides the identity and number of clients on the internal network from examination by an external network user.

Proxies work by listening for service requests from internal clients and then sending those requests on the external network as if the proxy server itself was the originating client. When the proxy server receives a response from the public server, it returns that response to the original client as if it were the originating public server. You can even use the proxy server to load balance similar to the NAT load balancing. As far as the user is concerned, talking to the proxy server is just like talking directly to the real server. As far as the real server is concerned, it's talking to a user on the host that is running the proxy server; it doesn't know that the user is really somewhere else.

The use of proxies does not require any special hardware, but something somewhere has to be certain that the proxy server gets the connection. This might be done on the client end by telling it to connect to the proxy server (Socks), or it might be done by intercepting the connection without the client's knowledge and redirecting it to the proxy server.

Socks is a protocol that a proxy server can use to accept requests from client users in a company's network so that it can forward them across the Internet. Socks uses sockets, a method for communication between a client program and a server program in a network. A socket is an end point in a connection. Sockets are created and used with a set of programming requests or function calls to represent and keep track of individual connections. A proxy must exist for each service. Protocols for which no proxy service is available cannot be connected through a proxy except by a generic TCP proxy service that would work similar to a NAT.

26

CONFIGURING THE CRYSTAL ENTERPRISE ARCHITECTURE FOR YOUR NETWORK ENVIRONMENT

Chapter 24, "Crystal Enterprise Architecture," introduced the components that make up the Crystal Enterprise architecture. However, before looking at how Crystal Enterprise can be configured to support the implementation of the firewall types described previously, it is necessary to review the architecture of Crystal Enterprise, concentrating on how the components that make up the complete product architecture communicate with each other. In fact, the mechanism employed to support server communications has a significant bearing on how Crystal Enterprise can be deployed with one or multiple firewalls.

Additionally, more detail needs to be provided about the relationship between the WC, the Web server, and the Web Component Server. This will be done in a later section; first, you will examine the core of Crystal Enterprise server communication—the Framework.

REVIEWING THE FRAMEWORK

From your investigation of the Crystal Enterprise architecture in previous chapters, you know that at the core of Crystal Enterprise is a communication layer called the Crystal Enterprise Framework. The Framework is made up of a collection of services, which provides a series of Business Intelligence–related functions implemented by one or more Crystal Enterprise services. It is, effectively, a CORBA bus integrating Enterprise information management facilities (Security, Deployment, Administration, and so on) with the CORBA 2 Open Standard services (Naming, Trading, Event, and so on). *Common Object Request Broker Architecture (CORBA)* is an architecture and specification for creating, distributing, and managing distributed program objects in a network. It allows programs in different locations to communicate in a network through an "interface broker."

Although CORBA is at the core of the Framework, it is hidden from Crystal Enterprise administrators and developers (and, therefore, does not form part of the discussion of administration in Chapter 27, "Administering and Configuring Crystal Enterprise"). No configuration needs be done with CORBA that would be done differently from any other TCP/IP application. Some definition of port numbers is all that is required as far as Framework Administration is concerned.

However, for the purpose of using firewalls one concept about CORBA needs to be understood—the IOR. The *IOR (Interoperable Object Reference)* is a unique identifier for an object and contains information about the CORBA object itself. For example, the Report Job Server appears to other CORBA clients using the Framework as an object that is available for those clients to use. Each time a server in the Framework requires the use of another server object, it requests information about that object. This information comes in the form of an IOR. The IOR includes the IP address and port to be used for returning messages—critical when working with firewalls.

To summarize, Crystal Enterprise uses CORBA for intra-server communication. Administrators and developers are not exposed to the technology, nor are they required to work with it; however, it can become important in terms of firewall configuration.

CRYSTAL ENTERPRISE AND TCP/IP COMMUNICATION

With standard TCP/IP communications, two servers that communicate with each other do so over a single point-to-point connection. The use of CORBA in the Crystal Enterprise Framework, however, lends a slightly different flavor. In an environment where many requests are to be served, traffic on a particular port can be overwhelming and slow the operations of the server—leading, obviously, to performance problems. Crystal Enterprise avoids this by listening on one port and sending on others. Within the Crystal Enterprise environment, therefore, communication consists of the opening and closing of multiple ports for a single request/service interaction. In Crystal Enterprise server-to-server communication, after the initial connection is complete, communication stops on this channel. Instead, another channel is established to send data back and forth, leaving the server that is listening on a given port free to service the next connection request quickly and efficiently.

UNDERSTANDING WEB CONNECTOR AND WEB COMPONENT SERVER COMMUNICATION

The gateways to the Crystal Enterprise information delivery environment are either the Web Component Server (WCS) in the COM environment, the Java application server in the Java environment, or the .NET application server in the .NET environment. These communicate via the CE-SDK to the Crystal Enterprise Framework. Because there are multiple configurations available with Crystal Enterprise depending on the platform and technologies used in each organization, a brief exploration clarifies the remainder of this chapter.

Three main types of configuration are possible at the application level of the Crystal Enterprise Architecture: the COM configuration, Java configuration, and .NET configuration. Note that *all* of these configurations could be connected to one Crystal Enterprise installation, allowing a diverse organization to leverage existing technology to write applications against one installation of Crystal Enterprise.

26

NOTE

> Crystal Enterprise supports three implementations of its SDK simultaneously. That means one implementation can support communication from Java, .NET, and COM environments at the same time. This enables organizations to leverage their inherent skill-sets when developing with Crystal Enterprise and also facilitates ongoing system availability through enterprise development standards changes (for example, moving from a COM-based shop to a J2EE-based organization).

The COM environment is common on Windows platforms and uses the Crystal Enterprise COM SDK, CSP or ASP pages, a Crystal Enterprise WCS, and a Crystal Enterprise Web Connector (WC) installed on the Web server. In this configuration two possible levels of communication are possible: the WC communicates with the WCS over TCP/IP, which in turn communicates with the Crystal Enterprise Framework; or ASP pages use the COM SDK, which communicates directly with the Framework.

The Java configuration installs by default in Unix environments, or can be installed when working with a Java Application Server in a Windows environment. Instead of a WC and WCS, the Java configuration uses a Crystal Enterprise Web Component Adapter (WCA) installed on the Application Server, and no WC or WCS. The Crystal Enterprise Java SDK also installs on the Application Server and causes the Application Server (for example, IBM's WebSphere or BEA's WebLogic) to communicate directly with the Crystal Enterprise Framework via TCP/IP.

The .NET environment uses .NET assemblies, which in turn directly communicate with the Framework via TCP/IP. In the .NET configuration no WCS, WC, or WCA are installed.

The remainder of this chapter discusses the COM configuration because it is the most complex. This discussion can easily be applied to the Java and .NET environments by considering that any IP and port configuration applied to the WCS should be applied to the initialization files for the Java Application Server. In .NET deployments, all port configurations are made within the various services as the Framework does not make outbound calls to the .NET server (in other words, IIS). The basic concepts for these alternate configurations, however, are the same.

The configuration for the WCA in the Java environment is done via modification of the file web.xml. This file can be found in Unix environments in the WEB-INF subdirectory of the webcompadapter.war file stored in the *crystal_root*/enterprise/JavaSDK/applications directory on Unix, or X:\Program Files\Common Files\Crystal Decisions\2.5\jars\ JavaSDK\applications on Windows. In this file you can set context parameters by entering XML such as

```
<context-param>
<param-name>viewrpt.groupTreeGenerate</param-name>
<param-value>true</param-value>
</context-param>
```

This chapter will deal primarily with setting IP addresses and ports, and so will involve setting the following two context parameters in the web.xml file:

- connection.cms sets the name and port number of the CMS. Equivalent to setting command-line argument -requestport for the WCS.

- connection.listeningPort defines the default ports that the WCA applets are running on. Equivalent to setting command-line argument -port for the WCS.

Thus, in any discussions in the remainder of this chapter, treat the Java Application Server and WCA together as equivalent to the WC in terms of network settings. Also, because the WCA carries out functions of the WCS, remember that no WCS will be installed.

→ For a detailed review of the application layer, **see** "Web Component Server," **p. 522**

If operating in a Java or .NET environment, you can draw a parallel between the WC and the application server. Because the application server communicates with the Framework, you will need to configure support for the application server to "talk" to the Framework the same way that you would configure the WC to "talk" to the WCS.

INTERACTION BETWEEN THE WCS AND THE WC

To demonstrate the interaction between the WC and the WCS, it's easiest to review the process of displaying a Crystal Report on a Crystal Viewer to examine exactly what traffic is being passed between the browser, Web server, WC, and the Crystal Enterprise report processing tier.

1. A request is made from the browser to the Web server for a specific report viewer. In this example, the user has clicked on a hyperlink (`http://<Server Name>/directory/viewrpt.csp&rptid=1863`), meaning that a request has been made to view a Crystal Report within the Crystal Viewer.

2. The WC on the Web server forwards the request to the WCS.

3. The WCS processes the CSP and calls the Crystal Enterprise SDK to invoke a report viewer object, which renders the report on the Page Server, passes the first page onto the Cache server, and then tells the WCS to send the appropriate HTML to the browser.

4. The viewer HTML is sent from the WCS to the WC, through the Web server, and to the user's browser.

For the purposes of the discussion of firewall configuration, there are essentially three discrete Crystal Enterprise entities that are likely to be deployed at different positions of a firewall architecture, seen in Figure 26.1. (The Web browser will be ignored because this is clearly outside the scope of the firewall.)

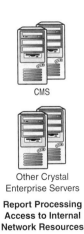

26

Figure 26.1
Crystal Enterprise has three levels at which security must be determined.

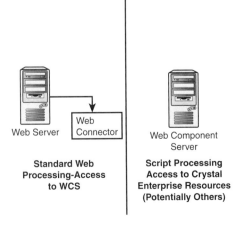

CMS

Web Server | Web Connector

Web Component Server

Other Crystal Enterprise Servers

Standard Web Processing-Access to WCS

Script Processing Access to Crystal Enterprise Resources (Potentially Others)

Report Processing Access to Internal Network Resources

Each of these entities is likely to require different levels of firewall protection determined by their closeness to the internal network.

In cases where you do not deploy a WCS (such as the Java, COM-SDK, and .NET scenarios) there are only two entities, however: the SDK running on the application server and the Crystal Enterprise services or daemons.

As previously mentioned, the barriers that a secure system provides are commonly broken down into distinct layers (with each layer defining a security measurement and effectively denoting an acceptable level of exposure). Each layer is identified by the communication from one network to another network via a firewall. Then, a detailed example involving Crystal Enterprise communication through a firewall will be provided as well as what the appropriate system settings should be and how the communication will be addressed at an IP/port level.

Figure 26.2 shows the most typical example of a firewall implementation. In this scenario, the browser-to-Web server communication is controlled through the standard firewall control, allowing only HTTP requests to be forwarded through to the Web server on port 80 (other services such as Telnet and mail might be permitted through other predefined ports as well). Clearly, Crystal Enterprise is not involved at this stage of the firewall. This does, however, represent the entry point into the resources managed by the target environment. From this point forward, internal network resources will be used; this interim environment is normally called the DMZ (or Demilitarized Zone). The DMZ, therefore, is a network added between a protected network and an external network.

Figure 26.2
Crystal Enterprise can be divided into tiers for firewall deployment.

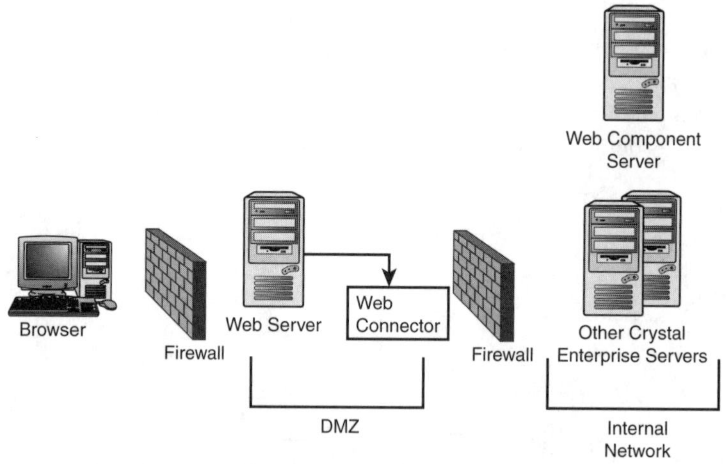

The architecture of Crystal Enterprise fits conveniently into this infrastructure. The separation of the WC from the WCS enables the WC to remain within the DMZ along with the Web server. Consequently, an additional firewall can easily be deployed to protect the requests forwarded through the WCS—this, after all, will be communicating directly to the other Crystal Enterprise servers and is a component on the Crystal eBusiness Framework. Alternatively, the various application server deployments (Java, COM, or .NET) would also reside in the DMZ on the application server.

Because the WC and WCS allow for support of URL-level requests to support legacy Crystal Enterprise applications, some enterprises choose not to implement the WC and WCS in an extranet environment. Instead the application-server deployment with the CE-SDK allows for application-level control of the interaction between the Web (application) server facilitating tighter security at this level. Please refer to Figure 26.3 for an illustration.

For instance, organizations might not desire any extranet access to the Crystal Management Console (CMC). By not installing the WC and WCS in the extranet DMZ, no access to the CMC can occur from the extranet, perhaps alleviating security concerns in an extranet environment where malicious attacks are routine.

Figure 26.3
This is how to configure a firewall in a non-WCS deployment.

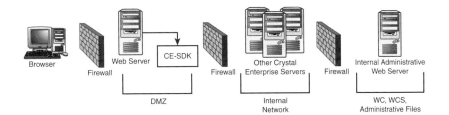

To examine the details of the communication of the WC to the WCS through the second firewall, the discussion will be broken down into two distinct portions: the initialization of the communication (a request for service), and servicing of the request once the communication has been established. This two-stage nature of communication was detailed in the eBusiness Framework in an earlier section in this chapter.

UNDERSTANDING INITIAL TCP/PORT PROCESSING

When the Web server receives a Crystal Enterprise resource request from a Web browser, it forwards the request to the WC or processes the request internally in the case of the SDK. For this example, assume that the Web server has an IP address of 10.55.222.241 (see Figure 26.4).

Figure 26.4
Browser requesting information from the Web server.

Web Server IP address: 10.55.222.241

The WC prepares to make a TCP connection to the WCS. A TCP connection request has four critical elements:

- Destination IP address (where it's going)
- Destination port (at which port/socket the request will be expected)
- Source IP (address of the sender, where to send return messages)
- Source port (port the sender will be listening on for a response)

The destination portion of this communication is determined by settings entered in the WC configuration dialog box in the Crystal Configuration Manager.

When making up the destination information, the WC reads this information from these settings. Because this is the machine name of the WCS, the IP address of the WCS is determined by network name resolution. The port destination takes less work—it's simply the number as entered in this dialog box. By default, this port is 6401. The only requirement is that this port number is the same as the WCS was set to use when the WCS started. The source portion of the requests are both determined by the Web server's operating system.

The Source IP is the IP address of the machine sending the request—the Web server. This IP address is determined by a request to the operating system. The port is also chosen by an operating system request. The WC asks for an available socket (or port) that is not in use. The operating system randomly chooses an unused socket. The WC begins temporarily listening on this port for a response from the WCS as soon as the initialization request is sent. It will only accept a response from the IP address of the WCS—any other requests at this port will be dropped. At this point, the TCP connection request is ready to be sent with this information:

- Source IP—IP address of the Web server machine as determined by a call to the operating system.
- Source port—Port deemed to be available by the operating system. This will be a port number higher than 1024.
- Destination IP—IP address of WCS as determined by network name resolution.
- Destination port—Port as entered into the WC Configuration dialog box in Crystal Configuration Manager. This must match the configured port for the WCS.

Assuming that the WCS has an IP address of 10.55.222.242 and that the assigned port (retrieved by an operating system call) is 3333, for this example, the completed request will be as follows (these are formatted as IP address:port):

- Destination IP—10.55.222.242:6401
- Source IP—10.55.222.241:3333

The WCS is constantly listening on its defined port for service requests (the default 6401 in your example, though another port could be used for listening if configured to do so).

When the WCS receives the TCP Connection Request from the WC, it begins to form a response. The response will have the same four primary components that the request had—a source port and IP and a destination port and IP. Embedded in this response is the IOR of the WCS. The IOR of WCS contains the IP address of the WCS, as well as the port number specified in the -requestport option.

NOTE

> When in a Java environment, the web.xml file configures the port of choice. When in the .NET environment, the port that the SDK uses to connect to the various services is determined by those services because no outgoing communication is necessary from the Crystal Enterprise Framework to the .NET application server and CE-SDK.

If the option is not specified, a free port is picked up at random by the CORBA library by asking the operating system for an available port. At this point, the WCS responds to the WC to complete the TCP connection. This TCP connection response will have this information:

- Source IP—IP address of the WCS as determined by a call to the operating system.
- Source port—A random port number, as determined by making a call to the operating system.
- Destination IP—The IP address as read from the Source IP address in the TCP Connection Request received from the WC.
- Destination port—The port as read from the source port in the TCP Connection Request received from the WC.

Assuming a randomly generated source port of 2345, you'll have the TCP connection confirmation of the following:

- Destination IP:port—10.55.222.241:3333
- Source IP: port—10.55.222.242:2345

While the WCS has been building its confirmation response, the Web server machine has been listening for the response on the chosen port.

The Web server/Connector will only accept packets from the IP to which it sent the request—this is for security. In this example, the operating system of the Web server machine has been listening on port 3333. When the TCP Connection Response/Confirmation is received, the OS of the Web server machine will determine whether it's from the correct location. If it is from the correct IP, it will accept the data and complete the TCP connection. The IOR is embedded inside this request, and the operating system passes it onto the WC for processing.

Now that all this work has been done to establish this connection, the WC immediately closes it. This was merely to establish that both client and server are up and running and accepting connections. The WC also received the IOR of the WCS in this short

26

connection. The listening port on the WCS resumes listening to other clients, and the work of sending IP packets back and forth will be done on a second TCP connection.

UNDERSTANDING SECONDARY TCP/PORT PROCESSING

It is in establishing the second TCP connection that Crystal Enterprise works differently from most TCP/IP applications. The WC reads the IOR of the WCS and acquires the IP address and port number from it. Using this port number and IP address a second connection is made—one that will be used for actually transferring the data. (A straight TCP/IP application doesn't have an IOR from which to read the IP and port of the server. It uses the source IP and port from the TCP connection confirmation to establish this second connection.) The Crystal Enterprise application uses the information in the IOR and discards the source IP and port from the TCP connection confirmation.

Continuing your example, upon reading the port and IP information from the IOR of the WCS, the WC initiates a second TCP connection. This request will use this information:

- Destination IP—The IP address of the WCS as reported in the IOR.
- Destination port—The port number to be used for communication as reported in the IOR. If the -requestport directive is used, it will be that port; otherwise, it will be a randomly generated port number (you will use this).
- Source IP—The IP address of the Web server.
- Source port—The port on the Web server to be used for this connection. This is determined by asking the operating system for an available port.

In this example, assume that the randomly generated destination port number is 2345 and the generated source port is 1061. You'll have the TCP connection confirmation of the following:

- Destination IP:port—10.55.222.242:4000
- Source IP:port—10.55.222.241:1061

When the WCS receives this request, it will respond to the WC to complete the connection. The address to which it will send this connection is 10.55.222.241:1061. This destination and port was determined by reading the source information of the incoming TCP connection request. This is where the WCS's connection response gets its destination. As demonstrated in the following list, this is really just the reversal of the information received from the WC. Completing your example, therefore, the WCS will communicate as follows:

- Destination IP:port—10.55.222.241:1061
- Source IP:port—10.55.222.242:4000

After the Web server/Connector machine receives the TCP connection response from the WCS, it is able to complete the TCP connection. Now that the TCP connection is made, IP packets will be sent back and forth on this channel. IP datagrams will be forwarded back and forth from the Web server (10.55.222.241:1061) to the WCS (10.55.222.242:4000), and vice versa, on these ports. The secondary connection, therefore, is the one that does nearly all the data transference.

Now that you have seen exactly how the IP/port allocation is determined in the Crystal Enterprise environment, you can look at a fully worked example applying a specific firewall technology. Initially, you will look at packet filtering and then apply NAT on top of this. Then this chapter briefly discusses how Crystal Enterprise would fit in with the application of a Proxy Server (Socks) firewall.

Deploying Crystal Enterprise with an IP Packet Filtering Firewall

Earlier this chapter noted that IP Filter firewalls restrict network traffic based on IP address and port number. Crystal Enterprise works well with IP Filter firewalls with the proviso that the IP address and TCP port number used by the servers are predetermined. This section discusses a scenario where the Crystal Enterprise WC/Web server and WCS has one IP Filter between the two of them and the WCS is separated from the rest of the Crystal Enterprise servers by a second firewall. In other words, it's the common firewall scenario you looked at in the previous section. This is illustrated in Figure 26.5.

Figure 26.5
IP Filtering–firewall definition.

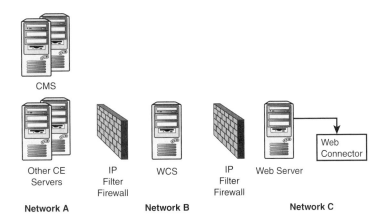

Let's look at two distinct parts of communication across the networks: first, the most external portion (that is, between Network C and Network B), and second, the communication between the WCS and the other Crystal Enterprise servers—the internal portion between Network B and Network A (see Figure 26.6).

Figure 26.6
Configuration with IP Filtering–external firewall.

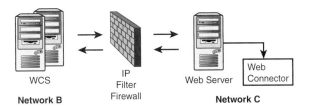

AN EXTERNAL PACKET FILTERING FIREWALL SCENARIO

Any requests of the WC machine would follow the same steps as described in the previous section. Initially, the WC would have to establish a TCP connection to the WCS. The WC would initiate this handshake communication. The IP Filter firewall would certainly stand to convolute this communication:

- Destination IP—The IP of the WCS as determined by network name resolution. The lookup would occur on the side of the Web server—usually by a DNS server in this zone.

- Destination port—The port to use for this communication is taken from the Registry—it's the value as entered in the WC Configuration dialog box in the Crystal Configuration Manager. By default, this is port 6401.

- Source IP:port—The IP:port of the Web server/WC machine as determined by a call to the operating system.

The network rules of this side of the firewall will quickly determine that the destination IP of this request will have to go through the firewall. Therefore, the network forwards this TCP connection request to the firewall. The firewall then evaluates the information within the request—the destination port and IP address, as well as the source IP and source port. The firewall must have rules that allow this connection to go through—it must accept requests for the WCS's IP from the WC's IP and the request must be on the specified port. At this point in the request, the firewall will have to allow traffic through it that follows this configuration:

- Source IP—The IP of the WC/Web server
- Source port—Any
- Destination IP—The IP of the WCS
- Destination port—6401 (or whichever is the WCS's listening port)
- Action—Accept

When the WCS receives this request, it must respond to it. It garners the information about where to respond from the information within the request. It takes the Source IP and Port and makes this the destination. Because this is a random port, the firewall must be configured to allow any ports to leave Network B and go to Network C. This is a generally accepted practice—strict port enforcement is done at the bastion host. Therefore, the firewall rules to complete this request should resemble the following:

- Source IP—Any IP from Network B
- Source port—Any
- Destination IP—Any IP outside the network
- Destination port—Any
- Action—Accept

When the connection request gets through the firewall, the network resolution will determine that the destination is in Network C. The request will hit the Web server/WC. At this point, there is a TCP connection between the two machines, going through the firewall. The WCS will send the WC its IOR and the WC will close this TCP connection.

The IOR contains the IP and port on which the second connection will be made. The port number in the IOR will be one of many values depending on the existence or nonexistence of the `-requestport` xxxx directive on the WCS's command line. If there is a `-requestport`, this is the value that will be in the IOR. If there isn't, it will be a random port as chosen by the WCS's operating system. Generally, a random port is not acceptable because administrators won't enable their firewall rules to accept any ports from a specific IP.

NOTE

> The Crystal Enterprise Administrator's Guide suggests that the use of the `-requestport` option is required with IP Filter firewalls.

When this second connection is made, the `-requestport` directive should be set to a fixed port number and this port number should be accepted if the IP is from the Web server/Connector machine. This second TCP connection information will look like this:

- Destination IP—The IP of the WCS as read from the IOR.
- Destination port—The port as read from the IOR, the recommendation being to use the `-requestport` directive to define this value.
- Source IP—The IP of the Web server/WC machine as determined by a call to the operating system.
- Source port—The free port as returned by a request to the operating system.

The firewall will evaluate this request and the port will have to be open. As an example, if the `-requestport` directive uses port 3333, the firewall rules will have to look like this:

- Source IP—The IP of the WC/Web server
- Source port—Any
- Destination—The IP of the WCS
- Destination port—3333 (or whichever is used with `-requestport` directive)
- Action—Accept

The WCS will respond to this request on whichever port the Web server/WC found to be available. This will be allowed through the firewall because any port is allowed from the internal network to the external. There will then be an established connection between the WCS and the WC, and IP packets will be sent on this channel. The configuration of the firewall rules for an IP Filter firewall between a WCS and WC are summarized in Table 26.1.

26

TABLE 26.1   FIREWALL CONFIGURATION RULES

Source	Destination	Port	Action
Network B	Any	Any	Accept
IP of WC	IP of WCS	6401, -requestport	Accept
Network C	Any	Any	Reject

NOTE

When the WCS is started with the `-requestport` switch, this port will have to be open going from Network B to Network C for the IP of the WCS.

AN INTERNAL PACKET FILTERING FIREWALL SCENARIO

There are several servers in the Crystal Enterprise environment with which the WCS communicates. It must communicate with the CMS as part of logon/security procedures, while the Cache Server will also be involved in a communication with the WCS for report viewing requests. (Additionally, the WCS will communicate with the Input File Repository Server, where the report objects are maintained when the thumbnail of a report is displayed on the Web page.) Obviously, traffic to each of these servers from the WCS will have to be allowed by the IP Filter firewall (see Figure 26.7).

Figure 26.7
Configuring an IP
Filtering–internal
firewall.

WCS   IP
           Filter   Web Server   Web
                        Connector
Network B   Firewall   **Network C**

First and foremost, the WCS will have to communicate with the CMS. The CMS provides the Name Service in the Crystal Enterprise environment. Without this service, the WCS will not be able to communicate with any of the servers. The CMS listens for requests on the port designated, shown in Figure 26.8 under the configuration tab in the Crystal Configuration Manager (the default value for this port is 6400).

Whenever the WCS needs to communicate with the Name Service of the CMS, it does so on port 6400 by default. The first time the WCS has to communicate with the Name Service is when it starts. When the WCS starts, it must register itself with the Name Service as part of its initialization process. This communication occurs on port 6400. A TCP connection occurs between the WCS and CMS for this to happen. The request will have the following information in it:

- Destination IP—The IP of the CMS as determined by network name resolution.
- Destination port—The port number of the CMS as defined in the SERVICES file.

- Source IP—The IP of the WCS as determined by a call to the OS of the WCS.

- Source port—A random available port as determined by a call to the OS of the WCS.

Figure 26.8
This screen shows CMS port configuration.

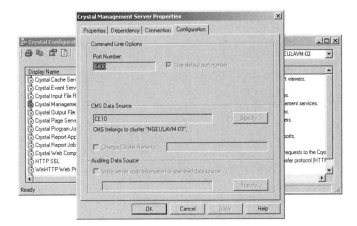

After the CMS receives this TCP connection request, it responds back to the WCS to complete the initial connection. This connection response contains the following information:

- Destination IP—The IP of the WCS as determined by reading the Source IP from the TCP connection request.

- Destination port—The port the WCS is using as determined by reading the Source Port from the TCP connection request.

- Source IP—The IP of the CMS as determined by a call to the OS of the CMS.

- Source port—A random port as determined by a call to the OS of the CMS.

After this initial connection is complete, the CMS sends the WCS its IOR. The WCS then closes the initial connection and establishes a connection to the CMS using the IP and port that is in the IOR. If the CMS is using the `-requestport` directive, this is the port that the WCS will use to initiate communication with the CMS. This second connection request will contain this information:

- Source IP—The IP of the WCS as determined by a call to the OS of the WCS.

- Source port—The port number of the WCS as determined by a call to the OS of the WCS.

- Destination IP—The IP of the CMS as read from the IOR that the CMS sent to the WCS in the initial connection.

- Destination port—The port the CMS put in the IOR. If using the `-requestport` directive, this is the port the CMS put in the IOR. Otherwise, it will be a port deemed available as per a request to the OS of the CMS.

26

The CMS responds to this request to complete the connection. This response contains the following information:

- Source IP—The IP of the CMS as determined by a call to the OS.

- Source port—A free port on the CMS as determined by a call to the OS of the CMS.

- Destination IP—The IP of the WCS as read from the Source IP of the connection request.

- Destination port—The port being used by the WCS as read from the Source Port of the connection request.

When this connection is complete, the WCS and CMS will hold it open and use it whenever communication between the two is required. From a firewall configuration perspective, two ports are involved in the communication between the CMS and the WCS: first, the port the CMS listens on—this is port 6400 by default—and second, the port that is established as the main communication channel between these two processes—this should be the value as defined by the -requestport directive. The "rules" for the firewall configuration can be defined as shown in Table 26.2.

TABLE 26.2   FIREWALL CONFIGURATIONS RULES (NETWORK A TO NETWORK B)

Source	Destination	Port	Action
Network A	Any	Any	Accept
WCS	CMS	6400, -requestport*	Accept
Network B	Any	Any	Reject

> **NOTE**
>
> When the CMS is started with the -requestport switch, this port will have to be open going from Network B to Network A for the IP of the WCS.

However, this is only one of three servers with which the WCS would need to communicate. Requests to the Input FRS and Cache Server would still need to be allowed through the firewall. The standard practice is when servers need to communicate with one another, they ask the Name Service for a copy of the IOR of the server they need to contact. To communicate with either the Input FRS or the Cache Server, therefore, the WCS needs to ask the CMS for information about the server to which it needs access.

When these servers start, they give the Name Service portion of the CMS a copy of their IOR. As the other servers require access to it, they ask the CMS for a copy of the IOR of the server they need information about. To determine the IOR of a given server, the WCS and CMS collaborate. When the WCS has a copy of the IOR of the particular server, it attempts to make a connection to the server using the information in the IOR. The information in the IOR contains both the IP address and the port to be used for communication and security information. If the `-requestport` directive is used, the port will be that defined port; otherwise, it's a random port. When working with firewalls, the preferred method is to use `-requestport` so you can control on which port traffic will be allowed in. As a conclusion, therefore, the firewall rules between Network B and Network A would need to be set up as shown in Table 26.3.

TABLE 26.3 FIREWALL CONFIGURATION RULES (NETWORK B TO NETWORK A)

Source	Destination	Port	Action
Network A	Any	Any	Accept
IP of WCS	IP of CMS	6400, `-requestport` for each of the servers (CMS, Input FRS, Cache Server)	Accept
Network B	Any	Any	Reject

The use of NAT within the IP Filtering firewall adds an additional level of complexity, something explored in the next section.

USING CRYSTAL ENTERPRISE WITH NAT

NAT takes IP Filtering one level further by masking the IP address of the internal server when its packet gets through the firewall. NAT makes it appear as if all traffic from inside the network comes from a different IP address. NAT hides internal IP addresses by converting all internal host addresses to the address of the firewall as packets are routed through the firewall. The firewall then retransmits the data payload of the internal host from its own address using a translation table to keep track of which ports/sockets on the exterior interface equate to which ports/sockets on the interior interface.

EXPLORING THE NAT AND CRYSTAL ENTERPRISE RELATIONSHIP

It has been established that within Crystal Enterprise, server-to-server communication takes the single TCP connection approach one step further. A second TCP connection is made when servers communicate in Crystal Enterprise (listen on one, communicate on another). When it comes to firewalls, it is important to recognize that two ports need to be open.

However, with translated IP addresses in the NAT instance, there is an additional concern because it is the IOR that tells the servers which IP to use; this is not directly retrieved from the packets themselves. This section explains what is required to make Crystal Enterprise work with a NAT firewall—the WC and WCS communication as an example.

When the WC communicates to the Web server, it is on the outside of the firewall. This is how it will be in most configurations and the assumption made during this chapter. The WC/Web server will reside in a DMZ and the rest of the servers inside the corporate

26

network. As before, when the WC needs to communicate with the WCS, it will send a TCP Connection request. To get there, it will need to resolve the name of the WCS machine. Because the WCS is inside the firewall, this can potentially create a problem with a NAT firewall. As you saw with the Telnet example in the previous section, generally the incoming rules for NAT firewalls only accept packets with destination IPs going to the firewall.

In the Telnet example, the client was inside the firewall and the outbound firewall rules allowed all IP destinations outside the wall, as well as any port (this is normal). The NAT firewall then altered the packet and sent it onto the Telnet server. The Telnet server responded back to the firewall. The firewall was expecting the response and allowed it through because it was expected. The NAT firewall altered the destination of this response back to the internal private IP of the Telnet client and routed it onto the Telnet client machine.

In Crystal Enterprise, the WC needs to send the initial TCP Connection request to the WCS. This is somewhat different from the Telnet application because the machine in the external network (the WC) is initializing the communication instead of the machine inside the network. Because the request didn't originate inside the firewall, the firewall isn't expecting any communication. When the WC resolves the machine name of the WCS to an IP address, this won't always be the IP as it exists on the internal network in a NAT environment. There are a number of options available where the features of NAT firewalls could be configured to work in this situation:

- The NAT firewall could be configured to allow packets whose destination is the firewall.
- The NAT firewall could be configured to allow packets whose destination is inside the firewall and have rules on which of these are allowed.
- The NAT firewall could use a group of IP addresses in the external network that each represents one IP address in the internal network.

There is still one outstanding question, however: To which IP address should the request be sent? Crystal Enterprise requires that the machine on the outside of the firewall be able to send packets to the private IP address of the WCS. It might be possible to get away with not using the private IP address for the initial connection; if the initial connection request was sent to a statically mapped IP address or to the IP address of the firewall itself, the firewall could inspect its destination and forward it on without issue.

Remember that the data that is sent in the initial connection from the WCS to the WC is the IOR of the WCS. The IOR contains the IP address and the port of the WCS. Moreover, this is the internal IP address of the WCS—it is not the address of the firewall or a static IP address of the firewall that is mapped to the internal IP address. To allow this traffic through, therefore, on a NAT firewall, the rule that needs to be in place for WC to WCS communication is that the packets to the internal IP address must be allowed through the firewall. (This might, of course, require further rules to route these packets on the firewall.)

The ports that are allowed through can be narrowed, of course. The destination port on which the WCS is listening and its request port need to be allowed through the firewall. In the end, the firewall rules with a NAT firewall are pretty much in line with what the firewall rules are on an IP Filter firewall. For example, Table 26.4 assumes the WCS is inside the network and the WC is external to the network.

TABLE 26.4   FIREWALL CONFIGURATION RULES (WCS INTERNAL AND WC EXTERNAL)

Source	Destination	Port	Action
Internal IP of WCS	External IP of WC	Any	Accept
External IP of WC	Internal IP of WCS	WCS listening port (6401 by default), -requestport	Accept
External Network	Internal Network	Any	Reject

If packets from the hosts on the external network sent to the internal IOP addresses are routed to the firewall and the firewall accepts the packets, the connection will be established successfully. Given that in many cases the external network is a DMZ and the firewall is a router on the LAN, this configuration is possible by adding static routes on the hosts in the DMZ to the firewall. Depending on network configuration, even static routes on the hosts won't be necessary if the firewall between the internal network and DMZ is the default route for all traffic.

CRYSTAL ENTERPRISE AND PROXY SERVERS

It is not the intention at this stage in the book to investigate how Crystal Enterprise can be configured to work with proxy servers in any great detail. This is covered in some depth in the Administrator's guide that accompanies Crystal Enterprise. However, some sample Socks configurations will be shown and there will be a brief discussion as to how Crystal Enterprise would operate effectively with each configuration.

Socks settings for each of the Crystal Enterprise servers are defined using the Crystal Configuration Manager (through the Connection tab).

SOCKS—THE WC AND WCS

Figure 26.9 illustrates the operation of Socks between the WC and the WCS.

Given this scenario, the Socks setting through the Crystal Configuration Manager should be the following:

- On WC, specify the Socks server at the WCS Configuration tab.
- On CMS, specify the Socks server at the Connection tab.

Access control rules on the Socks server should be set to something similar to that shown in Table 26.5.

26

Figure 26.9
Socks configuration—
WC to WCS.

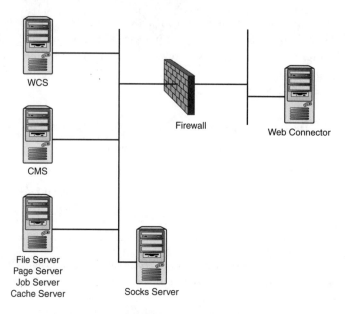

TABLE 26.5 SOCKS CONFIGURATION (WC TO WCS)

Source	Destination	Port	Action
WC	WCS	6401 -requestport	Accept
Otherwise			Reject

There are a couple of points worth noting:

- Although the WC connects to WCS, the Socks server information is set up on CMS rather than on WCS. This is because the WCS will obtain the Socks setting from CMS.

- The initialization from WC to WCS port 6401 uses the host name for the WCS in the Socks request. Therefore, the Socks server must be able to resolve the host name for WCS. For example, if the WC and WCS use NetBIOS names and the Socks server is a Unix box that doesn't support NetBIOS names, it is necessary to ensure the Socks server can resolve the same name as specified by the WC; that is, by using a local host's file.

FIREWALL CONFIGURATION: SOCKS—WCS AND CMS

Figure 26.10 illustrates the operation of Socks between the WCS and the CMS.

In this instance, the Socks setting at Crystal Configuration manager should be the following:

- On WCS, specify the Socks server at the CMS Configuration tab.
- On CMS, specify the Socks server at the Connection tab.

Figure 26.10
Socks configuration–
WCS to CMS.

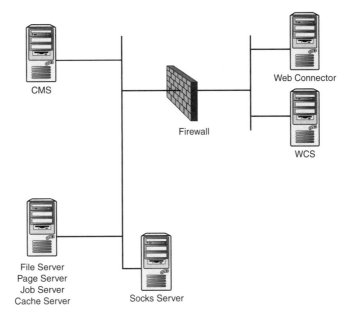

Access control rules on the Socks server should be set to something similar to that shown in Table 26.6.

TABLE 26.6   SOCKS CONFIGURATION (WCS TO CMS)

Source	Destination	Port	Action
WCS	CMS	6400 -requestport	Accept
WCS	Other Enterprise Servers	Default ports -requestports	Accept
Otherwise			Reject

Please note that when WCS makes the initial connection to CMS on port 6400, it will pass the host name to the Socks server. Thus, the Socks server must resolve the CMS hostname.

SOCKS—MULTIPLE CRYSTAL ENTERPRISE SERVERS

Figure 26.11 illustrates the operation of Socks between multiple servers in the Crystal Enterprise environment.

When multiple Socks servers are deployed in the network, the Crystal Enterprise Socks setup can facilitate the traversal of them. However, due care and attention should be taken in how the Socks servers are placed and traversed. In general, the Crystal Enterprise servers see these Socks servers as a chain, and the setup in the Crystal Console Manager should specify how to traverse them from the outermost to the innermost link.

In this instance, the Socks setting at Crystal Configuration Manager should be the following:

- On WC, specify the Socks server B at the WCS Configuration tab
- On WCS, specify the Socks server A at the CMS Configuration tab
- On WCS, specify the Socks server B at the Connection tab
- On CMS, specify the Socks server B followed by A at the Connection tab

Figure 26.11
Socks configuration–
multiple servers.

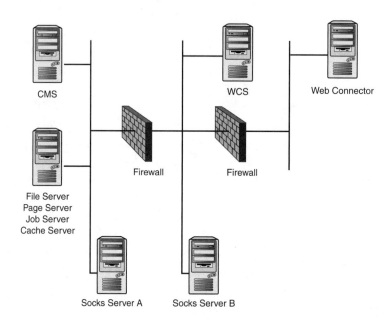

Access control rules on the Socks server should be set to something similar to that shown in Table 26.7.

TABLE 26.7 SOCKS CONFIGURATION (MULTIPLE SERVERS)

Source	Destination	Port	Action
WC	WCS	6401 -requestport	Accept
WCS	CMS	6400	Accept
WCS	Other Enterprise Servers	default ports -requestports	Accept
Otherwise			Reject

The point to note is that in the IOR for the CMS, the Socks server chain B-A is embedded. However, because the WCS has been configured with a local Socks server B, the program will do a comparison of these two Socks server lists and deduce that WCS only needs to go through A to reach the CMS.

ADMINISTERING AND CONFIGURING CRYSTAL ENTERPRISE

In this chapter

INTRODUCTION

This chapter reviews the administration tools for Crystal Enterprise, including best practices and other important information related to the management of the Crystal Enterprise system. Also covered are common system administration tasks such as adding new users, groups, folders, and reports, as well as configuring various Crystal Enterprise server components. The primary application for managing the Crystal Enterprise objects and components is the *Crystal Management Console* (CMC). A supplement to the Crystal Management Console is the *Crystal Configuration Manager*, a Windows-based application for managing certain server functions. The reason for a separate Crystal Configuration Manager is because the CMC is a Web-based management application. If the primary Web server to which Crystal Enterprise is tied were to become unavailable, the Crystal Configuration Manager provides backup server management capabilities.

NOTE

> Although this chapter deals with the out-of-the-box Crystal Enterprise administrative functions, the Crystal Enterprise Software Development Kit provides programmatic access to the capability provided through the CMC.

USING THE CRYSTAL MANAGEMENT CONSOLE

Holding true to the zero-client model of Crystal Enterprise for end-user applications, the Crystal Management Console (CMC) is a DHTML-based tool for managing and configuring the Crystal Enterprise system. The CMC provides Crystal Enterprise administrators with an intuitive way to manage any type of system object, including users, groups, reports, servers, and folders.

You can start the CMC by clicking the Crystal Management Console link in the Crystal Enterprise Launchpad. Initialize the Crystal Enterprise Launchpad by clicking Start, Programs, Crystal Enterprise 10, Crystal Enterprise Admin Launchpad. The Launchpad provides a link to the CMC. Visiting the URL directly can also start the CMC. The URL for the Crystal Management Console looks similar to `http://yourservername/crystal/enterprise10/admin/en/admin.cwr`, shown in Figure 27.1.

NOTE

> If this is the first login to Crystal Enterprise, the Administrator password is set to blank. You should change this as soon as possible.

After logging into the CMC, the Crystal Enterprise administrator is presented with a desktop-style screen from which all CMC functions can be accessed. Icons linking to frequently accessed CMC functions are prominently displayed. They include

- Organize Folders
- Organize Objects

- Organize Groups
- Organize Users
- Organize Server Groups
- Organize Servers
- Define Calendars
- Define Events
- Manage Settings
- Manage Crystal Applications
- Manage License Keys
- Manage Authentication

Figure 27.1
Only those with some administration rights can log on to the CMC.

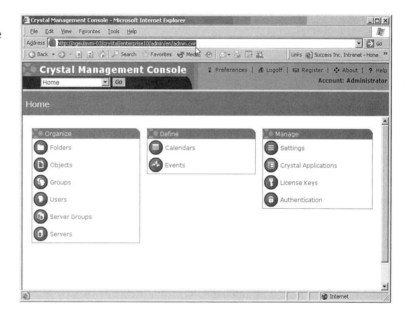

These common procedures, in addition to several others, can also be accessed by clicking the CMC drop-down menu in the upper-left corner of the screen. The Crystal Enterprise administrator can return to the main CMC screen at any time by clicking the Home link at the top of every page (see Figure 27.2).

This chapter groups the previously listed common system functions into broader groups because tasks such as managing groups and users are intertwined. This first group of sections focuses squarely on the CMC because a bulk of administration time takes place there.

The first section, "Managing Accounts," includes sections on managing users and groups. The second section, "Managing Content," covers objects and folders. The third section, "Introducing Servers," reviews individual server configuration for all the Crystal Enterprise servers and server groups. The last section on the CMC, "Managing Crystal Enterprise System Settings," covers management of system settings and authorization.

A subsequent section to these shifts gears to focus on the CMC.

Figure 27.2
All CMC functions can be accessed from the main screen.

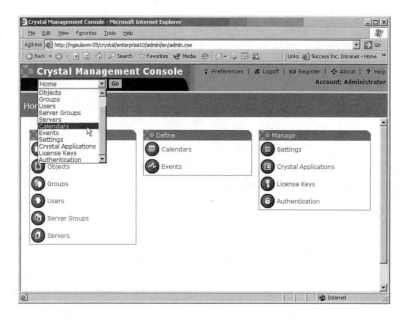

MANAGING ACCOUNTS

The most common use of the CMC is to manage user accounts. Although this chapter provides a review of managing user accounts, this should always be combined with an effective user-management strategy appropriate for your organization. For example, managing users is best accomplished through an effective group inheritance model, where object restrictions are never assigned to individual users, but rather to groups. When users are placed as members within those groups, they inherit the restrictions of the group. Often a single *system of record*, such as an LDAP or Active directory system, establishes one set of uses and groups that the entire organization and all software can use, greatly speeding user administration.

NOTE

> Rights are not assigned to users or groups, but to the objects within Crystal Enterprise themselves (Reports and Folders). This is explained later in the chapter.

This section reviews all the various components that factor into account management, which includes users and groups.

MANAGING USERS

To access Crystal Enterprise resources, a physical end user must possess a username. Upon initial installation, by default, Crystal Enterprise creates the Administrator user and the Guest user only.

The Guest account is a generic account meant for use in a scenario where certain global reports contain public information that could be accessed by anyone using Crystal Enterprise. Without an assigned username, a user can log on only as an administrator (if they know the password) or a guest (provided the Guest account remains enabled).

NOTE

> The Administrator and Guest accounts are required for proper system functionality. The Guest account can be disabled by the system administrator; however, it should not be deleted.

All Crystal Enterprise permissions ultimately originate from, or apply to, individual user accounts/usernames. In light of this, one of the most important aspects of system administration is the creation of new user accounts or mapping accounts from the system of record. Whether adding one user or several hundred, the Crystal Management Console makes this process fast and intuitive. To begin adding new users, click the New User icon displayed on the main CMC screen (see Figure 27.3).

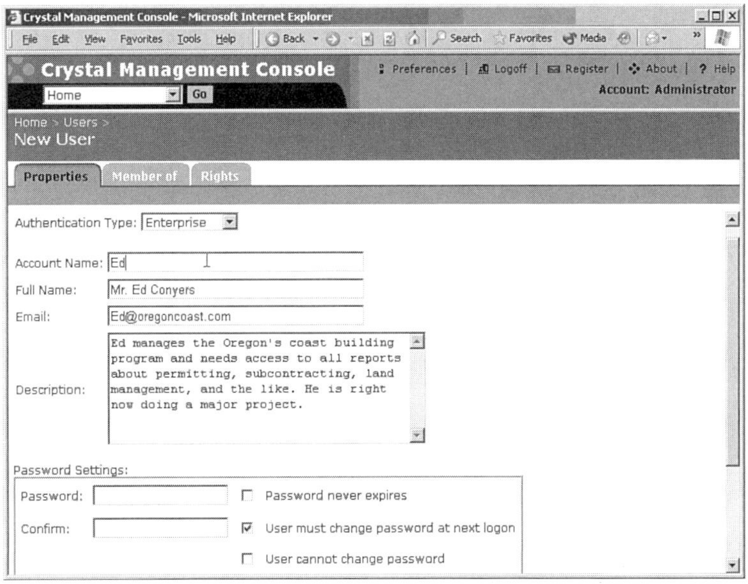

Figure 27.3
The initial CMC page for adding a new user.

In the Account Name field, enter a unique name that the user enters to log on to Crystal Enterprise. Generally, usernames are entered as a single word in lowercase (for example, Ed for Ed Conyers). If the Crystal Enterprise administrator prefers, the username can contain mixed-case letters as well as spaces. Crystal Enterprise is not case sensitive to usernames.

Next, enter the user's proper name in the Full Name field. The full name can contain mixed-case letters and spaces. A freeform text description can be included.

The Crystal Enterprise administrator can also specify a password in the Password Settings dialog; however, it's not necessary because users can be forced to change their passwords the first time they log on. Checking Password Never Expires exempts the username from the Crystal Enterprise global password expiration rules (discussed later in this chapter). Selecting User Cannot Change Password prevents end users from changing their passwords in the future.

The Connection Type radio buttons enable the Crystal Enterprise administrator to indicate whether the username will capture a concurrent user license or a named user license when logged in to Crystal Enterprise. A concurrent user license is not absorbed unless the user is logged in to Crystal Enterprise.

After the user's session ends, a default of 20 minutes, the concurrent license is released. This means that another user within Crystal Enterprise can log in to Crystal Enterprise and use the concurrent license. A named license is relinquished only when the username is deleted or changed to use a concurrent license. An in-depth discussion of license keys is covered later in this chapter in the Authorization section of the CMC.

After the required information for creating a new user is provided, click the OK button at the bottom of the screen. The new user is created. Refresh the User Properties screen. Note that the User Properties screen reload is the only confirmation that the new user was successfully added to the system.

After the User Properties screen has been reloaded, two new options appear at the bottom of the page. The Authentication setting enables you to specify whether the user's password validation will be processed by Crystal Enterprise, LDAP, Windows NT, Active Directory, or even perhaps a system such as SAP via the Crystal Enterprise Solution Kit for SAP. By default, Crystal Enterprise handles authentication internally. The Account Is Disabled option disables an account without deleting it. Although the account can always be enabled again in the future, this is useful for employees who might take a leave of absence from the company.

Before leaving this screen, a new feature to version 10 should be covered. The Rights tab at the top of the User screen can confuse a new administrator into thinking that he can grant the user whose profile he is looking at certain system rights. Actually the opposite is true! The Rights tab, which appears on *almost every object in Crystal Enterprise*, supports a new feature called Delegated Administration, which enables different users to administer different portions of one Crystal Enterprise system. Use the tab to specify which users or groups have access to this object; in this case to the particular user you are looking at. So if you only enable access to this user's profile for the Administrator's group, another user logging onto the CMC will not see the user at all. In this way you can have administrators in different departments or functional areas do their own system maintenance without seeing the information of other groups or departments.

A list of all the users in the system, including the Crystal Enterprise administrator, can be accessed by selecting Users from the CMC drop-down menu (see Figure 27.4).

Figure 27.4
All user-management functions are accessible from the Users screen.

From the Users screen, you can search for specific usernames, edit an existing username, add a new user, or delete an existing user. To delete a username, place a check mark in the corresponding box on the right side of the screen. You can select more than one username. After a minimum of one username has been selected in this manner, click the Delete button at the top of the screen. The Crystal Management Console then prompts to confirm deletion of the user account. Again we see a Rights icon as well—again this is to specify which user/group has the rights to see this portion of the administrative console.

MANAGING GROUPS

A user *group* is a collection of Crystal Enterprise users with one or more logical characteristics in common. For example, the users in the Marketing department should be grouped together based on the fact that they all belong to the same business division. Because these users work together, they are more likely to share the same reports. Creating groups such as marketing enables the system administrator to globally assign permissions to a broader audience.

Groups are useful for classifying users according to their job function and report needs. In most cases, it's advisable to create a series of logical user groups to reduce the complexity of managing permissions in Crystal Enterprise.

TIP

> Globally managing permissions for user groups is significantly less complex than trying to manage permissions for each individual user. However, there might be situations in which it's desirable to make an exception to a group's security policy for a minimum number of users within that group. Crystal Enterprise has the flexibility to make object restriction exceptions on a user-by-user basis.

Crystal Enterprise contains three default user groups:

- Administrators
- Everyone
- New Sign-Up Accounts

THE ADMINISTRATORS GROUP

The Administrators group is for system administrators only. Users who belong to this group have full, unrestricted access to Crystal Enterprise, including the capability to manage servers using the CMC. Administrators can run any report and access any report folder. *Use discretion when adding users to this group.*

THE EVERYONE GROUP

The Everyone group contains all users by default. When new users are created, they are automatically enrolled in the Everyone group. The Everyone group is useful for globally setting permissions for all Crystal Enterprise users.

NEW SIGN-UP ACCOUNTS

New Sign-Up Accounts is a special group that contains users who have created their own new accounts through the Register option in the Web Desktop. Note that this capability can be disabled.

CREATING NEW USER GROUPS

To create a new user group, click the New Group icon on the home CMC page (see Figure 27.5).

In the Group Name field, enter the group name exactly as it should appear in Crystal Enterprise. The group name field accepts upper- and lowercase, spaces, and punctuation. A freeform text description is optional. After the required information has been provided, click OK to create the group.

After clicking OK, the group creation screen should momentarily reload. This indicates that the group was created successfully. The Crystal Enterprise administrator now has access to three new tabs at the top of the screen: Users, Subgroups, and Member Of, shown in Figure 27.6.

Figure 27.5
Creating new user groups is a fundamental system administration task. It's often helpful to seek input from business users when formulating user group names and hierarchies.

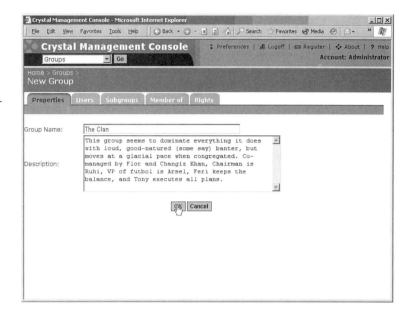

Figure 27.6
New group management options are made available after the group has been created.

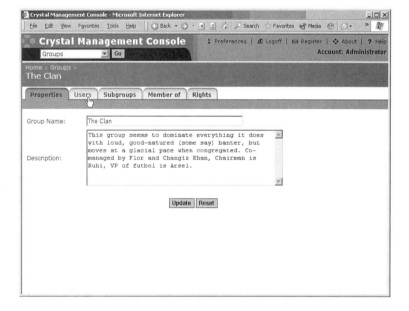

ADDING USERS TO A GROUP

Creating a group name is the first step in configuring a new group. By default, the new group does not contain any users. You must click the Users tab to add users to the group (see Figure 27.7).

Figure 27.7
Initially, the Users tab is empty. New users can be added to the group by clicking on the Add/Remove Users button.

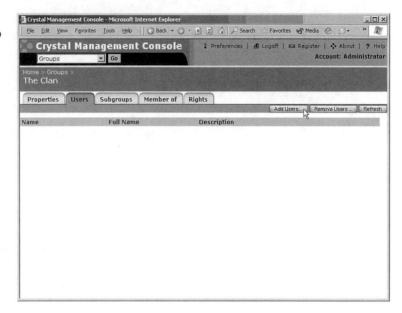

The Users tab does not contain any users initially. To add users to the new group, click the Add Users button at the top of the screen. A list of all Crystal Enterprise users appears on the left side of the screen, as shown in Figure 27.8. Highlight the users to add to the group. You can select several, noncontiguous names by holding down the Ctrl key when clicking. After the desired usernames are highlighted, click the Add button to verify the selection. Highlighted users are moved from the Available list to the Users list. When satisfied with the selections, click OK to commit, as shown in Figure 27.9.

Figure 27.8
All Crystal Enterprise users appear in the list box on the left.

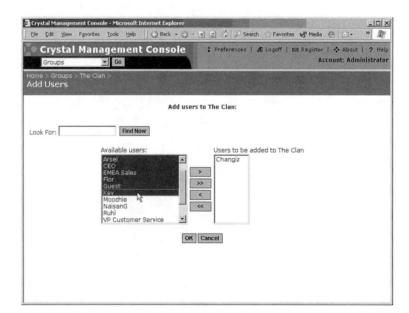

To select a range of users, click the topmost username in the desired range. Then, while holding down the Shift key, click the bottom username in the range. All users between the top and bottom names are selected.

Figure 27.9
Any changes to the group membership are not committed until the Crystal Enterprise administrator clicks OK.

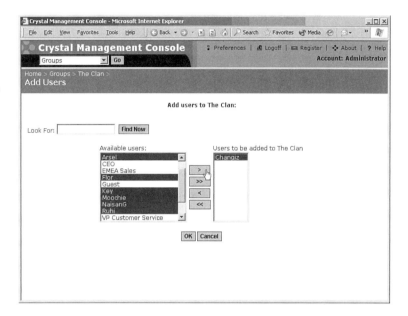

The CMC returns to the Users tab after the changes have been committed. The Users tab immediately reflects the membership of the group, as shown in Figure 27.10. Keep in mind that Crystal Enterprise enables a single user to be a member of multiple groups, so it's possible for users to belong to other groups, such as the Everyone group.

CREATING SUBGROUPS

Now that the group has users, you can create subgroups. As the name implies, a *subgroup* is a child of the parent group. Subgroups can be used to further define user roles and permissions at a more detailed level. A top-level group can contain several subgroups, and those subgroups can also contain subgroups, as Figure 27.11 shows. The benefit is that permissions need not be applied at a user level, even though they can be. Even if an individual user's needs might seem unique, there is always the distinct possibility that someone else could come along with similar requirements. Creating subgroups minimizes individual user permission/restriction management.

Click the Subgroups tab to add new subgroups.

Click the Add/Remove Subgroups button to designate a new subgroup. The Add/Remove Subgroups page works just like the Add or Remove Users screen. All available groups are listed in the list box on the left.

27

Figure 27.10
The new group now contains several users.

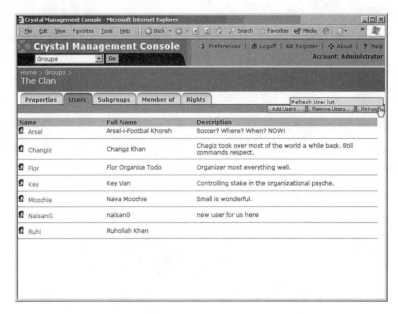

Figure 27.11
The Subgroups tab identifies any child groups that belong to the current parent group.

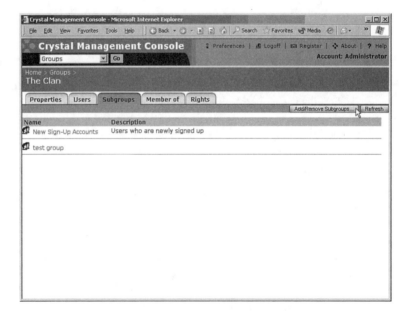

To be clear, a subgroup is not a special kind of group, but rather an ordinary group that has a hierarchical relationship established with another group. Like parent or top-level groups, subgroups are created by using the New Group option on the main CMC screen.

If a subgroup needs to be created (that is, it doesn't exist yet), you need to create the new subgroup in the same manner as other groups would be created, from the New Groups screen. Figure 27.12 shows a list of groups where the intended subgroup has already been defined.

Figure 27.12
SubgroupOne has already been created and you can move this into a parent group. (Note that the name can be anything –"SubgroupOne" is used to clarify the relationship in this text.)

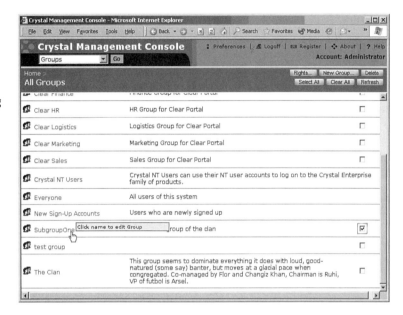

NOTE

Any group can also be a subgroup. This can get a bit messy with respect to restrictions because overlapping inherited security can be confusing. Try to keep things streamlined by using naming conventions and inherited permissions. This lowers administrative cost and Total Cost of Ownership.

Add the subgroups to the parent group and click OK to commit the change to the system database (see Figure 27.13). The CMC returns to the subgroup listing screen, which now reflects the new subgroups.

This particular subgroup tree is only one level deep. It's possible to create subgroups of subgroups for more granular management of users. For example, a few regional subgroups (East, Central, and West) could be added to the North America Sales subgroup. To do this, you only need to click the name of the subgroup, and then repeat the preceding steps to add another subgroup.

27

Figure 27.13
The subgroup
SubgroupOne is
added to two existing
subgroups.

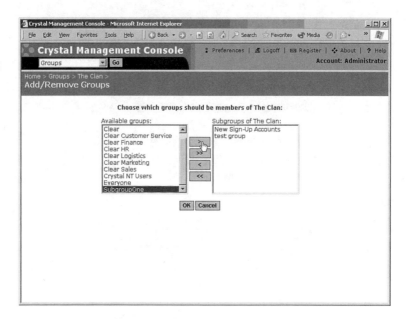

MANAGING CONTENT

Managing content means managing all the various objects, for instance Crystal Reports, Excel and Word files, programs, packages, and Crystal Analysis Professional reports that are published to Crystal Enterprise. As discussed in earlier chapters, all of these are referred to as *content*.

The management of content implies a host of tasks, from organizing items into various container folders to applying restrictions (or *rights*) to the actual objects. If not planned correctly, content management can be one of the most time-consuming tasks for a Crystal Enterprise administrator. Again, with delegated administration, this task can be distributed to various subject matter experts around the organization, saving the IT department this type of work, which often involves knowledge of a particular department's requirements in detail.

The flexible Crystal Enterprise architecture accommodates almost any content-management scheme. However, there are some general guidelines to follow when determining the best approach to content management. A content management scheme consists of a folder/subfolder tree that can be defined within Crystal Enterprise and the associated permissions on those folders.

An effective content-management scheme should have the following characteristics:

- Both descriptive and easy to understand folder and report names
- A standard report naming convention consistently applied throughout the system
- Strictly controlled object access that adheres to the organization's business rules

- A folder hierarchy that facilitates rapid end-user navigation to every report object
- Reliable reports with accurate database logon information

MANAGING OBJECTS

Objects in Crystal Enterprise are published into the object store. Objects, when published into Crystal Enterprise, are managed through the CMC. This chapter uses the terms *report* and *object* interchangeably because most object are, in fact, reports.

This book has already provided some object publishing and management review. The Publishing Wizard, a Windows-based application for publishing reports to Crystal Enterprise, primarily publishes most content through the Save As functionality of Crystal Reports or Crystal Analysis. This chapter reviews object publishing and management from the CMC perspective.

It's also important to note that the object type determines the options and properties available to the Crystal Enterprise system administrator. For instance, because Crystal Analysis Professional reports cannot be scheduled like Crystal Reports, no scheduling options are displayed when administering a Crystal Analysis Professional report.

Because Crystal Reports are the most widely used report type, this chapter focuses primarily on that object type.

PUBLISHING OBJECTS FROM THE CMC

→ For more information on objects in Crystal Enterprise, **see** "Content Plug-ins," **p. 512**

To add a new report to Crystal Enterprise, start the CMC and, from the home page, select Objects, and then the New Object button as shown in Figure 27.14.

Figure 27.14
The New Object function enables you to add a new object to Crystal Enterprise.

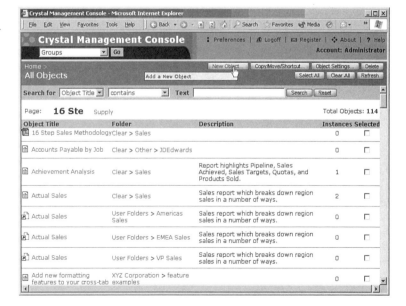

After selecting New Object, the New Object dialog launches, shown in Figure 27.15. To add a report, choose to add that type of object on the left, and then type the path and filename of the report in the File Name box, or click the Browse button to locate the report file.

Figure 27.15
The New Report dialog enables you to add objects to Crystal Enterprise from an external directory location. Supported objects are listed on the left.

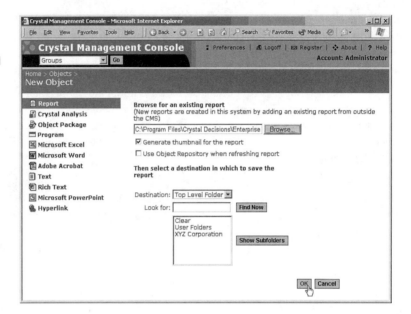

After selecting the report filename, indicate whether a thumbnail image of the report should be generated and displayed. A report *thumbnail* is a snapshot of page one of the report. This feature is currently available for Crystal Reports only. A thumbnail is merely a property of the report object, something that can be called programmatically or displayed only as an option. The Crystal Enterprise Web Desktop is a good example of an application that uses the report thumbnail.

The Generate Thumbnail for the Report option is useful for visually identifying reports, and it's recommended that the Crystal Enterprise administrator leave the setting enabled.

Because the Generate Thumbnail for the Report option only applies to Crystal Reports objects, the report must be saved with the Save Preview Picture option at design time. This must be enabled in the Crystal Reports application by clicking File, Summary Info.

While enabling this option in Crystal Reports, it's highly recommended that the Title, Author, and Comments fields be filled in because this information is available to users in Crystal Enterprise applications for report identification and searching. All these properties are stored in the Crystal Enterprise system database and can be leveraged for more specific report discovery.

The Summary Info dialog must be completed during report creation for the thumbnail (or report description details) to be available inside Crystal Enterprise.

The Use Object Repository when refreshing report option, new for version 9 of Crystal Enterprise, refreshes the repository objects added to the report with the most current objects. For instance, if the report designer had dragged a copyright text field onto the report, and the check box was enabled, Crystal Enterprise would check to see that the copyright text was the latest version stored in the repository and update it if a later one is available.

The final step to adding a new report to Crystal Enterprise is to select the desired enterprise folder that contains the report. This is done using the Destination option at the bottom of the New Report screen. Simply highlight the folder that should house the new report and click OK. The Crystal Enterprise administrator can also navigate to subfolders by highlighting the parent folder and clicking the Show Subfolders button.

CONFIGURING REPORT PROPERTIES

The CMC now displays a report Properties tab, shown in Figure 27.16. The Report Title is indicated at the top of the screen. This is the actual name that Crystal Enterprise displays when users browse for the report. The report name is actually taken from the report's Title field, which can be edited in the Summary Info dialog screen in Crystal Reports. The Crystal Enterprise administrator can override the default title by manually typing a different title. Report titles can contain upper- and lowercase characters, as well as spaces.

NOTE

Use a consistent naming convention for all reports, and make the report titles reasonably descriptive. This reduces object management issues when dealing with hundreds or thousands of distinct reports.

Figure 27.16
The Properties screen displays the report title, description, and other pertinent details.

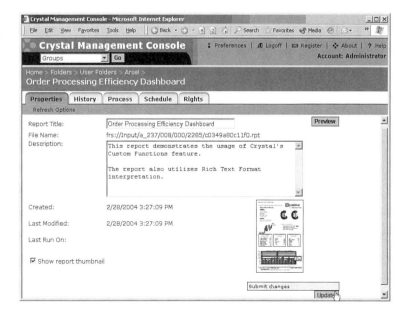

The File Name field indicates the true path and location of the actual file as it is managed by the File Repository Server (FRS). This information is controlled by Crystal Enterprise and *cannot* be edited. It's displayed as a reference for troubleshooting purposes.

The Description field can be used to add a detailed paragraph to note any special information about the report. The Description field is displayed in the Web Desktop, and it also will be parsed by the Web Desktop report keyword search feature.

NOTE

> Developers sometimes use the Description field as a catchall for keywords about the report that can be searched by a Crystal Enterprise application. Although this might be effective for a small number of reports, it can adversely affect system performance when you're dealing with large numbers of reports and is not recommended.

The Folder Path, at the top of the screen immediately above the title of the report, shows the folder structure that contains this report. Each word can be clicked to navigate to that folder. To move this object, you would first go to the containing folder, and then choose the Copy/Move/Shortcut button.

The upper-right corner of the report Properties tab contains a Preview button. The Preview button runs the report immediately on the first available Page Server. This option is useful for verifying database connectivity for the report without opening the Web Desktop.

The bottom of the report Properties tab, shown in Figure 27.17, allows the Crystal Enterprise administrator to enable the report thumbnail image using the Show Thumbnail check box. Be aware that the report must be designed with the Save Preview Picture option enabled for this setting to take effect, in addition to the settings required in Crystal Reports discussed earlier.

If any changes are made to the report Properties tab, you need to click the Update button at the bottom of the screen to commit the modifications to the system. After clicking Update, the Properties tab refreshes; this indicates that the changes were successfully committed to the system database.

On the Properties tab, just below the word Properties, links to navigate to the Refresh Options and Links appear. Clicking on the Refresh option navigates to an area where you can designate which properties of the report you want to refresh from the Object Repository or the report stored in the Crystal Enterprise system. Clicking on Links brings you to a display of the managed links in this report object so that you can verify that the links are valid. The actual links should be managed within Crystal Reports.

REVIEWING REPORT HISTORY

In addition to the report Properties tab, several other tabs pertain to the report. The first is the History tab. The History tab, shown in Figure 27.18, displays all instances of the report, including completed instances—successful or otherwise—pending (queued) instances, recurring instances, currently running instances, and paused instances. The Crystal Enterprise administrator can use this screen to manage all instances of this report.

Figure 27.17
Additional options in the report Properties tab–the links subsection.

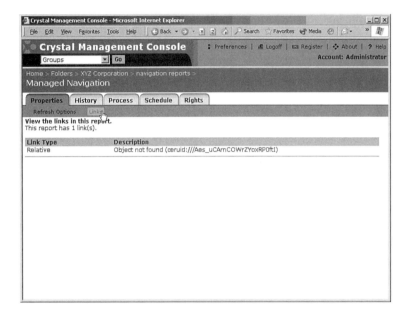

Figure 27.18
The History tab lists all instances of the report.

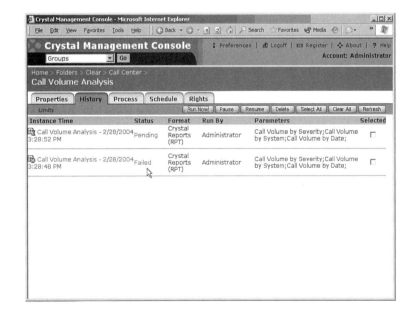

Recall that a report instance is a version of the parent report that has been scheduled and run at a specific point in time. The instance might have certain parameters that were specified at the time of scheduling, so very few assumptions about the report instance can be made without verifying this information. Fortunately, Crystal Enterprise stores the schedule time, scheduling user, start time, end time, and so on, as properties of the instance.

NOTE

> Although the number of report objects and instances stored and managed within Crystal Enterprise is, in theory, unlimited, the hardware dedicated to the CMS, CMS Database, and FRS plays a major role in determining true system scalability.

To see the details of instances (including error messages for failed instances), click the instance date/time stamp, shown in Figure 27.19, or the instance status message.

Figure 27.19
The instance's properties can be reviewed in the CMC.

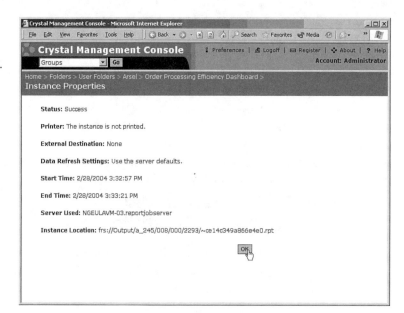

The upper-right corner of the History tab displays a row of action buttons. These include the following:

- Run Now—Schedules a new instance of the report for immediate processing.
- Pause—Pauses, but does not cancel, processing of any selected pending or running instances.
- Resume—Releases any selected paused instances so the report can continue processing.
- Delete—Permanently removes selected instances from Crystal Enterprise.

A large Crystal Enterprise deployment might generate thousands of report instances every day. Over time, the accumulation of old report instances unnecessarily consumes system resources. Crystal Enterprise has instance-limit controls for automatically managing the expiration (deletion) of old report instances. There is a global instance expiration setting in the Settings section of the CMC (discussed later in this chapter). The global expiration limits apply to all report instances in Crystal Enterprise, unless the system administrator defines exceptions on a report-by-report basis.

If a report is scheduled and a format other than Crystal Reports is specified, it's still stored in the Crystal Enterprise system database as a report instance. This means that report instances could be Microsoft Excel spreadsheets, Word documents, and so on. Crystal Enterprise provides a series of server plug-ins that enable objects to be stored in the system database that are not of type Crystal Reports or Crystal Analysis Professional.

MANAGING OBJECT LIMITS

Exceptions to the global instance expiration limits are defined on the Limits tab for each report. The Limits tab, shown in Figure 27.20, enables the Crystal Enterprise administrator to override the global or folder instance expiration limits for the current report only. In the upper-left corner of the Limits tab is an option to Delete Excess Instances When There Are More Than N Instances of an Object. You can use this option to trigger old report instances to be deleted when the specified threshold has been exceeded.

Figure 27.20
The Limits tab can be used to configure report instance expiration rules for the current report object. Object-level expiration limits take precedence over folder and global limits.

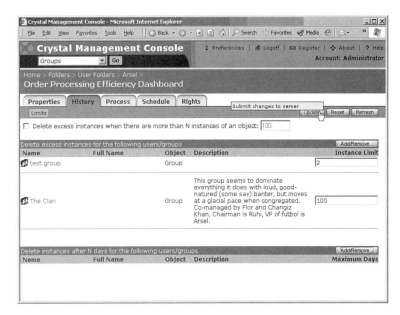

This setting applies to all users and user groups unless an exception is made in the Delete Excess Instances for the Following Users/Groups section of the Limits tab. The Crystal Enterprise administrator can click the Add/Remove button in this tab to add overriding expiration limits for specific users or user groups. The user/group expiration limits take precedence over any global or folder expiration limits.

THE PROCESS TAB

Within the Process tab, there are several sub-tabs. These sub-tabs allow you to set the options for how reports are processed.

SERVERS AND PROCESSING OPTIONS   Clicking on the Process tab navigates to the processing servers page. The Default Servers to Use for Scheduling area controls which server group executes the report.

Server groups are useful for categorizing servers by geographic region or processor speed. The server group options are useful for ensuring that reports are executed on a Crystal Enterprise Job Server that is in close physical proximity to the database server. For example, reports scheduled in Paris against the Paris sales database should be executed by a Job Server that is on the same network segment as the Paris database to maintain maximum report performance. Server groups can also be used to direct high-priority reports to servers with the most processing power.

For example, this option could be used to force the CFO's weekly financial reports to execute on the fastest server in the company. (A detailed discussion of server groups appears later in this chapter.)

The Use the First Available Server option is enabled by default and should remain enabled in most cases. This allows the report to be processed by the first available Job Server. However, the Crystal Enterprise administrator can direct Crystal Enterprise to use a specific server group when possible by enabling the Give Preference to Servers Belonging to the Selected Group option. If this option is enabled, Crystal Enterprise forces the report to execute on the first available Job Server in the group. If no Job Server is available, the report is executed by the first available Job Server outside the specified server group.

The option to Only Use Servers Belonging to the Selected Group causes the report to execute only on Job Servers within the specified group. Crystal Enterprise queues the scheduled instances of the report for the first available Job Server in the specified group. If no server is available, the report remains in the queue until one becomes available.

NOTE
> Be aware that the option to Only Use Servers Belonging to the Selected Group restricts Crystal Enterprise's capability to intelligently designate a Job Server for the report, and might cause scheduled instances of the report to remain in the job queue longer than normal. Exercise caution when enabling this feature.

In similar fashion, viewing and modification servers designate preferences for real-time viewing and report modification. Finally, default values on the PageServer and Report Application Server (RAS) regarding how often to refresh data versus caching can be overridden for any object, enabling you to tailor settings for more and less time-sensitive reports, for instance.

DATABASE SETTINGS   The Database subsection contains database logon information for the report, shown in Figure 27.21. Although the database information, such as server name, is stored in Crystal Enterprise by default, database logon information is not stored and can only be added on this tab by the system administrator.

When a user attempts to run a report that does not already have database logon information provided, Crystal Enterprise prompts the user to type the database username and password. Note, however, if the Crystal Enterprise administrator has already configured database logon information for the report, the user is not required to enter any additional passwords. This is the preferred method for running reports that do not rely on database-level security.

Figure 27.21
The Database subsection enables you to manage database logon information for the report object. Storing the logon information along with the report enables users to run the report without knowing a database username and password.

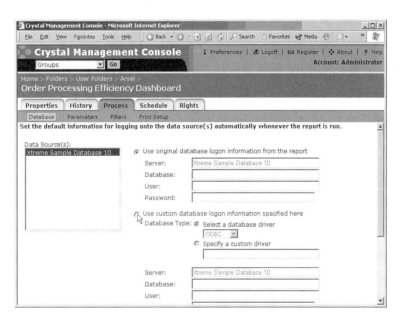

To configure database login information, click the Database link and highlight the report data source to configure first. All report data sources appear in the Data Source(s) list box. Most reports only have one data source; however, reports that contain subreports or multiple databases might have more than one data source. Note that each data source must be configured independently.

To store database logon credentials with the report, highlight a data source and fill out the database, logon name, and password for the data source. Remember to click the Update button to confirm the changes. If the report has multiple data sources, you are required to highlight each data source and provide the proper logon information. Database logon information is encrypted in the Crystal Enterprise system database, and it cannot be accessed by end users, even by querying the system database directly.

Enabling the Prompt the User for New Value(s) When Viewing option causes Crystal Enterprise to confirm the default database logon information each time the report is viewed.

If a database has changed, the Use Custom Database Logon Information Specified Here option should be checked, and the relevant information added. This feature, new to Crystal Enterprise 10, enables flexibility in changing databases even after an object enters the Crystal Enterprise system. Should batch maintenance of database connections be required, a script file can change these settings via the CE-SDK. Please see Chapter 36, "Creating Enterprise Reporting Applications with Crystal Enterprise Part II," for more information.

MANAGING OBJECT PARAMETERS

The Parameters subsection options, shown in Figure 27.22, can be used to provide default values for parameters in the report. Specifying default parameter values can reduce the number of steps required for a user to schedule a report. Of course, users can always override the default values if they want. To specify a default value for a parameter, click the parameter value listed in the Value column. Unspecified values are indicated as [EMPTY].

Figure 27.22
The Parameter subsection can be used to store default values for report parameters. Users have the capability to override the default values with their own values.

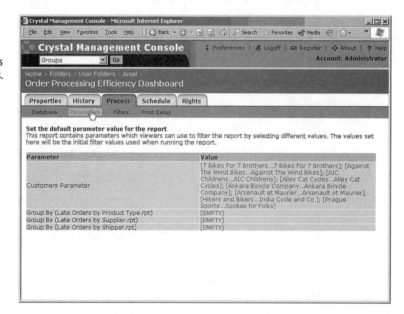

The Crystal Enterprise administrator might select a default value for a parameter from the drop-down list of default parameter values (see Figure 27.23). The values that appear in the drop-down list were provided at the time of report creation in Crystal Reports. If the desired values do not appear, the Crystal Enterprise administrator can type a new value by clicking the Edit button. Certain types of parameters, such as range parameters, can accept both a beginning and ending default value.

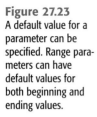

Figure 27.23
A default value for a parameter can be specified. Range parameters can have default values for both beginning and ending values.

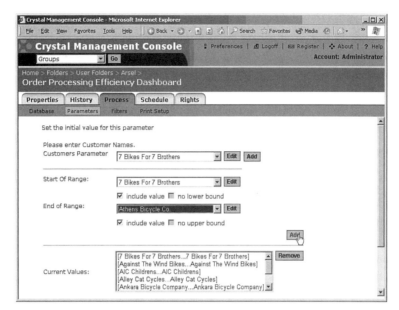

The Clear the Current Parameter Value(s) option erases the parameter's current default values, while the Prompt the User for New Value(s) when Viewing option ensures that users are reminded to confirm or modify the default parameter values each time the report is run. Any changes made to the Parameters area must be confirmed by clicking the Update button.

The benefit of using parameters with reports in Crystal Enterprise is that the user is prompted for value entry if the report is run or scheduled. No special programming is required, regardless of the report viewer in use.

FILTERS   The Filters subsection enables you to set the default record selection expression for the report, shown in Figure 27.24. The default record selection is normally adopted from the original report file. In most cases, the default selection expression should be left intact, but it can be useful to override this feature for specific purposes. With a proper understanding of Crystal syntax, you can modify the Record Selection Formula or Group Selection Formula manually.

At the bottom of the Filters tab is a section for indicating which Processing Extensions the report uses. A *Processing Extension*, discussed in Chapter 24, "Crystal Enterprise Architecture," is an optional programmatic library for controlling the display of report data. Processing Extensions were new to Crystal Enterprise 8.5 but are now largely superseded by Business Views in Crystal Enterprise 10. (Refer to Chapter 18, "Crystal Reports Semantic Layter—Business Views," for a complete discussion of Business Views.)

PRINT SETUP   Although previous versions of Crystal Enterprise managed print settings through the Destinations area, Crystal Enterprise 10 exposes these controls via the Process tab on the Print subsection. Crystal Enterprise 10 enables you to print the scheduled report by checking the Print in Crystal Reports Format option and specifying the details on the

27

printer. Note that the printing occurs from the Job Server, so any network and other permissions must be configured on the appropriate Job Server(s). Note that this modality allows the job to be scheduled to the printer and a destination in the same run, thereby letting you schedule to an archiving system, for instance, which has a printer driver as its front-end image acquisition method.

Figure 27.24
The Filters subsection can be used to override the report's preconstructed record selection expression. You need a solid understanding of Crystal Reports record selection expression syntax to modify the default filter.

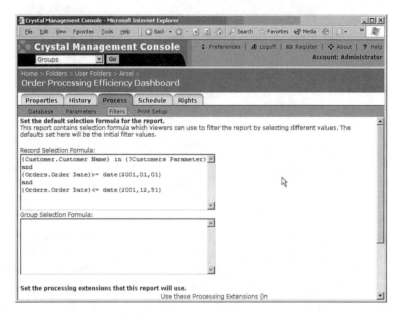

The bottom of this section enables you to set whether you want to use the print options stored in the report itself during report creation, the default printer options, or set custom options for that object.

MANAGING OBJECT PROCESSING SCHEDULES

The Schedule tab enables you to schedule the report to run at selected times (see Figure 27.25). The CMC provides this feature as a matter of convenience so the administrator doesn't have to refer to the Web Desktop for scheduling. When scheduling a report, the number of retries allowed (and the retry interval in seconds) can be specified before the report instance is marked as failed.

New in Crystal Enterprise 10, the calendar option schedules based on calendars stored in the system. A fuller discussion of calendars follows later in this chapter.

NOTIFICATION   Crystal Enterprise 10 offers two methods of notification around specific jobs, in addition to the general audit logging options available in the system. The notification can audit on successful and failed jobs, and e-mail notification can also be sent, perhaps to an administrator's pager to call attention to a particular failure or success.

Figure 27.25
The Schedule tab provides the same report scheduling functionality as the Web Desktop.

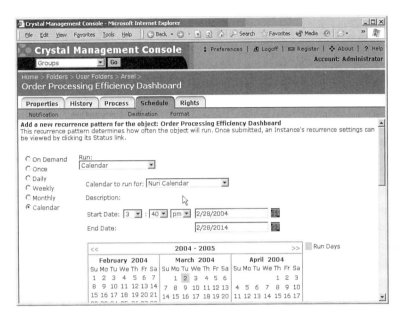

ALERT NOTIFICATION   Many organizations today work to streamline management practices and manage against goals. Thus management by exception increases daily in popularity. To fulfill the potential of this method, Crystal Enterprise sends e-mails when alerts have been triggered on reports, enabling users to receive notification when measured values are out of bounds and trigger a report alert, making it simple to manage actual results in real-time. Note that a link back to the triggering report can be composed at the bottom of the screen.

→ For a description of how to create alerts in reports, **see** "Adding Alerting to Your Reports" **p. 255**

DESTINATIONS   Crystal Enterprise version 10 supports scheduling to destinations. You can specify a default destination, shown in Figure 27.26, for the report output on the Destination subarea. The default destination is the Crystal Enterprise FRS. This is generally the preferred destination for all report instances because the report maintains its status as a managed object within Crystal Enterprise.

However, the administrator can configure Crystal Enterprise to output the report's instances to a network folder using the Unmanaged Disk option, for example. Crystal Enterprise also supports FTP (File Transfer Protocol), which is useful for transmitting the report instances to a remote destination, such as an archiving system. Another option, Email (SMTP) is a popular solution for distributing reports as an e-mail attachment.

NOTE

> The Crystal Enterprise Job Server must have a destination enabled for destination scheduling features to work. Job Server destinations are configured from the Servers section of the CMC, covered later in this chapter

27

Figure 27.26
Destinations enable you to specify a default output location for all new scheduled instances of the report. Supported destinations include network shares, FTP, and SMTP e-mail.

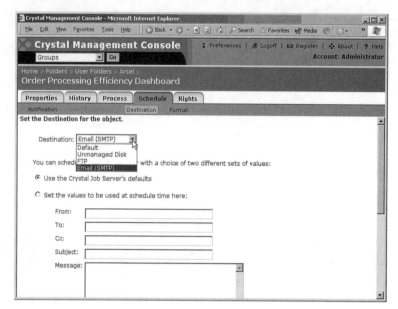

DETERMINING REPORT FILE FORMATS

Not to be confused with the format or look and feel of a report, report formats imply a file format. The Format subsection, shown in Figure 27.27, enables you to specify a default output format for the report. Keep in mind that certain cosmetic report formatting features might not be supported by every export format. Also, proprietary Crystal Report features, such as drill-down and on-demand subreports, are supported only in the native Crystal Report format. These special features are ignored when exporting a report to a non-Crystal format.

OBJECT RIGHTS

The Rights tab, shown in Figure 27.28, is used to grant report access/restrictions to different users and user groups. By default, report objects inherit the same rights as their parent folder.

TIP

> Much like managing groups is more effective than managing individual users, it's much easier to set restrictions for those groups by folder rather than by report objects themselves.

The Rights tab lists all the users and groups with permissions explicitly defined for the current report object. Note that if a group is not listed, permissions have not been defined for the group.

Figure 27.27
Use the Format sub-section to specify the default output format for the report. Popular output formats include Excel, Adobe Acrobat PDF, Word, and CSV (Character-Separated Values).

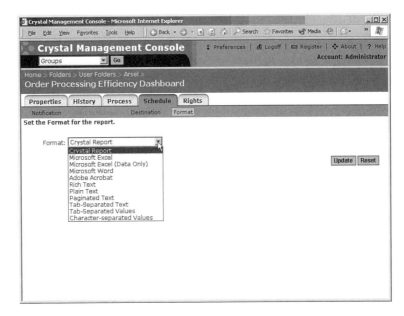

Figure 27.28
Report privileges are assigned on the Rights tab. The Crystal Enterprise administrator can use rights to define permissible actions for each user and user group.

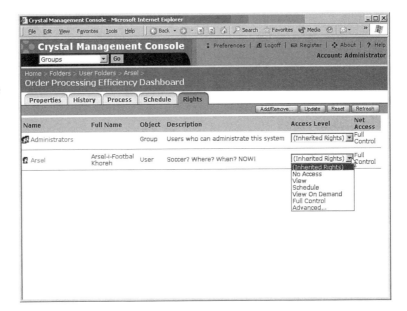

The *Everyone* group and the *Administrators* group are automatically attached to all new objects and folders in the system, and cannot be removed. Note that the rights build on each other: A lower bullet in this list includes the rights above it.

Each user or group can be assigned one of the following rights:

- Inherited Rights—The user or group inherits the parent folder's rights. This is the default setting for all new objects.

- No Access—The user or group is not aware of the object's existence. Note that this setting also would hide this object from any delegated administrators based on the new delegated administration feature.

- View—This setting enables the user or group to view instances scheduled by other users. On-demand viewing and scheduling is not available.

- Schedule—Allows the scheduling of the object as well as the previously listed rights.

- View on Demand—The user or group has View rights in addition to the capability to run the report on demand.

- Full Control—The user or group is granted all privileges except the capability to delete, hold, and release their own instances.

- Advanced—This option enables you to set detailed, specific permissions for the user or group, and is generally reserved for only the most complex security models.

In most organizational security models, the Everyone group is assigned the No Access privilege, or the parent folder's permissions are set to No Access for the Everyone group. Doing so prevents users from accessing an object unless access is specifically granted through another user group.

Permissions in Crystal Enterprise are cumulative. In other words, the net rights of a user are equal to the sum of the permissions granted to the user. To further clarify this point, consider the permissions scenario in Table 27.1.

TABLE 27.1 DERIVING NET SALES FOLDER PERMISSIONS FROM GROUP MEMBERSHIP

Group	Folder	Assigned Rights
Everyone	Sales	No Access
Sales	Sales	Run
Management	Sales	Full Control

Because permissions are cumulative, the net rights of each user are equal to the sum of the rights assigned to each group to which the user belongs (see Table 27.2).

A user's net permissions are determined by combining the rights they inherit from their group memberships. By combining permissions derived from group memberships, Crystal Enterprise enables a user to have access to the Sales folder as long as at least one of their group memberships permits it. Table 27.2 illustrates why the user Nicole is allowed Full Control of the Sales folder, even though the Everyone group is denied access as defined in Table 27.1.

User	Everyone	Sales	Management	Net Permissions
Navar	X	X	X	Full Control
Garbo	X			No Access
Kevvan	X	X		Run
Arsel	X		X	Full Control

TABLE 27.2   GROUP MEMBERSHIPS AND THEIR NET PERMISSIONS FOR THE SALES FOLDER

DIFFERENT OBJECT TYPES

Crystal Enterprise 10 includes support for several new object types (refer to Figure 27.15 for a complete list). Note that each of these objects has more or fewer configuration areas depending on the inherent type of object. For instance, a program object can be scheduled, while a Word document cannot.

MANAGING FOLDERS

Without exception, each report object in Crystal Enterprise must reside inside a folder. A folder in Crystal Enterprise is analogous to a folder on a Windows-based workstation or server. Many objects can populate a single folder, and folders can be nested inside other folders.

In general, the Crystal Enterprise folder hierarchy and report management behaves just like a standard network file system. The difference between the folder hierarchy in Crystal Enterprise and a standard network folder hierarchy is that any information about the folders is stored in the Crystal Enterprise system database, which can be queried to retrieve object information.

You can access folder management tasks by selecting Folders from the CMC's drop-down menu and clicking Go. The Folders screen in Figure 27.29 appears with a listing of all top-level folders in the folder hierarchy tree. You can click a folder name to see a list of all the reports the folder contains.

NOTE

> The Users folder contains a private subfolder for each Crystal Enterprise user. These personal folders store users' favorite reports, if an application such as the Web Desktop allows for it.

27

To add a new top-level folder, click the New Folder button. On the Properties tab, shown in Figure 27.30, type the folder name. The folder name can include spaces and should be descriptive for end users because they often navigate folders themselves. The Crystal Enterprise administrator can also type a freeform description. After entering a new folder name, click the OK button to commit the change to the system database. Four additional tabs for configuring the folder are now available.

Figure 27.29
The Folders screen displays all top-level Crystal Enterprise folders. You can navigate to the entire folder hierarchy from here.

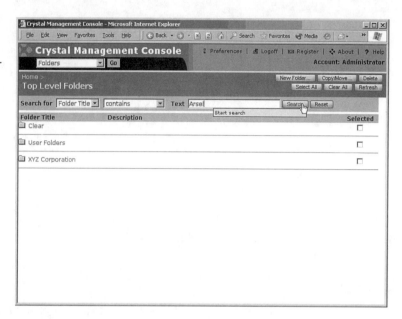

Figure 27.30
From the New Folder screen you can create a new folder, add reports and subfolders, specify instance expiration limits, and set folder rights.

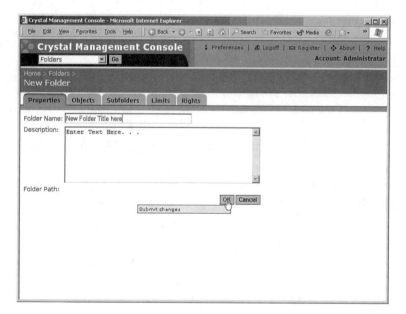

ADDING OBJECTS TO FOLDERS

Use the Objects tab, shown in Figure 27.31, to add new objects to the folder or copy, move, shortcut, and delete objects. Administrators often also use folders to navigate to objects via this route.

Figure 27.31
The Objects tab is used to add new reports to a folder. You can also manage existing objects from this screen.

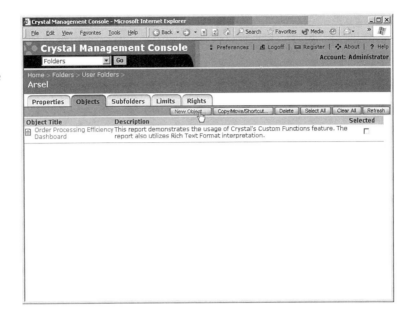

NOTE

The Copy function duplicates an object and assigns the duplicate object a slightly different filename on the FRS; the Shortcut function creates a duplicate report listing that points to the same filename on the FRS (similar to Windows file shortcuts). The Move function relocates the report to another folder.

The Subfolders tab in Figure 27.32 enables you to create and manage subfolders of the current top-level folder. Subfolders are useful for subcategorizing reports. Each subfolder can also have one or more child folders. Like a file system, the nesting of folders can traverse as many levels as necessary to convey the hierarchy of an organization.

FOLDER LIMITS

The Limits tab, shown in Figure 27.33, controls instance expiration limits for reports contained within the folder. Note that report object limits (if specified) take precedence over folder limits. Folder limits only take precedence over global limits.

NOTE

Report object limits take precedence over folder limits, and folder limits take precedence over global limits.

The Rights tab, shown in Figure 27.34, is used to control access to objects. The rights provided at the folder level are the same as those provided on the object level. (Refer to object rights for a definition of each option.) Instead of trying to manage rights for each individual report object, it's usually easier to secure reports by specifying rights at the folder level only. Report objects always inherit the rights of their parent folder, unless exceptions are configured at the object level shown in Figure 27.34.

Figure 27.32
You can use the Subfolders tab to add one or more subfolders to a top-level folder. In turn, each subfolder can have one or more subfolders (nested subfolders).

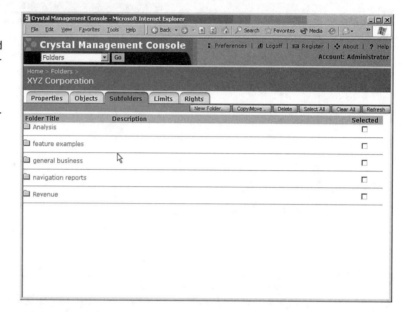

Figure 27.33
Like report objects, folders can be configured to override the global instance expiration limits.

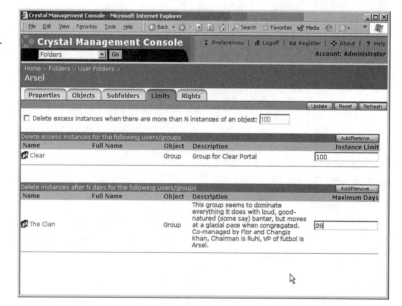

Figure 27.34
Any rights specified on the Rights tab are inherited by new objects. Unless an object has object-level rights specifically configured, it inherits the rights of its parent folder.

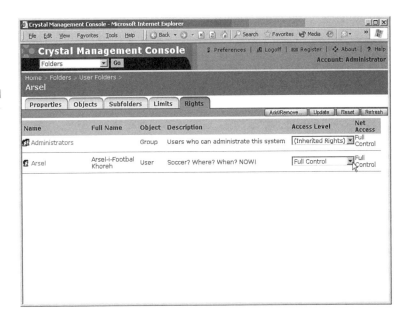

Note that with the addition of Delegated Administration, the CMC hides folders depending on folder rights. For instance, if an HR analyst logs on to the CMC, he does not see the Sales folder if the Sales folder Rights are set to disallow the HR analyst view rights. If a user doesn't have folder rights, he doesn't see any Folder information at all.

INTRODUCING SERVERS

Crystal Enterprise is built on the Crystal Enterprise Framework. At a high level, the Framework provides a communications bus between the various services or daemons that make up Crystal Enterprise.

Services or daemons, in the Windows or Unix environments respectively, are compartmentalized processes that perform a specific task. The use of individual services affords fault-tolerance (service redundancy), load-balancing, scalability, and greater system reliability. Crystal Enterprise uses the generic term "server" to refer to these services or daemons; for instance "Job Server." For simplicity, this book uses the product nomenclature: that is, server. The reader should realize that servers in this case are not physical machines. Please see Chapter 24 for additional discussion on this topic.

CONFIGURING SERVERS

Managing Crystal Enterprise servers is straightforward with the CMC. You can use the CMC to stop, start, restart, and manage various services from almost any location on the network.

To manage servers, select Servers from the CMC drop-down menu. Figure 27.35 shows a standard list of Crystal Enterprise servers in the CMC. Buttons in the upper-right corner enable you to start, stop, restart, delete, disable, or enable any server on the framework. Additionally, the Crystal Enterprise administrator can specify the order of the servers list by clicking on the column heading to specify a sort order.

Figure 27.35
All configured servers (services) in Crystal Enterprise can be managed from the CMC.

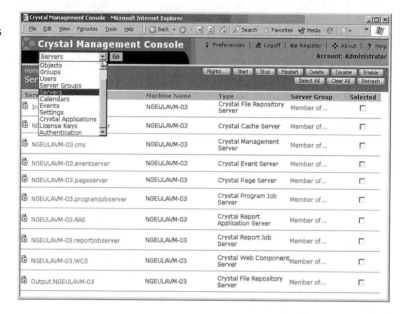

NOTE

A disabled server cannot be started until it is enabled, even if the machine is rebooted. Disabling a server can be useful for, among other things, temporarily interrupting the server's availability while maintenance tasks or hardware repairs are performed.

Clicking on each server navigates to the server settings area. The Properties tab provides server-specific management controls. The metrics tab shows a wide range of information about the performance of the server and the physical machine on which it resides (see Figure 27.36). The Rights tab again provides a way for delegated administration to take place because the system administrator can allow area administrators to have access to certain servers but not others. Finally the Auditing tab, when available, determines which features on each server are audited (see Chapter 24 for a complete discussion of auditing capabilities).

MANAGING THE WEB COMPONENT SERVER

The Web Component Server (WCS) has several configuration options available from the Properties tab shown in Figure 27.37. To access this tab, click the WCS name on the main Servers page.

Figure 27.36
Performance and
server resource data
is displayed on the
Metrics tab for each
Crystal Enterprise ser-
vice. This information
can be used to moni-
tor the activity of each
service.

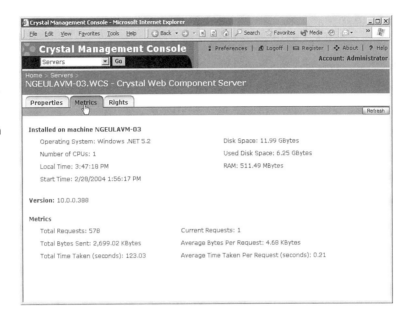

Figure 27.37
The Properties tab for
the Crystal WCS fea-
tures several options
for controlling logging
and report viewer
availability.

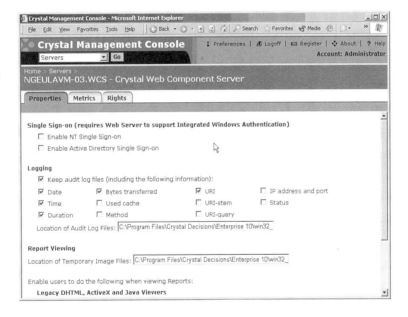

Various logging options for recording WCS activity are also displayed. Generally these
should be left unchanged except for specific troubleshooting purposes. Excessive logging
consumes system resources unnecessarily.

NOTE

> The WCS logs can be an excellent source of data for system auditing, such as which users are viewing certain reports. Consider building a Crystal Report from the WCS logs. Business Objects provides some prebuilt WCS log reports as well.

Options for managing report viewer availability and behavior are located at the bottom of the Web Component Server Properties page. These options enable a Crystal Enterprise administrator to specify which actions (drill-down, print, zoom, export, search, and so on) users can perform in the different report viewers.

Remember to click either Update or Apply to commit the changes. Changes to the WCS configuration do not take effect until the WCS service is restarted.

MANAGING THE CACHE SERVER

To adjust the settings for the Cache Server, click the Cache Server name from the main Servers screen. The Properties tab shown in Figure 27.38 appears for the Cache Server. The Location of Cache Files field contains the path to the actual cached report files. This path is local to the Cache Server machine. The Maximum Cache Size Allowed field specifies the maximum size of the cache directory. When the threshold has been exceeded, Crystal Enterprise deletes the oldest, least-used cache files first. Preserving old cache files is not critical because missing cache files can be rebuilt on-the-fly, transparent to the user.

Figure 27.38
The Crystal Cache Server's Properties tab enables you to control the cache performance.

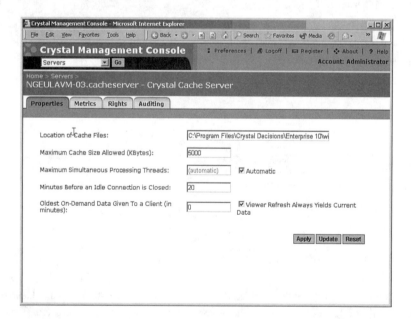

The Maximum Simultaneous option restricts the number of application threads that can be spawned concurrently by the cache server. A processing thread is responsible for converting .rpt pages into cache pages. In most cases, it's not necessary to adjust the automatic setting.

The Minutes Before an Idle Connection option causes the cache server to release a stale cache page from RAM to make room for other cache pages. The cache page is still physically stored on the disk, but it's no longer kept in RAM. By default, cached pages that have not been requested for 20 minutes are released from RAM and will have to be reloaded from the disk if they are requested again.

Oldest On-Demand Data controls the persistence of cached pages for on-demand reports. For example, assume that John requests an on-demand copy of the World Sales Report at 3:00 p.m. A few minutes later, at 3:04 p.m., Jane requests an on-demand copy of the World Sales Report with exactly the same parameters and record selection formula as John specified—an identical report in every way. In this case Crystal Enterprise serves Jane the same cached pages that John loaded only moments before. This has the benefit of giving Jane the fastest possible response time while relieving the database and Page Server of additional processing work. By default, on-demand cached pages expire after 20 minutes.

Keep in mind that users have the option to hit the database and rerun the report by clicking the Refresh button within the report viewer. The Viewer Refresh Always Yields option causes the report to be rerun against the database, not the cached data, if the user clicks the Refresh button within the report viewer. Normally, this option should remain enabled to give users the flexibility to "freshen" the report data at their convenience.

MANAGING THE EVENT SERVER

The Event Server, as explained in Chapter 24, is designed to allow Crystal Enterprise to interact with events external to the system. Events are conditions that trigger report processing to occur. The Crystal Event Server polls the system at set intervals to determine whether any configured events have been triggered. This is shown in Figure 27.39.

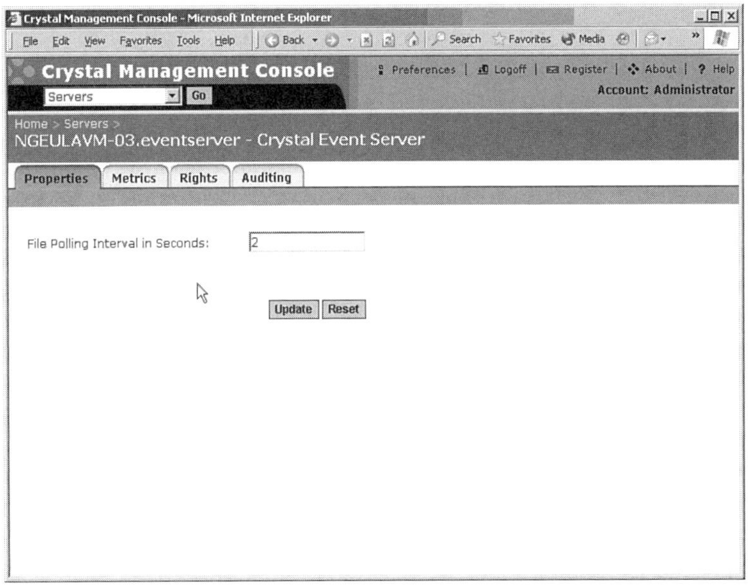

Figure 27.39
The Event Server periodically polls the system to check for triggered events. Setting a short poll interval value could negatively affect system performance.

The File Polling Interval in Seconds option enables you to control the frequency of the Event Server's polling process. A lower value results in faster recognition of triggered events, but it also expends CPU cycles that might otherwise be devoted to more important tasks. A value of 10–60 seconds between system polls is generally acceptable.

MANAGING THE PAGE SERVER

The Crystal Page Server handles on-demand report requests. The Properties tab of the Page Server has several options for controlling Page Server performance, as shown in Figure 27.40. The Maximum Simultaneous Processing Threads setting controls the maximum number of concurrent application threads allowed. On-demand reports consume a minimum of one processing thread; if all available threads are busy, Crystal Enterprise queues any excess threads for processing on a first-come, first-served basis.

Figure 27.40
The Crystal Page Server is responsible for processing on-demand report requests.

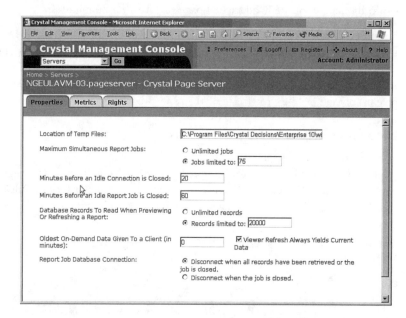

The Minutes Before an Idle Connection Is Closed option affects the persistence of open Page Server jobs. For example, if a user starts to view an on-demand report and walks away from her desk without closing the report viewer, the job is left open until the specified period of inactivity has passed. If the user does not request any new pages within the default 20-minute window, the job is closed. New page or drill-down requests reset the 20-minute job expiration timer.

MANAGING THE JOB SERVERS

The Maximum Jobs Allowed setting in Figure 27.41 affects the maximum number of reports that the Job Server can execute simultaneously. A setting of five concurrent report jobs is generally considered a harmonious balance between report throughput and server resources. Each concurrent report thread consumes significant system resources, not only in CPU cycles, but also in temporary disk space use, RAM overhead, and database resources. A robust multiprocessor machine with 2GB of RAM can comfortably process 10 jobs simultaneously. However, most servers run best with five or fewer concurrent jobs.

Figure 27.41
The Job Server processes scheduled jobs only. You can specify the number of jobs the Job Server can simultaneously process.

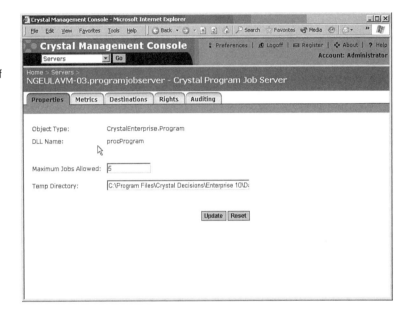

MANAGING THE CRYSTAL MANAGEMENT SERVER

The Crystal Management Server (CMS) is responsible for object and user security as well as scheduling of jobs. The CMS is the brain of Crystal Enterprise.

In addition to its role in enforcing object permissions, the CMS monitors and records the processing status of every scheduled job. The Properties tab of the CMS displays a listing of all currently connected users, as well as the number of sessions opened by each user ID (see Figure 27.42). Note that most of the time, a user ID has only one session open. However, it's possible for two people to log in with the same user ID from different computers, in which case the user ID would reflect two concurrent sessions. Each session consumes a license until the user logs off, or the session is released after 20 minutes of inactivity.

Possibly the most critical feature of the CMS is clustering. Crystal Enterprise includes out-of-the-box clustering capability for the CMS. This means that without any special hardware, two physical CMS servers can be clustered together. If one becomes unavailable, the other CMS supports authentication requests and scheduling tasks. CMS clustering is reviewed in the "Managing Crystal Enterprise System Settings" section of this chapter.

27

Figure 27.42
The CMS handles object and user security, as well as management of report instances.

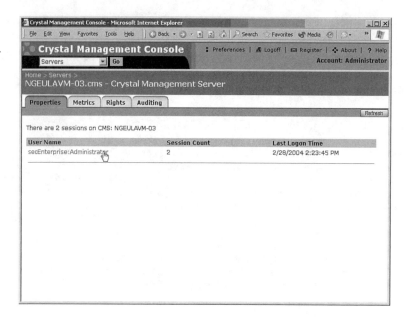

MANAGING THE INPUT/OUTPUT FILE REPOSITORY SERVERS

File Repository Servers (FRS) are services that manage the storage and retrieval of report files from the file system. Crystal Enterprise has an Input FRS and an Output FRS. Both FRS systems store report files using a proprietary naming convention. For example, the report template for the World Sales Report might be named 73422e16f293d0.rpt by the Input FRS. Any instances of the World Sales Report would be assigned a similarly cryptic name by the Output FRS. Both FRS servers store name translation information in the CMS system database, enabling users to see the true English name of a report instead of the cryptic file system name.

The Properties tab in Figure 27.43 for the Input and Output FRS has two configuration options. The Root Directory field stores the path of the physical file repository on the server's file system. This path is local to the FRS server. The Input FRS stores .rpt templates in one folder, whereas the Output FRS stores .rpt instances in another folder. Both servers also have a Maximum Idle Time option that controls the amount of time that an idle .rpt file remains cached in the FRS memory. When the idle time expires, the .rpt files are dropped from the memory cache and must be loaded from disk if required again.

MANAGING SERVER GROUPS

A large Crystal Enterprise deployment can have several physical Page and Job Servers spread over a wide area network. Some of the servers might have more processing power than others, and some might be located in specific regions such as San Francisco and New York. In multiple-server environments, it's often advantageous to categorize servers into specific groups. Server groups are helpful for managing processing just as user groups help manage permissions.

Figure 27.43
The Input and Output File Repository Servers have the same Properties tab settings. Note that a special tab called Active Files displays any .rpt files currently in the memory cache.

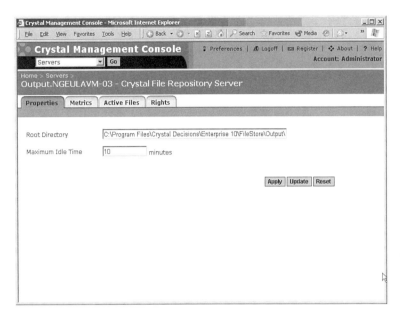

After a server group has been created, the Crystal Enterprise administrator can configure reports to process on specific server groups. For example, the CEO's personal reports could be configured to execute on a server group that contains one or more high-powered Job/Page Servers. This would ensure that the CEO's reports always process on the most powerful servers available, and thereby finish running as quickly as possible. Without server groups, the CEO's reports might get routed to a slower Job/Page Server, and the CEO would end up spending more time than necessary waiting for critical information. Server groups are also useful for forcing reports to execute on a Job/Page Server that is in close proximity to the report's database server.

To create a server group, select Server Groups from the drop-down menu in the CMC. Click New Server Group, and then type the name of the server group in the Server Group Name field. An optional Description for the server group can also be entered. Click the OK button to add the new server group to Crystal Enterprise. Figure 27.44 shows a server group.

MANAGING CALENDARS

The predecessor to Crystal Enterprise included a very popular feature for scheduled processing: business calendars. Simply put, this feature allows processing to take place based on specific calendars. Calendars can be configured by administrators and then selected by users for scheduling purposes.

Click on the *Calendars* icon from the home page of the CMC to enter the Calendars area.

27

NOTE

> The Calendars area has a rights button at the upper right to set delegated administration privileges. Setting permissions here controls access to this area in the CMC.

Figure 27.44
Server groups are configured like user groups. You can create groups and add servers to them. A server can reside in more than one group, and a group can also have several subgroups.

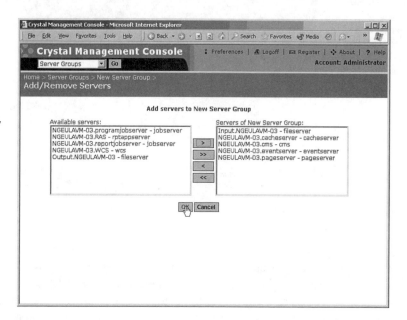

You can add new calendars or manage current calendars here. Like most objects in Crystal Enterprise, you see a simple *Properties* tab and *Rights* tab, which operate like the other tabs of those titles. The *Dates* tab, however, provides the heart of the functionality by allowing the administrator to configure a calendar. By clicking on months to enter that month, then clicking on days to select/de-select a day, the administrator sets days on which processing should occur. By simply clicking on a day you change the current setting, clicking on a row or column header selects that area. The drop-down at the top also exposes other calendar configuration types to allow tailoring to another calendaring option—for instance, a quarterly fiscal calendar with a set alternating number of weeks in a "fiscal month" that does not align with calendar months. That way you could configure a financial report to run on the first day of every quarter or fiscal month, for instance.

After calendars are configured, the administrator or end users would schedule reports using the Calendar option from the scheduling page.

MANAGING EVENTS

Although I touch on Events in the discussion of servers, the administrator must set up events before they can schedule against them. The Events link from the home page navigates to the Events area, where you can add new events. There are three types of events. The File event polls for a certain file in a certain location to appear. The Schedule event polls for success or failure of another scheduled object. The custom event provides a programmatic hook that can be triggered by a program written against the SDK to provide a programmatic interface into the scheduling system. Once created, events can be used for scheduling as per the previous section.

MANAGING CRYSTAL ENTERPRISE SYSTEM SETTINGS

The Crystal Enterprise Settings area contains a number of systemwide settings that aren't specific to a particular server. Information on system properties, metrics, clustering, instance limits, and user rights are available in this section. To configure system settings, select Settings from the Crystal drop-down menu in the CMC.

MANAGING AUTHENTICATION

There are two key components to managing Crystal Enterprise authentication:

- Licensing
- Authentication

The first one is a less technical topic but still important to understand. The second is discussed in subsequent sections.

MANAGING LICENSING

The License Keys tab displays important information about each license key (see Figure 27.45). Highlight a license key to display specific information about the key. Crystal Enterprise supports three types of licenses: named licenses, concurrent licenses, and processor licenses.

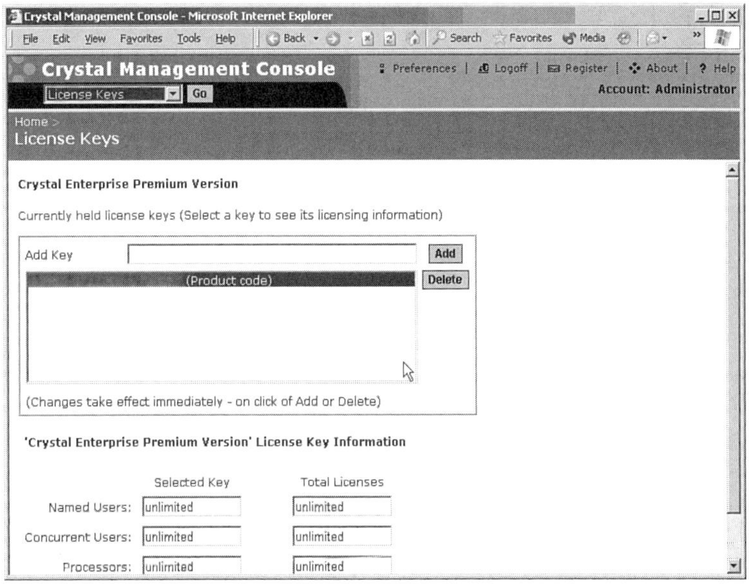

Figure 27.45
The License Keys tab provides information about each of the Crystal Enterprise license keys.

27

NOTE

> The license certificate keys determine the number and type of licenses available (name user or concurrent access). During the initial install of Crystal Enterprise, a license key was entered. Additional licenses can be added to Crystal Enterprise from the License Keys tab on the Authentication section of the CMC.

Crystal Enterprise gives you the flexibility to mix and match named and concurrent license types. *Named licenses* are assigned to specific users. Any number of named licenses can be simultaneously logged in to the system.

Concurrent licenses permit an unlimited number of named users to be added to the Crystal Enterprise, but only a certain number of those users can access the system simultaneously.

Processor licenses enable an unlimited number of both named and concurrent users for a specific processor. Processor licenses are most efficient in high-powered server environments where the server CPU is robust enough to support a large number of concurrent users.

It's best to contact Business Objects and discuss the optimum licensing strategy for your organization.

MANAGING AUTHENTICATION

The different types of authentication that can be leveraged with Crystal Enterprise are also found under the Authorization portion of the CMC.

Crystal Enterprise provides several authentication models for providing secure report access, including Native Crystal Enterprise authentication, Windows NT Authentication, Active Directory authentication, and LDAP authentication. Crystal Enterprise supports single sign-on for both the Windows NT and Active Directory methods, so users won't have to constantly enter credentials after exiting and reentering the system.

The reason Crystal Enterprise supports more security models than its own is simple: If an IT organization has already implemented an existing security model, why re-create certain entities such as user accounts and passwords?

Fortunately, none of these options is mutually exclusive; they can all be used simultaneously. This can cause some management headaches, so proceed with caution. Every topic in this chapter up until this point has used native Crystal Enterprise security as an example.

This does not imply that if Windows Active Directory authentication is used, for example, that administration is done exclusively from Active Directory. It simply implies that objects such as user accounts and passwords can be maintained within Active Directory, yet Crystal Enterprise feeds off those existing accounts when users try to retrieve reports. The configuration of Crystal Enterprise groups and objects, as well as relevant restrictions to those objects, are still created and configured from the CMC, in the same way that this chapter has shown. This is reviewed in greater detail later.

To configure system authentication settings, select Authentication from the drop-down menu in the CMC.

CRYSTAL ENTERPRISE AUTHENTICATION   Crystal Enterprise provides its own native security model. This means that Crystal Enterprise is not dependent on a foreign, third-party security database to configure and restrict access to any system function, object, or entity. The Crystal Enterprise authentication model is the default model. To leverage another security database, select the appropriate tab.

Selecting the Enterprise tab, shown in Figure 27.46, enables you to enforce password rules when using Crystal Enterprise authentication. You can use this tab to control the frequency that users are forced to change their passwords, as well as the length of the passwords and whether or not the password must contain mixed-case letters.

Figure 27.46
You can set Crystal Enterprise password expiration rules on the Enterprise tab. This tab only applies to the Crystal Enterprise native authentication method, not LDAP or Windows NT.

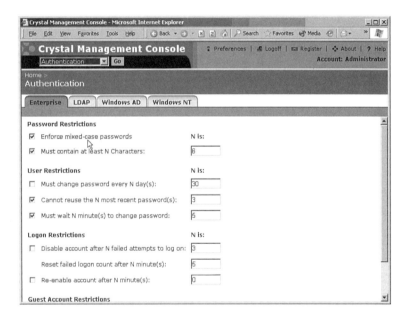

In general, the password options offered are similar to those provided by the Windows NT and Solaris operating systems.

DIRECTORY SERVER AUTHENTICATION THROUGH LDAP   Selecting the LDAP tab enables a system administrator to configure LDAP connectivity to a directory server, as shown in Figure 27.47. LDAP (Lightweight Directory Access Protocol) enables a network administrator to maintain a central directory server for managing user access to a variety of applications and operating systems. Crystal Enterprise can be configured to work with a variety of directory servers via LDAP. Crystal Enterprise support for LDAP was designed and tested to the LDAP version 3 specification.

Crystal Enterprise can tie into an LDAP server for User and Group information. Folder and Object permissions (that is, authorization) are still defined within Crystal Enterprise.

27

When Crystal Enterprise is tied to an LDAP server, equivalent Crystal Enterprise accounts are either created, if they don't already exist, or aliased if they do exist. The Crystal Enterprise system must have references to users and groups inside the system such that report object restrictions can be configured. User passwords are not stored in Crystal Enterprise. When using LDAP, it's the job of the directory server to verify passwords. Any time a user attempts to access Crystal Enterprise resources, a password confirmation request is sent to the directory server. If the user authenticates properly, Crystal Enterprise then compares the user's group membership and associated privileges assigned to those groups in Crystal Enterprise.

Figure 27.47
Configuring LDAP enables Crystal Enterprise to connect to a Directory server, such as Netscape iPlanet, and leverage existing usernames and passwords.

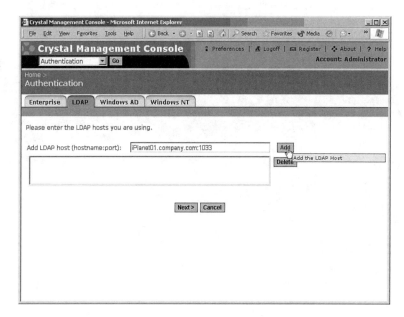

If, for example, a large number of users and groups were added to the directory server and the Crystal Enterprise administrator needed to configure Crystal Enterprise security settings, clicking the Update button on the LDAP page forces synchronization.

WINDOWS NT OR ACTIVE DIRECTORY AUTHENTICATION   Crystal Enterprise provides the capability to tie in user authentication to the Windows NT or Active Directory security model. If the primary network operating system and application authentication method in an organization is Windows NT or Active Directory, this feature can be a useful timesaver. Although there are material differences between the methods, they are similar enough to be discussed as Windows authentication.

Windows authentication can be configured from the Windows AD or NT tabs, as shown in Figure 27.48. To enable Windows authentication, select the Is Enabled option. Enter the name of the Default Domain. The default domain should be the same domain that contains the majority of the Windows users that will also be Crystal Enterprise end users.

Figure 27.48
Selecting the Windows AD tab enables you to configure Crystal Enterprise to support Active Directory authentication.

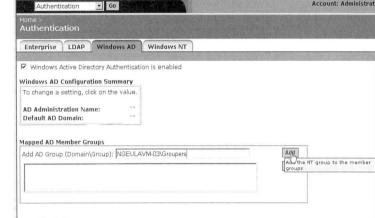

Users who do not have accounts in the specified default domain need to specify their domain name each time they log in to Crystal Enterprise.

The Mapped Member Groups section enables specification of which Windows user groups are permitted to access Crystal Enterprise. Any Windows users who belong to mapped Windows member groups are able to log in to Crystal Enterprise using single sign on.

Users who are not a member of at least one mapped Windows group will not be able to access Crystal Enterprise unless the administrator has specifically created a Crystal Enterprise user ID for them in the CMC. To import a new Windows group to Crystal Enterprise, type in the name of the Windows group (preceded by the group's domain or machine name) and click the Add button. Remember to click the Update button when you're finished adding or removing Windows groups.

The bottom of the Windows tab has two additional options for configuring NT integration. Assign Each Added Windows Alias to an Account with the Same Name forces Crystal Enterprise to match imported Windows usernames with existing Crystal Enterprise usernames. If Crystal Enterprise already has a username with the same name as an incoming Windows username, the two usernames are mapped to each other so that a duplicate account name is not created. In other words, an alias is created.

On the other hand, the Create a New Account for Every Added Windows Alias option causes Crystal Enterprise to add a new Crystal Enterprise username for each incoming Windows username. If a duplicate username exists in Crystal Enterprise, an alias is not created; instead, a new username is created with a slightly different name. When the group is added, navigate to the Manage Groups section of the CMC. Note that \\NGEULAVM-03\RUHI

27

is now listed as a group within Crystal Enterprise. Selecting this user group allows access to the same options as a native Crystal Enterprise group.

MANAGING CRYSTAL APPLICATIONS

New to Crystal Enterprise 10, the configuration of applications via a central location simplifies system administration. For instance, setting default colors or preferences (even setting a custom logo for the Web desktop!) can be accomplished from this location. As more applications, such as the Ad-Hoc application, are installed, these applications also add to this section.

By default, the Web Desktop area appears to allow configuration of the Web Desktop's preferences (see Chapter 23 for more information on the Web Desktop, and Chapter 21 for more information on the Ad-Hoc Application). These settings become global for this installation.

USING THE CRYSTAL CONFIGURATION MANAGER

The Crystal Configuration Manager (CCM) is a Windows-based tool installed on the Crystal Enterprise server by default (see Figure 27.49). A CCM script (ccm.sh) is also available for the Unix version of Crystal Enterprise. Although the "interface" discussion that follows does not apply to the ccm.sh, all the capabilities are present and can be accessed. Please refer to your Crystal Enterprise documentation for specific command-line options.

Figure 27.49
The CCM enables you to restart and configure Crystal services as well as configure the Web Connector.

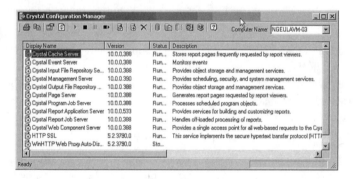

The Crystal Enterprise administrator can use the Crystal Configuration to start and stop Crystal Services on the local machine or remote machines, as well as configure the Web Connector, CMS database, and Audit database, and add and register new servers to the Framework.

TIP

> You can use the CCM to administer several Crystal Enterprise servers remotely by changing the computer name.

To start the CCM, click Start, Programs, Crystal Enterprise 10, Crystal Configuration Manager. When the CCM loads, it displays a list of all Crystal Enterprise services running on the current machine, as well as the World Wide Web Publishing Service and associated services if the machine runs Microsoft IIS. The name of the current machine is indicated in the upper-right corner of the CCM. To administer another Crystal Enterprise server, type in a new server name and press Enter. The drop-down box of server names maintains a list of each server visited. A Crystal Enterprise administrator can also click the Browse for Computer icon to select a different machine.

To start, stop, pause, or restart Crystal services, highlight a service name, and then click the appropriate icon at the top of the screen. Note that you can also select several Crystal services at once by using the Shift or Ctrl select methods. One interesting fact about the CCM is the use of command-line options to start various Crystal Enterprise servers. To view the command line used to start up a given server, such as the Web Component Server, right-click the service name and choose Properties. Notice that the dialog title Command Line shows the server startup command as well as potential parameters supplied to the server service.

Starting up servers from a command line can be a useful approach to solving or troubleshooting problems that might arise. More will be discussed on server startup command lines later.

To view the properties of a service, right-click on the service and select Properties from the drop-down menu. Note that the Crystal Enterprise administrator must stop the service first to make changes to the service's properties. From the Properties dialog, the Crystal Enterprise administrator can change the NT account used to run the service, and also view the service's dependencies. Depending on the service, the administrator might also be able to specify a communication port, although the default port is normally acceptable.

The Crystal Enterprise administrator can also use the CCM to add or remove instances of a service. To remove a service, highlight the service name, and then click the delete icon at the top of the screen. To add a new instance of a service, click the Add Server icon. A wizard walks you through the steps of adding the new service.

CONFIGURING THE WEB CONNECTOR

The Web Connector resides on the Web server, intercepting .csp, .cwr, and .cwi requests and passing them on to the Web Component Server. To configure the Web Connector, start the CCM and be sure it's connected to the machine that has the Web Connector installed on it (this machine is always a Web server). Click the Configure Web Connector icon to start the configuration process.

A list of all configured WCS machines appears in the Web Component Servers box. If there is more than one Web Component Server, the Crystal Enterprise administrator must be sure that each one is listed here. If a Web Component Server is not listed, the Web Connector is not able to forward Crystal Enterprise requests to that server. To add a new WCS, click the Add button and type in the WCS Host Name. The WCS Host Name is the

27

same as the machine name on which the WCS resides. The Crystal Enterprise administrator also needs to specify a port number; the default port is 6401. If a SOCKs server must be specified, click the Specify SOCKS button. After you have finished typing in the required WCS information, click OK to add the new WCS to the available Web Component Servers box (see Figure 27.50).

Figure 27.50
Each Web Component Server must be identi-fied to the Web Connector. If a Web Component Server has not been identi-fied to the Web Connector, it is not used.

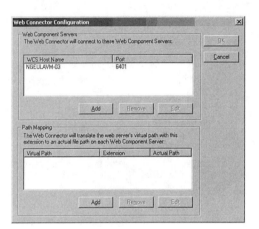

CONFIGURING CMS CLUSTERING FROM THE CONFIGURATION MANAGER

The CCM is also the location where the Crystal Enterprise CMS can be clustered. Clustering in Crystal Enterprise does not require any special hardware; it's software based. The CMS is the only server for which clustering is required because other servers, such as the Job Server, are managed from the CMS.

Crystal Enterprise could have two or more physical Job Servers and the CMS will actively load balance report processing tasks between those servers. If a Job Server fails, that CMS no longer sends report processing requests to that physical server.

As for CMS clustering, a few things are required for it to work:

- The CMS System database must be in a supported format such as Microsoft SQL Server. MSDE is not sufficient.
- Multiple CMS servers must be available.
- All CMS servers must connect to the same CMS database, and the connectivity options to the database must be identical.
- Multihomed CMS servers are supported, but special consideration is required. Refer to the Crystal Enterprise admin guide for more information on multihomed server sup-port.

After ensuring the system is properly configured and a backup of the CMS system database is complete, open the CCM, right-click on the CMS service, and choose Properties. Select the Configuration tab and check the Enable CMS Clustering box. The Clustering Wizard walks through the steps required to complete the CMS cluster. Afterward, the cluster name can be changed.

NOTE

> Crystal Enterprise refers to CMS clusters with the server name of the first server in the cluster preceded by the @ symbol. For example, @Era0441863 would be a CMS cluster name.

Command-line options can be specified by right-clicking the services, and then changing the command line. Note that the server must be stopped first.

NOTE

> Refer to the Crystal Enterprise Admin guide for a complete listing of all the various server command-line arguments that can be leveraged at server startup.

27

CUSTOMIZED REPORT DISTRIBUTION— USING CRYSTAL REPORTS COMPONENTS

CHAPTER 28

JAVA REPORTING COMPONENTS

In this chapter

OVERVIEW OF THE CRYSTAL REPORTS JAVA REPORTING COMPONENT

Business Objects has had a commitment to Java developers for quite some time. Crystal Reports version 9 included a Java edition of the Report Application Server Software Development Kit (SDK), and Crystal Enterprise version 8.5 had a Java edition of the Crystal Enterprise SDK. Both of these solutions consisted of a processing tier of non–Java-based services and then an application tier of Java-based objects that acted as the entry point to those services. The theme here was around multitier, large-scale, enterprise applications. This might sound quite natural to some Java developers, who would argue that's what Java is for.

In the version 10 suite of products, the Report Application Server and corresponding Java SDK have been moved out of the Crystal Reports product line and into the Crystal Enterprise product line. This makes it clear that all servers are part of the Crystal Enterprise offering. However, without any other changes this would leave the Crystal Reports product without any Java-based developer components. Because developers have always been important to Business Objects—especially Java developers—the Business Objects folks have spent a significant amount of time building a new offering in version 10 for Java developers: the Crystal Reports Java Reporting Component.

The key word in the name of the Java Reporting Component is "component." There is a clear distinction between the Crystal Reports–based developer solutions and the Crystal Enterprise–based developer solutions. This is based around the distinction between components and servers. Crystal Reports provides reporting components and Crystal Enterprise provides reporting servers. The following sections describe some of the key differences between components and servers.

COMPONENTS RUN ON THE WEB APPLICATION SERVER

Components are self-contained and reside on the Web application tier. They are single tier in that there is no separation between the programmatic interface and the report processing. Although they can be run on multiple machines in a Web application server farm, they themselves are individual components and have no built-in mechanism to load balance or share state.

Although this kind of deployment architecture is initially attractive to many Java developers, many eventually find that the report processing degrades the performance of the Web application server to an unsatisfactory level. Keep in mind the size of your user audience before deciding to do all report processing on the Web tier.

COMPONENTS ARE GENERALLY LESS SCALABLE

Although the actual report processing of a single report is generally done just as fast with a component as it is done with a server, the capability to scale the components differs. Although a farm can be created, components running on different machines are not aware of each other and thus don't have the smarts to figure out which component is least busy or has some information that is needed by another server. In general, the servers provide a more scalable, extensible solution for high-volume reporting. Obviously, cost can be a factor because the server solutions have higher licensing costs, so do your research about the product capabilities before you start development.

COMPONENTS ARE 100% PURE JAVA

Besides product line differentiation, the other reason Business Objects created the Java Reporting Component was so it would have a 100% pure Java reporting engine. Although the server solutions have a pure Java SDK, the Java Reporting Component consists entirely of native Java code. This is attractive to both Java purists and also partners who embed Crystal Reports technology inside Java-based applications, and finally for customers wanting to deploy a reporting component on a Unix platform. Providing a 100% pure Java reporting engine means Business Objects rewrote a portion of the Crystal Reports engine into Java. Because this was not a total port of the functionality, some reporting features are not available. However, in practical terms, most reports off standard relational data will run just fine.

UNDERSTANDING THE JAVA REPORTING COMPONENTS ARCHITECTURE

Now that you know why Business Objects created the Java Reporting Component and how it differs from some of the server solutions, you will move on to learning more about the components. The Java Reporting Component has three main pieces to it, as shown here:

- A report engine
- Report viewer controls
- Helper tag libraries

The report engine is the component that processes the reports. Its job is to load the report template (.rpt file), run the query to the data source, process the report's pages, and communicate with the report viewer controls to provide the information they need to render the reports. The main report viewer is an HTML viewer control that is used to display the report's output in JSP pages or servlets. The other viewer control is used to view the reports in other formats such as Rich Text Format (RTF) or PDF. Finally, there are helper tag libraries that make the process of using the report viewers easier by wrapping up their logic into a simple tag that can be inserted into JSP pages. Also of note is that the Java Reporting Component has integration with both Borland JBuilder and BEA WebLogic; more will be discussed on what this integration provides later in this chapter.

From an architecture point of view, all these components reside on the Java application server. The officially supported application servers are

- BEA WebLogic 7 (SP1)
- BEA WebLogic 8.1

28

- IBM WebSphere 5.0 (Fix-pack 2)
- Tomcat 4.1.27

NOTE

If the exact application server or version of application server you are targeting is not listed here, it does not necessarily mean that the Java Reporting Component will not work there. It just means that it was not one of the configurations explicitly tested by Business Objects, and although not "officially supported," chances are you will be able to use it. If you are unsure, contact Business Objects to see if they are aware of any issues with that particular application server. There are customers using other application servers such as JBoss in production today.

Although the Java Reporting Component comes with some JSP and servlet samples, the actual API is simply raw Java classes. These classes can be used inside of JSPs, servlets, EJBs, or other Web-based technologies. The advantage here is that there is no dependency on any particular version of the J2EE specifications such as servlets or struts. You might have noticed that desktop applications have not been mentioned thus far. This is because there is not currently a desktop viewer control (that is, based on the AWT or Swing frameworks). Because the viewer controls that exist are dependent on a Web framework being in place—they require servlet-based objects in order to work—there is currently no way to view reports in desktop applications. At the time of this writing, Business Objects has expressed interest in producing a desktop report viewer for the Java world at some point in the future. Check back with the company if you're interested. In the meantime, a good solution for delivering reports inside desktop applications is to host a Web browser applet inside of a Java form.

DIFFERENCES WITH THE JAVA REPORTING ENGINE

Although there are clear advantages to having a 100% pure Java reporting engine, the developers at Business Objects had to rewrite it from scratch. Anytime a large software component such as the Crystal Reports engine is rewritten, there are bound to be some differences, at least in the first version. Some of those differences are conscious decisions made by Business Objects to limit the scope of the development to meet the target release date. Other differences surface because of development platform differences: Java versus native Windows. The result is that some features are not currently supported by the report processing engine included with the Java Reporting Component. The following sections address some of these issues.

SUPPORTED FILE FORMATS

The first and most important limitation is that only version 9 and 10 report files are supported. This doesn't mean that reports designed in version 8.5 or earlier are useless, but it does mean they have to be converted to version 9. To make this process easier, you can download a Report Conversion Utility from the Business Objects Web site. It can open up reports in batch, make any necessary changes, and save them into a version 9/10 file format. New reports can be created using the standard Crystal Reports 10 designer.

TIP

> The file format has not had any major changes between version 9 and 10 of Crystal Reports. If you have report files created in version 10, you can generally use them in version 9 applications.

THE JAVA REPORTING ENGINE USES JDBC

Another difference related to the Java platform is the way queries are run against the database. Although the Windows world has many different data access technologies, Java has just one: Java Data Base Connectivity (JDBC). Previously, Crystal Reports did not support JDBC, but a new JDBC driver is available for version 10 as a Web site download.

NOTE

> At the time of this writing, the version 10 JDBC driver was not yet available but should be available for download shortly from the Business Objects Download Center found at `http://www.businessobjects.com/products/downloadcenter/`. Check the Web site for a status update.

For any new reports that you develop, choosing JDBC is generally the best approach. You will save yourself time and effort this way. The Crystal Reports JDBC driver shows up as "JDBC (JNDI)" in the Crystal Reports data explorer when creating a new report. It has two ways to connect to a data source: through a JDBC URL or a JNDI reference. This can be problematic at times because there are several steps involved in setting up your environment for JDBC access. Make sure you take your time going through the steps and double-check the changes you are making.

When connecting via a JDBC URL, you need to specify two items:

- Connection URL: a standard JDBC URL that specifies a data source
- Database classname: the fully qualified classname of the JDBC driver

The best way to figure out what these two values should be is to consult the documentation for the JDBC driver you'd like to use. The following bullets provide sample connection information for connecting to SQL Server using the SQL Server JDBC Driver. Figure 28.1 shows this information being used from the Crystal Reports designer.

28

- Connection URL: `jdbc:microsoft:sqlserver://abc:1433` (where *abc* is the name of the server running on port 1433)
- Database Classname: `com.microsoft.jdbc.sqlserver.SQLServerDriver`

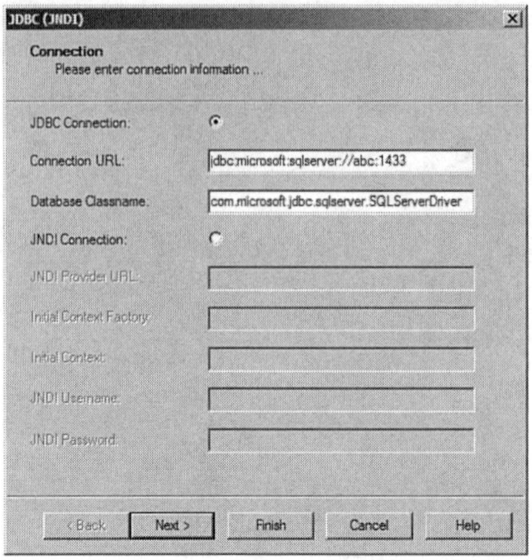

Figure 28.1
Connect to a JDBC
data source through
the Crystal Reports
designer.

Before you try to connect, you need to modify a configuration file. This file, `CRDB_JavaServer.ini`, can be found at the following location:

`\Program Files\Common Files\Crystal Decisions\2.5\bin\`

You should make the following changes:

- Set `PATH` to where your Java Runtime Environment (JRE) is, for example, `C:\jdk1.4\bin`.

- Set `CLASSPATH` to the location of the JDBC driver you want to use, and also include `C:\Program Files\Common Files\Crystal Decisions\2.5\bin\CRDBJavaServer.jar`.

- Set `IORFileLocation` to a location where the driver can write temporary files; make sure this location exists.

The other method of connecting to JDBC is through a JNDI reference. *JNDI (Java Naming and Directory Interface)* is a Java standard around resolving names and locations to resources in complex environments. In the case of the Crystal Reports JDBC driver, it is used to store JDBC connection strings. Connecting via JNDI has a few key benefits. First, the person creating the reports doesn't need to know the exact server name; he only needs to know an "alias" given to it in JNDI such as "FinanceData." Second, if that connection information were to change, no report change would be needed, only a change in the JNDI directory. Lastly, JNDI supports connection pooling which the Crystal Reports JDBC driver can take advantage of. As a recommendation, if you have an available JNDI server, use it to define all your database connections; this will save you time and effort later on.

Any existing reports you deliver through the Java Reporting Component will be converted on-the-fly to JDBC. This conversion is configurable using JNDI. To set up a configuration mapping, register a JDBC connection in a JNDI directory under the same name as the existing report's data source. For example, an existing report is connecting via ODBC to Oracle. With the same name as the ODBC DSN name, create a JNDI entry for a JDBC connection to the same Oracle server. When the report is run, it looks to JNDI and resolves the connection to the Oracle server.

CONFIGURING THE APPLICATION SERVER

Although building Web applications in Java is meant to be independent of application servers, the J2EE standard tends to be interpreted differently for each vendor's application server. Because of this, each application server has a different way of performing Web application configuration. The general rule is that there is a folder structure like this:

```
\webApplicationFolder
    \WEB-INF
        web.xml
        \lib
        \classes
```

When setting up the Java Reporting Component for a given Web application, the following steps are required:

- Copy all the Java Reporting Component .jar files from `C:\Program Files\Common Files\Crystal Decisions\2.5\java\lib` into the lib folder.

- Copy all the third-party .jar files from `C:\Program Files\Common Files\Crystal Decisions\2.5\java\lib\external` into the lib folder.

- Copy CrystalReportEngine-config.xml from `C:\Program Files\Common Files\Crystal Decisions\2.5\java` to the classes folder.

- Copy the crystalreportviewer10 folder from `C:\Program Files\Common Files\Crystal Decisions\2.5` to the Web application folder (webApplicationFolder in the previous example).

- Add the following entry to the web.xml file:

```
<context-param>
    <param-name>crystal_image_uri</param-name>
    <param-value>crystalreportviewers10</param-value>
</context-param>
```

There are two additional steps required if you intend to use the Crystal tag libraries:

- Copy crystal-tags-reportviewer.tld from `C:\Program Files\Common Files\Crystal Decisions\2.5\java\lib\taglib` to the WEB-INF folder.

- Add the following entry to the web.xml file:

```
<taglib>
    <taglib-uri>
        /crystal-tags-reportviewer.tld
    </taglib-uri>
        <taglib-location>
            /WEB-INF/crystal-tags-reportviewer.tld
        </taglib-location>
    </taglib>
```

28

DELIVERING REPORTS IN WEB APPLICATIONS

Report viewing is done primarily through the HTML report viewer included with the Crystal Reports Java Reporting Component. This report viewer is a control that runs inside a JSP or servlet. Its job is to get the information the report engine produces for a given page of a report and render that data to HTML format into the page's response stream.

The programmatic entry point to the report viewer is a class called `CrystalReportViewer`. This class is found in the `com.crystaldecisions.report.web.viewer` package. It can be instantiated as follows:

```
CrystalReportViewer viewer = new CrystalReportsViewer();
```

Make sure you add the class's package name in the import attribute of the page clause like this:

```
<%@ page import="com.crystaldecisions.report.web.viewer.*" %>
```

This is the main class you use to render reports to HTML. Its two main methods used to view reports are `setReportSource` and `processHttpRequest`. These methods are outlined in the following sections.

THE setReportSource METHOD

This `CrystalReportViewer` object's `setReportSource` method is used to indicate to the viewer which report it should display. Specifically, it accepts an object that implements the IReportSource interface. The Java Reporting Component's engine supplies this object. There are generally three steps involved in setting the report source.

The first step is to create a `JPEReportSourceFactory` object found in the `com.crystaldecisions.reports.reportengineinterface` package. As the name implies, this object's job is to create report source objects. This object has one relevant method: `createReportSource`. Its definition is as follows:

```
IReportSource createReportSource(object reportPath, Locale userLocale)
```

The `reportPath` argument should be a string consisting of the filename of the report file (.rpt). With the Java Reporting Component, the path from where the report file should be loaded is configured in the CrystalReportEngine-config.xml file. This XML configuration file has a <reportlocation> element that indicates the location of the report files relative to the location of the config file. The default value for the reportlocation is ..\.., which (if the config file was in the classes folder as outlined in the previous section) would point to the webApplicationFolder folder. It's a good idea to create a reports folder inside the Web application's folder and store all your reports there. Then change the report location setting to ..\..\reports. Then when reports are referenced in the call to `createReportSource`, you only need to pass the name of the report, not the folder location.

The second argument to `createReportSource` is a Locale object. Generally, you should pass in `request.getLocale()`. This means that whatever the user's locale is, it is passed down to the report engine so any locale-specific formatting can be applied.

THE processHttpRequest METHOD

After the viewer is told which report it needs to view, the only other method left to call is the processHttpRequest method. This method kicks off the actual report processing and renders the report to HTML. Its definition is as follows:

```
void processHttpRequest(HttpServletRequest request,
                        HttpServletResponse response,
                        ServletContext context,
                        Writer out)
```

The first argument passed in is the current servlet's request object. The report viewer uses this to access the HTTP request's form data where the viewer holds its state information such as what page it was showing, what level of drill-down, and so on. Also stored in the form data is the piece of data that indicates what action is to be performed. For example, the user might have clicked the Next Page button, or might have also drilled down. You simply pass in the servlet's request object.

The second argument is the response object. The report viewer uses this object to access the page's response stream so it can write the HTML output of the report. Here, you simply pass the servlet's response object.

The third argument is the servletContext, which is used to access the servlets container. Generally, you pass getServletConfig().getServletContext() for this argument. The final argument is a Writer. You generally pass null here unless you want to provide your own Writer.

Listing 28.1 shows these concepts all brought together in a JSP page that displays a report.

LISTING 28.1 VIEWING A REPORT IN HTML

```
<%@ page contentType="text/html;charset=UTF-8"
    import="com.crystaldecisions.reports.reportengineinterface.*,
            com.crystaldecisions.report.web.viewer.*"  %>

<%
// name of report file
String reportFile = "Income_Statement.rpt";

// create the JPEReportSourceFactory
JPEReportSourceFactory rptSrcFactory = new JPEReportSourceFactory();

// call the createReportSource method
Object reportSource = rptSrcFactory.createReportSource(reportFile,
                                              request.getLocale());

// create the report viewer
CrystalReportViewer viewer = new CrystalReportViewer();

// set the report source
viewer.setReportSource(reportSource);
```

28

continues

Listing 28.1 Continued

```
// tell the viewer to display the report
viewer.processHttpRequest(request,
                          response,
                          getServletConfig().getServletContext(),
                          null);

%>
```

The output of this page is shown in Figure 28.2. All content for the report consists of HTML elements, keeping all formatting and layout preserved. Every once in a while you will find a discrepancy in the report output between the designer and the HTML viewer, but the advantages of the HTML viewer generally outweigh the disadvantages. Besides drilling down or hyperlinking from the report's main content, a toolbar along the top provides a way for the end user to interact with the report. Buttons for page navigation as well as printing and exporting are present. When a command is performed by the user such as navigating to the next page or drilling down, the report viewer using a JavaScript function causes a form post to occur back to the same page. Both the current state and the new command are sent as part of the form's post data. The JSP or servlet reruns and the new state of the report is again rendered back to HTML.

Figure 28.2
This is the HTML report viewer in action.

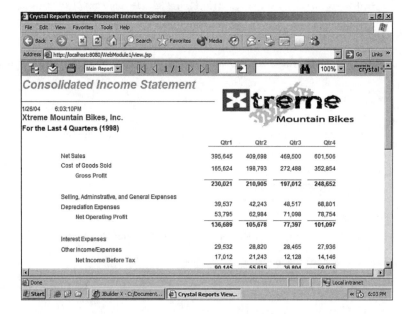

There is a collection of methods that the CrystalReportViewer object exposes that can be used to customize how the viewer looks and behaves. For the full list of methods, consult the API documentation; however, the following sections cover some of the more useful types of customizations.

CUSTOMIZING THE TOOLBAR

Each button or set of buttons on the report viewer toolbar can be individually turned off and on. These are done by a set of simple methods that accept a Boolean argument. They are listed here:

- `setHasToggleGroupTreeButton(boolean)`

- `setHasExportButton(boolean)`

- `setHasPrintButton(boolean)`

- `setHasViewList(boolean)`

- `setHasRefreshButton(boolean)`

- `setHasPageNavigationButtons(boolean)`

- `setHasGotoPageButton(boolean)`

- `setHasSearchButton(boolean)`

- `setHasZoomFactorList(boolean)`

- `setHasLogo(boolean)`

Finally, the entire toolbar can be turned off by calling `setDisplayToolbar(boolean)`. If the toolbar is turned off, the user does not have a way to interact with the report such as navigating pages. To facilitate this, there are other methods on the `CrystalReportViewer` object that can be called to drive the page navigation, including `showFirstPage`, `showPreviousPage`, `showNextPage`, `showLastPage`, and `showNthPage`. Similar methods exist to re-create the functionality of most of the other buttons as well. In general, the methods related to toolbar customization are almost self-explanatory.

CUSTOMIZING THE GROUP TREE

The group tree's width can be set via the `setGroupTreeWidth` method. To change the formatting of the group tree's text, change the CSS styles defined in the default.css file found in crystalreportviewers10/css. Alternatively, the entire group tree can be hidden by passing false to the `setDisplayGroupTree` function.

USING THE CRYSTAL TAG LIBRARIES

Now that you understand how the report viewer works, it's beneficial to understand some of the ways that it can be used in a more productive manner. Java tag libraries are a great way to accomplish this. A *tag library (taglib)* is an HTML-like tag that can be embedded inside a JSP page; it has some compiled code logic behind it that knows how to render itself to HTML. The beauty of a tag library is that you don't need to clog up your JSP page with a bunch of code; you simply need to insert the tag. When Business Objects created the HTML report viewer, they were wise enough to create some Java tag libraries alongside it. This is not to say you could not create your own tag libraries to suit your own needs, but the ones provided with the product will probably meet most requirements.

28

Refer to the Application Server Configuration section in this chapter for steps to configure the Crystal tag libraries. After you've finished the setup, you can start adding the tags to your page. The first step in using the tag is to add the taglib directive to the top of your JSP page. This directive looks like this:

```
<%@ taglib uri="/crystal-tags-reportviewer.tld" prefix="crviewer" %>
```

This indicates to the JSP page that any time it finds a tag prefixed with crviewer, it should look in the crystal-tags-reportviewer.tlb file to find out how to work with that tag.

There are two tags that must be added to the JSP page: viewer and report. Listing 28.2 shows a simple page using the viewer and report tags.

LISTING 28.2   USING THE TAG LIBRARIES

```
<%@ taglib uri="/crystal-tags-reportviewer.tld" prefix="crviewer" %>
<crviewer:viewer viewerName="" reportSourceType="reportingComponent">
  <crviewer:report reportName="Income_Statement.rpt"/>
</crviewer:viewer>
```

The viewerName and reportSourceType attributes of the viewer tag are required. The viewerName can be set to blank unless there are multiple viewer tags on the same page, in which case you'll need to name them uniquely. There is only one report source type supported in the Java Reporting Component, which is "reportingComponent." Inside the viewer tag, you'll see a report tag. For the reportName attribute, pass in the name of the report you want to display. The output of this page would be exactly the same as the output of the previous code example using inline Java code. The advantage of this page is that it is cleaner and simpler. To customize the viewer, rather than writing code, simply add attributes to the viewer tag. For example, adding the following attribute to the viewer tag hides the group tree:

```
displayGroupTree="false"
```

There are many other attributes supported. Consult the documentation for a full list but the general rule is that most methods on the CrystalReportViewer object have a corresponding tag library attribute.

EXPORTING REPORTS TO OTHER FILE FORMATS

You've learned so far how the CrystalReportViewer object can be used either in code or as a tag library to view reports in HTML format. This is useful for having a quick look at a report online, but users often require the capability to save the report to their own machine either for their own reference or so they can send the report elsewhere. Exporting is a perfect solution to this. The Java Reporting Component supports exporting reports to both Adobe PDF and RTF. There are two ways exporting can be done: via the export button on the toolbar and via code.

28

EXPORTING VIA THE TOOLBAR BUTTON

By default, the export button on the report viewer's toolbar is hidden. To enable it, either set the `displayToolbarExportButton` attribute to true if you are using the tag library or call the `setHasExportButton` method if you are using the viewer directly.

NOTE

> Even though you instruct the viewer to show the export button, you might find that it is still now showing up. This is most likely because you have not told the viewer that it owns the whole page. This is done via the `setOwnPage` method or `isOwnPage` attribute for the viewer or tag library, respectively.

When the Export button is clicked, a pop-up window appears asking the user which document format she would like to export the report to and which pages she would like to export to. This is shown in Figure 28.3.

Figure 28.3
Export a report through the report viewer.

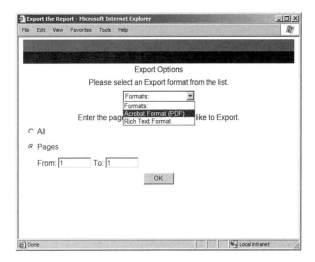

When the user clicks OK, the browser sends back the report in the requested format. Figure 28.4 shows the Income Statement report from the previous examples, exported to PDF.

EXPORTING VIA CODE

There are a few reasons why you might want to export via code. Perhaps you always want to deliver reports in PDF or RTF format instead of using the report viewer at all. Or perhaps you want to control the user interface for exporting. In any case, this section describes how to export using the `ReportExportControl`.

28

Figure 28.4
Here is a report exported to the PDF format.

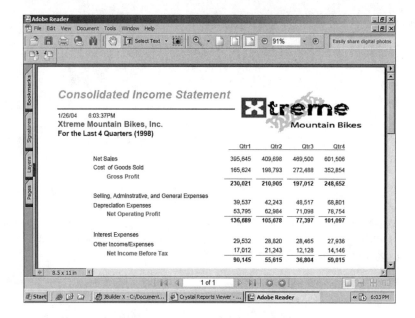

NOTE

Although some developers find it attractive to bypass the Crystal Report HTML viewer, and instead use either PDF or RTF as the primary way to deliver reports, this is often not the best way to go. Exporting is one of most processor-intensive operations and thus should be used sparingly if possible. In addition, when you export reports you lose all the interactive functionality like drill-down and group tree navigation. Use exporting where appropriate.

The `ReportExportControl` is the Java object used to render reports to both PDF and RTF. Because it is derived from the same class as the `CrystalReportViewer` object, it has many of the same properties and methods. The two main methods used in the report viewer—`setReportSource` and `processHttpRequest`—are used in exactly the same way in the `ReportExportControl`. Also, when exporting there is an additional method that is required: `setExportOptions`. This method is used to tell the `ReportExportControl` which export format should be used, and optionally, which pages should be exported.

The argument that is passed into the `setExportOptions` method is an object of type `ExportOptions`. This is found in `com.crystaldecisions.sdk.occa.report.exportoptions` package. With it, you call the `setExportFormatType` method passing in one of the following values:

- `ReportExportFormat.PDF` (for PDF)
- `ReportExportFormat.RTF` (for RTF)

NOTE

> Although the `ReportExportFormat` object has additional export formats not mentioned here such as MSExcel and Text, these are not currently available with the Java Reporting Component. These show up because the `ExportOptions` object is a shared object between other Crystal products that do support those export format types.

Listing 28.3 pulls this all together and shows a JSP page that exports a report to PDF format.

LISTING 28.3   EXPORTING VIA THE REPORTEXPORTCONTROL

```
<%@ page contentType="text/html;charset=UTF-8"
import="com.crystaldecisions.reports.reportengineinterface.*,
        com.crystaldecisions.report.web.viewer.*,
om.crystaldecisions.sdk.occa.report.exportoptions.*"  %>
<%

// name of report file
String reportFile = "Income_Statement.rpt";

// create the JPEReportSourceFactory
JPEReportSourceFactory rptSrcFactory = new JPEReportSourceFactory();

// call the createReportSource method
Object reportSource = rptSrcFactory.createReportSource(reportFile,
                                                request.getLocale());

// create the report viewer
ReportExportControl exporter = new ReportExportControl();

// set the report source
exporter.setReportSource(reportSource);

ExportOptions exportOptions = new ExportOptions();
exportOptions.setExportFormatType(ReportExportFormat.PDF);
exporter.setExportOptions(exportOptions);

// tell the viewer to display the report
exporter.processHttpRequest(request,
                            response,
                            getServletConfig().getServletContext(),
                            null);

%>
```

There are a few additional options that you might find useful. The first is the capability to specify which page numbers should be exported. This enables you to export just a small number of pages from a very large report. This is accomplished by creating either the `RTFWordExportFormatOptions` or `PDFExportFormatOptions` objects and calling their `setStartPageNumber` and `setEndPageNumber` methods. The resulting object is passed into the `setFormatOptions` method of the `ExportOptions` object. The code snippet shown in Listing 28.4 illustrates this.

LISTING 28.4   SPECIFYING PAGE NUMBERS WHEN EXPORTING

```
ExportOptions exportOptions = new ExportOptions();
exportOptions.setExportFormatType(ReportExportFormat.PDF) ;

RTFWordExportFormatOptions rtfOptions = new PDFExportFormatOptions();
rtfOptions.setStartPageNumber(1);
rtfOptions.setEndPageNumber(3);
exportOptions.setFormatOptions(rtfOptions);

exporter.setExportOptions(exportOptions);
```

The other option related to exporting is whether the resulting exported report should be sent back to the browser as an attachment or inline. When sent as an attachment, the browser pops up a dialog asking the user if he would like to save or open the file. This is useful if you think most of your users will want to save the file to their machines. The default behavior is for the report to open inside the browser window in either the Adobe or Microsoft Word embedded viewer. This is controlled via the `setExportAsAttachment` method of the `CrystalReportViewer`. This method simply takes a Boolean value, which determines whether the file should be an attachment.

PRINTING REPORTS FROM THE BROWSER

Viewing reports in electronic form is very valuable but as much as the "paperless office" is talked about, people still need to print reports to printers. The Java Reporting Component has the capability to print reports via the print button on the viewer's toolbar. Like the Export button, for the Print button to show, the viewer must be set to own the page via the `isOwnPage` attribute or `setOwnPage` method of the `CrystalReportViewer` object. When this button is clicked, a window opens asking the user which pages they want to print. This dialog is shown in Figure 28.5.

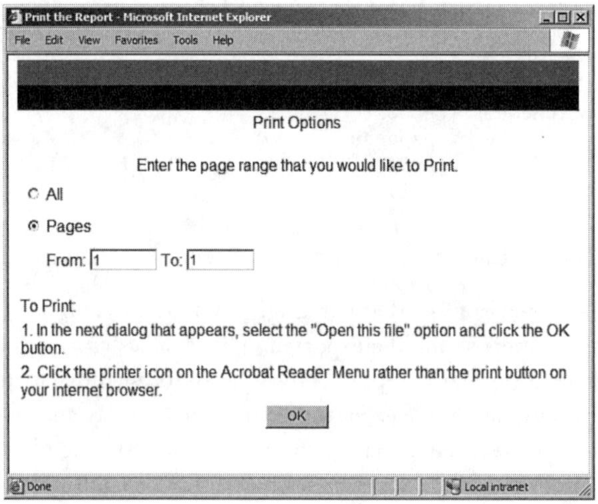

Figure 28.5
Print a report using the report viewer.

When the user clicks the Print button, the report opens in the Adobe PDF viewer, from which the user can then click Adobe's Print button. This prints the report to the user's printer.

COMMON PROGRAMMING TASKS

The different delivery mechanisms for the report viewer have been discussed. Now let's look at some of the common programming tasks that go along with delivering reports. This includes passing parameters to the report viewer and setting or changing the data source. The following sections will discuss these topics.

PASSING PARAMETERS

One of the most common programming tasks with any Crystal product is to pass parameters to the report viewer. This really isn't a hard task but developers often find this difficult because of a lack of proper examples in the product documentation. This chapter will attempt to provide concrete examples. Typically, reports are designed to be dynamic and so have multiple parameters that drive how the report functions. There are two ways to handle parameters: either have the report viewer prompt the user for the parameters automatically or pass the parameter values via code. Which method you choose is determined largely by whether you want the users to pick their own parameter values themselves.

Using the automatic parameter prompting requires no extra code or configuration. Simply view a report using either the viewer class or tag library and a default parameter prompting screen is displayed. Alternatively, you can pass the parameter values by code. This involves creating a series of objects as outlined below.

The first step in passing parameter values is to create an instance of the Fields class. This is a container class for parameter fields. This and the other objects are found in the com.crystaldecisions.sdk.occa.report.data package. Next, create an instance of the ParameterField object. To determine which parameter you are setting values for, call the setName method passing in the name of the parameter. Then to set the parameter values, create an instance of the Values class, which is a container for parameter value objects. Finally, create a ParameterFieldDiscreteValue object and call the setValue method to pass in the actual parameter value. This collection of objects is then passed to the report viewer via the setParameterFields method. Listing 28.5 shows a parameter being passed.

LISTING 28.5   PASSING A SIMPLE PARAMETER

```
Fields fields = new Fields();
ParameterField param = new ParameterField();
param.setName("Country");
Values vals = new Values();
ParameterFieldDiscreteValue val = new ParameterFieldDiscreteValue();
val.setValue("Canada");
```

continues

LISTING 28.5   CONTINUED

```
vals.add(val);
param.setCurrentValues(vals);
fields.add(param);
viewer.setParameterFields(fields);
```

Because there tends to be a bunch of objects you need to create, a nice way to handle this is to wrap up the parameter logic into a function. Listing 28.6 provides a sample function like this.

LISTING 28.6   A SAMPLE PARAMETER-HANDLING FUNCTION

```
public ParameterField createParam(string name, object value) {
    ParameterField param = new ParameterField();
    param.setName(name);
    Values vals = new Values();
    ParameterFieldDiscreteValue val = new ParameterFieldDiscreteValue();
    val.setValue(value);
    vals.add(val);
    param.setCurrentValues(vals);
    return param;
}
```

After you have a function like this in place, passing parameters looks as simple as in Listing 28.7.

LISTING 28.7   CALLING THE SAMPLE PARAMETER-HANDLING FUNCTION

```
Fields fields = new Fields();

field.add( createParam("Country", "Canada") );
field.add( createParam("Product Line", "Widgets") );

viewer.setParameterFields(fields) ;
```

SETTING DATA SOURCE INFORMATION

Setting data source information works very similar to the way setting parameters works. There is a collection of objects that you create, which then gets passed to the report viewer. In this case, the method used is setDatabaseLogonInfos. This method takes a ConnectionInfos object, which is found in the com.crystaldecisions.sdk.occa.report.data package. The ConnectionInfos class is a container class for any data source information for a given report. Each connection's information is held in an object called ConnectionInfo. This object has setUserName and setPassword methods for passing credentials. Also, each ConnectionInfo has a collection of properties associated with it called a *property bag*. The property bag contains information such as server name, database name, connection type, and so on. The property bag stores information in a name/value pair structure. There are variations as to what items are held in the `ConnectionInfo`, but the best way to figure it out is to look in the Set DataSource Location dialog from the Crystal Reports designer. There you can see which items are associated with a connection. Listing 28.8 shows how to pass logon information for a report.

LISTING 28.8 PASSING DATA SOURCE CREDENTIALS

```
ConnectionInfos connections = new ConnectionInfos();

ConnectionInfo connection as new ConnectionInfo();
connection.setUserName("Ryan");
connection.setPassword("123BAC");

connections.add(connection);
viewer.setDatabaseLogonInfos(connections);
```

DEVELOPING WITH A VISUAL DEVELOPMENT ENVIRONMENT

Not only has Business Objects delivered a full Java reporting offering with the Crystal Reports Java Reporting Component, but it also provides integration with some of the major Integrated Development Environments (IDEs) in the market to drive developers to build applications with the Java Reporting Component more quickly. The vendors Business Objects is currently working with on IDE integration are BEA and Borland. The integration consists of the following:

- **An integrated project item for reports.** This enables developers to add a report to their projects easily. It launches the Crystal Reports designer to edit the report automatically.

- **A report viewer wizard.** This is a visual wizard that walks users through the process of adding the report viewer tag to their JSP page.

Figure 28.6 shows the integration info BEA WebLogic Workshop and Figure 28.7 shows the integration into Borland JBuilder X. There are various other plug-ins to the IDEs as well that can be explored, such as automatically importing the Crystal libraries and configuring the web.xml.

For more information on IDE integration into these and other developer tools, visit the Business Objects Web site.

Figure 28.6
The Java Reporting Component integrated into BEA WebLogic Workshop.

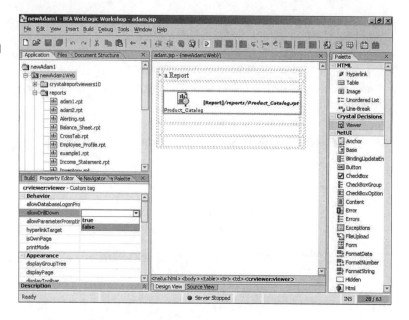

Figure 28.7
The Java Reporting Component integrated into Borland JBuilder X.

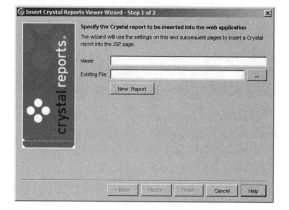

TROUBLESHOOTING

VERSION 10 JDBC DRIVER

I can't seem to find the version 10 JDBC driver.

This is not yet available at the time of this writing but should be available soon. You can check for status updates on this by visiting the Business Objects Download Center at http://www.businessobjects.com/products/downloadcenter/.

CHAPTER 29

CRYSTAL REPORTS .NET COMPONENTS

In this chapter

29

UNDERSTANDING MICROSOFT'S .NET PLATFORM

Crystal Decisions has a long partnership history with Microsoft. This has continued with Microsoft's .NET platform. This chapter provides an overview of the various .NET reporting technologies that are available both within Visual Studio .NET and with Crystal Reports 10.

Microsoft .NET is a next-generation platform that enables developers to create programs that transcend device boundaries and harness the connectivity of the Internet. .NET and the tools and languages that compose it are the foundation for building Windows-based components and applications, creating scripts, developing Web sites and applications, and managing source code.

Many of the terms used in this chapter are specific to the Microsoft .NET solution or the Visual Studio .NET development environment. Before you learn the Crystal components, review some of the key .NET technologies that are relevant to Crystal Reports developers:

- XML Web Services: A *Web Service* is a unit of application logic providing data and services to other applications. Applications access Web Services via ubiquitous Web protocols and data formats such as HTTP and XML, with no need to worry about how each Web Service is implemented. Web Services combine the best aspects of component-based development and the Web, and are a cornerstone of the Microsoft .NET programming model.

- ASP.NET: *ASP.NET* is a set of technologies in the Microsoft .NET Framework for building Web applications and XML Web Services. ASP.NET pages execute on the server and generate markup such as HTML, WML, or XML that is sent to a desktop or mobile browser. ASP.NET pages and ASP.NET XML Web Services files contain server-side logic (as opposed to client-side logic) written in Visual Basic .NET, C# .NET, or any .NET-compatible language.

- ADO.NET: *ADO.NET* is an evolutionary improvement to Microsoft *ActiveX Data Objects (ADO)* that provides platform interoperability and scalable data access. Using *Extensible Markup Language (XML)*, ADO.NET can ensure the efficient transfer of data to any application on any platform.

- SOAP: *SOAP (Simple Object Access Protocol)* is a lightweight and simple XML-based protocol that is designed to exchange structured and typed information on the Web. The purpose of SOAP is to enable rich and automated Web services based on a shared and open Web infrastructure.

For more detailed information on the Microsoft .NET solution, refer to Microsoft's Web site at http://msdn.microsoft.com/library/default.asp.

UNDERSTANDING THE DIFFERENT CRYSTAL .NET COMPONENTS

There have been multiple releases of both Visual Studio .NET and the Crystal .NET Components. This has created some confusion in the marketplace. In an attempt to clear this up, the following section describes the history of the various Crystal .NET products. Way back in 1993—a long time ago in the computing industry—Crystal signed an agreement with Microsoft to include Crystal Reports version 2 with Visual Basic 3.0. This relationship continued over the years as the Microsoft developer community embraced Crystal Reports technology. Late in the year of 2000, when Microsoft began to create the next generation of its development platform, it again looked to Crystal Decisions to provide the reporting solution. The Crystal folks ran full speed ahead with this project and embraced all the new technologies composing the .NET development platform.

In March of 2002, Visual Studio .NET shipped with a new product as part of the install: Crystal Reports for Visual Studio .NET. This was a special edition of Crystal Reports targeted at the .NET developer. It was seamlessly integrated with both the Visual Studio .NET integrated development environment (IDE) and the .NET Framework. It provided report viewer controls for both the Windows Forms and Web Forms application frameworks, a managed report engine object model, and a report designer integrated into the Visual Studio .NET IDE.

Another variant of the Crystal Reports .NET product came about when Microsoft released Visual Studio .NET 2003 (code named Everett). This was a point release of Visual Studio .NET and again included an updated edition of Crystal Reports for Visual Studio .NET. There were no new features per se, but the latest patches and updates were included. Many developers today have one of these Crystal Reports editions and believe that they have the most recent and complete Crystal Reports release. This is not true.

Subsequent to that release, Crystal Decisions updated its .NET offering by adding new features such as additional report viewer controls, more functionality through its API, and support for more data sources. This functionality was bundled with the Crystal Reports 9 release. Therefore, Crystal Reports 9 Advanced Edition served as an upgrade to Crystal Reports for Visual Studio .NET. Finally, version 10 again includes upgrades to the .NET components that shipped with version 9. The rest of this chapter covers the functionality of the .NET components included with Crystal Reports 10.

AN OVERVIEW OF THE CRYSTAL REPORTS 10 .NET COMPONENTS

Crystal Reports 10 provides developers working within Visual Studio .NET with a fast, productive way to create and integrate presentation-quality, interactive reports to meet the

29

demands of their application's end users. Crystal Reports 10 enhances the .NET platform by allowing you to

- Create reports from virtually any data source
- Deliver interactive, graphical report content in rich-client (Windows Forms), zero-client environments (Web Forms), or any device through an XML Web Services model
- Save time and write less code by leveraging existing Crystal Reports and report creation knowledge within .NET projects

To accomplish this, Crystal Reports 10 provides a broad offering of .NET technologies for delivering reports inside .NET applications. The following sections cover each component at a high level. They are

- The Report Designer
- The Report Engine Object Model
- The Windows Forms Viewer
- The Web Forms Viewers

THE REPORT DESIGNER

Like the original Crystal Reports for Visual Studio .NET product, Crystal Reports 10 provides an integrated report designer inside of the Visual Studio .NET development environment. This edition of the report designer enables you to create and edit reports from within the comfort of Visual Studio .NET. Figure 29.1 shows the report designer in action.

Figure 29.1
This is a report being designed in the Visual Studio .NET Report Designer.

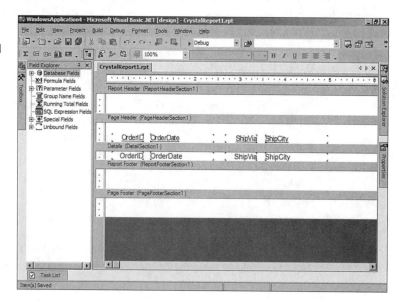

To add a new report to a project, select Add New Item from the Project menu. Select Crystal Reports from the Add New Item dialog. The filename you use here maps to the name of the report file as well as the name of the class created behind the scenes for the report (called the code-behind class).

NOTE
Many of you may be familiar with the Visual Basic report designer that was part of the Report Designer Component package made for Visual Basic 6.0. This new Visual Studio .NET report designer is the evolution of that component and works in a very similar manner.

After selecting Crystal Reports from the Add New Item dialog, the Report Wizard will be displayed. Select Using the Report Wizard or As a Blank Report to create a new report from scratch. The From an Existing Report option provides the capability to import any existing Crystal Report file (.rpt) and use the Visual Studio .NET report designer to make further modifications. This is a great way to leverage any existing work an organization has put into Crystal Reports. A report that is added or imported into a Visual Studio .NET project is just a standard RPT file. This means the standalone report designer can also be used to edit the report. The Visual Studio .NET Report Designer supports almost all the features of the standalone report designer and can be used to create everything from simple tabular reports to highly formatted professional reports. Although the feature set of these two editions of the designer are almost exactly the same, there are a few things for which the standalone designer is good, namely being able to preview the report without having to run the application.

TIP
A quick way to launch the standalone designer from within Visual Studio .NET is to right-click on a report in the Solution Explorer and select Open With. In the dialog that opens, select crw32.exe. This is the executable for the standalone report designer. This usually proves to be a better method to build reports anyway because you have a built-in preview screen to see what your report looks like before running.

Even though the capability of the two editions of the designers are similar, there are some differences in the way the designer works. This is not meant to be inconsistent, but rather to adapt some of the standalone report designer tasks to tasks that Visual Studio .NET developers would be familiar with. Ideally, the experience of designing a report with the Visual Studio .NET report designer should be like designing a Windows Form. The following sections cover these differences.

UNDERSTANDING THE REPORT DESIGNER'S USER INTERFACE CONVENTIONS

Several user interface components work differently in the Visual Studio .NET report designer. One of the first things you'll notice is that the section names are shown above each section on a section band as opposed to being on the left side of the window. However, the same options are available when right-clicking on the section band. This actually takes up less real estate and tends to be preferred by developers.

The Field Explorer resides to the left of the report page by default but can be docked anywhere as per most Visual Studio .NET tool windows. The Field Explorer can be easily shown or hidden by clicking the Toggle Field View button on the designer toolbar. Other explorer windows found in the standalone designer such as the Report Explorer and Repository Explorer are not available in the Visual Studio .NET report designer.

> **NOTE**
>
> Reports that contain objects linked to the Crystal Repository are fully supported; however, no new repository objects can be added to the report without using the standalone designer.

The menus that you would normally find in the standalone report designer can be found by right-clicking on an empty spot on the designer surface. The pop-up menu provides the same functionality.

THE PROPERTY BROWSER

To change the formatting and settings for report objects in the standalone designer, users are familiar with right-clicking on a report object and selecting Format Field from the pop-up menu. This would open the Format Editor, which would give you access to changing font, color, styles, and other formatting options. In the Visual Studio .NET report designer, this scenario is still available; however, there is an additional way to apply most of these formatting options: via the Property Browser.

The Property Browser is a window that lives inside the Visual Studio .NET development environment. It should be very familiar to developers as a way to change the appearance and behavior of a selected object on a form or design surface. In the context of the report designer, the property browser is another way to change the settings (properties) for report objects. In general, any setting that is available in the Format Editor dialog is available from the property browser when that object is selected. This generally proves to be a faster and better way to set properties than using the Format Editor. To see which properties are available for a given object, click to highlight the object, and then check out the Property Browser window shown in Figure 29.2.

The property names are listed on the left and the current values are listed on the right. To click a value simply click on the current value and either type or select from the drop-down list.

One property to pay attention to is the Name property. This becomes relevant in the next section when you learn how to use the Report Engine Object Model to manipulate the report on the fly at runtime. This is the way to reference that object in code.

Figure 29.2
Using the Property
Browser window to
modify a report
object's settings.

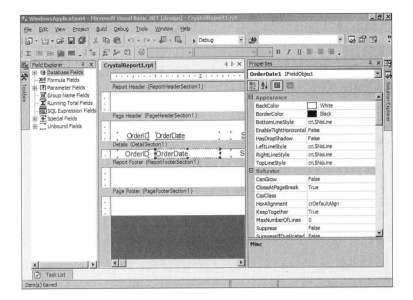

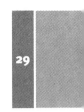

THE REPORT ENGINE OBJECT MODEL

The Report Engine Object Model is the .NET programmatic entry point to the Crystal Reports engine. It provides a collection of objects, methods, and properties that enable you to process, save, export, and print reports. While doing that, you are able to manipulate the report by modifying parameter values, database credentials, sorting, and grouping. The Report Engine Object Model (hereafter referred to as the object model) consists of a standard .NET assembly called CrystalDecisions.CrystalReports.Engine.dll. As the name of the dll implies, the namespace for all the objects contained in this dll is CrystalDecisions. CrystalReports.Engine. Because this is a standard .NET assembly, the object model contained within it can be used from any .NET programming language or tool. All sample code within this chapter uses the Visual Basic .NET language, but any .NET-compliant language could, of course, be used. Keep in mind that although the object model is pure "managed" code, the underlying report engine is not. This means you can't perform a pure "xcopy" deployment that Microsoft likes to advertise that all .NET applications can do.

There are many objects and thus capabilities in the object model. This chapter does not explain all of them but rather covers the most common scenarios. For a complete reference of all objects, properties, and methods, consult the Crystal Reports 10 documentation that is installed to the MSDN Help Collection. Some of you may be skeptical about the product documentation because in the past it was very sparse. However, there is much more information in the documentation in version 10 than ever before; have a look through it and you will be impressed.

OPENING REPORTS

The main object you use when working with the object model is the ReportDocument object. It is the root object in the object model hierarchy and forms the entry point to opening reports. The first step in opening reports is to create a new instance of the ReportDocument class. Then to open a report file, call the Load method. This method takes a single parameter, which is a string that points to the RPT file. An example of this is as follows:

```
Dim Report As New ReportDocument
Report.Load("C:\My Reports\Sales.rpt")
```

NOTE

> One common way to handle file paths is to use Application.StartupPath to determine the current location of the Windows Forms executable and reference report files relative to there.

The other way to load a report is to use a strongly typed report object. A *strongly typed report object* is an object automatically generated when a report is added to the Visual Studio .NET project. This object (sometimes called *code-behind*) is specific to the report file both in its class name and properties. For example, a report added to the project called InvoiceReport.rpt would in turn have a class called InvoiceReport. Instead of calling the Load method, a developer only needs to create an instance of the InvoiceReport class. This class knows how to locate the report. In the case of strongly typed reports, instead of having an external RPT file, the report file is compiled into the application executable. The report is loaded out of the application's resources from there. Whether you use a ReportDocument (untyped report) or a strongly typed report, the rest of the object model is the same.

EXPORTING REPORTS

One of the most common uses of the object model is to run a report and export it to another file format. In past versions, exporting required a good sized chunk of code. Fortunately exporting in version 10 is very easy with the updated object model. First, a ReportDocument object needs to be created and a report loaded into it. After that is done, several exporting methods are available to you:

- ExportToDisk: This is the simplest way to export a report; it accepts an argument to indicate the export format type to use and a filename to export to. This method is useful when you just need to export a file to the disk.

- ExportToStream: This method only accepts a single argument—the export format type. The return value of this method is a System.IO.Stream object. This is actually a MemoryStream object so you can cast it to a MemoryStream if need be. This method is useful when you intend to send the exported report elsewhere as a stream without having to write to an intermediate disk file. It's best to call the steam's Close method when finished with the stream to release memory.

- **ExportToHttpResponse:** This method is similar to the ExportToStream method in that it is intended to be used when the resulting report is streamed back to the user. However, this method accepts as an argument the ASP.NET HttpResponse object and automatically streams the exported report back to the Web browser handling the mime type and response stream for you.

- **Export:** This method is the master Export method. It accepts an object called ExportOptions as an argument that describes the export format type and destination type. You can think of this as the "long-hand" way of exporting but it does allow for a few additional options such as e-mail and Exchange destinations and page range options.

A common argument to all these exporting methods is the export format type. This is specified using the ExportFormatType enumeration found in the CrystalDecisions.Shared namespace. It's generally a good idea to add a reference to CrystalDecisions.Shared.dll because you will find many common objects used in the object model located in this assembly. The following list describes the members of the ExportFormatType enumeration:

- Excel: Microsoft Excel format

- ExcelRecord: A variation of the Microsoft Excel format that just exports the data, not the formatting

- HTML32: HTML for Netscape Navigator or other non-common browsers

- HTML40: HTML for Microsoft Internet Explorer

- PortableDocFormat: Adobe PDF format

- RichText: Microsoft's Rich Text Format (RTF)

- WordForWindows: Microsoft Word format

- Text: Plain text format

- CrystalReport: Standard Crystal Reports (RPT) format

> **TIP**
>
> When exporting to Crystal Reports format, a standard RPT file is created; however, the report has saved data. This is quite useful because you can run a report once and export to Crystal Reports format and then have many people view that report using the saved data. In this scenario, only one hit is made to the database even though many people are viewing the report. This is similar to creating a report instance in the Crystal Enterprise environment. This feature can be used to affect a greater scalability by introducing a "report instance" delivery model.

A common scenario for exporting would be processing many reports in a batch job. This is a great use of the object model. To help you do this effectively, I'll share a few tips here. First, you need to clean up to make sure memory is released, and second, use multiple threads to maximize the time available for processing reports. The report engine object model is thread safe. Listing 29.1 illustrates a multithreaded report processing class. Listing 29.2 shows how this class could be called.

LISTING 29.1 MULTITHREADED BATCH PROCESSING CLASS

```
Imports System.Threading
Imports CrystalDecisions.Shared
Imports CrystalDecisions.CrystalReports.Engine

Public Class BatchProcessor
    Private ReportList As New ArrayList
    Private OutputFolder As String
    Private BatchCounter As Integer

    ' Call this method to add a report to the list of reports
    ' to be processed by the batch processor
    Public Sub AddReportJob(ByVal ReportPath As String)
        ReportList.Add(ReportPath)
    End Sub

    ' This runs an individual report job
    Private Sub ProcessNextReportJob(ByVal Index As Object)
        Dim report As New ReportDocument
        Dim outputFileName As String

    ' Load the report based on index
        report.Load(ReportList(Index))
    ' Construct an output filename
        outputFileName = "Report" & Index & ".pdf"
    ' Call the ExportToDisk method
        report.ExportToDisk(ExportFormatType.PortableDocFormat, _
                            OutputFolder & "\" & outputFileName)
    ' Make sure to clean up the report object
        report.Close()

    ' Decrement a counter of remaining jobs
        BatchCounter = BatchCounter - 1
    End Sub

    Public Sub ExecuteBatch(ByVal OutputFolder As String)
        Me.OutputFolder = OutputFolder

        BatchCounter = ReportList.Count

        ' Grab the current time
        Dim startTime As DateTime = DateTime.Now

        ' Start the batch job
        Dim i As Integer
        For i = 1 To ReportList.Count
        ' Use the .NET ThreadPool class to handle the multiple requests
            Dim wc As New WaitCallback(AddressOf ProcessNextReportJob)
            ThreadPool.QueueUserWorkItem(wc, i - 1)
        Next
```

```
        While BatchCounter > 0
            Thread.Sleep(250)
        End While

        Dim elapsedTime As TimeSpan = DateTime.Now.Subtract(startTime)
        MessageBox.Show("Batch completed in " + _
                        elapsedTime.Seconds.ToString() & " seconds")
    End Sub

End Class
```

LISTING 29.2   CALLING THE BATCH PROCESSOR

```
Dim bp As New BatchProcessor

bp.AddReportJob("C:\Temp\Reports\Report1.rpt")
bp.AddReportJob("C:\Temp\Reports\Report2.rpt")
bp.AddReportJob("C:\Temp\Reports\Report3.rpt")
bp.AddReportJob("C:\Temp\Reports\Report4.rpt")
bp.AddReportJob("C:\Temp\Reports\Report5.rpt")
bp.AddReportJob("C:\Temp\Reports\Report6.rpt")
bp.AddReportJob("C:\Temp\Reports\Report7.rpt")
bp.AddReportJob("C:\Temp\Reports\Report8.rpt")
bp.AddReportJob("C:\Temp\Reports\Report9.rpt")
bp.AddReportJob("C:\Temp\Reports\Report10.rpt")

bp.ExecuteBatch("C:\Temp\Output")
```

PRINTING REPORTS

Although the fantasy of a paperless office floats around our heads, the reality today is that no matter how much technology for viewing reports is produced, people will always want to print them. Along these lines, the object model supports printing reports to printers. This is accomplished by calling the ReportDocument's `PrintToPrinter` method. It takes the following arguments, which determine basic print settings:

- `nCopies`: An integer representing the number of copies to print
- `collated`: A Boolean value indicating whether the printed pages should be collated
- `startPageN`: An integer representing the page number on which to start printing
- `endPageN`: An integer representing the page number on which to end printing

In addition to these printing options, there is another set of more advanced options. These options are in the form of properties and are contained in the ReportDocument's `PrintOptions` object:

- `PaperSize`: An enumeration of standard paper sizes, such as Letter or A4
- `PaperOrientation`: An enumeration to indicate the orientation of the paper, such as Portrait or Landscape
- `PageMargins`: A `PageMargins` object containing integer-based margin widths

- `PageContentHeight`/`PageContentWidth`: Integer-based width and height for the main page area
- `PaperSource`: An enumeration containing standard paper tray sources such as upper and lower
- `PrinterDuplex`: An enumeration containing duplexing options for the printer
- `PrinterName`: A string representing the name of the printer device or print queue

NOTE

Keep in mind that whatever account the report engine object model is running under needs access to the printer when the `PrintToPrinter` method is invoked. Sometimes when the object model is used in ASP.NET, it is running under a Guest-level account, which does not have access to the machine's printers. If this is the case, you need to install and grant access to the printers for that account.

DELIVERING REPORTS WITH THE WINDOWS FORMS VIEWER

After reports are imported into or referenced from a Visual Studio .NET project, the next obvious step is to have a way to view those reports. This section covers report viewing in Windows Forms applications.

Windows Forms is the new .NET technology for building rich-client applications. It is the evolution of the COM and ActiveX platform that Crystal Reports was so popular in. When it comes to .NET, Crystal Decisions decided to write a native .NET control based on the Windows Forms technology. This control is simply called the Windows Forms Viewer. It's corresponding class name is `CrystalDecisions.Windows.Forms.CrystalReportViewer`.

Like other Windows Forms controls, this control ultimately inherits from the `System.Windows.Forms.Control` class. It has many public methods and properties that enable you to drive the appearance and behavior. In addition to these runtime capabilities, the Windows Forms Viewer has design-time support to increase the efficiency and ease of using the control. The control can be found in the toolbox on the Windows Forms tab. You can see what the control looks like after being dropped onto a form in Figure 29.3.

THE `ReportSource` PROPERTY

Although there are many properties and methods, the `ReportSource` property is key. It is this property that is used to indicate to the viewer which report it should display. Because the `ReportSource` property's data type is object, it can accept multiple types of values, the most common of which are listed here:

- Filename: The full path to an RPT file as a String object.
- Report object: An instance of a `CrystalDecisions.CrystalReports.Engine.ReportDocument` class. This report should already have been loaded by calling the ReportDocument's `Load` method.

■ Strongly typed report object: An instance of a strongly typed report object derived from `ReportClass`.

Figure 29.3
A Crystal Report displayed in the Windows Forms Viewer control.

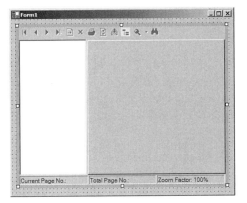

The following code shows VB.NET examples of setting these types of report source objects:

```
' #1 - A filename as a string
Viewer.ReportSource = "C:\Program Files\My Application\Reports\Sales.rpt"

' #2 - a ReportDocument object
Dim Report = As New ReportDocument()
Report.Load("C:\Program Files\My Application\Reports\Sales.rpt")
Viewer.ReportSource = Report

' #3 - A strongly-typed report object
Dim Report As New SalesReport()
Viewer.ReportSource = Report
```

If the viewer is visible when the `ReportSource` property is set, it displays the report immediately. If the viewer is not visible yet, that is, the form has not been shown yet, the viewer waits until it is shown onscreen to display the report. After a report source is provided to the viewer, it maintains that report until the viewer is destroyed or another report source is passed into it.

Because the viewer can generically accept report filenames and report objects, a single viewer can be reused for viewing multiple reports. One of the ways you could handle this is to create a form dedicated to report viewing. This form would contain the Windows Forms viewer. To easily invoke this form and pass in a report source, make the viewer a public variable and then create a shared method to accept a report source as an argument. An example of this function is shown here:

```
Public Shared Sub Display(ByVal ReportSource As Object)
    Dim newForm As New ReportViewerForm()
    newForm.Viewer.ReportSource = ReportSource
    newForm.ShowDialog()
End Sub
```

29

After this is in place, to invoke the report viewer from anywhere in the application, use the following code:

```
strReportPath = ...
ReportViewerForm.Display(strReportPath)
```

CUSTOMIZING THE WINDOWS FORMS VIEWER

There are many properties and methods of the report viewer that can be used to customize its appearance. The first level of customization is to show or hide the individual components of the viewer. The group tree on the left side can be shown or hidden via the DisplayGroupTree Boolean property. The toolbar works the same way via the DisplayToolbar property.

In addition to hiding the entire toolbar, each button or button group on the toolbar has corresponding properties that allow them to be individually hidden or shown. These properties can be found in the property browser or accessed via code. They all start with Show, such as ShowExportButton, ShowPrintButton, and so on. The names should be self-explanatory.

TIP

> There is a status bar at the bottom of the viewer that does not have a corresponding show/hide property. It tends to not add a lot of value and end up more of an annoyance than anything. A trick to hide this status bar is to drop a panel control onto the form and drop the viewer onto the panel. Set the viewer's Dock property to Fill so that the viewer always sizes itself to the size of the surrounding panel. Then set the DockPadding.Bottom property of the viewer to -20. This sizes the height of the viewer to 20 pixels more than the panel, effectively hiding the status bar below the extents of the panel. Keep in mind that any methods and properties that need to be accessed from the report viewer after you've done this need to be accessed via the panel object's controls collection. Figure 29.4 shows the report viewer with no group tree, no toolbar, and the status bar hidden.

Figure 29.4
The Report Viewer is shown here with its status bar hidden.

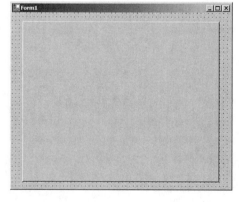

Another property that can be used to change the behavior of the report viewer is the EnableDrillDown property. Setting this Boolean property to false disables the user from performing any drill-down operations. Finally, the SelectionFormula and ViewTimeSelectionFormula properties can be used to create and append filters to the report. Keep in mind that the filtering is actually done by the report engine, but the report viewer simply exposes the property and then sends the information down to the report engine. The SelectionFormula property should be used when creating or overwriting a selection formula. To append to an existing formula, use the ViewTimeSelectionFormula property, which automatically appends using an AND operator.

DELIVERING REPORTS WITH THE WEB FORMS VIEWER

An equivalent viewer to the Windows Forms Viewer exists for ASP.NET-based applications; it's called the *Web Forms Viewer*. This is an ASP.NET control derived from the WebControl class. This means that it is a server-side control that renders only HTML to the client browser. No special controls, applets, or files are required on the client in order to view reports with the Web Forms Viewer.

Like the Windows Forms Viewer, the Web Forms Viewer can be found in the Visual Studio .NET toolbox and is called CrystalReportViewer. It is found in the CrystalDecisions.Web namespace and the CrystalDecisions.Web.dll assembly. Many objects used in the Web Forms Viewer are contained in the CrystalDecisions.Shared namespace. The Web Forms Viewer has many properties and methods that control how it displays reports. This section covers these.

The first step to using the viewer is to drop it onto a Web Form from the toolbox. From there, properties can be set via the property browser or via the code-behind for the ASPX page. The first relevant property for the Web Forms Viewer is the ReportSource property. The nice thing is that the types of objects that can be passed into the ReportSource property are exactly the same as the types of objects that can be passed into the Windows Forms Viewer's ReportSource property. For more information on the ReportSource property, refer to "The ReportSource Property" section earlier in this chapter on this topic.

After the ReportSource property is set, you can run the application. When the page is processed, the viewer is created; it processes the report specified in the report source, and then renders the output of the report page to HTML, which gets written to the response stream for the page. Figure 29.5 shows what the Web Forms Viewer looks like in action when rendering a report.

The next section describes some of the common properties used to customize the appearance and behavior of the report viewer.

Figure 29.5
A Crystal Reports is shown being displayed through the Web Forms Viewer control.

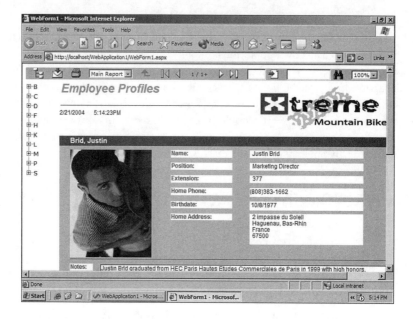

CUSTOMIZING THE WEB FORMS VIEWER

The first level of customization is to show or hide the main components of the report viewer. The DisplayGroupTree and DisplayToolbar properties show and hide the group tree and toolbar, respectively. PageToTreeRatio is a handy property that enables you to set the width of the group tree as a ratio to the width of the rest of the page. The default value is 6. To show or hide individual toolbar buttons, there is a collection of properties beginning with Has such as HasExportButton and HasRefreshButton. Using these properties, you can control each button or button group on the toolbar to meet your needs. In addition, the toolbar buttons themselves are standard gif files contained in the following directory:

```
C:\Program Files\Common Files\Crystal Decisions\2.5
➥\crystalreportviewers10\images\toolbar
```

These gif files can be changed using any graphics editing program or even replaced by entirely new images assuming the filenames are kept the same. Finally, there is a style sheet associated with the Web Forms Viewer that can be overridden to change the viewer's colors, fonts, alignment, borders, and more. By default, the viewer looks for the css file in the following location:

```
/crystalreportviewers10/css/default.css
```

This location translates to the following physical path:

```
C:\Program Files\Common Files\Crystal Decisions\2.5
➥\crystalreportviewers10\css\default.css
```

You can either modify this default.css file or create multiple copies of the css files, effectively having several "skins" for the viewer, and dynamically point the viewer to one of the css files based on a user preference. The css file location is set via the `CssFilename` property of the Web Forms Viewer.

By default, the viewer renders one page of the report at a time, just like the report designer would do. However, sometimes users find that it would be easier to have all the report's content contained on a single Web page. You can do this by setting the `SeparatePages` property to false instead of its default value of true. When this is done, the viewer renders each page under one another, effectively producing a single Web page with the entire report's data.

DATABASE CREDENTIALS

One of the nice things about the version 10 Crystal Report Viewers as opposed to previous versions is that if the report needs database credentials, it prompts the user for this information. Figures 29.6 and 29.7 show the Windows Forms and Web Forms Viewers database credential prompting.

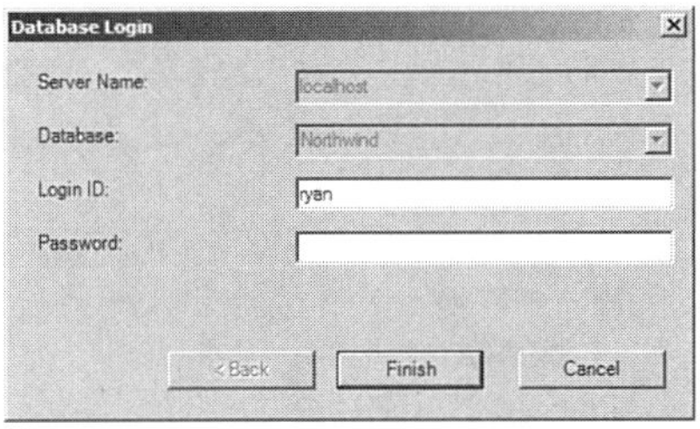

Figure 29.6
The Windows Forms Viewer prompts for database credentials.

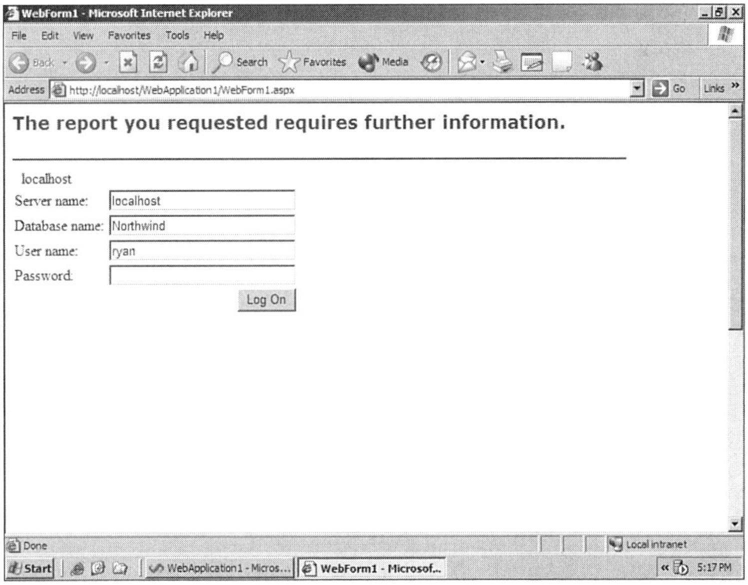

Figure 29.7
The Web Forms Viewer prompts for database credentials.

Although this is a nice feature, you will often want to suppress this and handle the database credentials themselves. The first reason to do this is to change the appearance or behavior of the database credential process. This could be as simple as customizing the look and feel of the user interface or perhaps changing the behavior in some way. For example, you could have the user prompted the first time but offer to save the credentials for later. This could be accomplished by writing the credentials to a cookie or database. The second reason for suppressing the viewer's prompting would be to set the credentials transparently behind the scenes, so the user won't need to enter them at all. The logic of the viewers is to determine whether credentials have been supplied through the viewer directly, and if not, to see if the corresponding report has them defined, and finally if not, to prompt the user. Therefore the solution to customizing or eliminating the database credential prompts is to simply set them before the report is viewed.

The easiest way to do this is to use the ReportDocument's SetDatabaseLogon method. This function is overloaded for several different argument types. There are really only two of them that you will use. The simplest version of SetDatabaseLogon accepts two strings: a username and password. Keep in mind that Crystal Reports stores the information required to connect to the database inside the RPT file, so unless you want to change the database, you only need to set the username and password. An example of this is shown in the following code:

```
Dim Report As New ReportDocument()
Report.Load("C:\Reports\Finance.rpt")
Report.SetDatabaseLogon("username", "password")
Viewer.ReportSource = Report
```

In this case, the Viewer object could be either a Windows Forms Viewer or a Web Forms Viewer because they both have the ReportSource property.

NOTE

When using the Web Forms Viewer, keep in mind that the viewer is stateless, that is, each time the ASPX page is processed, the credentials need to be set unless you are caching the ReportDocument object somewhere.

The other version of the SetDatabaseLogon method takes four string arguments: username, password, server name, and database name. This is useful for taking reports based off a test database and pointing them to a production database. Simply pass in the server name and database name you want the report to use, like this:

```
Report.SetDatabaseLogon("username", "password", "SERVER01", "SalesDB")
```

SETTING PARAMETERS

Parameter fields work almost exactly the same as database credentials. Both viewers prompt for parameters if they are required by the report but not supplied by the developer. These parameter prompting screens are shown in Figures 29.8 and 29.9.

Figure 29.8
The Windows Forms
Viewer prompting for
parameter values.

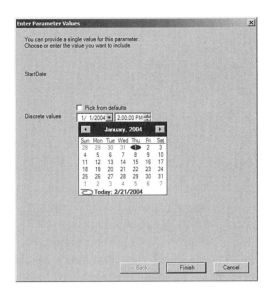

Figure 29.9
The Web Forms
Viewer prompting for
parameter values.

Again, the parameter prompting screens are useful but sometimes don't fit the look and feel of the application or simply need to be suppressed entirely. Another common usage of customized parameter prompting screens is to have the parameter pick lists values come directly from the database so they are always up to date. To do this you would use the ReportDocument object to set the parameters before passing it to the viewer to display. This is done via the ReportDocument's SetParameterValue method. There are three versions of this method:

- SetParameterValue(index As Integer, val As Object) is used to set a parameter value by index.

- SetParameterValue(name As String, val As Object) is used to set a parameter value by name.

- SetParameterValue(name As String, val As Object, subreport As String) is used to set a parameter for a subreport by parameter name and subreport name.

29

An example of this is

```
Dim Report As New ReportDocument()
Report.Load("C:\Reports\Orders.rpt")
Report.SetParameterValue("Geography", "North America")
Report.SetParameterValue("Start Date", DateTime.Now)
Viewer.ReportSource = Report
```

For parameters that accept multiple values pass in an array of those values.

UNDERSTANDING THE REPORT APPLICATION SERVER BRIDGE

An important change has occurred to the report engine object model in version 10 of Crystal Reports. In fact, you might not even have realized this change has taken place after using Crystal Reports 10 for quite some time; however, it's important to understand. The object model that was previously supplied with the various .NET offerings that Crystal Decisions has produced has talked directly to the Crystal Reports print engine. In version 10, the object model talks to the Report Application Server, and then in turn to the Crystal Reports engine. Although there is no immediate noticeable changes to the way the engine operates, this is an important change for two key reasons:

■ The Report Application Server exposes more functionality than the report engine object model discussed thus far, and this additional functionality can now be leveraged from the report engine object model.

■ Because the Report Application Server is a part of the Crystal Enterprise framework, any application using the Crystal Reports 10 report engine object model and viewers is now very easily upgradeable to Crystal Enterprise.

As for the first point, the Report Application Server's API is available through the standard report engine object model. To access it, use the ReportClientDocument property of the ReportDocument object. The ReportClientDocument is the equivalent to the ReportDocument for the Report Application Server. It includes the capability to not only open and change reports, but also to create reports from scratch, add new report objects, add new data sources, and so on. For more information on the Report Application Server, consult Chapter 31, "Introduction to Crystal Enterprise Embedded."

TROUBLESHOOTING

APPLICATION DEPLOYMENT WITH XCOPY

I am having problems using xcopy to deploy applications.

Although the object model is pure "managed" code, the underlying report engine is not. This means you can't perform a pure "xcopy" deployment that Microsoft likes to advertise that all .NET applications can do.

PRINTING REPORTS

I can't seem to print a report.

Sometimes when the object model is used in ASP.NET, it is running under a Guest-level account, which does not have access to the machine's printers. If this is the case, you need to install and grant access to the printers for that account.

CHAPTER 30

COM REPORTING COMPONENTS

In this chapter

UNDERSTANDING THE REPORT DESIGNER COMPONENT

Crystal Decisions has long viewed the Component Object Model (COM) development platform as one of the key areas it needed to embrace to become successful. Although there were other popular developer platforms in the market, the trend for development projects concerning information delivery was to use Visual Basic. This was because of its good mix of power and simplicity. Now part of the Business Objects product line, Crystal Reports 10 mirrors these attributes and delivers a powerful yet productive reporting solution. This chapter covers Crystal Decisions reporting solutions for the COM platform, specifically, the Crystal Report Designer Component.

Although the chapters covering the Java and .NET components focused primarily on Web-based applications, this chapter concentrates on desktop applications because that is the focus of the Crystal Decisions COM Components. Desktop applications, although still popular today, were what started it all. These are standalone applications that run on a single tier and are installed locally on a user's machine. These applications are most commonly built using Visual Basic, but are also sometimes built using Visual C++ or Delphi.

→ For more information on Java, **see** "Overview of the Crystal Reports Java Reporting Component," **p. 654**

NOTE

> All sample code in this chapter uses Visual Basic 6 syntax, but can easily be adapted to other languages that support COM. For sample code in other languages, visit the Business Objects support site at `http://support.businessobjects.com`.

Many development environments support Microsoft's COM technology. *COM (Component Object Model)* is a standard technology used for exposing Software Development Kits (SDKs) in the Windows world. It implies a set of objects with properties and methods. Much of Microsoft's own SDKs are based on COM. It follows that the recommended Crystal Reports SDK for desktop applications would also be based on COM. Its name is the Report Designer Component, and it consists of the following pieces:

- A report designer integrated into the Visual Basic environment
- An object model built around the report engine used for manipulation of the report
- A report viewer control used for displaying reports inside an application

The following sections describe each of these components in more detail.

BUILDING REPORTS WITH THE VISUAL BASIC REPORT DESIGNER

The Visual Basic report designer enables developers to create and edit reports from within the comfort of the Visual Basic environment. Figure 30.1 shows the report designer active inside Visual Basic.

Figure 30.1
Here a report is
shown being editing
in the Visual Basic
report designer.

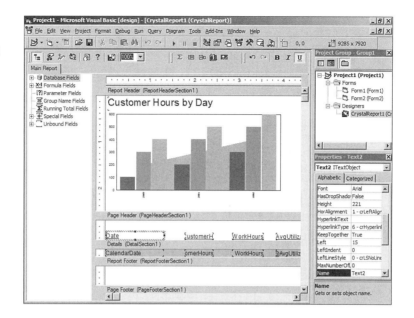

To add a new report to a project, select Add Crystal Reports 10 from the Project menu
inside Visual Basic.

NOTE

If Add Crystal Reports 10 is not showing on the Project menu, go to the Project,
Components menu, and on the Dialog tab, make sure Crystal Reports 10 has a check
beside it. If you turn this on, it permanently appears on the Project menu.

From the dialog that opens, select Using the Report Wizard or As a Blank Report to create
a new report from scratch. The From an Existing Report option provides you with the
capability to import any existing Crystal Report file (.rpt) and use the Visual Basic report
designer to make further modifications, a great way to leverage any existing work an organization has put into Crystal Reports. A report that is added to a Visual Basic project is saved
as a .dsr file, which is a container for the actual .rpt file along with some other information.
At any point, you can click the Save to Crystal Report File button on the designer's toolbar
and save the report out to a standard RPT file, so in effect reports can easily go both ways:
in and out of Visual Basic. Because the Visual Basic report designer is based primarily on
the same code-base as the standalone Crystal Reports designer, the RPT file format is the
same. You can also import existing reports from past versions into the Visual Basic report
designer.

The Visual Basic report designer supports almost all the features of the Crystal Reports
designer and can be used to create everything from simple tabular reports to highly formatted, professional reports. However, even though the capabilities of these two editions are

similar, there are some differences in the way the designer works. This is not meant to be inconsistent, but rather to adapt some of the Crystal Reports tasks to tasks with which Visual Basic developers are familiar. Ideally, the experience of designing a report with the Visual Basic report designer should be like designing a Visual Basic form. The following sections cover these differences.

UNDERSTANDING THE USER INTERFACE CONVENTIONS

Several user interface components work differently in the Visual Basic report designer. One of the first things you might notice is that the section names are shown above each section on a section band as opposed to being on the left side of the window. However, the same options are available when right-clicking on the section band. This tends to be more convenient anyway.

The Field Explorer resides to the left of the report page. Although it cannot be docked, it can be shown or hidden by clicking the Toggle Field View button on the designer toolbar. Other Explorer windows found in the standalone designer such as the Report Explorer and Repository Explorer are not available in the Visual Basic report designer.

NOTE

> Reports that contain objects linked to the Crystal Repository are fully supported; however, no new repository objects can be added to the report without using the standalone designer.

The menus that you would normally find in the standalone Crystal Reports designer can be found by right-clicking on an empty spot on the designer surface. The pop-up menu provides the same functionality.

MODIFYING THE REPORT USING THE PROPERTY BROWSER

To change the formatting and settings for report objects in the standalone designer, users are familiar with right-clicking on a report object and selecting Format Field from the pop-up menu. This opens the Format Editor, which gives access to changing the font, color, style, and other formatting options. In the Visual Basic report designer this scenario is still available; however, there is an additional way to apply most of these formatting options: the Property Browser.

The Property Browser is a window that lives inside of the Visual Basic development environment. It should be very familiar to Visual Basic developers as a way to change the appearance and behavior of a selected object on a form or design surface. In the context of the report designer, the Property Browser is another way to change the settings (properties) for report objects. In general, any setting that is available in the Format Editor dialog is available from the property browser when that object is selected. To see which properties are available for a given object, click on it, and check out the Property Browser window shown in Figure 30.2.

Figure 30.2
Changing a report object's settings via the Property Browser is shown here.

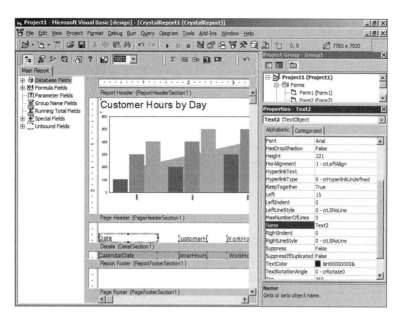

The property names are listed on the left and the current values are listed on the right. To choose a value, simply click on the current value and either type or select from the drop-down list.

One property to pay attention to is the Name property. This becomes relevant in the next section when you learn how to use the Report Engine Object Model to manipulate the report on the fly at runtime. This is the way to reference that object in code. Also of note is that the properties shown in the Property Browser map to the same properties that are available programmatically via the object model. If you see a property there, this means it is also available to be changed dynamically at runtime.

UNBOUND FIELDS

The Field Explorer in the Visual Basic report designer has an extra type field not found in the standalone report designer. These are called unbound fields. There is one type of unbound field for each data type. These fields are used to build dynamic reports. Because they do not have a predefined database field mapped to them, they provide a way to change the locations of fields on the report by using some application logic. The reason they each have their own data type is so that type-specific formatting can be applied such as the year format for a date object, or the thousands separator for a numeric object. Unbound fields are revisited later in this chapter.

NOTE

> When you create an unbound field, it also shows up as a formula in the Formula Fields list. This is because a formula is used behind the scenes of an unbound field. The best practice is not to edit this as a formula field.

PROGRAMMING WITH THE REPORT ENGINE OBJECT MODEL

The object model is the main entry point to the Crystal Reports engine for desktop applications. As mentioned earlier, it is based on COM and can be used from any COM-compliant development environment. Although the main library's filename is craxdrt.dll, the more important thing to know is that it shows up in the Project References dialog as Crystal Reports ActiveX Designer Runtime Library 10.0, as shown in Figure 30.3. After a reference is added to this library, a new set of objects will be available to you. These objects are contained in a library called CRAXDRT. To avoid name collisions, it's probably a good idea to fully qualify all object declarations with the CRAXDRT name, for example, Dim Param As CRAXDRT.ParameterField.

Figure 30.3
Reference the Report Designer Component's Object Model in the References dialog.

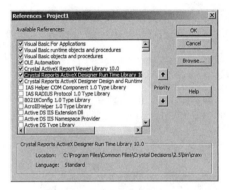

NOTE

When adding a Crystal Report to your project, a reference is automatically added to this library for you. You can use the CRAXDRT library right away.

In addition to many other features, the object model provides the capability to open, create, modify, save, print, and export reports. This section covers some of the more common scenarios a developer might encounter.

The main entry point to the object model is the Report object. This object is the programmatic representation of the report template and provides access to all the functions of the SDK. There are three ways to obtain a Report object:

- Load an existing RPT file from disk
- Create a new report from scratch
- Load an existing strongly typed report that is part of the Visual Basic project

The first two methods involve the Application object. Its two key methods are NewReport and OpenReport. As the name implies, the NewReport method is used to create a blank report and the `OpenReport` method is used to open an existing report. Creating a new report is useful if the application needs to make a lot of dynamic changes to the report's layout on the fly. This way all report objects can be added dynamically.

> **NOTE**
>
> Although many purist developers are tempted to not use any predefined report templates (RPT files) and create all reports on the fly, this tends to be overkill for most projects. There is a lot of work in having to programmatically make every single addition to a report. It's usually a better plan to have some RPT files as part of the application and then make some small modifications at runtime.

30

The other option is to use the `OpenReport` method, which takes a filename to an RPT file as a parameter. This opens an existing report. When using this method, the RPT files must be distributed along with the application. The advantage of having these externals files is that you can update the reports without updating the application.

The last method is to use a strongly typed report. A strongly typed report is one that is added to the Visual Basic project and turned into a DSR file. Whichever name you give that report, a corresponding programmatic object exists with the same name. For example, if you save a report as BudgetReport.DSR, you can create that report programmatically with the following code:

```
Dim Report As New BudgetReport
```

There are several advantages to using strongly typed reports. First, all report files are bound into the project's resulting executable so no external files are available for users to modify and mess up. Second, not only is the name of the report strongly typed (BudgetReport in the previous example), but also the section and report objects. For example, if you have a text object acting as a column header and you want to modify this at runtime, it's very easy to access the object by name like this:

```
Report.ColumnHeader1.SetText "Some text"
```

The long-handed way of doing this would look something like this:

```
Dim field as CRAXDRT.FieldObject
Set field = Report.Sections("PH").ReportObjects(3)
Field.SetText "Some text"
```

Not only is this last method longer, you'd also have to refer to the report object by index instead of name, which can become problematic. The following sections discuss some of the common tasks that are performed after a Report object is obtained.

EXPORTING REPORTS TO OTHER FILE FORMATS

A very common requirement for application developers is to be able to export a report through their application. Not only do developers want a variety of formats, they want the export to happen in a variety of ways, for example, having the user select where to save the report, saving to a temp file and then opening it, e-mailing it to somebody else, and so on.

By being creative with exporting, you can create some very powerful applications. The Report Designer Component object model provides a very flexible API to meet these broad needs. This section covers the basics of exporting.

There are two components to exports: the format and the destination. The developer specifies both of these through the `ExportOptions` property of the `Report` object.

Setting the format options involves two steps. The first step is to choose which format you want to export to. Sometimes an application provides the user a list of export formats and lets him choose, other times the export type will be hardcoded. In any case, simply setting the `FormatType` property of the `ExportOptions` object specifies this. This property accepts a number. For example, to export to PDF, pass in 31. Remembering which number represents which format is tough so there are some enumerations with descriptive names that make this easier.

NOTE

> For a full list of enumerations, consult the Crystal Reports Developers Help file and look at the `CRExportFormatType` enumeration in the Visual Basic object browser.

To help you get started, here are some of the more popular export format enumeration values:

- PDF: `crEFTPortableDocFormat`
- Word: `crEFTWordForWindows`
- Excel: `crEFTExcel97`
- HTML: `crEFTHTML40`
- XML: `crEFTXML`

Generally, all you need to do to set the format options is set the `FormatType` property. However, many of the format types have some additional options. For example, when exporting to Excel there is an option to indicate whether you want the grid lines shown. To handle these extra settings, there are some other properties off the `ExportOptions` object whose names begin with the format type. In the Excel grid lines example, the property is called `ExcelShowGridLines`. For PDF, there are `PDFFirstPageNumber` and `PDFLastPageNumber` properties that indicate which pages of the report you want exported to PDF. You can determine what options are available by checking out the Crystal Reports Developer Help file and looking at the `ExportOptions` object.

After the format is set up, you need to tell Crystal Reports where you want this report to be exported. This is called the *export destination*. The most common destination is simply a file on disk but there are destinations such as e-mail or Microsoft Exchange folders where reports can be automatically sent. The export destination is set via the `DestinationType` property of the `ExportOptions` object. Some example values are listed here:

- File: `crEDTDiskFile`
- E-mail: `crEDTMailMAPI`
- Exchange: `crEDTMicrosoftExchange`

Check out the `CRExportDestinationType` enumeration to see the other available options. Like the format, the destination has a set of additional options. The most obvious one is when setting the destination to a file (`crEDTDiskFile`), you would need to specify where you want this file and what its name should be. This is accomplished by setting the `DiskFileName` property. Other properties on the `ExportOptions` object are available such as the `MailToList` property, which is used to indicate who the report should be mailed to if the e-mail option is selected as the destination.

The final step in exporting is to call the `Report` object's `Export` method. It takes a single parameter: `promptUser`. If this is set to true, any options previously set on the `ExportOptions` object are ignored and a dialog appears asking the user to select the format and destination. This can be useful if you want the user to have the capability to use any export format and any destination. If you would like a more controlled environment, you can set `promptUser` to false. When this is done the previously selected values from the `ExportOptions` object are respected and the export is done without any user interaction besides a progress dialog popping up while the export is happening. This progress dialog can also be suppressed by setting the `Report` object's `DisplayProgressDialog` property to false. Listing 30.1 provides an example of a report being exported to a PDF file without any user interaction.

LISTING 30.1 EXPORTING TO PDF

```
Dim Report As New CrystalReport1

' Set export format
Report.ExportOptions.FormatType = crEFTPortableDocFormat

' Set any applicable options for that format
' In this case, set to only export pages 1-2
Report.ExportOptions.PDFFirstPageNumber = 1
Report.ExportOptions.PDFLastPageNumber = 2

' Set export destination
Report.ExportOptions.DestinationType = crEDTDiskFile

' Set any applicable options for the destination
' In this case, the filename to be exported to
Report.ExportOptions.DiskFileName = "C:\MyReport.pdf"

' Turn all user interface dialogs off and perform the export
Report.DisplayProgressDialog = False
Report.Export False
```

PRINTING REPORTS TO A PRINTER DEVICE

Although it's helpful to view reports onscreen and save some paper, many times reports still need to be printed. To accomplish this, there is a collection of methods for printing reports available from the Report object. The simplest way to print a report is to call the PrintOut method passing in true for the promptUser parameter as shown here:

```
Report.PrintOut True
```

This opens the standard Print dialog that enables the user to select the page range and then click OK to confirm the print. The limitation to this is that the pop-up dialog does not enable the user to change the destination printer. Because this is a common scenario, this method isn't used very often. Instead, the PrinterSetup method is called. This method pops up a standard printer selection dialog that enables the user to change the paper orientation or printer.

Keep in mind that calling the PrinterSetup method does not actually initiate the print; it only collects the settings to be used for the print later on. Luckily it does indicate via a return value whether the user clicked the OK or Cancel button. Listing 30.2 shows an example of how to use the PrinterSetup method to set printer options.

LISTING 30.2   PRINTING A REPORT INTERACTIVELY

```
' Call PrinterSetup to set printer, paper orientation, and so on
If Report.PrinterSetupEx(Me.hWnd) = 0 Then
    ' If the return value is 0, the user did not click Cancel
    ' so go ahead with the print
    Report.PrintOut False
End If
```

To print a report without any user interaction, call the PrintOut method passing in false for the promptUser parameter. Options such as pages and collation can be set with the additional argument to the PrintOut method. To change the printer, call the SelectPrinter method. This accepts the printer driver, name, and port as parameters and performs the printer change without any user interaction. Listing 30.3 illustrates a silent print.

LISTING 30.3   PRINTING A REPORT SILENTLY

```
' Call PrinterSetup to set printer, paper orientation, and so on

' Set paper orientation
Report.PaperOrientation = crLandscape

' Set printer to print to
'    pDriver -- for example: winspool
'    pName -- for example: \\PRINTSERVER\PRINTER4
'    pPort -- for example: Ne00:
Report.SelectPrinter pDriver, pName, pPort

' Initiate the print
Report.PrintOut False
```

SETTING REPORT PARAMETERS

Often reports delivered through an application need to be dynamically generated based on a parameter value. If a report with parameters is viewed, exported, or printed, a Crystal parameter prompting dialog pops up and asks the user to enter the parameter values before the report is processed. This parameter prompting dialog requires no code. The use of the object model comes into play when a developer wants to set parameters without user interaction. This is done via the `ParameterFieldDefinitions` collection accessed via the `Report` object's `ParameterFields` property. If all parameter values are provided before the report is processed, the parameter dialog is suppressed.

30

Parameters can be referenced by name or by number. To reference by name, call the `ParameterFields` object's `GetItemByName` method passing in the name of the parameter you want to access. This returns a `ParameterField` object. Alternatively, use the indexer on the `ParameterFields` object; for example, `ParameterFields(1)`. When referencing by index, the parameters will be stored in the same order they appear in the Field Explorer window in the report designer. After a `ParameterField` object is obtained, simply call the `AddCurrentValue` method to set the parameter's value as shown in Listing 30.4.

LISTING 30.4 SETTING PARAMETERS

```
Dim Application As New CRAXDRT.Application
Dim Report As CRAXDRT.Report

' Open the report from a file
Set Report = Application.OpenReport("C:\MyReport.rpt")

Dim p1 as ParameterField
Set p1 = Report.ParameterFields.GetItemByName("Geography")
p1.AddCurrentValue("Europe")


Dim p2 as ParameterField
Set p2 = Report.ParameterFields(2)
p2.AddCurrentValue(1234)
```

If the parameter accepts multiple values, simply call the `AddCurrentValue` method multiple times. For range parameters where there is a start and an end value, use the `AddRangeValue` method.

Sometimes a developer wants to prompt the user to enter some or all of the parameters but they want to control the user interface. Much information about the parameter can be obtained by reading its properties:

- `ParameterFieldName`: Name of the parameter
- `ValueType`: The data type of the parameter (string, number, and so on)
- `Prompt`: The text to use to prompt for this parameter

Also, by using the `NumberOfDefaultValues` property and `GetNthDefaultValue` method, a developer can construct her own pick-list of default parameter values that is stored in the report.

NOTE

> For more information on the other properties and methods available on the `ParameterField` object, consult the Crystal Reports Developer Help file and look for the `ParameterFieldDefinition` object.

SETTING DATA SOURCE CREDENTIALS

Although the sample reports that come with Crystal Reports 10 use an unsecured Microsoft Access database as their data source, most real-world reports are based on a data source that require credentials (username, password) to be passed. Also, it's very common to want to change data source information such as the server name or database instance name via code. This section covers these scenarios.

Unlike parameters, there is no default-prompting dialog for data source credentials. They must be passed via code. The server name, location, database name, and username are all stored in the report. However, the password is never saved. A report will fail to run if a password is not provided.

Most reports only have a single data source but because it is possible for reports to have multiple data sources that in turn would require multiple sets of credentials, setting credentials isn't something that's done on a global level. Credentials are set for each table in the report. Tables are represented by an object called a `DatabaseTable` inside the object model. The following code snippet illustrates the hierarchy required to get at the `DatabaseTable` object.

```
Report
    Database
        DatabaseTables
            DatabaseTable
```

Tables are accessed by their index, not their name. The indexes in the object model are all 1-based and are in the order you see them in the Field Explorer in the report designer. To access the first table in the report, you could do this:

```
Dim tbl as DatabaseTable
Set tbl = Report.Database.Tables(1)
```

After the correct `DatabaseTable` object is obtained, use the `ConnectionInfo` property bag to fill in valid credentials. If you do only have one data source in the report, but multiple tables from that data source, you need not set credentials for each one. The information is propagated across all tables. Listing 30.5 illustrates setting the server name, database name, username, and password for a report based off an OLEDB data source.

LISTING 30.5   SETTING DATA SOURCE CREDENTIALS

```
' Provide database logon credentials (in this case
' for an OLEDB connection to a SQL Server database)
Dim tbl as CRAXDRT.DatabaseTable
Set tbl = Report.Database.Tables(1)
tbl.ConnectionInfo("Data Source") = "MyServer"
tbl.ConnectionInfo("Initial Catalog") = "MyDB"
tbl.ConnectionInfo("User ID") = "User1"
tbl.ConnectionInfo("Password") = "abc"
```

Each type of data source has its own set of properties. OLEDB has a Data Source, which is the server name whereas the Microsoft Access driver has a Database Name, which is a file-name to the MDB file. The ConnectionInfo property bag is introspective so you can loop through and determine what properties are available.

MAPPING UNBOUND FIELDS AT RUNTIME

Earlier in this chapter you saw that a new type of field called an unbound field can be added to the report with the Visual Basic report designer. Using the object model, these unbound fields can be mapped to database fields in the report at runtime. This is done two different ways: manually or automatically.

The manual method is to use the SetUnboundFieldSource method of the FieldObject. This method takes a single parameter, which is the name of the database field to be mapped in the Crystal field syntax, such as {Table.Field}. If a strongly typed report is being used, that is, a report added to the Visual Basic project, the UnboundField objects can be referenced as properties of the Report object. For example, an unbound field object given the default name of UnboundString1 can be referenced like this:

```
Report.UnboundString1.SetUnboundFieldSource "{Customer.Customer Name}"
```

If a report is loaded at runtime, there are no strongly typed properties so the FieldObject needs to be found under the Section and ReportObjects hierarchy. The following example gets a reference to the first unbound field in the details section:

```
Dim fld As FieldObject
Set fld = Report.Sections("D").ReportObjects(1)
fld.SetUnboundFieldSource "{Customer.Customer ID}"
```

The automatic method is to simply call the Report object's AutoSetUnboundFieldSource method. This assumes that any unbound fields to be mapped are named to match a database field. Initially this might seem strange because the whole point of an unbound field is that the developer doesn't know which database field it will be mapped to at design time. However, this automatic method is valuable when the database table doesn't exist at design time, and instead is added at runtime based on some dynamic data.

USING THE CODE-BEHIND EVENTS

One of the reasons that the report is saved as a DSR file instead of just an RPT file is that the DSR file contains some code that is attached to the report file. This code, often called *code-behind*, is event-handing code for several events that the report engine fires. The following list describes events that are fired and their corresponding uses:

- `Initialize (Report)`: Fired when the report object is first created. This event can be useful for performing initialization-related tasks.

- `BeforeFormatPage/AfterFormatPage (Report)`: Fired before and after a page is processed; can be useful for indicating progress.

- `NoData (Report)`: Fired when a report is processed but no records were returned from the data source. Sometimes a report with no records is meaningless and thus should be skipped or the user should be warned; this event is a great way to handle that.

- `FieldMapping (Report)`: Fired when the database is verified and there has been a schema change; this event enables you to remap fields without user interaction.

- `Format (Section)`: Fired for the rendering of each section. This is useful for handling the detail section's event and performing conditional logic.

DELIVERING REPORTS USING THE REPORT VIEWER

In the previous section, only printing and exporting were mentioned as options for delivering reports. You might have been wondering how to view reports onscreen. This section will cover using the report viewer to view reports. This report viewer control is usually referred to as the ActiveX viewer, or the Crystal Reports Viewer Control. It is an ActiveX control, which means that in addition to being able to be dropped on to any Visual Basic form—like the other components of the Report Designer Component—it can be used in any COM-compliant development environment. Its filename is CRViewer.dll. Figure 30.4 depicts the ActiveX viewer displaying a report from a Visual Basic application.

Figure 30.4
A Crystal Report is shown here being displayed in the ActiveX viewer.

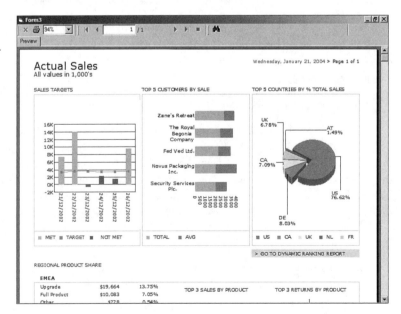

The ActiveX viewer works in conjunction with the object model and report engine to render the report to the screen. The object model talks to the report engine to process the report, and then the ActiveX viewer asks the object model for the data for an individual page. After this data is received by the viewer, it displays the report page onscreen. The following code snippet illustrates how to view a report with the report viewer control:

```
Dim Application As New CRAXDRT.Application
Dim Report As CRAXDRT.Report

Set Report = Application.OpenReport("C:\MyReport.rpt")
CRViewer.ReportSource = Report
CRViewer.ViewReport
```

The ActiveX control has many properties and methods that enable you to customize its look and feel. To turn off the toolbar at the top of the viewer control, simply set the `DisplayToolbar` property to false. To turn off the group tree, set the `DisplayGroupTree` property to false. This can result in a very minimalist viewer. In addition, the control has a full event model that notifies you when certain actions are performed, such as a drill-down or page navigation. For more information on the ActiveX viewer control, consult the Crystal Reports 10 developer help file.

USING THE OBJECT MODEL TO BUILD BATCH REPORTING APPLICATIONS

So far this chapter has focused on on-demand reporting, meaning that reports are processed as they are requested and they generally go away when the viewing or printing is completed. One of the biggest uses of the Report Designer Component today is for batch reporting; that is, running a large number of reports at once. This section covers some features and best practices relevant to batch reporting.

WORKING WITH REPORTS WITH SAVED DATA

When using the standalone report designer, you might have noticed an option on the File menu called Save Data with Report. This enables a report to be saved with the last returned dataset so that it can be viewed again without connecting to the database. Reports with saved data are in effect an offline report.

Applications using the Report Designer Component can both create and view reports with saved data. This enables you to run a batch of reports and then be able to view them at any point later. This can be useful for reports based on queries that take a long time to run, or also for achieving an archiving process for reports.

Creating a report with saved data is very simple. You just export to the Crystal Reports format by using the `crEFTCrystalReport` identifier. All exported reports have saved data. You can control where this report is saved and archive it for later.

Viewing a report with saved data doesn't actually require any code at all. The logic of the report engine is: If the report has saved data, use it and only hit the database again if the user clicks the Refresh button or the developer forces a refresh by calling the `DiscardSavedData` method off the `Report` object. You can always tell which copy of the data is being used from examining the `DataDate` property of the `Report` object.

Hopefully you can imagine how applying this principle to batch reporting would be powerful. A set of reports could be run overnight, producing another set of reports with saved data that can be viewed offline.

LOOPING THROUGH REPORTS

Another scenario that is relevant to batch reporting is looping through a set of reports. A common example is running either one report many times with different parameters (such as a bank statement) or running a large collection of reports all at once (such as financial statements).

These scenarios can be accomplished by using external report files and writing a loop that opens a report, prints or exports it, and then closes it. The best way to close a report is to set the Report object to `Nothing`:

```
Set Report = Nothing
```

This releases the COM object and releases the report job from memory.

Also, the `CRAXDRT` library is thread safe, which means that multiple threads can be calling into it at the same time. If a large number of reports need to be processing in a very small amount of time, you can spawn as many as five simultaneous threads that are all running reports at the same time.

TROUBLESHOOTING

ADD CRYSTAL REPORTS 10

"Add Crystal Reports 10" is not showing on my Project menu.

If you don't see "Add Crystal Reports 10" on the Project menu, go to the Project, Components menu, and on the Dialog tab make sure Crystal Reports 10 has a check beside it. If you turn this on, it permanently appears on the Project menu.

PART VII

CUSTOMIZED REPORT DISTRIBUTION— USING CRYSTAL ENTERPRISE EMBEDDED EDITION

CHAPTER 31

INTRODUCTION TO CRYSTAL ENTERPRISE EMBEDDED EDITION

In this chapter

INTRODUCTION TO CRYSTAL ENTERPRISE EMBEDDED EDITION

The Report Application Server (RAS) is a set of components that enable developers to take advantage of the report-design capabilities of the Crystal Reports engine. These components enable developers to build applications that include report design, modification, and viewing functionality and can be accessed through a Web browser. RAS is the replacement and evolution of previous single threaded object models and Crystal Products such as the Report Designer Component (RDC) and the Crystal Reports Print Engine (CRPE).

In version 10 of the Crystal Suite of Business Objects products, the standalone RAS is called the Crystal Enterprise Embedded edition. RAS is built using client/server technology. The server components consist of the application logic that interfaces with the reporting print engine. The client components consist of the RAS Software Developer's Kit (SDK) that communicates with the RAS via TCP/IP and the Viewers SDK that exposes a number of report viewers each suiting particular application needs. The RAS is a multithreaded server with both .NET/COM and Java object models.

The RAS and Viewers SDKs are discussed in greater detail in Chapter 32, "Crystal Enterprise—Viewing Reports," and Chapter 33, "Crystal Enterprise Embedded—Report Modification and Creation." This chapter introduces the sample applications provided around Crystal Enterprise Embedded and provides some configuration information.

UNDERSTANDING CRYSTAL ENTERPRISE EMBEDDED EDITION

Crystal Enterprise Embedded edition (the RAS by itself) is used in a standalone mode to deliver Crystal Report's creation, modification, and viewing functionality over the Web. In its simplest description, it can be thought of as an open Report Engine with a published object model and viewer controls. Crystal Enterprise Professional and Premium editions were introduced in Part V, "Web Report Distribution—Using Crystal Enterprise." Each of these advanced editions of Crystal Enterprise can also leverage the powerful report exploration (creation and modification) functionality of the RAS and object model. In these advanced editions, the RAS is effectively plugged into the Crystal Enterprise infrastructure or backbone and managed as any of its other services. Figure 31.1 displays the basic RAS standalone architecture.

In this standalone case, the installation is limited to a single RAS for the custom applications written to interact with. The RAS accesses reports on the server based on a central location specified in the RAS Configuration tool (see the next section for more detail). You can however have multiple installations of standalone RAS that share a central network location where the reports reside. Keep in mind that it is generally not a good idea to have the report located somewhere other than the RAS server—applications opening reports on this server require the server components to load the involved report and to create a local copy of it. The network traffic associated with pulling the .rpt file from a location on a different server results in application performance degradation.

Figure 31.1
The RAS architecture provides programmatic access to report creation and modification.

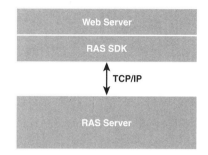

USING THE CRYSTAL CONFIGURATION MANAGER

The Crystal Configuration Manager (CCM) provides a point of access for setting the different options around the Crystal Enterprise Embedded (or RAS) installation. It is accessed through the Microsoft Start, Programs, Crystal Enterprise menu path and is highlighted in Figure 31.2.

Figure 31.2
The CCM for the RAS provides access to key settings.

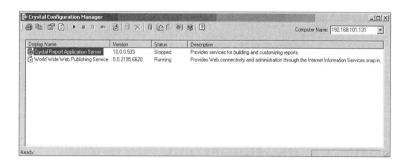

The default report location along with other RAS server settings can be accessed by stopping the RAS service in the CCM and then selecting Properties through the Properties button or the right-click menu on the service.

SETTING DATABASE PARAMETERS

After having accessed the Crystal RAS Properties dialog box, click on the Parameters tab and ensure the Option Type drop-down box has the Database option selected as shown in Figure 31.3. In this dialog, you can set the number of records that are brought back in reports by default or the number of records accessed in one batch. You can also set how many records are accessed and brought back when you expose the Browse Field functionality in your applicaton(s).

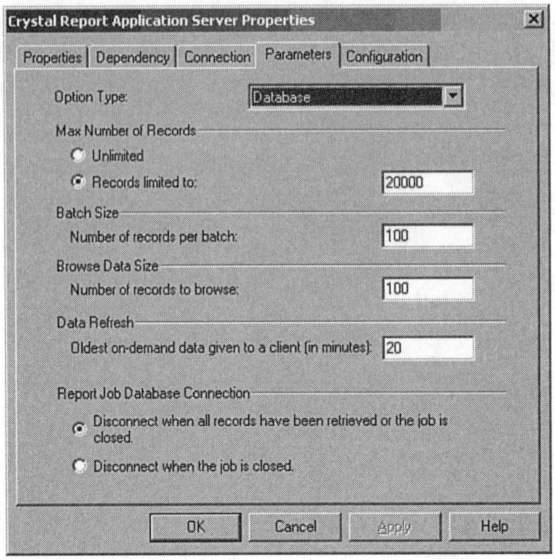

Figure 31.3
Setting the RAS
Database options.

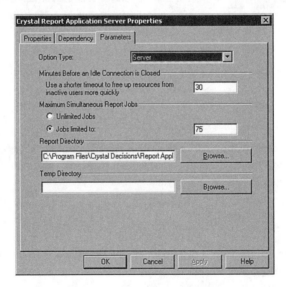

SETTING SERVER PARAMETERS

On the same Parameters dialog, after choosing Server for the option type you are shown the dialog displayed in Figure 31.4. Here you can set the location of your reports, the number of simultaneous jobs, and a number of minutes before an idle job is closed. Keep in mind as you change these settings you need to restart the RAS service for them to take effect.

Figure 31.4
The Parameters tab
of the RAS properties
dialog enables you to
set key RAS options
such as report loca-
tion, simultaneous
job maximums, and
user timeout.

NOTE

> The RAS also exposes caching capabilities that enable multiple users to view the same copy of a cached report. This ultimately increases the number jobs the RAS can handle at any given point. Keep in mind however that if your reports contain subreports these are not cached.

CRYSTAL ENTERPRISE EMBEDDED EDITION SAMPLES

There are a number of sample applications that ship as part of Crystal Enterprise Embedded (RAS standalone). This section describes these sample applications. It is important to note that the purpose of these examples is to demonstrate the basic capabilities of RAS in action and to provide sample starting points for further application development. In some cases you will find these immediately useful for allowing your users to perform simple tasks like viewing reports, setting report data sources at runtime, changing the selection formula at runtime, or passing parameters to reports. In the majority of cases, it is expected you will be able to leverage the concepts and sample code as starting points into developing your own rich and more full-featured applications.

31

REPORT PREVIEW SAMPLE

The Report Preview Sample is an application that demonstrates report viewing using Crystal Enterprise Embedded's RAS (see Figure 31.5). The frame on the left represents the directory structure as it appears starting at the root of the default RAS reports directory. By default, this directory is c:\program files\crystal decisions\report application server10\ reports. After a report is selected to view, it appears inside the bottom-right frame. The top-right frame lists report viewers that are available with RAS. You can toggle between the viewers available by selecting the desired option in this frame.

Figure 31.5
The Report Viewer Sample provides a good starting point for a report viewing application and also provides sample code.

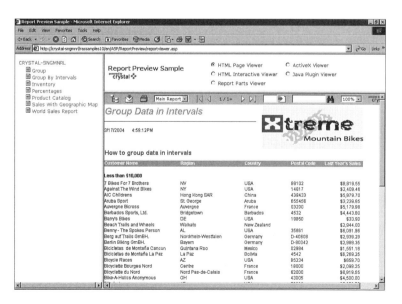

Additional information on the report viewers for RAS and their programmatic hooks and controls is provided in the next chapter.

THE SIMPLE DISCRETE PARAMETER SAMPLE

The Simple Discrete Parameter example shown in Figure 31.6 provides a demonstration of a report running with parameters. As previously discussed in this book, there are often cases where reports are required to run with parameters against the database. Some of these parameters might be passed in without the report consumer even being aware of them (for example, global environment variables to set a user's preferred language for report viewing). Other types of parameters require user input where the user is presented with a list of values to choose from and a report is run using those selected values and limits the resultset displayed in the report.

Figure 31.6
The Simple Discrete Parameters example provides a good starting point for a report viewing application using parameters.

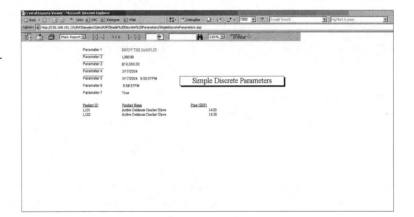

THE DATABASE LOGON SAMPLE

The Database Logon example illustrates the capability for the end user to supply his own logon credentials to the report when it is retrieving data from the database. This scenario is commonly found in implementations where users should only be able to see data that pertains to them and user-level database security has been set up. An example of this might include a sales executive for the eastern region and his counterpart for the western region viewing the same pipeline report—each executive only needs to view information for his specific geographies. When either of them views the report, they are prompted to supply logon information (see Figure 31.7) to continue and this information is passed to the database and the appropriate user-level security is applied there.

THE DATA SOURCE LOCATION SAMPLE

The Set Data Source Location sample demonstrates the task of setting the location of the database to be used for the involved report at runtime. This example might be useful in scenarios where you need to run the same report against different environments (such as Development, Testing and Quality Assurance [QA]). Another practical example would be in the scenario where different versions of identical databases are kept across an organization. You might want to enable the application users to decide what data source to dynamically run the report against (for example, different regional databases). In this case, a custom Web page could be developed to let the user make the desired choice and then use the RAS functionality to connect the report to the selected database.

Figure 31.7
The Database Logon example provides a good starting point for understanding database logons and Crystal Reports.

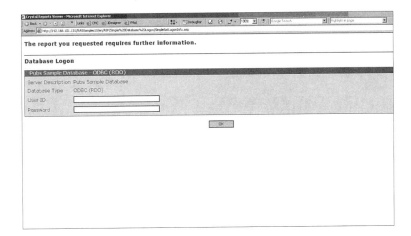

Examples discussed in this section are included with the out-of-the box installation of the RAS (Crystal Enterprise Embedded in version 10) and can be leveraged by reusing the source code distributed as part of the installation.

DHTML REPORT DESIGN WIZARD

When RAS is installed and licensed as part of Crystal Enterprise Professional or Premium editions, it presents a DHTML wizard application through Crystal Enterprise that enables end users to create new or modify existing reports that are published in Crystal Enterprise. This integrated Crystal Enterprise action provides the end user with a series of dialogs that step through common report creation/modification tasks like adding fields, groups, filters, sorts, charts, and the application of report templates to existing reports stored in the Crystal Enterprise system.

Take a closer look at the wizard user interface. When you select the modify action on a given report, a dialog is displayed (see Figure 31.8) that enables you to select fields to be included in the newly modified report.

After you have selected the fields you want, click the Next button to open a Grouping dialog (see Figure 31.9) that enables the end user to specify groupings to be included in the report.

If at least one group has been selected for the newly modified report, a Summaries dialog is presented next (see Figure 31.10). This enables the addition of summaries to the new report. To accomplish this, an end user defines the type of summary field (such as Sum, Average, Count, Max, or Min), the field to perform the summary on, and the group to calculate the involved summary on. Clearly, multiple summaries can be added to the newly created report in this dialog. Note that different types of summaries are presented based on the type of field selected (for example, Sum does not appear if a string field is selected).

Figure 31.8
The Field Selection dialog of the Modify Report Wizard enables user selection of fields from an existing Business View or Crystal Report.

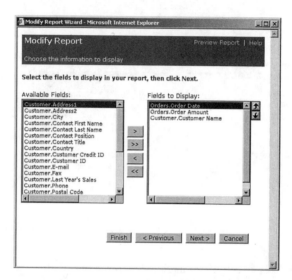

Figure 31.9
The Group Selection dialog of the Modify Report Wizard enables end users to add or change report groupings.

After you click the Next button, you are presented with a choice to override the default group sorting that is added when grouping the data in the report. Group sorting can be based on the actual Group names or the Summary fields that are calculated for that group.

When performing the sort on the latter, you can specify Top and Bottom N sorts or an All Records sort through the drop-down boxes in the dialog. Also in this dialog, you can specify the sort order for the detail level fields included in the detail section of the report (see Figure 31.11).

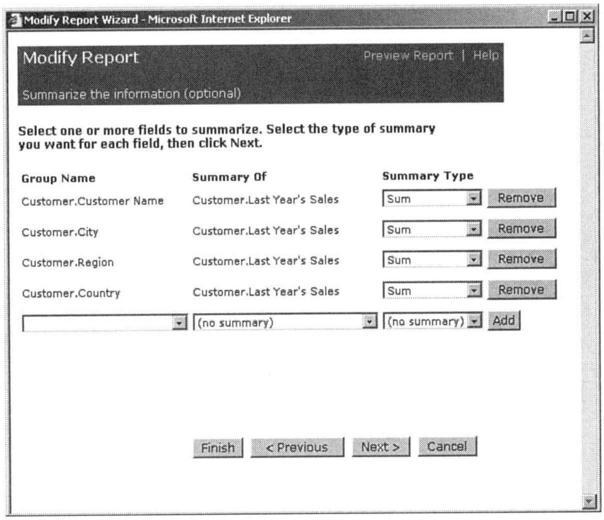

Figure 31.10
The Summary Selection dialog of the Modify Report Wizard enables the end user to add or change field summaries to reports.

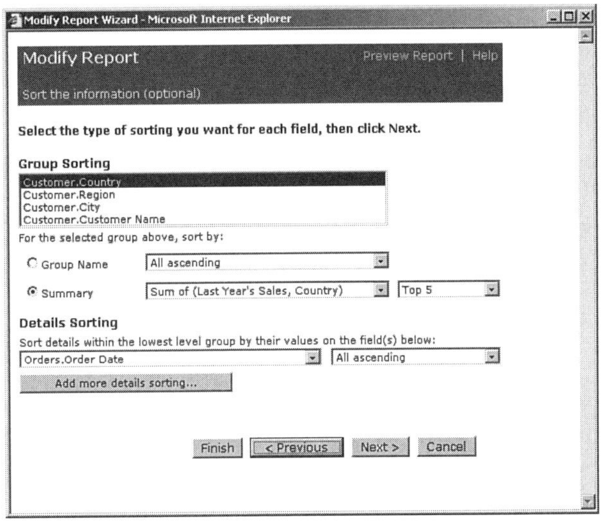

Figure 31.11
The Sorting Selection dialog of the Modify Report Wizard enables end users to add or change field sorting on the report.

The next step is the option to apply record filters. *Filters* are used to limit the data that the report displays. This dialog enables you to see any filters that are already defined and append new filters through the provided text box or the provided drop-down boxes.

NOTE

It is important to note that although the default wizard uses the AND operator to join multiple filters, a small customization to this wizard would enable the end user to specify the operator on multiple joins. As you move through the following two chapters, it should become more clear how this type of customization would take place.

The RAS-based DHTML wizard also enables the end user to place a chart in the report header or footer section. The Chart Type is selected in the dialog presented in Figure 31.12 and the end user can customize the chart by adding a title to the chart and specifying the summary data that is actually charted (see Figure 31.13).

Figure 31.12
The Filter Selection dialog of the Modify Report Wizard enables the end user to select filters for the modified report.

31

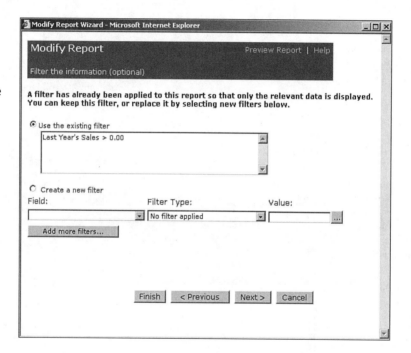

One last screen that is presented for optional use is the report template specification screen. In this dialog, you can apply an existing report template to the newly created report. Report templates were covered in Chapter 14, "Designing Effective Report Templates."

After the report is defined to fit your needs, you can preview it immediately using the Preview Report link on any of the DHTML wizard screens. If the newly modified report is of sufficient value to keep as a new report, you can save the report in any Crystal Enterprise folder that you have been granted access to within the Crystal Enterprise Professional/Premium security model.

Figure 31.13
The Charting
Selection dialog of
the Modify Report
Wizard.

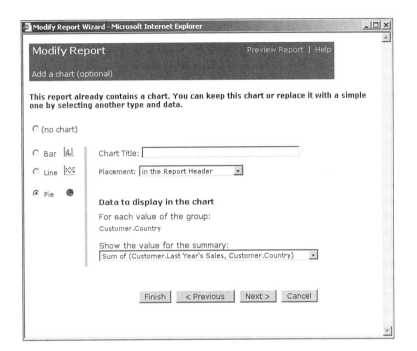

LEVERAGING THE OPEN SOURCE NATURE OF THE SAMPLE APPLICATIONS

It is worth pointing out as a reminder that all the functionality that is provided through the step-wise DHTML Report Design Wizard just described is provided through a single application called the Crystal Reports Explorer in version 10. (In previous versions it was called the Crystal Ad-Hoc Application and is often still referenced as such.) This application is provided with Crystal Enterprise Premium or Crystal Enterprise Professional with the Report Explorer Add-in.

For more information, see Chapter 21, "Ad-Hoc Application and Excel Plug-in for Ad-Hoc and Analytic Reporting."

It is also instructive to understand that both the DHTML Report Design Wizard and the Crystal Reports Explorer introduced in Chapter 21 are simply working examples of the Crystal Enterprise Embedded (or RAS) functionality in action. These applications are provided open-source and provide great starting points for rapid application development and customization. The next two chapters introduce the RAS object models and their capability to integrate report creation and modify functionality into either Java or .NET/COM-based applications.

Troubleshooting

Distributing Through the Web

I want to distribute Crystal Reports through the Web but I need to scale beyond the built-in simultaneous request limit of 3 provided with Crystal Reports Advanced.

Install Crystal Enterprise Embedded and either use one of the sample Web reporting applications or include programmatic access to the object model in your applications.

In cases where there have been legacy applications written in previous versions of the Crystal product set that make use of the Report Designer Component (RDC) or the Crystal Print engine (CRPE), Crystal Enterprise Embedded edition should be considered the logical migration path. This is particularly true when you're developing applications that require Web access. This version of the product leverages the advantages of the client/server architected components in RAS that are specifically written for the Web. In the following two chapters the common Crystal Viewers SDK and the functionality in the RAS SDK are presented in increasing detail.

CHAPTER 32

CRYSTAL ENTERPRISE—
VIEWING REPORTS

In this chapter

VIEWING REPORTS OVER THE WEB

This chapter introduces programmatic access to viewing reports over the Web through the Crystal Enterprise SDKs. It is important to note that these viewers and the means to programmatically access them have been made consistent across the Business Objects Crystal product line—including Crystal Reports, Crystal Enterprise Embedded, and Crystal Enterprise Professional and Premium editions. This consistency across products enables a seamless and rapid migration through the different versions of the Crystal product suite as developer's application requirements grow. These SDKs are provided in Java, .NET, and COM flavors and provide rich functionality that can be integrated into both intranet and extranet targeted applications.

This chapter introduces the different Crystal Report viewer components and explains how to set them up for inclusion in your custom applications. The following topics are covered:

- Introduction to the Crystal Report viewers
- Understanding the report source
- Implementing the Page viewer and toolbar buttons
- Implementing the Part viewer
- Implementing the Interactive viewer and toolbar buttons
- Implementing the Grid viewer and toolbar buttons
- Using the Export Control

INTRODUCTION TO THE CRYSTAL REPORT VIEWERS

The Crystal Report viewers that ship with Report Application Server break into four different categories to suit the need of a variety of applications: the Page viewer, Part viewer, Interactive viewer, and Grid viewer. Although all four viewers offer unique capabilities, they share a common API and set of basic features. Each viewer allows the developer to indicate which report to display, supply database logon credentials, apply report parameters, and export the report. All four viewers are exposed as server-side controls and as a result, output dynamic HTML that is rendered in any Web browser. No special software is required on the client's machines to view reports using any of the viewers.

Listed below is a short description about each report viewer:

- Page viewer: The standard report viewer component. It displays reports in a paginated fashion. A toolbar along the top allows access functions like page navigation, printing, exporting, zooming, and text searching.
- Part viewer: A report viewer component that renders just individual elements of a report. This is useful for portal-style applications where only a small portion of the screen is reserved for report viewing.

- Interactive viewer: Looks and acts identical to the Page viewer but exposes an extra toolbar button that provides an additional user interface for doing data-level searching within the report.
- Grid viewer: A viewer component that just displays the data from the report in a grid without any layout or formatting applied.

The means with which all of these viewers interact with the reports themselves is a mechanism called the report source. The following section describes the report source in detail.

UNDERSTANDING THE REPORT SOURCE

Because the Crystal Report viewer components are shared across both the Crystal Enterprise Embedded Edition and the Crystal Enterprise Professional/Premium editions, there must be a common interface defined so the viewer can display reports generated using both types of report processing engines. This interface is called the *report source*. The report source is an object that both the Embedded edition and Professional/Premium editions supply that the viewer in turn communicates with to render the reports to the various forms of HTML.

There are three types of report sources:

- Standalone Report Application Server: This is packaged as the Crystal Enterprise Embedded Edition.
- Clustered Report Application Server: This is packaged as part of Crystal Enterprise Professional/Premium edition. This is the Report Application Server running as a service on the Crystal Enterprise framework.
- Page Server: This is the primary report processing service as part of the Crystal Enterprise framework.

NOTE

> Because of the special functionality of the Interactive and Grid viewers, they do not work with a Page Server–based report source.

The Java code in Listing 32.1 illustrates the first scenario where a report source object is obtained from the standalone Report Application Server.

LISTING 32.1   OBTAINING A REPORT SOURCE FROM A REPORT FILE

```
//First you must create a new ReportClientDocument object
ReportClientDocument reportClientDoc = new ReportClientDocument();

//After the ReportClientDocument is created, you then need to
//specify the report file that is to be used as the report
```

continues

LISTING 32.1   CONTINUED

```
//source:
String path = "C:\\Program Files\\Crystal Decisions\\Report Application Server" +
             " 10\\Reports\\Sample.rpt";
reportClientDoc.open(path, openReportOptions._openAsReadOnly);

//Finally use the openReportSource method to return the report source object
IReportSource reportSource = reportClientDoc.getReportSource();
```

> **NOTE**
>
> All the code listings provided in this chapter are provided in JSP/Java. Although the .NET/COM and the Java flavors of the RAS SDK share identical functionality, there are obviously language nuances associated with each of them. Code samples for additional language flavors are available for download from the www.usingcrystal.com Web site.

Listing 32.2 illustrates obtaining a report source when using the Report Application Server as part of Crystal Enterprise. Notice that the same ReportClientDocument object is used. The difference is in how the ReportClientDocument object is obtained.

→ For more information on using the IEnterpriseSession as associated Crystal Enterprise objects, **see** "Establishing a Crystal Enterprise Session," **p. 767**

LISTING 32.2   OBTAINING AN EnterpriseSession OBJECT

```
//Retrieve the IEnterpriseSession object previously stored in the user's session.
IEnterpriseSession enterpriseSession =
        (IEnterpriseSession) session.getAttribute("EnterpriseSession");

//Use enterpriseSession object to retrieve the reportAppFactory object
IReportAppFactory reportAppFactory =
        (IReportAppFactory) enterpriseSession.getService("", "RASReportFactory");

//Open the report document by specifying the report ID
ReportClientDocument reportClientDoc = reportAppFactory.openDocument(reportID,
   0, Locale.ENGLISH);

//Finally use the openReportSource method to return the report source object
IReportSource reportSource = reportClientDoc.getReportSource();
```

An alternative way to do this is shown in Listing 32.3.

LISTING 32.3   ALTERNATIVE METHOD TO OBTAIN AN EnterpriseSession OBJECT

```
//Retrieve the IEnterpriseSession object.
IEnterpriseSession enterpriseSession =
        (IEnterpriseSession) session.getAttribute("EnterpriseSession");

//Use the IEnterpriseSession object's getService method to get
```

32

```
//an IReportAppFactory object.
IReportSourceFactory reportFactory =
        (IReportSourceFactory) enterpriseSession.getService("",
            "RASReportFactory");

//Use IReportAppFactory object's openReportSource method, passing it
//the report ID to return the reportSource object
IReportSource reportSource = reportFactory.openReportSource(reportID,
        Locale.ENGLISH);
```

Listing 32.4 illustrates obtaining a report source object from the Page Server service from Crystal Enterprise Professional/Premium.

LISTING 32.4 UTILIZING THE PAGE SERVER TO OPEN A REPORT

```
//Retrieve the IEnterpriseSession object previously stored in the user's session.
IEnterpriseSession enterpriseSession =
        (IEnterpriseSession) session.getAttribute("EnterpriseSession");

//Use the getService method of the EnterpriseSession object to obtain an
//IReportAppFactory object:
IReportSourceFactory reportFactory =
        (IReportSourceFactory) enterpriseSession.getService ("",
"PSReportFactory");

//Finally use the openReportSource method to return the report source object
IReportSource reportSource = reportFactory.openReportSource(reportID,
        Locale.ENGLISH) ;
```

IMPLEMENTING THE PAGE VIEWER

The first viewer component to be covered is the Page viewer, as illustrated in Listing 32.5. To use this viewer, you will create its CrystalReportViewer object. It, along with all the other viewers, exposes a method called setReportSource that accepts a valid report source object as obtained from the description in the previous section. Finally, again like the other viewers, it has a processHttpRequest method that accepts references to the current servlet context. This method does the actual rendering to HTML.

LISTING 32.5 VIEWING A REPORT OVER THE WEB

```
//To create a Java report viewer you need to instantiate a CrystalReportViewer
//object. To create a CrystalReportViewer object:
CrystalReportPartsViewer viewer = new CrystalReportViewer();

//Obtain a ReportSource object. Set the viewer's report source by calling its
//setReportSource method.
viewer.setReportSource(reportSource);

//When you have created and initialized a Java report page viewer, you call
//its processHttpRequest method to launch it in a Web //browser.
viewer.processHttpRequest(request, response, getServletContext(), null);
```

Figure 32.1 shows the output of this code.

Figure 32.1
A report being displayed in an HTML page viewer.

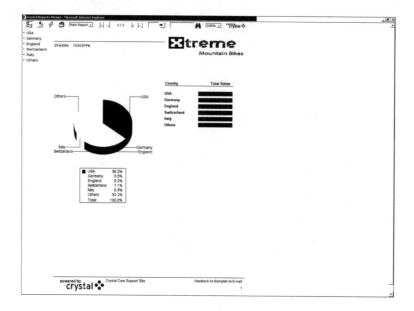

All viewers including the Page viewer share a number of toolbar elements. These properties can be programmatically toggled and are displayed in Table 32.1. All the viewer properties must be set before calling the `ProcessHTTPRequest` method that displays the selected report. For example, to ensure the Crystal logo is displayed when the involved report is viewed, the code line

```
Viewer.HasLogo(true);
```

needs to be included in the code before the `processHTTPRequest` method is called.

As the different viewers are introduced and discussed later in this chapter, some additional elements pertinent to the viewer being discussed will be displayed in that section's table.

TABLE 32.1 TOOLBAR ELEMENTS (PAGE VIEWER)

Property	Property Description
HasLogo	Includes or excludes the "Powered by Crystal" logo when rendering the report.
HasExportButton	Includes or excludes the export button when rendering the report.
HasGotoPageButton	Includes or excludes the Go to Page button when rendering the report.
HasPageNavigationButtons	Includes or excludes the page navigation buttons when rendering the report.

Property	Property Description
HasPrintButton	Includes or excludes the Print button when rendering the report.
HasRefreshButton	Includes or excludes the Refresh button when rendering the report.
HasSearchButton	Includes or excludes the Search button when rendering the report.
HasToggleGroupTreeButton	Includes or excludes the Group Tree toggle button when rendering the report.
HasViewList	Specifies whether the viewer should display a list of previous views of the report.
SetPrintMode	Set printing to use PDF or Active X printing (0=pdf, 1=actx).
HasZoomFactorList	Specifies zoom factor for displayed report.

IMPLEMENTING THE PART VIEWER

The Part viewer works much the same way as the Page viewer—in fact, much of the code is exactly the same, except for the type of viewer object that is created. Listing 32.6 assumes that the report to be displayed has an initial report part defined in the report itself.

LISTING 32.6   VIEWING A REPORT USING THE REPORT PART VIEWER

```
//To create a Java report part viewer you need to instantiate a
//CrystalReportPartsViewer object:
CrystalReportPartsViewer viewer = new CrystalReportPartsViewer();

//Obtain a ReportSource object. Set the viewer's report source by calling its
//setReportSource method
viewer.setReportSource(reportSource);

//After you have created and initialized a Java report part viewer, you
//call its processHttpRequest method to launch it in a Web browser.
viewer.processHttpRequest(request, response, getServletContext(), null);
```

If a report part is not defined for a report, or if the default part needs to be overridden, Listing 32.7 provides code that can be used to manipulate the ReportParts collection. Figure 32.2 shows the output of this page being displayed in a Web browser.

LISTING 32.7   SPECIFYING REPORT PART NODES

```
//To create a Java report part viewer you need to instantiate a
//CrystalReportPartsViewer object:
CrystalReportPartsViewer viewer = new CrystalReportPartsViewer();

//After you have created the CrystalReportPartsViewer object,
//you must specify the report parts that you want to display when the
```

continues

LISTING 32.7   CONTINUED

```
//viewer is launched.  To specify the report parts that you want the
//viewer to display Create a ReportPartsDefinition object.
ReportPartsDefinition partsDefinition = new ReportPartsDefinition();

//Get the collection of ReportPartNodes that belong to the
//ReportPartsDefinition.
ReportPartNodes reportPartNodes = partsDefinition.getReportPartNodes();

//Create a corresponding ReportPartNode object for each report part that
//you would like the viewer to display. Add these objects to the
//ReportPartNodes collection. Part1 is being used here as the default
//Report Part to display
ReportPartNode node0 = new ReportPartNode();
node0.setName("Part1");
partsDefinition.getReportPartNodes().add(node0);

//Obtain a ReportSource object. Set the viewer's report source by calling
//its setReportSource method
viewer.setReportSource(reportSource);

//Call the viewer's setReportParts method, passing it the ReportPartsDefinition.
viewer.setReportParts(partsDefinition);

//After you have created and initialized a Java report part viewer,
//you call its processHttpRequest method to launch it in a Web browser.
viewer.processHttpRequest(request, response, getServletContext(), null) ;
```

Figure 32.2
The Report Part viewer displaying a report part.

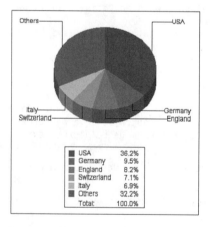

IMPLEMENTING THE INTERACTIVE VIEWER

The Interactive viewer works almost exactly like the Page viewer. In fact, the Interactive viewer component derives from the Page viewer component, so it inherits all the base functionality. What it adds is a new toolbar button that enables an advanced searching User Interface inside the viewer. This is useful for larger reports and for end users requiring advanced searches where simple text string searching is not suitable. The Interactive viewer allows the report to be filtered using a specified record selection criteria.

Listing 32.8 shows a report being viewed by the Interactive viewer. Note that the
setOwnPage method is called to indicate that the viewer owns the entire page, which is generally a good thing to do when using this viewer.

LISTING 32.8   USING THE REPORT PART VIEWER IN CODE

```
//To create a Java interactive viewer you instantiate a
//CrystalReportInteractiveViewer object:
CrystalReportInteractiveViewer viewer = new CrystalReportInteractiveViewer();

//Set the viewer's report source by calling its setReportSource method
viewer.setReportSource(reportSource);

//Enable the Advanced Search Wizard.
viewer.setEnableBooleanSearch(true);

//Set the setOwnPage property to true. The setOwnPage property should always
//be set to true for the interactive viewer.
viewer.setOwnPage(true);

//After you have created and initialized a Java interactive viewer,
//you call its processHttpRequest method to launch it in a Web browser.

viewer.processHttpRequest(request, response, getServletContext(), null);
```

Figure 32.3 shows a report being displayed in the Interactive viewer and the advanced
searching UI being used.

Figure 32.3
The Interactive
viewer in action.

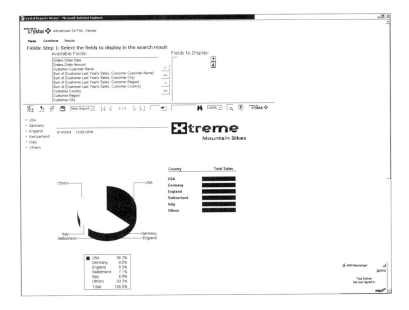

All viewers including the Interactive viewer share a number of toolbar elements. These
properties can be programmatically toggled and are displayed in Table 32.2. All the viewer

properties must be set before calling the `ProcessHTTPRequest` method that will display the selected report. For example, to ensure the Crystal logo is displayed when the involved report is viewed, the code line

```
Viewer.HasLogo(true);
```

needs to be included in the code before the `processHTTPRequest` method is called.

TABLE 32.2   TOOLBAR ELEMENTS (INTERACTIVE VIEWER)

Property	Property Description
HasLogo	Includes or excludes the "Powered by Crystal" logo when rendering the report.
HasExportButton	Includes or excludes the Export button when rendering the report.
HasGotoPageButton	Includes or excludes the Go to Page button when rendering the report.
HasPageNavigationButtons	Includes or excludes the page navigation buttons when rendering the report.
HasPrintButton	Includes or excludes the Print button when rendering the report.
HasRefreshButton	Includes or excludes the Refresh button when rendering the report.
HasSearchButton	Includes or excludes the Search button when rendering the report.
HasToggleGroupTreeButton	Includes or excludes the Group Tree toggle button when rendering the report.
HasViewList	Specifies whether the viewer should display a list of previous views of the report.
SetPrintMode	Set printing to use PDF or Active S printing (0=pdf, 1=actx).
HasZoomFactorList	Specifies zoom factor for displayed report.
HasBooleanSearchButton	Includes or excludes the toggle Boolean search button when rendering the report. Unique to Interactive viewer.
HasHeaderArea	Includes or excludes the header area when rendering the report. Unique to Interactive viewer.
HasPageBottomToolbar	Includes or excludes the page bottom toolbar. Unique to Interactive viewer.

IMPLEMENTING THE GRID VIEWER

The final viewer to be covered in this chapter is the Grid viewer. The Grid viewer (shown in Figure 32.4) differs more from the other viewers in that it does not render the report's presentation onscreen. Instead it looks at the dataset associated with the report (that is, the query result after the report engine has done its magic) and displays that data in a tabular fashion. This opens up some very interesting scenarios if you use your imagination.

NOTE

> You can override the style of the grid table by defining a stylesheet that maps to the styles used by the grid object. Consult the documentation for more information on this.

Listing 32.9 shows a report being displayed using the Grid viewer.

LISTING 32.9 DISPLAYING A REPORT IN THE GRID VIEWER

```
//To create a Java grid viewer you need to instantiate a GridViewer object.
//To create a GridViewer object:
GridViewer viewer = new GridViewer();

//Set the viewer's report source by calling its setReportSource method
viewer.setReportSource(reportSource);

//After you have created and initialized a Java grid viewer object, you call
//its processHttpRequest method to display the results in the Web page
viewer.processHttpRequest(request, response, getServletContext(), null);
```

Figure 32.4
The Grid viewer in action.

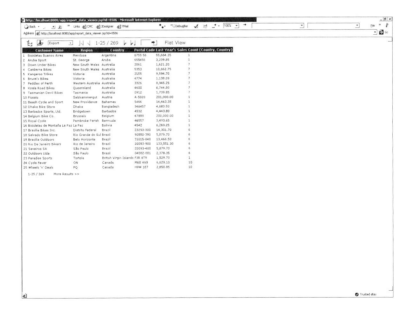

All viewers including the Grid viewer share a number of toolbar elements. These properties can be programmatically toggled and are displayed in Table 32.3. All the viewer properties must be set before calling the ProcessHTTPRequest method that will display the selected report. For example, to ensure the Crystal logo is displayed when the involved report is viewed, the code line

```
Viewer.HasLogo(true);
```

needs to be included in the code before the processHTTPRequest method is called.

TABLE 32.3   TOOLBAR ELEMENTS (GRID VIEWER)

Property	Property Description
HasLogo	Includes or excludes the "Powered by Crystal" logo when rendering the report.
HasExportButton	Includes or excludes the Export button when rendering the report.
HasGotoPageButton	Includes or excludes the Go to Page button when rendering the report.
HasPageNavigationButtons	Includes or excludes the page navigation buttons when rendering the report.
HasPrintButton	Includes or excludes the Print button when rendering the report.
HasRefreshButton	Includes or excludes the Refresh button when rendering the report.
HasSearchButton	Includes or excludes the Search button when rendering the report.
HasToggleGroupTreeButton	Includes or excludes the Group Tree toggle button when rendering the report.
HasViewList	Specifies whether the viewer should display a list of previous views of the report.
SetPrintMode	Set printing to use PDF or Active X printing (0=pdf, 1=actx).
HasZoomFactorList	Specifies zoom factor for the displayed report.
DisplayNavigationBar	Specifies whether the viewer should display the navigation bar at the bottom of the grid. Unique to Grid viewer.
DisplayRowNumberColumn	Specifies whether to display the row number column. Unique to Grid viewer.

Property	Property Description
DisplayToolbarFindRowButton	Includes or excludes the Find Row button when rendering the toolbar. Unique to Grid viewer.
DisplayToolbarGroupViewList	Specifies whether the viewer should display the view list. Unique to Grid viewer.
DisplayToolarSwitchViewButton	Includes or excludes the Toggle Grid View button. Unique to Grid viewer.
EnableGridToGrow	Specifies whether the viewer should enable the Grid to Grow. Unique to Grid viewer.
GridViewMode	Specifies the viewer View mode. Unique to Grid viewer.
MatchGridandToolbarWidth	Specifies whether the table should align with the toolbar. Unique to Grid viewer.
TableStyle	Specifies the style class of the table. You can apply a css style class to the grid table that shows records. You do so by stating: `Gridviewer.TableStyle="cssclass";` Unique to Grid viewer.
ToolbarStyle	Specifies the style class of the toolbar. You can apply a css style class to the grid toolbar. You do so by stating: `Gridviewer.ToolbarStyle="cssclass";` Unique to Grid viewer.

32

USING THE EXPORT CONTROL TO DELIVER REPORTS IN OTHER FORMATS

So far all the scenarios that have been discussed in this chapter have involved displaying reports in dynamic HTML format. Although this is a great report delivery method for most scenarios, there are times when reports need to be exported to various other file formats. Although this can be accomplished by using the ReportClientDocument object model, there is an easier way to do this: using the Export control.

Listing 32.10 shows how the Export control would be used to export a report to PDF. Notice that the Export control has the concept of the report source of the processHttpRequest method.

LISTING 32.10   EXPORTING A REPORT VIA CODE

```
//Instantiate a ReportExportControl object
ReportExportControl exportControl = new ReportExportControl();

//After you have created the ReportExportControl object, you must
//specify the export format that you want to export the report to. To
//specify the export format create an ExportOptions object:

ExportOptions exportOptions = new ExportOptions();

//Specify the export format by calling the ExportOptions object's
//setExportFormatType method, passing it the integer constant that
//represents the chosen format:
exportOptions.setExportFormatType(ReportExportFormat.PDF);

//To initialize an Export control in a Crystal Enterprise environment set
//the control's report source by calling its setReportSource
method.exportControl.setReportSource(reportSource);

//Call the control's setExportOptions method, passing it an ExportOptions object
exportControl.setExportOptions(exportOptions);

//You may also want to call the setExportAsAttachment method, passing it the
//Boolean value true. The Export control will then display a dialog box
//that allows users of your Web application to save the exported report before
//they open it: exportControl.setExportAsAttachment(true);

//To initialize an Export control in an unmanaged RAS environment set the
//control's report source by calling its setReportSource method and passing
//the method a reference to a report source object.
exportControl.setReportSource(reportSource);

//Call the control's setExportOptions method, passing it an ExportOptions object
exportControl.setExportOptions(exportOptions);

//You may also want to call the setExportAsAttachment method, passing it the
//Boolean value true. The Export control will then display a dialog box
//that allows users of your Web application to save the exported report before
//they open it:
exportControl.setExportAsAttachment(true);

//After you have created an export control, you call its processHttpRequest
//method to complete the export.
exportControl.processHttpRequest(request, response, getServletContext(), null) ;
```

Figure 32.5 shows a report being exported to PDF.

Figure 32.5
Using the Export control to export a report to PDF.

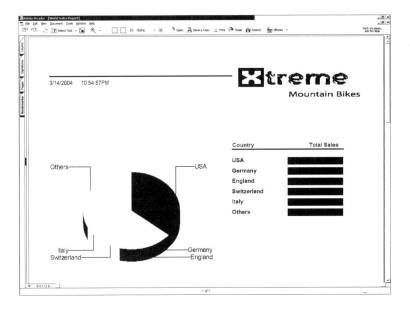

TROUBLESHOOTING

REPORT VIEWING PERFORMANCE IS SLOW

What efficiencies can I add to increase the performance of my application?

Caching a report source in the session variable allows it to be used multiple times efficiently. When a report source is not cached, the process of creating a new report source multiple times becomes fairly expensive. Furthermore, caching a report source allows reports with or without saved data to be refreshed.

Listing 32.11 shows how to store and retrieve the report source object from session state.

LISTING 32.11   CACHING A REPORT SOURCE OBJECT

```
//To store the report source in a session variable
request.getSession().settAttribute("RptSrc",reportSource);

//To retrieve the report source from a session variable
rptSrc = request.getSession().getAttribute("RptSrc");
```

THE VIEWER NEEDS TO WORK IN A PAGE WITHOUT A FORM ELEMENT

How can I control how the viewer interacts with a surrounding form?

If your Web page contains only the viewer and nothing else, several things can be done that can simplify the report viewing implementation. The viewer is capable of generating complete HTML pages and can set the appropriate page properties depending on the viewing context. Setting the setOwnPage property to true provides several benefits. Allowing the viewer to handle the surrounding HTML content reduces the amount of code you need to add to your Web page and allows the viewer to automatically determine certain settings. It correctly sets the content-type and charset information for the page. This ensures that pages containing international characters will be displayed correctly. When setOwnPage is set to true, you must use the processHttpRequest method to display the report instead of getHtmlContent. The processHttpRequest method must be used because using getHtmlContent has the same effect as setting setOwnPage to false, negating any of the benefits gained from setting setOwnPage to true. If your Web page does not contain any controls that require post back, you should set the setOwnForm method to true. Doing so allows the viewer to handle the view state information automatically. The view state is used to perform client-side caching of information about the current state of the report. If you have other controls on the page, you must set setOwnForm to false and handle the view state information manually.

THE CHARACTER SET IS DISPLAYING INCORRECTLY

How can I indicate which unicode character to set should be used for the report viewing session?

To send characters from a Web page to a Web browser, you must use the correct encoding. Always specify the correct content-type and character set for all your Web pages. If your Web page returns content to a standard HTML browser, the following lines will ensure that the correct character set is defined. The contentType and charset directives let the browser know how the returned HTML page is encoded. UTF-8 is the recommended standard character set if it is available for your target client browser. For more information, consult the Release Notes or the vendor for your target client browser.

CHAPTER **33**

CRYSTAL ENTERPRISE EMBEDDED— REPORT MODIFICATION AND CREATION

In this chapter

INTRODUCTION

This chapter covers the capability of the Report Application Server (RAS) SDK to create and modify reports. Topics include

- RAS environments
- Loading report files
- RAS component locations
- Installing the RAS SDK
- Exception handling
- Programming with the RAS SDK

DEPLOYING RAS ENVIRONMENTS

The RAS functions in two different environments—either as a standalone report processing and modification server or as a service of the Crystal Enterprise framework.

USING RAS IN A CRYSTAL ENTERPRISE ENVIRONMENT

Crystal Enterprise provides a framework for delivering enterprise reporting. RAS adds the capability for users to modify reports stored in Crystal Enterprise. In this scenario, the Crystal Enterprise framework manages the RAS. Multiple instances of the RAS can be added and Crystal Enterprise will load balance between them.

→ For additional information on the Crystal Enterprise Framework, **see** "The Server Tier: Introduction to the Crystal Enterprise Framework," **p. 510**

USING RAS IN A STANDALONE ENVIRONMENT

Even without Crystal Enterprise, the capabilities of RAS can be leveraged. In this scenario the RAS SDK modifies unmanaged reports (reports stored on the file system rather than in Crystal Enterprise) so you refer to the RAS as an unmanaged server.

NOTE

> The core functionality of the RAS is the same regardless of the environment it is running in. The rest of this chapter assumes the RAS is running in unmanaged mode as a standalone server.

LOADING REPORT FILES

Crystal Report (.rpt) files must first be placed in a folder designated as the Report Directory for the RAS. The RAS interacts only with reports in this folder and its subfolders. An "access denied" error results from attempting to access reports outside of this folder.

The RAS Configuration Manager sets the Report Directory. In a default installation, the Report Directory points to the location of the sample reports folder.

After setting the report directory, there are several ways to designate a report file.

For example, the ras prefix can be used:

```
ras://D:\directory\reportname.rpt
```

The location on the RAS machine of reportname.rpt is given by this string.

It is not necessary to always key in the ras prefix because it is assumed by default; for example, c:\reportname.rpt is assumed to be a path on the RAS machine.

The rassdk prefix also can be used like this:

```
rassdk://c:\directory\reportname.rpt
```

Where RAS SDK is running on the machine, generally the Web application server, this string gives the location of reportname.rpt.

Because reports must be serialized and sent to the RAS for processing each time they are accessed, reports stored outside the RAS slow down performance. Therefore, to improve performance it is highly recommended that a local folder is used on the RAS machine for the Report Directory.

LOCATING RAS COMPONENTS IN A NETWORK ARCHITECTURE

Though the default installation places both the RAS SDK and RAS on the local machine, they can be installed on separate computers.

SPECIFYING SEPARATE RASs

The server attribute of the clientSDKOptions.xml file defines the location of the RAS. This file is created in the jar folder under Program Files\Common Files\Crystal Decisions during the RAS installation. This file can be modified to indicate the location of the RAS when installed separately. This can also be done programmatically using the RAS SDK, which will be illustrated by examples later in the chapter.

The location of the clientSDKOptions.xml file can be specified either statically, by setting a classpath that points to the file, or dynamically, by specifying the location of this file. Load balancing can be enabled where there are multiple RASs by specifying the location of all the RASs on the network in the clientSDKOptions.xml file.

SETTING A STATIC LOCATION

Adding the file path of the file clientSDKOptions.xml to the Web application server's CLASSPATH environment variable specifies the location of the file statically. The file path might also need to be added to the CLASSPATH on the local system. More information

33

regarding adding classpaths might be found on the Web server's documentation information.

DEPLOYING RAS IN A DYNAMIC LOCATION

The location of the clientSDKOptions.xml file can be specified at runtime. From the JSP or Java files use the Java method `setProperty` from the System class. Set the system property indicated by the ras.config key to the specified directory as follows:

```
system.setProperty("ras.config","c:/temp")
```

This specifies that to locate RAS servers, the clientSDKOptions.xml file in `c:/temp` will be used. Using the web.xml file (located by default in the `\WEB-INF\` directory of your Web application) to specify the location of the clientSDKOptions.xml will avoid hard-coding the location for the clientSDKOptions.xml file throughout your program.

INSTALLING THE RAS SDK

As mentioned previously, the RAS SDK JAR files can be found in the jar folder by default. Copy the RAS and Crystal Enterprise .jar files to the appropriate folder on the application server being used. If you are using Apache Tomcat, for example, move the .jar files to the Web application's `WEB-INF\lib` folder. Configuring a Web server to access the SDK JAR files might take additional steps, detailed in the installation help files provided with the RAS.

BEST PRACTICES IN RAS EXCEPTION HANDLING

Options for displaying and logging exception information can also be specified. These tasks can be performed by modifying the web.xml file (located by default in the `\WEB-INF\` directory of your Web application) as follows.

DISPLAYING EXCEPTIONS

Three options exist for displaying exception information to the user. Setting the `crystal_exception_info` parameter to one of the following values determines how exceptions are handled:

- `short`—The exception information is displayed without the accompanying stack trace.
- `long`—The exception information is displayed with the accompanying stack trace.
- `disable`—The exception information is not displayed; the user must handle the exception.

The following code shows an example of the exception display configuration:

```
<context-param>
    <param-name>crystal_exception_info</param-name>
        <param-value>long</param-value>
    <description>
        Options for displaying exception information.
```

```
        If this parameter is not set, the default value is short.
        It can be one of the following values: short, long, disable.
    </description>
</context-param>
```

The `crystal_exception_info` parameter is short by default. Modifying exception.css specifies the style and formatting of short messages.

LOGGING EXCEPTIONS

The option to turn exception logging either on or off can be set with the `crystal_exception_log_file` parameter. The exception information output to the log file will be in the long format regardless of the setting of the `crystal_exception_info` parameter. The following code shows an example of the exception logging configuration:

```
<context-param>
    <param-name>crystal_exception_log_file</param-name>
        <param-value>c:\temp\webreportingexception.log</param-value>
    <description>
        Set this parameter to log the exception in long form
        to the file specified.
        The value is the full path of the log file.
    </description>
</context-param>
```

When setting the parameter to the desired path of the log file, by default, exceptions are not logged.

THE RAS SDK IN ACTION

This section covers the common programming tasks associated with the RAS SDK. Although the SDK provides many capabilities, some of the following tasks are common to most programming exercises and are central to the SDK.

INITIALIZING AN RAS SESSION

Initiating a session with the RAS is the first step in programming with the RAS SDK. In this step, a specific RAS can be specified for use; otherwise, the system selects one from the RASs listed in the clientSDKOptions.xml file using a round-robin method. Initializing a RAS session by specifying a machine name at runtime is shown in the following code:

```
//Create a new Report Application Session
ReportAppSession reportAppSession = new ReportAppSession();
//Create a Report Application Server Service
reportAppSession.createService("com.crystaldecisions.sdk.occa.report.
➥application.ReportClientDocument");
//Set the RAS server to be used for the service. You can also use "localhost"
➥if the RAS server is running on
your local machine.
reportAppSession.setReportAppServer("MACHINE_NAME");
//Initialize RAS
reportAppSession.initialize();
//Create the report client document object
```

```
ReportClientDocument clientDoc = new ReportClientDocument();
//Set the RAS Server to be used for the Client Document
clientDoc.setReportAppServer(reportAppSession.getReportAppServer() );
```

All ReportClientDocument objects created from the same ReportAppSession communicate with the same RAS.

OPENING A REPORT

A report can be opened first by creating a new ReportClientDocument object and specifying the ReportAppServer. Then the open method can be used to open a report. This method takes two parameters:

- The absolute path and filename of the report
- A flag indicating how the file will be opened

See the OpenReportOptions class for valid report options.

NOTE

> Reports are loaded from the report folder found at \Program Files\Crystal Decisions\Report Application Server 10\Reports\ by default.

The following code opens a report:

```
try
{
    reportClientDocument.open("C:\MyReports\GlobalSales.rpt", 0);
}
catch (ReportSDKException e)
{
    // Handle the case where the report does not open properly.;
}
```

The previous chapter explained how to view reports using RAS. Creating and modifying those reports using the RAS SDK will be the focus of the remainder of this chapter.

ADDING FIELDS TO THE REPORT

A report can be modified after creating and opening a ReportClientDocument by using the report's controllers. The only way to modify reports and ensure that the changes are synchronized with the server is to use controllers. Although the report's fields can be accessed directly through the DataDefinition property, any changes made will not be committed. This section explains how to add a field to a report.

IDENTIFYING THE FIELD TO ADD

A field is usually selected by name. The DatabaseController can be used to retrieve the object that represents this field given a database field's name or its table's name. Another method of accessing a table's fields is using the ReportClientDocument's Database property. Here you use the DatabaseController.

The DatabaseController contains a collection of database tables that are available to the report and might be accessed using the getDatabaseController method of ReportClientDocument. Each table contains a collection of DBField objects.

NOTE
> All tables and fields that are listed by DatabaseController.getDatabase() are not retrieved when the report is refreshed; that is, they are available for report design but might not actually be part of the report's data definition.

A method called findFieldByName is shown in the following sample code snippet. This method returns a field given its fully qualified field name in the form: <TableAlias>.<FieldName>. The table alias is used as a qualifier and it is assumed that a period is used to separate the table alias from the field name.

```
IField findFieldByName(String nameOfFieldToFind, ReportClientDocument
➥reportClientDocument)
{
    //Extracts the field name and the table name.
    int dotPosition = nameOfFieldToFind.indexOf(".");
    String tablePartName = nameOfFieldToFind.substring(0, dotPosition);
    String fieldPartName =
        nameOfFieldToFind.substring(dotPosition + 1,
➥ nameOfFieldToFind.length());

    ITable table = null;

    // Uses the DatabaseController to search for the field.
    try
    {
        Tables retreivedTables =
            reportClientDocument.getDatabaseController().getDatabase().
➥getTables();
        int tableIndex = retreivedTables.findByAlias(tablePartName);
        table = retreivedTables.getTable(tableIndex);
    }
    catch (ReportSDKException e)
    {
        return null;
    }

    // Finds the field in the table.
    int fieldIndex =
        table.getDataFields().find(fieldPartName,
➥FieldDisplayNameType.fieldName, Locale.ENGLISH);
    if (fieldIndex == -1)
    {
        return null;
    }
    IField field = table.getDataFields().getField(fieldIndex);

    return field;
}
```

33

This method uses the following key methods:

- `Tables.findByAlias` finds the index of a particular table when given its alias. Given the index, the desired `Table` object can be retrieved from the collection.
- `Fields.find` finds the index of a field in a table's `Fields` collection when given the name of the field.

ADDING A FIELD TO THE REPORT DOCUMENT

After you obtain the `Field` object that you want to add, the field can be added to the report so that it is processed and displayed when the report is run. This is done via the `DataDefController`, which is used to modify the report's data definition and contains a sub-controller called the `ResultFieldController`. This subcontroller is used for modifying fields that have been placed on the report and that are processed at runtime. The fields that are shown on the report belong to the `ResultFields` collection. A new database field will be added to the `ResultFields` collection in this step.

NOTE

> The `ResultFields` collection can contain other types of field objects such as parameter fields, formula fields, and summary fields in addition to `DBField` objects. Like `DBFields`, the `ResultFieldController` can add these fields to a report. Unlike `DBFields`, only the `DatabaseDefController`'s `DataDefinition` property, and not the `DatabaseDefController`'s `Database` property, can retrieve these fields.

A field being added to the `ResultFields` collection is shown by the following code:

```
/*  * Because all modifications to a report must be made with a controller,
    * the resulting field controller is used to add and remove each field.
    */
ResultFieldController resultFieldController =
    reportClientDocument.getDataDefController().getResultFieldController();
// Adds fieldToAdd. -1 indicates the end of the collection.
resultFieldController.add(-1, fieldToAdd);
```

The parameter -1 indicates that the field is to be placed at the end of the collection. As a result of this code, the new field displays on the report and is processed when the report is refreshed.

DETERMINING ALL FIELDS USED IN THE REPORT

The fields that have been added to a report are stored in the `ResultFields` collection and can be retrieved using the following sample method:

```
Fields getUsedDatabaseFields(ReportClientDocument reportClientDocument)
{
    Fields usedFields = new Fields();

    /*
```

```
 * The DataDefinition's ResultFields collection
 * contains all the fields that have been placed
 * on the report and which will be processed
 * when the report is refreshed.
 */
Fields resultFields = null;
try
{
    resultFields = reportClientDocument.getDataDefinition().
➥getResultFields();
}
catch (ReportSDKException e)
{
    return null;
}

/*
 * Because the ResultFields collection contains
 * many different kinds of fields, all fields except
 * for database fields are filtered out.
 */
for (int i = 0; i < resultFields.size() - 1; i++)
{
    if (resultFields.getField(i).getKind() == FieldKind.DBField)
    {
        // Adds the database field to the collection.
        usedFields.addElement(resultFields.getField(i));
    }
}

return usedFields;
}
```

With the full name of the field, you can use a `DatabaseController` to retrieve the `DBField` object.

33

REMOVING A FIELD FROM THE REPORT

When you've found the field you want to remove, use the `ResultFieldController` to remove it as follows:

```
// Removes fieldToDelete.
resultFieldController.remove(fieldToDelete);
```

In this code, `fieldToDelete` is a `DBField` object. After the field is removed from the result fields using this method, the report ceases to display the field.

CREATING A NEW REPORT

A new report can be created by first creating an empty ReportClientDocument as shown:

```
ReportClientDocument reportClientDocument =
    reportAppFactory.newDocument(Locale.ENGLISH);
```

NOTE

> Because the `newDocument` method of `ReportClientDocument` is provided for deployments that use an unmanaged RAS to access report (.rpt) files, it should not be deployed when using a Crystal Enterprise RAS. Instead, when deploying with Crystal Enterprise, the `IReportAppFactory.newDocument` method should be used as in the previous code.

Because the report is not actually created until tables are added, after creating an empty `ReportClientDocument`, details such as the new report's tables and the fields used to link them should be added.

RETRIEVING A REPORT'S TABLES

However, before adding the tables to the new report, the table objects must first be retrieved from the source report. This can be accomplished in two ways: using the `DatabaseController` object and using the `Database` object, both of which are available from the `ReportClientDocument` object. The ensuing code iterates through all the tables in an open report and prints the tables' aliases:

```
Tables tables = reportClientDocument.getDatabase().getTables()
for (int i = 0; i < tables.size(); i++)
{
    ITable table = tables.getTable(i);
    out.println(table.getAlias());
}
```

ADDING TABLES TO THE REPORT

Because controllers are the only objects that can modify the report's object model, a controller must be used to add tables to a report. The following code retrieves the report's `DatabaseController` and adds a table.

```
DatabaseController databaseController;
try
{
    databaseController = reportClientDocument.getDatabaseController();
    databaseController.addTable(sourceTable, new TableLinks());
    databaseController.addTable(targetTable, new TableLinks());
}
catch(ReportSDKException e)
{
    throw new Exception("Error while adding tables.");
}
```

The `addTable` method of the `DatabaseController` adds a table to the report. The `addTable` method takes two parameters:

- The `Table` object you want to add
- A `TableLinks` object that defines how the table being added is linked with other tables

LINKING TABLES

Tables must be linked after they have been added to the report. To link two tables, first create a new `TableLink` object, set the properties of the `TableLink`, and then add the `TableLink` to the report definition.

Linking two tables using an equal join is illustrated by the following code:

```
// Create the new link that will connect the two tables.
TableLink tableLink = new TableLink();

/*
 * Add the source field name and the target field name to the SourceFieldNames
 * and TargetFieldNames collection of the TableLink object.
 */
tableLink.getSourceFieldNames().add(sourceFieldName);
tableLink.getTargetFieldNames().add(targetFieldName);

/*
 * Specify which tables are to be linked by setting table aliases
 * for the TableLink object.
 */
tableLink.setSourceTableAlias(sourceTable.getAlias());
tableLink.setTargetTableAlias(targetTable.getAlias());

// Add the link to the report. Doing so effectively links the two tables.
try
{
    databaseController.addTableLink(tableLink);
}
catch(ReportSDKException e)
{
    throw new TutorialException("Error while linking tables.");
}
```

These newly linked tables can be used as the report's data source. However there have been no visible objects added to the report, so when the report is refreshed, it will be blank.

ADDING GROUPS

To add a group, you must know which field is being grouped on. For information on working with fields, see the "Adding a Field to the Report Document" section earlier in this chapter. Because not all fields can be used to define a group, use the `canGroupOn` method of `GroupController` to check whether a field can be used for grouping. If `canGroupOn` returns true, the field is an acceptable field to use for grouping. The next example demonstrates a function that adds a new group to a report:

```
// Uses the sort controller to remove all the report's sorts.
Sorts sorts = dataDefController.getDataDefinition().getSorts();
SortController sortController = dataDefController.getSortController();
for (int i = 0; i < sorts.size(); i++)
{
    sortController.remove(0);
}
```

33

Here the group was added to the end of the Groups collection by setting the index to -1, which means that the new group becomes the innermost group. When a new group is added, a new sorting definition is also added which will sort the records according to the group's condition field and group options. An additional reflection of adding the new group is the group name field appearing on the group's header. Fields added to the group header are not added to the ResultFields collection. When the group is removed, the group name field is also removed.

ADDING SORTING TO THE REPORT

Using the SortController adds a new sorting definition to a report. The SortController can add any kind of sorting definition, including a Top N sort. Adding a Top N sort requires that a summary has first been added.

Next you demonstrate how to add a sort to the report by taking a Fields collection and adding a sorting definition based on each field in the collection:

```
void addNewGroup(ReportClientDocument reportClientDocument,
➥ Fields newGroupFields)
throws ExampleException
{
    try
    {
        // Create a new, empty group.
        IGroup group = new Group();

        // Iterate through every field in the given Fields collection.
        for (int i = 0; i < newGroupFields.size(); i++)
        {
            IField field = newGroupFields.getField(i);

            // Set the field that will define how data is grouped.
            group.setConditionField(field);


            GroupController groupController =
                reportClientDocument.getDataDefController().
➥getGroupController();
            groupController.add(-1, group);
        }
    }

    // If any part of the above procedure failed, redirect the user
➥to an error page.
    catch (ReportSDKException e)
    {
        throw new ExampleException("Error while adding new groups.");
    }
}
```

When the new Sort object is added, it is added to the end of the collection, indicated by the -1 argument, which designates that the records will be sorted on this field after all other sorting definitions. The SortDirection class indicates the direction of the sort. The static objects SortDirection.ascendingOrder and SortDirection.descendingOrder are the only values that can be used for a normal sort. The other values are used for a Top N or Bottom N sort. See Adding a Top N sorting definition in the SDK documentation for additional details.

ADDING SUMMARIES TO THE REPORT

The SummaryFieldController adds a new summary field. To determine if a field can produce a summary, the SummaryFieldControllers method canSummarizeOn is called. Here you add a summary to a group:

```
void setSorting(ReportClientDocument reportClientDocument, Fields
➥fieldsToSortOn)
throws ExampleException
{
    try
    {
        DataDefController dataDefController = reportClientDocument.
➥getDataDefController();

        // Create a new Sort object
        ISort sort = new Sort();

        // Iterate through the fields
        for (int i = 0; i < fieldsToSortOn.size(); i++)
        {
            IField field = fieldsToSortOn.getField(i);

            // Add the current field to the result fields.
            dataDefController.getResultFieldController().add(-1, field);

            // Set the field to sort on.
            sort.setSortField(field);

            // Define the type of sorting. Ascending here.
            sort.setDirection(SortDirection.ascendingOrder);

            //Get Sort Controller.
            SortController sortController =
                dataDefController.getSortController();

            sortController.add(-1, sort);
        }
    }

    // If any part of the above procedure failed, redirect the user to
➥an error page.
    catch (ReportSDKException e)
    {
        throw new TutorialException("Error while setting sort.");
    }
}
```

33

After creating a summary field, set the following properties before adding it:

- `SummarizedField`—The field used to calculate the summary.
- `Group`—The group for which the summary will be calculated.
- `Operation`—The operation used to calculate the summary. One of the static objects defined in the `SummaryOperation` class.

WORKING WITH FILTERS

Filters are used in record selection and group selection. The filter is initially a string written in Crystal formula syntax. The record selection formula is then parsed into an array of `FilterItems` stored in the Filter object's `FilterItems` property. The string is broken up into data components and operator components that act on the data. These components are stored as `FieldRangeFilterItem` and `OperatorFilterItem` objects respectively, which are stored in the `FilterItems` collection in the same order that they appear in the formula string. Re-ordering the objects in the array changes the functionality of the formula. In summary, the `FieldRangeFilterItem` is an expression that is joined with other expressions using an `OperatorFilterItem`.

For instance, consider a simple record selection formula such as

`{Customer.Name} = "Bashka Futbol" and {Customer.Country} = "USA".`

This results in only the records that have a name equal to `"Bashka Futbol"` and a country of the USA. The result is stored in the `FreeEditingText` property. After this string is parsed, the `FieldRangeItems` collection contains two `FieldRangeFilterItem` objects because there are two data items used to filter the records. The `OperatorFilterItem` is used to indicate how two primitive expressions are combined, so it is now equal to and.

The `FieldRangeFilterItem` contains three properties:

- `Operation`—This property indicates the operation performed in the primitive expression; in both cases, it is the equals operator.
- `RangeField`—The `RangeField` property indicates the comparator field used in the expression. Because not all fields are suitable to filter records and groups, use the `canFilterOn` method in the `RecordFilterController` and the `GroupFilterController` to determine whether a field can be used for a particular filter.
- `Values`—The `Values` property indicates the comparison values in the expression. In this example, it is the strings "USA" and "Bashka Futbol". This property has one `ConstantValue` object that stores "USA".

After the file is opened, and the filters parsed, the `FreeEditingText` property that stores these strings is cleared and the `FilterItems` populated. Conversely, if the formula is too complex, the `FilterItems` collection property remains empty and the `FreeEditingText` property populated. When altering a filter, you have two options: modify the `FreeEditingText` property or the `FilterItems` property.

If you use only one property to modify the filter, the other will not be automatically updated, however. For instance, you would modify the `FreeEditingText` property, but this will not necessarily be parsed again to repopulate the `FilterItems`. You should use only one of these properties per session.

Use a controller to ensure that modifications are saved. The `GroupFilterController` and the `RecordFilterController` modify the group formula and record formula respectively.

CREATING A `FieldRangeFilterItem`

A `FieldRangeFilterItem` contains a primitive comparison expression. Its most relevant properties are

- `Operation`
- `RangeField`
- `Values`

The `Operation` and `RangeField` properties usually contain a constant. However, the `Values` property stores either `ConstantValue` objects, which don't need evaluation (such as 1, 5, or "Stringiethingie"), and `ExpressionValue` objects, which do need evaluation (such as "WeekToDateSinceSun," 4/2, and so on).

The following section of code defines the expression {`Customer.ID` > 2}. Note how it creates a new `ConstantValue` object for the number 2 and adds it to the `Values` collection:

```
//  Create a new range filter item.
FieldRangeFilterItem fieldRangeFilterItem = new FieldRangeFilterItem();

// Assume the customerDBField has been retrieved from a table
fieldRangeFilterItem.setRangeField(customerDBField);

// Set the operation to >
fieldRangeFilterItem.setOperation(SelectionOperation.greaterThan);
fieldRangeFilterItem.setInclusive(false);

// Create a constant value and add it to the range filter item
ConstantValue constantValue = new ConstantValue();
constantValue.setValue(2);
fieldRangeFilterItem.getValues().addElement(constantValue);

//  Create a filter and add the field range filter item
IFilter filter = new Filter();
filter.getFilterItems().addElement(fieldRangeFilterItem);
```

All fields cannot be used in a filter formula (for example, you can't use BLOB fields). Use the `canFilterOn` method, which is located in either the `RecordFilterController` or the `GroupFilterController`, to verify that a field can be filtered on. You must also verify that the constant data type is the same as the field. In the previous example, `constantValue` must not be a variant and corresponds to the data type used in the comparison.

33

CREATING A `OperatorFilterItem`

The following example assumes the same expression as defined in the preceding example, but concatenates to the filter using the OR operator. Assume the filter would look like this: `{Customer.ID} > 2 OR {Customer.name} = "Arsel"`. To the code above you would add:

```
OperatorFilterItem operatorFilterItem = new OperatorFilterItem();
operatorFilterItem.setOperator("OR");

filter.getFilterItems().addElement(operatorFilterItem);
filter.getFilterItems().addElement(fieldRangeFilterItem);
```

The `filterItems` parameter is a `FilterItems` collection. It stores `FilterItem` objects. In the two examples, both a `FieldRangeFilterItem` object and an `OperatorFilterItem` object were added to this collection. Both of these objects inherit from `FilterItem`, making this possible.

ADDING A FILTER TO THE REPORT

After defining the filter, you add it to the report. Filters can be used in two places: group selection and record selection. The `GroupFilterController` and `RecordFilterController`, which can be accessed via the `DataDefController` object, modify their respective filters.

You can also obtain the filters from the `GroupFilter` and `RecordFilter` properties in the `DataDefinition`, although they can only be modified with a controller.

`FilterController` provides these methods for modifying a filter:

- `addItem`—This method adds an expression or an operator to the existing filter.
- `modify`—This method replaces the current filter with a new or modified one.
- `modifyItem`—This method modifies a filter element.
- `moveItem`—This method moves the filter element around the filter array.
- `removeItem`—This method deletes a filter element.

In the following code, the modify method is used because a new filter has already been defined. Assume that there is a `ReportClientDocument` object and that you have opened a report already:

```
FilterController groupFilterController =
reportClientDocument.getDataDefController.getGroupFilterController();
groupFilterController.modify(filter) ;
```

WORKING WITH PARAMETERS

Parameters enable end users to enter information to define the report behavior. Parameters have specific data types just like any other field: string, number, date, and so on. Parameters also are divided into two basic types: discrete and ranged. A discrete parameter value is one that represents a singular value such as 9, "Nur", 1863, True, and so on. Ranged values represent a particular span of values from one point to another such as [9..95], [4..6], ["Alpha","Omega"]. The lower bound value of the range must be smaller than the upper bound. Some parameters support more than one value: They effectively contain an array containing many values.

Parameters have default values and the user can be forced to select from them. You can also provide default parameters but allow users to enter their own values. Default values are stored in the `ParameterField.DefaultValues` property. Selected values are stored in the `ParameterField.CurrentValues` property.

Parameters support many more features than those covered here. For a complete list of features, see the `ParameterField` class in the SDK documentation.

READING PARAMETERS AND THEIR VALUES

The parameters are exposed in the SDK by the `DataDefinition`'s `ParameterFields` class. The `ParameterFields` class inherits from the `Fields` class. For example the name of a parameter is obtained using this method:

```
Fields parameterFields = reportClientDocument.getDataDefinition().
➥getParameterFields();
ParameterField parameterField = (ParameterField)parameterFields.getField(0);
parameterField.getDisplayName(FieldDisplayNameType.fieldName, Locale.ENGLISH);
```

The `getDisplayName` method is used for UI purposes and so is not a unique identifier. The `getFormulaForm` method can be used to retrieve a unique identifier. `getDisplayName` and `getFormulaForm` are not documented under the `ParameterField` class because they are inherited from `Field`.

Because parameter values might be either discrete or ranged, and default values might only be discrete, there are two different objects to represent these: `ParameterFieldDiscreteValue` and `ParameterFieldRangeValue`. Both of these objects inherit from `ParameterField`. You must understand the type of the parameter to know what kind of parameter values it contains. For example, the following code determines if the parameter is of a ranged or discrete type:

```
// Check to see if the value is range or discrete
IValue firstValue = parameterField.getCurrentValues().getValue(0);
if (firstValue instanceof IParameterFieldRangeValue)
{
    IParameterFieldRangeValue rangeValue =
➥ (IParameterFieldRangeValue)firstValue;
    toValueText = rangeValue.getEndValue().toString();
    fromValueText = rangeValue.getEndValue().toString();
}
else
{
    IParameterFieldDiscreteValue discreteValue =
➥ (IParameterFieldDiscreteValue)firstValue;
    discreteValueText = discreteValue.getValue().toString();
}
```

Check the parameter's type before you try to print the parameter's values. You must determine the type so you can retrieve the correct field. Trying to access the `EndValue` of a discrete value will cause a runtime error because no `EndValue` exists. The previous code

example determines whether the parameter value is an instance of
`IParameterFieldRangeValue` to determine what kind of values it will have. For parameters
that support both discrete and ranged values, however, you must verify the type of the parameter by using `getValueRangeKind` method. The following code checks the parameter type
and calls a secondary function to handle the correct type and build a table of parameters:

```
ParameterValueRangeKind kinda = parameterField.getValueRangeKind();
if (kinda == ParameterValueRangeKind.discrete)
{
    table += createDiscreteParameterTableData(parameterField, key);
    key += 1;
}
else if (kinda == ParameterValueRangeKind.range)
{
    table += createRangeParameterTableData(parameterField, key);
    key += 2;
}
    else if (kinda ==  ParameterValueRangeKind.discreteAndRange)
{
    table += createDiscreteRangeParameterTableData(parameterField, key);
    key += 3;
}
else
{
    table += "<td>Parameter kind not known</td>";
}
```

CHANGING PARAMETER VALUES

The `ParameterFieldController`, which can be found in the `DataDefController`, enables you
to change parameters. To modify a parameter field in the report, you copy the field, modify
the copy, and then have the controller modify the original based on changes made to the
copy. For instance here you demonstrate this by changing a default discrete value:

```
ParameterField newParamField = new ParameterField();
parameterField.copyTo(newParamField, true);
newParamField.getCurrentValues().removeAllElements();

// Check the type of the parameter
ParameterValueRangeKind kinda = parameterField.getValueRangeKind();

// If it is discrete
if (kinda == ParameterValueRangeKind.discrete)
{
    // Get the parameter's value
    String textFieldText = request.getParameter("textField" + key);

    // Convert this value to the right format
    String discreteValueText =
(String)convertToValidValue(newParamField, textFieldText);

    // Modify the copy of the parameter field with the value above.
    ParameterFieldDiscreteValue discreteValue =
➥new ParameterFieldDiscreteValue();
    discreteValue.setValue(discreteValueText);
```

```
    newParamField.getCurrentValues().add(discreteValue);

    key += 1;
}
```

ADDING A PARAMETER

Use the `ParameterFieldController` to add new parameters. You do this the same way as adding any other fields to the report: A new field is created, its fields are set, and it is added using a controller. Here you define a new, discrete, string parameter and add it using the controller:

```
IParameterField paramField = new ParameterField();

paramField.setAllowCustomCurrentValues(false);
paramField.setAllowMultiValue(false);
paramField.setAllowNullValue(false);
paramField.setDescription("Here we go dude!");
paramField.setParameterType(ParameterFieldType.queryParameter);
paramField.setValueRangeKind(ParameterValueRangeKind.discrete);
paramField.setType(FieldValueType.numberField);
paramField.setName("YourNewParameter");

reportClientDoc.getDataDefController().getParameterFieldController().
⮕add(parameterField);
```

Adding a parameter using the Parameter field controller does not place the parameter on the report, so the user is not prompted for the parameter when the report is refreshed. To prompt the user, either use it in a filter, or add it by using the `ResultFieldController`.

TIPS AND TRICKS FOR PARAMETER HANDLING

Handling parameters involves many important details. When using parameters keep the following points in mind:

- Parameter values must match the type of the parameter.
- Any values for the parameter should respect the parameter mask.
- Ensure that you know what type of values you are reading: Are they discrete or ranged?
- Set the bound type on a range value before adding it to the parameter.
- Ensure that the upper bound of a range value is greater than the lower bound.

Failing these tests results in a runtime error.

CHARTING OVERVIEW

The `ChartObject`, which represents a chart in the RAS SDK, inherits variables and methods from the `ReportObject`. Remember that the report that you open is represented by the `ReportClientDocument`, not the `ReportObject`.

The `ChartObject`'s properties determine the chart's appearance and where it shows on the report.

33

Here you focus on three `ChartObject` properties:

- `ChartDefinition` indicates the chart type and the fields charted. The chart type can be a Group or Details type.

- `ChartStyle` specifies the chart style type (such as a bar chart or a pie chart) and the text that appears on the chart (such as the chart title).

- `ChartReportArea` is where the chart is located (for example, the report footer).

The following two sections show how you can use these `ChartObject` properties to create a chart. You must first specify the fields on which you want your chart to be based on. To do this, create a `ChartDefinition` object, which will then be added to the `ChartObject` with the `ChartDefinition` property.

DEFINING THE FIELDS IN A CHART

The `ChartDefinition` object determines the type of chart that appears in the report and sets the fields to be displayed. A simple, two-dimensional chart displays two types of fields:

- `ConditionFields`—The fields that determine where to plot a point on the x-axis.

- `DataFields`—The fields that determine what to plot on the y-axis.

Below the chart added is a Group type (see the `ChartType` class), so the `ConditionFields` and `DataFields` that are being charted on are group fields and summary fields respectively.

ADDING ConditionFields

Add the first group field in the `Groups` collection to a `Fields` collection. This field is retrieved with the `ChartDefinition`'s getConditionFields method.

```
ReportClientDocument's DataDefinition:
// Create a new ChartDefinition and set its type to Group
ChartDefinition chartDef = new ChartDefinition();
chartDef.setChartType(ChartType.group);

Fields conditionFields = new Fields();
if (!dataDefinition.getGroups().isEmpty())
{
    IField field = dataDefinition.getGroups().getGroup(0).getConditionField();
    conditionFields.addElement(field);
}
chartDef.setConditionFields(conditionFields);
```

> **NOTE**
> Adding two groups as `ConditionFields` enables you to create a 3D chart. Because one value is required for the x values, the next value drives the z-axis.

ADDING DataFields

After you have added `ConditionFields` to the `ChartDefinition`, add the `DataFields`. In a Group type chart, the `DataFields` are summaries for the group fields that you added as `ConditionFields`.

Adding `DataFields` is similar to how you added `ConditionFields`. For example, you use the name of the summary field that the user has selected to locate the desired field in the `SummaryFields` collection and add this field to a `Fields` collection. You then accessed the summary field with the `ChartDefinition`'s `DataFields` property:

```
Fields dataFields = new Fields();
for (int i = 0; i < dataDefinition.getSummaryFields().size(); i++)
{
    IField summaryField = dataDefinition.getSummaryFields().getField(i);
    if (summaryField.getLongName(Locale.ENGLISH).equals(summaryFieldName))
    {
        dataFields.addElement(summaryField);
    }
}
chartDef.setDataFields(dataFields);
```

Here you use the `LongName` of the summary field. The `LongName` contains the type of summary, for example, a sum or a count, and the group field that it applies to. For example

```
Sum of (Customer.Last Year's Sales, Customer.Country)
```

In general you will want to use a field's `LongName` instead of its `ShortName` or Name to avoid confusion as the `ShortName` or Name might be the same for several fields.

CREATING A ChartObject

After the fields are defined, they are added to the `ChartObject` with the `ChartDefinition` property. The following code uses the `ChartObject`'s `ChartStyle` property and `ChartReportArea` to specify the chart style type, the chart title, and the location of the chart:

```
ChartObject chartObject = new ChartObject();
chartObject.setChartDefinition(chartDefinition);

String chartTypeString = request.getParameter("type");
String chartPlacementString = request.getParameter("placement");
String chartTitle = request.getParameter("title");
if (chartTitle.equals(""))
{
    chartTitle = "no title at all!";
}

ChartStyleType chartStyleType = ChartStyleType.from_string(chartTypeString);
AreaSectionKind chartPlacement =
➥AreaSectionKind.from_string(chartPlacementString);

// Set the chart type, chart placement, and chart title
chartObject.getChartStyle().setType(chartStyleType);
chartObject.setChartReportArea(chartPlacement);
chartObject.getChartStyle().getTextOptions().setTitle(chartTitle);
```

33

```
// Set the width, height, and top
chartObject.setHeight(5000);
chartObject.setWidth(5000);
chartObject.setTop(1000);
```

In this example, the first chart that you add will appear 50 points below the top of the report area in which the chart is located. (These fields are measured in twips, and 20 twips = 1 font point, so 1000/20 = 50 points.) Adding another chart to the same report area places it over the first chart because the formatting for report objects is absolute. The first chart remains hidden until the second chart is removed.

ADDING A CHART TO THE REPORT

Now add the chart using the ReportObjectController's add method. This method takes three parameters: the ChartObject, the section to place it in, and the position in the ReportObjectController collection where you want to add the chart. An option of 1 for the index adds the chart to the end of the array. Return the ReportObjectController by the ReportDefController's getReportObjectController method:

```
reportDefController.getReportObjectController().add(chartObject,
➥chartSection, 1);
```

NOTE

> If you want to modify an existing chart, you can use the clone method to copy the chart, make the desired changes, and then call the modifyObject method using the original chart and the newly modified chart as parameters.

PART **VIII**

CUSTOMIZED REPORT DISTRIBUTION— USING CRYSTAL ENTERPRISE PROFESSIONAL

INTRODUCTION TO THE CRYSTAL ENTERPRISE PROFESSIONAL OBJECT MODEL

In this chapter

UNDERSTANDING THE CRYSTAL ENTERPRISE OBJECT MODEL

Crystal Enterprise was designed from its inception to be extensible. Rather than provide a "black box" product, the folks at Business Objects made sure that they had a layer on top of the core Crystal Enterprise (CE) services that consisted of a Software Development Kit (SDK). A developer armed with a bit of Crystal Enterprise knowledge can customize the look, feel, and functionality of the product or simply create his own solution from scratch. This chapter provides an introduction to using the Crystal Enterprise SDK to extend the out-of-box product to meet new requirements and challenges.

Previous chapters introduced the core Crystal Enterprise services. These services, including the CMS, Page Server, and Job Server, each perform a set of reporting-related functions. Also, it has been illustrated how clicking through the Web Desktop and Crystal Management Console applications makes these services perform their jobs. Perhaps what hasn't become apparent yet is that there is a layer between the CE services and the applications you've seen. This layer consists of the Crystal Enterprise SDK. Each and every feature that CE supports is available via its SDK—the SDK is the entry point for driving CE to do its job. When the Search button in Web Desktop is clicked, or the Add User button is clicked in the Crystal Management Console, those applications are making a call to the Crystal Enterprise SDK, which in turn talks to the various services to perform the requested operation.

For some people, using the Web Desktop application out of the box is sufficient. Others do some minor customization of Web Desktop to provide a familiar corporate look and feel by modifying some style sheets and/or image files. When users want to modify the behavior of the application, they turn to changing the actual code behind the application using the SDK.

Although customizing Web Desktop can be a productive way to meet a particular set of a project's requirements, sometimes the user interface and functionality of Web Desktop is overkill. In this case, it is often better simply to create a new application from scratch rather than modify the existing Web Desktop application. Also, a project's scope is often larger than simply reporting and thus there is a surrounding application that is being developed. In this case, whether Web Desktop meets the requirements or not, the developer probably starts from scratch because the reporting module needs to fit into the architecture, process flow, and look and feel of the surrounding application.

A key factor when integrating into surrounding applications is the development platform used for that application. The popular development platforms today are Crystal Server Pages (CSP), Active Server Pages (ASP), Java Server Pages (JSP) and Java servlets, and finally Microsoft's .NET platform (ASPX). To meet the needs of an organization using any or all of these development technologies, the Crystal Enterprise SDK is provided in three flavors:

34

- COM for CSP and ASP
- Java for JSP and servlets
- .NET for ASP.NET

For the purpose of the SDK introduction, the next few sample code listings in this chapter are in ASP using the COM SDK. Near the end of the chapter the Java and .NET SDKs are visited to explain some concepts specific to those technologies.

NOTE

> Business Objects has announced the deprecation of CSP. This means that although applications using CSP still function, at some point in the future this functionality will be removed. The recommendation is that any new applications that are being developed use ASP instead of CSP. Because the same COM SDK is used in both ASP and CSP, the same functionality is available.

ESTABLISHING A CRYSTAL ENTERPRISE SESSION

The first step in interacting with Crystal Enterprise from an SDK perspective is to establish an active session with CE. This is done via the SessionMgr (Session Manager) object. The result of logging on is an EnterpriseSession object, which provides an entry point into all the SDK operations. There are several ways the logon can happen; the following sections describe these methods.

LOGGING ON TO CRYSTAL ENTERPRISE WITH A USERNAME AND PASSWORD

This is a fairly straightforward two-step procedure. First, the SessionMgr object must be created. Then its Logon method must be invoked, passing in four parameters:

- Username
- Password
- CMS name
- Authentication type

As discussed in Chapter 24, "Crystal Enterprise Architecture," Crystal Enterprise has several different types of authentication modes it supports, including the following:

- Crystal Enterprise authentication (secEnterprise)
- Windows NT authentication (secWindowsNT)
- LDAP authentication (secLDAP)
- Active Directory (secWinAD)

→ For more information on types of supported authentication modes, see "Authentication," p. 515

34

To indicate which authentication mode to use, pass in the authentication type identifier—listed above in parentheses as the last argument to the Logon method. The return value of the Logon method is an EnterpriseSession object. Listing 34.1 shows a sample code listing that logs on a user named Ryan, with a password of 123 to a CMS named CMS1 using Crystal Enterprise authentication.

LISTING 34.1   LOGGING ON USING ENTERPRISE AUTHENTICATION

```
<%
'Create the session manager
Set sessMgr = Server.CreateObject("CrystalEnterprise.SessionMgr")
'Log on to the system
Set sess = sessMgr.Logon("Ryan", "123", "CMS1", "secEnterprise")
%>
```

Listing 34.1 was made to be simple and easy to follow but in the real world, it wouldn't be a good practice to hard-code the username and password. Listing 34.2 illustrates how a developer might prompt the user to type in their username and password. LogonPrompt.htm provides the user interface for the logon, and it performs a form post to Logon.asp to perform the logon (see Listing 34.3).

LISTING 34.2   LOGONPROMPT.HTM PROVIDES THE USER INTERFACE

```
<html>
<body>
<form method=post action=Logon.asp>
Username: <input type=text name=username>
<br>
Password: <input type=password name=password>
<br>
<input type=submit value=Logon>
</form>
</body>
</html>
```

LISTING 34.3   LOGON.ASP PERFORMS THE ACTUAL LOG-ON STEP

```
<%
usr = Request.Form("username")
pwd = Request.Form("password")

Set sessMgr = CreateObject("CrystalEnterprise.SessionMgr")
Set sess = sessMgr.Logon(usr, pwd, "CMS1", "secEnterprise")
%>
```

The interactive logon is better than a hard-coded logon, but still not always ideal, especially if it's running as a reporting module inside a surrounding application that the user has already logged in to. A desirable behavior would be to log the user on behind the scenes. This is accomplished by simply reading the username and password from a location such as a database, encrypted cookie, or Session variable as shown in Listing 34.4.

LISTING 34.4   EXTRACTING THE USERNAME AND PASSWORD FROM SESSION VARIABLES

```
<%
usr = Session("username")
pwd = Session("password")

Set sessMgr = Server.CreateObject("CrystalEnterprise.SessionMgr")
Set sess = sessMgr.Logon(usr, pwd, "CMS1", "secEnterprise")
%>
```

TIP

> The name of the CMS will likely change because an application often is moved from
> environment to environment (that is, from developer's machine to test server to produc-
> tion server). A good practice is when calling the Logon method, don't hard-code the CMS
> name but rather read it from a variable stored somewhere: a Registry key, a configura-
> tion file, and so on. This way, the code doesn't need to be modified when moving to a
> different environment.

LOGGING ON TO CRYSTAL ENTERPRISE USING SINGLE SIGN ON

Although the previous examples were simple and effective, a Crystal Enterprise administrator most likely does not want to create accounts manually for every user and have her log
on using Crystal Enterprise Authentication. Instead, it is likely that Crystal Enterprise will
be pointed to an external security mechanism such as Active Directory. In this case, the
application can still pass the Active Directory username and password as arguments to the
Logon method as shown in Listing 34.5.

LISTING 34.5   LOGGING ON USING ACTIVE DIRECTORY AUTHENTICATION

```
<%
Set sessMgr = Server.CreateObject("CrystalEnterprise.SessionMgr")
Set sess = sessMgr.Logon("RyanM", "abcxyz", "CMS1", "secWinAD")
%>
```

Although this works, the probable desirable behavior is to log the user on without having to
hard-code credentials or having the user type them in. Instead the user is logged on silently
based on the current user account logged onto the client's workstation. This is called *Single
Sign On*. From an SDK perspective, Single Sign On is very simple: pass blank strings for the
username and password, as shown in Listing 34.6.

LISTING 34.6   LOGGING ON USING SINGLE SIGN ON

```
<%
Set sessMgr = Server.CreateObject("CrystalEnterprise.SessionMgr")
Set sess = sessMgr.Logon("", "", "CMS1", "secWinAD")
%>
```

34

This is simple from a coding point of view, but there is some server configuration needed before this runs successfully. The Crystal Enterprise documentation has a section on Single Sign On and provides step-by-step instructions on what settings to change, but at a high level, they are listed here:

- Turn off anonymous access in IIS for the virtual directory from which the ASP page is running

- Turn on Windows NT (NTML) authentication in IIS for the virtual directory from which the ASP is running

NOTE

Single Sign On is only supported with the Windows NT (secWindowsNT) and Active Directory (secWinAD) authentication modes. It is not supported with LDAP (secLDAP).

HANDLING THE EnterpriseSession STATE

So far, the sample code in this chapter has consisted of just a single ASP page. In a real-world application, there would be many ASP pages involved. Based on standard rules of ASP, all objects created during the processing of the page are destroyed when the page has finished delivering its output. Because the EnterpriseSession object represents a Crystal Enterprise session, the session is lost and terminated when this object is destroyed. If another ASP page needed to access the Crystal Enterprise SDK, it would need a way to access the Crystal Enterprise session that was used previously. There are multiple ways to handle this.

The first approach to solving this problem would be to store the EnterpriseSession object in an ASP Session variable that could be accessed later. This is shown in Listings 34.7 and 34.8.

LISTING 34.7 STORING THE EnterpriseSession OBJECT IN A SESSION VARIABLE

```
<%
Set sessMgr = Server.CreateObject("CrystalEnterprise.SessionMgr")
Set sess = sessMgr.Logon("Ryan", "123", "CMS1", "secEnterprise")
Set Session("CE-Session") = sess
%>
```

LISTING 34.8 RETRIEVING THE EnterpriseSession OBJECT FROM A SESSION VARIABLE

```
<%
Set sess = Session("CE-Session")
%>
```

This approach is easy to implement and can work given the following conditions:

- ASP Session state is turned on for the Web server.

- The Web server is running on a single machine. ASP Session state generally works only on a single machine, not a Web farm.

- The user base is small enough to be able to handle the server memory consumed by the session variables.

When the application gets larger and there are reasons why Session variables are not attractive or possible, you can use the last method of logging on: a logon token.

LOGGING ON TO CRYSTAL ENTERPRISE WITH A LOGON TOKEN

If an ASP Session variable was not used, each ASP page would need to log on again using the username and password. This would be an expensive operation from a performance perspective. A better way to handle this would be to log the user on and then ask Crystal Enterprise to generate a token that can be used to log on again later. This token could be stored in a cookie, hidden form field, or on the query string.

Using a logon token is a two-step process. First, the token needs to be generated. This is done using the LogonTokenMgr object. Listing 34.9 creates a token and stores it in a cookie.

LISTING 34.9   STORING A TOKEN IN A COOKIE

```
<%
Set sessMgr = Server.CreateObject("CrystalEnterprise.SessionMgr")
Set sess = sessMgr.Logon("Ryan", "123", "CMS1", "secEnterprise")
token = sess.LogonTokenMgr.DefaultToken
Response.Cookies("CE-Logon-Token") = token
%>
```

When control passes to a new ASP page, the token can be retrieved from the cookie and used to log on. Instead of using the Logon method, the LogonWithToken method is used (see Listing 34.10).

LISTING 34.10   RETRIEVING A TOKEN FROM A COOKIE AND LOGGING ON AGAIN

```
<%
Set sessMgr = Server.CreateObject("CrystalEnterprise.SessionMgr")
token = Request.Cookies("CE-Logon-Token")
Set sess = sessMgr.LogonWithToken(token)
%>
```

In Listing 34.9, the token is generated by accessing the DefaultToken property of the LogonTokenMgr object. This is the simplest way to generate a token but doesn't provide

34

control over how long that token can be used. A more granular way of generating a token is to call the `CreateLogonTokenEx` method. It takes the following parameters:

- `MachineName`: The name of the machine the SDK is running from, that is, the Web server
- `NumMinutes`: The number of minutes for which the logon token is valid
- `NumLogons`: The number of times the logon token can be used before it becomes invalid

Listing 34.11 shows this in action.

LISTING 34.11   CREATING A RESTRICTED TOKEN

```
<%
Set sessMgr = Server.CreateObject("CrystalEnterprise.SessionMgr")
Set sess = sessMgr.Logon("Ryan", "123", "CMS1", "secEnterprise")
token = sess.LogonTokenMgrEx.CreateLogonToken("WEB1", 60, 25)
Response.Cookies("CE-Logon-Token") = token
%>
```

QUERYING THE CRYSTAL ENTERPRISE REPOSITORY

So far this chapter has covered the process of establishing and maintaining a Crystal Enterprise session. After that is done, the next logical step is to perform some kind of action on something stored in Crystal Enterprise. Some examples of this might be listing all reports in the system, listing all report instances in a folder called "Sales," or viewing a report called "District Forecast." As it turns out, all things stored in Crystal Enterprise are stored as objects.

Starting at the most granular level, the `InfoObject` is an abstraction of an object that is persisted in the Crystal Enterprise system. An `InfoObject` contains information about itself, such as its name, description, type, and so on. Examples of the different types of `InfoObjects` that can exist on a Crystal Enterprise system are

- Reports (Crystal Report)
- Report instances
- Analytical reports (Crystal Analytical Report)
- Folders

→ For a discussion of InfoObjects, **see** "Object Scheduling," **p. 519**

An `InfoObjects` collection is, not surprisingly, a collection of `InfoObject` objects. After an `InfoObjects` collection is obtained, you can enumerate through it to get each `InfoObject` contained within.

The `InfoStore` object is the key object that enables retrieval, scheduling, and modification of reports as well as creation of new `InfoObjects` collections. To retrieve an `InfoObjects` collection from the `InfoStore` object, the `Query` method is called, passing in a SQL-like query statement.

INFOSTORE QUERIES

The high-level syntax of this statement is as follows:

```
SELECT [Properties] FROM [Table] WHERE [Condition]
```

Properties begin with `SI_`, for example, `SI_ID`, `SI_NAME`. They describe the object's properties. Generally, `CI_INFOOBJECTS` is the table that is used for all queries. The `WHERE Condition` can be used to filter to a collection of objects coming back.

> **NOTE**
>
> To get the `InfoStore` object, the user must be logged on first and the application must have reference to the `EnterpriseSession` object. The user's rights determine what `InfoObjects` can be accessed by the `InfoStore` object.

The following list describes some of the more useful properties that can be queried for:

- `SI_ID`: The unique identifier of the object
- `SI_NAME`: The name associated with the name, a report title for a report, or a folder name for a folder
- `SI_PARENTID`: The unique identifier of the parent object, a report's parent object is the folder object that contains the report, a folder's parent object is its parent folder, and so on
- `SI_PROGID`: The type of object; some examples of valid values are CrystalEnterprise.Report, CrystalEnterprise.Folder, and CrystalEnterprise.Pdf
- `SI_OWNER`: The name of the user who owns that object

Given these properties, the following list shows some sample queries that use these properties.

- `SELECT SI_ID FROM CI_INFOOBJECTS WHERE SI_NAME = "Budget"` retrieves the ID of a report named Budget
- `SELECT SI_ID, SI_NAME FROM CI_INFOOBJECTS WHERE SI_OWNER = "Neil"` retrieves all reports in the system that are owned by Neil
- `SELECT SI_NAME, SI_PROGID FROM CI_INFOOBJECTS WHERE SI_PARENTID = 456 AND SI_PROGID = "CrystalEnterprise.Report"` retrieves all report objects stored in the folder with an ID of 456

NOTE

> A very useful tool provided with Crystal Enterprise enables system administrators and developers to directly query the system without writing code. The Query Builder is available under the Client Samples section of the Crystal Enterprise Desktop Launchpad. To try it out, start the Query Builder and enter a query into the query window. After it is entered, click the Submit Query button. Notice that the logon information supplied to the Query Builder application affects the returned resultset. Try using a specific user account with restrictions to a particular folder or object. Note that information for those objects is not returned in the query.

Effectively querying the Crystal Enterprise repository is one of the most crucial pieces related to application performance when a large number of objects are present in the Crystal Enterprise system. Clearly, using SELECT * FROM CI_INFOOBJECTS is not an ideal query. Just as with any other relational database, using efficient queries to retrieve data is a best practice and often can be the culprit when experiencing poor Crystal Enterprise application performance.

LISTING REPORTS AND FOLDERS

Listing 34.12 queries Crystal Enterprise for all reports. After it has the collection of reports back, it loops through each one and prints out its name into the resulting ASP page. Figure 34.1 shows the output of this ASP page.

LISTING 34.12   LISTING REPORTS FROM CRYSTAL ENTERPRISE

```
<%
Set sessMgr = Server.CreateObject("CrystalEnterprise.SessionMgr")
Set sess = sessMgr.Logon("Ryan", "123", "CMS1", "secEnterprise")

Set iStore = sess.Service("","InfoStore")

Set infoObjects = iStore.Query("SELECT SI_NAME FROM CI_INFOOBJECTS WHERE
SI_PROGID='CrystalEnterprise.Report'")

For i = 1 to infoObjects.Count
    Set infoObject = infoObjects(i)
    Response.write infoObject.Properties("SI_NAME") & "<br>"
Next
%>
```

On a relatively empty system, listing all reports in a single list might be feasible; however, in larger implementations, showing all reports is generally not a great idea for a couple of reasons. There might be too many for a user to search though, and it is an expensive operation to bring back all report objects, where perhaps the user only wanted to look at a few of them in the list. Some more efficient ways of listing reports are to show them in their folder structure. Listing 34.13 starts at the root folder in the system and shows only objects at that level. A hyperlink is used to refresh the page with a different folder level and thus drill-down into that folder's contents.

Figure 34.1
The output of Listing 34.11 shows all reports held in Crystal Enterprise.

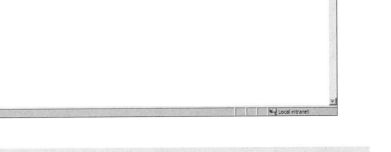

LISTING 34.13 PROVIDING A FOLDER-BY-FOLDER REPORT LISTING

```
<%
' Note: for simplicity, no session handling is done, the logon
' operation is performed on each page hit
Set sessMgr = Server.CreateObject("CrystalEnterprise.SessionMgr")
Set sess = sessMgr.Logon("Ryan", "123", "CMS1", "secEnterprise")

Set iStore = sess.Service("","InfoStore")

parentID = Request.QueryString("ParentID")
If parentID = "" Then
    parentID = "0"
End If

Set infoObjects = iStore.Query("SELECT SI_ID, SI_NAME, SI_PROGID FROM " & _
                            "CI_INFOOBJECTS WHERE SI_PARENTID=" & parentID)

For i = 1 to infoObjects.Count
   Set infoObject = infoObjects(i)

   objectName = infoObject.Properties("SI_NAME")
   objectID = infoObject.Properties("SI_ID")

   If infoObject.Properties("SI_PROGID") = "CrystalEnterprise.Folder" Then
           Response.Write "<a href='tree.asp?parentID=" & objectID & "'>" & _
                        objectName & "</a><br>"
   Else
        Response.Write objectName & "<br>"
   End If
Next
%>
```

34

With some creativity, using only the ID, Name, ParentID, and ProgID properties, a great number of user interfaces can be produced. They might show reports by folder, by name, by type, and so on.

RETRIEVING REPORT INSTANCES

As previously covered in this book, when Crystal Enterprise has finished processing a report, the resulting report with its snapshot of data is stored as an instance in the Crystal Enterprise system. To retrieve these instances, it's necessary to query the system.

Like a folder and its content, hierarchically, a report and its instances have a parent-child relationship. It's possible to retrieve the instances of a report by querying for objects with SI_PARENTID property equal to the report object's ID.

Given a report with ID of 234, entering the following query retrieves its instances:

```
SELECT SI_ID FROM CI_INFOOBJECTS WHERE SI_PARENTID = 234
```

VIEWING REPORTS

Naturally, simply printing out a list of reports isn't all that useful if they can't be viewed. This section focuses on viewing reports. Report viewing is also done via the Crystal Enterprise SDK, specifically, through an object called the CrystalReportViewer. This viewer object, like the other SDK objects, resides on the server. Its job is to render reports to a paginated HTML output. Generally, an ASP page is created and this page is passed in some kind of identifier to determine which report to display (see Listing 34.14).

LISTING 34.14   VIEWING A REPORT IN HTML

```
<%
' Logon
Set sessMgr = Server.CreateObject("CrystalEnterprise.SessionMgr")
Set sess = sessMgr.Logon("Ryan", "123", "CMS1", "secEnterprise")

' Get the name of the report from the query string
reportID = Request.QueryString("reportID")

' Retrieve the report source object given the ID
Set reportSource = sess.Service("", "PSReportFactory").OpenReportSource(reportID)

' Create and set up the viewer object
Set viewer = CreateObject("CrystalReports.CrystalReportViewer")
viewer.EnterpriseLogon = sess
viewer.ReportSource = reportSource

' Instruct the viewer to render the HTML output into the response stream
viewer.ProcessHttpRequest Request, Response

%>
```

34

The first part of Listing 34.13 establishes a session to Crystal Enterprise. The second part then extracts the reportID item off the query string and stores it in the reportID variable. Next, like the InfoStore, the PSReportFactory is retrieved via the EnterpriseSession object. The PSReportFactory (or Page Server Report Factory) is an object that represents the Page Server service. It has an OpenReportSource method that takes the report ID as an argument. When this method is invoked, the page server opens the report and loads it ready for processing. Next, the CrystalReportViewer object is created and two things are passed into it: the active Crystal Enterprise session, and the reportSource object, which represents the report the page server has open. Finally, the ProcessHttpRequest method of the viewer object is called, which instructs the Page Server to execute the first page of the report and return its output. The viewer then converts that output into HTML and writes that into the page's response stream. The end result is a page with the first page of the report displayed. Figure 34.2 shows the output of one of the sample reports.

Figure 34.2
The output of Listing 34.14 shows a report displayed in HTML.

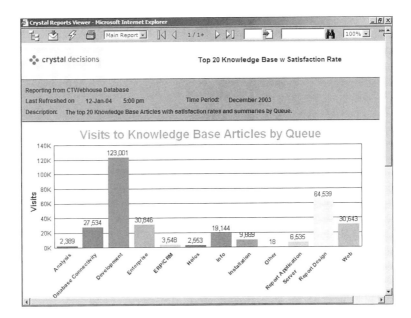

NOTE

> When querying the InfoStore for a given report by name, if you want only report objects and not report instances, include the WHERE SI_INSTANCE=0 condition in the query. This tells the InfoStore to only bring back reports that are not instances. Remember, the report keeps the same name when it's scheduled.

Because the report output can be written anywhere into the response stream, many possibilities of report presentation are available. Sometimes the only content on an ASP page is a report, other times it can be residing along with page headers, footers, navigation panels, or other images and text.

34

THE CRYSTAL ENTERPRISE JAVA SDK

For those developers wanting to program on the Java platform, an equivalent SDK is available. This section provides information specific to the Java SDK. Although the Java SDK is intended for use in J2EE/Web applications, there are no prebuilt servlets, JSP pages, or EJBs as part of the SDK. Instead, a set of Java classes is provided. This offers the most flexibility because developers can write any combination of Java servlets, JSP pages, EJBs, or other kinds of Java applications that use the Crystal Enterprise Java SDK classes. The examples provided in this section are JSP pages.

ACCESSING THE JAVA SDK

The Crystal Enterprise Java SDK consists of a set of Java classes packaged up in a set of .jar files. These .jar files can be found in the following directory:

```
\Program Files\Common Files\Crystal Decisions\2.5\jar
```

→ For more information on Java, **see** "Understanding the Java Reporting Components Architecture,"
p. 655

Most Java application servers have the following folder structure for Web applications:

```
\ApplicationFolder
    \WEB-INF
        \lib
        \classes
        \src
```

To make the classes contained in these .jar files available for use, copy them to the lib folder.

The documentation (JavaDocs) for the SDK can be found at the following location:

```
\Program Files\Crystal Decisions\Enterprise 10\Web Content\Help\sdk\
➥html\java_docs.zip
```

The naming convention for the Java SDK is almost exactly the same as the COM SDK, which makes it easy to understand for those developers working on multiple development platforms. The exception to the naming is that rather than dealing with Java objects directly, interfaces are exposed. These interfaces begin with the letter I, such as IEnterpriseSession, IInfoStore, and so on.

In Java, all classes are organized into namespaces. The namespace for the Crystal Enterprise Java SDK classes all begin with com.crystaldecisions.sdk. There are more granular namespaces beneath that. For example, the ISessionMgr and IEnterpriseSession classes are contained in the com.crystaldecisions.sdk.framework namespace. For a list of all namespaces and the classes contained in them, consult the JavaDocs.

Listing 34.15 is a JSP version of the previously provided report viewing page.

34

LISTING 34.15   VIEWING A REPORT IN A JAVA SERVER PAGE

```
<%@ page import="com.crystaldecisions.sdk.framework.*" %>
<%
// Log on to CE
ISessionMgr sessMgr = CrystalEnterprise.getSessionMgr();
IEnterpriseSession sess = sessMgr.logon("Ryan", "123", "CMS1", "secEnterprise");

// Get the name of the report from the query string
String reportID = request.getParameter("reportID");

// Retrieve the report source object given the ID
IReportSourceFactory factory =
    (IReportSourceFactory)sess.getService("PSReportFactory");
IReportSource reportSource = factory.OpenReportSource(reportID);

// Create and set up the viewer object
CrystalReportViewer viewer =  new CrystalReportViewer();
viewer.setEnterpriseLogon(sess);
viewer.setReportSource(reportSource);

// Instruct the viewer to render the HTML output into the response stream
viewer.processHttpRequest(request, response, getServletContext());
%>
```

For more examples, visit the Developer Zone on the Business Objects Web site at
http://www.businessobjects.com/devzone.

ACCESSING THE .NET SDK

Business Objects has been supporting Microsoft's .NET development platform since its
inception when Crystal Reports for Visual Studio .NET was created. This has continued
with Crystal Enterprise 10, which provides a full .NET SDK equivalent to the COM SDK.
This SDK is intended for use within Microsoft Visual Studio .NET but can also work in
other tools such as Borland C# Builder. This section covers content specific to the .NET
SDK.

The .NET SDK consists of a set of .NET classes. Like Java, these classes are organized into
namespaces. The Crystal Enterprise .NET SDK is contained in the
CrystalDecisions.Enterprise namespace. The naming of all the objects is exactly the same
as the COM SDK, for example, SessionMgr, EnterpriseSession. The .NET assemblies (.dll
files) that make up the SDK can be found in the following folder:

`\Program Files\Common Files\Crystal Decisions\2.5\managed`

Unlike Java, there is no need to copy these files anywhere in order to be able to program
with them. A developer simply needs to open the Project References dialog and select which
assemblies they want to use. Although there is only a single namespace, there are multiple
physical .dll files. The naming convention is CrystalDecisions.Enterprise.*Module*.dll

34

where *Module* is one of a set of modules that compose the full Crystal Enterprise SDK. Some common assemblies a developer uses include the following:

- CrystalDecisions.Enterprise.Framework.dll
- CrystalDecisions.Enterprise.InfoStore.dll
- CrystalDecisions.Web.dll

Notice that CrystalDecisions.Web.dll does not conform to the naming convention of the other assemblies. This is because it is a shared component across Crystal Reports and Crystal Enterprise.

→ For more information on the CrystalDecisions.Web.dll assembly and the CrystalReportViewer Web control, **see** "Delivering Reports with the Web Forms Viewer ," **p. 687**

The C# code sample in Listing 34.16 is an ASPX page version of the report viewing page that has been used previously in this chapter.

LISTING 34.16 Viewing a Report in HTML

```
<%@ Page Register TagPrefix="cr" Namespace="CrystalDecisions.Web" %>
<%@ Import Namespace="CrystalDecisions.Enterprise" %>
<html>
<head>
<script runat="server">

public void Page_Load()
{
        // Log on to CE
        SessionMgr sessMgr = new SessionMgr();
        EnterpriseSession sess = sessMgr.logon("Ryan", "123", "CMS1",
                                                "secEnterprise");

        // Get the name of the report from the query string
        String reportID = Request.QueryString["reportID"];

        // Retrieve the report source object given the ID
        InfoStore iStore = sess.GetService("InfoStore");
        InfoObject reportSource = iStore.Query("SELECT * FROM CI_INFOOBJECTS " +
                                                "WHERE SI_ID = 123")[1];

        // Create and set up the viewer object
        viewer.EnterpriseLogon = sess;
        viewer.ReportSource = reportSource;
}
</script>
</head>
<body>
<form runat="server" method=post action="ViewReportInASPX.aspx">
// Instruct the viewer to render the HTML output into the response stream
<cr:CrystalReportViewer id=viewer runat="server">
</form>
</body>
</html>
```

In addition, the .NET SDK has some components that the COM and Java SDKs do not: visual components for rapid Crystal Enterprise development. These components, found in the CrystalDecisions.Enterprise.WebControls namespace are visual components that can provide a drag-and-drop method of constructing a Crystal Enterprise application. Figure 34.3 shows the Crystal Enterprise .NET Web Controls in action.

Figure 34.3
The Crystal Enterprise .NET Web Controls in action.

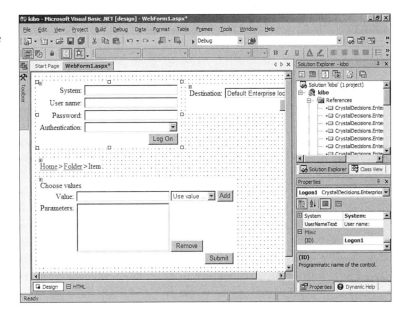

The following list provides a brief explanation of some of the Web Controls:

- Logon: Provides a visual control that automates the process of building a logon credential UI.

- Identity: Abstracts the details of managing sessions across multiple pages away from the developer.

- Items: Simplifies queries to the Crystal Enterprise InfoStore repository by hiding the actual SQL-like query and instead providing a programmatic interface.

NOTE

There are several more Crystal Enterprise Web Controls. For more information on these controls, consult the Crystal Enterprise .NET documentation, which is installed into the MSDN documentation framework.

34

TROUBLESHOOTING

SINGLE SIGN-ON

I can't seem to get Single Sign On to work.

Single Sign On is only supported with the Windows NT (secWindowsNT) and Active Directory (secWinAD) authentication modes. It is not supported with LDAP (secLDAP).

CHAPTER 35

CREATING ENTERPRISE REPORTS APPLICATIONS WITH CRYSTAL ENTERPRISE PART I

In this chapter

ADVANCED SCENARIOS WITH THE CRYSTAL ENTERPRISE OBJECT MODEL

In Chapter 34, "Introduction to the Crystal Enterprise Professional Object Model," you learned how to log on to Crystal Enterprise, present a list of available reports, and view those reports. This chapter and Chapter 36, "Creating Enterprise Reporting Applications with Crystal Enterprise Part II," cover more advanced functionality with the object model that comes into play when building robust enterprise reporting applications. This chapter covers the following topics:

- Scheduling
- History
- InfoObject properties
- Searching
- Alerting
- Crystal Analysis reports
- Program objects
- Events

NOTE

> Chapter 34 introduced you to the Crystal Enterprise Software Development Kit (SDK) and provided sample code in Active Server Pages (ASP) using the COM SDK. To provide insight into the Java SDK, this chapter provides all code samples as Java Server Pages (JSP) using the Java SDK.

SCHEDULING REPORTS

There are many reasons why you would want to use the Crystal Enterprise scheduler. The most obvious case is when you want to run a report at a reoccurring time and make it available for a large number of users. However, the value of the scheduler is more than just time-based report processing. Often, the scheduler can be used for efficiency reasons. Being able to schedule a report once while incurring a single hit to the database, but allowing a large number of users to view the report instance, is a powerful thing. It decreases the number of queries to the database, which could affect the number of database licenses required. At the same time, because a cached copy of the data is stored with the report instance, the performance of viewing the report instance is much better than viewing the report in an on-demand mode. When you understand this basic scheduling principle and the Crystal Enterprise scheduling API, you can create a highly efficient and effective reporting system. This section provides that scheduling API knowledge.

Because the Crystal Enterprise SDK is a unified object model, it's not surprising to learn that the scheduling API is built into the core object model. Scheduling a report is pretty straightforward; you simply call the `schedule` method of the IInfoStore interface, passing in a collection of reports to be scheduled. You'll remember from the previous chapter that reports are stored as objects inside Crystal Enterprise. They are accessed via the `IInfoObject` interface. Multiple objects are stored in the `IInfoObjects` collection. Therefore the `schedule` method takes an `IInfoObjects` collection as a single argument. For most cases, this collection only contains a single object; however, it's possible to schedule a batch of reports at the same time.

The process for scheduling a report is generally a three-step process. First, the report's corresponding `IInfoObject` interface needs to be retrieved, next the scheduling information needs to be filled into the object, and finally the schedule method needs to be called. Chapter 34 described how to retrieve an object's `IInfoStore` interface, but as a review, the following code snippet illustrates querying the InfoStore for a report object:

```
IInfoStore iStore = (IInfoStore) ceSession.getService("InfoStore");
IInfoObjects results = iStore.query("SELECT * FROM CI_INFOOBJECTS WHERE " +
    "SI_NAME='World Sales Report' AND SI_INSTANCE=0");
IInfoObject report = (IInfoObject) results.get(0);
```

This code uses `SI_INSTANCE=0` in the `WHERE` clause of the query to ensure that the report object and not the report instance is brought back. This is important when you start scheduling reports because the report instance has the same report name as the report object, so querying by name does not necessarily give you the object you are looking for.

After an IInfoObject is obtained, its `getSchedulingInfo` method should be called to obtain an `ISchedulingInfo` interface. Use this interface to define the settings for the scheduled job. At a high level, these settings are as follows:

- The date and time for the scheduled job
- If and how the job should reoccur
- Any events that job should wait for or fire
- Which format the job should output to
- Notification settings
- A server group preference

The following sections cover these settings in detail.

WORKING WITH SCHEDULE DATE AND TIMES

The most obvious attribute of a scheduled job is when that job should execute. The job can be either set to run immediately or at a predetermined date and time. Setting a job to run immediately is as simple as calling the `setRightNow` method of the `ISchedulingInfo` interface. The following code snippet shows a report scheduled to run immediately:

```
IInfoObjects results = iStore.query("SELECT SI_ID FROM CI_INFOOBJECTS WHERE " +
    "SI_NAME='World Sales Report' AND SI_INSTANCE=0");
IInfoObject report = (IInfoObject) results.get(0);
ISchedulingInfo sched = report.getSchedulingInfo();
```

35

```
sched.setRightNow(true);
iStore.schedule(results);
```

Because there is no immediate feedback that the report has been scheduled, open the report's properties in the Crystal Management Console and click the History tab. Here you can see the report's scheduling history, specifically the exact time the report was scheduled and its completion status. This provides the verification that the code actually scheduled the report properly. This is shown in Figure 35.1.

Figure 35.1
Viewing a report's history in the Crystal Management Console.

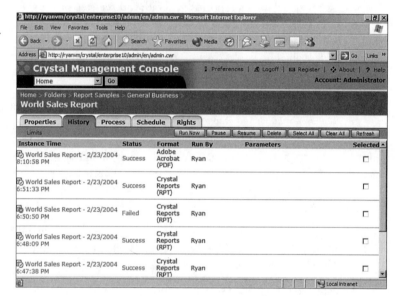

Scheduling a report to run immediately might seem like a useless task. Some people might wonder why the report would not just be viewed on-demand. There are sometimes limitations around the size and complexity of reports that you want to have viewed on-demand; often the browser or application server will timeout the HTTP request because the page server took longer than required to bring back the results of the report. In this case, a common feature for developers to implement is something colloquially referred to as "fake on-demand." In a fake on-demand scenario, when the user chooses to view a report, the script actually schedules the report for the user and either provides an auto refreshing page that polls for the completion of the report, or provides the capability to e-mail the report to the user when completed.

For the traditional schedule scenario, you want to specify when the job should run. This is done via a standard Java Date object. Keep in mind that the date and time are relative to whichever time zone the Crystal Enterprise servers are running on, which could be different from an end user's time zone in a geographically distributed Crystal Enterprise implementation. To set the schedule date and time, pass a Date object to the setBeginDate method of the ISchedulingInfo interface as shown in the following code snippet:

```
ISchedulingInfo sched = report.getSchedulingInfo();
SimpleDateFormat dateFormat = new SimpleDateFormat();
Date beginDate = dateFormat.parse("10/01/2004 07:00 AM");
sched.setBeginDate(beginDate);
iStore.schedule(results);
```

Although this example might seem fairly simple, a developer could use the scheduling API to create a complex scheduling interface like the one found in the Crystal Management Console. This is shown in Figure 35.2.

Figure 35.2
Scheduling a report through the Crystal Management Console.

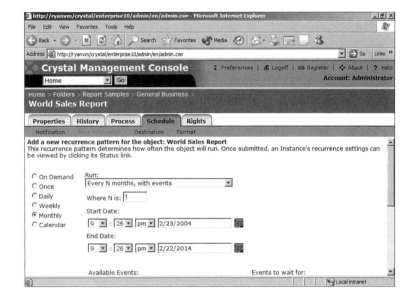

CREATING REOCCURRING SCHEDULES

Sometimes a report needs to be scheduled as a one-time event, but more commonly, a report needs to be scheduled at a set date and time, and then reoccur at some interval thereafter. The Crystal Enterprise scheduler supports the basic reoccurrences daily, hourly, weekly, and monthly. In addition it provides some advanced occurrences such as Nth day, first Monday of the month, or last day of the month. Finally, it enables administrators to define a business calendar that is a custom daily schedule based on some business rule. There are several methods used to define the schedule reoccurrence. The first method that must be called is the ISchedulingInfo interface's setType method. This accepts a CeScheduleType enumeration value. The default value is CeScheduleType.ONCE. To set a reoccurring schedule, pass in one of the following values:

- CeScheduleType.DAILY (daily reoccurrence)
- CeScheduleType.HOURLY (hourly reoccurrence)
- CeScheduleType.WEEKLY (weekly reoccurrence)

35

- `CeScheduleType.MONTHLY` (monthly reoccurrence)

- `CeScheduleType.NTH_DAY` (monthly reoccurrence on the Nth day of the month)

- `CeScheduleType.FIRST_MONDAY` (monthly reoccurrence on the first Monday of the month)

- `CeScheduleType.LAST_DAY` (monthly reoccurrence on the last day of the month)

- `CeScheduleType.CALENDAR` (a customized list of days)

- `CeScheduleType.CALENDAR_TEMPLATE` (a predefined list of days stored in a business calendar template)

After you set the type of reoccurrence, depending on which type you used, there are several methods you can use to define the intervals. The simplest scenario is a daily reoccurrence. To indicate which day to begin and what time of day to run the report, call the `setBeginDate` method. To set the date to end the daily schedule, call the `setEndDate` method. The following code snippet shows a report being scheduled each day at 8:00 a.m. from June 1st to June 15th:

```
ISchedulingInfo sched = report.getSchedulingInfo();
sched.setType(CeScheduleType.DAILY);
SimpleDateFormat dateFormat = new SimpleDateFormat();
Date beginDate = dateFormat.parse("06/01/2004 08:00 AM");
Date endDate = dateFormat.parse("06/15/2004 08:00 AM");
sched.setBeginDate(beginDate);
sched.setEndDate(endDate);
iStore.schedule(results);
```

This is a simple example because only the start and end dates need to be specified. In the following example, the report is scheduled hourly:

```
ISchedulingInfo sched = report.getSchedulingInfo();
sched.setType(CeScheduleType.HOURLY);
SimpleDateFormat dateFormat = new SimpleDateFormat();
Date beginDate = dateFormat.parse("06/01/2004 12:00 AM");
Date endDate = dateFormat.parse("06/15/2004 12:00 AM");
sched.setBeginDate(beginDate);
sched.setEndDate(endDate);
sched.setIntervalHours(1);
iStore.schedule(results);
```

In this case, in addition to the start and end dates, you should set an interval that indicates how many hours should pass in between the scheduled jobs. In the previous example, the report is scheduled every six hours.

When working with weekly schedules, it's assumed that the report runs the first day of the week at the specified time. This can be done by simply setting the schedule type to WEEKLY and providing a start and end date as follows:

```
ISchedulingInfo sched = report.getSchedulingInfo();
sched.setType(CeScheduleType.WEEKLY);
SimpleDateFormat dateFormat = new SimpleDateFormat();
Date beginDate = dateFormat.parse("01/01/2005 08:00 AM");
```

35

```
Date endDate = dateFormat.parse("01/30/2005 08:00 AM");
sched.setBeginDate(beginDate);
sched.setEndDate(endDate);
iStore.schedule(results);
```

The other way to do a weekly schedule is to specify individual days of the week to run the report. In this case, even though it's a weekly-type schedule, you need to define a custom schedule by setting the schedule type to CALENDAR. When using the calendar type, you need to call the getCalendarRunDays method of the ISchedulingInfo interface to obtain the ICalendarRunDays interface. Through this interface you can add any day combination you want. It has an add method that accepts eight arguments indicating day, week, month, and so on. In this case, only the day of week argument is used so set the rest to -1. The following example schedules the report every Monday, Wednesday, and Friday from January 1st to 30th:

```
ISchedulingInfo sched = report.getSchedulingInfo();
sched.setType(CeScheduleType.CALENDAR);
ICalendarRunDays days = sched.getCalendarRunDays();
days.add(-1, -1, -1, -1, -1, -1, 2, -1);
days.add(-1, -1, -1, -1, -1, -1, 4, -1);
days.add(-1, -1, -1, -1, -1, -1, 6, -1);
SimpleDateFormat dateFormat = new SimpleDateFormat();
Date beginDate = dateFormat.parse("01/01/2005 08:00 AM");
Date endDate = dateFormat.parse("01/30/2005 08:00 AM");
sched.setBeginDate(beginDate);
sched.setEndDate(endDate);
iStore.schedule(results);
```

Working with monthly schedules is fairly simple. First, set the schedule type to MONTHLY and provide start and end dates, and optionally call the setIntervalMonths method to indicate that the report job should be run every Nth month.

Finally, working with business calendars is quite simple. The real work is in creating the calendar, but luckily this is a task that can be performed visually through the Crystal Management Console shown in Figure 35.3. Business calendars are stored as InfoObjects just like everything else in the Crystal Enterprise repository. However, business calendars are stored in the CI_SYSTEMOBJECTS table instead of the CI_INFOOBJECTS table. To create a scheduled job based on a business calendar, first look up the ID of the business calendar object, and then call the setCalendarTemplate method of the ISchedulingInfo interface as shown in the following code:

```
IInfoObjects calResults = iStore.query("SELECT SI_ID FROM CI_SYSTEMOBJECTS " +
    "WHERE SI_NAME='Each Quarter End'");
IInfoObject cal = (IInfoObject) calResults.get(0);
ISchedulingInfo sched = report.getSchedulingInfo();
sched.setType(CeScheduleType.CALENDAR_TEMPLATE);
sched.setCalendarTemplate(cal.getID());
iStore.schedule(results) ;
```

35

Figure 35.3
Defining a business calendar in the Crystal Management Console.

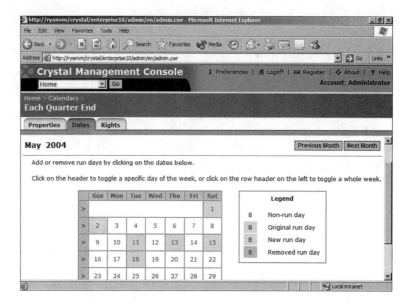

EVENT-BASED SCHEDULING

A scheduled job can work with events in two ways: A job can wait to run until an event is triggered or it can be the one that triggers events upon success or failure of itself. Jobs using events keep the same scheduling rules with respect to dates and times and reoccurrences; however, the start dates don't imply when the report starts processing, but rather when the report starts listening for the event. The most common scenario around events is needing to wait for a data warehouse load to complete before a job is run. There are several steps involved in setting up this scenario. First, an event needs to be created. This can be done via the Crystal Management Console or programmatically. The next chapter discusses how to create events programmatically. Next, use the ISchedulingInfo to set up the preferred date/time and reoccurrence settings. Then call the getDependencies method to obtain the IEvents interface. Finally, call the add method passing in the ID of the event object. This object is found in the SI_SYSTEMOBJECTS table like the business calendars. The following code snippet shows scheduling a report to start listening for an event called "Data Warehouse Load" at 2 a.m. every morning for November:

```
IInfoObjects eventResults = iStore.query("SELECT SI_ID FROM CI_SYSTEMOBJECTS" +
    " WHERE SI_NAME='Data Warehouse Load'");
IInfoObject event = (IInfoObject) eventResults.get(0);
ISchedulingInfo sched = report.getSchedulingInfo();
IEvents events = sched.getDependencies();
events.add(event.getID());
sched.setType(CeScheduleType.DAILY);
SimpleDateFormat dateFormat = new SimpleDateFormat();
Date beginDate = dateFormat.parse("11/01/2004 02:00 AM");
Date endDate = dateFormat.parse("11/30/2004 02:00 AM");
```

```
sched.setBeginDate(beginDate);
sched.setEndDate(endDate);
iStore.schedule(results);
```

In this case, the report is waiting for the data warehouse load event to be triggered, but perhaps there are multiple steps to this load and multiple events. This is fine because a scheduled report can listen for multiple events to be fired. Simply call the IEvents add method for each event that needs to be listened for.

The other way to work with event-based scheduling is to have a completed report job trigger an event either on success or completion. That event could in turn kick off other actions in the system. From a programmatic standpoint, this works exactly the same way as event dependencies except, instead of calling the ISchedulingInfo's getDependencies method, the getDependants method is called. Keep in mind that events added to a schedule's dependants can only be schedule events, not file or custom events. The following code snippet schedules a report but triggers a Weekly Report Completed event upon successful completion:

```
IInfoObjects eventResults = iStore.query("SELECT SI_ID FROM CI_SYSTEMOBJECTS" +
    " WHERE SI_NAME='Weekly Report Completed'");
IInfoObject event = (IInfoObject) eventResults.get(0);
ISchedulingInfo sched = report.getSchedulingInfo();
IEvents events = sched.getDependants();
events.add(event.getID());
sched.setType(CeScheduleType.WEEKLY);
SimpleDateFormat dateFormat = new SimpleDateFormat();
Date beginDate = dateFormat.parse("06/01/2004 08:00 AM");
Date endDate = dateFormat.parse("06/15/2004 08:00 AM");
sched.setBeginDate(beginDate);
sched.setEndDate(endDate);
iStore.schedule(results) ;
```

SCHEDULING TO A DESTINATION

By default when a report is scheduled inside Crystal Enterprise, the resulting file is stored inside the Crystal Enterprise repository. In addition to this, scheduler has the capability to write the report to an arbitrary folder on the machine, e-mail the report to an individual or group, and upload the file to another machine via ftp. The destination is set as part of the scheduled job. From the ISchedulingInfo interface, there is a getDestination method that is used to get access to the IDestination interface. The setFromPlugin method accepts a handle to a destination type object called an IDestinationPlugin. Don't worry about the code required to create the plug-in object, which is covered in the next chapter. The types of destination plug-ins are

For more information on the code required to create the plug-in, see Chapter 36, "Creating Enterprise Reporting Applications with Crystal Enterprise Part II."

35

- CrystalEnterprise.DiskUnmanaged (arbitrary folder location)
- CrystalEnterprise.Smtp (e-mail)
- CrystalEnterprise.Ftp (FTP server upload)

The following code shows a report being scheduled once to the Temp folder of the machine:

```
ISchedulingInfo sched = report.getSchedulingInfo();
sched.setRightNow(true);
IDestination dest = sched.getDestination();
IDestinationPlugin disk = getDestinationPlugin(iStore,
    "CrystalEnterprise.DiskUnmanaged");
IDiskUnmanagedOptions options =
    (IDiskUnmanagedOptions) disk.getScheduleOptions();
options.getDestinationFiles().add("C:/Temp/");
dest.setFromPlugin(disk);
iStore.schedule(results);
```

Each type of destination has its own corresponding set of options. In the case of the DiskUnmanaged destination, it has an object called IDiskUnmanagedOptions that accepts a folder location as well as optional credentials used to access that folder. The Smtp destination has an ISMTPOptions object that specifies mail routing information. Finally, the Ftp destination has an IFTPOptions object that specifies server, port, credentials, and the target folder:

```
ISchedulingInfo sched = report.getSchedulingInfo();
sched.setRightNow(true);
IDestination dest = sched.getDestination();
IDestinationPlugin smtp = getDestinationPlugin(iStore, "CrystalEnterprise.Smtp");
ISMTPOptions options = (ISMTPOptions) smtp.getScheduleOptions();
options.setDomainName("domain_name");
options.setServerName("smtp_server_name");
options.setPort(25);
options.setSMTPAuthenticationType(ISMTPOptions.CeSMTPAuthentication.NONE);
options.setSMTPUserName("domain\username");
options.setSMTPPassword("password");
options.setSenderAddress("email@address.com");
options.setSubject("The report '%SI_NAME%' ran successfuly");
dest.setFromPlugin(smtp);
iStore.schedule(results);
```

Note that in the call to the setSubject method, the string uses the %SI_NAME% variable. Crystal Enterprise replaces this placeholder with the name of the report. This means that the code can be written fairly generically.

USING CRYSTAL ENTERPRISE NOTIFICATIONS

In addition to being able to trigger alerts upon completion of a scheduled job, there are multiple notifications that can be set up. These are typically targeted for the consumption of Crystal Enterprise administrators as opposed to end users. There are two types of notifications: audit notification and e-mail notification.

There are two audit notifications that can be turned on: one for the success of a report job and one for the failure of a report job. When either of these audit notifications is enabled and a job finishes, a record is written to the auditing database indicating the job name, time, status, and so on. To enable audit notifications, call the getNotifications method of the

ISchedulingInfo interface. This returns an INotifications interface. Using this interface, the setAuditOption method can be called, passing in a member of the CeAuditOnResult enumeration. The valid values are

- CeAuditOnResult.NONE (no audit notification)
- CeAuditOnResult.SUCCESS (audit notification enabled for a successful job)
- CeAuditOnResult.FAILURE (audit notification enabled for a failed job)
- CeAuditOnResult.BOTH (audit notification enabled for either success or failure of a job)

The following example schedules a report and enables audit notification for a successful job:

```
ISchedulingInfo sched = report.getSchedulingInfo();
sched.setRightNow(true);
INotifications notify = sched.getNotifications();
notify.setAuditOption(INotifications.CeAuditOnResult.SUCCESS);
iStore.schedule(results);
```

Email notification works in a similar manner. It can be enabled for both successful and failed jobs. To enable email notification, obtain the INotifications interface as described previously like you would do for auditing. From there, you can call the getDestinationsOnSuccess or getDestinationsOnFailure methods to obtain the IDestinations interface. You might recognize this interface as the same one used to configure schedule destinations. To enable email destinations using the Report Job Server's default email settings, you can simply call the IDestinations's add method passing in CrystalEnterprise.Smtp as shown here:

```
ISchedulingInfo sched = report.getSchedulingInfo();
sched.setRightNow(true);
INotifications notify = sched.getNotifications();
IDestinations dest = notify.getDestinationsOnSuccess();
dest.add("CrystalEnterprise.Smtp");
iStore.schedule(results);
```

If you want to customize the e-mail settings such as the recipients, subject line, and so on, you can call the getScheduleOptions method and get access to the ISMTPOptions interface.

SCHEDULING TO A SERVER GROUP

There are several reasons why a Crystal Enterprise system might be broken up into server groups. Servers could be split up by geography, or by the database server they access. If this is the case, it's often a requirement when scheduling that the report job run on a server in a specific server group. This is programmatically set via the ISchedulingInfo interface. The setServerGroup method can be called to indicate which server group to use. It accepts an integer that is the ID of the server group. The ID can be obtained by an InfoStore query. In addition, the setServerGroupChoice enables the developer to specify an additional level of control. It accepts a member of the GroupChoice enumeration as described here:

- GroupChoice.FIRST_AVAILABLE: Use the first available server, regardless of which server group it belongs to.

35

- `GroupChoice.PREFERRED`: Use a server in the specified server group if possible, but otherwise fall back to the next available server.

- `GroupChoice.SPECIFIED`: Use only servers in the specified server group.

The following code schedules a report using a preferred server group of `'Vancouver Servers'`:

```
IInfoObjects serverGroupResults = iStore.query("SELECT SI_ID FROM CI_SYSTEMOBJECTS
WHERE SI_NAME='Vancouver Servers'");
IInfoObject serverGroup = (IInfoObject) serverGroupResults.get(0);

ISchedulingInfo sched = report.getSchedulingInfo();
sched.setRightNow(true);
sched.setServerGroup(serverGroup.getID());
sched.setServerGroupChoice(ISchedulingInfo.GroupChoice.PREFERRED);
iStore.schedule(results);
```

All the settings around scheduling discussed this far in this chapter have been accessed via the `ISchedulingInfo` interface. These options are directly tied to the actual scheduling process. However, there are some other options that are relevant when scheduling that are accessed through the `IReport` interface. They are as follows:

- Output format
- Database credentials
- Parameter values
- Selection formula

SCHEDULING TO A SPECIFIC FORMAT

The location of the output format setting is slightly strange in that it really is only relevant in the context of scheduling, so it might make more sense in the `ISchedulingInfo` interface, but instead it's found in the `IReport` interface. The `IReport` interface is obtained by casting from an `IInfoObject` interface. The following code obtains the `IReport` interface for an InfoObject:

```
IInfoObjects results = iStore.query("SELECT SI_ID FROM CI_INFOOBJECTS WHERE" +
    " SI_NAME='World Sales Report' AND SI_INSTANCE=0");
IInfoObject infoObject = (IInfoObject) results.get(0);

IReport report = (IReport) infoObject;
```

After this interface is obtained, there are many methods available. The following sections focus on the relevant settings for scheduling.

To set the output format, call the `getReportFormatOptions` method, which returns an `IReportFormatOptions` interface. With this interface, the `setFormat` method can be called that accepts a member of the `CeReportFormat` enumeration. The following values are allowed:

35

- `CeReportFormat.CRYSTAL_REPORT`: The default value, keeping the report in its native format

- `CeReportFormat.EXCEL`: Microsoft Excel format

- `CeReportFormat.EXCEL_DATA_ONLY`: A variation of the Microsoft Excel format, which exports the data from the report without the formatting

- `CeReportFormat.PDF`: Adobe PDF format

- `CeReportFormat.RTF`: Microsoft Rich Text Format (RTF)

- `CeReportFormat.TEXT_CHARACTER_SEPARATED`: Character separated value (CSV) format

- `CeReportFormat.TEXT_PLAIN`: Plain text format

- `CeReportFormat.TEXT_PAGINATED`: A variation of the plain text format that adds pagination

- `CeReportFormat.TEXT_TAB_SEPARATED_TEXT`: Tab-separated text format

- `CeReportFormat.WORD`: Microsoft Word format

The following code snippet schedules a report to Word format:

```
IReport report = (IReport) infoObject;
IReportFormatOptions format = report.getReportFormatOptions();
format.setFormat(IReportFormatOptions.CeReportFormat.WORD);
iStore.schedule(results) ;
```

SETTING DATABASE CREDENTIALS

If you have tried to use some of the code samples thus far, you might have found that your reports were failing to run when scheduled. One of the causes of this is a lack of database credentials. Keep in mind that Crystal Reports stores all the connection information for the database inside the report *except* the password. Therefore, this needs to be set at runtime. The easiest way to do this is to type it in manually in the Crystal Management Console and save it with the InfoObject (shown in Figure 35.4). However, sometimes there are many reports and this manual step becomes unrealistic. In this case, the report's credentials can be set programmatically.

To set a report's credentials, call the `getReportLogons` method of the `IReport` interface. This returns a Crystal Enterprise collection interface called `ISDKList`. The reason there is a collection of report credentials is that some reports point to multiple data sources that each have their own respective credentials. These reports are rare though, so assume a collection of only one element. Calling the `get` method returns an `IReportLogon` interface. Here you can call the `setUserName` and `setPassword` methods as shown in the following code:

```
IInfoObjects results = iStore.query("SELECT * FROM CI_INFOOBJECTS WHERE " +
    "SI_NAME='World Sales Report' AND SI_INSTANCE=0");
IInfoObject infoObject = (IInfoObject) results.get(0);
IReport report = (IReport) infoObject;
ISDKList list = report.getReportLogons();
IReportLogon logon = (IReportLogon) list.get(0);
logon.setUserName("username");
```

35

```
logon.setPassword("password");
ISchedulingInfo sched = infoObject.getSchedulingInfo();
iStore.schedule(results);
```

Figure 35.4
Setting database credentials through the
Crystal Management
Console.

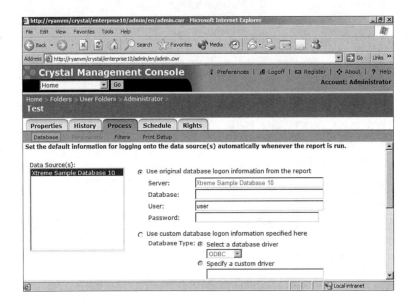

There are other methods available from the IReportLogon method such as
setCustomServerName and setCustomerDatabaseName that enable you to point the report at a
different database and server at schedule-time if required.

PASSING PARAMETERS TO THE REPORT

Many of today's reports have parameters defined in them. This allows reports to be
dynamic and adaptable. When reports are scheduled, any parameters defined in the report
need to have a value unless a default value is already defined. Like database credentials,
parameter values can be manually typed in from the Crystal Management Console on the
Process tab. However, I describe how to accomplish this programmatically here.

From the IReport interface, call the getReportParameters method. This returns a collection
of IReportParameter objects. There is one object in the collection per parameter values
required for the report. After the IReportParameter interface is obtained, there is a
getCurrentValues method that needs to be called. This returns an IReportParameterValues
interface. There are two types of parameter values that can be added via this interface: a
single value or a range value. As the name implies, a single value is an individual parameter
value.

A range value, on the other hand, is two values that form upper and lower bounds. Range
parameters are common in date ranges. For this example, assume a single value is being

added. This is done by calling the addSingleValue method. This returns yet another interface called IReportParameterSingleValue. To set that actual value, call the setValue method.

NOTE

> Even though the argument to the setValue method is of type String, this does not mean that other types of parameter values can't be set. When setting other parameter types, simply send in a string version of their value. For example, the string "100" can be passed in for a numeric parameter value or the string "True" could be passed in for a Boolean value.

The following code snippet schedules a report passing in the value "Canada" for the first parameter defined in the report:

```
IReport report = (IReport) infoObject;
List params = report.getReportParameters();
IReportParameter param = (IReportParameter) params.get(0);
IReportParameterValues vals = param.getCurrentValues();
IReportParameterSingleValue val = vals.addSingleValue();
val.setValue("Canada");
ISchedulingInfo sched = infoObject.getSchedulingInfo();
iStore.schedule(results);
```

NOTE

> Parameters are stored in the report parameters collection in the same order that they are shown in the Crystal Reports field explorer.

The code example above hard-coded the value but a more generic approach might be to prompt users to enter a value when they create the scheduled job. Sometimes users cannot remember the exact spelling or value they should use for a parameter. Along these lines, the IReportParameter interface exposes a collection of pick list values that were created at report design time. This makes it easy for a developer to provide a list of values for the end user. Listing 35.1 provides a JSP page that fills a drop-down box with pick list values for a parameter.

LISTING 35.1 PROMPTING FOR A PARAMETER

```
<%@ page import="java.util.*,
                com.crystaldecisions.sdk.framework.*,
                com.crystaldecisions.sdk.occa.infostore.*,
                com.crystaldecisions.sdk.plugin.desktop.common.*,
                com.crystaldecisions.sdk.plugin.desktop.report.*" %>

<html>
<body>
<form method=POST action=schedule.jsp>
Select a country to use for the scheduled report:
```

35

continues

LISTING 35.1   CONTINUED

```
<select name=country>
<%

ISessionMgr sessMgr = CrystalEnterprise.getSessionMgr();
IEnterpriseSession ceSession = sessMgr.logon("Ryan", "123", "CMS_NAME",
                              "secEnterprise");
IInfoStore iStore = (IInfoStore) ceSession.getService("InfoStore");
IInfoObjects results = iStore.query("SELECT * FROM CI_INFOOBJECTS WHERE " +
    "SI_NAME='Parameter Report' AND SI_INSTANCE=0");
IInfoObject infoObject = (IInfoObject) results.get(0);

IReport report = (IReport) infoObject;
List params = report.getReportParameters();
IReportParameter param = (IReportParameter) params.get(0);
IReportParameterValues vals = param.getDefaultValues();
for (int i=0; i<vals.size(); i++) {
    IReportParameterSingleValue val = (IReportParameterSingleValue) vals.get(i);
    out.println("<option value=" + val.getValue() + ">" +
            val.getValue() +"</option>");
}
ceSession.logoff();
%>
</select>
<input type=submit value=Select>
</form>
</body>
</html>
```

Figure 35.5 shows the output of this page.

Figure 35.5
Prompting for a parameter before scheduling.

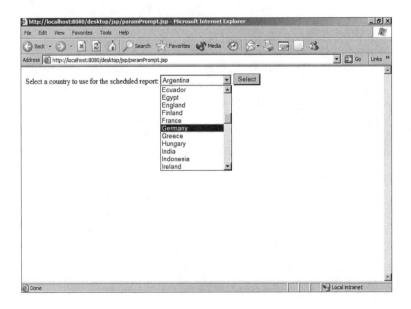

SELECTION FORMULA

Most reports have some kind of record selection formula used in the report processing to reduce the number of records returned to the report. This is a key factor in maximizing report performance. The selection formula often needs to be dynamic. It can be set programmatically via the IReport interface. There are two methods for doing this: setRecordFormula and setGroupFormula. These set the record selection formula and group selection formula, respectively. These methods accept a string argument, which is the formula expressed in the Crystal Reports formula language syntax. The following example schedules a report with a modified record selection formula:

```
IReport report = (IReport) infoObject;
report.setRecordFormula("{Products.Category} = 'Widgets' AND +
{Product.Status}='In Stock'");
ISchedulingInfo sched = infoObject.getSchedulingInfo();
iStore.schedule(results);
```

TROUBLESHOOTING

PROBLEMS WITH CRYSTAL ENTERPRISE AUDIT NOTIFICATION

I can't seem to enable the audit notifications.

Try this: call the getNotifications method of the ISchedulingInfo interface. This returns an INotifications interface. Using this interface, the setAuditOption method can be called, passing in a member of the CeAuditOnResult enumeration.

CREATING ENTERPRISE REPORTING APPLICATIONS WITH CRYSTAL ENTERPRISE PART II

In this chapter

QUERYING THE CRYSTAL ENTERPRISE INFOSTORE

The previous chapter focused on some of the advanced scenarios with the Crystal Enterprise Object Model. Most of these scenarios focused around creating scheduled report jobs and the associated settings. This chapter continues the coverage of advanced Crystal Enterprise Object Model scenarios and covers the following topics:

- The InfoStore
- Alerting
- Program Objects
- Crystal Analysis Reports

In Chapter 34, "Introduction to the Crystal Enterprise Professional Object Model," the concept of an InfoStore query was introduced. This is the programmatic entry point into the Crystal Enterprise Repository where all items such as reports, folders, users, and groups are stored. These items are all represented as objects called InfoObjects. From the COM, .NET, and Java object models, a query can be defined that retrieves objects and their corresponding properties. This section covers some of the advanced scenarios when dealing with InfoStore queries.

THE QUERY BUILDER SAMPLE APPLICATION

There is a sample application that comes with Crystal Enterprise 10 that is very useful when working with InfoStore queries. It's called the Query Builder. There is a link to it from the User Launchpad or you can find it at the following location:

`http://CESERVER/crystal/enterprise10/websamples/en/query/`

The Query Builder application (shown in Figure 36.1) provides a simple text box that you can type InfoStore queries into.

When you click the Submit Query button, it runs the query and displays the results in a simple table. Also, it enables you to type in a user account to use to execute the statement. This is very useful for testing different levels of security. For example, logging on as one user should bring back different reports than logging on as another user. The nice thing is that any valid InfoStore query can be used here, including queries that return objects like users, groups, and servers. Figure 36.2 shows the results of running a query retrieving the name of all reports in the system (SELECT SI_NAME FROM CI_INFOOBJECTS WHERE SI_PROGID='CrystalEnterprise.Report').

This is an indispensable debugging tool for developers. If a query is returning an error through your application, copy and paste it into the Query Builder and make sure it runs successfully there before worrying about any application coding problems.

OPTIMIZING YOUR QUERIES

It's important to understand that when running an InfoStore query, the query command that is passed in is not the actual query that is run against the Crystal Enterprise repository database. The Crystal Enterprise InfoStore query is a *meta-query*, meaning that it is meant to be simple and high-level but when run, gets translated into a more complex query against the repository, which has a different database schema. The main reason for this kind of design is to abstract the developer away from the actual raw data source and instead provide an application-level interface to get at the underlying information.

Figure 36.1
The Query Builder sample application being used to run an InfoStore query.

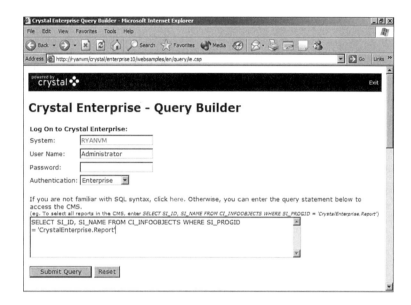

Figure 36.2
Viewing query results in Query Builder.

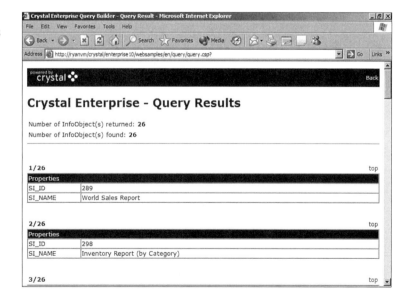

Although the InfoStore query is a meta-query and not the actual database query, the syntax and structure of the queries passed in are still a performance factor. There are three basic rules of query optimization:

- Reduce the "width" of your query—bring back only those properties that you need
- Reduce the "length" of your query—bring back only the objects (records) you need
- Reduce the frequency of queries

The first step is to reduce the width of your queries. When looking at example applications and sample code, you often see the SELECT * clause being used in InfoStore queries. Although this is a short and easy way to write a query, the result can be greatly degraded performance. As any developer familiar with basic database concepts understands, the general theory of querying a database is to bring back as little data as possible. The same principle applies here. Performing a "SELECT *" query actually returns upward of 60 properties, and some of those properties even have subproperties. To see this for yourself, run the query SELECT * FROM CI_INFOOBJECTS WHERE SI_PROGID='CrystalEnterprise.Report'. You might think you are only bringing back a list of reports, but there is a lot of metadata stored in the Crystal Enterprise repository about each report.

Using "SELECT *" queries would almost certainly result in a large number of unused properties and thus wasted bandwidth. Because performance is always a factor is any large-scale enterprise software deployment, it's important to understand which properties you need and only bring those back. For example, the following query only returns the ID and name of reports and folders:

```
SELECT SI_ID, SI_NAME FROM CI_INFOOBJECTS
```

For reference, consult the Crystal Enterprise developer documentation and look for the Query Language Reference section. This contains a topic collection called InfoObject properties that provides a description of every single InfoObject property. This is useful for determining which properties are needed as opposed to just using a "SELECT *".

> **TIP**
>
> The SI_ID property is always returned, even if it is not specified in the SELECT clause. You don't need to ask for it explicitly although it's usually a good idea just for clarity.

When looking at reducing the "length" of your queries—that is, keeping the number of records returned to a minimum—you'll need to employ the use of the WHERE and TOP N clauses. These standard SQL constructs work pretty much the way you would expect.

The WHERE clause is used to filter the records returned from the query. Ideally, if you only need to obtain information about a single object, use a WHERE clause such as

```
WHERE SI_ID=123
```

If properties for a single object are needed, try to use the WHERE clause to filter on the SI_ID (ID) or SI_NAME (name) of the object. If all reports at a certain level of the folder structure need to be brought back, use the SI_PARENTID property in the WHERE clause. The following sample query returns all reports at the root level of the folder structure:

```
SELECT SI_NAME FROM CI_INFOOBJECTS WHERE SI_PARENTID=0
```

The other common type of operation is to bring back all objects of a certain kind, for example, all reports, users, events, and so on. This is where the SI_PROGID property should be used in the WHERE clause, as shown in the following example that returns a list of all usernames:

```
SELECT SI_NAME FROM CI_SYSTEMOBJECTS WHERE SI_PROGID='CrystalEnterprise.User'
```

In addition to using a WHERE clause to filter the query, a big performance gain can be made by only filtering on indexed properties. The following properties are indexed in the Crystal Enterprise repository database:

- SI_CUID
- SI_GUID
- SI_HIDDEN_OBJECT
- SI_ID
- SI_INSTANCE_OBJECT
- SI_NAME
- SI_NAMEDUSER
- SI_NEXTRUNTIME
- SI_OWNERID
- SI_PARENTID
- SI_PLUGIN_OBJECT
- SI_PROGID
- SI_RECURRING
- SI_RUID
- SI_RUNNABLE_OBJECT
- SI_SCHEDULE_STATUS
- SI_UPDATE_TS

These indexed properties are used as actual fields in the Crystal Enterprise repository. All other properties are stored in a single binary data field in the repository. This means if a query is passed to the InfoStore with a WHERE clause using an indexed property, that WHERE clause can be used in the actual repository database query. This is the ideal situation. Alternatively, if a non-indexed property such as SI_DBNEEDLOGON is used, the query against the repository database must be run without a WHERE clause, thus bringing back extra records and then the InfoStore component must make a pass through the records and filter out the unnecessary ones. If there are large numbers of reports, folders, user, or other similar types of objects present in Crystal Enterprise, filtering on a non-indexed property can result in a performance bottleneck.

The TOP N clause is used for limiting the results of a query. The N would be replaced by a number, for example, TOP 10 returns the top 10 records. If no ORDER BY clause is used, the TOP N clause simply returns the first N values it finds. This can be useful for preventing a large query that would affect performance. An example of this is allowing the user to search for a report by name or keyword. If the system were to have several thousand reports, then depending on the search term used, a search could potentially bring back far too many results. This is analogous to performing a Google search for a word like "crystal." It would bring back too many results for a user to really be able to review.

By default, if a TOP N clause is not used, the InfoStore limits the results to 1,000. Effectively, the InfoStore inserts a TOP 1000 clause into all queries. You can determine if the list of objects returned has been truncated due to a TOP N by comparing the number of objects in the result collection (InfoObject's Count property) with the real number of records resulting from the query (InfoObjects's ResultCount property). If the Count is less than the ResultCount, the object collection has been truncated.

If there is a valid reason to run a report and return more than 1,000 objects, you can specify an arbitrary number in the TOP N clause such as TOP 5000. If you want to change the default limit of 1,000 to a different number, lower or higher, modify the InfoStoreDefaultTopNValue Registry key values found in the following location:

HKLM\Software\Crystal Decisions\10.0\Enterprise\CMS\Instances*MACHINENAME*.cms

The *MACHINENAME* is the name of the Crystal Enterprise CMS server. This needs to be configured for each instance of the CMS.

The other way the TOP N clause can be used is to rank the objects being returned. This is done by using an ORDER BY statement. The following query returns the name and start time of all scheduled jobs ordered by the start time in descending order.

```
SELECT SI_NAME, SI_STARTTIME FROM CI_INFOOBJECTS WHERE
    SI_PROGID='CrystalEnterprise.Report' AND SI_INSTANCE_OBJECT=1
    ORDER BY SI_STARTTIME DESC
```

This query essentially provides a log of scheduled reports. However, you can imagine how this list could get very large with a large system with many reports and many schedules. By adding the TOP 25 clause, only the last 25 scheduled reports would be returned.

The final principle to InfoStore query optimization is to reduce the number of overall queries to the database. Typically this is done by using some little-known InfoObject properties that can answer a question and eliminate the need for an additional query to find out that answer.

A typical scenario is to call a recursive function to display reports in the system. Typically the process is started by running a function like the following:

```
SELECT SI_ID, SI_NAME, SI_PROGID FROM CI_INFOOBJECTS WHERE SI_PARENTID=0
```

This would return a collection of objects that could be a report, folder, or favorites folder that exist as children of the object with an ID of 0, which is the root folder. After that, a function could be recursively called that would list objects in each subfolder. Sometimes this statement would run and that folder would have no children objects. In this case, that query could have been avoided if the SI_CHILDREN property was brought back. This property is a number representing the number of children objects that exist for a given InfoObject. If the value were 0, there would be no need to run a query to retrieve the children. This property also works for reports and instances. A report with four instances returns an SI_CHILDREN value of four. It's also a nice feature to show this number in the user interface to indicate how many objects are below a certain level.

Another property that is useful for reducing additional queries is the SI_INSTANCE_OBJECT property. It is a Boolean value that indicates whether the current object is a report instance. Because this is an indexed property, it could be used in the WHERE clause to limit the results to only report instances or perhaps the opposite: only report objects.

OBJECT IDENTIFIERS

Thus far in this book, the SI_ID property has been used as the unique identifier of a report. This is valid, but the ID is technically only unique to the current Crystal Enterprise deployment. You might find that a report when moved from the development to production environment will have a different SI_ID. Depending on how your application works, this might be a concern. In a very generic application, the only ID hard-coded anywhere should be the ID of the root folder in Crystal Enterprise, which is always 0. However, sometimes the ID is hard-coded or perhaps stored somewhere outside of Crystal Enterprise. If this is the case, the SI_CUID property can be used as a unique identifier. This property is a globally unique identifier within a Crystal Enterprise cluster, so that when reports are moved from one deployment to another, the SI_CUID property stays the same. Keep in mind that this value is a string instead of a number and contains alphanumeric data, so it needs to be handled appropriately. To see what the SI_CUID values are for your current reports, run the following statement in the Query Builder:

```
SELECT SI_NAME, SI_CUID FROM CI_INFOOBJECTS WHERE
    SI_PROGID='CrystalEnterprise.Report'
```

HIERARCHICAL PROPERTIES

So far the InfoObject properties that have been discussed have been simple string, date, or numeric properties. There are some types of properties that exist in the InfoStore that need to provide more than a single value. For example, to return a list of parameters (prompts) defined in the report, instead of having properties such as SI_PROMPT1, SI_PROMPT2, SI_PROMPT3, and so on there is simply an SI_PROMPTS property that contains information for multiple prompts. Hierarchical properties generally map to an object in the Crystal Enterprise object model, in this case, the ReportParameters collection.

As an example, the SI_FILES property returns a list of files that are stored with an InfoObject. To retrieve the hierarchical properties, SI_FILES must be included in the SELECT clause:

```
SELECT SI_NAME, SI_FILES FROM CI_INFOOBJECTS WHERE
    SI_PROGID='CrystalEnterprise.Report'
```

Its values can be accessed via the Files collection attached to the InfoObject. Obviously there is more than one piece of data retrieved to make up the collection, but that is handled behind the scenes. Consult the documentation for a list of query properties and which object collections they map to.

Report-Specific Properties

When dealing with report objects specifically, there are two additional categories of properties that are available. They are processing information and scheduling information. Notice they map to the ISchedulingInfo and IProcessingInfo interfaces from the previous chapter on scheduling. These properties are accessed by the SI_PROCESSINFO and SI_SCHEDULEINFO prefixes, respectively. The following example retrieves the name and record selection formula via the SI_NAME and SI_RECORD_FORMULA properties:

```
SELECT SI_NAME, SI_PROCESSINFO.SI_RECORD_FORMULA FROM CI_INFOOBJECTS WHERE
    SI_PROGID='CrystalEnterprise.Report'
```

These properties do need to be prefixed or they will not work. There is a full list of these processing info and scheduling info properties in the Crystal Enterprise documentation. Look for the Query Language Reference section. The following is a list of some of the more useful properties.

Processing Info (SI_PROCESSINFO):

- SI_LOGON_INFO: A hierarchical property containing the logon credential information for a report
- SI_PROMPTS: A hierarchical property containing the definition and metadata for each parameter defined in a report
- SI_RECORD_FORMULA: The record selection formula for a report

Scheduling Info (SI_SCHEDULEINFO):

- SI_STARTTIME: The start time for a scheduled job
- SI_ENDTIME: The end time for a scheduled job
- SI_OUTCOME: The resulting status for a scheduled job, this maps to values in the CeScheduleOutcome enumeration
- SI_SUBMITTER: The username of the user who submitted the scheduled job

Advanced Searching

Based on the material provided so far, you should be able to add searching capability to your application by using the WHERE clause to limit results returned. As an example, the following query would return all reports that are called Sales Report:

```
SELECT SI_ID FROM CI_INFOOBJECTS WHERE SI_NAME='Sales Report'
```

Although this is useful, the user would need to know the exact name of the report, which somewhat defeats the purpose of the search. This section describes some advanced methods for providing more robust searching within a Crystal Enterprise-based application.

Up until this point in the coverage of InfoStore queries, all conditions used in the WHERE clause have used the = operator. In fact there are several additional types of operators:

- Not equal to: !=
- Greater than: >
- Less than: <
- Greater than or equal to: >=
- Less than or equal to: <=
- Textual wildcard match: LIKE
- Negative textual wildcard match: NOT LIKE
- In a list of values: IN
- Not in a list of values: NOT IN
- Between the range of two values: BETWEEN

These operators are type-sensitive as you would expect from standard database query operators. As an example, the LIKE operator works against string items only, and the equality operators work only against numeric data. Most of these are self-explanatory but some require some additional information.

The LIKE operator is a great way to handle searching for reports by a keyword or partial report name. Its syntax is as follows:

```
<property> LIKE <pattern>
```

The pattern can contain the following wildcard characters:

- % matches any string of zero or more characters (not case-sensitive). The condition SI_NAME LIKE '%budget%' returns all reports with the word budget in them. The condition SI_USERFULLNAME LIKE 'Lisa%' returns all usernames that begin with Lisa.
- _ matches any single character. The condition SI_NAME LIKE 'Team _' matches Team A, Team B, Team C, and so on.
- [] matches any single character between a specified range. The condition SI_NAME LIKE '200[1-3] Budget' matches reports with the names 2001 Budget, 2002 Budget, and 2003 Budget.
- [^] performs a negative match on any single character between a specified range. The condition SI_NAME LIKE '200[^3] Forecast' matches reports with the names 2001 Forecast, 2002 Forecast, and so on, but not 2003 Forecast.

As you can see, the LIKE operator is quite powerful and can be used to provide some robust searching. This becomes important as the number of reports, folders, and users grows.

The IN operator is useful for querying for reports from a known list of IDs or names. The syntax for the IN operator is

```
<property> IN (<values>, <value>, ...)
```

Some examples of using the IN operator are shown here:

```
SELECT SI_NAME FROM CI_INFOOBJECTS WHERE SI_ID IN (223, 732, 442, 334, 743)

SELECT SI_ID FROM CI_SYSTEMOBJECTS WHERE SI_PROGID='CrystalEnterprise.User'
    AND SI_NAME IN ('jsmith', 'sbecker', 'mblouin')
```

Finally, the BETWEEN operator is a quick way to express a range condition. The syntax is as follows:

```
<property> BETWEEN <value> and <value>
```

Some examples of using the BETWEEN operator are listed here:

```
SELECT SI_NAME FROM CI_INFOOBJECTS WHERE SI_ID BETWEEN 250 and 260

SELECT SI_ID FROM CI_INFOOBJECTS WHERE SI_PROGID='CrystalEnterprise.Folder'
    AND SI_CHILDREN BETWEEN 1 AND 20
```

CUSTOM INFOOBJECT PROPERTIES

You've probably figured out so far that when InfoStore queries are run, any properties listed in the SELECT clause are available from the InfoObject's Properties collection. This is a properties() method in the Java object model and a Properties collection in the COM and .NET object models. Assume the following query was run against the InfoStore:

```
SELECT SI_NAME, SI_DESCRIPTION FROM CI_INFOOBJECTS WHERE
    SI_PROGID='CrystalEnterprise.Report'
```

At this point, the following JSP code could be used to access the SI_DESCRIPTION property:

```
IInfoObject infoObject = (IInfoObject) results.get(0);
IProperties props = infoObject.properties();
IProperty prop = props.getProperty("SI_DESCRIPTION");
out.println(prop.getValue());
```

You might have noticed that there is an add method on the IProperties interface. This means you can add any number of properties and subproperties yourself. The following code adds a property called Project to the report, so that reports can be tied to specific projects.

```
IInfoObject infoObject = (IInfoObject) results.get(0);
IProperties props = infoObject.properties();
IProperty newProp = props.add("Project", "Project X", IProperty.DIRTY);
iStore.commit(results);
```

After this custom property is set, a developer can retrieve this property at any time to display to the user. The new property 'Project' can be used in the InfoStore query like this:

```
SELECT SI_NAME, Project FROM CI_INFOOBJECTS WHERE SI_ID=289
```

This new property can even be used in the WHERE clause to perform a filter as shown here:

```
SELECT SI_NAME FROM CI_INFOOBJECTS WHERE Project='Project ABC'
```

Note that custom properties are not indexed so are not optimal to filter on, but can be useful when used appropriately.

CREATING AND RESPONDING TO CRYSTAL ENTERPRISE ALERTS

Crystal Enterprise generally provides a successful platform for building and delivering reports over the Web. Although successful implementations and wide user adoption are always a good thing, one of the challenges that comes with that is that as more reports get published to the system, it becomes more of a challenge to wade through the mounds of information to quickly find the answers users need. A trend that has recently been growing faster than ever is dashboards. A *dashboard* is typically a page or series of Web pages that provide a summary of many different measures and metrics defined inside a business. One of the most popular ways to represent information on a dashboard today is in the form of alerts. An alert is a flag that is triggered when a value falls above or below a threshold. Typical examples of this could be headcount rising above a certain number, sales weekly revenue dropping below a certain level, or average call center wait times rising above a preferred level. An alert is defined inside a Crystal Report template and when scheduled, any alerts that are triggered surface themselves through the Crystal Enterprise Object Model. Typically, a user would boot up her computer in the morning and visit the dashboard page to see any alerts that she needs to respond to. This section describes how to provide this list of alerts.

FINDING TRIGGERED ALERTS

Alerts are triggered during a scheduled report job. This means that when querying for alerts, you should query only report instances. The following query returns the name and corresponding triggered alerts from any report instances that have at least one triggered alert:

```
SELECT SI_NAME, SI_ALERTS FROM CI_INFOOBJECTS WHERE SI_ALERTS != NULL
```

The only type of object that can have an alert is a report, so when including a condition like SI_ALERTS != NULL, there is no need to filter on SI_PROGID as well. Figure 36.3 shows the output of the previous query when run in the Query Builder application.

As you can see, the SI_ALERTS property is a hierarchical property. It has a subproperty called SI_NUM_ALERTS and then depending on the number of alerts triggered, it has an SI_ALERT1 property, SI_ALERT2 property, and so on. That property is another hierarchical property that contains the alert name and message in the SI_ALERT_NAME and SI_ALERT_MESSAGE properties, respectively.

DISPLAYING ALERTS

One of the things you will find right away is that although there is a way to get all the reports that have run and had alerts triggered, there is no way to determine what alerts are defined on reports that have not been triggered yet. So instead of providing a "triggered/not triggered" type of interface, you can only present a list of alerts that have been triggered. A good way to do this is to simply create a listing called "Alerts of the day" and display the SI_ALERT_MESSAGE value. Because this is attached to an InfoObject, you know the corresponding ID of the report, so it would be a good idea to make the message a hyperlink to the report itself. This enables the user to click on the alert to drill to the detail of what happened.

Figure 36.3
Viewing any triggered alerts

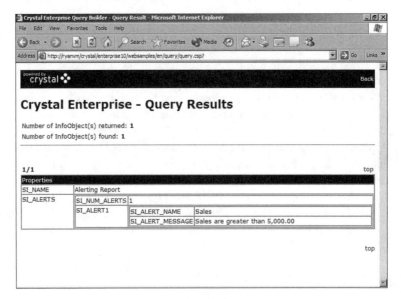

Also, if a report runs every day you don't want duplicate alerts so you would want to filter for any alerts fired that day. Let's say the scheduled reports run at 2 a.m. each morning. You might use the following query to only retrieve the alert for the current day:

```
SELECT SI_NAME, SI_ALERTS, SI_ENDTIME FROM CI_INFOOBJECTS WHERE
    SI_ALERTS != NULL AND SI_ENDTIME >= '2004/02/29.2.00'
```

CREATING SCHEDULABLE PROGRAM OBJECTS

As the depth and breadth of business intelligence (BI) platforms like Crystal Enterprise grow within organizations today, one of the key challenges is the interoperability of the core BI platform with the rest of the surrounding infrastructure. There are many services that the BI platform might need to work with such as ETL tools, databases/data warehouses, Web servers, portal servers, and security and directory servers. One of the ways that Crystal Enterprise can work with these external technologies is through Program Objects.

A Program Object is a small program or link to a program published as a standard object to Crystal Enterprise. It has its own name, location in the folder structure, security permission, and all the other attributes you'd expect from a standard Crystal Enterprise object. From a programmatic perspective, it is represented by an InfoObject. Generally Program Objects are only scheduled, not viewed on-demand. They are processed by the Program Job Server instead of the Report Job Server. Figure 36.4 shows creating a Program Object from the Crystal Management Console.

Figure 36.4
Creating a Program
Object.

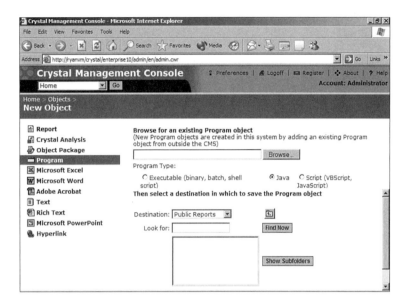

There are three types of programs that can be run via a Program Object: an executable, a script file, or a Java program. When creating a Program Object, you simply point to the location of the file. When creating the scheduled job, you can specify arguments to the program. The types of executable files supported are .exe, .bat, and .sh. The types of script files supported are .vbs and .js. The more interesting type of Program Object is a Java program. To write a Java program that can be scheduled within Crystal Enterprise, you must implement the IProgramBase interface found in the com.crystaldecisions.sdk.plugin. desktop.program package. This interface only has a single method called run. It receives as arguments to the method: a valid IEnterpriseSession, a valid IInfoStore, and a String array consisting of the program's arguments as defined at schedule time. This is useful because you can use these objects to gain access to Crystal Enterprise without having to pass in credentials. Listing 36.1 provides an example Java Program Object that when scheduled, accepts a username as an argument and deletes all object instances that are owned by that user (in other words, all the objects that the user scheduled).

LISTING 36.1   DELETEINSTANCES.JAVA

```
import com.crystaldecisions.sdk.plugin.desktop.program.IProgramBase;
import com.crystaldecisions.sdk.framework.IEnterpriseSession;
```

continues

Listing 36.1   Continued

```java
import com.crystaldecisions.sdk.exception.SDKException;
import com.crystaldecisions.sdk.occa.infostore.*;
import java.util.Date;

public class DeleteInstances implements IProgramBase
{
    public void run(IEnterpriseSession session, IInfoStore iStore,
                    String[] args) throws SDKException
    {
        String query;
        IInfoObjects infoObjects;

        Date now = new Date();
        query = "SELECT SI_ID, SI_NAME, SI_ENDTIME FROM CI_INFOOBJECTS WHERE" +
                " SI_PROGID = 'CrystalEnterprise.Report' AND " +
                "SI_INSTANCE_OBJECT=1 AND SI_OWNER = '" + args[0] + "'";

        System.out.println("Executing at " + now);
        System.out.println("Deleting all instances owned by '" + args[0] +
                           "' on " + session.getCMSName());
        System.out.println("query: " + query);

        infoObjects = iStore.query(query);

        System.out.println(infoObjects.getResultSize() +
                          " instance(s) found for '" + args[0] + "' on " +
                          session.getCMSName());

        if (infoObjects.getResultSize() > 0)
        {
            int infoObjectsReturned = infoObjects.getResultSize();

            for (int i=infoObjectsReturned-1; i > -1; i--)
            {
                IInfoObject infoObject = (IInfoObject)infoObjects.get(i);
                IProperty props = infoObjects.properties();
                System.out.println((infoObjectsReturned - i + 1) +
                    ".) Deleting Instance #" + infoObject.getID() + " (" +
                    infoObject.getTitle() + " - " +
                    props.getProperty("SI_ENDTIME").getValue() + ")" );
                infoObjects.delete(infoObject);
            }

            System.out.println("Committing Delete Action");

            iStore.commit(infoObjects);
        }

        System.out.println("Exiting");
    }
}
```

Because a Java Program Object needs to implement an interface defined in the Crystal Enterprise Java libraries, you need to include those libraries in the classpath when compiling the program. The specific files you need to reference are

- cesession.jar
- ceplugins.jar
- cecore.jar
- celib.jar

These and the rest of the Crystal Enterprise Java libraries can be found in the following directory:

```
\Program Files\Common Files\Crystal Decisions\2.5\java\lib
```

Figure 36.5 shows the output of scheduling the DeleteInstances Java Program Object and passing in Administrator as the username to delete instances for.

Figure 36.5
The output of the DeleteInstances scheduled job.

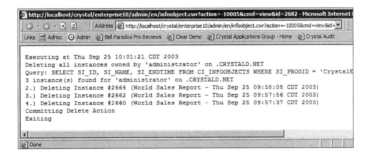

There are many uses for Java Program Objects. Because the implementation for the program is defined by the developer the only limits are the creativity in which it is used. Some typical examples of Program Objects are

- Performing maintenance-like actions on the Crystal Enterprise system, such as deleting unused instances, archiving instances to another location, creating auditing snapshots, and so on.
- Running external applications such as database or data warehouse loads, queries, extraction transformation and loading (ETL) tools.
- Scheduling arbitrary programs to run such as virus checkers.

Performing data warehouse loads can be a great use of a Program Object. In the previous chapter you learned how to create a scheduled report job (or scheduled report package job) that waited for an event to be triggered before it ran. If you were to create a Program Object that launched a data warehouse load, you could create a "schedule event" attached to the Program Object. The end result would be that a report or collection of reports would wait until a successful execution of the data warehouse load was done before running the report off that warehouse. This ensures the reports don't run too early before the

36

warehouse load is complete and also ensures that if the warehouse load fails, the reports don't run at all.

ADDING CRYSTAL ANALYSIS REPORTS TO YOUR APPLICATION

Thus far, the chapters on the Crystal Enterprise Object Model have focused on delivering relational Crystal Reports. This section discusses delivering Crystal Analysis reports in custom Web applications.

N O T E

> Crystal Reports can report off OLAP data sources such as Microsoft SQL Server Analysis Services as well. However, Crystal Reports provides OLAP Reporting as opposed to what Crystal Analysis provides, which is OLAP Analysis. If all you need is to view snapshots of a cube's data, Crystal Reports is the best solution. However, the real power of building OLAP cubes is in the explorative analysis that can be performed. Instead of simply answering the "what" and "when" and "who" questions, that OLAP analysis provided by Crystal Analysis can answer the "how" and "why" questions.

DISCOVERING CRYSTAL ANALYSIS REPORTS

The first thing you should understand when learning about working with the Crystal Enterprise object model and Crystal Analysis is that the Crystal Analysis report files (.car files) are hosted as InfoObjects just like all other objects in Crystal Enterprise. The object type for these reports is CrystalEnterprise.Analysis. The following is an InfoStore query that returns all Crystal Analysis reports stored in a given system:

```
SELECT SI_ID, SI_NAME FROM CI_INFOOBJECTS WHERE
    SI_PROGID='CrystalEnterprise.Analysis'
```

As you can see the `SI_ID` and `SI_NAME` properties apply to Analysis reports the same way as they do to Crystal Reports. Some other InfoStore properties that are applicable to Crystal Analysis are

- `SI_UPDATE_TS`: The date and time when the Analysis report was created.
- `SI_DESCRIPTION`: A description attached to the Analysis report. This can only be set programmatically.

Unlike Crystal Reports, Analysis reports cannot be scheduled. However, a user can create a saved view of a Analysis report. A saved view is simply a certain viewpoint and state of the report that is saved as another InfoObject. Like Crystal Report instances, saved views are children of the original report in the Crystal Enterprise repository. The following query would be used to return only reports and not saved views:

```
SELECT SI_ID FROM CI_INFOOBJECTS WHERE SI_PROGID='CrystalEnterprise.Analysis'
    AND SI_SAVED_VIEW=0
```

Notice that the `SI_SAVED_VIEW` property is used much the same way as the `SI_INSTANCE_OBJECT` property is used for Crystal Reports.

VIEWING REPORTS

Unlike Crystal Reports, Crystal Analysis does not have the corresponding object or component that is used to view reports. Instead reports are viewed by redirecting to a URL with a certain syntax that indicates which report to view and some other information. This URL is handled by the Web Component Server, which calls out to the Crystal Analysis engine to display the report. This ends up being a much easier solution anyway. The report can be loaded into a frame if needed as well. The URL used to view Crystal Analysis reports is as follows:

```
http://SERVER/crystal/infoobject.cwr
```

This infoobject.cwr URL accepts the following arguments along the query string:

- id: This required item indicates the InfoObject ID of the report to display. This can either be the ID of the Crystal Analysis report or the ID of a saved view.

- wcslogontoken: This required item is a URL-encoded logon token obtained from the LogonTokenMgr object. Tokens were discussed in detail in Chapter 34.

- action: A required query string item. This should always be set to 0.

- page: An optional item that indicates which page number is to be displayed. By default, page 1 is shown if this item is omitted.

NOTE

> Any of these items can also be passed via an HTTP form post to hide their values from the end user.

A sample URL is provided here:

```
infoobject.cwr?id=243&action=0&wcslogontoken=CRYSA:84g323fms3adgmeh&page=1
```

Figure 36.6 shows the result of this URL.

PASSING PARAMETERS TO CRYSTAL ANALYSIS REPORTS

A new feature to Crystal Analysis is parameterized reports. A parameter can be used to set the cube location, page, member set, or member. When viewing a report that has a parameter defined and using the URL from the previous example, the Crystal Analysis report viewer would pop up a message asking the user to type in a value for the parameter. Often it's preferable to bypass that parameter prompting screen and pass the parameter value to the viewer directly. This is done via the `promptex` query string item.

The syntax for the `promptex` query string item is as follows:

Single value: `promptex-NAME=VALUE`

Multiple value: `promptex-NAME=KEY%3DVALUE,KEY%3DVALUE,...`

Figure 36.6
Viewing a Crystal
Analysis report.

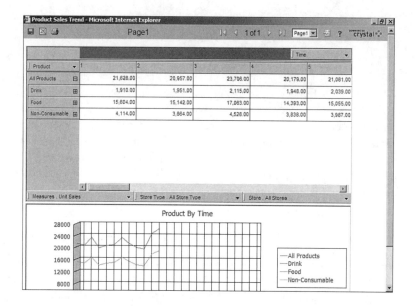

For single value parameters, use the first syntax, replacing NAME with the name of the parameter as defined in the Crystal Analysis designer, and VALUE with the value required. The following example would pass the value 2004 to the Year parameter:

```
promptex-Year=[Time].[2004]
```

Some other examples are listed here:

- Setting the page number:
  ```
  promptex-PageNo=4
  ```
- Setting a memberset parameter:
  ```
  promptex-ProductsMembers=[Products].[Meat],[Products].[Dairy]
  ```

TROUBLESHOOTING

ACCESSING THE CRYSTAL MANAGEMENT CONSOLE

I am trying to access the Crystal Management Console (CMC) but there are connection errors.

Make sure you are using the proper machine name in the browser's address bar when connecting to the CMC. It's often tempting to use localhost instead of the machine name but this will not work properly with Crystal Enterprise.

Using SQL Queries in Crystal Reports

In this appendix

A

The SQL Commands feature was introduced in Chapter 1, "Creating and Designing Basic Reports." For those users who are unfamiliar with *SQL (Structured Query Language)*, this appendix serves as an introduction and helps enable the creation of SQL commands. For those users who are familiar with SQL, this appendix serves as a refresher with some important tips pertaining to the use of SQL with the new SQL Commands feature. This chapter provides the following:

- A review of SQL Commands
- An introduction to SQL

REVIEW OF SQL COMMANDS

With reports based on tables, views, or stored procedures, Crystal Reports does the background work of generating a database query. This query incorporates the fields you have used in the report, any sorting or filtering you've applied, and even some calculations. This is one of the strengths of Crystal Reports—you don't need to be an expert at writing SQL to use the product. All that complexity is abstracted away from the user designing the report. However, sometimes the person developing the report is familiar with the SQL language, and perhaps is also the database administrator. In situations like this, people often want to write their own query for several reasons, including the following:

- An already defined query, which has the required fields, is in use elsewhere.
- The user wants to optimize her query beyond what Crystal Reports provides out-of-the-box.
- The user wants to perform a complex query that is beyond what Crystal Reports automatically generates; for example, a union query.

The SQL Commands feature is meant to address these needs. Rather than adding a table or view to a report, you can add a SQL command. This command represents a SQL query that you will type in. After this SQL command is created, it is treated just like a table in that it contains fields that can be used in the report and can be linked to other tables or SQL commands.

AN INTRODUCTION TO SQL

As its name implies, SQL is used to express a database query. SQL has facilities for defining which fields should be returned from the query, if and how the query should be filtered and sorted, and so on. Although SQL is an industry standard language, various specific versions and editions of the standard are implemented by SQL-based databases. Crystal Reports does not use just a single syntax, but rather is robust enough to handle most major SQL language derivations. The rest of this appendix walks you through the SQL Language and points out specific areas that are of concern to Crystal Reports. Although it doesn't focus on a specific version of SQL, it does point out differences where appropriate.

THE SELECT STATEMENT

Even though the name implies that SQL is only about querying databases, most implementations also enable you to insert, delete, and update records inside the database. Each of these distinct actions has its own command: SELECT (query), INSERT, UPDATE, and DELETE. Although SQL commands allow any valid SQL statement that returns records to be used, SELECT statements are generally the only statements to be used. However, there are situations in which other statements can be used in addition to a SELECT statement. One example of this is running an INSERT statement to create a record to log the fact that the report is being run. This section focuses on describing the SELECT statement from SQL.

A basic SELECT statement has the following syntax:

```
SELECT field-list
FROM table-list
```

SELECT statements always begin with the word SELECT. The general convention is to capitalize all SQL keywords used in the query to make it clear which is SQL and which is a table or field name. The list of fields to include is a comma-separated list of field names, such as "Name, Age, Gender." To include all fields in the specified table(s), use an * instead of listing individual field names. If the name of a field contains a space, the field name should be surrounded by a quote character (`'field name'`). Various SQL implementations allow different quotes, but most of them support ' (single quote) as a quote character. The list of tables follows the same convention: They are separated by commas and are optionally enclosed in a quote. Any extra whitespace or carriage returns are usually ignored by the database. The following is a sample SQL statement using the Xtreme Sample Database:

```
SELECT `Customer Name`, City, Country
FROM Customer
```

Notice that quotes were only used for the Customer Name field because it was the only field with a space in the name. However, as a general convention, quote all your field and table names to be safe. The same statement could be written like this:

```
SELECT 'Customer Name', 'City', 'Country'
FROM 'Customer'
```

Depending on the type of database, table names can also be prefixed with the associated database name, for example, MyDatabase.MyTable. When using a qualified name such as this, you need to quote both names separately; that is, `'MyDatabase'.'MyTable'`.

NOTE

> When you're using a SQL command in Crystal Reports, the fields that you specify in the field-list part of the SELECT statement determine which fields will be available to you inside your report. Although it's easy to use a SELECT * ... statement, keep in mind that you could be bringing back fields that aren't used and increasing processing time and required bandwidth. It's better to specify individual fields. You can always add or remove a field after the SQL command is created by opening the Database Expert, right-clicking on the Command object, and selecting Edit Command from the context menu.

A

In the previous examples, data was being returned for each customer. However, if you wanted to return a list of countries, you might use a query such as the following:

```
SELECT 'Country'
FROM 'Customer'
```

Although this wouldn't return incorrect results, it would return redundant results because there is more than one record that contains the same country name. To work around this, use the DISTINCT keyword, which filters out all duplicate records:

```
SELECT DISTINCT 'Country'
FROM 'Customer'
```

FILTERING RECORDS

By learning a basic SELECT statement, you have the capability to return any or all fields. But so far, the query would return all records stored in that table. This section builds on what you've learned up to now by introducing a new clause in the SQL statement. If you're not sure why you would want to filter records, consider that an "average" corporate data source might contain millions of records of data, and without being more specific in a query, you are putting an undue load on the database server as well as overwhelming business users with more data than they need.

The WHERE clause enables you to specify which records should be included in the query. If the WHERE clause is omitted (as it has been in the examples thus far), all records from the table are returned. Specifying a WHERE clause can limit these records to a more relevant subset. The syntax of a SQL statement with a WHERE clause is as follows:

```
SELECT field-list
FROM table-list
[WHERE condition]
```

NOTE

> Square brackets that enclose any component of the SQL statement indicate that component is optional and need not be included in the SQL statement.

The condition can be any equality expression. Fields from the table can be used in the condition, as well as text literals and numbers. Let's look at a few examples:

```
SELECT 'Customer Name', 'City'
FROM 'Customer'
WHERE 'Country' = 'USA'
```

The preceding SQL statement returns all customers who have a Country of USA. Notice that in this statement a text literal is used ('USA'). Text literals are surrounded by a text delimiter. The most common delimiter is the single quote, as used here.

Conditions can be combined together with ANDs and ORs, as shown in the following example:

```
SELECT 'Order ID', 'Order Date'
FROM 'Orders'
```

```
WHERE 'Order Amount' > 2000 AND
       'Customer ID' = 123
```

NOTE

> Sometimes it's appropriate to use a SQL statement that has a hard-coded (static) number or string. However, it's often more common to use parameters in the place of such values. That way, the report can be reprocessed with different values showing diverse information without having to modify the SQL Command each time a change is needed. To create a parameter in SQL syntax, click the Create button in the Create SQL Command dialog and substitute the parameter name in place of the hard-coded value.

SORTING RECORDS

Like filtering, sorting can be performed by Crystal Reports on your local workstation. However, it's always faster to have the database itself perform the operation because a typical database server has far more processing power than your desktop PC. This section introduces another clause to the SQL statement that enables you to specify the order in which the records are returned.

The ORDER BY clause is used to specify sorting. The syntax is as follows:

```
SELECT field-list
FROM table-list
[WHERE condition]
[ORDER BY field-list [ ASC | DESC ] ]
```

The ORDER BY clause comes last in the SQL statement and is followed by a comma-separated list of fields. The records returned from the query will be sorted first by the first field specified, and then by the second, and so on. By default, fields are sorted in ascending order (from smallest to largest, or A to Z); but by adding ASC or DESC after the field name, you can specify either ascending or descending (largest to smallest, or Z to A) sort order.

The following SQL statement sorts the records by country, and then by region:

```
SELECT *
FROM 'Customer'
ORDER BY 'Country' ASC, 'Region' ASC
```

The preceding example is sorting alphabetically. The following example shows where sorting is done on a numeric field. This query returns a list of customers in the order of highest sales first.

```
SELECT 'Customer Name', 'Last Year's Sales'
FROM 'Customer'
ORDER BY 'Last Year's Sales' DESC
```

JOINING MULTIPLE TABLES

So far, we've only used a single table, but of course multiple tables can be used. You might have already tried a statement like this:

```
SELECT 'Customer Name', 'Order ID'
FROM 'Customer', 'Orders'
```

This might seem correct initially, but this query most likely won't return what you are looking for. Although only 2,192 records are in the Orders table, this query will return more than 500,000 records and, with a larger database, could actually bring down the database server! This is because for each record in the Customer table, the entire set of records in the Orders table is included. In other words, the database doesn't know how to match up the records between the tables. If more than one table is used, a join should be applied that indicates how to match up the tables. There are various syntaxes for joins, but the simplest is to add a WHERE clause to the SQL statement (shown as follows), which produces an equal join:

```
SELECT field-list
FROM table1, table2
WHERE table1.field = table2.field
```

This type of join applied to the previous sample query would look like this:

```
SELECT 'Customer Name', 'Order ID'
FROM 'Customer', 'Orders'
WHERE 'Customer'.'Customer ID' = 'Orders'.'Customer ID'
```

Notice that because there is a Customer ID field in both the Customer and Orders tables, when that field is referenced in the WHERE clause, it is prefixed with the table name so as not to be ambiguous.

ALIASING

One beneficial feature of SQL is the capability to give fields and tables more meaningful names. Often fields are defined in the database with non-meaningful names such as ACTID instead of Account ID, and it would be useful to rename, or alias, this name.

Aliasing is straightforward: After the field that you want to alias, simply append 'AS field-name', where *field-name* is the new name for the field. Here's a working example:

```
SELECT 'Customer Name', 'Region' AS 'State'
FROM 'Customer'
WHERE 'Country' = 'USA'
```

In this example, because the records are being filtered to only include customers from the USA, it can be inferred that that the Region field will contain the State (where other countries such as Canada might use the Region field for the province). Because of this, the field is aliased to State. Note that the alias name need not be contained in quotes unless it has a space, but as stated earlier, it's good practice to always quote field names.

CALCULATED FIELDS

It's often a requirement to display data on the report that doesn't exist directly in the database—that is, data inferred or calculated based on other fields in the database. Although Crystal Reports provides a full formula language for defining these "formulas," when using SQL only, you need to follow its rules and limitations. SQL does have the capability to handle basic expressions like this. An expression, or calculated field, is specified in the SELECT part of the SQL statement just like any other field. Consider the following example, which uses an expression to concatenate a first and last name field together:

```
SELECT 'Customer Name', 'Contact First Name' + ' ' + 'Contact Last Name'
FROM 'Customer'
```

If you were to use this SQL statement in a SQL command, the correct field values are returned; however, the calculated field would be named something slightly cryptic like Expr1001. It's clear to you that this field represents a Contact Name, but the database can't easily infer that. To correct this problem, draw on the aliasing concept explained in the previous section. The corrected SQL statement is here:

```
SELECT 'Customer Name',
       'Contact First Name' + ' ' + 'Contact Last Name' AS 'Contact Name'
FROM 'Customer'
```

In addition to textual expressions, you can perform mathematical expressions as well. The following SQL statement uses a calculated field to determine the tax paid based on sales:

```
SELECT 'Customer Name', 'Last Year's Sales',
       'Last Year's Sales' * 0.07 AS 'Tax Paid'
FROM 'Customer'
```

For more information on what kind of expressions can be used in your SQL command, consult the documentation for your database.

UNION QUERIES

In the Xtreme Sample Database, each table represents a certain type of object, but often multiple tables represent the same type of object. For example, rather than having a single table called Orders, you might have multiple tables called Orders2001, Orders2002, Orders2003, which each contain the orders for a particular year as indicated by the table name. If you only want to report off one of those tables at a time, you don't need to do anything special. But, if you'd like to consolidate those together into a single query result, you must use a union query.

> **TIP**
>
> Union queries were not inherently supported by Crystal Reports in previous versions. However, the introduction of SQL Commands in Crystal Reports version 9 enables you to use this feature fully.

The syntax for a union query is as follows:

```
SELECT statement
[ UNION
SELECT statement ]
```

Here is a SQL statement with a UNION clause combining some fictitious order tables:

```
SELECT * FROM 'Orders2001'
UNION
SELECT * FROM 'Orders2002'
UNION
SELECT * FROM 'Orders2003'
```

These tables can be unioned together because they have the same table structure. You are not able to perform a union on two tables with different fields.

GROUPING

Grouping enables records to be grouped together based on a specified field, and then summarized using a given summary operation. Note that grouping in a SQL command will not allow a drill-down to the detail records. The syntax for grouping is as follows:

```
SELECT field-list
FROM table-list
[WHERE condition]
[GROUP BY field-list]
[ORDER BY field-list [ ASC | DESC ] ]
```

The following example groups all customers by country and summarizes the sales:

```
SELECT 'Country', SUM('Last Year's Sales') AS 'Total Sales'
FROM 'Customer'
GROUP BY 'Country'
```

Two components to grouping exist in a SQL statement. The first is the summary operation—that is, SUM, COUNT, AVG, and so on. This operation determines which field will be summarized and in what way. The second component is the GROUP BY clause, which specifies for which field the data should be summarized—in other words, on which field the data should be grouped.

INDEX

authentication
    applications, 515-516
    CMS (Crystal Management
        Server), 515-516
    Crystal Enterprise,
        463-464, 767
    managing (CMC)
        Active Directory,
            644-646
        LDAP, 643-644
        licensing, 641-642
        Native, 643
        user accounts, 602
        Windows NT, 644-646
authorization, CMS (Crystal
    Management Server), 516
Auto-Complete feature, 103
automatic conversion
    functions, 112
automatic parameter
    passing, 669
automatic totals, worksheets,
    396-397
Automatic Totals tab, 433
Autosave feature, 49
axes, cross-tabs, 232
Axes tab (Chart Expert),
    196-197

B

Background Color option
    (Border tab), 157
backups, migration
    preparations, 357
bar charts, 203
barcode conversion
    functions, 113
Basic formula syntax,
    282-283
Basic syntax, 100
batch report exporting,
    681-683
batch reporting, Report
    Designer Component,
    709-710
batch scheduling, CMS
    (Crystal Management
    Server), 520
BEA WebLogic Workshop,
    IDE (Integrated
    Development
    Environments) integration,
    671

Boolean tab, 159
Border Color option (Border
    tab), 157
Border tab, 157
Borland JBuilder X, IDE
    (Integrated Development
    Environments) integration,
    671
Box command (Insert
    menu), 220
boxes
    formatting reports, 220-221
    text, 420
braces ({})
    formula fields, 82
    formula languages, 283-284
    parameter field objects, 139
Browse Field option (Set
    Default Values dialog box),
    133
Browse Table option (Set
    Default Values dialog box),
    133
browsers
    client tier, 508-509
    OLAP Connection, 327,
        378
    Property, 678
Business Element Wizard,
    373
Business Elements
    component, 372-373
Business Objects
    Developer Zone Web site,
        779
    Web site, 696
Business Objects Universe,
    363
business pain, identifying,
    543
business tiers, Business
    Views, 363-364
Business View command
    (File menu), 373
Business View Manager, 362
    Business Elements
        component, 372-373
    Data Connection
        component, 366
    Data Foundation
        component, 367
        custom functions, 372
        filters, 368-371
        formulas, 368-369

    parameters, 369
    SQL Expressions,
        368-369
    Dynamic Data Connection
        component, 366
    Repository Explorer,
        364-366
Business View Manager
    command (Tools menu),
    351
Business Views (BV), 553
    benefits, 360-362
    business tiers, 363-364
    Business View Manager
        Business Elements
            component, 372-373
        Data Connection
            component, 366
        Data Foundation
            component, 367-372
        Dynamic Data
            Connection
            component, 366
        Repository Explorer,
            364-366
    client tiers, 363
    data tier, 374
    missing, troubleshooting,
        357
    overview, 360
    performance considerations,
        362-363
    joining, 362-363
buttons, layout
    Chart Expert, 192-193
    Map Expert, 200
BV. *See* Business Views

C

CA (Crystal Analysis), Excel
    plug-in
    connecting, 454-458
    installing, 454
cache
    Crystal Enterprise
        Embedded Edition, 717
    managing, Cache Server,
        529
cache pages, converting to
    .rpt pages, 634
Cache Server
    cache management, 529
    constraints, 529
    managing, 634-635
    sizing, 558

J

.jar files, Java SDK access, 778

Java
CE-SDK (Crystal Enterprise Software Development Kit), 510
classes, Java Reporting Component, 656
code, Java Reporting Component, 655
configuration, Crystal Enterprise architecture, 578
data sources, 319-320
running, Program Objects, 813-815
servlets, 766

Java Database Connectivity (JDBC), Java Reporting Component, 657-659

Java Naming and Directory Interface (JNDI), JDBC connections, 658

Java Reporting Component
application servers, 655-656, 659
Crystal tag libraries, 663-664
helper tag libraries, 655
IDEs (Integrated Development Environments), 671
Java classes, 656
Java code, 655
overview, 654
programming, 669-671
report engines, 655
report viewer controls, 655-656
reports
exporting, 664-668
printing, 668-669
running, Web application servers, 654
scaling, 654
version comparisons, 656-659
viewing reports
group trees, 663
processHttpRequest method, 661-662

report viewer toolbar, 663
setReportSource method, 660

Java SDK (Crystal Enterprise SDK), 778-779

Java Server Pages (JSP), 766

Java Viewer, 495

Java Virtual Machine (JVM), 495

JDBC (Java Database Connectivity), Java Reporting Component, 657-659

JDBC driver version 10, locating, 672

JNDI (Java Naming and Directory Interface), JDBC connections, 658

Job Servers
managing, 636
Program Job Server, 527
Report Job Server, 525-527
sizing, 560-561

join type links, 33

joins
Full Outer, 34
Inner, 33
large data sets, 362-363
Left Outer, 34
multiple tables, 823-824
Not Equal, 34
tables, 367, 751
types, 33-34

JSP (Java Server Pages), 766

justification, rotated text, 223

JVM (Java Virtual Machine), 495

K-L

Key Performance Indicators, cubes, 382

keyword searches, 286

labeling, data-point (charts), 197

labels
customizing, OLAP Expert, 338
Data Labels tab, 206-208
summaries, cross-tab, 240

Labels tab (chart grid options), 209

languages
code, 696
formulas, 100
Basic syntax, 282-283
brackets, 283-284
characters, 284
Crystal syntax, 282-283
multilanguage text, custom functions, 123-126

Latest Report Changes node (Performance Information tool), 260

layering report objects, 159-162

Layers menu, 211

layout buttons
Chart Expert, 192-193
Map Expert, 200

Layout section
Chart Expert, 192-193
Map Expert, 200

Layout tab
Chart Options menu, 206
Section Expert, 179-180

LDAP (Lightweight Directory Access Protocol)
authentication, 642, 767
Crystal Enterprise authentication, 643-644
security plug-ins, 515-516

Left Outer join, 34

legacy mainframe data, COM connections, 315

legends
charts, 197
maps, 204

Length Limit option (Set Default Values dialog box), 134

libraries
CRAXDRT, 700, 710
references, 700
UFL (User Function Libraries), 354
user function library, 250

licenses, 641-642

Lightweight Directory Access Protocol. See LDAP

Line command (Insert menu), 220

Line Style option (Border tab), 157

lines, formatting reports, 220-221

link operator, 33

R

range functions, Date and Time formulas, 107

range value parameters, passing, 796

ranged maps, 203

Rapid Map Creation feature, 201

RAS (Report Application Server), 438, 467, 714. *See also* Crystal Enterprise Embedded Edition
  clustered (report source), 727
  deployment, 742
  exceptions, 744-745
  functions, 742
  performance, 743
  .rpt files, loading, 742-743
  sizing, 559-560
  specifying locations, 743-744
  Standalone (report source), 727

RAS SDK
  charts, 759-762
  filters, 754-756
  installations, 744
  parameters, 756-759
  reports
    creating, 749-750
    fields, 746-749
    filters, 755
    groups, adding, 751
    opening, 746
    sorting, 752-753
    summaries, adding, 753-754
    tables, 750-751
  sessions, initializing, 745

RDBMS (Database Management System), 533

RDC (Report Designer Component), 714

readability
  formulas, 115
  improving, report sections, 186

record selection formulas, 82, 97
  creating, 248
  database operations, 251-253
  dates, editing, 248-250

displaying, 248
  overview, 248
  parameter fields, 138-140
  SQL Expressions, 253-255
  strings, 250-251

Record Sort Expert command (Report menu), 84

Record Sorting Expert, accessing, 60

records
  filtering, 721, 822-823
  sorting, 83-85, 823

references, libraries, 700

Refresh Report Data command (Report menu), 49

refreshing
  object properties, 614
  reports, 137, 223

relative positioning, cross-tabs, 236-237

reliability, Crystal Enterprise, 466-467

remote terminal access, 571

Remove, Remove All option (Set Default Values dialog box), 134

reoccurring report schedules, creating, 787-789

reordering groups, 67-68

Repeat on Horizontal Page option (Common tab), 156

report alerts
  alert messages, 255
  alert names, 255
  alert triggers, 255-256
  creating, 256-257
  editing, 256-257
  viewing, 257, 260-262

Report Application Server. *See* RAS

Report Conversion Utility, downloading, 657

Report Custom Functions, 96

report definition folders, 441

Report Definition node (Performance Information tool), 260

report design explorers, 22-24

Report Designer, 676-677, 696
  batch reporting, 709-710
  Property Browser, 678
  user interface, 677

Report Designer Component (RDC), 714

Report Engine Object Model, 679
  code-behind, 707-708
  data source credentials, 706-707
  parameters, setting, 705-706
  Report object, 700-701
  ReportDocument object, 680
  reports
    exporting, 680-683, 701-703
    printing, 683-684, 704
  unbound fields, 707

report engines, Java Reporting Component, 655

Report Expert Wizard, 18

report experts. *See* Report Wizard

Report Explorer, 23

Report Gallery, 35-45

report instances, 554, 772, 776

Report Job Servers, 525-527

Report menu, 22

Report menu commands
  Group Sort Expert, 131
  Record Sort Expert, 84
  Refresh Report Data, 49
  Selection Formulas, Group, 87
  Selection Formulas, Record, 82, 141, 248
  Template Expert, 298

Report object, 700-701

report objects
  combining, 159-162
  designing, 148-150
  layering, 159-162
  modifying, 151-155
  overlapping, 162
  positioning/sizing, 146-150

Report Options menu, 432-433

report pages, configurations, 163-164

UsingCrystal.com

UsingCrystal.com is the accompanying site for this book, <u>Special Edition Using Crystal Reports 10</u>. In addition to providing a central area for supporting download samples, the site provides additional material not covered in the book based on new Crystal features or new productivity-enhancing tips and tricks. It is a great place for consultants, companies, and third party value-add vendors to interact and meet each other.

- Download the sample reports from this book
- Download the code snippets from this book
  - v   Downloads User ID is 'UsingCrystal' and
  - v   Downloads Password is 'BusinessObjects'

- Access Crystal Reports, Crystal Enterprise, and Crystal Analysis tips and tricks from the UsingCrystal community of consultants and experts.
- Become a registered member of the UsingCrystal community and share your expertise on the world's most used Business Intelligence tools.

- <u>Consultants –</u> Register your skills for clients to review and access posted client implementation requirements.
- <u>Companies –</u> Review resumés of Crystal consultants for your posted Crystal reporting and business intelligence implementation projects. Browse a library of value-add utilities and programs provided by third parties.
- <u>Value Add Partners – Sub</u>mit your value-add utilities and programs for review by potential clients.